The Balkans in Transition

THE BALKANS IN TRANSITION

ESSAYS ON THE DEVELOPMENT OF
BALKAN LIFE
AND POLITICS
SINCE THE EIGHTEENTH CENTURY

EDITED BY Charles and Barbara Jelavich

ARCHON BOOKS 1974

Library of Congress Cataloging in Publication Data
Jelavich, Charles, ed.
    The Balkans in transition.
    Reprint of the ed. published by the University of Cali-
fornia Press, Berkeley, in series: Russian and East European
studies.
    Papers presented at a conference held at the University
of California, Berkeley, June 13-15, 1960, and sponsored by
the Center for Slavic and East European Studies.
    Includes bibliographical references.
    1. Balkan   Peninsula—History—Congresses. I. Jela-
vich, Barbara (Brightfield), Joint ed. II. California. University. Center for Slavic and East European Studies.   III.
Title. IV. Series: Russian and East European Studies.
DR36.J4 1974   914.96′03   73-22373
ISBN 0-208-01431-4

Printed in the United States of America

The following papers were presented at a conference given at the University of California, Berkeley, on June 13, 14, and 15, 1960, on the subject "The Transformation of the Balkans since the Ottoman Era." The purpose of the meeting was to discuss developments common to the Balkans as a whole and not characteristic only of some individual states—the emphasis was thus on the areas of unity and agreement. Albania, Bulgaria, Greece, European Turkey, Jugoslavia, and Rumania were included; Hungary was discussed only in "The Geopolitics of the Balkans." Generally speaking, the contributions cover the years from the mid-eighteenth century to the Second World War, although some of the authors have found it necessary to extend these limits.

The topics selected do not, of course, exhaust the subject. A second similar conference could be held and, it is hoped, will be held in the future to treat such intriguing additional topics as: Byzantium and its legacy in the Turkish and nationalist periods; the role and influence of the Habsburg Empire as distinct from the West, the influence of music and folklore in the Balkans, and the role of the military in Balkan politics.*

In preparing the papers the authors were asked to be deliberately provocative and interpretive in order to stimulate discussion and fur-

---

* Two essays which were presented and discussed at the conference have not been included in this volume: James F. Clarke, "Education and National Consciousness in the Balkans" and Alexander Gerschenkron, "Some Aspects of Industrialization in Bulgaria, 1879–1939." The latter essay was included (with an appendix "Industrialization in Bulgaria, Basic Data and Calculations" in a collection of essays by the author, *Economic Backwardness in Historical Perspective* (Cambridge, Mass.: Harvard University Press, 1962).

ther research. The request that the conclusions be based on a study of all Balkan countries led to practical difficulties. Few scholars know the languages of all the states and even those who do find it difficult to follow the literature of their field of specialization in every country. Another problem was the uneven development of scholarly research in the different subjects. For example, until recent years research in history was confined to dynastic, political, and diplomatic questions to the neglect of economic, social, and cultural influences. In anthropology, education, and sociology much still needs to be done.

In attendance at this conference were 75 scholars representing anthropology, economics, geography, government and politics, history, language, literature, music, sociology, and Turcology. Most participants came from American universities and colleges, but there were also representatives from England, Finland, Germany, Greece, and Jugoslavia.

The papers were distributed before the conference met, thereby permitting each participant to read them beforehand. Each paper was discussed by several designated commentators and, after a rebuttal by the authors, an open discussion followed. The authors were subsequently provided with transcripts of the comments, and each was at liberty to modify or revise his paper.

The conference, the first of its kind in the United States, was sponsored by the Center for Slavic and East European Studies of the University of California, Berkeley. The conference itself was made possible through the financial support of the Joint Committee on Slavic Studies of the American Council of Learned Societies, the Social Science Research Council, and the Institute of International Studies of the University of California, with the Joint Committee providing the major share of the funds.

The transliteration presented problems, since no one system has been developed for the different Balkan languages which is acceptable to all scholars. To provide a degree of uniformity to the volume, the editors have in general followed the Library of Congress system for the Slavic languages, and have adopted a modified form of modern Rumanian, Turkish, and Greek. In proper names the form used in the country of national origin has been taken except where a generally recognized Western spelling exists. It is thus Belgrade, not Beograd,

and Jassy, not Iaşi. The editors and not the authors are responsible
for the transliterations and spellings.

The editors wish to express their particular appreciation to Professors Peter K. Christoff and Jozo Tomasevich of San Francisco State
College and to Professor Wayne S. Vucinich of Stanford University
for their valuable coöperation in the formulation of the basic idea of
the conference and for their assistance in the many details associated
with the meetings. Professor Harold Kirkpatrick of the University
of Nevada and Mr. Frederick Kellogg aided greatly in the organization and administration of the conference. Mrs. Eileen Grampp and
Mrs. Kathleen Tucker, secretaries of the Center for Slavic Studies,
University of California, gave generously of their time and efforts.
Our special appreciation is due Mr. Myron Greene who prepared the
index and assisted in many other respects. In the final preparation of
this manuscript for publication, Mr. Max E. Knight of the University
of California Press gave outstanding editorial advice and showed his
usual patience and understanding of the many problems connected
with a collection of this kind. In conclusion, it should be mentioned
that since the majority of these papers were completed before the
meeting in June, 1960, publications concerning these topics and developments in the Balkan countries after that date have not been included.

January, 1963   C. & B. J.

CONTENTS

INTRODUCTION

Charles and

Barbara Jelavich

Despite the multitude of works available on the various Balkan countries few attempts have been made to write on Balkan problems from the point of view of the entire peninsula. Among the Balkan historians, in particular, localism and regionalism have been emphasized to the virtual exclusion of a view of the area in general. This development is best illustrated in Jugoslavia, where before 1941 only one significant work, Vladimir Ćorović, *Istorija Jugoslavije* [*History of Jugoslavia*] was produced as against a wealth of research on Serbia, Croatia, Slovenia, Dalmatia, Bosnia-Hercegovina, Montenegro, Macedonia, and the Vojvodina. Moreover, much that has hitherto been written has been strongly influenced by the intense nationalism of the nineteenth century and by the legacy of conflict among the Balkan peoples themselves. History has nurtured a tradition of emphasis upon diversity and conflict.

Yet despite this condition the Balkan peninsula does represent a unity in its historical, social, economic, political, and cultural development, especially since the era of liberation from Ottoman control. Although the national groups offer much contrast, and although generalizations valid for all peoples are often difficult to make, the papers presented in this volume are in this direction. The foundation for the basic unity of the peninsula is shown in the contribution on the common historical tradition of the Balkan peoples. Situated at the crossroads of Europe and Asia, the area was the birthplace of two of the world's greatest civilizations—the ancient Greek and the Byzantine. By the sixteenth century the peninsula had fallen under Ottoman control. In the late eighteenth and early nineteenth centuries the peoples shared in the common goal of seeking to overthrow Ottoman domination and to establish national states with representative governments. Again in the present day they are joined by a mutual desire to escape from foreign rule and to achieve the material standards of life enjoyed by the Western nations.

Certainly of the greatest significance to the course of developments in the Balkans and to the shaping of a common mold of life were the long years of Ottoman administration, an experience in which all Balkan nations participated. Under Muslim rule each religious group was organized as a *millet* (religious unit). The Orthodox were regarded as belonging to one religious body, and national distinctions were disregarded. The Patriarch at Constantinople thus provided the political as well as the spiritual leadership of the subject peoples. This unity was broken only in the era of national liberation when the traditional national Orthodox churches became instruments of local patriotism and turned against both the Ottoman Empire and the Ecumenical Patriarchate.

Ottoman influences over the long years of occupation naturally affected the daily life of the Christian peoples—the food they ate, the clothes they wore, the language they spoke, and, most important, their habits of mind. In every Balkan state the local population developed an attitude of distrust toward authority and of indifference toward the concept of civil responsibility. Moreover, the corruption and deception in political life, a condition which characterized Ottoman rule, was accepted as normal and natural. This tragic lesson gained from Ottoman statecraft remains even today a legacy of past history despite the immense political changes of the past century.

In addition to their common experience of Ottoman rule, the Balkan peoples were united in the nineteenth century in their pursuit of a similar goal—national liberation and the modernization of their political, economic, and social life. Although the struggle for these aims resulted in the political fragmentation of the peninsula and in war and discord, the movements throughout the Balkans had basically similar characteristics. For instance, in all the states foreign influences played a major role both in the practical achievement of national independence and in the type of government established in the new states. Tsarist Russia, more than any other country, was responsible for the physical liberation of the Balkan peoples because it was the Russian armies that broke the military power of the Ottoman Empire. In both

Russia and the West it was believed that the racial, religious, and cultural ties between Russia and the Balkan states were sufficiently strong to assure Russian domination once Turkish rule was overthrown. Initially the policies of Russia and her great power adversaries were conditioned by this assumption.

However, once the immediate weight of Turkish occupation was removed, the Balkan states found that Russia had little to offer outside of military assistance. Not tsarist autocracy, but Western liberal constitutional government was the political pattern adopted by the new states. Besides, the attainment of the level of Western economic development and the standard of living enjoyed there became a goal of Balkan aspirations. Modernization could only be attained through the study of Western science and technology. Thus, although Russian aid on the battlefield was accepted, it was the civilization of Western and Central Europe that the Balkan leaders attempted to introduce into their lands and to graft on to a native culture that was basically Byzantine but modified by centuries of Muslim domination.

Of the two goals of the nineteenth century, liberation and modernization, only the former was attained. Modernization thus remains the problem of the present era. Today the Balkan states have adopted different means of achieving this common aim. They are now divided not only into three great political groupings but into the same number of economic divisions. Greece is the only state that has retained her prewar economic pattern, and this because of financial aid from the West, especially from the United States. Jugoslavia is following a road to socialism and economic independence, but also with economic support from the capitalist world. In contrast, Bulgaria and Rumania (and in theory at least, Albania) are adapting their economies to the Soviet model. The Balkans thus offer the example of three competing economic systems. However, whereas before 1941 Russia had little to offer the outside world in science and technology, her later spectacular advances, particularly in rocket and space research, have placed her, at least in the eyes of the people of the area, on an equal footing with the West. The latter, therefore, no longer has a monopoly on the exportation and dissemination of scientific and technological knowledge.

A common pattern in the Balkans since the age of Ottoman domination can also be found in the realm of literature and education.

Once the control of the Orthodox Church over the schools was removed, the secular governments turned to the West for the models
for their new systems. Students and future teachers went preferably
to Western universities for their education and brought home similar
experiences and standards to be utilized in the educational institutions
of their own nations. In the same manner, the literary efforts of the
Balkan peoples passed through a romantic-nationalistic phase at the
time of the struggle for national independence, to the more recent
emphasis on general social and economic conditions. Again this work
was strongly influenced by European movements in general.

In the modern period all Balkan states have shared in another
characteristic development and one which has earned for them the
reputation of being the tinder box of Europe. Weak and divided
among themselves they have become an area of power conflict. Although throughout the nineteenth and twentieth centuries various
schemes were proposed aiming at some sort of Balkan federation, no
idea of unity was sufficiently powerful to override the traditional local
nationalism. Consequently, in the nineteenth century the Balkan states
became pawns in the quarrels between the great empires, Russia,
Austria, Germany, and Britain, with France and Italy also involved.
At present this situation is modified only in the sense that the struggle
is now between two blocs, Soviet Russia and the West.

Although foreign influence in these areas has frequently been
measured by nonmilitary criteria, the decisive fact has always been
force. The Turks imposed Ottoman domination through their superior
arms; communism was imposed through Soviet military intervention.
Tito's policy of independent socialism is largely successful because of
the direct military aid offered by the United States. Peace was achieved
and prevails in Greece today because of American arms. Thus all
Balkan states are semidependent areas whose fate is determined directly or indirectly by the great powers.

In addition to the discussion of the common traditions of the
Balkans, the contributions emphasize the problem of transition. Here
again the pattern is similar. All Balkan peoples sought the road to
modernization, and all encountered similar difficulties. The predominantly rural and backward Ottoman economic system had offered
little experience in the adoption of new ways of life. In this respect
the difficulties that arose were similar to those encountered by the

underdeveloped areas in the entire world. Moreover, some aspects of Balkan tradition made transition to other forms difficult. With a historical heritage of a basically Byzantine civilization, influenced by Ottoman domination, the peoples could not readily understand the ideological principles of the West, although they were willing to adopt the outward aspects. They desired the power and wealth of the industrial nations, but they endeavored to achieve their goals without destroying their own qualities and characteristics. This feeling remains today. Whereas all Balkan peoples seek to acquire the material rewards of the more developed societies, none wish to see their own traditions, customs, and standards submerged in the process of modernization.

THE GEOPOLITICS OF

THE BALKANS

Huey Louis Kostanick

From the southeastern part of Europe a jagged, mountainous peninsula stretches out into the Eastern Mediterranean basin between the Adriatic and Black Seas. This peninsula is separated from Asia Minor by the narrow waters of the Turkish Straits, a strategic gateway separating Europe from Asia.

This is the Balkans, a complex and picturesque region of diverse physical landscapes and equally diverse peoples. Over the centuries, these lands and peoples have faced severe political upheavals and disastrous conquests. The long history of suppression and strife has left a bitter legacy of mutual animosity and distrust between nations and between peoples. Too often overemphasis of local cultural and political differences has triumphed over more sensible movements of coöperation and mutual aid in the face of common problems. Indeed, so marked has been the historical turbulence of the area that the term "to Balkanize" has come to mean fractionization into small inimical units.

Yet these difficulties have not been due to internal frictions alone but have also been engendered in great part by the political aspirations and military conquests of foreign powers during centuries. To the Balkans came the Romans and later the Turks, to be followed by Austrians, Russians, and British, and, in more recent times, by Germans, Italians, Frenchmen, and finally by Americans.

In geopolitical terms, the Balkans have been historically an unstable area of friction and conquest, thus posing two basic questions: why so much internal friction and fragmentation and why such a continuous history of foreign occupation and intervention? The answers lie in the

complex interplay of geography and history, a situation in which the
Turkish Empire played a key role because of its long occupation of
the Balkans from the fourteenth century into the first decades of the
twentieth. In this period Balkan nationalism was born; in it the present
Balkan states grew into their present territories and developed their
present unfulfilled territorial ambitions.

The word "Balkan" means "mountain" in Turkish. The name is well
chosen, because the peninsula is dominated by massive mountain
chains and knots from the Dinaric Alps of the northwest and S-curved
Carpathians and Transylvanian Alps of the northeast to the Pindus
chains of Greece.

These mountains are broken by a few natural gateways, formed by
river valleys, that connect the Danubian Plain with the Eastern Mediterranean. The most direct route is the Morava-Vardar Corridor that
extends southward from Belgrade at the confluence of the Danube and
the Sava rivers to Salonica on the Aegean Sea. This route also gives
access eastward to Istanbul (Constantinople) from Niš in the Morava
Valley through the Sofia basin and from there down the Maritsa River
to Thrace and the Golden Horn.

Thus, although the peninsula itself is a jumble of mountainous valleys and cul-de-sacs that unquestionably produce local internal isolation for the peoples of the Balkans, the network of passageways has
provided ready access for foreign invaders into and across the Balkans.
It is this geographic paradox of being a facile passageway in a maze
of mountains, that, combined with strategic location at the crossroads
of Europe, Asia, and Africa, lies at the heart of the geopolitics of the
Balkans.[1]

Viewed in its fullest extent as a political bloc of seven countries
(Albania, Bulgaria, Greece, Hungary, Jugoslavia, Rumania and Turkey), the Balkans forms an area of 632,000 square miles (1,639,000
square kilometers)[2] with a population of nearly 90,000,000. But viewed
as a geographical region including European Turkey but excluding
Turkish Asia Minor, the Balkans is a much smaller area of 345,000
square miles (895,300 square kilometers) with a population of 65,000,-
000. (See Table 1.)

---

[1] See Robert Lee Wolf, *The Balkans in Our Time* (Cambridge, Mass.: Harvard
University Press, 1956), pp. 11–20.

[2] For this particular Balkan conference, Hungary, Bessarabia, and northern
Bukovina have been excluded.

THE BALKANS, 1961

MAP 1

These countries have many similarities and common problems. All have essentially the same peasant cultures, which, although they include linguistic and religious differences, contain virtually the same basic philosophies. All have predominantly agricultural economies.

Yet these factors of unity have been submerged in a sea of disunity that has characteristically engulfed the Balkans, and has made the region a zone of perennial conflict accurately dubbed the "powder keg" of the world. The effects of such disunity are evident both internally and externally. Internally, there is political fragmentation into numerous states, which, small as they are, face within themselves critical regional and ethnic frictions, that are further aggravated by

TABLE 1

POPULATION AND AREA

Country	Date of census	Population	1958 Estimate	Annual percentage increase (1953–58)	Area (square miles)
Albania	October, 1955	1,391,499	1,507,000	3.0	11,022
Bulgaria	December, 1956	7,613,709	7,728,000	1.0	42,768
Greece	April 1951	7,632,801	8,173,000[a]	0.9	51,182
Hungary	January, 1960	9,977,870[b]	9,857,000	0.6	35,919
Rumania	February, 1956	17,489,450	18,059,000	1.4	91,698
Jugoslavia	March, 1953	16,991,449	18,189,000	1.3	98,766
Turkey	October, 1955	24,064,763[c]	25,932,000	2.7	301,381[c]
European	October, 1955	1,979,000	2,128,000		9,068
Asiatic	October, 1955	22,143,000	23,804,000		287,117
TOTALS					
Including European Turkey only		63,018,541	65,641,000		345,639
Including Asiatic Turkey		85,161,541	89,445,000		632,736

[a] Estimate of questionable reliability. [b] Provisional figure. [c] These figures do not exactly total up the individual figures for European and Asiatic Turkey in the *Yearbook*.
SOURCE: United Nations, *Demographic Yearbook, 1959* (New York: United Nations, 1960), pp. 120–124.

an astonishing melange of territorial disputes and claims. Externally, disunity is evidenced by the multifarious alliances that have been made with diverse and often antipathetic foreign powers and by past conquest and foreign occupation.

BASES OF TERRITORIAL CONFLICT

One of the most important seeds of conflict is the diverse pattern of historical development of the Balkan states, which were formed in their present structure only in 1919 after centuries of control as parts of the Ottoman, Austro-Hungarian, and Russian empires. During that long struggle for independence and recognition, strong animosities were engendered over territories occupied and then lost to each other as the fortunes of war and empire changed. Thus was born the thorny web of "problem areas" that enmeshes the Balkans and prejudices Balkan actions in peace and in war. In addition, the conflict in influences and aspirations of foreign powers have led to actions inside and outside the Balkans which strongly and directly affected Balkan affairs.

This essay focuses on the problem areas of the Balkans. Yet one event of Balkan history had so critical an effect on subsequent Balkan problems that it needs be spotlighted first. That event was the Congress of Berlin in 1878 where the great powers of Europe drastically revised the Treaty of San Stefano that had partitioned Ottoman lands earlier in the same year. The Congress of Berlin made of Bulgaria an irredentist nation that in the Balkan Wars and in both World Wars sought to rectify the losses sustained at the congress.[3] (See Map 2.)

The Treaty of San Stefano had been signed in March, 1878, between a defeated Turkey and a victorious Russia. Under the treaty, the sultan recognized the independence of Serbia, Montenegro, and Rumania, but Albania, although given autonomy, was to remain a nominal part

---

[3] These events have been the subject of numerous subsequent studies. For detailed analyses see W. N. Medlicott, *The Congress of Berlin and After: A Diplomatic History of the Near Eastern Settlement, 1878–1880* (London: Methuen, 1938) and Robert Howard Lord, "The Congress of Berlin" in *Three Peace Congresses of the Nineteenth Century* (Cambridge, Mass.: Harvard University Press, 1919), pp. 47–69. Also H. B. Sumner, *Russia and the Balkans, 1870–1880* (Oxford: Clarendon Press, 1937).

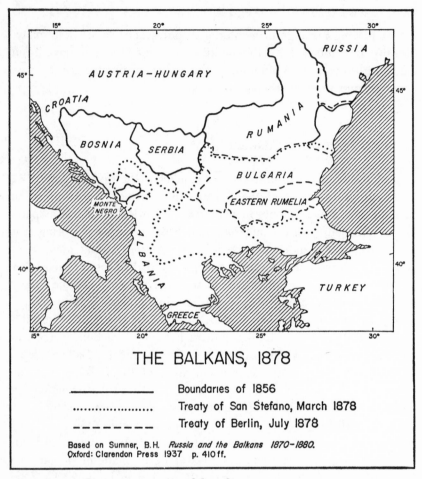

THE BALKANS, 1878

————————	Boundaries of 1856
····················	Treaty of San Stefano, March 1878
– – – – – –	Treaty of Berlin, July 1878

Based on Sumner, B.H. *Russia and the Balkans 1870–1880.*
Oxford: Clarendon Press 1937 p. 410 ff.

MAP 2

of the Ottoman Empire. The greatest change was the creation of Bulgaria, whose borders coincided roughly with those of Tsar Simeon's medieval empire, although Bulgaria was to be given only autonomy and not complete independence.

Actually the Bulgars had done little to win the war, but Russia felt that formation of a sizable Bulgarian state would give Russia a position of control in the Balkans, thus advance Russia's ambitions for control of the Turkish Straits. The new Bulgaria was given northern Thrace, although the Aegean coast of Thrace remained in Turkish hands. A Bulgarian exit to the Aegean Sea was provided by giving Bulgaria most of Macedonia including the mouth of the Vardar and the mouth of the Mesta, although excluding Salonica. Westward the boundaries were extended beyond Lake Ohrid and northward along the crest of the Šar Planina.

There were provisions concerning other Balkan states but this particular creation of a Greater Bulgaria aroused the ire of Britain and Austria-Hungary both of which, for reasons of their own, had attempted to prevent such a development over the course of a century.

The Treaty of Berlin was signed in July of 1878, drastically revising the provisions of San Stefano. Greater Bulgaria was destroyed by returning the lands adjacent to the Aegean to the Turks and by creating a Turkish-ruled province of Eastern Rumelia. This loss was not compensated in the minds of the Bulgarians by creation of the autonomous state of Bulgaria between the Danube River and the Balkan mountains.

Thus the Treaty of Berlin provides a classical example of the internal geopolitical effects of foreign events. In a similar fashion the Treaty of Trianon of 1920, which dismembered the "Greater Hungary" of the Austro-Hungarian Empire, also made of Hungary a discontented "revisionist" state with territorial conflicts with each of her neighbors.[4] (See Map 3.)

In addition to the dissension created by history, strategic importance is a critical factor in the development of Balkan problem areas. Although strategic values change, some routes have retained their basic value over centuries. The outstanding examples of such persistency are the Morava-Vardar Corridor for land communications and the Bosphorus and Dardanelles for sea communications. This is why Macedonia and the Straits have been critical areas for so long.[5]

No less significant is the role of Balkan ethnic complexity, which

---

[4] For a Hungarian point of view see C. A. Macartney, *Hungary* (London: Earnest Benn, 1934).

[5] For a stimulating hypothesis of the relationship of state policy conditions and geographical proximity see Howard E. Koch, Jr., Robert C. North, and Dina A. Zinnes, "Some Theoretical Notes on Geography and International Conflict," *The Journal of Conflict Resolution*, IV (March, 1960), 4–14. This uses the Balkans as a specific example.

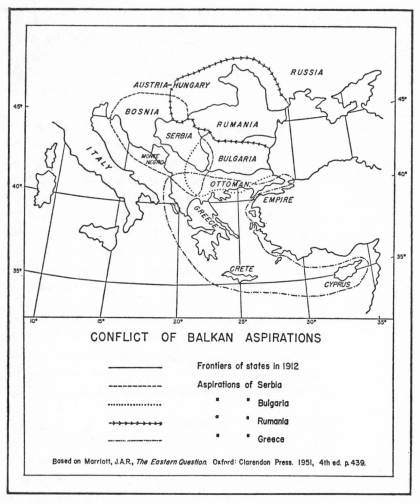

CONFLICT OF BALKAN ASPIRATIONS

———————	Frontiers of states in 1912
– – – – – – –	Aspirations of Serbia
••••••••••••••••	" " Bulgaria
→–→–→–→–→	" " Rumania
–••–••–••–••	" " Greece

Based on Marriott, J.A.R., *The Eastern Question.* Oxford: Clarendon Press. 1951, 4th ed. p. 439.

MAP 3

Permission received to use this map published in *The Journal of Conflict Resolution*, Vol. 4, March, 1960, p. 6.

stems from the long series of racial invasions of the Balkans and the isolation and protection afforded by mountain barriers. Such intermixture of peoples and of cultural traits makes boundary delimitations most difficult and can be used to support irredentist claims.

Economic value also has some significance, although it has played a secondary role.

PROBLEM AREAS OF THE BALKANS

The problem areas of today are a result of the interaction of these basic factors. They remain constant sources of disunity among Balkan nations and no permanent solutions have yet been found. During periods of amity between countries, territorial problems lie dormant and are temporarily amicably resolved or tolerated. But in times of crisis, both local and international, territorial aspirations are revived and another phase is added to the struggle over territories. It is precisely this feature of changeability of attitude that makes it so necessary to under-

MAP 4

stand individual areas in their relation to Balkan national issues, especially in the present international situation in which the Balkans are a
contact point of the two major powers and could conceivably again
set the world afire. (See Map 4.)

In reference to ethnic statistics on problem areas, a strong word
must be expressed about the "numbers game." In support of individual
claims, contestants seem invariably to support their contentions with
statistics, which at times seem to have been miraculously conjured by
sympathetic genii. Such statistics become even more suspect when
one attempts to rationalize the separate tabulations, especially of
ethnic composition. In many cases, this is impossible. Therefore it is
best to adopt a somewhat sanguine approach to the problem by caution and a healthy scepticism of the definitive value of the statistical
table—a procedure which to the uninitiated in the ways of the Balkans
may seem unscientific and even sinful in these days of belief in the
scientific reliability of the statistical table, especially if carried out to
two decimal points. In the discussions of the problem areas which
follow, statistics have been used to demonstrate points of view rather
than to be evidence of incontrovertible proof of the existing ethnic
structure.

Macedonia

Macedonia is the classical hotspot of the Balkans, an area historically
contested by Bulgarians, Serbs, Greeks, Albanians, and Turks. Occupied by various peoples from an early day, it achieved fame in ancient
history as the seat of empire of Alexander of Macedon and in Biblical
days for the journeys of St. Paul in answer to the poetic appeal, "Come
over unto Macedonia and help us!"—a cry that has echoed for many
centuries.

Macedonia came into prominence in the eighteenth century as a
result of the rise of nationalistic movements by the Bulgars, Greeks,
and Serbs for the control of Macedonia. Although initially proclaimed
as an effort to secure independence for' the Macedonians, the "Macedonian Question" was soon transformed into individual ambitions for
political annexation and control of Macedonia by the neighboring
states, as well as non-bordering states such as Rumania and Italy.[6]

[6] See Huey Louis Kostanick, "Macedonia—A Study in Political Geography"
(doctoral dissertation, Worcester: Clark University, 1947).

The early decades of the nineteenth century saw the upsurge of nationalist movements in the Balkans aimed at wresting eventual independence from the Ottoman Empire or at gaining greater ethnic recognition with attendant political, religious, and economic privileges from the Sublime Porte. Since these objectives were both based upon ethnic distinction, intensified effort was focused upon criteria for ethnic identification and upon geographic distribution of ethnic groups in the Balkans. Associated with this was the sharpened interest of the rest of Europe in the "Eastern Question"—the future of the Ottoman Empire and the disposition of Ottoman territories.

The result was a rash of ethnographic studies of the Balkans purporting to show their "true" ethnic structure. Most of the studies, whether published in text or as maps, were tendentious. Indeed one can say that the maps were only as good as the intentions of the map maker—and in most cases the map maker started out to prove that his cause was the just one and that his ethnic group was in the dominant position.[7] As might be expected, Macedonia as a coveted area of controversial ethnic composition was a prime target for ethnic claims.

Out of these efforts came two significant results. The first was a newer and more realistic knowledge of the ethnic structure of the Balkans and of ethnic geographic distribution. The other, of international rather than regional scope, was a clarification of primary ethnic criteria in relationship to political identification and affiliation.

Under the Ottoman Empire, religion was the key factor in political identification. When the Turks took over the Balkans they granted official recognition to the Orthodox Church as a *millet,* or national-religious community, which could treat directly with the Sublime Porte for the welfare of its adherents. In the earlier period of Turkish rule, the Serbian Patriarchate of Peć and the Bulgarian Patriarchate of Ohrid had also been recognized but both had been abolished in the eighteenth century. Therefore all Orthodox Christians were considered to be part of the *Rumi millet* or Greek Orthodox Church and hence politically Greeks. For this reason, the battle for national consciousness and national independence of the Serbs, Bulgarians, and Rumanians included the attempt to establish separate churches to gain recognition as *milleti* other than Greek. This caused a struggle not

[7] See H. R. Wilkinson, *Maps and Politics: A Review of the Ethnographic Cartography of Macedonia* (Liverpool: University Press, 1951).

only with the Turks but with the heads of the Greek Orthodox Church in Constantinople, commonly called the Phanariote for the district in which the Greek bishops lived.

The Serbs were the first to gain autonomy in 1829, when Turkey gave recognition to the Serbian principality under the Treaty of Adrianople. For the Bulgarians the critical period came in 1870–1872 when the Bulgarian Exarchate was finally established as a *millet*. This was followed by the creation of a "Greater Bulgaria" at the Treaty of San Stefano where most of Macedonia was included—only to be lost again at the Treaty of Berlin and not to be reöccupied except temporarily in the Balkan Wars and in the First and Second World wars. But for Bulgaria, Macedonia thus became its "terra irredenta," unredeemed but not forgotten.

With the establishment of separate countries and separate churches the older focus on religion as the major index of political affiliation gave way to language and to a lesser extent to customs and historical affiliation.

The end of the First World War saw Macedonia divided among four Balkan states. Of its approximately 26,150 square miles, about half (13,300 square miles) went to Greece. Jugoslavia gained nearly as much (10,100 square miles), but Bulgaria obtained only a small area (2,600 square miles) and Albania annexed but a tiny strip along its eastern border. (See Map 4.)

Geographically, Macedonia is an ill-defined region of the Vardar (Axios) and Struma river basins on the northern shores of the Aegean Sea. It is primarily a mountainous region cut by valleys of the Vardar and Struma. Its southern part is formed by the broad coastal plains along the northern Aegean. Climatically, this is a transition region between the continental climate of the interior and the true Mediterranean climate of the shores of the north Aegean. Thus it has the cold, snowy winters of the interior and the dry summers of the coastal regime. Economically, it is one of the most valuable agricultural areas of the Balkans, an excellent producer of wheat and other grains, tobacco, fruits and vegetables. It also has great strategic value as the crossroads of the north-south Morava-Vardar Corridor and the east-west *Via Egnatia*. Its largest city, Salonica,[8] is the best port on the northern Aegean coast, a port which could serve as an excellent com-

---

[8] P. Risal, *La Ville Convoitée* (Paris: Perrin, 1918).

mercial Mediterranean outlet for the interior were it not for the barrier effect of boundaries and divergent political philosophies. Its Jugoslav counterpart is Skoplje (Macedonian: Skopje), the largest city and capital of Jugoslav Macedonia.

Ethnically, Macedonia is a border zone of Bulgars, Serbs, Greeks, Albanians, and Turks. Its transitional character is best evidenced by the majority group, the Macedonian Slavs, who have cultural traits of both the Serbs and the Bulgars and have historically been associated with both the Greeks and the Turks.

Strategic value, historical rights, and ethnic relationship were the key points of contrasting claims. The Bulgarians lay historical claim to Macedonia on grounds of early empires, especially that of Tsar Simeon, and of the Treaty of San Stefano of 1878, which created "Greater Bulgaria." The Bulgarians also insisted that the "Macedonians" were in truth Bulgarians ethnically in reference to language and customs. For example, Macedonians like Bulgarians use the personal pronoun "As" for "I" rather than the Serbian "Ja." During the Turkish rule of Macedonia, Bulgarian influence was quite strong, exerted not only through the usual churches of the Bulgarian Exarchate but also through the institution of Bulgarian schools. An element of terror was added through the dreaded acts of the infamous I.M.R.O. (Internal Macedonian Revolutionary Organization) bands, that included some who sought the creation of an independent Macedonia and others that talked of independence but actually sought annexation by Bulgaria because I.M.R.O. was supported by Bulgarian funds. Until the Second World War Bulgaria insisted that Macedonia was an integral unit, that the Macedonians were Bulgars and that all of Macedonia should be part of Bulgaria.

The Serbs also used language and customs as proof of Serbian affinity, ranging from Macedonian grammar to the existence of the *zadruga*, or communal family, in Macedonia. Historical claims were expressed, based on the fourteenth-century empire of Tsar Stepan Dušan, who used Skoplje as his capital. These Serb claims were dramatically invalidated in the Second World War by Tito's recognition of the Macedonians of Jugoslavia as a separate ethnic group and by the subsequent creation on August 2, 1944, of the "People's Republic of Macedonia," which became one of the federal republics of Jugoslavia.

The Greek case was based upon historical claims to Macedonia

dating back to Alexander of Macedon and early Macedonian tribes, as
well as the long Byzantine period of Balkan rule. During the Turkish
period, the Greeks pointed out, and quite correctly, that the peoples
of Macedonia were mainly adherents of the Greek Orthodox Church
until the creation of the Bulgarian and Serbian churches. To race,
history, and religion, the Greeks added the political and social concepts of "lack of a national consciousness" of "Slavophone" peoples
who were "Greek at heart."

These were the classical arguments used by each in their battle to
annex Macedonia until the final partition of Macedonia after the First
World War. These arguments were pursued in numerous tendentious
publications issued in the Balkans and in other countries of Europe
from Britain to Russia.

But after the First World War, two events signally changed the
Macedonian situation. The first was an exchange of minorities following 1923 between Greece and Turkey, Greece and Bulgaria, and
Jugoslavia and Bulgaria. The most significant exchange took place in
Greek Macedonia, where the Turkish minority was replaced by Greek
immigrants from Turkey. In addition, 96,000 Bulgars left, although
80,000 Slavs elected to stay in Greece and become Greek citizens.[9]
Thus Greek Macedonia became thoroughly Hellenized with the remaining Macedonian Slavs as a distinct minority. Nonetheless Bulgarian sources dispute such statistics with the claim that in the immediate postwar period following the Second World War there were
still more than 258,000 Slavs remaining.[10] Thus Bulgaria has continued
to press its claim to Greek Macedonia in spite of the dramatic ethnic
shift that has taken place.

The second event was the creation in 1944 of the People's Republic
of Macedonia as one of the federal units of Jugoslavia. This gave
recognition to the Macedonians as a separate Slavic group within
Jugoslavia with the right of using "Macedonian" as an official language
and of teaching the language in Macedonian schools, and of publishing newspapers, periodicals, and books in this language.

---

[9] Stephen P. Ladas, *The Exchange of Minorities: Bulgaria, Greece and Turkey*
(New York: Macmillan, 1932), p. 721.

[10] Makedonski Nauchen Institut, *Makedoniia kato prirodno i stopansko tsialo*
[*Macedonia as a Geographical and Economic Unit*], (Sofia: 1945), p. 239.

During the period of early postwar friendship between Bulgaria and Jugoslavia in 1944 when there was even discussion of uniting Bulgaria and Jugoslavia in a "Balkan union," it seemed possible that Bulgarian Macedonia (Pirin Macedonia) might be merged with Jugoslav Macedonia as a separate federal unit.[11] But as the idea of such a union quickly cooled, Bulgaria clamped a tight hold on Pirin Macedonia to the dismay of the Jugoslav Macedonians and, in an attempt to stave off any possibilities of the annexation of Pirin Macedonia into the Jugoslav Macedonian Republic, Bulgarian official policy on the existence of Macedonians was changed completely with the new insistence that there were no "Macedonians" in Pirin Macedonia, only Bulgarian citizens. Yet, in an entirely inconsistent argument, Bulgaria continued to lay claim to Greek Macedonia, both on ethnic and strategic grounds.

In 1947, this impasse between Bulgaria and Jugoslavia was again temporarily eased when the Bulgarians permitted Jugoslav Macedonians to sell books and teach in Pirin Macedonia, although still resisting Jugoslav efforts to annex the Bulgarian portion. But this amicable state was soon blasted apart violently in 1948 by Jugoslavia's expulsion from good standing in the Communist elite of Eastern Europe. Since that time both nations have launched virulent polemics toward each other over their respective treatment of Macedonians.

A recent example of the antipathy of the two former friends is illustrated by the appearance of Jugoslav articles in *Borba* of Belgrade and in *Nova Makedonija* of Skopje in May, 1961, that 5,000 "Aegean Macedonians" who had been living in Poland since 1949, presumably as refugees from the Greek civil war, had been deported from Poland to Bulgaria, where they had been resettled in Pirin Macedonia near the Greek border.[12] As was to be expected, this aroused the ire of Greece against Bulgaria, bringing another crisis in their mutual relations and reviving the problem of Macedonia.

The reaction of Greece has been to accuse both the Bulgarians and the Jugoslave of wanting to annex Greek Macedonia and of falsifying the whole problem of a united Macedonia. One of the current Greek arguments is that

[11] For an excellent discussion of the Communist views of Macedonia during 1945–1949 see Elisabeth Barker, *Macedonia: Its Place in Balkan Power Politics* (London: Royal Institute of International Affairs, 1950).

[12] *East Europe*, X (July, 1961), 2, 9, 29, 41, and 45.

The term "Macedonia" is to-day a geographical term only, it is not an ethnological one. Ever since the ancient Macedonians, together with all the other Greek phylae, merged into the great Hellenism of Hellenistic, Roman and Byzantine times there has not existed a separate Macedonian nation; neither is the term conceivable to represent a nation to-day. By the will of History the soil of that great ancient Macedonia is now divided among three peoples; Greeks, Yugoslavs and Bulgarians, each part having been attached to each of the three Balkan States respectively, through a series of international Treaties.[13]

In the same publication the author maintains that use of the term "Macedonians" for the Slavs of Jugoslav Macedonia is deliberately misleading and that they should be called "Bugari" or Bulgarians, an item undoubtedly calculated to arouse the ire of Jugoslavs who would want to have the term Bulgarian applied least of all. To further cement the claim of a Hellenized Greek Macedonia, the statement is made:

As is well-known, the Macedonia included at present in the Greek realm is inhabited by 1,700,000 people (census of 1951). Out of these only a few thousands speak Slavic and all are conscious of being Greek; for those who were conscious of being Slav left Greece of their own free will after the Treaty of Neuilly.[14]

The clearest recognition of the Macedonians as an ethnic group has come from Jugoslavia. The census of 1953 lists 893,247 Macedonians of a total population of 16,936,573.[15] Of a total of 1,304,514 in the People's Republic of Macedonia, 860,699 were listed as Macedonians and 35,112 as Serbs, but only 920 Bulgarians and 848 Greeks.[16] (See Table 2.)

Thus today Macedonia is a divided land with each segment displaying a different ethnic structure. Greek Macedonia is the largest area, and there is no doubt that the population of 1,700,000 consists primarily of Greeks. As Greece does not officially recognize the Macedonians

---

[13] Nic. P. Andriotes, *The Confederate State of Skopje and Its Language* (Athens: 1957). Similar ideas are expressed by the same author in Society for Macedonian Studies, Institute for Balkan Studies, "History of the Name 'Macedonia,'" *Balkan Studies* (Thessaloniki: 1960), I, 143–148.

[14] "History of the Name 'Macedonia,'" p. 43.

[15] Savezni Zavod za Statistiku, Federativna Narodna Republika Jugoslavija, *Popis Stanovništva, 1953* [*Population Census, 1953*], Knjiga I: *Vitalna i Etnička Obeležja* [Volume I: *Vital and Ethnic Characteristics*], (Beograd: 1959), p. 51. Hereafter cited as *Popis Stanovništa*.

[16] *Ibid.*, pp. 82–83.

TABLE 2

ETHNIC COMPOSITION OF THE PEOPLE'S REPUBLIC OF MACEDONIA,
JUGOSLAVIA

(1953 Census)

Macedonians	860,699
Turks	203,938
Albanians	162,524
Serbs	35,112
Gypsies	20,462
Vlachs	8,668
Croats	2,770
Montenegrins	2,526
Slovenes	983
Bulgarians	920
Greeks	848
Russians	672
Others	...
TOTAL	1,304,514

SOURCE: Federal Bureau of Statistics. The Federated People's Republic of Jugoslavia, *Census of Population, 1953*. Vol. I, Vital and Ethnic Statistics (Belgrade, 1959), pp. 82–83.

as a separate ethnic group, it is difficult to ascertain the probable number of Macedonians. According to the Greek census of 1951, 41,017 people were listed in all of Greece as Slavic by "mother tongue" but only 10,346 were classified as Slavic "by language usually spoken." [17] One estimate of the number of Macedonian Slavs in Greek Macedonia just before the Second World War was 120,000.[18] In all probability a reasonable estimate for today would be about 125,000.

Similarly the Bulgarian government does not list Macedonians as a separate group. A prewar estimate was 220,000 Slavs in Bulgarian Macedonia;[19] 1956 census statistics issued by Bulgaria list 282,000 persons as the population of Blagoevgrad (formerly Gorna Dzhumaia, capital of Pirin Macedonia) department, which corresponds to Bulgarian Macedonia.[20] (See Table 3.) Hence a reasonable estimate would be 250,000 Macedonians.

---

[17] *Statistical Yearbook of Greece, 1958* (Athens: 1959), p. 21.

[18] Barker, *op. cit.*, p. 12.

[19] *Ibid.*

[20] *Razvitiye Narodnogo Khozaistva Narodnoi Respubliki Bolgarii* [*Development of the National Economy of the People's Republic of Bulgaria*], (Moskva: Vneshtorgizdat, 1958), p. 16.

TABLE 3

Population of Bulgaria and Blagoevgrad (Gorna Dzhumaia) Okrug
(Estimated)

Year	Bulgaria	Blagoevgrad Okrug
1947	7,067,000	254,000
1948	7,139,000	257,000
1949	7,210,000	260,000
1950	7,271,000	264,000
1951	7,285,000	266,000
1952	7,307,000	268,000
1953	7,384,000	271,000
1954	7,467,000	276,000
1955	7,548,000	283,000

SOURCE: U.S. Joint Publications Research Service, *Statistical Yearbook of the People's Republic of Bulgaria, 1956* (New York, 1958), p. 12. This is an American translation of *Statisticheski Godishnik na Narodna Republika Bulgariya* (*Sukrateno Izdanie*), *1956*, published by the Tsentralno Statistichesko Upravlenie pr. Minister-skiya Suvet (Sofia, 1956).

For Macedonia as a whole, then, the estimated population would be a grand total of 3,300,000, of whom about 1,235,000 are Macedonian Slavs.

Thus Macedonia as a divided region still poses a Balkan problem and will continue to be so because of the irreconcilable views of the contestants. It would not be improper to hold that the specific aims and claims of the contestants are not necessarily related to the actual situation existing in Macedonia of today or of the past, but are more attuned to the political exigencies of the moment. Thus it can be held for Macedonia, and indeed for most of the other Balkan problem areas, that the geopolitics of the Macedonian question are more political than geographical and that the intensity of the conflict is directly related to the amity or enmity of political relationships. A fair analysis of present-day Macedonia would be that the most important feature underlying the problem is strategic control of the Morava-Vardar Corridor with its exit to the Aegean Sea and that the ethnic problem of the Macedonians has supplied a handy vehicle for the individual territorial aspirations of the contestants.

It is within this framework of political aspiration versus geographical reality that the problem areas of the Balkans must be viewed.

Trieste and Istria

The problem of Trieste and Istria is similarly based upon strategic geographical location of control of major passageways from the interior to the sea. (See Map 5.) Trieste is a charming city of some 275,000 people[21] situated on a narrow plain backed by high, dry karstic mountains at the head of the Adriatic Sea. An excellent seaport, the city is the best natural outlet to the Mediterranean Sea for the Hun-

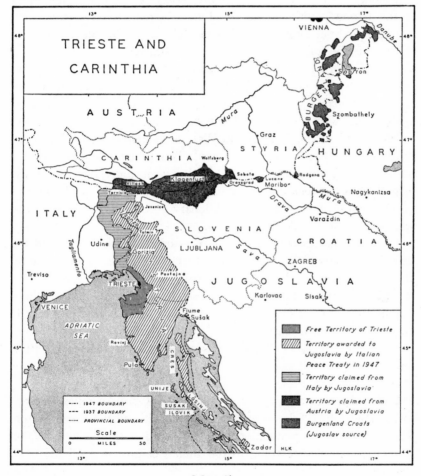

MAP 5

---

[21] According to the census of November 4, 1951, the population of Trieste was 270,164 (*The Statesman's Year-Book, 1960,* p. 1166).

garian basin and Central Europe.[22] It is linked to the interior by a
number of passes through the Dinaric Alps, such as the historically
famous Kruševica (Pear Tree) Pass and the present-day route of the
Postumia Gate followed by both railroad and road between Trieste
and Ljubljana.

During the long reign of Austria-Hungary by the Habsburg monarchy, Trieste was favored economically and developed as a major
port with good railroad connections to Vienna.

Although under Austrian hegemony, Trieste and the adjoining parts
of the Istrian peninsula and the Julian March region to the north
were peopled not by Austrians but by Italians and the Slavic Slovenes
and Croats. Because of the large group of Italians, these areas (called
Venezia Giulia by the Italians), Dalmatia to the south, and Trentino
in the west were viewed as *Italia Irredenta* (unredeemed Italy) by
Italian nationalists. Foremost among these was the poet Gabriele
D'Annunzio, who was born in Dalmatia in 1863 but schooled in Italy.

At the end of the First World War the Austro-Hungarian Empire
broke up and Jugoslavia was created. This precipitated the difficult
problem of establishing a boundary between Jugoslavia and Italy.
Negotiations between the two were interrupted in 1919 by the seizure
of Fiume (Rijeka) by an expeditionary force led by D'Annunzio,
which successfully occupied Fiume.

As was to be expected, both sides pressed claims to Trieste and the
neighboring territory. Italy argued that Trieste was predominantly
Italian-populated and that strategically and economically Trieste
should be part of Italy. Jugoslavia based her claims on the ethnographic principle of Slav predominance in the rural area and on the
Jugoslav need for a maritime outlet to the Adriatic. After long negotiations, the Treaty of Rapallo was signed on November 12, 1920,
although agreement over Fiume was not reached until the Pact of
Rome of January, 1924.

Under these agreements, Italy gained 3,500 square miles of territory that included Trieste, the Istrian peninsula and the Julian March.
These lands had a population of nearly a million, of whom 467,000
were Jugoslavs.[23] According to the Italian census of April 21, 1936,

---

[22] The best detailed study of the Trieste problem is A. E. Moodie, *The Italo-
Yugoslav Boundary* (London: George Philip, 1945).

[23] *Ibid.*, p. 191.

the population of Venezia Giulia was approximately 975,000.[24] Italian ethnic statistics of the area listed 525,000 Italians and 420,000 Slavs, of whom 280,000 were Slovenes and 140,000 Croats.[25]

During this interwar period the Italians made strong efforts to Italianize the Slavic groups. Family names were changed to Italian forms; towns, villages, and street names were Italianized and children in schools were taught in Italian. But the Jugoslavs continued to press their claims that the area was predominantly Slav-populated, with Slovenes in the north and Croats in the south, and that there was even a Slav majority in the cities of Trieste and Fiume.[26]

Economically, the separation of Trieste and Fiume by political boundaries from the economic hinterland had severe repercussions on both cities. Although it was the hope of Italy that Trieste would maintain its position as an economic outlet for Central Europe, trade seriously declined due to various factors, such as political difficulties between Jugoslavia and Italy, the general world depression of the thirties, and the shift of Central European trade to Germany and the North Sea ports.[27] Fiume similarly stagnated because the Jugoslavs deliberately developed the adjacent Jugoslav town of Sušak as a port and also exported goods through other Dalmatian ports, such as Šibenik and Split.

At the end of the Second World War in 1945, the Jugoslavs reasserted claims to Trieste and again used the justification that Trieste was needed by Jugoslavia as an economic outlet and that the Jugoslav hinterland could substantially revive Trieste's economic position.[28]

A peace treaty with Italy was finally concluded in 1947. Under its provisions, most of the Julian March and the Istrian peninsula were

---

[24] *Annuario Statistico Italiano, 1941,* p. 14. Population of 194,431 cited in *Memorandum of the Government of the Democratic Federative Yugoslavia concerning the Question of the Julian March and the Yugoslav Territories under Italy,* 1945, pp. 10–11.

[25] Ferdinando Milone, *Il Confine Orientale* (Napoli: Mario Fiorentino, 1945), pp. 47 and 65–66.

[26] *Memorandum concerning the Question of the Julian March and Other Yugoslav Territories under Italy,* pp. 10–11.

[27] Moodie, *op. cit.,* pp. 215–220.

[28] *Memorandum concerning the Question of the Julian March and Other Yugoslav Territories under Italy,* pp. 12–18, and Anton Melik, *Trieste and North Jugoslavia* (Ljubljana: Research Institute, 1946).

awarded to Jugoslavia.[29] This territory totaled 2,850 square miles with a population of over 500,000.[30] But Jugoslavia still claimed an additional 728 square miles with a population of 199,900, plus the newly created Free Territory of Trieste.[31]

The Free Territory of Trieste established by the Italian peace treaty was to be under the jurisdiction of the Security Council of the United Nations. The Free Territory had an area of approximately 300 square miles.[32] According to an Italian census of 1936, this area had a population of 343,000, of whom 248,000 were in the commune of Trieste.[33]

Under the treaty, Trieste was to be a Free Port operated by an International Commission, and the Free Territory was to have its own currency and, in effect, its own autonomy. In reality, the concept of the Free Territory was never implemented because Trieste became a political pawn in the existing international situation of cold war between East and West. Jugoslavia at that time was a satellite of the Soviet Union, and it was felt by the West that if the Free Territory were dominated by Communist groups Trieste would become another Russian victory. Conversely the Russians and the Jugoslavs felt that if Western groups would come into power, Trieste would fall to Italian persuasion.

The resulting stalemate led to military occupation for nine years:[34] The Free Territory was divided into two zones, Zone A of 84 square miles and Zone B of 217 square miles. Zone A, which included Trieste and the northern part, was placed under the military government ad-

---

[29] For a discussion of the contrasting views of the U.S., United Kingdom, France, and the U.S.S.R. see Wolff, *op. cit.*, pp. 304–313.

[30] An estimate of 700,000 is listed in Frank Lorimer, "Population Changes in Europe, 1938–1947," *Economic Bulletin for Europe*, I: 1 (1949), 11.

[31] Anton Melik, *Jugoslavija* (Ljubljana: Ljubljanska Tiskarna, 1949), p. 7.

[32] *The Statesman's Year-Book, 1955*, p. 1416. Leonard Unger, "The Economy of the Free Territory of Trieste," *Geographical Review*, XXXVII (Oct., 1947), 588, says 276 miles. *The World Almanac, 1951*, p. 349, cites 320 square miles.

[33] Unger, *op. cit.*, p. 593.

[34] For Italian claims during this period see Giorgio Roletto, *Trieste ed i suoi Problemi: Situazione—Tendenze—Prospettive* (Trieste: Eugenio Borsatti Editore, 1952). For Jugoslav views see Edvard Kardelj, *Trieste and Yugoslav-Italian Relations* (New York: Yugoslav Information Center, 1953) V. Sedmak, and J. Mejăk, *Trieste, the Problem Which Agitates the World* (Beograd: Edition Jugoslavija, 1953) and *Who Should Have Trieste?* (Ljubljana: Tiskarna Ljudske Pravice, 1953) issued by the Institute for Questions of Nationality at the University of Ljubljana.

ministration of the United States and the United Kingdom. Zone B, under Jugoslav military government, included the southern part of the Territory along the Istrian peninsula. In Zone A, a census of August, 1953, listed a total of 297,003, of whom 257,858 were Italians and 39,145 Slovenes.[35] A Jugoslav census of Zone B in 1945 gave a total of 67,461 persons, of whom 30,789 were Slavs and 29,672 Italians.

The Jugoslavs immediately included Zone B into general Jugoslav administration creating a new frontier at the Zone A border of Zone B. In Zone A, American and British troops occupied the city and created a somewhat false prosperity with the influx of military expenditures.

Again the resulting stalemate satisfied no one, but following the political breach in 1948 between Jugoslavia and the Soviet Union, a new solution was tried. On October 5, 1954, a Memorandum of Understanding was signed between the United States, United Kingdom, Jugoslavia, and Italy which terminated military government in the two zones. United States and British forces were withdrawn from Zone A on October 25, 1954, and the zone placed under the administration of the Italian government essentially as a part of Italy. A small strip of Zone A was added to Zone B, which became a part of Jugoslavia under ordinary civil administration.[36] These arrangements were approved, in essence, by the Security Council, thus establishing a new phase of the Trieste question, although not creating a final solution because Jugoslavia continues to lay claim to the city, although most of the Julian March and the Istrian peninsula are now in Jugoslavia. Thus the question of Trieste, as that of Macedonia, has not been definitively settled.

Italian Losses in World War II

In addition to the loss of territory in Istria, Italy was forced to relinquish her possessions along the Dalmation coast of Jugoslavia as well as ceding strategic Adriatic islands to Albania and Aegean islands to Greece, thus removing the last vestiges of Italian rule in the Balkans. (See Maps 4 and 5.)

Jugoslavia gained the islands of Cherso (Cres) and Lussin (Lošinj)

---

[35] *The Statesman's Year-Book, 1955*, p. 1416.
[36] *Ibid.*

just south of the Istrian peninsula. Actually these are part of the off-shore group of islands that fringe the Dalmatian coast of Jugoslavia and were peopled mainly by Jugoslavs. According to the Jugoslav census of 1953, these combined islands have an area of approximately 200 square miles with a population of 12,508.[37]

The small island groups of Lagosta (Lastovo) and Pelagosa (Pala-gruza) were similarly ceded to Jugoslavia. The island of Lagosta (see Map 4), given to Italy at the Treaty of Rapallo in 1920, had a strategic position for Italy near the Jugoslav islands of Vis, Korčula, and Mljet. According to an Italian census of 1931, the population included 1,558 persons.[38] The Jugoslav census of 1953 lists the population as but slightly higher, 1,721.[39]

Of greater significance than these small islands was the cession of Zara (Zadar), an urban enclave on the Dalmatian coast. This district of approximately 43 square miles was predominantly Italian-popu-lated, with a reported population of 22,000 in 1936.[40] In 1953 the population of the two administrative districts of Zadar and Zadar Vanjski was 25,606.[41]

Italy also lost the strategic island of Saseno (Sazanit), which guards the eastern end of the 45-mile-wide Strait of Otranto between Albania and Italy and also commands the Albanian port of Valona (Vlonë). This island, less than four square miles in area,[42] was occupied by Italy in the First World War and was legally assigned to Italy by the Italo-Albanian Treaty of August 3, 1920.[43] Reportedly, Saseno, previ-ously an Italian submarine base, was used as a Russian submarine base in the period after the Second World War until 1961, thus pro-viding the unusual situation of a Russian military facility in the Adri-atic.

Besides, Italy ceded the Dodecanese Islands in the eastern Medi-terranean. These had been seized by the Italians in 1912 following a

---

[37] *Popis Stanovništva*, 1953, XIII, 107.

[38] *Enciclopedia Italiana*, XX, 379.

[39] *Popis Stanovništva*, 1953, XIII, 132.

[40] Istituto Centrale di Statistica del Regno d'Italia. *Annuario Statistico Italiano, 1941* (Roma, 1941), p. 14.

[41] *Popis Stanovništva*, 1953, XIII, 182.

[42] *The World Almanac, 1951*, p. 334.

[43] *Enciclopedia Italiana* (Roma: 1936), XXX, 885.

war with Turkey, although the islands were populated predominantly by Greeks—100,000 Greeks and 12,000 persons of other nationalities.[44] In spite of Greek protests, the islands were ceded to Italy by the Treaty of Lausanne in 1923. Strategically situated in the eastern Mediterranean near Turkey, Cyprus, and the Middle East, the Dodecanese include approximately fifty islands, although only fourteen, containing an area of 1,305 square miles,[45] are permanently settled. Of particular concern to the Turks is the island of Castellorizzo, which lies only a few miles off the Turkish coast. The Dodecanese were awarded to Greece at the Paris Conference of Foreign Ministers on June 27, 1946, and were formally taken over on March 7, 1948. According to a census of October 19, 1947, the population numbered 115,343[46] and in 1951 was reportedly 121,480 persons.[47]

The result of these cessions was to remove Italy as a Balkan power after the Second World War but Italy has continued to press for the return of the former Italian territories on the Adriatic coast.

Jugoslav Claims to Austrian Carinthia, Styria, and Burgenland

At the end of the Second World War, the new Jugoslav regime headed by Tito asserted various claims to neighboring territories from both Italy and Austria as had the former Jugoslav regime at the end of the First World War following the creation of the Jugoslav state. With regard to the claims against Italy, Jugoslavia was quite successful. But in regard to claims against Austria, the Jugoslavs failed.

On the northwest, Jugoslavia is hemmed in by picturesque mountain ranges that because of their height and ruggedness might suggest "natural boundaries" separating not only political units but also ethnic groups. This, however, is not the case because Austrians and Slovenes were intermixed in a wide area making exact boundary delimitation difficult.

Thus in both Carinthia and Styria Jugoslavs could claim ethnic

---

[44] Isaiah Bowman, *The New World: Problems in Political Geography* (New York: World Book Company, 1928), pp. 402–403.

[45] *The Statesman's Year-Book, 1950,* p. 1076.

[46] United Nations, Statistical Office, Department of Economic and Social Affairs, *Demographic Yearbook, 1948* (Lake Success: 1949), p. 82.

[47] *Statistical Yearbook of Greece, 1958,* p. 15.

kinship. Jugoslavia was awarded a part of Styria by the Treaty of St. Germain of September 10, 1919, which also provided for a plebiscite in the Klagenfurt area of Carinthia.[48] The plebiscite, divided into two zones, included 755 square miles and a population of 127,000.[49] Although the southern zone was predominantly Slovene-populated, Austria got 59 percent of the vote,[50] thus precluding the necessity of a vote in the northern zone which otherwise might have become an enclave in Austria.

Jugoslav claims were reasserted at the Council of Foreign Ministers on February 18, 1946. Jugoslavia demanded 954 square miles of Carinthia, which she maintained included 120,000 Slovenes of a total population of 180,000. Three border areas of Styria—Soboth (*Sobota*), Leutschach (*Lučane*), and Radkersburg (*Radgona*)—were also claimed with a combined area of 50 square miles and a total population of 10,000, including 6,000 Slovenes.[51]

In addition, the Jugoslavs asked that the Burgenland Croats, numbering 70,000 according to Jugoslav statistics, be given special autonomous rights under Austria or that there be an exchange of minorities if the Carinthia and Styria areas were assigned to Jugoslavia.[52]

Regardless of the value of Jugoslavia's claims, there was little chance that there would be favorable action in terms of boundary rectification because of the agreement in Moscow in 1943 of the four major Allies that Austria would be restored to its pre-Anschluss borders. And even though the Soviet Union offered some support to Jugoslav demands, even this political help failed following Jugoslav-Russian difficulties in 1948 with the result that in 1950 Marshal Tito publicly soft-pedaled such claims. The final denouément to Jugoslav aspirations came in 1955 when on May 15 the Austrian State Treaty was signed, based on the borders of January 1, 1938. Jugoslavia's ac-

[48] Robert J. Kerner, *Yugoslavia* (Berkeley and Los Angeles: University of California Press, 1949), p. 101.

[49] Sarah Wambaugh, *Plebiscites Since the World War* (Washington, D.C.: Carnegie Endowment for International Peace, 1933), I, 179.

[50] *Ibid.*, pp. 198–200.

[51] *The Question of 200,000 Yugoslavs in Austria: The Slovene Carinthia and the Burgenland Croats* (Beograd: 1947).

[52] *Memorandum du Gouvernement de la Republique Federative Populaire de Yougoslavie concernant la Carinthie Slovène, les régions frontalières slovènes de Styrie et les Croates du Burgenland* (Beograd: 1946), p. 8.

ceptance of this treaty officially ended Jugoslavia's demands for outright annexation.[53]

Nonetheless Jugoslavia continues to display marked interest in Austrian treatment of the Slovene minority in the Klagenfurt plebiscite area estimated by Jugoslavs to contain 35,000 to 70,000 Slovenes. Austrian authorities claim a smaller minority. In the 1951 Austrian census, people were grouped according to the *Umgangssprache*, or language of normal daily use, under nine linguistic headings, these being German, Slovene, Windish (a Slovene dialect) and six combinations of the three. Of a total of 175,000 people in the plebiscite area, only 7,000 were listed as speaking Slovene only.[54] Obviously the ninefold classification masked rather than clarified the question of ethnic status because a continuing battle over the teaching of Slovene as well as German in some schools indicates that this small showing is not indicative of the actual number of the minority group.

Hungarian Claims against Jugoslavia

Not only has Jugoslavia asserted territorial claims against her neighbors, her neighbors have also pressed territorial demands against her. The most important of these is the Hungarian protest over the loss of part of the Vojvodina, the fertile plains of the northern Jugoslav state.

By the Treaty of Trianon of June 4, 1920, Hungary lost Baranja between the Drava River and the Danube, Bačka between the Danube and the Tisa, and the Banat east of the Tisa and north of the Danube. Jugoslavia got Baranja and Bačka, and, in addition, one-third of the Banat as a military bridgehead for the defense of Belgrade. The rest of the Banat went to Rumania. These three areas of Jugoslavia cover 7,200 square miles. In 1921 they had a population of 1,380,000.[55] On their fertile lands, indeed the most productive of all Jugoslavia, there was a great ethnic mixture of Serbs, Germans, Hungarians, and Rumanians as well as smaller minority groups. The German element was concentrated in the Banat, numbering 130,000 in

---

[53] Richard R. Randall, "Political Geography of the Klagenfurt Basin," *Geographical Review*, XLVII (July, 1957), 416.

[54] *Ibid.*, p. 417.

[55] F. N. Petrov, *Balkanskie strany* [*The Balkan States*], (Moskva: OGIZ, 1946), p. 51.

1931, compared to 300,000 Serbs.[56] The Hungarians were concentrated in northern Bačka, which in 1931 included 200,000 Hungarians (Magyars).[57]

These three areas of Jugoslavia were occupied militarily by Hungary in 1941 and more than 18,000 Hungarians were reportedly settled in the Bačka and Baranja, consisting primarily of Szekler repatriates from the Rumanian Bukovina, which was also occupied by Hungary.[58]

Under the postwar rearrangement of Jugoslav administrative areas in 1946, Baranja, Bačka, and the Jugoslav Banat were included in the newly created autonomous district of the Vojvodina in the Republic of Serbia.[59] The autonomous district has an area of 8,400 square miles. According to the census of March 15, 1948, it had a population of 1,661,632; in 1953, this had risen to 1,712,619.[60]

In comparative terms, the area of the present Autonomous District of the Vojvodina had a population in 1931 of 1,643,359,[61] of whom 392,000 or 22.5 percent were Hungarians and 358,604 or 20.6 percent were Germans,[62] whereas in 1953, there were 435,345 Hungarians, a sizable increase over 1931, but only a remainder of 35,290 Germans. This demonstrates the decimation of the German minority group in the Vojvodina as a result of the Second World War.

Actually within the past decade there has been a return movement from western Europe of former German residents who have found a ready welcome in the Vojvodina. To replace the many Germans who left, the Jugoslav government initiated a mass resettlement of Jugoslavs, especially Macedonians and Montenegrins, from the less hospitable regions of the south. But this has not proved very successful because many returned to the mountains because they could not adjust to life on the open plains, even though theoretically they had a higher standard of living in the Vojvodina. Reportedly between 1946

---

[56] Joseph B. Schechtman, *European Population Transfers, 1939–1945* (New York: Oxford University Press, 1946), p. 240.

[57] Kerner, *op. cit.*, p. 102.

[58] Eugene M. Kulischer, *The Displacement of Population in Europe* (Montreal: International Labor Office, 1943), Studies and Reports, Series O (Migration), No. 8, pp. 86 and 434–435.

[59] Melik, *op. cit.*, p. 395.

[60] *Popis Stanovništva*, 1953, XIII.

[61] Melik, *op. cit.*, p. 395.

[62] *Ibid.*, p. 405.

and 1949 60,000 were resettled in the area.[63] Such settlement added newer minority groups to the Vojvodina, such as the Macedonians and Montenegrins, to the older Slovaks, Czechs, Rumanians, and even smaller groups of Greeks and Turks. (See Table 4.) The two largest

TABLE 4

ETHNIC STRUCTURE OF THE AUTONOMOUS DISTRICT OF THE
VOJVODINA, JUGOSLAVIA
(Census of March 31, 1953)

Serbs	874,346
Hungarians	435,345
Croats	128,054
Slovaks	73,460
Rumanians	57,236
Germans	35,290
Montenegrins	30,561
Ruthenians- Ukrainians	23,043
Macedonians	11,689
Gypsies	11,525
Slovenes	6,025
Czechs	3,480
Bulgarians	3,706
Russians	3,318
Albanians	965
Jews	893
Poles	749
Greeks	451
Turks	388
Italians	196
Austrians	69
Vlachs	25
Others	...
TOTAL	1,712,619

SOURCE: Federal Bureau of Statistics. The Federated People's Republic of Jugoslavia, *Census of Population, 1953*. Vol. I, Vital and Ethnic Statistics (Belgrade, 1959), pp. 62–63.

non-Slavic groups are the Hungarians and the Rumanians. While at the moment they do not pose a serious internal problem, they could be used as pawns should a serious battle break out between Jugoslavia and her neighbors to the north and east. In any event, there is

---

[63] *Ibid.*

no doubt that the Jugoslavs would resist any attempts at annexations of any part of the Vojvodina.[64]

Hungary's Claims against Rumania

As might be expected, Hungary also lays claim to the Rumanian Banat because of the large number of Hungarians living there. (See Map 4.) The Rumanian Banat is as complex ethnically as the Jugoslav Banat. Hungarians and Jugoslavs occupy the lowland areas of the Hungarian plain, while the Rumanians are concentrated in the Transylvanian foothills to the east.[65] The Rumanian Banat has an area of 7,200 square miles and in 1930 had a population of 939,958.[66] (See Table 5.)

TABLE 5

ETHNIC STRUCTURE OF THE RUMANIAN PROVINCES OF
BANAT, CRIȘANA-MARAMUREȘ, AND TRANSYLVANIA
(Rumanian Census of December 29, 1930)

	Banat	Crișana-Maramureș	Transylvania
Rumanians	511,083	844,078	1,852,719
Hungarians	97,839	320,795	934,642
Germans	223,167	67,259	253,426
Jugoslavs	40,503	2,171	668
Czechoslovaks	14,096	23,580	9,110
Jews	11,248	88,825	78,626
Gypsies	17,919	15,895	75,342
Ruthenes	3,885	23,569	2,153
Others	...	...	...
TOTAL	939,958	1,390,417	3,217,988

SOURCE: Central Institute of Statistics. *Statistical Yearbook of Rumania, 1939 and 1940* (Bucharest: 1940), pp. 60–61.

To the north of the Banat is the province of Crișana-Maramureș with the towns of Oradea and Satu-Mare. This province is similarly

[64] For a Jugoslav discussion of minorities in Jugoslavia see Ljubiša Stojković and Miloš Martić, *National Minorities in Yugoslavia.* (Beograd: Jugoslavija, 1952).

[65] Walter Fitzgerald, *The New Europe* (New York: Harper, 1946), p. 96.

[66] *Anuarul Statistic al României, 1939 și 1940* [*Statistical Yearbook of Rumania, 1939 and 1940*], pp. 60–61. For detailed Rumanian statistics on these areas see Sabin Manuila, *Aspects Démographiques de la Transylvanie* (Bucarest: 1939).

valuable for its agricultural production and has a complex ethnic structure similar to that of the Banat. (See Table 5.) Its area is 8,200 square miles; it had a population of 1,390,417 in 1930.

But of greater importance to the Hungarians is the question of mountainous Transylvania, which has an area of 24,000 square miles. In 1930 there was a population of 3,217,988 of whom 934,642 were Hungarians. The Hungarian historical and ethnic claims are based on the Szeklers who settled in the central basins of Transylvania in the thirteenth century and have remained a distinct, unassimilated ethnic group, just like the German Saxons of western Transylvania.

During the Second World War Hungary occupied these three areas of Rumania under the Vienna Award of August 30, 1940, under which 17,500 square miles of northern Transylvania were awarded to Hungary with provisions that there be voluntary population exchanges of Hungarians and Rumanians between northern and southern Transylvania. This precipitated a mass flight of about 200,000 Rumanians from north Transylvania. Under the Soviet-Rumanian armistice, the area was restored to Rumania in March, 1945, creating a return mass flight of Hungarians to Hungary.[67]

Actually the war solved neither the problem of the Hungarian minority nor that of the German minority in Rumania. According to the census of 1956, of a total population of 17,489,450, 1,587,675 or 9 percent were reported as Hungarians by nationality and 384,708 or 2 percent as Germans.[68] The minority groups live in the same territories as before, although statistics now appear according to the new administrative districts following the adoption of the new constitution of 1952. At that same time the Rumanian government gave recognition to the problem of the Hungarian minority by creation of the Autonomous Magyar District as one of the 16 administrative provinces (Regiunea), following the pattern of the Soviet Union. (See Table 6.)

At the present time, both Rumania and Hungary are sister "people's republics" closely linked to the Soviet Union. So long as this condition prevails the lid can be kept down on Hungarian claims to northwestern Rumania. But should conditions change, the Rumanians might again find themselves cut off into a rump state as during the

[67] Schechtman, op. cit., pp. 425–433.
[68] Anuarul Statistic al R.P.R., 1959 [Statistical Yearbook of the People's Republic of Rumania, 1959], (Bucureşti: I. V. Stalin, 1959), pp. 72–73.

TABLE 6

Ethnic Structure of Selected Rumanian Provinces
(Census of February 21, 1956)

	Total population	By nationality	By mother tongue
Banat Area			
Timișoara Province	1,195,871		
Rumanians		768,650	775,067
Hungarians		147,427	160,616
Germans		173,733	179,519
Jugoslavs		44,683	41,739
Others		...	...
Crișana-Maramureș Area			
Oradea Province	858,743		
Rumanians		584,399	581,913
Hungarians		243,828	253,939
Germans		9,571	9,233
Jugoslavs		73	40
Others		...	...
Baia Mare Province	712,567		
Rumanians		469,499	461,150
Hungarians		198,093	214,541
Germans		6,264	6,111
Jugoslavs		22	15
Others		...	...
Transylvania Area			
Cluj Province	1,259,073		
Rumanians		963,748	974,280
Hungarians		257,974	262,014
Germans		8,335	8,332
Jugoslavs		73	44
Others		...	...
Autonomous Magyar Region Province	731,387		
Rumanians		146,830	144,624
Hungarians		565,510	575,737
Germans		3,214	3,209
Jugoslavs		37	24
Others		...	...
Stalin (Brașov) Province	901,708		
Rumanians		616,220	633,062
Hungarians		108,751	111,087
Germans		148,343	148,761
Jugoslavs		114	65
Others		...	...
Hunedoara Province	572,963		
Rumanians		502,257	510,984
Hungarians		37,048	38,265
Germans		18,795	17,641
Jugoslavs		207	151
Others		...	...

SOURCE: *Statistical Yearbook of the Rumanian People's Republic, 1959*, pp. 72–73.

Second World War. The Rumanians well remember that although Transylvania and the other areas occupied by Hungary were eventually returned to them, northern Bukovina and Bessarabia occupied by the Russians are now parts of the Soviet Union.

Bessarabia and Northern Bukovina

One of the most important geopolitical changes in the Balkans associated with the Second World War was the introduction of the Soviet Union as a Balkan power by Soviet seizure of northern Bukovina and Bessarabia from Rumania. (See Maps 1, 4, and 6.)

These two territories have an area of 19,355 square miles and a

MAP 6

combined population of 3,700,000 of whom about half were Rumanians and only 10 percent Russians.[69]

The acquisition of Bessarabia was an important strategic, political, and economic asset to the Soviet Union. The fertile plains of the area offer a direct route into the Balkans and through the Danubian gateway into Central Europe. Because of her new position on the Danube, the Soviet Union declared herself a Danubian country with the right to participate as a riparian member in the Danubian Conference held at Belgrade in 1948. At this conference, a new international Danubian Commission was organized, which excluded all nonriparian nations, particularly Great Britain and the United States, who expressed strong interest in continued internationalization of the Danube.[70] By controlling the northern (main) channel of the Danube Delta, Russia is in virtual control of the Danube–Black Sea trade.

The annexation of northern Bukovina was the means of gaining control of railroad and road connections through the Carpathian mountains to the newly-annexed areas of Polish Galicia and Czechoslovak Ruthenia to the north and west. The Hungarian revolution of 1956 was crushed by Soviet troops that moved in through Ruthenia. Thus by these two annexations the Soviet Union moved southward into the Balkans; gained a controlling position at the mouth of the Danube; and consolidated her new position in the Hungarian plain in Ruthenia.[71]

As a border zone of ethnic mixture of Rumanians, Ukrainians, Russians, and numerous others, Bessarabia and Bukovina had been a source of controversy since Russian conquest of Bessarabia in 1812 and Austrian conquest of Bukovina in 1775. (Bessarabia was retaken in 1856 but lost again to Russia in 1878.) These territories were annexed by Rumania in 1919, but were occupied by Russia in 1940 and ceded to Russia directly by the Soviet-Rumanian Agreement of June 28, 1940. They were retaken by German and Rumanian forces and held from 1941 to 1944, when they were reoccupied by the Russians.

---

[69] *The World Almanac, 1947*, p. 490.

[70] U.S. Department of State, "Soviet Domination of the Danube Conference," *Documents and State Papers* (Nov. and Dec., 1948), I, 487–513. Also David Cattell, "The Politics of the Danube Commission under Soviet Control," *The American Slavic and East European Review*, XIX (Oct., 1960), 381–394.

[71] Huey Louis Kostanick, "The Significance of Geopolitical Changes in Eastern Europe," *Education*, LXXII (Feb., 1952), 381–389.

The Rumanian Peace Treaty of February 10, 1947, reaffirmed the 1940 boundaries.

Bessarabia.—This region between the Prut and the Dniester (Dnestr) rivers, has an area of 17,325 square miles.[72] It is a rolling-plains region with deep and fertile *chernozem* soils that make it a productive farmland of grains and vegetables and an orchard of fruits. In its southern expanses along the Danube and the Black Sea coast are marshes and sloughs that, although poor for crop farming, are excellent sources of fish and caviar.

After the First World War, it was estimated that the population of Bessarabia totaled approximately 2,700,000 with 1,000,000 Rumanians (Moldavians), 900,000 Ukrainians and 300,000 Jews as the principal groups.[73] The Rumanian census of 1930 lists a total of 2,864,402, with

TABLE 7

ETHNIC STRUCTURE OF BESSARABIA AND NORTHERN BUKOVINA
(Rumanian census of December 29, 1930)

| | Bessarabia | | Northern Bukovina[a] | |
	Population	Percent	Population	Percent
Rumanians	1,610,757	56.2	136,184	29.8
Russians	351,912	12.3	4,877	1.0
Ruthenes, Ukrainians	314,211	11.0	213,762	45.0
Jews	204,858	7.2	66,569	12.8
Bulgars	163,726	5.7	100	—
Germans	81,089	2.8	28,576	5.8
Gypsies	98,172	3.4	399	—
Others	...	...	...	...
TOTAL	2,864,402	100.0	476,088	100.0

[a] Northern provinces of Cernăuti and Storojinet.
SOURCE: *Statistical Yearbook of Rumania, 1939 and 1940* (Bucharest: 1940), pp. 60–63.

1,610,757 Rumanians and 666,123 Russians and Ukrainians. (See Table 7.) The Rumanians were concentrated in the hill lands of central Bessarabia and the Slavic groups in northern Bessarabia and in the plains of the south.

[72] For a personal account of Bessarabia in the twenties see Charles Upson Clark, *Bessarabia* (New York: Dodd, Mead, 1927).

[73] Bowman, *op. cit.*, p. 371.

The Second World War created major losses of the German, Hungarian, and Jewish minorities in Bessarabia. The entire German group was evacuated under the Soviet-German agreement on transfer of minorities signed in Moscow on September 5, 1940. German sources had estimated that there were 85,000 Germans, but the number evacuated was 93,548, which was 8,500 more than their own estimate and 12,500 more than the Rumanian estimate. This excess group undoubtedly included assimilated people who had not been officially listed as Germans and also non-Germans who wished to take advantage of the opportunity to leave the area.[74] It was similarly reported that the entire Hungarian minority of 829 people was repatriated to Hungary under an exchange agreement made between Hungary and Rumania in 1940.[75]

The history of the Jewish minority was different. The Jewish population of Bessarabia was increased in 1940 by refugees who had fled from Rumania to Soviet territory to escape Nazi terror and seizure. But, with the occupation of the area by the Germans and Rumanians, many fled eastward into the Ukraine. Others were later forced to move into the Rumanian-occupied section of the Ukraine, called Transnistria.[76] After the Second World War many returned to Bessarabia from other parts of the Soviet Union; the Soviet census of 1959 reported 95,000 Jews in the Republic of Moldavia, forming 3.3 percent of the population.[77]

Northern Bukovina.—This area has an area of 2,035 square miles which was about half of the new territory assigned to Rumania by the Treaty of St. Germain-en-Laye in 1919. The 1930 Rumanian census listed a total of 476,088 for the two northern provinces of Cernăuti (Chernovtsy) and Storojinet. (See Table 7.)

Under the Soviet-German agreement on transfer of minorities, 44,-441 Germans were reported to have been evacuated from northern Bukovina, thus ending the German problem in the area.[78] As in Bessarabia, the Jewish population was forced to flee into the Ukraine during the Rumanian-German occupation in 1941; undoubtedly many

---

[74] Schechtman, *op. cit.*, pp. 184–185, and Kulischer, *op. cit.*, p. 16.

[75] Schechtman, *op. cit.*, p. 436.

[76] Kulischer, *op. cit.*, p. 106.

[77] *Izvestia*, February 4, 1960, p. 2.

[78] Schechtman, *op. cit.*, p. 184.

later returned, but no specific data have been available on the ethnic structure of northern Bukovina in the postwar period. In 1940 northern Bukovina and Bessarabia were incorporated into the Ukrainian Soviet Socialist Republic and into the newly formed Moldavian Soviet Socialist Republic. The Ukraine also annexed the Khotin province of northern Bessarabia and the Akkerman (Belgorod Dnestrovski) and Ismail provinces of southern Bessarabia, which total 5,000 square miles and had a population of 1,050,000 in 1940. The new Moldavian Soviet Socialist Republic was created in 1940 from the former Moldavian Autonomous Soviet Socialist Republic within the Soviet Union and the remaining portion of Bessarabia, which included 11,200 square miles and a 1940 population of 2,100,000.[79]

The Moldavian Soviet Socialist Republic of the Soviet Union has an area of 13,012 square miles and a 1959 population of 2,885,000. The largest group was the Moldavians, 1,887,000 in number, forming 65.4 percent of the population. These were followed by the Ukrainians, 421,000 or 14.6 percent and the Russians, with 293,000 or 10.2 percent.[80] (See Table 8.) Thus Moldavians form the majority in the People's Republic.

For some idea of a possible estimate of the number of Moldavians in northern Bukovina, now called Chernovtsy Province of the Ukraine, the census of 1959 lists the province population as 776,000. The number of Moldavians in the Ukrainian S.S.R. is given as 239,000.[81] In all probability most of these live in Chernovtsy Province. Actually some Moldavians also live in Odessa province near the borders of the Moldavian S.S.R. and in much smaller number in Kirovograd and Nikolaevskii provinces of the Ukraine.[82]

In addition to the Moldavians in the Moldavian S.S.R. and Ukrainian S.S.R., 64,000 of them were reported in the Russian Soviet Federated Socialist Republic, thus accounting for virtually all 2,214,000 Moldavians in the Soviet Union as given in the 1959 census.

The Soviet use of the term "Moldavian" instead of "Rumanian"

---

[79] Frank Lorimer, *The Population of the Soviet Union: History and Prospects* (Geneva: League of Nations, 1946), p. 187.

[80] *Izvestia*, February 4, 1960, p. 2.

[81] *Ibid.*

[82] Akademiia Nauk Ukrainskoi SSR, Institut Ekonomiki, *Ukrainskaia SSR* [*The Ukrainian People's Republic*], (Moskva: Gosudarstvennoe Izdatelstvo Geograficheskoi Literaturi, 1957), p. 157.

TABLE 8

ETHNIC STRUCTURE OF THE MOLDAVIAN S.S.R. AND THE UKRAINIAN S.S.R.
(Census of January 15, 1959)

Total population of the Soviet Union	208,827,000
Total number of Moldavians (Rumanians) in U.S.S.R.	2,214,000

Ethnic group	Moldavian S.S.R.		Ukrainian S.S.R.	
	Population	Percent	Population	Percent
Moldavians (Rumanians)	1,887,000	65.5	289,000	0.6
Ukrainians	421,000	14.6	31,852,000	76.1
Russians	293,000	10.2	7,400,000	17.7
Gagauz	96,000	3.3	0	0.0
Jews	95,000	3.3	840,000	2.0
Bulgarians	62,000	2.1	219,000	0.5
White Russians	0	0.0	291,000	0.7
Poles	0	0.0	363,000	0.9
Others	...	...	...	...
TOTAL	2,885,000	100.0	41,869,000	100.0

SOURCE: *Izvestia*, February 4, 1960, p. 2.

reflects the political overtones involved in Soviet annexation of Rumanian territories and a sizable Rumanian minority, while calling
Rumania a sister "people's republic." The Soviet government has attempted to build the notion that the people of the annexed areas are
not "Rumanians" but constitute a different ethnic group. All forms of
propaganda have been bent to this end not only in the Soviet Union
but in Rumania as well where the Rumanian government is forced
to give open recognition to the Republic of Moldavia and to visiting
Soviet "Moldavian" cultural groups of singers and dancers; indeed, it
has even given publicity to the spurious idea that Rumanians are
formed of two peoples, the Moldavians and the Wallachians.[83] For
the Soviet Union this focus on "Moldavian" nationality might be used
later as attempted justification for annexation to the Moldavian S.S.R.
of more or all of the remaining Moldavian territory in Rumania, an
event that would prove even more disenchanting to the Rumanian
people than the existing annexations have been. Aside from the mi-

[83] For a discussion of this see Wolff, *op. cit.*, pp. 458–459.

nority problem which can easily be handled within the framework of Soviet minority policy, the Moldavian S.S.R. is an economic asset constituting the "garden" of the Soviet Union with its picturesque and productive orchards and vegetable plots.[84] Because of their economic and strategic value there is little hope for Rumania that these lands will be returned.

Settlement of the Problem of Southern Dobrudja

In contrast to these still contested losses, the cession of southern Dobrudja to Bulgaria helped solve a long-standing problem between Rumania and Bulgaria. (See Map 4.) In the Congress of Berlin in 1878, northern Dobrudja was ceded to Rumania and southern Dobrudja to Bulgaria. The Treaty of Bucharest of 1913 awarded southern Dobrudja to Rumania, but Bulgaria occupied it during the First World War, although it was returned to Rumania by the Treaty of Neuilly.

During the Second World War, Bulgaria joined the Axis forces, and, aided by Germany, forced the cession of southern Dobrudja under the Treaty of Craiova of August 23, 1940.

Southern Dobrudja, a fertile, wheat-producing plateau area south of the Danubian Delta on the Black Sea, had in fact been peopled mainly by Bulgarians. The second largest ethnic group was not the Rumanians but Turks who had lived in the area for centuries.

The ceded districts of Durostor and Caliacra comprised an area of 2,982 square miles with a population of 378,344.[85] According to the Rumanian census of 1930, there were 77,728 Rumanians, 143,209 Bulgarians and 129,025 Turks.[86] But under the minority-exchange agreement it was reported that 100,000 Rumanians left southern Dobrudja, of whom 65,000 were resettled in northern Dobrudja, 60,000 Bulgarians were repatriated[87] from northern Dobrudja, although the 1930

---

[84] For a detailed description see A. L. Odud, *Moldavskaia SSR* [*The Moldavian People's Republic*], (Moskva: Gosudarstvennoe Izdatelstvo Geografischeskoi Literaturi, 1955) and S. Levit, N. Mohov and A. Odud, *Moldavskaia SSR* [*The Moldavian People's Republic*], (Moskva: Izdatelstvo Adademii Nauk SSSR, 1959).

[85] Schechtman, *op. cit.*, pp. 404–405.

[86] *Anuarul Statistic al Rumâniei, 1939 și 1940* [*Statistical Yearbook of Rumania, 1939 and 1940*], pp. 58–59.

[87] Schechtman, *op. cit.*, pp. 406–412.

census listed only 42,000 Bulgarians in the districts of Constanţa and Tulcea.[88]

Despite the contradiction in statistics, the Dobrudja question seems to have been satisfactorily resolved between Rumania and Bulgaria. In the 1956 Rumanian census only 900 Bulgarians were reported still in Constanţa province, which included all of northern Dobrudja.[89]

The Expulsion of Bulgarian Turks

Although Bulgaria welcomed the addition of southern Dobrudja, the addition of more than 100,000 Turks to 500,000 already in Bulgaria helped create a serious ethnic problem for Bulgaria—a problem not of economic or cultural but of political significance for the Communist regime which took over soon after the Second World War.

Actually the Turkish minority in Bulgaria before the Second World War had been in many respects a model minority group because of their consistent support of the Bulgarian government and their feeling of friendship with the Bulgarians. For those who wanted to emigrate to Turkey a voluntary exchange agreement was signed between Bulgaria and Turkey on October 18, 1925. Until 1940 only 10,000 to 12,000 Turks emigrated to Turkey annually under this agreement, except during the depression years of the middle thirties when the total fell to less than 1,000 per year. As might be expected, there was also little migration during the Second World War.[90]

When the Communists took control of Bulgaria in 1944, the government officially discouraged emigration. But where previously the Turks had enjoyed minority rights of religion and of Turkish language schools as well as special privileges in local government, these were revoked by the Communist government, and even the Muslim religion was attacked as were Turkish customs and continued use of the Turk-

---

[88] Detailed statistics are listed in Sabin Manuila, *La Population de la Dobroudja* (Bucarest: Institut Central de Statistique, 1939).

[89] *Anuarul Statistic al R.P.R., 1959* [*Statistical Yearbook of the People's Republic of Rumania, 1959*], pp. 72–73.

[90] Huey Louis Kostanick, *Turkish Resettlement of Bulgarian Turks, 1950–1953*, University of California Publications in Geography, Vol. 8, No. 2 (Berkeley and Los Angeles: University of California Press, 1957) and "Turkish Resettlement of Refugees from Bulgaria, 1950–1953," *The Middle East Journal*, IX (Winter, 1955), 41–52.

ish language instead of Bulgarian. Equally painful were harsh economic measures aimed at establishing collective farms, especially in the rich and fertile Dobrudja, where Turks owned and farmed most of the wheat lands.

Turkish resistance to such measures were so strong that in 1950 the government reversed its policy and began to ease emigration restrictions. Despite severe limitations on the amount of personal property that could be taken out, voluntary emigration rose to a new total of over 3,000 persons per month.

Then in August, 1950, the Bulgarian government announced mass expulsion for the Turks. Despite Turkish diplomatic protests thousands of Turks were transported to the Turkish border at Svilengrad. Because of diplomatic incidents regarding Bulgarian attempts to include Gypsies among the Turks, Turkey closed her border from October 7 to December 2, 1950. But the border was again opened following the institution of greater security measures by the Turks. During the major mass emigration period of 1950–1951, more than 150,000 Turks entered Turkey from Bulgaria, leaving 450,000 who form about 6 percent of the Bulgarian population.[91]

These refugees of Communist oppression were resettled in Turkey under an excellent scheme of the newly organized Land and Settlement Administration. It was a propitious time for such resettlement because the Turks were at that time actively participating in the Korean War and therefore resettlement aid was viewed both by the government and by the Turkish people as a patriotic effort. Such resettlement was also helped by the cultural factor that the Turks of Bulgaria were so similar to the Turks of Turkey in language, religion, and customs that no serious ethnic problems were presented.

Nonetheless the government felt that a security problem could easily arise if there were Communist elements among the emigrants, therefore all refugees were settled in the western half of Turkey and none in the sensitive regions of eastern Turkey bordering the Soviet Union, which had at different times pressed Soviet claims to the annexation of the Turkish areas of Kars and Ardahan.

Since 1951, the Bulgarian government has again discouraged Turkish emigration, but should another mass expulsion take place Turkey

[91] *The Worldmark Encyclopedia of the Nations, 1960* (New York: Harper, 1960), p. 99.

would find herself in a more difficult position to undertake such mass resettlement than in the previous program, on both economic and political grounds. Thus Bulgaria continues to have a somewhat less than amicable relationship with her southeastern neighbor over the sizable Turkish minority in Bulgaria. Her problems with her neighbors to the south and west, however, are even more acute.

Bulgarian Claims in Greece

Like Hungary, Bulgaria has long sought revision of her frontiers, and, in addition to the Dobrudja controversy, has made direct claims to territories in Greece and Jugoslavia on strategic, economic, ethnic, and historical grounds—one might say the whole gamut of possible justification.

Bulgarian aspirations to Greek territories date back to the Treaty of San Stefano of 1878, when Bulgaria included most of Macedonia and had an outlet to the Aegean Sea through Thrace. The Congress of Berlin of 1878 returned these areas to Turkey and, since that time, Bulgaria has continued to press claims to these areas, and gained temporary wartime control of them in the Balkan Wars of 1912–1913, the First World War, and the Second World War, but at present retains only a small portion of Macedonia, the Pirin area.

Bulgaria has long stressed the need of an outlet to the Aegean Sea particularly through western Thrace along the valley of the Maritsa River which debouches into the Aegean as the present boundary between Greece and Turkey. Access could also be gained through the Struma Valley in eastern Macedonia. In 1919, the Treaty of Neuilly recognized this need by providing for an economic concession of a permanent lease of a zone at the port of Alexandroupolis (Dedeagatch), but this was not acceptable to Bulgaria. The Greeks therefore maintain that Bulgaria does not in truth need such an economic outlet but that instead Bulgaria wants to annex western Thrace itself.[92] They cite as additional evidence that the Bulgars similarly refused to use the free port established in Salonica in 1925, although it was profitably used by Jugoslavia.

---

[92] *La Question du Débouche Bulgare à la Mer Égée* (Athènes: Imprimerie Jean Vartsos, 1928) and George E. Mylonas, *The Balkan States* (St. Louis: Public Affairs Press, 1947), pp. 183–185.

In addition to its strategic situation on the Aegean just west of the Turkish Straits, western Thrace does indeed have economic value. Its fertile plains, stretching along the Aegean coast at the foot of the high mountains that mark the Greek-Bulgarian border, are an excellent producer of wheat, tobacco, and grapes, all of high commercial value. This province of Greece includes 3,314 square miles and in 1951 had a population of 336,954.[93]

The question of the Bulgarian ethnic minority in Thrace and Macedonia had been raised in 1919, and presumably had been settled by the emigration of the Bulgarians who wished to do so under the Reciprocal Emigration Treaty of November 27, 1919. But when Bulgaria occupied Thrace on April 21, 1941, many thousands of Greeks fled or were deported to other parts of Greece and some 122,000 Bulgarians were reported settled in Thrace and eastern Macedonia. Under the Bulgarian armistice of October 28, 1944, however, these Bulgarians were returned to Bulgaria.[94] After the war, many Greeks returned to Thrace but again there was local displacement of population because of the guerrilla warfare which enveloped northern Greece until 1950. As a result of these drastic population movements the population of Thrace actually declined from 359,923 in 1940 to 336,954 in 1951.[95] Without question this area is now predominantly populated by Greeks, but there is still a sizable group of Turks and even a number of Bulgarians.

Because of such Bulgarian claims and consequent Bulgarian occupation of Thrace and Macedonia in the Second World War, the Greeks asserted a postwar counterclaim to southern Bulgaria, maintaining that for military security of a "natural frontier" a strip of thirty to fifty miles wide should be annexed along the entire northern border of Greece.[96] Newspaper reports at that time indicated that Greece would demand 4,150 square miles of Bulgaria that would have included 250,000 Bulgarians.[97] But under the Bulgarian Peace Treaty of February 10, 1947, these claims were not recognized.

---

[93] *Statistical Yearbook of Greece, 1958,* p. 15.

[94] Schechtman, *op. cit.,* pp. 415–424.

[95] *Statistical Yearbook of Greece,* 1958, p. 15.

[96] William Hardy McNeill, *The Greek Dilemma* (London: Victor Gollancz, 1947), p. 207.

[97] Ona K. D. Ringwood and Cyril E. Black, "Territorial Problems of the Axis Satellites," *Foreign Policy Reports,* XXII (May 1, 1946), 52.

Bulgarian Claims in Jugoslavia

To the west, Bulgaria still eyes Jugoslav Macedonia with misgivings and in addition seeks the return of four small areas along the western border taken by Jugoslavia under the Treaty of Neuilly of 1919. These were annexed on grounds of protection from Bulgarian attack of the vital Belgrade-Salonica railway even though it meant inclusion of Bulgarians in Jugoslavia. In the north, a part of the Timok valley was annexed. The Caribrod area, with 21,000 Bulgarians and the Bosilgrad area, with 22,000 Bulgarians gave Jugoslavia control of border mountain passes, but in so doing the new boundary was advanced to within thirty miles of Sofia, the Bulgarian capital. In the south, Bulgaria also lost the Strumitsa area, which became additionally an irredentist part of Jugoslav Macedonia.[98]

Greek Claims to Southern Albania (Northern Epirus)

Since the formation of Albania in 1912, Greece has reiterated her claims to southern Albania, which the Greeks call northern Epirus. These claims are based on grounds of military security and on ethnic grounds that Greeks form the major element of the population.[99] Northern Epirus is a mountainous territory of 2,500–3,000 square miles with a population of 228,000 according to Greek estimates.[100]

Long subject to Turkish rule and a border mixing zone of Albanians and Greeks, it is difficult to ascertain nationality on the basis of either language or religion because during the centuries many people have become bilingual, while in terms of religion some are Moslems while others as Christians may belong to either the Greek Orthodox or Albanian Orthodox churches. Furthermore, under Turkish rule before establishment of an Albanian Orthodox Church all were members of the Greek Orthodox Church.

In the Peace Conference of 1919, Greek assertions that there was a Greek majority in northern Epirus were denied by the Albanians,

---

[98] Bowman, *op. cit.*, p. 387, and Kerner, *op. cit.*, p. 102.

[99] Ph. A. Philon, *The Question of Northern Epirus* (Washington, D.C.: Greek Government Office of Information, 1945).

[100] Edith Pierpont Stickney, *Southern Albania or Northern Epirus in European International Affairs, 1912–1923* (Stanford University Press, 1926), p. 1.

who were given the area as part of the Albanian state.[101] In return the Albanians asserted that the northern part of Greek Epirus was in fact Albanian-populated and should be included in Albania.[102] Since Greek Epirus has 3,570 square miles with a 1951 population of 330,543 the Greeks have not taken such Albanian demands lightly, hence Greece continues its battle for northern Epirus even though there is little hope for success in its demand.

Albania's Claim to Kosovo-Metohija

In the formation of Albania's northern frontiers political considerations overrode ethnic considerations with the result that in the subsequent creation of Jugoslavia at the end of the First World War a large Albanian minority was included in the new state along the borders of Albania and in the famous plain of Kosovo. Until the Second World War, the Albanians suffered many repressions and indignities in this area, generally given the name of Kosovo, both because of their difference of language and because most of them were Moslems. In addition large numbers of Serbs were settled in an effort to change the ethnic structure of the region, whose lands were valuable for grains and fruits as well as for timber and as grazing lands for the ubiquitous Balkan sheep.

In the Second World War, the Albanians aided by the Germans occupied the area but were forced to return it to Jugoslavia at the end of the war. At that time Tito, creating a new federated Jugoslavia on the basis of ethnic distinctions, established the autonomous area of Kosovo-Metohija of 4,127 square miles in the Republic of Serbia as recognition of the Albanian predominance in the area.[103] According to the Jugoslav census of 1953, of a total of 754,245 Albanians in Jugoslavia, 524,559 were in Kosovo-Metohija[104] and the remainder were mostly in other areas along the Albanian border. They have again been permitted the right to use the Albanian language and to have Albanian schools but locally much ill-will still prevails between the Albanians and the Serbs, although under the present oppressive re-

---

[101] Mylonas, op. cit., pp. 114–118.
[102] Stickney, op. cit., p. 95.
[103] Popis Stanovništva, 1953, 1, 50.
[104] Ibid., p. 66.

gime in Albania, the Albanians of Kosovo-Metohija would undoubtedly prefer to remain in Jugoslavia. Thus by creating an autonomous area the Jugoslavs hope to head off any future claims by Albania, even though at present any such claims would seem to have as little chance of fulfillment as Albanian claims to northern Greece.

Greece and the Cyprus Question

Forty-four miles off the coast of Turkey in the eastern Mediterranean is the island of Cyprus, third largest island in the Mediterranean with an area of 3,572 square miles. Following its capture by the Turks in 1571, Turkish families permanently settled on the island but remained separate from the Greeks, who formed the majority of the population, although Cyprus had never been part of the Greek state. Because of its strategic position in the eastern Mediterranean, especially in reference to the Suez Canal, the British took administration of the island through a treaty with Turkey in 1878. When war with Turkey began in 1914, the British annexed the island as a direct colony and in 1925 gave it the legal status of a Crown Colony.[105]

Because of the large Greek population on the island,[106] Greece has for centuries been a source of attraction, and the Cypriot Greeks have sought union with Greece (enosis). In the 1930's a serious disturbance for enosis broke out with the result that local political autonomy was sharply curtailed and legislative powers placed in the hands of the governor.

After the Second World War, demands for political union with Greece were renewed and the British began talks with local leaders for constitutional reform. These reforms were not only unacceptable to the Greeks who formed nearly 80 percent of the island's population of 558,000 but were also the signal for increasing discontent and concern on the part of the Turks who formed 18 percent of the population of Cyprus. (See Table 9.) In support of the Turkish minority the Turkish government began to demand partition of the island on an ethnic basis. By 1955 the Greek Cypriots were conducting an open

---

[105] The Statesman's Year-Book, 1960, p. 234.

[106] For an excellent description of the ethnic situation see Alexander Melamid, "The Geographical Distribution of Communities in Cyprus," The Geographical Review, XLIV (July, 1956), 355–374.

TABLE 9

ETHNIC STRUCTURE OF CYPRUS

(By religion)

Religion	1921	1931	1946[a]	1956[a]
Greek Orthodox	244,887	296,573	361,199	416,986
Muslim	61,339	64,238	80,548	92,642
Others	4,489	7,148	8,367	19,251
TOTAL	310,705	347,959	450,114	528,879

[a] Excluding military and camps.
SOURCE: *The Statesman's Year Book, 1960*, p. 235.

terrorist campaign not only against the British but against Turks and even fellow Cypriots accused of an insufficient feeling of *enosis*. In 1959 the difficulties were surprisingly solved by an agreement, signed in London by the prime ministers of Great Britain, Greece, and Turkey and accepted by the 558,000 Greek and Turkish Cypriots, that Cyprus should become an independent nation. On August 16, 1960, Cyprus became a new state,[107] with Archbishop Makarios as president of the republic. Then again in a surprise movement on March 17, 1961, Cyprus was accepted as a new member of the Commonwealth of Nations.[108]

Thus the colony returned full circle back to close political ties with Britain but this time as a full-fledged member of the Commonwealth. To further cement its place in British military defense, as part of the independence agreement, 99 square miles of Cyprus were ceded to Britain as sovereign military bases so that Britain still has a strategic seat in the eastern Mediterranean even though the Suez Canal passed from British to Egyptian control.

The Straits Question

No discussion of Balkan problem areas would be complete without reference to Soviet demands to greater control of the Turkish Straits. This vital passageway of the Dardanelles, Sea of Marmara, and the

[107] *The Worldmark Encyclopedia of the Nations, 1960*, pp. 241–242, and the *World Almanac, 1961*, p. 348.
[108] British Information Services, *British Record* (March 23, 1961), Supplement, p. 4.

Bosphorus, serves a dual role as an international waterway between the Mediterranean and Black Seas, and as an area of strategic importance to the countries of the Black Sea and to those countries with interests in the eastern Mediterranean.

Controlled by the Turks, the Straits have for centuries been a long-sought prize for the Russians, who never succeeded in gaining military control of it. After the defeat of Turkey in the First World War, Turkey was obliged to demilitarize the Straits, which were then placed under the administration of an International Commission. But in 1936 a new convention was signed at Montreux whereby Turkish rights to militarize the Straits were fully restored and the International Commission abolished.

The controversy over control of the Straits refers to military fortifications and not to simple commercial passage. The principle of free passage of merchant ships of all nations in time of peace is recognized by the Montreux Convention, but limitations are made on the passage of capital ships in peace time and of warships of belligerent states in wartime in which Turkey should be neutral.

The Straits issue was raised by the U.S.S.R. at the Potsdam Conference of July, 1945. The Soviet demands included greater limitations on the warships of non-Black Sea powers and proposals for joint Soviet-Turkish defense of the Straits and for control of the Straits by Black Sea powers only.[109] This proposal aimed at excluding all extra-regional powers was similar in purpose to later restriction of participation on the Danube Commission to riparian powers, which meant exclusion of the United States, Great Britain, and France. The Soviet proposals were rejected by Turkey which has continued to fortify the Straits even to the extent of an antisubmarine net stretched across the Black Sea entrance of the Bosphorus, but there is little doubt that such proposals will again be made.

Problem Area Characteristics

In total the problem areas of the Balkans encompass a combined territory of more than 120,000 square miles and a population of more

---

[109] Cyril E. Black, "The Turkish Straits and the Great Powers," *Foreign Policy Reports*, XXIII (Oct. 1, 1947), 174–182, and H. N. Howard, *The Problem of the Turkish Straits*, Department of State Publication 2752, Near Eastern Series 5, (Washington, D.C.: 1947).

than 19,000,000. Considering that the Balkans have an area of 340,000 square miles and a population total of 65,000,000, this means that problem areas amount to more than a third of the land area of the Balkans and affect a fourth of the people. Every state of the Balkans is directly involved in territorial or ethnic problems, either with other Balkan neighbors or with non-Balkan nations.

Certain conclusions seem warranted as to features which charac-

TABLE 10

BALKAN TERRITORIAL CHANGES AND PROBLEM AREAS

Area	Square miles	Population	Population date
Macedonia; Greece, Bulgaria, Jugoslavia	26,150	3,300,000	1961[a]
Free Territory of Trieste	300	365,000	1953[a]
Istria, Jugoslavia	2,850	500,000	1947–49[a]
Jugoslav claims to Italy	728	200,000	1949[a]
Cres-Lošinj, Jugoslavia	200	12,508	1953
Lastovo-Palagruza, Jugoslavia	...	1,700	1953
Zadar, Jugoslavia	43	25,600	1953
Saseno, Albania	4	...	
Dodecanese Islands, Greece	1,305	121,500	1951
Carinthia, Austria	954	180,000	1946
Border Areas of Styria, Austria	50	10,000	1946
Burgenland Croats, Austria	...	70,000	1946
Banat, Bačka, Baranja; Jugoslavia	7,200	1,500,000	1953[a]
Banat, Rumania	7,200	1,200,000	1956
Crişana-Maramureş, Rumania	8,200	1,500,000	1956
Transylvania, Rumania	24,000	3,450,000	1956
Bessarabia, U.S.S.R.	17,325	3,000,000	1961[a]
Northern Bukovina, U.S.S.R.	2,035	700,000	1961[a]
Southern Dobrudja, Bulgaria	2,982	380,000	1947[a]
Bulgarian Turks (expelled)	...	250,000	1951
Thrace, Greece	3,314	337,000	1951
Southern Bulgaria	4,150	250,000	1946
Caribrod, Bosilgrad, Strumica; Jugoslavia	...	50,000	1928
Northern Epirus, Albania	2,500	225,000	1961[a]
Epirus, Greece	3,570	330,000	1951
Kosovo, Jugoslavia	4,500	600,000	1961[a]
Cyprus	3,572	558,000	1959[a]
TOTAL	123,132	19,116,308	

[a] Estimated.

terize these contested territories. All are frontier lands, thus pointing up boundaries as focal points of friction. Again, with only a single major exception, that of the Straits question, all are areas of ethnic complexity where the presence of a certain ethnic group offers ethnic grounds for irredentist claims, weak as they may be. Most of the problem areas also are said to have strategic value or to constitute a natural military frontier, claims which at times seem farfetched, as the Greek demand for the annexation of southern Bulgaria as a "natural frontier" of Greece. Besides, the problem areas have often changed hands politically, which establishes the factor of historical possession as justification for territorial demands. Curiously enough economic value has seldom been cited as justification for a demand, perhaps because this might seem to be too weak a justification, but has often been used as a reason why an area should not be relinquished.

Above all of these characteristics emerges the signal conclusion that the key factor is state nationalism, and that territorial demands and conflicts rise and fall according to changes in national policies.

The question naturally arises what could be done to alleviate some of the problems. The element most amenable to change would seem the ethnic one. It would appear that minority exchanges could take place under reciprocal agreements and would be mutually beneficial. Some such exchanges have produced positive results, in particular the Greek-Turkish exchange of the early twenties, but other attempts at expulsion of minorities have only produced greater friction as in Bulgarian attempts to expel the Turks in the middle of this century. Still, the trend toward homogeneity within each of the Balkan states is unmistakable. It is the result of losses of the recent two World Wars, of voluntary and involuntary migrations, and of population exchanges. This trend would in time give less creditability to irredentist claims, but in view of the persistence of the same problems in the course of centuries, one is forced to the conclusion that ethnic relationships are not the real problems, but are more truly simply overt justifications for expansion of a nation's lands.

Certain geographical relationships appear as consistent patterns in the web of territorial claims. Bulgaria has constantly sought an exit southward to the Aegean through Macedonia and western Thrace. In similar fashion, Jugoslavia also aimed at southward expansion to the

Aegean through Macedonia and at expansion westward along the shores of the Adriatic. Hungary has dreams of reoccupying the lowlands of the Danubian basin and of even gaining the mountains of Transylvania and by so doing to restore the glory of the Hungarian position in the old Austro-Hungarian Empire.

Yet these internal geopolitical patterns of nationalistic aspirations form but part of the total geopolitical world of the Balkans because foreign nations have also had direct interests in the Balkans and have directly intervened to secure by peace or war what they wanted. Indeed had it not been for the interventions of the foreign powers, Balkan relations probably would have progressed more smoothly.

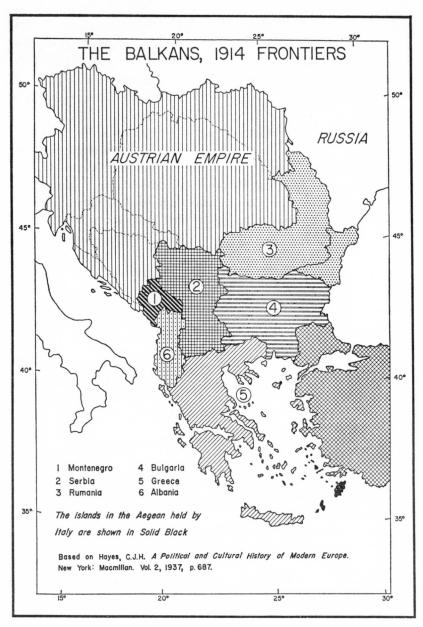

THE BALKANS, 1914 FRONTIERS

RUSSIA

AUSTRIAN EMPIRE

③

②

①

④

⑥

⑤

1 Montenegro   4 Bulgaria
2 Serbia   5 Greece
3 Rumania   6 Albania

The islands in the Aegean held by

Italy are shown in Solid Black

Based on Hayes, C.J.H. *A Political and Cultural History of Modern Europe.*
New York: Macmillan. Vol. 2, 1937, p. 687.

MAP 7

Bibliographical Note

Much has been written about the geopolitics of the Balkans, although rarely under that title. The Balkans have attracted constant attention during the past two centuries on the part of many writers. Many of the publications are both analytical and informative. Some might even be given the euphemistic label of "objective," but these few gems pale into insignificance beside the spate of tendentious and misleading literature that continues even at present. Yet it must be recognized that one man's truth is but another man's propaganda. Hence even these oft fallacious tracts serve the useful purpose of demonstrating a particular point of view. Without doubt it is often the tendentious items that make for interesting reading, such as the dramatic threats of IMRO or the appeals for nationalism.

The materials dealing with the various aspects of Balkans geopolitics fall into several categories. The greatest number are concerned directly with territorial aspirations and problem areas of the Balkans. These may be private works or governmental publications. The second category focuses on the historical development of Balkan states both in reference to the growth of nationalism and to the interests and actions of the foreign powers involved in Balkan affairs. These might in the main be characterized as political or regional histories. Another major group of source materials is formed by governmental statistical publications, ranging from the again available "statistical yearbooks" to a variety of statistical periodicals. These often constitute a rich source of comparative data, although one should always be cautious in interpreting printed statistics too literally. Attention should also be called to the usefulness of geographic regional texts on Europe, which usually contain background information of a general nature and specific discussions of national problems and problem areas. Similarly, textbooks in political geography and geopolitics also contain analyses of Balkan geopolitics.

In terms of a geographical approach to problem areas the classical text is Isaiah Bowman's *The New World: Problems in Political Geography* (New York: World Book Company, 1928). Although now out of date, *The New World* is still a sound reference for the historical development of present-day Balkan problem areas and supplies an equally sound pattern of area analysis usable at present. Another classical study is Marion I. Newbigin, *Geographical Aspects of Balkan Problems* (New York: Putnam, 1915), a highly readable account of the Balkans up to the First World War.

A. E. Moodie, *The Italo-Yugoslav Boundary: A Study in Political Geography* (London: Philip and Son, 1945), is another excellent analysis of a specific problem area, namely Trieste and the Julian March.

In reference to Macedonia, two valuable sources are H. R. Wilkinson, *Maps and Politics: A Review of the Ethnographic Cartography of Macedonia* (Liverpool: University Press, 1951) and Elisabeth Barker, *Macedonia: Its Place in Balkan Power Politics* (London: Royal Institute of International Affairs, 1950). The former is a historical study based on maps, the latter a popularized survey of political events of the last few decades. Though slightly pro-Bulgarian, N. H. Brailsford, *Macedonia: Its Races and Their Future* (London: Methuen, 1906) is an excellent historical reference.

Another valuable regional study is Edith Pierpont Stickney, *Southern Albania or Northern Epirus in European International Affairs, 1912–1923* (Stanford University Press, 1926).

Several geographical works are of interest. The classical Balkan work is Jovan Cvijić, *La Péninsule balcanique, geographie humaine* (Paris: A. Colin, 1918), later translated into Croatian by Borivoje Drobnjaković as *Balkansko Poluostrvo i Južnoslovenske Zemlje* [*The Balkan Peninsula and the South-Slav Lands*], (Zagreb: Hrvatski Stamparski Zavod D. D., 1922). This is a historical treatment of major population movements in the Balkans and is still useful although some of his ideas are now questioned. Among recent publications in the Balkans two outstanding texts are Anton Melik, *Jugoslavija: Zemljepisno Pregled* [*Jugoslavia: A Geographical Review*], (Ljubljana: Ljubljanska Tiskarna, 1949; 2d ed., 1958, in Slovene) and *Geografia Economica A.R.P.R.* edited by Mihail Hașeganu (Bucureşti: Editura Ştiinţifică, 1957).

Recent materials on the geography of the Balkans are included in a number of geography texts. The best treatments are W. Gordon East and A. E. Moodie, *The Changing World: Studies in Political Geography* (New York: World Book Company, 1956), *Military Aspects of World Political Geography* (Maxwell Air Force Base: Air University, 1959), Lewis M. Alexander, *World Political Patterns* (Chicago: Rand McNally, 1957), and George W. Hoffman, *A Geography of Europe* (New York: Ronald Press, 2d ed. 1961). Also useful is the Oxford Regional Economic Atlas volume *The U.S.S.R. and Eastern Europe* (London: Oxford University Press, 1956).

Statistical materials have become more available in recent years, but there are still significant lacunae on ethnic data and population movements in the Balkans. All countries are again publishing statistical yearbooks, and all except Albania have issued census statistics within the past decade, especially Jugoslavia which has published a number of volumes on data of the 1953 census. In addition to the publications issued by the individual countries, valuable sources are the *Demo-*

graphic Yearbook (New York: Statistical Office of the United Nations, Department of Economic and Social Affairs); the old stand-by, *The Statesman's Year-Book* (London: Macmillan); and that recent arrival *The Worldmark Encyclopedia of the Nations* (New York: Harper, 1960). W. S. and E. S. Woytinsky, *World Population and Production: Trends and Outlook* (New York: The Twentieth Century Fund, 1953) is an excellent source for comparative statistics.

THE OTTOMAN VIEW

OF THE BALKANS

Stanford J. Shaw

Any effort to evaluate the Ottoman state of mind on any matter can be attempted only with great trepidation, since it must be gleaned from many sources as widely divergent as was Ottoman society itself. To understand the position of the lands and peoples of the Balkans in the structure of Ottoman government and society and in the Ottoman mind, we must first make a preliminary examination of the Ottoman view of government and society as a whole, and in fact decide to whom among the heterogeneous and multilingual elements which composed Ottoman society we can in truth apply the term "Ottoman" itself.

THE OTTOMAN VIEW OF GOVERNMENT AND SOCIETY

By Ottoman theory, the principal attribute of sovereignty was the right of the sovereign sultan to hold as Imperial Possessions (*havass-i humayun*) all sources of wealth in his empire together with authority sufficient for him to exploit them for his own benefit. The entire structure of Ottoman society and government was based on this essential presumption.

Sources of wealth in the Ottoman Imperial Possession were produced directly by cultivation, trade and commerce, on which taxes were levied to exercise the imperial right, and indirectly in the form of fees charged for services performed by members of the sultan's government. To exploit these sources, Ottoman state and society were organized into units called *muqata'a,* or "leasing," which were superimposed over each. Every *muqata'a* was placed in the hands of an agent of the sultan, whose primary duty was to exploit it for the benefit of the sultan's Treasury (*hazine-i amire*), and whose scope of authority was limited to that necessary for him to fulfill this obligation, although within it his authority was absolute. So the sphere of Ottoman government and of the individuals who composed it was limited to functions involved with the basic attribute of Ottoman sovereignty, the exploitation of the wealth of the sultan. The *muqata'a* was the basic unit of Ottoman government from its foundation until the nineteenth century *Tanzimat* reform movement. Every government position was a *muqata'a*, for every office in some way had at least one source of revenue, either actual tax payments or fees which each official had the right to collect in return for the performance of his official duties. There were three basic kinds of *muqata'as*, three types of government positions, according to the purpose for which the holding was assigned and the degree to which each holder was required to deliver all or part of his revenues from that *muqata'a* to the imperial Treasury.

Those *muqata'as* whose holders were given the full revenues for their own profit without having to deliver any part of them to the Treasury were called *timars*, or "fiefs," and their holders were called *timarli*. These *timars* were given in return for administrative or military service not directly connected with the exploitation of the *timar* itself. The revenues of the *timar* type of *muqata'a* were assigned as the equivalent of salary to the holder, who thus was being required to collect his own salary from one of the sources of Treasury revenue.

Those *muqata'as* whose holders were given a portion of the revenues in return for their service of administering the *muqata'a* and sending the balance of its revenues to the Treasury were called *iltizams*, or "tax farms," and their holders were called *multezims*. Since the duties of the *multezim* were limited to the exploitation of the source of wealth in his *muqata'a* and did not include additional administrative or military duty, he was given only part of its revenues as payment for this service and had to surrender the balance as part of the service itself.

The third kind of *muqata'a* was the *emanet*, whose holder was called *emin*, or "steward." The *emin* was fully compensated for his service of exploiting and administering his *muqata'a* by direct salary from the Treasury. So he had to turn over to the Treasury the full fruits of his collections and did not benefit directly from them as did the *timarli* in full and the *multezim* in part. The *emanet* thus was the closest equivalent of the modern government office but was by far the least prevalent form in the Ottoman system, and for the most part it was limited to the easily accessible urban sources of government revenue.

To administer the Imperial Possessions through the *muqata'a* system, the Ottoman sultan maintained a class of slaves (*kul;* pl., *kullar*) whose lives were devoted to his service. Throughout Ottoman society the slave held the status of his master, so the slaves of the sultan became the ruling class of Ottoman society and were called *Osmanlilar*, or "Ottomans." In traditional Ottoman society, to be accepted as a member of the ruling class a person needed three basic attributes: (1) He had to profess loyalty to the sultan and his state and devote his life to their service; (2) he had to accept and practice the Muslim religion and the system of thought and action which was an integral part of it; and (3) he had to know and practice the complicated system of customs, behavior, and language which was known as the "Ottoman Way." Those who were not members of the Ottoman ruling class were considered to be members of the subject class and were called rayahs (*re'aya*). A person was considered to be a rayah because he lacked any of the attributes required of an Ottoman. He might be a Christian or a Jew; he might be a Muslim, but Arab-speaking. Or he might even be a Muslim Turk, but untrained in the Ottoman mores of social behavior, the Ottoman culture, or the very complex Ottoman version of the Turkish language. So in the traditional Ottoman system of the sixteenth and seventeenth centuries, there was a system of social mobility based on the possession of definable and attainable attributes. Persons in the rayah class could rise into the Ottoman class by acquiring these attributes and persons in the Ottoman class could become rayahs by losing or failing to practice them. Rayahs could be Muslims, and they could be far wealthier than members of the Ottoman class, but they were still not Ottomans and could not share in the benefits and obligations of that class unless they acquired all its attributes.

Each of these two classes had its distinct privileges and functions in the Ottoman system. The members of the ruling Ottoman class had the right to share in the revenues of the Imperial Possessions. In return for that right, they were slaves of the sultan, and their lives and properties were at his disposal. Their duty was to govern and defend the empire, that is, to exploit and defend the imperial sources of wealth. The duties of government were limited to this; anything not connected with it was considered to be outside the scope of the ruling class and was left to the rayahs to organize as they wished. This concept of the scope of government thus excluded many things which today are considered to be basic parts of the functions of government, such as the maintenance of transportation, public health, social security and public works, and the regulation of individual rights and duties and relations between individuals. All these were left to the rayahs. But the primary duty of the rayah subject class was to produce the wealth which was the source of imperial revenue, by farming the land and engaging in trade or industry, so that the *muqata'as* superimposed over these sources of wealth would continue to produce revenue to support the sultan and the members of his Ottoman ruling class.

Both the Ottoman and the rayah classes had their own internal systems of organization to carry out the functions assigned to them, and of education to train new members possessing the necessary attributes.

The Ottoman ruling class was divided on a functional basis into four classes (*sinif*). The imperial class (*mülkiye*), headed by the sultan, was in charge of supervising Ottoman society and maintaining its traditional structure and operation. The military class (*seyfiye*) was in charge of expanding and defending the imperial sources of wealth. The administrative class (*qalemiye*) was in charge of directing the operation of the *muqata'a* system, and thus was the basic administrative organ of the Ottoman system. The religious class (*diniye*) was in charge of interpreting, teaching, studying, and expounding the Ottoman religious law, and later was also in charge of the bulk of local and district administration.

To carry out these functions on the provincial level, the empire was divided into administrative provinces called *eyalet* at first, and later *vilayet*. There were two basic kinds of provinces in the Ottoman system. In the *timar* provinces, the bulk of the revenues from trade, industry and agriculture were divided into *timar* fiefs and were given

to Ottoman soldiers and administrators in return for their service to
the government. In such provinces, the local and district duties and
functions of administration were carried out by these *timar* holders,
and the provincial revenues went to them rather than to the government treasury. So the *timar* provinces provided primarily service
rather than revenue to the central Treasury and caused it hardly any
expense.

In the *iltizam* provinces, the administration of sources of revenue
was apportioned in *iltizams*, or "tax farms." In these provinces, the
multezims supervised the exploitation of the wealth and collected
revenues. The ruling, military, and administrative functions on the
provincial and district levels—in other words the regulation and direction of the *multezims*—were carried out by officers sent by and
responsible to the appropriate classes of the Ottoman ruling class in
Istanbul. But in this case, the Treasury and the *multezims* shared the
revenues of the province, and the Treasury had to pay the Ottomans
sent to these provinces either by salary or by the assignment of *timars*
in other provinces. These same provinces were also divided into judicial districts (*nahiye*), in each of which members of the religious
class were sent to carry out their functions, which in addition to their
religious and cultural activities, later also came to include much of
the duties of administration and police on the local and district levels
in both the *timar* and *iltizam* provinces.

Each of these four divisions of the Ottoman ruling class maintained
its own system of recruiting new members both from within and outside of the Ottoman system. In the sixteenth and seventeenth centuries
recruits came from three principal sources: about 75 percent of the
new members were children of existing members of the Ottoman class;
about 20 percent came from the rayah class, of whom approximately
half came from the Muslim rayahs and half from the Christian rayahs
by means of the *devshirme* system of recruitment. Approximately five
percent came from persons entirely outside the Ottoman system, new
slaves imported from Georgia, the Caucasus, and the Sudan, and converts from the non-Ottoman portions of Christian Europe. Persons
coming from outside the Ottoman class entered it in one of two ways:
Those who entered it as adults acquired all the attributes required
for membership and then secured an alliance (*intisab*) with an existing member who sponsored his entrance and placement in the Otto-

man class. In this case the new member and his descendants were called *donme,* or "convert." Those who entered it as youths usually were recruited for membership by the sultan through the *devshirme* system, thus by alliance with the sultan rather than with an individual member of the Ottoman ruling class, and so these new members and their descendants were called *devshirme* men.

The rayah class of subjects also had its internal organization to carry out the functions left to it by the ruling class. The basic determinant of division in the rayah class was religion. Each religious group was organized into a relatively self-contained and internally autonomous community called *millet,* which was allowed to maintain its own traditional laws and internal administrative organization under the direction of its religious leader, who thus was made a civil as well as religious authority. It was the semiautonomous *millet* system which enabled the Ottoman class to exploit the wealth produced by the rayahs with the least possible resistance and friction, so it was a basic factor in Ottoman stability and success. At the peak of Ottoman power, the Muslims who were not members of the ruling class were considered to be rayahs organized into a Muslim *millet* just as much as were the Christians. In fact, the Muslim *millet* did hold a position of superiority over the other *millets* because it was the only one which practiced the same religion and laws as did the ruling Ottoman class, and which had an organic connection with it in the person of its director, *the Sheyh ul-Islam,* who also was the director of the Ottoman religious class.

So, the Ottoman system was an attempt to organize society to produce the maximum possible wealth for the sovereign. The ruling class of Ottomans exploited the imperial sources of wealth through the *muqata'a* system, and the subject rayahs produced wealth for the ruling class while retaining their old institutions, laws, and traditions under the cloak of the *millet* system. It was through the *muqata'as* and *millets* that alien customs and laws and forms of action and government were introduced into and retained in the Ottoman system. But these were essentially Islamic forms inherited from pre-Ottoman Muslim states and civilizations in the East, so they provided an Islamic veneer to the many non-Muslim elements which were preserved in the empire, especially in the Balkans. And the Ottoman mind, in considering the Balkans as well as other elements in the system thought of

them only in terms of how they fitted into this pattern and contributed
to the goal of Ottoman organization. In the Ottoman mind, there was
no idea of "the Balkans" as a concept of society or administration, and
the word itself appeared very rarely in Ottoman texts, and then only
in its most limited geographical meaning. It was only in terms of the
provincial and local *muqata'as* into which the Balkans were divided
that the Ottomans in some cases and under some conditions focused
their attention on them as distinct entities in the Ottoman world.
Likewise on the personal level, the Ottoman mind did not conceive of
"Balkan peoples" any more than they did of "Arab peoples." Each
individual had a certain status in life depending on his class, rank,
religion, and occupation, and it was in terms of these that he was
considered.

THE TRADITIONAL OTTOMAN VIEW OF THE BALKANS

The position of the Balkans in the traditional Ottoman system and in
the Ottoman mind was governed principally by four historical factors:

The Gazi Tradition as the Basis of Loyalty to the Sultan

When the Ottoman principality first appeared in history as an independent entity in thirteenth-century Bithynia, it was smaller and
weaker than its Turkish neighbors in Anatolia. But alone of them, it
was in a geographical position to take direct advantage of the decay of
the Byzantine and Serbian empires. It was the lure of conquest of
these infidel lands which enabled the early Ottoman sultans, rather
than their Turkish neighbors in Anatolia, to attract into their service
the unsettled nomadic Turkoman tribes and unemployed urban workers who were unable to find their place in the urban Turkish states of
fourteenth-century Anatolia. As a result of this, throughout the remaining centuries of the Ottoman Empire, the continued maintenance
of Ottoman rule in the infidel lands of the Balkans always remained the
most important and basic factor of loyalty to the sultan by the Turkish
elements of the Ottoman subject class. The Ottoman sultans recognized and maintained this tradition by emphasizing their role as
gazis, "warriors of the Faith," against the infidels. It was primarily as

THE OTTOMAN VIEW OF THE BALKANS 63

"*gazi* son of *gazi*" that they were described in official documents, rather than as *padishah* (sultan) or caliph, the latter title in fact being used officially for the first time only in the late eighteenth century. Rule of the Balkans therefore provided an integral part of the traditional base of loyalty to the Ottoman sultans, and it was for this reason that the Ottomans hung on so long and tenaciously to lands which, as we will see, had little financial or military value to the empire after the middle of the seventeenth century.

Identification of the Balkans with the Timar System

At the time the Ottomans conquered the Balkans, the financial needs of the Ottoman Treasury were abundantly provided for by the booty of conquest, and it was primarily men who were needed to conquer and rule large new territories. Since the fourteenth and early fifteenth centuries were an age when the central Ottoman administrative machinery was at best embryonic and inefficient, the motive of personal profit in the decentralized *timar* fief system was found to be more effective than central administration and, thus, the most efficient means of producing soldiers and administrators from the conquered lands. Hence the Balkan lands were given out as fiefs and provided a relatively small amount of revenue in cash or kind to the imperial Treasury.

But in the late fifteenth and sixteenth centuries, when eastern Anatolia and the Arab provinces were conquered, conditions were quite different. The central Ottoman administrative machinery was more efficient and able to control the operation of the *muqata'a* system. The feudal cavalry based on *timars* was militarily obsolete and the Treasury was in need of cash revenues to pay an increasing number of infantry, soldiers, and administrators who were being compensated by salaries rather than by *timars*. As a result, the eastern provinces, as they were conquered, were organized primarily into *iltizams*. So within the traditional Ottoman administrative structure, the Balkan provinces were always identified with the *timar* system and the service which it was supposed to provide, while the eastern provinces, while not entirely devoid of *timars* in their border areas, were primarily connected with the *iltizam* system, and provided the bulk of the revenues of the imperial Treasury, both in cash and kind.

The Balkan Timars *as the Bases of Political Power*

The great Ottoman conquests in the Balkans were made primarily by
members of the old Turkish aristocracy, descendants of the ruling
families of the pre-Ottoman Turkish principalities in Anatolia who
had entered the service of the Ottomans, and it was to the members
of this Turkish aristocracy that the bulk of the newly conquered
Balkan lands were given as *timars* in the fourteenth and early fifteenth
centuries. A primary element of the Ottoman policy of conquest was
always an effort to reduce opposition to a minimum by absorbing the
conquered native notables into the Ottoman system. It was found that
the most effective method of absorbing members of the old Turkish
Anatolian noble families was that of giving them new positions and
estates of value equal to those they held before, but situated in the
Balkans, far away from their old family principalities in Anatolia. So
the *timars* in the conquered Balkan lands provided the Turkish aristocracy in the Ottoman Empire with the revenues which formed the
backbone of its position in Ottoman society.

As the Balkan conquests continued, the Turkish aristocrats secured
such large Balkan estates and revenues, that by the start of the fifteenth century the Ottoman sultans were no more than first among
equals, and the Turkish aristocracy exercised a deciding influence in
Ottoman government and military affairs through its leading family,
the *Jandarli*. So in this early period, the members of the Turkish
aristocracy looked on the Balkans as the basis of their financial and
political position.

After 1450, the Ottoman sultans sought various means to strengthen
their personal power and regain control of the Ottoman system from
this Turkish aristocracy. The principal source of power which they
developed against the Turkish aristocracy was the old Balkan ruling
families, first as vassals and later as fully absorbed members of the
Ottoman class. Initially, in the fourteenth century, in order to secure
a minimum of local Balkan resistance against the advancing Ottoman
armies, portions of the Balkans were left as autonomous provinces
under their old ruling families, who in return provided tribute and
military service to the Ottoman sultans. Where the lands were taken
directly into the Ottoman system, as much as 50 or 60 percent of the

timars into which they were divided were given to Christians. The Christian *voynuks* in Bosnia, Serbia, Bulgaria, Thessaly, Macedonia, and Albania were incorporated into the Ottoman army, usually without any requirement of conversion, and they provided the sultans with troops to counter the increasingly independent power of the Turkish aristocracy at the same time as the latter was increasing its own financial power through new conquests in the Balkans.

But the vassal system proved to be unsatisfactory as a means of developing a major base of power, since the loyalties were at the most tenuous and temporary. So after Tamurlane's victory over Bayazid I at the Battle of Ankara (1402) and the temporary dissolution of the Ottoman Empire during the interregnum (1402–1413), as part of the process of restoration and reconquest, the vassal system was eliminated by Mehmed I (1413–1421) and his successors, and in its place two means were employed to establish a firmer base of Balkan support of the sultan against the power of the Turkish aristocracy. On one hand, as the Balkans were reconquered, Balkan vassals were fully incorporated into the Ottoman system. They often retained some of their Balkan patrimonies, but to them were added great *timar* estates in western Anatolia, and when they became Muslims and adapted the Ottoman way they became full Ottomans eligible to attain the highest positions open to members of the ruling class. Most of the great Balkan families and smaller *timar* holders converted to Islam during the sixteenth century not as the result of Ottoman pressure, but in consequence of their realization that this was a necessary first step on the road to becoming full Ottomans. Those of the old ruling classes who were not assimilated into the Ottoman ruling class, like the Christian mercenaries who served as Ottoman auxiliaries until the start of the sixteenth century, thereafter were reduced to the status of rayahs.

On the other hand, the *devshirme* system was developed as a means to recruit members of the non-Muslim *millets* into the Ottoman class, both to fill the need for new manpower in an expanding empire and to provide the sultan with a more numerous and obedient base of support than even that provided by the assimilated Balkan noble families.

During the Ottoman conquest, there usually was no policy of forced conversion of the Balkan peasants. Under the late Byzantine emperors, the central government had lost most of its control over the great landed nobles, who were able to misrule and overtax at will. But with the Ottoman conquests, a strong centralized government was reëstablished in the Balkans, and while the *timar* system essentially incorporated the old Balkan feudal systems, Ottoman law strictly controlled the relations between the feudal *timar* holders and the peasants. The old feudal requirements of forced labor and obligations to provide wood, hay, and straw for the lord were replaced by one simple tax called *chift resmi*. The Ottoman judges, as local representatives of the ruling class, were able to use their positions to make the *timar* holders obey the law. So the Balkan peasantry and church remained intact, and it was only the Balkan nobility which eventually was assimilated into Ottoman society.

As with the nobles, so with the peasants: it was not Ottoman policy to force conversion, since it was felt that such an effort would disrupt the main purpose of Ottoman government, the collection of taxes. It was only under Bayazid II (1481–1512), and especially with Selim I (1512–1520) and thereafter that the entry into the Ottoman state of the fanatical *ulema* class of the newly conquered Arab provinces and an Ottoman reaction to the increased Franciscan missionary activity in the Balkans (supported by the Habsburgs and Venetians as a political weapon) caused the Ottomans to adopt coercive measures against the Christians in Serbia, Albania, and Danubian Bulgaria. This development culminated during and after the reign of Murad IV (1623–1640). After that time the Muslim *millet* was raised in status to a lower element of the ruling class, while thereafter the term rayah came to be limited to the non-Muslim subjects, to whom thereafter increasingly coercive measures were applied. But long before this, it was out of these non-Muslim rayah *millets* of the Balkans that the Ottoman sultans developed the *devshirme* system and the *devshirme* class as a second source of power independent from that of the Turkish aristocracy.

The *devshirme* system of recruiting was a traditional means of securing new manpower in the pre-Ottoman Turkish states of the Near East and Central Asia, and it was used under the Ottomans as early as the late fourteenth century. But it was developed on a large scale only after the conquest of Constantinople as a means to create a class of converts dependent entirely on the sultans for their revenues and position, and thus more loyal and obedient to the sultans than the relatively independent feudal Turkish and Balkan aristocrats and their descendants. The members of the old Balkan aristocracies previously absorbed into the Ottoman class joined with those newly entered through the *devshirme* system to form a distinct group within the Ottoman class. To counter the power of the Turkish aristocracy, members of this *devshirme* class were given greatly increased financial and military strength in the form of salaries and other revenues available from the Treasury and of *timars* taken from members of the Turkish aristocracy for one reason or another. The internal political history of the Ottoman Empire from 1453 to 1566 was primarily a story of struggle for power in the Ottoman ruling class between the members of these two groups—the Turkish aristocracy with financial and military power based on *timars* held primarily in the Balkans, and the *devshirme* class with financial power based on Treasury revenues from the newly conquered Anatolian and Arab provinces. As a result of this rivalry, after the conquest of Constantinople (Istanbul), the addition to the empire of new Balkan lands and territories was looked upon with increasing opposition and fear by the members of the Turkish aristocracy, who saw quite rightly that the revenues and *devshirme* men which these new conquests were introducing into the Ottoman class would submerge their power even more beneath the rising *devshirme* power.

Decline of the Timar *System and*
Triumph of the Devshirme *Class*

The changing position of the Balkans in the Ottoman system and of the corresponding Ottoman view of the Balkans was related directly to changes in the *timar* system and the political triumph of the *devshirme* class in the late sixteenth century. When the *timar* system was first developed, the persons to whom the fiefs were given, no matter what their origins or rank, had to provide in return to the Ottoman state military or administrative service in amounts directly proportional to the revenues received from the *timars*. But during the sixteenth century, various military and economic developments made obsolete both the mounted feudal cavalry and the *timar* system on which it was based.

Militarily, this development was connected with the introduction of gunpowder and fire weapons. The new rifles were too heavy to be carried and used efficiently on horseback; the stationary cannon could not be coördinated with the fast-moving cavalry; and the use of cannon and rifles by infantry required a type of training and discipline which could be applied only to troops kept permanently together, not scattering periodically to the sources of their revenue as the *timar* cavalrymen had been required to do. In other words, well-trained and maneuverable salaried infantry units using cannon and rifles became far more effective than cavalry with their disorganized mass charges and bows and arrows. One of the chief reasons for the rapid Ottoman success in the Balkans as in the East was the Ottoman willingness to accept such effective new weapons and techniques and the development of the Janissaries and a whole series of infantry corps specifically to use them.

Until the time of Mehmed II (1451–1481), these corps were manned principally by Christian mercenaries recruited from the Balkans. After his accession they were manned by *devshirme* converts to whom they were given in order to secure a more orderly, regular, and obedient source of manpower, and also to give a military backing to the *devshirme* class which was being developed as a political weapon against the Turkish aristocracy. From 1453 to 1566 the Janissaries and the other new infantry and artillery corps gradually replaced the feudal cavalry as the backbone of the Ottoman army. In regard to the Balkans, this development had three important results:

1) Militarily, the development and use of the infantry corps armed with fire weapons and modern tactics gave the Ottomans military supremacy over lingering resistance in the Balkans and enabled them to beat back the efforts of the Crusader and Habsburg armies sent to regain the Balkans during the sixteenth and seventeenth centuries. Thus, militarily at least, the *devshirme* class was an element of strength in the Ottoman system.

2) Politically, it meant that the *devshirme* class, composed primarily of descendants of the Balkan noble and rayah classes, was closely allied with the growing permanent salaried corps armed with the most modern weapons and tactics, while the Turkish aristocracy was tied to a landed cavalry corps whose military value was becoming increasingly obsolete. As a result, after the start of the seventeenth century—and only then—the *devshirme* class emerged supreme within

the Ottoman ruling class. While the Turkish aristocracy was not destroyed, it no longer had the financial and military power necessary for it to be an equal in the political struggle for power in the empire. This meant essentially a triumph of the Balkan Christian convert element as political masters in the Ottoman ruling class and the relegation of the Turkish aristocracy to a subordinate position.

3) Administratively and economically, the decline of the feudal cavalry as a military weapon, and of the Turkish aristocracy as a military and political power made the *timar* system itself obsolete as a means of supporting military and administrative service. This coincided with a great increase of population and inflation of Ottoman coinage during the sixteenth century, which made land a much more profitable and secure source of income than it had previously been. The coincidence of these factors caused the Ottomans gradually to abandon the distribution of *timars* in return for service, and to distribute them instead simply as sources of revenue for members of the *devshirme* class. With the decline of the Turkish aristocracy, the *devshirme* obtained control over the sultan and the empire through monopoly of the positions in the imperial and military classes. Members of the Turkish aristocracy thereafter managed to maintain predominance although not monopoly in the administrative and religious classes, but this gave them no more than a passive power of supervision in the Ottoman system as a whole. Most sultans became puppets in the hands of the leaders of the *devshirme* party, who were able as a result to force the establishment of a new kind of *muqata'a* called *malikane,* which was virtually private property, could be bought and sold and left in inheritance, and in return for which only nominal fees and no service was required for the Treasury. As a result, most of the *muqata'as* in the Balkans were rapidly transformed into *malikane* holdings held by members of the *devshirme* class. So the Balkan provinces after the seventeenth century provided the Ottoman Empire with little service and less revenue and did little more than support the power of a *devshirme* class which increasingly milked the Ottoman system for its own benefit. Admission to the Ottoman class and appointments to positions and revenues were made for reasons of politics rather than ability, and the inevitable result was disintegration of administrative efficiency and honesty. Essentially, it was the triumph of the Balkan element in the Ottoman ruling class through the *devshirme*

system which led to the breakdown of the financial and administrative system of the Ottomans and caused the subsequent decline of the empire. So long as the sultans were able to control the Ottoman system by balancing off the Balkan-Christian *devshirme* element against the Turco-Islamic aristocracy, they were able to control and use both for the benefit of the empire. But once one obtained supremacy, it was able to use the sultans and the empire for its own benefit, and decline resulted.

THE VIEW OF THE BALKANS BY OTTOMAN REFORMERS

Throughout the centuries of decline, there were two main classes of Ottomans working to revive and restore the empire. These were (1) the Turkish members of the Muslim rayah class, resident chiefly in Anatolia and led by members of the Turkish aristocracy who had been dispossessed of their properties and positions in Constantinople by the *devshirme* class, and (2) members of the Turkish aristocracy still remaining in the Ottoman ruling class, who were raised to positions of predominance on occasion by the few strong sultans who managed to rise to power during the years of decline.

The Turkish rayahs and their Turkish aristocratic leaders reflected their dissatisfaction by virtually continuous *Jelali* revolts in Anatolia from the middle of the sixteenth until well into the nineteenth century. The Ottoman chronicles and administrative materials of the time are filled with reports of *Jelali* declarations of Turkish resentment against "foreign" *devshirme* predominance in Istanbul as the major cause of Ottoman decline. The common view of these Turkish rayah reformers was on one hand scorn of the Balkans for providing the source of *devshirme* power, but on the other hand constant affirmation that a principal object of reform should be the restoration of Ottoman control in the Balkans, since their rule was still felt to be an important basis of Muslim loyalty to the Ottoman sultans, and their revenues a necessity for Ottoman revival. They sought to eliminate the *timar* system in the Balkans and replace it with *iltizams* administered by members of the Turkish aristocracy. At the same time, the *devshirme* would be entirely eliminated from the Ottoman ruling class and the empire would be made a Turkish state instead of a cosmopolitan political unit.

Within the Ottoman ruling class, there were three main streams of reform during the centuries of Ottoman decline:

The first was a traditionalist stream, beginning with Sultan Murad IV (1623–1640), reaching its peak under the Köprülü grand vezirs in the late seventeenth century, and culminating in the reforms of Selim III (1789–1807) at the start of the nineteenth century. These traditionalist reformers were confident that the Ottoman decline could be ended and the lost territories regained if only the old Ottoman institutions and techniques were restored to the perfect state which they were considered to have attained in the sixteenth century, although under this guise of adherence to tradition they did occasionally introduce innovations of one sort or another. New military techniques and forms of organization of demonstrated superiority were occasionally added beside the old, but the old institutions and techniques were essentially left as they had been in the time of Ottoman grandeur. In particular, these reformers tried to restore the old Ottoman social and institutional systems. Within the ruling class, they wished to retain the *devshirme* system, but they also intended to restore the power of the Turkish aristocracy so they could balance each other off. In the subject class the Christian and non-Christian rayahs would be divided into semiautonomous and obedient *millets* as before, and the supremacy of the Muslim *millet* would be retained. In the Balkans, the original operation of the *timar* system would be restored, with hereditary rights eliminated and possession allowed only in return for service to the state.

These reformers were almost completely unsuccessful because they did not see that Europe had in fact developed techniques of organization and action in every field of life which were far superior to anything which the Ottomans had at their peak, and that even if the old Ottoman institutions were restored they would not have the same supremacy in relation to eighteenth- and nineteenth-century Europe that they had earlier. They did not understand that European techniques and institutions could not operate successfully so long as the old Ottoman institutions remained beside them to parallel, oppose, and limit their operation, that the new institutions could not be introduced in isolation from the entire context of thought and action in which they had successfully developed in Europe. They failed in the Balkans because the traditional Ottoman social system remained the basis of their thought and action. They could no more understand the effect of nationalism on the non-Turkish subjects of the empire than they could its manifestation in the Turkish nationalism then being expounded by the Turkish rayah bands of Anatolia. National sentiment simply did not fit in with the order of society conceived of by even the most enlightened Ottomans of the time. They did not understand that nationalism had made impossible the maintenance of a *millet* system which had worked for centuries, no matter how much autonomy was to be given to each *millet* under the new system. So the tide of Balkan separatism continued unchecked by the efforts of even the most successful of the traditionalist reformers. And their efforts to retain the *devshirme* as an element of Ottoman society caused them to be opposed also by the Turkish nationalists of Anatolia, although in fields other than this, the goals of the two groups were basically the same.

The second stream of Ottoman reform was that of the "men of the *tanzimat*," who first arose under Mahmud II (1808–1839) and continued their activities until the end of the reign of Abd ul-Hamid II (1876–1909). These *tanzimat* reformers were essentially agents of the Ottoman ruling class, trying to save its autocratic social and political position by modernizing the instruments of its rule, the administration and the army. They were aware of the reasons for the repeated failures of the traditionalist reformers, and so they were quite willing to destroy or radically change the old Ottoman institutions and replace them with new ones imported from the West. It was the crisis entailed in the loss of the bulk of the Balkan provinces in the first part of the nineteenth century which enabled the men of the *tanzimat* to introduce and apply this extreme concept of reform in place of the mild traditional type which preceded it, but so far as the Balkans were concerned, the men of the *tanzimat*, like the traditionalist Ottoman reformers, could not offer the social changes needed to combat the attraction of nationalism. Indeed, all they could offer was a restoration of the old social system. During the *tanzimat*, the empire continued to be ruled by an autocratic ruling class led by the sultan. The subject class had to continue to obey his decrees as before, and was excluded from all direct participation in the process of government. The *millet* system was retained and restored, with the exception that equality under the law and legal guarantees of individual life and property were given to the members of the non-Muslim *millets*. The *tanzimat* tried to restore the equality of all *millets*, Muslim and non-Muslim alike, an equality which had existed until the start of the seventeenth century.

Only in the fields of the administration and the army did the men of the *tanzimat* depart from the policies of the traditionalist reformers. Here the old institutions were entirely destroyed and replaced by the new. To the ruling class was added a newly created group of expert bureaucrats and officers educated in the new arts and sciences developed in the West. To facilitate their rule and imposition of the new systems, centralized control was established. The indirect *muqata'a* system was replaced by direct rule by officials paid by and responsible directly to the central government in Istanbul. But for the Balkan provinces still remaining in the Ottoman Empire, this meant the elimination of what little autonomy they had possessed under the old system and the imposition of Ottoman techniques and methods more completely than ever had been attempted even at the peak of Ottoman power.

So the men of the *tanzimat* understood Balkan nationalism even less than their predecessors. They failed in the empire as a whole because they did not foresee that the technical and institutional reforms they were introducing to rescue an autocratic ruling class would eventually produce a demand for social and political reform and an end to the autocratic position of the class they were trying to save. They failed in the Balkans because, like the traditionalist reformers, they retained the Ottoman mentality at least to the extent that they did not understand the effect of nationalism on the *millet* system. They considered Balkan efforts to maintain or secure autonomy or independence to be as reactionary as the rantings of the conservative *ulema* and others who opposed the reforms of the *tanzimat*. To them Balkan nationalism was no more than the treason of rebellious rayahs, and so they could make no provision to appease or contain it and thus save the empire.

The third and final stream of reform in Ottoman society was that of the Young Ottoman intellectuals and their political successors and allies, the Young Turks, who arose in the last half of the nineteenth century. These men were products of the new technical class of expert Ottomans produced by the *tanzimat*. But they discarded the essential object of the *tanzimat*—the preservation of the old social system and introduction of technical and physical reforms by an autocratic upper class—and demanded political and social equality among the subjects of the sultan and constitutional limitations on the ruling class, in other words an end to its absolute and autocratic power. In fact, this meant an end to the very distinction between the ruling and subject classes as it was known in traditional Ottoman thought.

In regard to the Balkans, the young Ottomans accepted the centralization of administration and reduction of autonomy which had been one of the characteristic policies of the *tanzimat*. They did not understand the significance of Balkan nationalism to the extent that they tried to reconcile the minorities and Balkan provinces for the loss of administrative autonomy by advocating an "Ottomanization" of the population, an end to the *millet* system and its replacement by a common citizenship for all subjects of the sultan regardless of religion, race and class in society. This group replaced the men of the *tanzimat* with the overthrow of Abd ul-Hamid II in 1909, but its efforts at Ottomanization were entirely rejected by the Balkan nationalists who demanded nothing more than full independence from the empire of all parts in which persons of their nationality formed a majority. As a result of this and the crushing defeats of the Balkan wars, Ottoman constitutionalism and modern Turkish reform in all aspects of society were forced into the channel of Turkish nationalism, an association which has remained until the present day in the modern Turkish republic.

Thus the Ottoman view of the Balkans varied according to the class and rank of the Ottoman, and the time. The Turkish aristocrats of the fourteenth century looked to the Balkans as the source of their power; those of the fifteenth century and thereafter saw them as the source of the *devshirme* power which was gradually replacing them in control of the Ottoman ruling class. The descendants of the Balkan ruling houses who were absorbed into the Ottoman system saw the Balkans first as a stronghold of their opponents, later as the main source of their financial and political power. Within the Ottoman administrative structure and the Ottoman mind as a whole, the Balkans evolved from a position where they provided the empire with administrative and military service through the *timar* system to one where they provided the Ottoman system with a degenerate *devshirme* class bringing the empire to administrative dissolution and chaos. It was only in its role as the location for the numerous comfortable summer estates owned by upper class Ottoman families regardless of descent or party that the Balkans continued to be preferred to the barren and hot hills of Anatolia. But to the Ottoman reformers, it was to the Balkans, or at least to those Balkan provinces still remaining in the empire, that reforms had to be applied as the primary and most essential means of restoring the strength of the empire.

BIBLIOGRAPHY

The basic concepts of Ottoman organization and the Ottoman mind developed in this essay are discussed in more detail in my two books, *The Financial and Administrative Organization and Development of Ottoman Egypt, 1517–1798* (Princeton, N.J., 1962) and *Ottoman Egypt in the Eighteenth Century: The Nizamname-i Misir of Ahmed Cezzar Pasha* (Cambridge, Mass., 1962). They are based primarily on study in three types of Ottoman source material—archives, chronicles, and Ottoman descriptive materials:

Archives

Ottoman administrative registers and documents held in the Ottoman archives of Istanbul and Cairo. These archives are described in Midhat Sertoglu, *Muhteva Bakimindan Başvekalet Arşivi[The Contents of the Prime Minister's Archives]*, (Ankara, 1956); Tahsin Öz, *Arşiv Kilavuzu [Guide to the Archives]*, (Istanbul, 1940); S. J. Shaw, "Archival Sources for Ottoman History: The Archives of Turkey," *Journal of the American Oriental Society*, LXXX (1960), 1–12, and "Cairo's Archives and the History of Ottoman Egypt," *Report on Current Research, Spring, 1956*, Middle East Institute (Washington, D.C., 1956), pp. 59–72; Jean Deny, *Sommaire des Archives Turques du Caire* (Cairo, 1930). Much official material was also published in the official Ottoman government newspaper, *Taqvim-i Veqa'i [Calendar of Events]* after 1831.

Chronicles

[1365–1493]   Uruc b. Adil, *Tevarih-i Al-i Osman* [*Annals of the Otto-man Dynasty*] in F. Babinger, ed., *Die frühosmanischen Jahrbücher des Urudsch* (Hannover, 1925).

[1285–1502]   Aşiq Paşa zade, *Tevarih-i Al-i Osman* [*Annals of the Ottoman Dynasty*], (Istanbul, 1914).

[13th century to 1597]   Ali (Mustafa b. Ahmed), *Kunh ul-Ahbar* [*The Essence of Events*], (Istanbul, 1860), 5 vols.

[13th century to 1485]   Mehmed Neşri, *Cihannuma* [*Picture of the World*], (unpublished).

[13th century to 1553]   Lutfi Paşa, *Tevarih-i Al-i Osman* [*Annals of the Ottoman Dynasty*], (Istanbul, 1925).

[13th century to 1520]   Hoca Saduddin, *Tac ut-Tevarih* [*The Crown of Annals*], (Istanbul, 1863), 2 vols.

[1591–1660]   Mustafa Naima, *Tarih-i Naima* [*Naima's History*], (Istanbul, 1865), 6 vols.

[1660–1721]   Mehmed Raşid, *Raşid Tarihi* [*Rashid's History*], (Istanbul, 1867), 5 vols.

[1721–1728]   Ismail Asim, Küçük Çelebi zade, *Asim Tarihi* [*Asim's History*], (Istanbul, 1867).

[1730–1740]   Mehmed Subhi, Mustafa Sami and Huseyn Şakir, *Tarih-i Subhi, Sami ve Şakir* [*Subhi, Sami and Şakir's History*], (Istanbul, 1783).

[1744–1747]   Suleyman Izzi, *Izzi Tarihi* [*Izzi's History*], (Istanbul, 1784), 2 vols.

[1747–1766]   Mehmed Hakim, *Hakim Tarihi* [*Hakim's History*], (unpublished).

[1766–1768]   Çeşmi zade Mustafa Reşid Efendi, *Çeşmizade Tarihi* [*Çeşmizade's History*], (Istanbul, 1959).

[1768–1791]   Sadullah Enveri, *Tarih-i Enveri* [*Enveri's History*], (unpublished).

[1787–1791]   Edib Mehmed Efendi, *Tarih-i Edib* [*Edib's History*], (unpublished).

[1794–1798]   Halil Nuri Efendi, *Nuri Tarihi* [*Nuri's History*], (unpublished).

[1752–1804]   Ahmed Vasif Efendi, *Mahasin al-Asar ve Haqayik al-Ahbar* [*The Beauties of Relics and the Truths of Histories*], (Cairo, 1830), 2 vols. The two published volumes cover only the years 1752–1774 and do no more than summarize *Hakim Tarihi*. Vasif's more valuable records of his own time, for the years 1774–1804 remain unpublished in five manuscript volumes.

[1791–1808]   Ahmed Asim, *Tarih-i Asim* [*Asim's History*], (Istanbul, 1867), 2 vols.

THE OTTOMAN VIEW OF THE BALKANS   77

[1808–1821]   Mehmed Ataullah Şani zade, *Şani zade Tarihi* [*Şani zade's History*], (Istanbul, 1875–1876), 4 vols.

[1821–1826]   Mehmed Esad Efendi, *Tarih-i Esad Efendi* [*Esad Efendi's History*], (unpublished).

[1774–1825]   Ahmed Cevdet, *Cevdet Tarihi* (first edition, Istanbul, 1856–1885; second revised edition, Istanbul, 1885–1887), 12 vols. each edition.

[1825–1876]   Ahmed Lütfi, *Tarih-i Lütfi* [*Lütfi's History*], (Istanbul, 1875–1902), 8 vols. The published volumes cover only the years 1825–1846. The unpublished nine volumes go on to 1876.

[1876–1922]   Abd ur-Rahman Şeref, *Tarih-i Devlet-i Osmani* [*History of the Ottoman State*], (Istanbul, 1899–1902), 2 vols.

Ottoman Descriptive Materials

Tayyarzade Ahmed Ata, *Tarih-i Ata* [*Ata's History*], (Istanbul, 1876–1877), 5 vols. A description of Ottoman palace organization in the nineteenth century, with some material on its historical development.

Ayn-i Ali Efendi, *Qavanin-i Al-i Osman der Hulasa-i Mazamin-i Defter-i Divan* [*Laws of the Ottoman Dynasty, Comprising a Summary of the Contents of the Council Register*], (Istanbul, 1864). Description of Ottoman administrative and financial structure in the seventeenth century.

Evliya Çelebi, *Seyahatname* [*Travel Account*], (Istanbul, 1928–1938), 10 vols. Exhaustive description of Ottoman society and government in the late seventeenth century. The parts on Thrace have been translated with notes by Hans J. Kissling, *Beiträge zur Kenntnis Thrakiens im 17. Jahrhundert* (Wiesbaden, 1956).

Gelibolulu Mustafa Ali, *Meva'idün-Nefa'is fi kava'idi'l-Mecalis* [*Trays of Rare Things on the Customs of the Assemblies*], (Istanbul, 1956). Description of the Ottoman Empire in the middle of the sixteenth century.

Hezarfen Huseyn Efendi, "Telhis ul-Beyan fi Qavanin-i Al-i Osman" ["Abstract of the Declaration on the Laws of the Ottoman Dynasty"]. Unpublished description of the Ottoman administrative and financial structure at the end of the seventeenth century. Summarized and discussed in Robert Anhegger, "Hezarfen Hüseyin Efendi'nin Osmanli Devlet Teşkilatina dair mülahazalari" ["Hezarfen Huseyn Efendi's Studies of the Organization of the Ottoman State"], *Türkiyat Mecmuasi*, X (1953), 365–393.

Qoçi Bey, *Qoçi Bey Risalesi* [*Qoçi Bey's Treatise*], (Istanbul, 1887). Proposals for Ottoman reform made in the mid-sixteenth century.

Lütfi Paşa, *Asafname* [*Letter of the Grand Vezir*], (first edition, Istanbul, 1909; second edition, ed. R. Tschudi, 1910). Proposals for reform made by the sixteenth-century Ottoman grand vezir and historian.

Sari Mehmed Paşa, *Nasaih ul-vüzera vel-ümera* [*Advice to the Ministers and Princes*], (ed. and tr. W. Wright as *Ottoman Statecraft*, Princeton, N.J., 1935).

Qanunname-i Sultani ber muceb-i Örf-i Osmani. [*The Sultanic Law Code, in Accordance with Ottoman Practice*]. Official fifteenth-century Ottoman law code. Edited and transliterated into modern Turkish by Robert Anhegger and Halil Inalcik, *Kanunname-i Sultani ber Muceb-i Örf-i Osmani* (Ankara, 1956). A photograph of the same text was published by F. Babinger as *Sultanische Urkunden zur Geschichte der osmanischen Wirtschaft und Staatsverwaltung am Ausgang der Herrschaft Mehmeds II., des Eroberers* (Munich, 1956).

Photographs and microfilms of all the unpublished manuscripts mentioned above are available at the Harvard University Library, Cambridge, Massachusetts.

Secondary Works

Babinger, Franz, *Beiträge zur Frühgeschichte der Türkenherrschaft in Rumelien* (Brünn, 1944).

Barkan, Ömer Lütfi, "Osmanli imparatorlugunda bir iskan ve kolonizasyon metodu olarak vakiflar ve temlikler" ["Foundations and Freeholds as Methods of Settlement and Colonization in the Ottoman Empire"], *Vakiflar Dergisi*, II (1942), 278–286.

Bistra A. Cvetkova, "L'évolution du régime feodal turc de la fin du XVIᵉ jusqu'au milieu du XVIIIᵉ siècle," Académie des Sciences de Bulgarie, *Etudes Historiques* (Sofia, 1960), pp. 171–206.

Djurdjev, Branislav, "Bosna," *Encyclopaedia of Islam: New Edition*, Leiden, I (1960), 1261–1275.

Gibb, H. A. R. and Harold Bowen, *Islamic Society and the West*, Vol. I: *Islamic Society in the Eighteenth Century* (2 parts, London, 1950–1958). Entirely supersedes Lybyer as a description of Ottoman government and society.

Gökbilgin, Tayyip, *XV. ve XVI. asirlarda Edirne ve Paşa Livasi* [*The Edirne and Paşa Districts in the Fifteenth and Sixteenth Centuries*], (Istanbul, 1952). Collection of Ottoman documents concerning the administrative, financial, and social systems in Adrianople and Pasha districts.

———. *Rumeli'de Yürükler, Tatarlar ve Evlad-i Fatihan* [*The Yuruks, the Tatars and the Evlad-i Fatihan Tribes in Rumelia*], (Istanbul, 1957). Ottoman documents concerning the settlement of Turkish tribes in the Balkans.

Heyd, Uriel, *Ottoman Documents on Palestine, 1552–1615* (Oxford, 1960).

Inalcik, Halil, "Arnawutluk," *Encyclopaedia of Islam: New Edition*, I (1960), 650–658.

————. "Balkan," *Encyclopaedia of Islam: New Edition,* I (1960), 998–1000.

————. *Fatih Devri üzerinde Tetkikler ve Vesikalar* [*Studies and Documents concerning the Age of Mehmed the Conqueror*], (Ankara, 1954).

————. "Ottoman Methods of Conquest," *Studia Islamica,* II (1954), 103–129. Summary of parts of the above.

————. *Süret-i Defter-i Sancak-i Arvanid* [*Copy of the Register of the District of Albania*], (Ankara, 1954). A fifteenth-century Ottoman cadastral register of Albania.

————. "Stefan Dușan'dan Osmanli Imparatorluğuna. XV asirda Rumeli'de hiristiyan sipahiler ve menşeleri," ["From Stefan Dushan to the Ottoman Empire. The Christian feudal cavalrymen and their origins in 15th century Rumelia"], *Fuad Köprülü Armagani. Mélanges Fuad Köprülü* (Istanbul, 1953), pp. 207–248.

————. "Timariotes chrétiens en Albanie au XVᵉ siècle," *Mitteilungen des Österreichischen Staatsarchivs,* IV (1952), 118–138. Summary of the above.

Levend, Agah Sirri, *Gazavatnameler ve Mihaloglu Ali Bey'in Gazavatnamesi* [*Accounts of Raids in the Name of Islam, with Mihaloglu Ali Bey's Raid Account*], (Ankara, 1956). Bibliography of the earliest Ottoman chronicles of the Balkan conquests, together with the text of one of the most important of these.

Lybyer, Albert H., *The Government of the Ottoman Empire in the Time of Suleiman the Magnificent* (Cambridge, Mass., 1913).

Mutafcieva, Vera P., "De l'exploitation féodale dans les terres de population bulgare sous la domination turque au XVᵉ et XVIᵉ siècle," Académie des Sciences de Bulgarie, *Etudes Historiques* (Sofia, 1960), pp. 144–170.

Nedkoff, Boris Christoff, *Die Gizya (Kopfsteuer) im Osmanischen Reich. Mit Besonderer Berücksichtigung von Bulgarien* (Sofia, 1942).

Nuri, Mustafa, *Netayic ul-Vuqu'at* [*The Results of Events*], (Istanbul, 1909), 4 vols.

Refik, Ahmed, *Türk idaresinde Bulgaristan (973–1255)* [*Bulgaria under Turkish Rule from 1565 to 1840*], (Istanbul, 1933).

Sudi, Suleyman, *Defter-i Muqtesid* [*Concise Register*], (Istanbul, 1891), 3 vols. Description of Ottoman administration in the nineteenth century.

Uzunçarşili, Ismail Hakki, *Osmanli Tarihi* [*Ottoman History*], (Ankara, 1947–1960), 4 vols. History of the Ottoman Empire from 1299 to 1789.

————. *Osmanli Devleti Teşkilatina Medhal* [*Beginning of the Organization of the Ottoman State*], (Istanbul, 1941). Study of Turkish administrative and financial organization in thirteenth-century Anatolia before the rise of the Ottoman state.

————. *Osmanli Devletinin Merkez ve Bahriye Teşkilati* [*The Central Organization and Naval Organization of the Ottoman State*], (Ankara, 1948).

————. *Osmanli Imparatorlugu Teşkilati, 1453–1575 senesine kadar* [*The Organization of the Ottoman Empire, from 1453 to 1575*], (Istanbul, 1936).

Wittek, Paul, "Yazijioghlu Ali on the Christian Turks of the Dobrudja," *Bulletin of the School of Oriental and African Studies*, XIV (1952), 639–668.

————. "Devshirme and shari'a," *Bulletin of the School of Oriental and African Studies*, XVII (1955), 271–278.

SOME ASPECTS OF

THE OTTOMAN LEGACY

Wayne S. Vucinich

Precisely what constitutes the Ottoman legacy in the Balkans is difficult to say. One should not ascribe, as is often done, everything negative in the lives of the Balkan peoples to the Ottoman heritage and
everything positive to the autochthonous cultures. Scholarship has long
established that the cultures of the Balkan peoples are eclectic consisting of Illyrian-Celtic-Greek-Roman-Slavonic components, to mention but a few, all molded under local conditions into distinctive national cultures. That the Ottoman influence figured in the evolution of
Balkan cultures is undeniable, but the extent of it is subject to different
interpretations.

Of special significance in the Balkans is the Byzantine tradition
which has persisted in part to the present. The Byzantine and Ottoman
traditions are intertwined, and some find it appropriate to lump the
two together, along with the Greco-Roman tradition, as "the great
tradition." In other words, the Ottoman heritage is, to an extent, the
Byzantine heritage. In the Greek world, attempts have sometimes been
made to distinguish between the two traditions, but to other peoples
in the Balkans this separation seems unreal. The question of origins
and individual cultural traits is one thing, while the question of cul-
ture-cluster is another. Individually, many Ottoman institutions and
their vestiges are clearly part of the Ottoman heritage. To call them
Byzantine would be like calling English institutions developed in the
United States Norman or Saxon; some of these institutions may have
had earlier origins, but they are still a part of the English heritage.

The appraisal of the Ottoman legacy in the Balkans is further complicated by matters normally belonging to the realm of semantics. How

does one define progress, for example, and how does one measure the *quality* of a culture? Lacking a precise measure of cultural inheritance, we can only look to the evidences of Ottoman influence which are apparent in the Balkans. On the basis of our observations we can then make some assessment of the degree and quality of this influence.

When considering the Ottoman legacy in the Balkans, however, one must seek out several factors: elements of culture other than Ottoman transmitted by the Turks; revitalization of traits which Ottoman and Balkan peoples inherited from the same sources; the survival of evidence that may be purely Ottoman; and, changes of existing cultural patterns under Ottoman influence. But before we can understand even the most obvious aspects of the Ottoman legacy in the Balkans, we must consider the nature of the Ottoman civilization and its impact on the cultures of the conquered peoples.

SOCIAL SIGNIFICANCE OF THE OTTOMAN CONQUEST

The importance and consequences of the Ottoman rule has long been a subject of keen interest to Balkan historians as they sought an explanation why their peoples, which were so advanced in the fourteenth century, had since then fallen far behind the rest of Europe. Nearly all historians agree that the Ottoman rule had devastating effects on the conquered populations, and that it was primarily responsible for the social lag of the Balkan peoples.[1]

Historians do not interpret in the same way every phase of Ottoman history and civilization. One group contends that the Ottoman rule was initially beneficent to the Balkan peoples because it ended feudal strife, provided much-needed peace, established a powerful centralized authority, and facilitated economic progress.[2] These historians

---

[1] Included in this group are such historians as G. Finlay, K. Paparrhegopulos, K. Jireček, E. Driault, S. Stanojević, F. Šišić, V. Ćorović, N. Iorga, V. Zlatarski, and P. Mutafchiev.

[2] A. Pogodin, *Istoriia Bolgarii* [*History of Bulgaria*], (St. Petersburg, 1910). K. Jireček, *Istorija Srba* [*History of Serbs*], 4 vols., translated by J. Radonić (Belgrade, 1922–1923). N. Iorga, *Geschichte des Osmanischen Reiches*, 5 vols. (Gotha, 1908–1913). V. Zlatarski, *Geschichte der Bulgaren*, 2 vols. (Leipzig, 1917–1918). S. Novaković, *Srbi i Turci XIV i XV veka* [*Serbs and Turks in the Fourteenth and Fifteenth Centuries*], (Belgrade, 1893).

SOME ASPECTS OF THE OTTOMAN LEGACY   83

argue that the Turks actually freed the Balkan masses from their own "despotic" ruler and "greedy" feudal lords, and that Ottoman feudalism was "less oppressive" than the variety it replaced. For this reason, they maintain, the Balkan peoples at first got along well with the Turks.[3] According to their view, the lag in the development of the Balkan societies did not stem directly from the Ottoman conquest; it was only after the Ottoman Empire began to decay at the end of the sixteenth century that the Balkan societies were retarded.

Other historians hold that the Ottoman conquest brought ruin to the Balkans from the beginning, because the Ottoman feudalism was less advanced than the Balkan feudal system, and that this accounted for social "involution" and cultural retrogression of the Balkan peoples.[4] One of these historians says that the Ottomans never adjusted to Europe and simply "did not belong to the Mediterranean world."[5]

A particularly negative interpretation of Ottoman history in the Balkans is championed by Marxist historians. They assert that Balkan feudalism (as part of a general European development) was representative of a "higher level" of socioeconomic relations, than Turkish feudalism which was in "a primitive and barbarian stage."[6] The Turkish conquest, according to P. N. Tretiakov, led the Bulgarian people into five hundred years of "unenlightened slavery"; it deprived them of national independence, disrupted their normal historical development, and, in general, impeded the growth of productive forces; after several centuries of Turkish rule the Bulgarians became one of "the most backward peoples" in Europe.[7] Other Soviet writers assess the effects of the Turkish conquest upon the Balkan peoples in a similar manner[8] and show strong contrasts between the Byzantine, Bul-

---

[3] V. Dvornikovič, *Karakterologija Jugoslovena* [*Characteristics of Jugoslavs*], (Belgrade, 1939), p. 310. D. J. Popović, "O Turcima u našoj prošlosti," ["About the Turks in Our Past"], *Srpski književni glasnik*, n. s. XXVI, No. 6 (1929), 451–453; No. 7 (1929), 534–539. M. Ninčić, *Istorija agrarnopravnih odnosa srpskih težaka pod Turcima* [*History of Agrarian-Legal Relations of Serbian Peasants under the Turks*], (Belgrade, 1902). Branislav Nedeljković, *Istorija baštinske svojine* [*History of* Baština *Ownership*], (Belgrade, 1930).

[4] Dvorniković, p. 307.

[5] Edouard Driault, *La Question d'Orient* (Paris, 1917), p. ii.

[6] V. Litskii in *Voprosy Istorii*, No. 2 (1948), 148–150.

[7] P. N. Tretiakov, ed., *Istoriia Bolgarii* [*History of Bulgaria*], 2 vols. (Moscow, 1954).

[8] S. A. Nikitin, ed., *Istoriia iuzhnykh i zapadnykh Slavian* [*History of Southern and Western Slavs*], (Moscow, 1957), pp. 102–113. I. S. Dostian, *Bor'ba serb-*

garian, and Serbian societies before and after the Ottoman triumph.[9] Jugoslav,[10] Bulgarian,[11] and Rumanian[12] Marxist historians interpret Ottoman history in essentially the same way as the Soviet historians. M. V. Levchenko[13] finds it incomprehensible that anyone can see

---

skogo naroda protiv turetskogo iga XIV–nachalo XIX v. [*The Struggle of the Serbian People against the Turkish Yoke from the Fourteenth to the Beginning of the Nineteenth Century*], (Moscow, 1958), pp. 28–55. *Bol'shaia sovetskaia entsiklopediia,* [*Grand Soviet Encyclopedia*], XLIII (1956), 495.

[9] *Vsemirnaia istoriia* [*Universal History*], III (1957), 743–744. Dostian, pp. 28–55.

[10] Branislav Djurdjev, "Osnovni problemi srpske istorije u periodu turske vlasti nad našim narodima" ["Basic Problems of Serbian History in the Period of Turkish Rule over Our Peoples"], *Istoriski glasnik,* Nos. 3–4 (1950), 107–108. By the same, "Prilog pitanju razvitka i karaktera tursko-osmanskog feudalizma: timarsko-spahiskog uredjenja" ["Contribution to the Question of Development and Character of Turko-Ottoman Feudalism: the Timar-Sipahi Order"], *Godišnjak istoriskog društva BiH,* II (1950), 19–82, hereafter cited as *GID.* Nedim Filipović, "Pogled na osmanski feudalizam sa naročitim obzirom na agrarne odnose" ["A Glance at Ottoman Feudalism with Special Consideration to Agrarian Relations"], *GID,* IV (1952), 5–146. By the same, "Odžakluk timari u Bosni i Hercegovini" ["Ocaklik Timars in Bosnia and Hercegovina"], *Glasnik zemaljskog muzeja,* V (1954–1955), 251–274.

[11] Vasil Kolarov, *Osvobozhdenieto na B'lgariia ot tursko rabstvo* [*Liberation of Bulgaria from Turkish Slavery*], (Sofia, 1948), p. 4. I. Mitev, *Kratka istoriia na B'lgarskiia narod* [*Short History of the Bulgarian People*], (Sofia, 1951), pp. 80–96. D. Kosev, ed., *Istoriia na B'lgariia* [*History of Bulgaria*], I (Sofia, 1954), pp. 303–305. Zhak Natan, *Istoriia ekonomicheskogo razvitiia Bolgarii* [*History of the Economic Development of Bulgaria*], (Moscow, 1949). Bistra Tsvetkova, *Prinos k'm izuchavaneto na turskiia feodaliz'm v b'lgarskite zemi prez XV–XVI v* [*Contribution to the Study of Turkish Feudalism in Bulgarian Lands in the Fifteenth to Sixteenth Centuries*], I (Sofia, 1954). By the same, "L'Évolution du régime féodal turc de la fin du XVIe jusqu'au milieu du XVIIIe siécle," *Etudes Historiques* (Sofia, 1960), pp. 171–206. Alexander Burmov, "Les Problèmes de la conquête de la Peninsule des Balkans par les Turcs," *ibid.,* pp. 135–143. Ivan Snegarov, *Turskoto vladichestvo prechka za kulturnoto razvitie na b'lgarskiia narod i drugite balkanski narodi* [*Turkish Rule as an Obstacle to Cultural Development of the Bulgarian People and Other Balkan Peoples*], (Sofia, 1958). V. Mutafchieva, "De L'exploitation féodale dans les terres de population bulgares sous la domination turque au XVe et XVIe s.," *Etudes Historiques,* pp. 145–168.

[12] E. Franches, "Klassovaiia pozitsiia vizantiiskikh feodalov v period Turetskogo zavoevaniia" ["Class Position of Byzantine Feudatories in the Period of Turkish Conquest"], *Vizantiiskii vremennik,* XV, (Moscow, 1959), 70–99.

[13] M. Levchenko, "Zavoevanie turkami Konstantinopolia v 1453 g. i istoricheskie posledovaniia etogo sobytiia" ["The Conquest of Constantinople by the Turks in 1453 and the Historical Consequence of that Event"], *Vizantiiskii vremennik,* VII (1953), 3–8.

something good in the conquest of Constantinople.[14] He rejects Bréhier's[15] views on the graduality and relatively peaceful nature of the Ottoman conquest and denies the thesis that the conquerors pursued a policy of religious toleration which promoted the fusion of the Turkish with the conquered peoples. Levchenko deprecates the contention of the Rumanian historian Iorga[16] that the Turkish victory gave the Balkan peoples peace, on the ground that such a contention implies the incapacity of the Balkan peoples to govern themselves. Levchenko suggests that a critical application of Marxist-Leninist methodology to historical sources reveals the fallacies of Western historians and of those Turkish writers who have succumbed to Pan-Turanian ideas.[17]

The salient points in the Soviet interpretations of Ottoman history are not new. Like many non-Marxist specialists, the Soviet commentators explain the inhibited evolution of the Balkans as the inevitable outcome of a retrogressive Ottoman social and economic system. But the ideological labels used in Soviet historiography for historical events and processes are indeed new. Likewise new is the attempt to minimize the importance of historical problems which do not fit into the Marxist theoretical system and to exaggerate those that do.

Despite variations in the interpretations of Ottoman history in the Balkans, no historian would deny that the protracted and diversified contact between the Turks and the local population helped to create a new civilization in which Ottoman influence was of paramount significance. The Ottoman legacy in the contemporary Balkans is many-sided, and its roots are deep and ramified.

SOCIAL INVOLUTION

While the Balkan kinship and quasi-kinship associations had resisted political and military unification during the Middle Ages, external

---

[14] For recent Greek interpretations of the final days of the Byzantine Empire, see *Le Cinq-Centiéne Anniversaire de la prise de Constantinople* (Athens, 1953). The symposium includes articles by A. Amentos, N. Moschopoulos, G. Kolias and A. P. Argyropoulos.

[15] L. Bréhier, *Le Monde byzantine: Vie et Mort de Byzance* (Paris, 1947).

[16] Nicolae Iorga, *Histoire de la vie Byzantine*, 3 vols. (Bucharest, 1934).

[17] Levchenko, "Zavoevanie turkami . . . ," pp. 3–8.

pressures gradually forced them to yield, by the time of Turkish ascendancy, they were either in a state of dissolution or had disappeared. The Ottoman conquest, however, led to the regeneration of such patriarchal institutions as the tribe,[18] the clan,[19] the joint family,[20] and the pastoral community.[21]

The Ottoman government might have wished to weaken local territorial and kinship organizations, but found it necessary to permit them as a means by which order could be maintained through the application of the principle of collective responsibility. In other words, since the patriarchal institutions gave support to feudal society, the Ottomans fostered them. Also, because of the absence of security of person and property, many other forms of social association flourished, some of which originated in the pre-Turkish period while others first came into being during Turkish rule.[22] This social setback was especially apparent in Serbian provinces where the tribal domains replaced particular administrative units (*župas*) of the medieval state. The *župa* Vrsinje, for example, became the domain of the Zupci tribe, and the *župa* Papratna the land of the Mrkovići tribe.[23]

Social organizations which had been substantially weakened through the emergence of the medieval states were infused with new life by the advent of the Turks. Henceforth, national life came to revolve around "small tribal cells" under the protection of the Church. The Church "insulated" the nation and culture of each individual Balkan people, and served as the nucleus for the rebirth of the state. To build a state after three to five centuries of Turkish rule was no small task; the Balkan peoples once again had to undergo the metamorphosis from a local and tribal to a state organization. This difficult process was

---

[18] Jovan Cvijić, *Le Péninsule Balkanique* (Paris, 1918), pp. 103–110.

[19] *Ibid.*

[20] V. Popović, *Zadruga: Istoriska rasprava* [*Zadruga: Historical Discussion*], (Sarajevo, 1921). By the same, "Zadruga, teorije i literatura" ["Zadruga, Theory and Literature"], *Glasnik zemaljskog muzeja*, XXXIII–XXXIV (1921–1922), 73–114. Literature on *zadruga* is very large. The latest to appear are two works by Émile Sicard: *Problèmes familiaux chez les Slaves du Sud* (Paris, 1941), and *La zadruga dans la littérature serbe* (*1850–1912*), (Paris, 1943).

[21] Cvijić, pp. 103–110. *Enciklopedija Jugoslavije* [*Encyclopedia of Jugoslavia*], (1962), V, 230–231.

[22] See Traian Stoianovich, "Factors in the Decline of Ottoman Society in the Balkans," *Slavic Review* (December, 1962).

[23] Vladislav Skarić, "Uticaj turskog vladanja na društveni život" ["The Influence of Turkish Rule on Social Life"], in *Knjiga o Balkanu*, II (Belgrade, 1937), 137.

strikingly illustrated by Montenegro,[24] which, after a long struggle, succeeded in building a state comprising "a strange mixture of tribal patriarchalism, feudal atavism, Turko-Oriental despotism, and modernistic reformism." [25]

After the conquest of Constantinople in 1453, the Orthodox Church was organized as a *millet* (community), actually *Rum milleti*—the Roman community—under the patriarch. The patriarch ranked in honor with the pasha as symbolized by the three *tuğs* (*horsetails*), and was given many rights, including his own court and prison and almost absolute jurisdiction over the faithful (*zimmîs*). The Turks provided this arrangement because of expediency and in accordance with earlier Islamic experience,[26] not because they wanted to enable various ethnic groups to "preserve their traditional institutions and practices under the veneer of common loyalty to the Sultan." [27] The notion that the *millet* system supplied non-Muslims with the "requisite conditions for developing their own cultures" is contradicted by the severe restraints placed by Muslim law and discriminatory legislation on the freedom of the people of a *millet* and the economic emasculation to which the *millets* were submitted.

No mutual influence or real cultural intercourse occurred between *millets*. The *millet* embraced neither a unified territory, nor a homogeneous ethnic group, nor peoples possessing the same political and legal status. It consisted of widely separated communities, isolated from each other, which enjoyed different social, political, and economic privileges and were weakly linked through ecclesiastical administration. Except for a few non-Muslims in major cities and the urban clergy, the people (peasants and nomads) or rural regions had practically no contact with cities or the outside world. The state did not provide for the enlightenment of the people of non-Muslim *millets* and discouraged most forms of learning. While the powerful ruling hierarchy of the Muslims could count on rich feudal landlords and state functionaries to establish educational institutions, the impoverished Christian communities largely depended on taxes and contribu-

---

[24] Dvorniković, pp. 859–860.

[25] *Ibid.*

[26] H. A. R. Gibb and Harold Bowen, *Islamic Society and the West* (London, 1957), I:2, 215–216. Philip Hitti, *History of the Arabs* (New York, 1951), p. 716.

[27] Stanford Shaw, "The Aims and Achievements of Ottoman Rule in the Balkans," *Slavic Review* (December, 1962).

tions of the *rayah* (subjects, flock, cattle) to build schools and churches. To be sure, Greeks, Armenians, Tsintsars, and Jews who lived in the major cities were exposed to learning. A few of them could also study abroad, buy favors, and attain high government positions. But the rest of the population was driven into the hills and mountains, relegated to the status of peasants, and cut off from cultural centers.

The *millet* system means isolation of ethnic and confessional social entities, and isolation meant stagnation. The contact between Christians and Muslims, between villages and cities, was limited. The non-Muslims were never able to mix freely in Muslim society. As subject infidels, they were socially ostracized and deprived of rights enjoyed by the ruling Muslim elite; they were economically oppressed and culturally starved. But while the *millet* system, like the kinship associations discussed above, enabled the Balkan peoples to preserve their traditions and ethnic individuality, it simultaneously retarded their social development.

The rebuilding of their states was an enormous problem for the Balkan peoples. At the beginning of the nineteenth century, they were largely illiterate peasants who had experienced only the Turkish method of rule. Among the Serbs, for example, particularism based on loyalty to the village, *knežina* (a village or district over which presided a *knez* or leader), and to the *nahija* (from Arabic: district) could not easily be overcome. The evolution of Serbia from an oriental patriarchal society to a modern state was slow. At the beginning of this development, the First Serbian Revolution (1804–1812) was hardly more than a peasant rebellion.[28] Karadjordje, who led the rebelling Serbs, behaved more like a peasant leader than a ruler of a state in formation. His successor, Prince Miloš (1815–1839), scarcely went beyond the role of an "oriental despot" and a "little sultan."[29] The incipient growth of the Serbian state can be largely attributed to the *nemačkari*—the more advanced Serbs from the Austrian-occupied

---

[28] For the latest Marxian interpretation of the First Serbian Revolution, see Miroslav Djordjević, *Politička istorija Srbije XIX i XX veka* [*Political History of Serbia in the Nineteenth and Twentieth Centuries*], Vol. I: *1804–1813* (Belgrade, 1956). Since the end of the Second World War much material on the Serbian revolution has been published. See Wayne S. Vucinich, "Marxian Interpretations of the First Serbian Revolution," *Journal of Central European Affairs*, XXI: 1 (1961), 3–14.

[29] Dvorniković, pp. 861–862.

territory on the other side of the Sava and the Danube. Greece and Bulgaria faced comparable difficulties in building their modern states, and they, too, depended on nationals influenced by Western ideas and educated abroad.

It took a long time for the remaining patriarchal social organizations to die out. In fact, they still survive as psychological remnants (in Albania, kinship organizations continue to be an important social force). This problem poses a challenge to scholars and government leaders alike. The particularism manifested in strong feelings of kinship and community membership seriously impedes national policies.

ATTITUDES, VALUES, AND CUSTOMS

The Ottoman Empire not only helped to perpetuate antiquated social organizations, but its peculiar social code and mode of government also produced many undesirable practices which outlasted it. Some of the worst features of Ottoman life (*baksheesh;* distrust of government) were inherited by modern Balkan states and still exist despite official efforts to stamp them out.

Centuries of Ottoman rule, religious discrimination, and feudal oppression caused the Christian subjects to acquire distinctive characteristics.[30] One of these is the eastern *yavaşlik* (Turkish: laziness, indecision, indifference), and another, the tendency toward submission as a means of survival. It can easily be detected in the attitude toward authority—apprehension combined with humility and acquiescence. Coupled with subservience is cleverness, which was expressed in attempts to get around obstacles, including authority, by using none-too-ethical (from the point of view of the authorities) and even illegal means. The notion still prevails in many Balkan circles that it is all right to cheat and steal from the government, an attitude with which even the Communist governments have not been able to cope despite stringent laws.

The peasant's suspicion of government—especially the police agent and the tax collector—can be traced to the long period of special conditioning under Ottoman rule. These are the institutions the peasant

---

[30] Jovan Cvijić, *Govori i članci* [*Speeches and Articles*], (Belgrade, 1931), I, 83.

abhorred and fought for centuries. The peasant shows the same kind of basic antagonism toward the city and despises the city *čaršija*[31] (Turkish: *çarşi*)—a group of merchants, artisans and speculators who came to control the economic and political life of the city. After the withdrawal of the Turks from the Balkans, the *čaršija* took on a national cast, but retained many features of their Ottoman precursors. For peasants, the dominant population in each Balkan country, the *čaršija* continued to connote a clique which exploited them economically and ruled them politically. The *čaršija* came to represent an unpatriotic and opportunistic group of people who had a common response to daily issues and behaved as a class conscious of its own interests. It survived in one form or another until the end of the Second World War in most Balkan countries.

Because their future has frequently been uncertain, the Balkan peoples developed a somewhat hedonistic attitude toward life. The Turkish governor in the Greek novel, *The Greek Passion*,[32] personifies this attitude and is a character likely to be better understood by Greeks than by Westerners. According to this view, the present counts more than yesterday or tomorrow and is here to be enjoyed. One must work only to gain leisure; work is, therefore, a means to leisure and not an end in itself. Work is generally not prized by the Balkan peoples, and yet when transplanted to the United States they quickly adopt most of the attitudes of Americans.

Many writers believe that fatalism, as stressed in the Koran[33] and so deeply rooted among Balkan Christians, is the product of Islamic influence. This fatalism is based on the predestination idea:[34] that everything has been preordained by Allah and that a mortal is powerless to change his destiny. The Christians unwittingly accepted the Koranic passage to the effect that upon everyone's forehead is written how long he shall live.[35] One still encounters people in the Balkans

---

[31] H. Kreševljaković, "Esnafi i orbti u Bosni i Hercegovini (1463–1878)" ["Esnafs and Crafts in Bosnia and Hercegovina"], *Zbornik za narodni život i običaje*, Jugoslavenska Akademija, I (Zagreb, 1935), II (Zagreb, 1951). V. Skarić, *Sarajevo i njegova okolina* [*Sarajevo and Its Environs*], (Sarajevo, 1937).

[32] N. Kazantzakis, *The Greek Passion* (New York, 1954).

[33] J. M. Rodwell, tr., *The Koran* (New York, 1933), Sura, III, 399; Sura LXXXVII, 40; Sura VIII, 376; Sura IX, 476; and others.

[34] *Ibid.*, Sura III, 400; Sura VI, 320; Sura XVI, 202; Sura XXXII, 191; and others.

[35] Skarić, "Uticaj turskog vladanja . . . ," p. 141.

who attribute everything that happens to *kismet* (Arabic via Turkish: fate) and that, therefore, little can be done to change the course of events. For a long time the Balkan peoples had nothing to look forward to, and in consequence acquired a world outlook of their own. But many characteristics of the Balkan man usually attributed to Turkish or Muslim influence may well be of earlier origin and, in some instances, merely revitalized after the Turkish conquest. The Balkan peoples must have believed in predestination (the cult of the written) before the coming of the Turks. Yet, there are practices that can be traced with a greater degree of certainty to the Muslim influence. One student of Ottoman society thinks, for example, that Christian mothers adopted the practice of breast-feeding their children for an unusually long period from Muslim mothers who did so in compliance with the Koranic invocation that "mothers shall suckle their children for two whole years." [36] He attributes to Muslim influence the references in the Serbian epics to mothers who breast-feed their children for many months and thereby endowed them with "superhuman physical strength." [37]

The same author also holds that the great respect for teachers and education in the Balkans was inspired by the Muslim Holy Book. But his contention that the Serbian saying, "May God save the teacher first and then the parents," comes from the Koranic passage which reads, "He who teaches me but a single letter, I shall be his slave" [38] is questionable. Respect for teachers and education is a phenomenon common in many other societies.

The Ottoman legacy to the Balkan peoples is also reflected in the treatment of women and children.[39] Although concubinage and other Byzantine practices had spread into the Balkans during the fourteenth century, the status of women in the medieval Balkans and in the Byzantine Empire substantially differed from that in the Ottoman Empire. Whereas women could ascend the throne and rule as queens and empresses in the former, this was not possible in the Ottoman Empire. The Orthodox Church often granted divorce to a woman on grounds of desertion or abandonment; the Muslim hierarchy never did.

---

[36] M. M. Pickthall, *The Meaning of the Glorious Koran* (The New American Library, 1954), Sura II, 233. Skarić, "Uticaj turskog vladanja . . . ," p. 141.

[37] Skarić, "Uticaj turskog vladanja . . . ," p. 141.

[38] *Ibid.*

[39] *Ibid.*, p. 135.

The institutions of polygamy and the harem, which were an integral part of Ottoman Muslim theocracy, had degrading effects upon women, who were generally treated as inferior beings. In deference to the ruling Muslim males and in compliance with prevailing Muslim practice, the Christian women in many places had to share the fate of their Muslim sisters. For the most part, they lived in social isolation, deferred to men with blind subservience, and in some districts adopted veils and other pieces of Muslim female dress. Until the Second World War, it was not unusual in Hercegovina to encounter an elderly Christian woman wearing the Muslim *dimije* (Turkish: *dimi;* Greek: *dimitos*), baggy female pants, instead of modern dress.

In many Balkan homes, the man rules with absolute authority, and the wife obeys him slavishly. As in Anatolia, in a Balkan village home Christian women can still be seen eating separately with the children and, when on a trip, walking laden with freight several steps behind their husbands. The woman finds it difficult to free herself from the tradition which, if not introduced by the Ottomans, was cemented during their rule. The Communist governments have had great difficulty in their attempts, through legal action and education, to raise the status of women (especially Muslim) to full equality with men.

The treatment of children (especially female) with indifference and inhumanity is also traceable to Ottoman influence. The children were brutally exploited for their labor power, particularly girls who married young and became "someone else's fortune." The children were taught to serve their parents and dedicate their lives to them. They were put to work in their teens and subjected to iron discipline. The vestiges of this kind of family relation have been disappearing rapidly in recent years. A new attitude toward women and children is emerging, and the liberation of children from parental domination is gaining momentum.

THE COFFEEHOUSE

Many social habits of varying importance have survived the Ottoman Empire in every region of the Balkan Peninsula. One of the most conspicuous gifts of the Ottomans to the Balkan peoples is the coffeehouse (Turkish: *kahvehane*). This institution, like the Ottoman cuisine, exists not only in the territories once part of the Ottoman state, but has expanded into adjacent districts never ruled by the Turks. The Balkan inns and restaurants which served wine and mead in medieval times were seriously hampered after the Ottoman conquest because of the Koranic interdict against wine. For this reason, the *kahvehanes* became the favorite rendezvous for the Muslims.

When coffee-drinking became general in the sixteenth century, a movement developed against this "Turkish poison." Despite protests by religious and state authorities, it spread from Constantinople into the provinces. By the end of the sixteenth century, even distant provincial cities, such as Sarajevo, had their *kahvehanes*.[40] The coffeehouses served as social centers where the Muslims gathered to exchange gossip, tell stories, and discuss the political and religious issues of the day. Here the bards (Turkish: *ozan, cögür, 'ashik*), who wandered about the country, came to sing and recite poetry in "the popular rhythm and in traditional forms" to the accompaniment of the old Turkish string instrument, *kobuz*.

Sometimes the *kahvehanes* became the hubs of intrigue and political plots. The men of learning (*ulema*), a body of scholars and teachers who safeguarded Islam and its principles, opposed the *kahvehanes* because the unruly and unorthodox elements often gathered in them. For this and other reasons the government issued stringent laws concerning the inns, coffeehouses, tobacco shops, baths, and even barbershops. Several sumptuary laws were enacted in the second half of the sixteenth century and during the seventeenth century.[41] In 1827, after quelling a Janissary mutiny, the Bosnian vezir Abdurahman closed down the *kahvehanes* because they served as the meeting places of insurgents.[42]

The function of the *kahvehane* changed little after Ottoman power expired. In place of the Turkish bard, a native Serbian bard, playing the one-string *gusle* came to the coffeehouse to sip coffee and to recite the national epic poems. Here the peasants and townspeople gathered to politicize, transact business, or merely socialize. Many an idle hour was spent in the *kahvehane*, and many a "dangerous

---

[40] *Ibid.*, p. 141.

[41] Traian Stoianovich, "Factors in the Decline of Ottoman Society in the Balkans," *Slavic Review* (December, 1962). Sir Paul Rycaut, *The History of the Turkish Empire from the Year 1677* (London, 1687), pp. 28, 32–38.

[42] Skarić, "Uticaj turskog vladanja . . . ," p. 141.

thought" germinated there. Even today a large number of *kahvehanes*, packed with leisurely and gossipy males, flourish in many parts of the Balkans. Whether it be the *kaffeneion* in the Greek parliamentary democracy or the *kafana* in Jugoslavia's Communist state, the institution remains a gathering place for the men of the town and village, and it often serves as a forum and place of entertainment. This Ottoman tradition has become so much a part of Balkan life that not only its name but a whole list of Turkish Arabic, and Persian words connected with it have been taken into the native languages.[43]

FOOD AND DIET

The Ottoman Turks left a lasting mark on the food and diet habits of most of the Balkan populations. The Ottoman (or Near Eastern) cuisine has not only outlived Ottoman political power, but has continued to develop and expand to Balkan districts that were only briefly under Ottoman rule. From the standpoint of the dietitian and the culinary artist, Near Eastern cuisine is superb. Ingredients are blended to produce nutritious and exquisite dishes. The excellence as well as the economy help explain the appeal and survival of the Near Eastern foods. Most items from which the principal dishes are made are produced locally.

How much of the Balkan menu is of Turkish origin and how much of Greek, Armenian, and other origins is still not definitely known. Patriots of each group claim the most popular dishes as their own people's invention. But it is safe to assume that foods which were not inherited or originated by the Turks were in a large measure introduced or popularized by them. Notice should be given to the Turkish, Arabic, and Persian names attached to many dishes and foods (including vegetables and fruit).[44] A study of the diet of the Balkan

---

[43] *Kahváji* (coffee color), *kahvàltija* (breakfast), *kàhvaparasi* ("just enough money" to pay for coffee), *kahvèdžija* (one who cooks coffee, owns a coffee shop, or enjoys coffee), *kahvènisati* (a Serbo-Croatian form of Turkish verb "to drink coffee"), *kahvenjaci* (a Serbo-Croatian word form for Turkish term for coffee dishes), *kàhve-odžak* (a place in a larger building where coffee is prepared, or a fireplace where coffee is made). Every dish used in making coffee and the word for sugar are also Turkish or Arabic and Persian by way of Turkish.

[44] *Kačamak* (a simple dish made out of maize flour), *kàjmak* (cream, collected from boiled milk), *ćevap* (meat cut in pieces and boiled), *sùtlijaš* (cold dish made

peoples at different stages of their history would shed light on their social and economic development under Ottoman rule.

IMPACT ON RELIGIOUS LIFE

The long period of restrictive existence and of affiliation with the Ottoman government undoubtedly hampered the theological (dogmatic) development of the Orthodox Church.[45] Once a source of great spiritual strength, the Church began to show signs of intellectual stagnation although it accomplished far more in the field of learning than is sometimes recognized. The Church was in no position to keep up with the intellectual and other developments in the world and was of necessity cocooned in medievalism. The Church was compelled to dedicate itself to preserving religious and cultural traditions and in this sense rendered a service to the faithful. The parish clergy, however, had to give more attention to saving the lives than the souls of the flock. This preoccupation with physical and material matters affected the lives of the clergy and the future of the Church.

In the period of native rule, the Church and the State were closely related. With the disappearance of the medieval Balkan states, it remained to the Church to maintain a link with the past. After 1453 the Greek Orthodox Church was allowed to continue and received official support.[46] The Ottoman system of rule helped to preserve and

---

of milk, rice, and sugar), *sàrma* (meat and rice wrapped in cabbage or grape leaves), *djùveč* (piece of meat, rice, potatoes, onions, and spices), *dòlma* (filled peppers and tomatoes), *halva* (special Oriental pastry), *baklava* (pastry resembling *strudel*), *rahatlokum* (Oriental candy), and so on.

[45] B. Djurdjev, "O uticaju turske vladavine na razvitak naših naroda" ["About the Influence of Turkish Rule on the Development of Our Peoples"], *GID*, II (1950), 19–82. By the same, "Uloga srpske crkve u borbi protiv osmanske vlasti" ["The Role of the Serbian Church in the Struggle against Ottoman Rule"], *Pregled*, I (Sarajevo, 1953), 42. Vasa Čubrilović, *Istorija političke misli u Srbiji XIX veka* [*History of Political Thought in Serbia in the Nineteenth Century*], (Belgrade, 1958), pp. 23–28. *Istorija naroda Jugoslavije* [*History of the Peoples of Jugoslavia*], (Belgrade, 1960), II, 98–105, 462–464, 531–535, 1256–1268.

[46] A. D. Kyriakos, *Geschichte der orientalischen Kirchen von 1453–1898* (Leipzig, 1902). Theodore Papadopoullos, *Studies and Documents Relating to the History of the Greek Church and People Under Turkish Domination* (Brussels, 1952). Georgiades Arnakis, "The Greek Church of Constantinople and the Ottoman Empire," *The Journal of Modern History*, XXIV: 3 (1952), 235–250. L. Hadrovics, *L'Église Serbe sous la domination Turque* (Paris, 1947).

strengthen the concept of unity of society and community. Consequently, the Church exercised a degree of power and enjoyed much prestige. This was true of the Serbian Patriarchate[47] and of other churches as well. The clergy made substantial contributions toward maintaining the national culture and saving the ethnic individuality of the faithful during the centuries of Turkish rule. With the cross in one hand and a knife in the other, they often led peasant rebellions against the Turks. The clergy constituted the bulk of national leadership during Ottoman domination. As a result the dividing line between politics and Church affairs after the liberation of the Balkan peoples was blurred, and the clergy sought to perpetuate the dual role to which it had become accustomed. The heads of both the Greek and Serbian churches were discontented over the loss of power to the secular authorities during the half-century or more after 1830; nevertheless, the prestige of the Church in national affairs steadily declined. A primary justification for the Church's existence, namely to save its followers and itself, was gone. The Church was unable to adjust and to concentrate on spiritual functions, and tended to give way to growing materialism. In the Balkan Communist states, one of the first major legal acts after 1945 was to confine the Church to purely religious functions.

Ottoman rule left its mark on Balkan religious life in still another way: the influence of Islam and Christianity upon each other. The Christian renegades, after conversion to Islam, retained some Christian customs. The Muslim converts of Gorane (Macedonia), for instance, have kept not only their native language but also some Christian saints and cling to some Christian fasting habits.[48] The days of St. Elijah (Ilija) and St. George are those most commonly retained by converts.[49] The Bosnian Muslims say that they celebrate Ilija until noon and Alija (Ali) after noon.[50] Curiously enough, both Christians and Albanian Muslims in the vicinity of the medieval Serbian monastery Dečani revere that shrine. The Christians in parts of the Balkans at one time

---

[47] Abolished soon after 1459, restored in 1557, and again abolished in 1766.

[48] M. Dj. Popović, "Balkanski narodi muhamedanske vere" ["Balkan Peoples of Muhammedan Faith"], Nova Evropa, VII (May 21, 1923), 450. T. Djordjević, "Preislamski ostatci medju jugoslovenskim Muslimanima" ["Pre-Islamic Survivals among Jugoslav Muslims"], Naš narodni život, VI (Belgrade, 1932), 26–56.

[49] St. Elijah, a pagan Slav god Perun. St. George (or St. Demetrius), the "Thracian horseman" (Dionysos).

[50] Skarić, "Uticaj turskog vladanja . . . ," p. 141.

called the object of their pilgrimage (the Holy Sepulchre in Jerusalem) the "Kaaba," a term designating the object of the Muslim pilgrimage in Mecca. The Christians who made the pilgrimage received the appellation "hadži" after the Muslim *hâjj*.[51]

ISLAMIZATION AND TURKIFICATION

Ottoman territorial expansion and ability to create a state in which the majority of people were not Ottomans has been possible largely by both voluntary and forced conversion to Islam. Many Balkan Christians voluntarily adopted Islam because they wanted to win privileges or, as the "Bosnian Bogomils," [52] because they saw in Islam a faith more akin to their own than either of the two Christian churches which persecuted them. The Ottomans offered their captives the alternative to become "slaves" or to become part of the ruling elite by adopting Islam. Many accepted Islam to preserve their social positions and to gain favors. The institution of *devshirme*, a levy of Christian boys into Ottoman government service and into conversion, was likewise an instrument of Islamization. Through Islamization the Turks swelled the Muslim population and also harnessed the conquered peoples into the service of the new state.

Despite the policy of segregation and the division of society into Muslim and non-Muslim, greater social mobility prevailed in Ottoman society than is generally believed. Frequent wars, epidemics, and insurrections caused significant demographic changes in the empire. From the beginning, the Turks adopted the policy of "sedentarization," by which nomadic and seminomadic peoples were settled as

---

[51] *Ibid.*

[52] The question as to whether the Bosnian Bogomils are really followers of the Manichean cult or schismatic Catholic or Orthodox believers is still a subject of heated polemics among historians. See, for example, J. Šidak, "Problem 'bosanske crkve', u našoj historiografiji od Petranovića do Glušca" ["The Problem of the 'Bosnian Church' in Our Historiography from Petranović to Glušac"], *Rad*, Jugoslavenska Akademija (Zagreb, 1937), pp. 37–182. D. Angelov, *Filosovskite vzgledi na bogomilite* [*Philosophical Views of Bogomils*], (Sofia, 1951). V. Glušac, *Istina o bogomilima* [*The Truth About Bogomils*], (Belgrade, 1945). D. Obolensky, *The Bogomils* (Cambridge, 1948). Vaso Čubrilović, "Poreklo muslimanskog plemstva u Bosni i Hercegovini" ["Origin of Muslim Nobility in Bosnia and Hercegovina"], *Jugoslovenski istoriski časopis*, I: 1–4 (1935), 352–367.

agriculturists or military auxiliaries (like the Vlachs). This method of "settlement and colonization," called *sürgün*, was not uncommon and was sometimes dictated by penal or by political, economic, and military needs.[53]

These people were settled mostly along the frontier and were constituted into auxiliary military units. Thousands of Serbs settled along the Austrian and Venetian frontiers or emigrated to border territories held by Austria and Venice. On several occasions, Austrian authorities invited the Serbs to settle on their side of the frontier and to join the frontier army on the basis of permanent preparedness for war with the Turks. Of great significance for the national future and immediate social dislocation were the two migrations of Serbs to southern Hungary and Austria led by patriarchs Arsenius III in the 1690's and Arsenius IV in 1739. These migrations extended the influence of the Church and planted Serbian colonies in the heart of Hungary and in Croatia.[54]

The mixing of the population in the Ottoman Empire led to an ethnic and cultural fusion. Little is known about the formation of modern Balkan tribes from different ethnic and social groups and the ethnogenesis of peoples. The transformation of the Vlachs and the fusion of the "old" and "new" peoples—of Illyrians, Romanized groups, and Slavs—are indeed important, but still obscure developments of Balkan social relations. Tribes which were partly Montenegrin and partly Albanian or those which were divided into families professing both Christianity and Islam epitomize the nature of Ottoman society. Protracted scrambling of Serbs and Croates in the frontier regions, on both sides of the Austro-Turkish and Turko-Venetian frontiers, homogenized them and facilitated eventual Jugoslav unification.[55] At the same time, the constant flow of people from the Dinaric region to the depopulated, fertile Serbian and Pannonian plains served to

---

[53] Bernard Lewis, *The Emergence of Modern Turkey* (London, 1961), p. 10. Ömer Lûtfi Barkan, "Les Déportations comme méthode de peuplement et de colonisation dans l'Empire ottoman," *Revue de la Faculté des Sciences Économiques de l'Université d'Istanbul*, XI (1949–1951), 67.

[54] For further significance of the subject, see Čubrilović's *Istorija političke misli*. Much has been written on the migrations. The most recent books are: Jovan Radonić i Mita Kostić, *Srpske privilegije od 1690 do 1792* [*Serbian Privileges from 1690 until 1792*], (Belgrade, 1954); and Rajko Veselinović, *Arsenije III Crnojević u istoriji i književnosti* [*Arsenius III Crnojević in History and Literature*], (Belgrade, 1949).

[55] *Ibid.*

rejuvenate the surviving indigenous element, to refresh the national tradition, and to revive the patriarchal social organization.[56]

After the Turkish conquest of Constantinople, the Greek nation declined in numbers.[57] Moreover, the "translocations of the inhabitants"[58] significantly altered the ethnography of Greece. In addition, the coasts of Greece were depopulated by the frequent measures taken by Ottoman authorities against Greeks who collaborated with their Christian enemies; these measures caused loss of life and dispersion of population. Under Turkish pressure, the Greek rural population "abandoned extensive districts to the Albanian race," which colonized the whole of Boeotia, Attica, Megaris, and several other districts. Large sections of Thrace, Macedonia, and Thessaly were settled by *Yürüks* (nomad Turkomans) or other Turkish elements.[59] Greeks emigrated to Apulia, Corsica, and to other parts of Europe.[60] The result of this decline of population, particularly in the seventeenth century was an ethnic distribution more favorable to Turks and Albanians.

A distinction must be made, therefore, between the minority of Turkish colonists and the majority of converted Muslims. Both served as instruments for spreading Turkish civilization in the Balkans. Most of the Turkish colonists settled in Macedonia, Bulgaria, Thrace, and the Dobrudja. A small group also settled in Bosnia. Wherever the Turks settled in the Balkans, they gave Turkish names to geographical locations, translated the existing names into Turkish, or merely gave them Turkish speech forms. The basic difference between the Turkish colonists and converts is that the colonists speak Turkish and the converts do not.[61]

Practically none of the Albanian Muslim population, estimated at 70 percent of the total of 1,393,000 (1955),[62] is of Turkish origin. They, as well as an additional 754,000 (1953) Albanians who constitute a minority in Jugoslavia,[63] together with an undetermined num-

---

[56] *Ibid.*
[57] George Finlay, *A History of Greece* (Oxford, 1877), V, 55.
[58] *Ibid.*, p. 58. See *ibid.*, III, 522, and IV, 266.
[59] *Ibid.*, V, 125–126.
[60] *Ibid.*
[61] T. Djordjević, "Preislamski ostatci . . . ," pp. 55–56.
[62] United Nations. *Demographic Yearbook*, 1955, p. 109.
[63] *Statistički godišnjak FNRJ*, 1955, Tables 3–5.

ber of recent refugees from Albania, are almost entirely converted Muslims. Approximately 2,083,000 (12.3 percent of the total population of 16,937,00 in 1953)[64] Jugoslav inhabitants, including the Albanian minority just mentioned, are likewise converted Muslims. Only 260,000 (1.5 percent) of the Jugoslav Muslim inhabitants are considered to be descendants of Turkish colonists, and many of them have emigrated to Turkey since the end of the Second World War.[65]

Bulgarian statistics and the ethnic breakdown of the Muslim population are incomplete. It is estimated, on the basis of the 1934 census, that more than 700,000 Muslims now live in Bulgaria (9.15 percent of the population of 7,600,000 [1956]). This figure takes into account the emigration of thousands of Turks from Bulgaria to Turkey after 1934, the expulsion of many thousands of Muslims (some of them probably Gypsies) to Turkey in 1951–1952, and the element of natural increase. The figure of 700,000 includes 440,000 Turks, 110,000 Muslim Gypsies, and 160,000 Pomaks (Islamicized Bulgarians and Macedonians).[66] According to a Soviet source, about 90,000 Turks "emigrated" to Turkey from Bulgaria in 1949–1950; the same source states that about 150,000 Gypsies live in Bulgaria, though some of these are Orthodox in religious persuasion and are labeled "Bulgarian Gypsies."[67]

As a result of the exchange of population with Turkey in the 'twenties, less than 150,000 Muslim Turks remain in Greece, representing a small percentage of the country's total population (estimated in 1956 at 8,062,000). European Turkey has a population of 2,000,000, which, whatever its original ethnic background, is considered Turkish today. Most Rumanian Muslims (180,000) live in the Dobrudja, and are divided into several ethnic groups—Tatar, Gypsy, and Turkish.

As yet no systematic study exists of individual Muslim groups (Pomaks, Apovci, Torbeši, Albanians, Bosnian Muslims, Tatars, Cherkess, Arabs, Gypsies, and others) in the Balkans, and the problem of Balkan Islamization. The Muslims are today considered the most backward segment of the Balkan population. Why Muslims, once the ruling elite, should find themselves in this unenviable position would be

[64] *Ibid.*, Tables 3–10.
[65] *Ibid.*
[66] L. A. Dellin, *Bulgaria* (New York, 1957), p. 77.
[67] E. B. Valev, *Bolgariia* (Moscow, 1957), p. 82.

a challenging subject for investigation; it would also be interesting to assess the Communist impact on Balkan Muslims. The Communist policies of social destratification and secularization, and the awakening of latent Slavic sentiments in Muslims, apparently have markedly affected the lives of Balkan Muslims. But in the meantime, the Balkan Muslims remain a lasting Ottoman legacy.

Besides the ethnic and cultural "Hellenization," "Slavonization," and "Albanization" which occurred in some districts, the processes of "Islamization" and "Turkification" also effected social change. In Greece, the Islamization of indigenous elements was slight, and the Muslim population primarily derived from Turkish and Albanian colonization. In Bulgaria and Jugoslavia (Macedonia, Bosnia), both the Islamization of Slavs and the colonization of Turks were extensive. The withdrawal of the Serbs from their "medieval cradle" in the Kossovo-Metohija region and the colonization of the region by Albanians shifted the Serbian ethnic center and significantly influenced the nation's future, just as earlier Slavic invasions influenced the destiny of Albanians and pressed them into the mountains. A few smaller groups, such as the *Dönme* (members of the Sabbatayan sect of Jews), also went over to Islam. The settlement of Spanish Jews in Turkish cities in the fifteenth century and the conversion of some of them to Islam yielded a competitive element which took over many branches of trade and industry in a hitherto Greek monopoly. The Jews became physicians, bankers, and merchants, and many of them occupied "a high social position."[68]

Just what classes of the population accepted Islam, and under what circumstances, has never been thoroughly investigated. Nor does a good study exist of the social relations between the born Muslims and converted Muslims (*Mawali*) or between the Muslims and non-Muslim scripturians (*zimmî*) and foreigners (*ecnebi*). Yet these categories of population greatly affected one another. The result is that a Christian and a Muslim peasant in the Balkans have more in common than either of them has with an Anatolian or Arabian counterpart.

The large Muslim population in the Balkans, made up mostly of converted Christians, is an important portion of the Ottoman legacy. During Ottoman rule, many of these converts regarded themselves as

---

[68] Finlay, V, 148–149.

Turks whom they imitated without adopting their language. At one
time, some converted Slavs wrote their language in Arabic script. In
the past, persons usually identified themselves by religion rather than
by nationality, and, since the Turks were Muslims, the converts also
identified themselves as Turks. It was Islam and not Turkish "national
identity" that separated the rulers from the ruled. The Turks thought
of themselves "almost exclusively as Muslims." Not until the nineteenth century did concepts of "a Turkish nationality" and "Otto-
manism" develop under European influence.[69]

TURKISH INFLUENCE ON BALKAN LANGUAGES

Turkish influence on the Balkan languages is conspicuous. An examination of the words which came into Balkan languages by way of the
Turks helps to explain the social and economic conditions under
which the subject peoples lived in the Ottoman Empire. Much work
has already been done on the subject,[70] and several good studies and
dictionaries of Turkish words and word forms in Balkan languages
have been published.[71] But a precise study of Turkish linguistic in-

---

[69] B. Lewis, "Turkey: Westernization," in G. von Grunebaum, ed., *Unity and
Variety in Muslim Civilization* (Chicago, 1955), p. 314.

[70] Franz Miklosich, *Die türkischen Elemente in den südost- und osteuropäischen
Sprachen* (Wien, 1884), 2 vols. The work was revised, expanded, and republished
in Vienna, 1888–1890. Otto Blau, *Bosnisch-türkische Sprachdenkmäler* (Leipzig,
1868). Useful despite some glaring errors. Vuk Stefanović Karadžić, *Srpske
narodne pjesme* [*Serbian Popular Songs*], (Belgrade, 1932).

[71] Abdulah Škaljić, *Turcizmi u narodnom govoru i narodnoj književnosti Bosne i
Hercegovine* [*Turkicisms in Popular Speech and Popular Literature of Bosnia
and Hercegovina*], 2 vols. (Sarajevo, 1957). The best collection of Turkicisms in
Serbo-Croatian; it includes 6,500 words of Turkish, Arabic, Persian, and some
other origins which entered Serbo-Croatian by way of Turkish. The author gives
only the words which are used in everyday speech. Vuk Stefanović Karadžić,
Srpski rječnik [*Serbian Dictionary*], (Wien, 1818; Belgrade, 1935). *Rječnik
hrvatskog ili srpskog jezika* [*Dictionary of Croatian and Serbian Language*], Jugoslavenska Akademija, A–S (Zagreb, 1880–1955). Ivan Esih, *Turcizmi. Rječnik
turskih, arapskih i perziskih riječi u hrvatskom književnomjeziku i pučkom govoru*
[*Turkicisms: Dictionary of Turkish, Arabic and Persian Words in Croatian Literary Language and Popular Speech*], (Zagreb, 1942); to be used with caution
because of numerous mistakes. Bratoljub Klaić, *Rječnik stranih riječi, izraza i
kratica* [*Dictionary of Foreign Words, Expressions, and Abbreviations*], (Zagreb,
1951). Author sometimes confuses Turkish with Arabic and Persian words. Gliša
Elezović, *Rečnik kosovsko-metohiskog dijalekta* [*Dictionary of Kosovo-Metohija*

fluence in the Balkans is still lacking. The problem is complicated because it requires a discussion of non-Turkish words, especially Arabic and Persian, which came into the Balkans by way of the Turks;[72] Arabic and Persian words which came into Balkan languages from the West; and Turkish words which entered Balkan languages (for example, through the Avars) before the Ottoman conquest of the Balkans.[73] Serbo-Croatian affords a good illustration of the extent and scope of Turkish influence. A systematic study of Turkish linguistic influence would clarify the picture of social and economic conditions under Ottoman rule.

Turkicisms are abundant in all Balkan literature, folklore, and everyday speech. Their character, however, vary from one region to another. Turkish and other Oriental words were spread among the Balkan people principally by Turkish military and civilian officials, local Muslims educated in Constantinople, and popular poetry. Educated persons, when unable to find corresponding native words for Islamic religious and institutional terminology, adopted Turkish (Arabic, Persian) terms and either fit them into Serbo-Croatian syntax or used them without change. Popular literature, especially the epic and lyric poetry which evolved during the Ottoman rule, contains a mass of Turkish words. The milieu in which oral poetry developed, and the events which inspired it, required the use of Turkish nomenclature. Without it, the poetry would have been "food without spices."[74] Through its use, the Turkish words were perpetuated and remain almost indispensable for this form of literature. Consequently the oral poetry, much of which has been collected and published, can

---

Dialect], Srpski dijalektološki zbornik, Srpska Kraljevska Akademija, I, Book 4 (Belgrade, 1932), II, Book 4 (Belgrade, 1935). Milan Vujaklija, *Leksikon stranih riječi i izraza* [*Lexicon of Foreign Words and Expressions*], (Belgrade, 1937, 1954). Nikola Vanchev, *Tursko-b'lgarski rechnik* [*Turko-Bulgarian Dictionary*], (Sofia, 1952). Stefan Mladenov, *Rechnik na chuzhdite dumi v b'lgarskiiat iazik* [*Dictionary of Foreign Words in the Bulgarian Language*], (Sofia, 1947).

[72] Škaljić, I, iv–x.
[73] P. Skok, "Južni Sloveni i turski narodi," ["South Slavs and Turkish Peoples"], *Jugoslovenski istoriski časopis*, II: 1–4 (1936), 1–15. By the same, "Prilozi proučavanju turcizma u srpskohrvatskom jeziku," ["Contributions to Investigation of Turkicisms in the Serbo-Croatian Language"], *Slavia*, IV (Prague, 1937–1938), 166–190.
[74] Škaljić, I, xi. Ivan Franjo Lukić i Lj. Hercegovac, *Narodne pjesme bosanske i hercegovačke* [*Popular Songs of Bosnia and Hercegovina*], (Osijek, 1858).

be considered today as a valuable source of linguistic and ethnographic information.

Because of centuries of association with the Turks, many Turkish words became so much a part of the native vocabulary that they could not be easily expurgated from it. Whenever a talk arose about ridding the language of foreign influences, distinguished Jugoslav linguists (Karadžić, Jagić, Maretić, and others) took a lenient position toward Turkicisms because they employed them freely in their own writings.[75] The Turkicisms seem not only to be tolerated, but often used in preference to a native word in order to stress a point or to flavor a sentence; sometimes they are used unwittingly. Jugoslav literary classics, daily newspaper articles, and public pronouncements are replete with Turkicisms. The two-story buses which the Sarajevo municipality purchased in London a few years ago were nicknamed the *čardaklija* (a Persian and Turkish word for a large room with a good view from the second floor).[76] To be sure, some Turkish words change their meanings in time. Thus the word rayah (subjects, cattle, flock) as used in Communist parlance has a connotation somewhat different from the accepted meaning.

Serbo-Croatian words borrowed from the Turks fall into two categories. In the first are words which have no substitute in Serbo-Croatian: foods (*baklava*, a special Oriental pastry; *halva*, several kinds of candy); fruit (*dud*, mulberry; *jeribasma*, a type of pear; *limun*, lemon); vegetables (*boranija*, string beans; *pazija*, type of greens); beverages (*boza*, a brew made from maize flour; *kafa*, coffee); clothing and footwear (*ćurak*, top cover worn by men; *firale*, sandals; *šarvale* or *šalvare*, baggy pants); utensils and furnishings (*ćilim*, rug; *džezva*, special copper coffee pot), *ibrik*, a water container with a nozzle); musical instruments (*saz*, a string instrument; *tambura*, another string instrument; *zurna* or *zurla*, a type of flute); and construction materials, horse equipment, arms, crafts, artisan and merchant terms, and words for several other things which had not been introduced in the Balkans until after the Turkish conquest (*šećer*, sugar; *duhan, tutun*, tobacco).[77] Many Jugoslav regions received their first maize, a Western product, from Egypt, which was an Ottoman province. Various

---

[75] Škaljić, I, xii.

[76] *Ibid.*, I, xii, 131.

[77] *Ibid.*, I, xii–xiii.

Jugoslav languages and dialects have almost a dozen words for maize and as many doublets. At least three names for maize indicate its Egyptian or Turkish origin, although these words have become obsolete.[78] In literary Greek the word for maize suggests its Arabic origin.[79] In Turkey itself, maize was introduced in the sixteenth and seventeenth centuries,[80] and the Turks call it *misir* (Egypt) and *misir bagdaj* (*bugdaj*).

The second category of borrowed words[81] includes those Turkish (Arabic, Persian) terms preferred to their Serbo-Croat equivalents. There are, for instance, a group of words which are so completely accepted that the Croats, Serbs,[82] Macedonians, and others have scarcely any feeling for their alien origin. Some borrowed words are used in everyday speech, but occur in literature only when needed for occasional stress or embellishment,[83] or they are used in one area but not in another,[84] or in literature but not in daily discourse.[85] Interestingly, the borrowed words may have different meaning from district to district. Furthermore, Turkicisms have been disappearing from Balkan languages at different rates. Finally, religious terminology, greetings, and personal names comprise another long list of Turkicisms still extensively employed.[86]

Turkish (Arabic, Persian) words are given a consistent Serbo-Croatian form. Words ending in *li* have been given the ending *ja* (*çakşirli, čakširlija*, the man who wears baggy pants); words ending in *e* have received the ending *a* (*akçe, akča*, Turkish silver money); words ending in *lik* and *siz* have the endings *luk* and *suz* (*terzilik, terziluk*, tailoring craft; *çiçeklik, čičekluk*, flower place; *çiraklik, čirakluk*, candle-holder; *edepsiz, edepsuz*, uneducated, uncultivated; *arsiz, arsuz*, shameless). Some words are taken over without change (*abdal*, a naive or stupid person; *adet*, custom; *ada*, island) and others after transformation of consonants (*bahce, bašča*, garden; *ikbal, igbal*, for-

---

[78] G. Elezović, "Kukuruz" ["Maize"], *Naš Jezik*, III:9–10 (1935), 272–277.

[79] *Aravositos, arapostaran*. In Western Macedonia the common word for maize is *čenka* (from *pšenka*, probably derived from the Greek *psome*, bread).

[80] Elezović, pp. 272–277.

[81] Škaljić, I, xiii.

[82] *Ibid.*, xiii–xiv.

[83] *Ibid.*, xxviii–xlv.

[84] *Ibid.*, xlv.

[85] *Ibid.*

[86] *Ibid.*

tune).[87] Many Turkish words were taken into Serbo-Croatian after simple changes of consonants or vowels (e.g., *gümrük, djumruk*, tariff; *güvec, djuveč*, dish containing meat, rice, potatoes, and spices; *katib, ćatib*, scribe; *kel-ćela*, head sores).

The Turkish verbs in use are given appropriate Serbo-Croatian prefixes (*na, o, po, pre, pri*). By adding prefixes to Turkish (Arabic, Persian) nouns, new words (*nebaht*, misfortune; *nerahat*, disturbed; *nevakat*, untimely; *kozbaša*, hay cutter; *habernosa*, woman gossip) are often created. Sometimes a special transformation occurs, as in the Arabic *rugábet* which became Serbo-Croatian *rugoba* (ridicule). Finally, the comparatives and superlatives of borrowed words are made by the usual addition of prefixes *naj* and suffixes *ji*; thus, *dertli* (sad) becomes *dertliji* and *najdertliji*.[88]

Turkish influence is waning in the Balkan languages. The jargon of the Communist revolutionaries and a vast new technological terminology are slowly replacing obsolete Turkish words. As the old economic and social practices and habits become discarded, many older words, whether native or Turkish, will fall into disuse.

LITERATURE, ART, AND MUSIC

The attitude of Balkan peoples toward their Ottoman masters, dominated by irreconcilable animosity, has found artistic expression in folk ballads. The simple and lucid epic poems glorify individual and collective acts of heroism in the struggle against the Turks.[89] During the long period of Turkish rule, epic poetry enabled the Serbs, for example, to preserve their national tradition and ethnic individuality and inspired them to struggle against their foreign masters. The Serbian epics consist of a cycle of songs which cluster around some great historical event or prominent personality. The epic poem is a "chronicle in verse" of past events, heroic deeds, and life under Ottoman rule. It records important and interesting incidents concerning the country and the people. Their composers unknown, they spread among

---

[87] *Ibid.*, xxvii–xlv.
[88] *Ibid.*, xliv.
[89] Antun Barac, *Jugoslavenska književnost* [*Jugoslav Literature*], (Zagreb, 1954), pp. 88–96. Čubrilović, *Istorija političke misli*, pp. 36–49.

the people and became a collective possession. The most popular epic or lyric is the decasyllabic poem. The poem is saturated with clichés and phrases created to describe specific activities and events. It is a rich source of historical and ethnographic information. Archaic words from the national language and Turkish nomenclature and terminology abound throughout the epic.

Sung by bards to the accompaniment of the *gusle,* the epics reminded the Serbs of their medieval states and promised them a better future. The clergy, *hajduks,* craftsmen, and ordinary men sang to the *gusle.* At home, at church gatherings, in the market place, or in an inn, people listened to the bard narrate about the great men and events of the past. Mixed with fiction, the epic poems relate facts of history and of religious and patriarchal life in the past. The poems describe the exploits of the legendary Kraljević Marko who cut down the Turks and collaborated with them, presumably for the benefit of the people. They recount the story of the Battle of Kossovo (1389) at which King Lazar chose the "heavenly" in preference to the "worldly" kingdom and lost his life in defense of his people and his faith. While describing the unbearable life of the oppressed people, the epic poems suggest plans for future struggle against the Turks, who are depicted as oppressors of the poor and weak.

Since the Serbs in the Ottoman Empire were mostly beyond the reach of the written and printed word, their popular literature was spread by word of mouth. The epic poems came to represent a unique form of culture.[90] The verses, containing all the people's experiences, thoughts, and hopes, were in "an eternal state of creation." New events produced new poems, which either replaced the old epics or modified them to fit the new situations. Touching upon everything of interest, the popular epics indiscriminately reflected "serious and humorous" as well as "important and unimportant" events.[91] But one basic recurring thread in the epics is the "revolutionary" anti-Turkish sentiment.[92]

Another cycle of epic poems commemorates the deeds of the *hajduks* (Turkish: *haydud,* bandit), and the *uskoks* (pirate), who went to the woods to wage guerrilla warfare against the Turks. Although

---

[90] *Istorija naroda Jugoslavije,* II, 749–758.
[91] Barac, pp. 89–90.
[92] Čubrilović, *Istorija političke misli,* p. 42.

their work was not always altruistic and patriotic, the *hajduks* and the *uskoks* came to be regarded as Robin Hoods who extolled the national cause and fought the Turks in defense of the oppressed Christians. The poem "Beginning of the Uprising against the Dahis" —unique in that its author (Filip Višnjić) is known—tells of the struggle against the Turks and the liberation of the Serbs in 1804. The author exalts contemporary heroes (particularly Karadjordje Petrović), and their bravery and patriotism.[93]

Because they are fewer and are considered to be of inferior artistic quality, the comparable Muslim epic poems of Bosnia and Hercegovina are little known. The Muslims had created their own heroes.[94] Whatever their other values, the epic poems and most of the oral literature also have a negative side, for they espouse a deep-seated hatred and religious bigotry. So significant is this problem in the contemporary lives of the Balkan peoples that in 1951 the Turkish and Greek governments signed an agreement by which they promised to "insure, within the limits permitted by respective legislation, that the textbooks published in the two countries do not contain inaccuracies relating to either of the two countries."[95]

But an agreement of this type can be enforced only with difficulty, for every bright page in the history of one nation is a tragedy for the other. In 1953, when the Turks celebrated the five-hundredth anniversary of the conquest of Constantinople, the Greeks offered prayers in their churches to those who had fallen in defense of the city. The impact of Ottoman rule upon the Balkan peoples will unquestionably survive the longest in historical annals, literature, and folklore.

The decorative arts of the Balkan peoples show Oriental, Ottoman, and indigenous influences. But apart from wood-carving, metalwork, and embroidery, which still persist, the decorative arts are losing out rapidly. Rug-weaving, indubitably influenced by Persian and Turkish styles, still thrives.[96] In Communist countries, the governments officially support arts and handicrafts. The Jugoslav rug makers, for ex-

---

[93] Barac, pp. 92–94. See also, Božidar Tomić, *Pjesme Filipa Višnjića* [*Songs of Filip Višnjić*], Belgrade, 1935), a collection of Višnjić's poems, and an introduction.

[94] Kosta Hermann, *Narodne pjesme Muslimana u Bosni i Hercegovini* [*Popular Songs of Muslims in Bosnia and Hercegovina*], 2d ed. (Sarajevo, 1933).

[95] *United Nations Treaty Series*, Vol. CLXXVIII (Brussels, 1953), No. 2333, Cultural Agreement, signed at Ankara, April 20, 1951, Article XIV.

[96] For a good article on rug-making in Jugoslavia, see *Enciklopedija Jugoslavije* (1956), II, 620–622.

ample, are organized into "socially" owned factories; they are supplied raw materials, and patterns, and their product is turned over to "socially" operated stores at stipulated prices. Although it may have economic advantages, this guided art is bound to stifle the creative genius of the native artist.

The resemblance between many artistic practices and social habits of the Balkan peoples and those of the Middle East, stems from cultural contacts between the Balkans and Middle Eastern peoples in the era that preceded the Turkish conquest of the Balkans. This early "Orientalization" and subsequent "re-Orientalization" under the Ottoman rule explains why the Turks and Balkan peoples have so much in common and understand each other so much better than they can understand a Western European. It is important, therefore, to distinguish between early Oriental artistic influences and the Byzantine and Turkish influences in Balkan art.

Ottoman architecture can still be found in the Balkans in religious institutions, in bridges, fountains, bath houses, and an occasional home. In some parts of Macedonia, especially in the small and retarded communities, whole blocks of buildings designed in Turkish style and erected during Ottoman rule are preserved.[97] Rarely is a new structure built in Turkish style, but sometimes a building in modern architecture is given an Arabic (Persian) name, such as the recently built *bezistan* in Belgrade.[98]

After liberation from the Turks, most important cities in the Balkans rapidly shed their Oriental character and acquired a modern look.[99] This process has been speeded up by the rapid growth of cities and urbanization which tend to obliterate the last urban vestiges of Oriental influence. Among the major cities, except for those in Turkish Thrace, parts of the erstwhile Turkish market places persist only in Skoplje and Sarajevo. The many minarets and the famous *baščaršija* (*baş çarşi*, the main market place) give Sarajevo an Oriental flavor that will long continue.[100]

---

[97] On Turkish architecture, see Dj. Sabo, "Arhitektura," *Narodna Enciklopedija*, I, 83–85.

[98] A Turkish and Persian word for a covered shopping center or market place.

[99] On Turkish cities and urban life, see H. Kreševljaković, "Gradska privreda i esnafi u Bosni i Hercegovini (od 1463 do 1851)," ["City Economy and Esnafs in Bosnia and Hercegovina"], *GID*, I (Sarajevo, 1949), 194–195.

[100] *Ibid.*

Most Balkan songs written in the Oriental vein have a plaintive and nostalgic air, and their lyrics constantly refer to death and frustrated love. The Orientalism in Balkan music has never been systematically investigated. Some believe that the Balkan Slavs obtained "the melancholy of the steppes" through their old racial and cultural ties with Eastern peoples, and that this element in music was later reinforced by the Byzantine and Turkish influences. The use of instruments of Middle Eastern origin in some Balkan regions is a further indication of Oriental musical influence.[101] The *lyra* (ancient Greek lyre) and the *bouzouki* (type of lute) are still played in Greece. The *bouzouki* is currently the center of renewed interest.

Experts assert that the Balkan peoples developed their peculiar music in the distant past, that they borrowed music from each other, and that their music was strongly influenced by Byzantine and Ottoman music. Yet, it is argued, each nation has its own music. We are reminded that just as the Balkan peoples did not adopt the Turkish language, neither did they take over the Turkish music.[102] In other words, the Turkish, Middle Eastern, and European elements in Balkan music did not change the essence of the local music, just as the Turkish and other foreign words "did not change" the Balkan languages. A patriotic ethnographer avers that, unlike artistic style and technique, the popular "spirit"[103] cannot be transplanted from region to region and be taken over from another people. What one often finds in Jugoslav songs, he writes, are Slavonic "archaisms" wrapped in "Oriental embellishment."[104] In reality, then, the music of the Balkan peoples is their own product which merely absorbed some Turkish elements.[105] Turkish music as such disappeared from the Balkans together with the Ottoman Empire.[106] The Turks never succeeded in imposing their own music upon the Balkan peoples, probably because they lacked a strong musical tradition.[107] The musical culture which they brought to the Balkans was one borrowed from the Arabs; in this way, some

---

[101] Dvorniković, pp. 396–398.

[102] V. R. Gjorgjević, "Turski elementi u našoj muzici," ["Turkish Elements in Our Music"], *Nova Evropa*, VII (May 21, 1923), 469–470.

[103] Dvorniković, pp. 376–394.

[104] Gjorgjević, pp. 469–470.

[105] *Ibid.*

[106] *Ibid.*

[107] Dvorniković, pp. 376–394.

Arabic scales found their way into folk music of the Balkan peoples. The Turkish music was shaped under the influences of Central Asian, Caucasian, Arabic, medieval Church, and Greek music. The so-called Doric, Eolic, and Phrygian modes often occur in Anatolian folk music. But the Turkish music clearly has its own distinctive ethnic flavor, and, whatever its origins, has influenced the Balkan folk music.

Probably no other Balkan songs are so beautiful and so rich in Oriental flavor as the *sèvdalinka*[108] (*sèvdàh*, Arabic for "love" and "desire for love") of Bosnia and the *dertliška* (*dèrtli*, Persian and Turkish for worry and grief) of Macedonia. The popular *sèvdalinka* is an expression of a man's and woman's emotional life and combines Slavic sentimentalism with Oriental passion. The melancholy *dertliška* song tells of concern over life and love, sadness and pain.

The songs of Bosnia and Macedonia display remarkable dynamism and have a great popular appeal. The *sèvdalinka* is favored in all Jugoslavia, and the Macedonian songs throughout Bulgaria and Jugoslavia. These songs are holding their own against invading American and Western music; their appeal has grown, and they are preferred in districts (Slovenia, Dalmatia) that were not ruled by the Turks.

CLOTHING

An expert eye can discern various early Oriental, Byzantine, pre-Slavonic, Turkish, and local influences in Balkan clothing.[109] After the Ottoman conquest, a "Turkification" of dress began. The type of clothing worn was not a mere copy of Turkish styles, but included local improvisations and sometimes was entirely indigenous in origin. Only a few Christians living in cities and engaged in trade and crafts wore clothes of Turkish style. That "Turkification" of clothing in general had been considerable is attested by the fact that many parts of the formal peasant national costume are known by Turkish words.[110]

---

[108] Gjorgjević, pp. 469–470.

[109] N. P. Kondakov, "Les Costumes orientaux a la cour de Byzance," *Byzantion*, I (1924), 10. Jovan Kovačević, *Srednjevekovna nošnja Balkanskih Slovena* [*Medieval Dress of Balkan Slavs*], (Belgrade, 1953), pp. 274–275.

[110] *Džamadan*, a kind of vest; *dolama*, coat with long sleeves; *šalvare*, baggy breeches; *toke*, metallic buttons or pieces of metal used for decorative purposes.

Practically every garment of the Montenegrin native dress has a Turkish (Persian, Arabic) name.

The Turks did not like to see Christians imitate them in clothing and, at various times, would not allow them to wear expensive and brightly colored clothes. The Christians were forbidden to wear garments in the "sacred" Muslim color of green.[111] This emphasis on Muslim exclusiveness intensified similar tendencies among the Christians. If the Muslim raised the wearing of the *fez* and *ferace* (veil worn by women) to the level of a cult, the Montenegrin lifted the wearing of his *zavrata* to the symbol of patriotism and faith. To a good Muslim, an acceptance of infidel headgear implies social degradation and religious betrayal. The Muslims, therefore, regulated the Christian dress and forbade the Christians to wear Muslim dress.

But there is still one important consideration: the Muslim clothing had a class connotation; it was the garb of the rulers. Consequently, the dress had socio-psychological implications. A desire to look like a Turk or to free oneself of social restrictions by wearing Turkish-styled clothes became deeply ingrained. It did not matter what the Ottoman intended to achieve (for example, avoid friction by discrimination in dress),[112] but rather what their policies produced. There were many instances of friction over clothing, just because it was discriminatory.

As the Ottoman rule weakened there was a tendency on the part of the Christians to assert themselves and to copy the Turkish clothing and jewelry. Looking like Turks was the means by which they hoped to lift themselves socially and demonstrate their freedom; it was the result of a long-suppressed desire for emancipation. Another probable reason was the likelihood that as time passed the Christian taste for clothing became "Turkified" and that Turkish clothing was more in harmony with the general environment.[113] Whatever the real reasons, the first impulse of liberated Serbs in 1804 was to don Turkish dress. Only after satiating their egos did they gradually adopt part Western and part local dress.

---

[111] See, for example, Pavle Vasić, "Srpska nošnja za vreme Prvog ustanka," ["Serbian Dress in Time of the First Serbian Uprising"], *Istoriski glasnik*, Nos. 1–2 (1954), 149–191.

[112] Wayne S. Vucinich, "The Nature of Balkan Society Under Ottoman Rule," *Slavic Review* (December, 1962), p. 637.

[113] Dvorniković, pp. 454.

After the political and cultural contacts with the West expanded, everything associated with the Turks came to be regarded as backward and alien. In the course of the nineteenth and twentieth centuries, the cities have become rapidly Westernized in clothing. A visitor in the 'seventies of the nineteenth century observed that the lower classes still wore "the baggy breeches, the loose jacket, and the red cap of Turkey, while the well-to-do citizens dressed in coats, and vests, and trousers from the slopshops of Vienna and Paris."[114] The influx of Western styles and vogues into the village has been slow, and, until recently, many villages clung in part or completely to their local garb, which exhibited strong Turkish influences. Today, the traditional native costumes are, by and large, museum pieces.

CONCLUSION

Never a homogeneous polity, the Ottoman Empire was an enormous and intricate network of social subsystems. The complex mosaic of Ottoman society, moreover, changed significantly from one period to another far more than is generally believed. At any one time, the empire amounted to vast congeries of discrete cultural and societal elements which shifted and related like the particles in a kaleidoscope. Not only did they differ one from the other, but they often displayed important variations within themselves. The dominant Ottoman Turkish society and the numerous subsocieties which functioned within the encompassing system of social relations preserved their distinctive characters and yet influenced each other. The long period of coexistence and intermingling has given the Turks and their erstwhile subjects many common characteristics and a similar outlook on life. The Ottoman Empire vanished, but its influence survived.

Ottoman influences have been thoroughly blended with the cultures of the Balkan peoples which have shown strong resilience to the challenges of modernity. While the Balkan peoples are discarding some Ottoman influences and grafting on their culture the elements of Western culture, they have not completely yielded to the latter. In other words, they are absorbing the new without entirely rejecting the old. The result is that the cultures of the Balkan peoples continue

---

[114] Thomas Knox, *Backsheesh!* (Hartford, Conn., 1875), pp. 72–73.

to bear a powerful autochthonous and Oriental, and specifically Ottoman, flavor. Side by side there exist and thrive folk and modern art,
music, and literature. Traditional habits of mind, social practices, and
much else remain very much a part of national life among each of
the Balkan peoples.

The modifications in physical environment and political and economic institutions have been the most apparent in de-Ottomanization
of the Balkans. The Ottoman material influence, though still visible,
began to disappear with the Ottoman recession into Asia. The territories first severed from Turkish rule—Hungary, Transylvania, Vojvodina, and Slavonia—show practically no physical influence from the
Ottoman era. Those which won their freedom at the beginning of the
nineteenth century (Serbia and Greece) have retained little evidence
of Turkish culture. The most rapid transformation occurred in Bulgaria after its liberation from Turkish rule in 1878, but, on account
of the large number of Muslim inhabitants, many examples of Ottoman civilization nevertheless survive. Where the Turks remained the
longest, such as in Bosnia-Hercegovina (until 1878) and in Macedonia and Albania (until 1912), and the Muslim population is most
heavily concentrated, the traces of the Turkish physical influence are
the strongest, and the degree of social backwardness the highest.

Official fostering in Communist countries of the so-called "socialist
culture," coupled with an accelerated industrialization which is in
progress, threaten many aspects of national culture in the Balkans,
but not the culture itself. The transformation of Balkan societies during the past century and a half, from Oriental communities to modern
polities with an Oriental flavor, is a fascinating chapter in modern
Balkan history.

THE ROLE OF RELIGION

IN THE DEVELOPMENT

OF BALKAN NATIONALISM

George G. Arnakis

Spyridon Trikoupis, the historian of the Greek Revolution, an enlightened Greek nationalist whose work is still regarded as a classic, notes
with chagrin the fact that the Catholic inhabitants of the Aegean
Islands (Syra, Tinos, Naxos, and Santorini), numbering about 11,000,
remained indifferent to the cause of national freedom, and even collaborated with the Turks against their fellow Greeks; and he concludes with the following generalization:

Blessed is the nation that professes one and the same faith. We
[Greeks] possess this blessing—thanks be to God—and cursed by the
nation is he who will conspire against the unity of the faith of the
Greeks, through alien teachings, no matter what the pretext, or whatever the means.[1]

The present essay was written in Greece and Italy, in the winter of 1959–60,
during the tenure of a Guggenheim Fellowship and a fellowship from the Research Institute of the University of Texas. To both foundations I am deeply
grateful.

[1] Spyridon Trikoupis, *Historia tēs Hellēnikēs Epanastaseōs* [*History of the Greek
Revolution*], 3d ed. (Athens, 1888), I, 125. The Greek constitutions of 1844,
1864, 1911, 1927, and 1951, all in Article 1, define the Orthodox Church as the
established church and declare that all other faiths are tolerated. An important
work on Greek religious policy and its background is S. Th. Lascaris, *Hē Katho-
likē Ekklēsia en Helladi* [*The Catholic Church in Greece*], (Athens, 1924). Perhaps the earliest indication of religious tolerance in the constitutional history of
modern Greece is in the *Nomikē Diataxis* of Eastern Continental Greece at the
outbreak of the Revolution. Article 1 states: "All the inhabitants of Greece who
believe in Christ are Greeks." Article 6 promises naturalization to all Christians,
regardless of church affiliation, after a residence of five years, if they have "good
character." Article 12 refers to those who "do not believe in Christ" as metics;
they can serve as soldiers but not as officers; otherwise their rights are broadly
described as "the same as those of the citizens." Andreas Z. Mamoukas, *Ta kata
tēn Anagennēsin tēs Hellados* [*Concerning the Rebirth of Greece*], (Piraeus,
1839), I, 43–45.

Trikoupis belonged to a distinguished family of Mesolonghi, and he played a leading part in the war of national independence and in the political life of Greece during the next two decades. Having lived several years in England before he embarked on his career as a historian, he was as Western in his views as anyone in the Balkans around the middle of the nineteenth century. A keen observer of society, a realist with a Thucydidean flavor in his style, he was able to grasp the significance of religion in the perpetuation of Greek national consciousness and in the development of modern Greek nationalism.

To Trikoupis, and practically to all Greek historians after him, religion—in this instance the beliefs and institutions of the Eastern Orthodox Church—was the power that welded heterogeneous elements into one ethnic group, and during the four or five centuries of Ottoman domination it served as an effective barrier against the further expansion of Islam. The Catholic Church played a similar, though less conspicuous, role in sections of the Balkans—such as Croatia and parts of Transylvania—where it embraced the majority of the people and was not involved in a struggle against Orthodoxy. Both churches, each one in her own domain, invoked the powers of heaven and hell and made full use of their hierarchy and institutions, in order to prevent their adherents from becoming absorbed by the Ottoman-Turkish world, through conversion to Islam. It is an undeniable fact that if the Greeks, Serbs, Croats, Rumanians, and Bulgarians had embraced the faith of Mohammed, they would have crossed the dividing line, and their Turkification would have followed their Islamization within a generation. Indeed, the Ottoman Empire, in those prenationalist days when the only political loyalties were to king and religion, recognized no barriers of race, language, color, or origin; it knew only the equality of Islam and the "inferiority" of the other revealed religions; it accepted Islam as the sole leveling and integrating factor in the *pax Ottomanica*;[2] and it sought constant self-renewal through the conversion and social elevation of virile peasant stock. The Christian peoples of the Balkans, on the other hand, had

---

[2] Arnold J. Toynbee, *A Study of History:* Abridgement of volumes i–vi, by D. C. Somerville (Oxford University Press, 1947), pp. 130, 177, 372, 536. Toynbee's term, adopted by L. S. Stavrianos' *The Balkans since 1453* (New York, 1958), pp. 112–115, is generally applicable to the Balkan scene, though I believe that the scene, under Turkish management, was not so attractive or so well-ordered as the term might imply.

no sociocultural bulwark on which to rally for their self-preservation, other than their religious heritage.

This phenomenon can best be studied in Greece, partly because the Greek people had a continuous historical tradition and partly because geographical and social conditions in the more exposed parts of the country helped a good segment of the people catch early glimpses of the spirit of Enlightenment and the French Revolution, both potent forerunners of the national awakening. Spyridon Trikoupis, Constantine Paparrhegopoulos, Spyridon Lampros, Paul Karolides, and Constantine Amantos—to mention those who are no longer living—were leaders in a long line of Greek historians who studied the various phases of modern Greek nationhood and analyzed the contributing factors of the Greek *risorgimento*, which bears a natural similarity to the Italian, Serbian, Rumanian, and Bulgarian experience.

Historians from outside the Balkans, unlike their Greek colleagues, were not always able to penetrate into the character of Balkan Christianity and see its impact on the growth of modern nationalism. Not least among the historians of postclassical Greece is the Scotsman George Finlay, who came to the country for the first time during the revolution and was connected with ties of friendship with Lord Byron, Captain Frank Abney Hastings, Dr. Samuel G. Howe, and the pleiad of militant Philhellenes of the 1820's. During his long life at Athens (from 1834 to his death early in 1876), Finlay took an active part in Greek affairs and became involved in various financial enterprises that ended in disappointment and frustration. As is natural to a man of his temperament, he did not keep his bias out of his voluminous *History of Greece since the Roman Conquest*. His references to John Kolettis, the leader of the "French" party, as "the Zinzar-Vlach," and his scathing remarks about other leaders of the Greek Revolution, are less justifiable than his fear of Russian penetration in the days of Palmerstonian diplomacy.[3] Fear of Russia, perhaps more than any other factor, prevented him from viewing the Greek Orthodox Church in an objective light. Hence, he frequently disparaged the role of religion in the development of modern Greece. Like certain political scientists and statesmen in the middle of the twentieth century, he did not always see what business clergymen had in Near Eastern politics.

---

[3] George Finlay, *History of Greece since the Roman Conquest* (Oxford, 1870), VI, 332–342; VII, 171, 185–186, 191, 195–197, 199.

As a correspondent of the London *Times* in Athens, Finlay wrote articles on current issues (such as "The Cretan Revolt of 1866–69") and he also prepared long, informative essays, or reports, intended for the *Saturday Review,* some of which have never been published in their entirety and are on file in the library of the British School at Athens. One of these reports bears the title "The Cretan Insurrection and Greek Nationality, 19 September, 1867." Discussing developments in Crete, Finlay makes the statement that "nearly one-third of the Greeks in the island are of the Mohammedan religion," and he keeps referring to "Greek Musulmans." As criteria of nationality he recognized only "language and literature."[4]

To anyone who looked at the Balkan scene from the inside, statements like Finlay's would sound paradoxical. They would be rejected in the light of overwhelming historical experience and contemporary actuality. A variety of cases may be cited to illustrate the primary influence of religion. We have Turkish-speaking Greeks, who are loyal to Greece because they are Orthodox Christians, and a long list of Vlach-speaking benefactors of Greece, all with a Greek consciousness, in the nineteenth century, are still familiar names in Athens. We also have Bulgarian-speaking Pomaks, who, being Muslims, are more sympathetically inclined toward Turkey than Bulgaria (most of them, it will be remembered, were expelled from Bulgaria and found refuge in Turkey in 1950 and after.)[5] We meet Greek-speaking Turks from Crete, settled in Turkey during the first quarter of the present century, after decades of national-religious struggles known as the Cretan revolutions; even today, with nearly four decades of peace intervening between Greece and Turkey, the Muslim Cretan, who may still speak Greek as his vernacular, will never call himself a Greek, but, using the Greek language, he will refer to himself as a *Tourko-Krētikós,* a Turkish Cretan. Similarly, on some islands of the Aegean, and even in the neighborhood of Athens, we may come across Albanian-speaking Greeks, whose ancestors fought for Greece in the 1820's, while other Albanian-speaking Orthodox Christians from Karystos on the

---

[4] "The Finlay Papers: Letters on Greek Affairs, 1867; Additional Material," pp. 3, 7, 9. I wish to express my thanks to Mr. Philip Sherrard, librarian of the British School at Athens, for permission to read the (unpublished) Finlay Papers.

[5] See Joseph B. Schechtman, "Compulsory Transfer of the Turkish Minority from Bulgaria," *Journal of Central European Affairs,* XII (1952), 154–169.

Euboea emigrated to Asia Minor and adopted Turkish as their vernacular. It is interesting to note, in this connection, that Castel Rosso,
the Frankish name of Karystos, survived in Turkish translation as
Kızıl Hisar, or Red Fortress, and the last Turkish-speaking Karystians,
or Castel Rossians, or Kızıl Hisarlıs, were expelled from Turkey, as
exchangeable Greeks, after the Greek defeat in 1922.[6]

From these examples it will appear that language is no criterion of
nationality: it sits lightly on the cultural equipment of our Balkan
peoples and it may accommodate itself to any new environment. Language usually carries with it what Finlay calls "literature"—not merely
the written records, which were scanty in an age of nonliteracy, but,
more significantly, the oral tradition (poems, fables, proverbs, songs)
that form part of a people's modes of expression.

In several instances the people's language did not fail to pay its
tribute to religion by adopting the alphabet of the church to which
the people belonged. Perhaps the best-known instance can be taken
from Asia Minor, which, though not a Balkan territory, was closely
connected with the Balkans as a part of the Ottoman Empire. In Asia
Minor the Turkish-speaking Greeks used the Greek alphabet, the alphabet of their church, to write their vernacular. Among the Greeks
these people are known as "Karamanlis" and their language and literature "Karamanlidika."[7] Similarly, the Greek Catholics of the Aegean Islands used the Latin alphabet in writing Greek, their mother
tongue, and their records and literature are known as Frango-Syrianá
or Frango-Chiótika. Much more impressive in bulk and content is the
literature of the Croats, who being Catholics, use the Latin alphabet,
while their Orthodox brothers, the Serbs, use the Cyrillic, just like the
Orthodox Russians and Bulgarians. In Albania, too, before the generalization of the Latin alphabet, the Orthodox Albanians wrote Albanian in the Greek alphabet, their Catholic neighbors in the Latin
and the Muslims in the Arabic script. At the other end of the peninsula, it was only the potent nationalism of the Rumanians, oriented

---

[6] To Mr. Nicholas Stavrinides, librarian of the Municipal Library at Heraklion,
Crete, I am indebted for this information, which happens to be true of his own
family background.

[7] A complete list of Karamanli books, with introductory information, has been
published by Père S. Salaville and E. Daleggio, under the title *Karamanlidika*
(Athens: Collection d'Institut Français, 1958). Vol. II is forthcoming.

toward Paris and Rome, that prevailed upon them, as late as the middle of the nineteenth century, and compelled them to adopt the Latin alphabet—a unique instance for an Orthodox people.

Thus, in contrast to the mutability of literature and language, religion, which addresses itself to the human soul, is characterized by a sense of loyalty that is devoutly meant to be perpetual. To the subjects of the sultan in the Balkans, when religion was lost, all was lost from one's ethnic and social identity. Reduced to its simplest terms, the terms that were fully grasped by Balkan mentality during the Turkish period, if one became a Muslim, he became a Turk; while a Christian who remained a Christian could also call himself a Greek, a Serb, a Vlach, a Bulgar, a Croat. The case of the Albanian nation, with its Orthodox, Catholic, and Muslim community, deserves special treatment.

THE TURKS OF THE BALKANS: ISLAMIZATION

The secret of the success of the Ottoman Empire in the Balkans lay in the power of the Turks to absorb non-Turkish groups and employ them in the army, navy, and administration. One way through which this was accomplished was the *devshirme*, the notorious tribute of children. While the majority of the recruits formed the *élite* corps— that is, the Janissaries—children with exceptional aptitudes were trained in the Palace School, founded by Mohammed the Conqueror, for higher administrative posts.[8] The government resorted to the *devshirme* periodically and in specified areas each time, during the fifteenth and sixteenth centuries. In the latter part of the sixteenth century, the Janissaries began to enlist their sons (celibacy was no longer the rule in their ranks) and an increasing number of recruits were born Muslims. The number of the entire force was probably less than one hundred thousand. The *devshirme* system fell into decay in the

---

[8] See Barnette Miller, *The Palace School of Muhammad the Conqueror* (Harvard University Press, 1941). For a brief account of the Janissaries, see H. A. R. Gibb and Harold Bowen, *Islamic Society and the West* (Oxford University Press, 1951), I, 1, 56–66, and the article by Cl. Huart in *Encyclopedia of Islam* (Leyden and London, 1927), II, 572–574. The most detailed treatment of the subject is Ismail Hakkı Uzunçarşili, *Kapukulu Ocakları* [*The Odjaks of the Slaves of the Gate*], (Ankara, 1943–1944) 2 vols.

seventeenth century, while the majority of the Janissaries entered service primarily for the sake of the stipend, and at the same time engaged in other profitable activities, ranging from *halva* production to racketeering. Hence, the once famous corps lost its original character and degenerated into a colorful and seditious confraternity, whose allegiance was as costly as it was precarious.[9]

During the three hundred years of its application, the *devshirme* had an indirect effect that outweighed its declared objective, which was the recruitment of personnel. This indirect effect, as H. A. Gibbons pointed out,[10] was the incentive that the system provided to the native Christians to keep their sons at the price of Islamization of the whole family. Less important as an inducement for the adoption of Islam was the desire of the peasants to avoid the head tax (*harach*), which, in fact, was not heavy beyond their endurance. Thus, in agricultural areas—Bosnia, Macedonia, Thessaly, Thrace, among others—the urge among the Christian peasants to keep their sons, who were more important to them than the faith of their forefathers, resulted in numerous conversions to Islam.

If statistical data were available, we could determine the percentage of the increase of Islamization during the years of the *devshirme* in the areas from which the tribute children were recruited. In the absence of statistics, the theory of Gibbons seems quite plausible, in view of the fact that Islamization was, indeed, extensive in rural areas in the fifteenth, sixteenth, and seventeenth centuries—that is, during the period when the *devshirme* was practiced—and at the same time Islamization was negligible in commercial and maritime centers, such as the Aegean Islands, which were exempted from the levy of children. The Balkan peasants, by adopting the faith of the "Ruling Institution"—to use Lybyer's apt term[11]—not only kept their sons near them, but, as a rule, safeguarded their possessions, especially their land.

---

[9] Walter L. Wright, Jr., *Ottoman Statecraft: The Book of Counsel for Vezirs and Governors, of Sari Mehmed Pasha, the Defterdar* (Princeton University Press, 1935), pp. 38–42, 113–115.

[10] Herbert Adams Gibbons, *The Foundation of the Ottoman Empire* (Oxford, 1916), pp. 118–119. Cf. G. Georgiades Arnakis, *Hoi Prōtoi Othōmanoi* [*The Early Osmanlis*] in *Texte und Forschungen zur byzantinisch-neugriechischen Philologie*, 41 (Athens, 1947), p. 100.

[11] A. H. Lybyer, *The Government of the Ottoman Empire in the Time of Suleiman the Magnificent* (Harvard University Press, 1913), pp. 36, 45–46, 57–58.

There is no doubt that all voluntary converts, whether they lived in the country or in the city, expected to better their lot by avoiding the pressures, the embarrassments, and the discriminations that they were subject to, as Christians. By accepting the faith of the *Herrenvolk* they figured out that they would augment their state. They would be exempt from the head tax; they would be better able to defend themselves from the arbitrary practices of the tax farmer; in case of dispute, they could count on a favorable hearing of their case in a court, which was not noted for its impartiality. In the city, the renegade had much more freedom to circulate; he could choose his residence; he could wear clothes of a style and color that befitted his superior status and not the drab attire of the Christian. He could even ride a horse—he could ride his horse down Main Street in the town, something that no Christian could do. In short, even without the *devshirme*, the pressures for abandoning Christianity in favor of Islam were too many and too real to be ignored.[12] If from time to time the renegade fell short of his expectations, if he did not become a *spahi*, or a tax farmer, or an administrator, if he was even looked down upon by the established Muslim-Turkish class, or was treated as a lowly character (despite Islam's equalitarianism), he could still derive some satisfaction when he compared himself with his Christian cousins and could hope that some day he or his progeny might become full-fledged Ottomans.

His Christian cousins continued living in the shadow of fear, not least being the fear about the future of their daughters. Down to the nineteenth century, the Turks and Islamized natives replenished their harems with as many attractive Christian women as inclination, fortune, and finances permitted. This practice, though by no means gen-

---

[12] See G. G. Arnakis, "The Greek Church of Constantinople and the Ottoman Empire," *The Journal of Modern History*, XXIV (1952), 235–250. Cf. H. A. R. Gibb and Harold Bowen, *Islamic Society and the West* (Oxford University Press, 1957), I, 2, 208. Constantine Amantos, *Scheseis Hellēnōn kai Tourkōn, 1071–1571* [*Relations of Greeks and Turks, 1071–1571*], (Athens, 1955), pp. 190–193, mentions, among other factors, the tendency of the Turks to accuse Christians of insulting the memory of Mohammed the Prophet, an offense which was punishable by death. In such cases, adoption of Islam was the only escape from death, but some Christians were determined to die rather than forsake Christ. An important work on these latter-day saints comes from the Archbishop of Athens, Chrysostomos Papadopoulos, *Hoi Neomartyres* [*The Neomartyrs*], 2d ed. (Athens, 1934).

eral, extending, as it did, over a period of four hundred years, resulted in the racial transformation of the Anatolian Turks, the conquerors, who were already a mixed race before they entered the Balkans. The Turks of the Balkans, so far as physical anthropology is concerned, are in no appreciable way different from their Christian subjects. As in the instance of the *devshirme*, the process of selection resulted in improving the human stock of the "master race" and depleting the biological resources of the Christian peoples, because the women admitted into Turkish harems, as a rule, and the children they bore to the Turks, automatically became Muslims and were absorbed by the Turkish people.

This intermingling rarely resulted in good relations between the Turks and their Christian subjects in the Balkans. Instances of brotherly coöperation across the barrier of religion—such as that of Mehmed Sökölü (Sokolović), the grand vezir, and Makarij Sokolović, the founder of the independent church of Serbia (1557)—are very rare in the annals of Balkan Islam.[13] The long-nourished resentment, on the part of the Christian relatives, over what was regarded as an arbitrary act, an outrage, or a deplorable accident, the insult to the family, the uncompromising attitude of the church, whose traditions were by no means dead—these and related factors created a gap between the convert and the first generation Turks, on one hand, and the native Christian community, on the other hand, or, to use different terms, between the ruling class and the subject people. From contemporary accounts it appears that the strife between Muslim converts and Christians was more bitter and more enduring in the Balkans than in Anatolia, where the conversions were of a much older date. The bloody feuds of the Bosnians and the Cretans were irreconcilable and costly largely because both sides spoke the same language. Memories of family ties, even the survival of the same family name in the Muslim branch, made the gap wider, the contact more painful.

The importance of the converts, or renegades, and their offspring, in the Ottoman Empire, needs no elaboration. Suffice it to note that,

---

[13] Charles Jelavich, "Some Aspects of Serbian Religious Development in the Eighteenth Century," *Church History*, XXIII (1954), 144–152, with important bibliography.

as L. S. Stavrianos points out,[14] of the forty-nine grand vezirs who served the sultans from 1453 to 1623, only five appear to have been of Turkish extraction. Eleven of them were Albanians, eleven Slavs, six Greeks, one Armenian, one Georgian, one Italian, and the rest were Christian-born men of unknown nationality. The majority, it will be seen, came from the Balkans. The situation was much the same until past the middle of the seventeenth century, though, quite naturally, we find an increasing number of second- and third-generation Turks in the highest posts. Through conversion, under different pretexts, the human resources of the Ottoman Turks were strengthened in direct proportion to the depletion sustained by the Christians.

However, all the process of Turkification that went on in the Balkans, during the Turkish era, cannot be explained in terms of forceful changes of faith or pressure of external circumstances. There is no doubt that numerous conversions, some of which took place as late as the eighteenth century, notably in Albania and Crete, were due to psychological factors, ranging from loss of faith (in what Christianity professed) to positive belief in Mohammed's finality of message. The part played by the various orders of dervishes—especially the more methodical Bektashi dervishes—must be given precedence, in view of the fact that the Balkans, from the Black Sea to the Adriatic, remained a fruitful field of missionary activity. Most of this activity was centered on Bektashi *tekkes*.[15] Albania is still the citadel of Bektashism, which is recognized, even under communism as a major religion (along with the Eastern Orthodox Church, the Roman Catholic Church, and Sunni Islam).[16]

What rendered Bektashism a mighty weapon of conversion was its broad scope, based on the mystical concept of the unity of existence and the denial of barriers of race, origin, status, or creed. The Bektashi dervishes persistently gave the impression that they accepted Christ more unreservedly than the other Muslims and gave Jesus Christ a rank among Islam's 124,000 prophets which was very close,

---

[14] *Op. cit.*, p. 501.

[15] See G. G. Arnakis, "Futuwwa Traditions in the Ottoman Empire: Akhis, Bektashi Dervishes, and Craftsmen," *Journal of Near Eastern Studies*, XII (1953), 232–247. The beliefs and practices of the Bektashis are described in John Kingsley Birge, *The Bektashi Order of Dervishes* (London, 1937).

[16] Stavro Skendi, *Albania* (New York, 1956), p. 294. G. G. Arnakis, "Albania," *Americana Annual 1958* (New York, 1958), p. 25.

if not equal, to that of Mohammed. The hybrid religion, with its mystical rites, was sure to attract the masses, whose theology was by no means clearly formulated at a time when even clergymen were illiterate. On the other hand, the Bektashis could adjust and readjust the dogmas they claimed to profess as circumstances demanded, because one of their cardinal beliefs was the belief in dissimulation (takiye), which in its daily manifestations, produced a deceitful labyrinth of confusion between spiritual essentials, modes of expression, techniques of approach, intentions, motives, loyalties, and every manner of socioreligious modality that favored the syncretism of the two faiths. Beyond this state of fluidity there was, to be sure, a hard core of beliefs that were built around the idea of the brotherhood of man and the fatherhood of God, who was, as in all Islam, merciful and compassionate and ready to forgive human foibles. To grasp the spiritual essence of God—taught the Bektashis—one would have to transcend the limits of the earthly sphere, and wine (banned by the Prophet together with all intoxicants) was a welcome uplifter of the human spirit, hence a vehicle of approach to God.

As the God of the Bektashis was broader in his sympathies, so were (in Muslim eyes) the saints of the Christian faith, whose worship was associated with mausoleums, sacred springs, and temples of both faiths. St. George, St. Demetrius, St. Nicholas, and the Virgin Mary were regarded with sincere reverence by the Bektashis, and Christians could recall many a Bektashi baba donating money for the oil of the lamps before the sacred icons, lighting candles to them, and giving other indications of Crypto-Christian predilections.[17] The devout of the countryside, Christians and Muslims, frequented the same miracle-working sites to find relief from various ailments. Human

[17] The best work on this subject is still F. W. Hasluck, *Christianity and Islam under the Sultans*, 2 vols. (Oxford University Press, 1929). The situation in the Balkans could not have been much different from that in Asia Minor, which is the main area in Hasluck's book. Since then, valuable material, unique of its kind, has been collected by the Center of Anatolian Studies (Centre d'Etudes d'Asie Mineure), founded and directed by Mme. Melpo Merlier, under French auspices, in Athens. During my stay in Greece, in 1960, it was my privilege to read part of the material dealing with the social institutions and religious traditions of Cappadocia and adjacent regions, and I should like to take this opportunity to express my thanks to Mme. Merlier and her devoted staff for the help they have given me. It is to be hoped that the Center will be able to publish a periodical to make this material available to international scholarship.

sympathy, borne out of common suffering, was the greatest common denominator that embraced both the Christian and the Muslim. During periods of drought, Christians and Muslims would pray for rain, and if the litanies of the Christians went unheeded, the good offices of Mohammed were solicited. If rain came, as an answer to the prayers of the Muslims, the Christians felt a strong urge to join the Muslim religion, admitting that Mohammed had proved his powers.

The cases of voluntary mass conversions that occurred in Albania in the eighteenth century indicate, perhaps, that Christianity was not deeply rooted among the Albanian tribes, but there is no doubt that the ground was prepared by the missionary activity of the Bektashis who taught that there was no unbridgeable difference between the two faiths. The conversions in Albania went on till the majority of the people became Muslims and are so to this day. The religious diversity of the Albanian people—Muslims, Orthodox, Catholic—deprived them of a solid foundation for nationalism and delayed their national awakening until 1878 and after.

THE EASTERN ORTHODOX CHURCH: PRESERVER OF NATIONALITY

To counteract Islamization and Turkification was the main role of the Church. Though the Orthodox Church, to which the majority of the Balkan peoples belonged, was under Greek administration, it still adhered to the doctrine of Christian universalism. It was the "ecumenical" Church, in the same way as the Byzantine Empire had been the ecumenical empire. The Church carried in her earthly body the heritage of the Byzantine Empire that was demolished by Mohammed the Conqueror in 1453.[18] Just like Islam, theoretically the Orthodox Church knew no racial or ethnic discriminations and insisted only on

---

[18] In 1953, five hundredth anniversary of the fall of Constantinople, D. A. Zakythenos, pointed out that Mohammed II preserved the Orthodox Church not merely because of the traditional policy of toleration, but also because he wanted to stress the claim of Ottoman succession to the Byzantine Empire. Professor Zakythenos spoke of "the strong attraction of the Orthodox Byzantine imperial tradition" to which the Ottoman Turks were subjected. *Hē Pentakosiostē Epeteios apo tēs Alōseōs tēs Kōnstantinoupoleōs* [*The Five Hundredth Anniversary of the Fall of Constantinople*], a book published by the journal *L'Hellénisme Contemporain* (Athens, May 29, 1953), pp. 95–96. George Th. Zoras analyzed the motives of the "collaborationism" of the church, in "Ideological and Political Orien-

the unity and purity of the faith. What mattered in those days was Christianity (of the Eastern rite), not loyalty to the nation, or ethnic-cultural traditions.

Ottoman policy, for the most part, was not hostile to the Orthodox Church. The reason is obvious. It was essential for the Turks to keep the Orthodox subjects of the sultan from uniting with the Catholic Church, which was associated with the struggle to drive Islam out of Europe.[19] It was, no doubt, with Turkish support that Gennadios Scholarios, the first patriarch after the Conquest, and his successors in the patriarchate, extended their jurisdiction over the non-Greek provinces of the Balkan Peninsula. For, in the eyes of the Turks, there was no essential difference between Greek and non-Greek Orthodox Christians, as long as they were all subjects of the sultan. This tendency not to discriminate between one Orthodox people and another made the incorporation of the seats of Slavic Orthodoxy, under Constantinople, seem easy and natural.

The first Slavic church to disappear was the Patriarchate of Trnovo, which is sometimes called "the National Church of Bulgaria." Recognized as a "patriarchate" by the ecumenical patriarch in 1235,[20] it ceased to exist in the 1390's, during the Ottoman conquest of Bulgaria, and its dioceses were formally brought under the jurisdiction of the Patriarchate of Constantinople in the pontificate of Gennadios Scholarios.

After Trnovo came the turn of Ohrid (Ahrid) and Peć (Ipek). The Archbishopric of Peć, founded in 1219, and elevated to the rank of "patriarchate" by Stepan Dušan in 1346,[21] was Serbian as much as

---

tation before and after the Fall," the first of a collection of his studies, *Peri tēn Alōsin tēs Kōnstantinoupoleōs* [*Concerning the Fall of Constantinople*], (Athens, 1959), pp. 59–64.

[19] Theodore H. Papadopoullos, *Studies and Documents Relating to the History of the Greek Church and People under Turkish Domination* [Bibliotheca Graeca Aevi Posterioris, 1], (Brussels, 1952), pp. 20–26.

[20] A. A. Vasiliev, *History of the Byzantine Empire, 324–1453* (University of Wisconsin Press, 1952), p. 526. For the background of Bulgarian resurgence, see Robert Lee Wolff, "The Second Bulgarian Empire: Its Origin and History to 1204," *Speculum*, XXIV (1949), 167–206. In B. J. Kidd, *The Churches of Eastern Christendom* (London, 1927), both Bulgaria (pp. 319–332) and Serbia (pp. 332–342) receive inadequate treatments.

[21] Vasiliev, *op. cit.*, p. 619. Gennadios, Metropolitan of Heliopolis and Theira, *Historia tou Oikoumenikou Patriarcheiou* [*History of the Ecumenical Patriarchate*], (Athens, 1953), I, 339–340.

Trnovo was Bulgarian, while Ohrid, farther south, had a mixed congregation, with a Slav majority.[22] Ohrid was associated with the name of Emperor Justinian, who established the archbishopric known as Ἀχρίδος καὶ Πρώτης Ἰουστινιανῆς (*Ochridae ac primae Justinianae*), as a tribute to his birthplace. Ohrid was never recognized as a "patriarchate" by the Mother Church, and it is a moot question if Peć was ever accorded that distinction.[23]

Peć and Ohrid were restored as independent churches, sometimes called "patriarchates," in the reign of Süleyman the Magnificent, and they maintained their privileged status, the former until 1766, the latter until 1767.[24] The causes of their abolition are not altogether clear, but they must be sought in the economic crisis that prevailed after the Austro-Turkish war of 1737–1739 and the depletion of human resources as a result of Islamization. The latter was particularly noticeable in Ohrid. On the other hand, the Turks, during the period of decline, showed a characteristic preference to deal with one central ecclesiastical authority, which, situated in the imperial capital, was easier to keep in line. In Turkish eyes, the Serbian Church was an object of suspicion because it had allied itself with the invaders, and its leader, Arsenius IV, had directed a new Serbian immigration to the Habsburg Empire. Organized under the Metropolitanate of Karlovac, the Serbs beyond the frontier (the *prečani*, that is, "those from beyond the river") were now able to foment trouble in the South Slav prov-

---

[22] H. Gelzer, *Der Patriarchat von Achrida* (Leipzig, 1902), pp. 6–16, 19. Gennadios, *op. cit.*, I, 261. For a discussion of the character of this church, see A. P. Péchayre, "L' Archevêché d' Ochrida de 1394 à 1767," *Echos d' Orient*, XXXIX (1936), 183–204, 280–323.

[23] Vasiliev (*op. cit.*, p. 619) states that the Patriarchate of Constantinople refused to recognize the Serbian Patriarchate. Only when the Serbian threat to Constantinople subsided before the Turkish advance, did the Greeks begin closer political and ecclesiastical relations with the Serbs and extended a limited recognition to the Serbian Church. See Michel Lascaris, "Le patriarcat de Peć a-t-il été reconnu par l'Eglise de Constantinople en 1375?" *Mélanges Charles Diehl* (Paris, 1930), I (*Histoire*), 171–175. Professor Lascaris concludes that the Serbian Church was not recognized as a patriarchate. Dr. Charles Jelavich and Dr. George Soulis directed my attention to further discussion in support of the Serbian thesis: George Ostrogorsky, *Seminarium Kondakovianum*, V (1932), 233 ff., and *Byzantion*, XII (1952), 159; Francis Dvornik, *Byzantinoslavica*, III (1931), 186–187; and V. Laurent, "L' archevêque de Peć et le titre de patriarche après l' union de 1375," *Balcania*, VII (1944), 303–310.

[24] Jelavich, *op. cit.*, p. 148.

inces, under the guise of religion, with aid from Russia or Austria or from both. It was, therefore, political considerations from the Turkish side and economic exigencies from the local Church, rather than intrigues of Patriarch Samuel, that dictated the action of the imperial government with regard to these two churches.[25]

After the disappearance of the Slavic patriarchates, the only independent Orthodox Church in the Balkan provinces of the Ottoman Empire was the bishopric of Montenegro, in which ecclesiastical and temporal authority were combined under the *vladika*, until the secularization of the princely office by Danilo in 1851. Montenegro could claim that it had never been a part of the Ottoman Empire and that it had always enjoyed independent status; whereupon Turkey's spokesmen would retort that all that the empire had granted to the Montenegrins was religious autonomy. Montenegro presents a very eloquent example of the role of the Church in the struggle for national liberation.

The patriarch of Constantinople organized the Slavic provinces as integral parts of the Ecumenical Patriarchate, thereby becoming the undisputed leader of the Orthodox Christians of the empire. He was the spiritual head of the twelve or thirteen million Orthodox Christians in the eighteenth century (roughly one-fourth of the inhabitants of the empire), and he also represented the patriarchs of Alexandria, Antioch, and Jerusalem, whose following had dwindled to negligible proportions. His Armenian colleague, recognized as patriarch since 1461, was only in theory his peer, having no more than a few hundred thousand Gregorian Armenians under his jurisdiction.

Despite their unquestionable preponderance, however, the Greek clergymen at Constantinople did not always handle the affairs of the Church with the adroitness or ingenuity that might have been expected

---

[25] Jelavich, *op. cit.*, pp. 148–149, points out that the Greek officials, who had meanwhile become the controlling influence at Peć, proposed the incorporation of that patriarchate into the Church of Constantinople. The motives of these clerics, however, could not have been nationalistic, since Greek nationalism, still in its nascent stage, did not invade the church, certainly not the Patriarchate of Constantinople, until the beginning of the following century. Theodore H. Papadopoullos (*op. cit.*, pp. 89–91), on the basis of documents, states that Patriarch Samuel accepted the abolition of the two autocephalous archbishoprics with great reluctance. For bibliography on the conflicting viewpoints, see Jelavich, *op. cit.*, p. 151.

of them. Their own squabbles weakened the position of the Patriarchate in front of the Sublime Porte, and relations between the two establishments were often critical. The courtesy shown to Gennadios by the
Conqueror was soon forgotten. Instead of the new patriarch receiving
an inaugural money gift from the sultan, as in 1454, the sultans and
the grand vezirs began to extract money from every new pontiff, as
they did from practically every new officeholder.[26] The top eccle-
siastic's position, as well as many lower ones, were offered to the
highest bidder. Ambitious bishops, who wanted to become patriarchs,
tried hard to make a fortune, and less ambitious men who found themselves on the patriarchal throne often had difficulty facing the exorbitant demands of Jewish and Armenian creditors. As a result, the
moral caliber of church leaders declined with the growing decay of
the Ottoman Empire. There is no doubt that many a bishop exploited
the people of his diocese, as he knew that his position was precarious
and money made the difference between success and failure. Thus,
extortion and corruption, starting at the Ottoman court, which was the
head of Near Eastern society, ran through the body of the Orthodox
Church, eating at the helpless peasantry, regardless of national origin.

This state of affairs, detrimental as it was to the spiritual character
of the Church, did not seem to undermine the traditional union of
the Balkan peoples. As subjects of the sultan and spiritual children of
the patriarch, the Christians of the Balkan Peninsula maintained a
sense of brotherhood, which grew in volume and intensity until the
time of Rhigas Pheraios. In his famous war song, the revolutionary
poet could appeal to all groups to rise and shake off the tyranny of
the sultans:[27]

> In the east and in the west, in the south and in the north,
> Let us all have one heart for the Fatherland.
> Bulgars and Albanians, Serbians and Greeks,
> Islanders and mainlanders, all with the same zeal,
> Let us girdle the sword for the cause of freedom!
>
> Souliotes and Mainotes, renowned lions,
> Till when will you sleep, imprisoned in your dens?
> Tigers of Montenegro, eagles of Olympus,

---

[26] See Arnakis, *The Journal of Modern History*, XXIV, 247–248.

[27] C. Fauriel, *Chants Populaires de la Grèce Moderne* (Paris, 1825), II, 24, 26.
New, complete edition in L. I. Vranoussis, *Rhigas* [Basikē Bibliothēkē, 10],
(Athens, 1953), pp. 391–393.

Champions of the Agrapha heights, become men with one soul!
Brother Christians of the Sava and the Danube,
Come forth, each with his weapons in his hands!

Strike! Let the root of the tyrant perish!
Light the flame that will spread
Throughout the Turk's domains from Bosnia to Arabia.
Raise high the banners of the Cross
And fall upon the enemy like thunderbolt!

Even then, during the era of the French Revolution, when a Balkan
Christian referred to himself as a "Christian" he meant "Eastern
Orthodox Christian," because all other kinds of Christians (with the
possible exception of the Croats as seen by some of the Orthodox
South Slavs) were commonly called "Franks." During the Ottoman
era, Orthodox Christendom eyed the "Franks" with much the same
feelings as it did the Turks.

In vain did the forces of Catholicism and Protestantism try to capture the Eastern Orthodox Church during the Wars of Religion and
after. The East displayed monolithic endurance. The advances of both
sides were repulsed effectively because, despite the many patriarchs
and bishops who rose and fell as heroes, or victims, of intrigue, the
fundamental rights that the Christian Church had enjoyed for centuries under Muslim rule were preserved from the beginning to the
end, and a sense of spiritual freedom made the church self-confident
to face any crisis.

In Constantinople, the Protestants and their friends were supported
by the embassies of Great Britain and Holland, while the Catholics,
led by the Jesuits, were under the protection of the French.

In the struggle for preëminence in the Balkans the initiative was
taken by the Protestant theologians of the University of Tübingen, who
approached Patriarch Jeremiah II with a Greek translation of the
Augsburg Confession, in 1574.[28] If Jeremiah endorsed the document,
the union of Protestantism and Orthodoxy could be presented as an

---

[28] George E. Zachariades, *Tübingen und Konstantinopel* [Schriftenreihe der
Deutsch-Griechischen Gesellschaft, Heft 7], (Göttingen, 1941), pp. 18–25.
Chrysostomos Papadopoulos, *Scheseis Orthodoxōn kai Diamartyromenōn* [*Rela-
tions of Orthodox and Protestants*], (Jerusalem, 1927), pp. 3–7. The first visit of
Stephen Gerlach to the patriarch occurred in October, 1573. The best monograph
on Jeremiah II is still C. N. Sathas, *Biographikon Schediasma peri Patriarchou
Ieremiou II* [*Biographical Sketch of Patriarch Jeremiah II*], (Athens, 1870).

accomplished fact. However, the correspondence of the patriarch and the Lutherans, which continued with long intervals till the end of 1581, revealed divergences of a doctrinal nature, the most important ones being the nonacceptance of the sacred tradition and of the saints by the Protestants and the Protestants' adoption of the *filioque,* which was rejected by the Orthodox. In the heat of the Thirty Years' War the Protestants, represented by the ambassadors of England and the Netherlands, won the ear of Patriarch Cyril Loukaris. But the intrigues of the Catholic party brought about the downfall of Cyril, who died a martyr's death in 1638.[29]

The opposition of the Orthodox Church to Protestantism and to Catholicism continued with various degrees of intensity. In 1582 a church council, convoked by Jeremiah II, declared itself against the reformed calendar of Pope Gregory XIII, considering it as insidious an influence as the "heresy" of Martin Luther. The Orthodox Church remained faithful to the Julian calendar until the twentieth century, a century and a half longer than Protestant England. Though the matter was basically nonreligious, it became the object of vehement controversy because it originated in the Vatican at the time of the crisis between the East and the West.

Despite the great efforts made by the Reformation and the Counter Reformation to win the "third bloc" that was Eastern Orthodox Christianity, only the borderland proved to be vulnerable. German Protestants converted some thousands of South Slavs, but most of them were originally Catholics and were later reconverted to Catholicism by the Jesuits, who operated from Dubrovnik. Farther east, Bishop Theophilos of Alba Iulia, at the close of the seventeenth century, signed a "confession" that brought approximately two hundred thousand Rumanians to the Catholic fold. They became the nucleus of the Uniate Church of Transylvania, where there was also a rival Calvinist congregation. At about the same time, the Croatian Jesuit Juraj Križanić strove to bring his fellow Yugoslavs to Catholicism,

---

[29] An important work on this great patriarch is that of Archbishop Chrysostomos Papadopoulos, published at Trieste, in Greek, in 1907. The second edition of the book appeared in Athens, posthumously, in 1939. In the same year and place, a committee of scholars, under the presidency of Emmanuel Tsouderos, published a 300th-anniversary volume entitled *Kyrillos ho Loukaris* (*1572–1638*). The Protestant point of view is presented in G. A. Hadjiantoniou, *Kyrillos Loukaris* (Athens, 1954), in Greek.

with nothing but meager results. By and large, the Eastern Orthodox Church remained firm in its neutral position, rejecting the "confession" attributed to Cyril Loukaris, and subscribing to the resolutions of the councils held at Jassy in 1642 and at Jerusalem in 1672.[30] The resolutions redefined the Orthodox faith in relation to Catholic and Protestant dogma. The importance of these documents exceeds the domain of theology. From the point of view of national history they may be regarded as the Magna Charta of the Balkan peoples.

To sum up: by maintaining a neutral position vis-à-vis Catholicism and the Protestant movement, the Orthodox Church contributed substantially to the transition of the Balkans from their mediaeval antecedents to the era of nationalism. In the same way that it protected Christianity from the encroachments of Islam, it kept the Christians of the Balkans from the confusion that tormented Europe during the Wars of Religion. Thanks to the conservative role of the church, the Christian peoples of the peninsula made good use of the Muslim empire as a political shelter, so that they could be free for their national awakening, in which Orthodox affiliations, linked up with the medieval background, played a very conspicuous part. This role of "preserving" the Balkans for the future was not less important than the struggle to combat Islamization.

THE RISE OF NATIONAL CHURCHES

The most serious challenge to the universalism of the Orthodox Church came, strangely enough, from Greece when that country won her independence in 1830. Count John Capodistrias, first president of independent Greece, suspected that a committee of bishops sent by the patriarch, in 1828, was actually a diplomatic delegation dispatched by the Sublime Porte to pressure Greece into submission, and his atti-

---

[30] Basil K. Stephanides, *Ekklēsiastikē Historia* [*Ecclesiastical History*], (Athens, 1948), pp. 649–652. The author tends to accept the "confession" as a genuine work of Loukaris but devoid of official character. Archbishop Chrysostomos rejects its authenticity (*op. cit.*, pp. 103–114, 167–170), and so does A. N. Diamantopoulos in the introduction of the same book (pp. ix–xxxiii) and in the anniversary volume (pp. 53–55). Hadjiantoniou (*op. cit.*, pp. 104–127) accepts it as genuine. Greek opinion was divided on the authenticity of the "confession"— e.g., Tsouderos (in *Eleutheron Bēma*, April 5, 6, 7, 8, 1939) rejected it, while D. S. Balanos (in the same daily, April 19) accepted it.

tude, despite his profound Orthodoxy, was one of opposition to the ecclesiastical organization whose head could be under the influence of the Turks.[31]

After the assassination of Capodistrias (1831), the Regency adopted the policy of Theoclitos Pharmakides, who advocated separating the Church of Greece from that of Constantinople on the principle that political independence carried with it ecclesiastical independence. One of the regents, Dr. George Maurer, a Bavarian archaeologist, introduced an adaptation of the Russian Church administration under Peter the Great, thereby making King Otho, who remained a Catholic to the end of his life, head of the Orthodox Church of Greece, and subjecting the religious hierarchy to civil rule. Though there were bishops that favored the new system, the majority of the clergy and laity felt sympathetically inclined toward the Patriarchate of Constantinople, which was the head of Greek society during the period of Ottoman domination and had offered many sacrifices (such as the martyrdom of Patriarch Gregory V) for the cause of Greek freedom.

The unilateral emancipation of the Church of Greece was denounced by the Ecumenical Patriarchate, and the rift continued from July 23/August 4, 1833, to 1850. Greek historians, especially Paul Karolides,[32] who took a longer and broader view of their nation, criticized the decision of the Regency as contrary to the Greek tradition and as a denial of the Byzantine background that had nourished the national consciousness after the fall of Constantinople. At best it was an evidence of localism, or particularism, that did not coincide with the *Megalē Idea* that was assiduously cultivated in Greece during the nineteenth century. The *Megalē Idea* advocated expansion in the Balkans and possibly in Asia Minor, union of all the Greeks under one administration, and, above all, revival of the medieval "glory" that was terminated in 1453. Otho and his queen adopted the *Megalē Idea* but their advisers did not grasp the significance of a united Orthodox Church under Greek auspices, a church harnessed to the chariot of Hellenism. The Ecumenical Patriarchate, too, failed to see in the little kingdom of Greece the successor of the Byzantine Empire. The prelates of Constantinople accepted a *modus vivendi* with the Turks, en-

---

[31] Trikoupis, *op. cit.*, IV, 212–213.

[32] *Historia tōn Hellēnōn kai tōn Loipōn Laōn tēs Anatolēs* [*History of the Greeks and Other Peoples of the* (*Near*) *East*], (Athens, 1922), II, 18–34.

trenched themselves behind the *millet* system and its privileges, and put forth their claim to universalism with a persistence that seemed to ignore the new trend for the creation of nation states and state churches. With the blessing of the Church of Constantinople, a new generation of Phanariotes, among whom Costakis Mousouros and Alexander Karatheodoris are best known, served the sultans loyally and prospered all the way from the reign of Abd ul-Medjid (1839) to the last days of Abd ul-Hamid (1909).

Relations between Greece and the Mother Church did not improve until 1849. At the end of that year the Greek minister in Constantinople (Rizos Neroulos) died, and the patriarch and the holy synod attended the funeral, a fact that created a favorable impression on the Greek government.[33] The latter had meanwhile assumed a constitutional character as a result of the revolution of September 3/15, 1843. The Greek government decorated Patriarch Anthimos IV, an honor which he accepted after securing permission from the grand vezir. The synod of the Church of Greece wrote to the patriarch expressing the hope of a rapprochement. But the patriarch refused to answer a document that came from an unrecognized institution. The Greek government then addressed itself to the patriarch, explaining the developments that led to the establishment of the Church of Greece and asking for its recognition (May 30/June 11, 1850).[34] Accordingly, after due consultation with the other patriarchates and autocephalous churches, and upon the decision of a grand synod held in Constantinople on June 16/28, 1850, the Ecumenical Patriarchate extended its recognition to the new autocephalous Church of Greece. The details were worked out in the next two years; and before the close of 1852, Hellenic localism, or better "statism," and Orthodox universalism were reconciled in a document that bore the Byzantine appellation of *Tomos*.[35]

Unlike the Church of Greece, the Church of Serbia became autonomous and autocephalous gradually and without much friction. In 1832, two years after Miloš was recognized as hereditary prince of Serbia, the bishop of Belgrade was elevated to the rank of metropolitan and the Serbians formally acquired the right to choose their bishops.

---

[33] Karolides, *Historia,* IV, 4–6.

[34] *Ibid.,* pp. 6–13.

[35] *Ibid.,* pp. 13–54. Pharmakides voiced his objections to the procedure followed. His thesis is discussed and criticized by Karolides, *ibid.,* pp. 16, 61–86.

At that time their church was described as autonomous but not auto-cephalous. After the Treaty of Berlin, the metropolitan of Belgrade became autocephalous, presiding over a Serbian holy synod (*Tomos* of October 20, 1879). The title of "Patriarch of the Serbs" was adopted after the First World War (1920), when the Church of Montenegro and the Metropolitanate of Karlovac united with that of Belgrade.[36]

The Church of Rumania, which according to Rumanian nationalist historians, had always been regarded as independent under the metro-politan of Hungro-Wallachia, followed a course similar to that of Greece.[37] Relations with Constantinople were strained, particularly because the property of the monasteries in the Danubian Principalities were nationalized and distributed to the peasants by Prince Cuza in 1863. The ensuing struggle delayed the recognition of Rumania's ec-clesiastical independence until May, 1885. The Patriarchate of Ru-mania was officially proclaimed in 1925.

The most problematic of all emancipations was that of Bulgaria. Constantine Jireček,[38] and others after him, belonging to the Bulgarian nationalist school, asserted that the Patriarchate of Constantinople was oppressive in Bulgaria and that a systematic attempt was made by the Greek clergy to Hellenize the Bulgarian people. Jireček speaks of Greek bishops burning Slavic books and replacing them with Greek ones. The Greek clergy is further accused of suppressing the Bulgarian language and cultural traditions, and thus bringing about the historical amnesia that characterized the Bulgarians until the nineteenth cen-tury.

The fairest estimate of the situation that prevailed in Bulgaria until the mid-1800's comes from L. S. Stavrianos:

"The charge of Greek domination in schools, churches, and culture, in general, is largely justified. But this domination was to a consider-able degree unavoidable because of the cultural disparity between Greeks and Bulgarians. A later generation of Bulgarian nationalists keenly resented the use of Greek in schools and churches and they assumed that their forebears had felt the same resentment. This as-

---

[36] See Matthew Spinka, "Modern Ecclesiastical Development," in Robert J. Kerner, ed., *Yugoslavia* (University of California Press, 1949), pp. 244–251.

[37] Kidd, *op. cit.*, pp. 345–351.

[38] *Geschichte der Bulgaren* (Prague, 1876), pp. 468–470, 513–520.

sumption is unjustified and is a good example of the common error of interpreting the past in terms of the present."[39]

The burning of Bulgarian manuscripts—an act which has been alleged rather than proved—could be attributed to ignorance of the Slavic language rather than to anti-Bulgarian sentiment. It will be recalled that Greek manuscripts were used to kindle the fire of many a monastic kitchen in various parts of the Greek-speaking world and during the Greek Independence War they were put to good use as material for cartridges. The Bulgarians, who constituted practically the entire lower clergy in what later (1864) became the Vilayet of the Danube, could be held responsible for the destruction of manuscripts as much as their Greek colleagues. For ignorance was widespread among the clergy of the entire Balkan Peninsula. Among the upper clergy and in the higher echelons of society in Bulgaria the Greek language was the accepted medium of communication. It was generally known that ambitious Bulgarians showed a preference for Greek learning during the long period when the term "Grecomaniac" had not acquired the significance that it did later. The influence of the Greek schools, which the Bulgarians attended in Constantinople, Bucharest, Jassy, and elsewhere, was paramount until the first decades of the nineteenth century. The curriculum of these schools emphasized the humanities—Classics, the Scriptures, and the Apostolic Fathers.[40] With their Hellenistic education, the bishops, many of them of Bulgarian peasant background, found their way to the imperial city, served in non-Bulgarian dioceses and at least four of them (Metroph-

[39] *Op. cit.,* p. 367.

[40] In his monumental work, *Historia toū Hellēnikou Ethnous* [*History of the Greek People*], 6th ed. (Athens, 1932), V, 2, 82, Paparrhegopoulos, thinking in terms of Greek nationalism, criticizes the Church of Constantinople and its schools for their failure to Hellenize the Bulgarians, a task for which—he thinks—circumstances were favorable during four centuries. On the other hand, Karolides (*op. cit.,* IV, 277–285) believes that the humanistic character of classical education inspired a desire for freedom for the individual and his nation. According to Karolides, every attempt to Hellenize a people through education would have been a utopia and an absurd anachronism. A middle position is presented by Gerasimos Konidaris, *Hē Hellēnikē Ekklēsia hōs Politistikē Dynamis en tēi Historiai tēs Chersonēsou tou Haemou* [*The Greek Church as a Civilizing Power in the History of the Balkan Peninsula*], (Athens, 1948), pp. 144–145. The author speaks of the dual—national and extranational—position of the Church and her responsibility to maintain a balance between the two roles.

anes III, Eugenios, Chrysanthos, and Agathangelos—the last three as late as the third decade of the nineteenth century) became patriarchs of Constantinople. They were not ecclesiastics of superior caliber, but neither their shortcomings nor their failures had anything to do with their Bulgarian origin. On the contrary, the circumstances tend to prove that their Greek colleagues in the synod had no compunctions in selecting Bulgarians, even mediocre clerics, to the supreme position. Without this spirit of tolerance, based upon the concept of Orthodox universalism, ecclesiastics like Hilarion of Macariopolis (Ilarion Makariopolski) and his fellow bishops, all champions of Bulgarian nationalism, could not have risen to their posts before 1870.

In the name of this universalism, the clergy, indiscriminate of ethnic origin, maintained its position of influence over the Bulgarian people. The abuses connected with ignorance and venality, already noted, undoubtedly did much to alienate the Church from its congregation in the time of national awakening. Bulgaria's nationalist leaders voiced the complaint that the Church imposed various dues (for baptisms, funerals, weddings, divorces, and ordination of clergymen). As far as we know, Orthodox bishops nowhere neglected the business of collecting funds to defray the cost of their imperial *fermans* and to set aside a respectable amount for their old age; they also collected money for the Patriarchate, which in this manner met its expenses and its obligations to the Turkish government. It is not surprising, therefore, that the bishops were wealthy, affording a contrast to the poverty and squalor of peasant life. Yet for this disparity, and the evils it gave rise to, Ilarion Makariopolski and Liuben Karavelov had less reason to be anti-Greek than the Serb Dositej Obradović (an enlightened monk) and the Greek Adamantios Korais (a classical philologist) had reason to be anticlerical, so long as the spirit of Orthodox universalism overshadowed national considerations and "ethnicism" (or "racism") was condemned by the Church.

In the same manner that ecclesiastical "statism" was introduced by Theoklitos Pharmakides in Greece, "ethnicism" was brought forth by the Bulgarian nationalists, who, unlike the Greeks, believed that ecclesiastical emancipation must precede political independence. An obvious advantage of this policy, from the Bulgarian standpoint, was the possibility of establishing control over the Slavic-speaking population of Macedonia. It was the belief of the nationalists that the Macedonian Slavs and the Slavophones of European Turkey would be attached to the Bulgarian National Church—the Exarchate—and would be recognized by the Ottoman government as part of the Bulgarian *millet*. They would thus be absorbed by the Bulgarian nation, with the connivance of the Turks, and become a part of Greater Bulgaria at the opportune moment. In the middle of the nineteenth century, the Turks were glad to see the Orthodox community (the *Rum millet*) divided into two hostile camps, such as the Patriarchists and the Exarchists, because imperial diplomacy had become aware not only of the danger of nationalism but also of the common ground on which the various Balkan nationalisms could meet—that is, the liquidation of the Ottoman Empire.

It is beyond the scope of the present discussion to go into the phases of the struggle for the establishment of the Bulgarian National Church, from 1860 to 1870, a struggle that led to the schism that lasted until 1945.[41] What matters here is the insistence of the Ecumenical Patriarchate on Orthodox universalism, the acceptance of the principle of establishing autocephalous churches only for independent nation-states, and the reiteration of the precedent that such independent churches can be constituted with the consent of all the patriarchates and the existing autocephalous churches. What is of equal import, as regards Ottoman policy toward the Church, is the abandonment of the tradition of a united Patriarchate for the Christian subjects of the sultan. The Russophile Turks of the reign of Abd ul-Aziz, the men who listened to Ignatiev's dictates, failed to grasp the significance of the religious policy of Mohammed the Conqueror. But the year 1870 was a far cry from the year 1454.

---

[41] The schism, which resulted in the excommunication of the Bulgarian clergy, was proclaimed in a grand synod on September 16–28, 1872, and was repealed on February 22, 1945. The Tomos, establishing the autocephalous Church of Bulgaria, was signed by Patriarch Maximos V on March 13, 1945. On May 10, 1953, the Bulgarian Church proclaimed itself a patriarchate, without the previous consent of the Church of Constantinople and the other Orthodox churches outside the Iron Curtain. The Patriarchate of Bulgaria considers itself as the continuator of that of Trnovo. See Konidaris, "The Repeal of the Bulgarian Schism" (in Greek), *Annual of the School of Theology of the University of Thessalonikē*, I (1953), 97–196. For earlier bibliography see Stavrianos, *op. cit.*, p. 913. In the last two years relations between the Bulgarian Church and the Greek churches have been normalized, with Bulgarian participation in the Pan-Orthodox Conference at Rhodes and the official visit of the Bulgarian Patriarch Cyril at the Ecumenical Patriarchate (March 17, 1962).

Bulgarian nationalism, with the irredentism that it carried in its train, thus challenged the universalism of the Church much more than Theoklitos Pharmakides and the extreme group of Hellenic "statists," who in their days had gone so far as to make the absurd statement that the Greek Revolution had been fought for the emancipation of the Greek Church from the Patriarchate as well as for the liberty of the Greeks from the sultan.[42] It was clear that the nation, nourished by the Mother Church for centuries, now asserted itself against her, and proclaimed its religious independence, with or without the blessing of the Patriarchate, which embodied not only the unity of the faith but also the tradition of Orthodox Christian brotherhood.

NATIONALITY ACROSS THE BARRIERS OF RELIGION:
ALBANIA AND JUGOSLAVIA

It is a remarkable coincidence that within the same decade of the 1870's, shortly before the Congress of Berlin, Albanian patriots—Orthodox, Catholic, and Muslim—began to speak in terms of a nationalism over and above the loyalties of religion. To an articulate group of Albanians, who were at first encouraged by Abd ul-Hamid, "being an Albanian" came first, and the religion they professed was now a secondary matter, a purely private affair.

The immediate objective of the new nationalist movement was to prevent Montenegro, Serbia, and Bulgaria from annexing parts of Albanian territory by virtue of the Treaty of San Stefano. In a meeting held at Prizren, in the district of Kosovo-Metohija, then a part of the Ottoman Empire, the nationalist leaders declared: "We make no distinction between creeds. We are Albanians." [43] They constituted themselves into an "Albanian League" for the term "league" they significantly borrowed the Turkish word *millet*), and they appealed to the Congress of Berlin to let all Albanian-speaking areas remain within the Ottoman Empire.

As this desire of the Albanian League was in tune with Ottoman

---

[42] Cited by Karolides, *op. cit.*, II, 25, IV, 61.
[43] See Stavro Skendi, "Beginnings of Albanian Nationalist and Autonomous Trends: The Albanian League, 1878–1881," *The American Slavic and East European Review*, XII (1953), 219–232.

interests, the Sublime Porte continued its favorable attitude until 1880. During the same period and later, Italy and Austria-Hungary, fearing the expansion of the Slavic states to the Adriatic littoral, encouraged Albanian nationalism, even armed resistance to the Montenegrins, on the morrow of the Treaty of Berlin. The Albanians of the north, both Muslim and Catholic bands, actually succeeded in driving the Montenegrins out of border towns ceded to Prince Nikola by the treaty.

In the south, the leader of the movement was Abdul Frashëri, a Bektashi.[44] Other members of the Frashëri family assumed prominent roles, Naim Frashëri and Sami Frashëri being the most important both in politics and in cultural activities.[45] Bektashism, which had previously been instrumental in the spread of Islam, was now a valuable link between the three religious groups. The Frashëris and their associates demanded the right to open Albanian schools to take the place of the Greek institutions that operated for the Christians and the Turkish ones that existed for the benefit of the Muslims.[46] For the first time in Balkan history, it was language, and not religion, that was to become the vehicle of national aspirations. With language as a criterion, the Albanians felt that they could claim parts of the areas of European Turkey which were objects of Greek and Serbian irredentism.[47] The Greeks and the Serbs at once reacted to Albanian expan-

---

[44] *Ibid.,* p. 221.

[45] See Stavro Skendi, "Beginnings of Albanian Nationalist Trends in Culture and Education, 1878–1912," *Journal of Central European Affairs,* XII (1953), 356–367.

[46] Skendi, *The American Slavic and East European Review,* XII, 226; *Journal of Central European Affairs,* XII, 363.

[47] Skendi, *The American Slavic and East European Review,* XII, 222–225. Cf. Constantine A. Chekrezi, *Albania: Past and Present* (New York, 1919), pp. 52–53, 90–100. On the basis of language, Albanian nationalists claimed as their own a good number of Greece's national heroes. See Chekrezi, *op. cit.,* pp. 25, 47–48. Nonetheless, a common language was not sufficient to cement an alliance between Muslim Albanians and Albanian-speaking Greeks, such as the Souliotes, during the Greek Revolution. Tahir Abbas, a Muslim Albanian, who came to Mesolonghi, while Ali of Yannina was hard pressed by the Turks, found out that the religious character of the Greek struggle was too pronounced to leave any room for coöperation of Muslims and Christians and advised his coreligionists to side with the imperial forces; see Trikoupis, *op. cit.,* II, 92. The importance of the Orthodox Church in Greece's War of Independence is recognized by Finlay, VI, 139, 144, 158.

sionism, and the Ottoman government, too, assumed a hostile position that entailed repressive measures against the new nationalists.[48]

After their leaders were exiled, the Albanians of Muslim faith reaffirmed their loyalty to the Ottoman Empire and continued serving it as soldiers and administrators until 1912. Likewise, the majority of the Orthodox was, as before, oriented toward Athens. Even those of Albanian ancestry were Hellenized to such a degree that it was hard to draw a line of distinction between a Greek of North Epirus and an Albanian of Orthodox persuasion. This was so not only in the closing years of the nineteenth but also in the beginning of the twentieth century. The Albanian government in the interwar period did much to absorb the Greeks into the Orthodox Albanian community, and it also made it clear that the Çams of South Epirus were not subject to the obligatory exchange of populations between Greece and Turkey, because these people were not Turks but "Albanians of Moslem faith." [49]

A similar readjustment occurred in the South Slav area after the incorporation of Bosnia and Hercegovina in 1918 and of Old Serbia and northern Macedonia in 1912. In Bosnia-Hercegovina, the Muslim element, which had retained its distinct character under Austria-Hungary (1878–1918), had gradually declined in number because of voluntary emigration to Turkey. For, as Muslims, they found it distasteful to live under a government of another faith. As a result, by 1921, about 65 percent of the population of the two provinces was Christian (43.7 percent Orthodox, 21.3 percent Catholic).[50] The Muslims were only 31.1 percent. Unlike Greece, however, Jugoslavia did not send her Muslims to Turkey—for one thing there were no Serbs in postwar Turkey with whom the Bosnians could be exchanged. So, whether they chose to call themselves Bosnians or by their tribal names, the Muslims grew accustomed to a Christian administration and even welcomed the idea of a "Jugoslav brotherhood," regardless of religion.[51]

---

[48] Skendi, *Journal of Central European Affairs,* XII, 363–364; *The American Slavic and East European Review,* XII, 229–230.

[49] During the Greek Civil War (1946–1949) the Çams, together with some of the defeated Greek Communists, left for Albania; and the Communist government of Albania embarked on a policy of forcible assimilation of the Greeks of North Epirus.

[50] See Wayne S. Vucinich, "Yugoslavs of Moslem Faith," in Kerner, ed., *Yugoslavia,* pp. 261–275. Statistics on p. 263.

[51] Dositej Obradović, about 150 years before, echoed this type of nationalism when he wrote: "A Turk of Bosnia and Hercegovina is called a Turk according

To defend their cultural heritage they instituted "the Jugoslav Muslim Organization," under the leadership of Mehmed Spaho. Politically, they usually supported whatever government was in power. Within the postwar federation and its Marxist program, they are identified as "Jugoslavs of Muslim faith." Memories of common origin and the use of a common vernacular are proving as effective among the Bosnians and the Hercegovinians as among the Albanians.

Less successful has been the merging of the Old Serbian and Macedonian Muslims with the other religious communities of their districts. Linguistically not all of these Muslims are assimilated. Those who speak Albanian (most of whom are concentrated in the autonomous region of Kosovo-Metohija) are likely to associate themselves ethnically with the Albanians of Albania, while another group retains its old cultural relationship with the Turks. A number of Macedonian Turks left for Turkey in recent years, many of them, no doubt, because of their opposition to communism. Just as in the instance of the Pomaks and the Dobrudja Turks, the Ankara government accepted the newcomers as repatriates.[52] Those of them who chose to remain in the Jugoslav area are undergoing a rapid Slavization.

If nationalism is not obliterated by communism, the Muslims of Jugoslavia will be the twentieth-century pioneers in the new national consciousness that transcends the lines of religion and stresses language, literature, and memories of common origin, just as Finlay did— though unrealistically and prematurely—in the case of the Cretans nearly a hundred years ago. This extrareligious nationalism is a relatively recent development: its absence determined the fate of the Muslim Cretans and the Anatolian Greeks as late as 1924.[53]

---

to his religion; but as for race and language, of whatever sort were his remote ancestors, of the same sort will be his latest descendants: Bosnians and Hercegovinians, so long as God's world endures. . . . When the real Turks return to their own vilayet, whence they came, the Bosnians will remain Bosnians." George R. Noyes, *The Life and Adventures of Dimitrije Obradović* (University of California Press, 1953), p. 135.

[52] Turkish policy in this respect goes back to the era of Mustafa Kemal Atatürk. See Schechtman, *Journal of Central European Affairs*, XII, 154, for official statements in 1934 and 1935.

[53] That a nationalism devoid of a religious basis is by no means strong in the Near East (including the Balkans) is illustrated by Lebanon, where Christian and Muslim citizens, of about equal numerical strength, faced the prospects of a civil war, which was basically a war of religion, in 1958. By the same token, it

The phenomenon of Albanian nationalists, seeking to unite in one loyalty people of three faiths that were mutually antagonistic, and, to a lesser degree, the experience of the Christians and Muslims in Jugoslavia, mark the end of the dominant role of religion as a shield for the national heritage of the Balkan peoples. The Church continued her mission as foster mother of the nationalities well into the twentieth century, and that was her historical function during the long period of Ottoman domination.

---

appears unlikely that there will ever be a Cypriote nation on independent Cyprus, where the people are about 80 percent Greek and less than 20 percent Turkish, each group with its nation-state in easy reach.

RUSSIA AND THE MODERNIZATION

OF THE BALKANS

Cyril E. Black

The Balkans, Russia, and the West

The transformation of the peoples of the Balkans from oppressed and backward subjects of the Ottoman Empire to citizens in independent national states in the throes of industrialization, is part of a larger story which started in the Middle Ages and is likely to continue for the foreseeable future. The term "modernization" is frequently used to describe this process, by which is meant the entire scope of change accompanying the revolutionary growth in man's control over his environment.

This process started in Western Europe as a revolution in science and technology, but soon became intertwined with political, economic, and social change. Political modernization has taken the form of the consolidation of the authority of national states at the expense of landowners, provincial magnates, the Church, and a variety of local authorities. Where national states already existed, as in England and France, the change was made with relatively little strife; where they did not, as in Germany and Italy, the process of national unification led to extensive upheavals. The movements in ideology and politics which stirred Europe between the fifteenth and eighteenth centuries are familiar enough, and the French Revolution has become a symbol of the dramatic turning point when the proponents of moderniza-

---

The author wishes to acknowledge his indebtedness to Ivo J. Lederer, David MacKenzie, and Stephen G. Xydis for bibliographical suggestions; to Robert L. Wolff and Nicolas Spulber for comments on matters of interpretation; and to the Center of International Studies at Princeton University for assistance in the preparation of the manuscript.

tion first began to gain decisive victories over the adherents of the traditional regimes on the European continent.

The essential change in economics has been the increase in the per-capita output of human labor as a result of technological innovations. Industrialization is no doubt the most dramatic result of modernization, but the impact of technological change has been scarcely less revolutionary in agriculture, communications, transportation, and in methods of doing business. Economic growth has been accompanied by rapid social change: urbanization, education, the growth of an industrial proletariat and of a professional and political elite, and so on. At the same time, there has been a transformation of popular beliefs from the folklore of rural life to the somewhat more sophisticated outlook of today.

To some extent the entire European world shared in this process, but the initiative was clearly taken by the peoples bordering on the North Atlantic and the new outlook spread only gradually to Central and Eastern Europe, and beyond. In the countries of Southeastern Europe this process has passed through several phases. In the initial phase, during the seventeenth, eighteenth, and nineteenth centuries, modern ideas gained influence and the peoples of this region became convinced that they could and should strive to attain the level of achievement of Western Europe. The Ottoman rulers themselves were influenced by these ideas, and they undertook significant modernizing reforms in their Balkan provinces. These reforms were too limited and too long delayed, however, to capture the imagination of local modernizers. The latter, who before long included practically the entire literate population, were convinced that independence from Ottoman rule was the prerequisite to systematic modernization. Nationalism must thus be regarded as a means to modernization, although it raised political issues of such complexity that for the more short-sighted leaders it became an end in itself to which the larger goals of modernization were subordinated.

National independence nevertheless remains the most convenient point of division between this introductory phase, when traditional political forms predominated, and a second, in which modern-minded leaders gained political control. The central struggle in his second phase was between the leaders interested primarily in national liberation and unification and those who wished to subordinate these traditional goals to economic and social development. This phase may be said to have begun in 1863 in Greece and in 1878 in Rumania, Serbia, and Bulgaria, and it was substantially completed by the end of the First World War. In Albania it did not start until 1912, and it ended in the course of the Second World War. One may also think in terms of a third phase, in which the problems of economic and social development form the central issue. In this phase the main political struggle hinges on the decision which of several alternative programs of modernization should be undertaken. In terms of domestic strife this phase is often the most violent. It is also the one in which the influence of foreign models is greatest. If one thinks of the goal of this third phase as the establishment of stable modern institutions and the achievement of a level of development similar to that of the advanced countries, it is clear that for the Balkan peoples this goal is not yet in sight.

It is within such a framework that one must approach the problem of the political, ideological, economic, and cultural influence of Russia on the modernization of the Balkans. To a significant degree, both Russia and the Balkan countries have turned to the West for ideas, institutions, and technology, and even today the announced goal of the Soviet rulers is to overtake the advanced countries, and at some more distant future time to surpass them. Any discussion of this problem must therefore take for granted the predominance of Western influence. This is not to say, however, that Russian influence was negligible. In an important sense, Russia has served as one of the channels through which Western ideas and institutions reached Southeastern Europe. Moreover, within Russia the Western heritage was reinterpreted and adapted to Russian traditions and needs, and in this new form was frequently in a position to compete in Southeastern Europe with more direct Western influences.

THE POLITICS OF POWER

The political influence exerted by Russia in the Balkans has reflected the importance of this area to Russian security. Southeastern Europe borders on Russia and has played a key role in the balance of power between Russia and rival great powers. This region also lies across Russia's land route to the Turkish Straits, which for more than a century was one of the vital channels of Russian commerce.

The stabilization of the Russian frontier in the region of the Dniester and Pruth rivers was the culmination of the slow conquest of the Ukrainian steppes from Turkey and Poland in the seventeenth and eighteenth centuries. The annexation of Bessarabia in 1812 kept within reasonable ethnic bounds the territorial expansion of tsarist Russia in Southeastern Europe, although the tsar's troops crossed the Pruth four times after 1812 and for a generation (1856–1878) southern Bessarabia was restored to Turkish sovereignty. The Revolution of 1917 brought no immediate change in Russian objectives in this regard. The loss of Bessarabia to Rumania was never recognized, and the province was reoccupied at a convenient juncture in 1940. In contrast to the reannexation of Bessarabia, the acquisition of northern Bukovina at the same time did represent a new extension of Russian sovereignty in the Balkans. In view of the smallness of the area, however, and the ethnic claim to it which Russia could make, this latter addition of territory did not constitute a substantial departure from Russia's traditional policy of keeping her formal Balkan frontier within general ethnic bounds.

Of much greater significance than the frontier issue has been the Russian aim of asserting a predominant political influence in the Balkans. Possibilities of realizing this objective were seen in the time of Peter the Great, but it was not until the reign of Catherine II that substantial progress was made. The breaking of the Turkish monopoly of the Black Sea and the Straits in the treaty of 1774, the terms of which were to afford Russia in future years many opportunities to intervene in the affairs of the Ottoman Empire, laid the foundations for the extension of Russia influence—achievements which provided a point of departure for Catherine's ambitious but illusory "Greek project" (1782). Henceforth Russia was to exert a steady political pressure in this region, which became an area of intense rivalry with the other great powers, and it was only the combined efforts of the latter that prevented her from completely dominating it. After the Revolution, the desire to exert a predominant political influence remained, although its ideological content was of course radically altered. At the first opportunity, the traditional policy sprang to life again, and after the Second World War Russia's political influence was reëstablished under conditions more favorable than before.

A somewhat more complex relationship was that between Russia's policy in the Balkans and her desire to guarantee free passage for her commerce through the Turkish Straits. It was not until the nineteenth century, when the export of grain from southern Russia increased until it constituted from a third to a half of all Russian exports, that Russia's concern regarding the Straits became a major motivating factor in her Balkan policy. Insofar as arrangements regarding the Straits were dependent on negotiations between Russia and Turkey, the exertion by Russia of military and political pressure in the Balkans frequently served as the opening gambit in her efforts to gain concessions from Turkey. Here the Revolution did represent more of a break in Russian policy, for the means used by the Soviet Union to further its interests at the Straits have on the whole had little to do with the Balkans. Even with the revival of Russian influence in that region in 1940, and the subsequent stationing of sizable units of Soviet armed forces within easy striking distances of Constantinople (Istanbul), Russia's interest in the Straits does not appear to play so great a role in her Balkan policy as it did in the century before the Revolution.

Russia has employed various methods to pursue her objectives in the Balkans. Whatever may have been Russia's ambitions at one time or another, the resort to military force has always been a major instrument of policy and the most successful means of extending her political influence in the Balkans and of exerting pressure on Turkey. Of the Balkan states only Albania received its independence without some military assistance from tsarist Russia. When, on the other hand, it was the tsar's policy to oppose popular uprisings, as in the Danubian Principalities in 1848–1849, it took Russian troops to do the job. Similarly, after the Revolution the Soviet regime found no solid basis for its influence before the Red Army arrived, and since that event its influence has been decisive in the areas where its military power has prevailed.

The occupation of important areas in the Balkans has been another serviceable means of attaining Russia's objectives. In her wars with Turkey, Russia has invaded the Balkans about ten times, and her troops have remained in prolonged occupation on eight occasions. Of these, seven were before the Revolution (the Danubian Principalities in 1769–1774, 1787–1792, 1806–1812, 1829–1834, and 1848–1851; the Ionian Islands in 1798–1807; Bulgaria in 1878–1879), and one after the advent of the Soviets (Rumania and Bulgaria after 1944). These periods of occupation have been decisive for the political development of the areas concerned, but they cannot be said to have aroused significant popular support. In the Danubian Principalities, the prolonged periods of Russian occupation before the Revolution were a major factor in giving the Rumanian people the administrative and spiritual unity which were essential prerequisites for the later political unification of Moldavia and Wallachia. The Russian occupation of Bulgaria in 1878–1879 was similarly decisive in the history of that country, for the Constitution of 1879 which Russia sponsored was to provide the framework for the course of the political development of the country for the next several generations.

The Soviet occupation of Rumania and Bulgaria after 1944 was even more decisive than the tsarist ventures. The Soviet authorities were more determined and self-confident than the tsarist, and less restricted by the rival interests of the other great powers. Exercising the rights accorded them in the armistice terms and working largely through local instruments, they used their occupation opportunities to great advantage and with profound results for the future. In Jugoslavia, on the other hand, Russian influence was based on ideology rather than on power, as the Soviet leaders discovered when they failed in their effort to intervene in the domestic affairs of the country. In Greece, Soviet policy supported a large-scale internal war (1944–1949) in an effort to overthrow the government. In all these various forms of political influence, the Soviet Union has drawn heavily on precedents established by tsarist Russia.

Diplomacy has also been an important means of implementing Russian policies in the Balkans and the Straits question. Both tsarist and Soviet Russia have found that the main obstacles to the achievement of their objectives in this region have not been the Turkish armies or Balkan nationalism, but rather the competing interests of the other great powers. Whenever Russia has come up against the great powers in this region she has turned to diplomacy rather than to force although the threat of the latter has always lurked in the background. The periods of greatest Russian influence in the Balkans, from 1815 to 1856 and since 1944, have been times in which the other great powers were unable or unwilling to exert pressure on Russia. Even in its periods of greatest influence, however, Russian policy has been tempered by the need to maintain normal relations with the rest of the world.

IDEOLOGIES OF MODERNIZATION

The study of the influence of Russian ideas as distinct from political power is complicated by the fact that there have often been two and sometimes three "official" policies emanating simultaneously from St. Petersburg, and later from Moscow. Not infrequently these ideological approaches have been advanced simultaneously or in rapid alternation. There have also been a number of unofficial trends of Russian thought—liberal, radical, populist, Marxist before 1917, and conservative since that date—which have been regarded as subversive by the Russian government but which nevertheless have constituted important Russian ideological influences. Indeed, the range of opinions emanating from Russia has been so wide that at one time or another all major programs of modernization implemented or even discussed in the Balkans have been subjected in some degree to Russian influence. At the risk of oversimplifying, the many trends of policy and thought involved in this process may be summarized in a roughly chronological order under the headings of conservatism, liberalism, and Marxism-Leninism.

From 1774 to 1856, at least, it appeared to be reasonable from the Russian point of view to promote the independence of the Balkan peoples within a framework of conservative domestic policies. In a situation in which Russia and Austria were the dominant European powers in this region, it was quite feasible to support national revolutions without stimulating political liberalism. The germ of weakness in such a policy lay in the growing influence of West European liberalism, which was in due course to become the dominant philosophy of Balkan national leaders. It was only after the Crimean War, however, and indeed not until the Congress of Berlin, that Russian-supported conservatism ceased to exert an influence on the Balkan political scene.

The provinces of Wallachia and Moldavia had the most frequent and direct contact with Russian policy, and here Russian support went initially to the boiars. After Russia's decisive intervention in the Principalities in 1828–1829, the major abuses of the Phanariotes were abolished but the *Réglement Organiques* sponsored by Count Kiselev established the basis for a virtual Russian protectorate which lasted until 1856. Similarly, in Greece, though under somewhat different political circumstances, Russian conservative influence was strongly felt. John Capodistrias had been a close associate of Alexander I before 1821, and the regime which he established in Greece was politically conservative even though Greece was a republic. The influence of Russia, as one of the three guaranteeing powers under the treaty terms of 1827, was perhaps even more directly felt during the reign of King Otho (1832–1862). Before his death in 1843 the popular leader Theodore Kolokotronis, who had served briefly in a Russian-led regiment in Corfu, headed the "Russian party" in Athens. In Serbia, Russia joined with the Habsburg monarchy in exercising a conservative influence, and intervened to prevent the adoption of "radical" political ideas on more than one occasion before the establishment of a fully sovereign constitutional government in 1878. In Montenegro, likewise, Russian influences served to support the efforts of the traditional regime to free itself from Turkish rule, in particular after the visit of Prince Nikola to St. Petersburg in 1868. In Bulgaria, the official Russian policy was reflected in the moderate outlook of such leaders as Ivan Seliminsky and Naiden Gerov, who had gone to Russia for their higher education. After the liberation of Bulgaria, under circumstances in which Russia had to work in conjunction with the other great powers, Prince Alexander Battenberg was supported by the tsar on the assumption that he would pursue conservative policies.

The force of Russian conservatism in Balkan politics waned rapidly after 1856, and the renewed Russian participation in Balkan affairs in the 1870's failed to reëstablish its former position of influence. It should nevertheless be noted that after 1917 an unofficial version of Russian conservatism reasserted itself briefly, especially in Bulgaria and Jugoslavia, as a result of the influx of Russian refugees. These adherents of tsarism in a number of instances occupied important positions, and exercised some influence on public opinion. Moreover, the fact that King Alexander of Jugoslavia was educated at the imperial court in St. Petersburg no doubt also affected his political outlook.

The impact of official Russia on the liberal programs of modernization which dominated Balkan politics from the 1860's until the 1930's
was immeasurably smaller than on the conservative programs of the
earlier period. Indeed, there was something incongruous about Russian support in the Balkans of institutions denied to the Russian people themselves, and both during and since the nineteenth century
students of the problem have hesitated to believe their sources. Yet
it is clear that after the Crimean War it was a vital Russian interest
to prevent the domination of the Balkans by another great power, and
it was more important to have friends among the Balkan liberal political leaders than to support conservative principles.

It is under these circumstances that Russia came rather hesitantly to
the point of supporting liberalism. The most dramatic expression of
this policy was the active sponsorship of a draft Bulgarian constitution in 1879 that was advanced by contemporary standards. This draft,
after some further liberalization by a Constituent Assembly, was
adopted with Russia's blessing and promptly put into operation. The
risks of this Russian experiment soon became apparent, however, and
it led first to confusion and then to disaster for Russian interests. The
initial confusion stemmed from a division of counsels within Russia.
Miliutin, the minister of war and a Panslav, calculated that by supporting political liberalism Russia would win the friendship of Bulgarian national leaders and prepare the way for a reassertion of Russian influence in the Balkans at the next opportunity. Indeed, the more
ardent Panslavs among his subordinates toyed with the idea of encouraging a new Bulgarian national uprising against the Western powers responsible for the defeat of the San Stefano program. On the
other hand Giers, the minister of foreign affairs, supported a policy of
moderation designed to keep Bulgarian nationalism in check and to
avoid giving offense to Britain and Austria.

While these two divergent policies were reconcilable in the spring
of 1879, before Bulgarian political forces had been fully set in motion,
the Russian government soon faced some difficult choices. First the
liberals were supported against Prince Alexander Battenberg, whose
loyalty to Russia was suspect. Then, after the assassination of Alexander II by Russian radicals whose views were suspiciously akin to
those of the Bulgarian liberals, Battenberg was permitted to set aside
the constitution and rule with the aid of Russian military officials. The

latter soon antagonized first the prince and then the liberals, and by
1886 the Russians were forced to abandon Bulgaria, losing most of
their friends and influence. Liuben Karavelov set forth concisely the
Russian dilemma when he predicted in 1870, in an oft-quoted statement, that "if Russia comes to liberate, she will be received with great
sympathy; but if she comes to rule, she will find many enemies." Although one can cite other examples in later decades of Russian support of liberal regimes—support of Geshov in Bulgaria in 1911–1913,
Pašić in Serbia throughout the first two decades of the twentieth century, and Bratianu in Rumania in 1916—these were all maneuvers in
world politics and were essentially devoid of ideological implications.

The irony of this ideological retreat on the part of official Russia
was that to some degree the Balkan liberalism dominant after 1878
had been nurtured under the influence of unofficial Russian ideologies.
If one interprets liberalism broadly to include the radical and populist strains of thought, one can trace the process by which the utili-
tarianism, romanticism, utopian socialism, liberalism, and nationalism
prevalent in Western Europe were absorbed and adapted by the Russian radicals and passed on through their writings and political movements to Balkan public opinion. The difficulties of tracing this type
of influence are many, for the Russian radicals were familiar with a
wide range of Western thought and the Balkan radicals in turn studied
both Western and Russian writings. If one considers also that both the
Russian and the Balkan radicals were less concerned with a discrimi-
nating analysis of these ideas than with their applicability to the political and social problems of their respective countries, one can see
how difficult it is to distinguish between specifically Russian and specifically Western influences. At the same time the difficulties of this
task should not be exaggerated, for there is considerable evidence of
direct Russian influence.

The first wave of unofficial Russian liberal and radical influences
may be traced to the Decembrists. The Society of United Slavs of
Kiev, in particular, included among its aims the liberation of all Slavic
peoples and the establishment of democratic governments united in a
federation. The Decembrists established a branch of their movement
in Kishinev and were in touch with the Philike Hetaeria in Odessa.
It is significant that Tudor Vladimirescu, as an officer of the Russian
army and through his contacts with the Philike Hetaeria, was familiar

with the views of the Decembrists. Alexander Ypsilanti and his colleagues in the Philike Hetaeria were also acquainted with advanced thought in Russia, although the aims and methods of their own organization were so misconceived that it is difficult to distinguish a recognizable ideology in their abortive efforts.

A second generation of Balkan liberals and radicals, most of whom were engaged primarily in revolutionary activity, but never reached the point of holding public office, received their education in Russia or came into close contact with Russian radicalism. It has been estimated that approximately five hundred Bulgarians were educated in Russia between 1856 and 1878, apart from the members of the substantial Bulgarian colony in Odessa, and an unknown number of Serbs and Rumanians also went to Russia for their higher education. Although some of these students no doubt returned to their countries as loyal admirers of the Russian government, most appear to have been inspired by Western liberalism and socialism as reflected in the writings of Pisarev, Chernyshevsky, Herzen, Dobroliubov, Bakunin, and Nechaev.

No doubt the most typical representative of this generation was Svetozar Marković. He studied in St. Petersburg in the 1860's, at a time when the influence of radicalism was in full blossom. Later, in Zürich, he met Bakunin on a number of occasions but did not become a member of the Bakuninist clique of Serbian students. Despite this exposure to Russian radicalism, Marković's philosophy drew primarily on West European progressive thought. In Bulgaria, such prominent leaders of the revolutionary movement as Liuben Karavelov and Khristo Botev also studied in Russia, and in their writings the Russian radical influence probably plays a proportionately larger role than in Marković. Their relations with the Russian radicals were frequently direct. Karavelov was personally acquainted with Herzen, Ogarev, Bakunin, and Nechaev, and his colleagues in the Bulgarian revolutionary movement were all familiar with their writings. Moreover the substantial number of Bulgarians who emigrated to such centers as Bucharest, Braila, and Odessa in the first half of the nineteenth century, came more or less directly into contact with the prevailing currents of Russian thought. In Rumania the radicals of this period drew much more directly on French thought, whereas in Greece and Albania there is even less evidence of Russian influence.

A later generation, in experience if not in years, is formd by radicals of the 1860's and 1870's who survived to become liberal statesmen later in the century. Of these, Nikola Pašić is doubtless the best known. Like Marković, he met Bakunin as a student in Zürich, and he was nurtured in his early years on Russian radicalism as well as on West European socialism and liberalism. In his later career as a statesman it was nevertheless these latter influences that predominated. He served as his country's diplomatic representative in St. Petersburg in 1893–1894, and as prime minister of his country in the prewar era he counted tsarist Russia as an ally, but under the circumstances this coexistence of an early admiration for Russian radicalism and a later reliance on the friendship of Russian tsarism is not so incongruous as it might seem. Similarly Petko Karavelov and Stefan Stambolov, who spent their student years in Russia and whose outlook reflected a characteristic blend of Western liberalism and Russian radicalism, went on to become liberal statesmen who looked primarily to the West for their political inspiration. These few examples are only the best known of an entire generation of Serbian and Bulgarian leaders who gained a significant share of their ideas about the modern world through the writings of the Russian radicals.

In the latter part of the nineteenth century the influence of Russian populism was much less prominent. In Rumania, where the agrarian situation somewhat resembled that in Russia, the Russian populist tradition had only a few representatives. Zemfiri K. Ralli-Arbore studied in Russia and later was intimate with Bakunin and Nechaev in Zürich. He exercised only a negligible influence in his home country, however. More prominent was Constantin Stere, a Bessarabian boiar who had served a term of exile in Siberia. He became one of the principal theorists of the Rumanian Peasant party in the early years of the twentieth century, and some characteristic aspects of Russian thought were reflected in his views. Two Russian populists emigrated to Bulgaria, Vladimir K. Debogori-Mokrievich and Boris Mintses, but they did not become prominent in the affairs of that country. Among Bulgarian political writers, Todor G. Vlaikov and Petko Todorov in particular were influenced by Russian populism, but the organized agrarian movement in Bulgaria gained its principal inspiration from the West. Alexander Stambolisky received his higher education in Germany, and the references in his principal theoretical work are exclusively to

Western authorities. Stjepan Radić, on the other hand, studied in Russia and throughout his life combined a characteristic Croatian Russophilism with his peasantist ideology. He visited Russia in the 1890's, and again in 1923, but the problems of the Croatian peasantry were very different from those in Russia, and it cannot be said that the solutions proposed by the Croatian Peasant party relied significantly on Russian models.

The Socialist movements which developed in the Balkan countries at the end of the nineteenth century had deep roots in the earlier radicalism, but were distinguished from it by their formal party structure and their concern for organized political action. These movements developed in three stages: from the founding of the Social Democratic parties to 1917, from 1917 to 1944, and since the latter date. From the start, Russian influence was significant. Serbian social democracy was strongly influenced by the legacy of Marković and, of its more prominent leaders, Vasa Pelagić, Mihailo Ilić, and Dragutin Popović had lived and studied in Russia and were close to the Socialist movement in that country. The leading Rumanian theorist of socialism was a Russian radical named M. I. Kats, who emigrated to Rumania in the 1870's and became prominent under the pseudonym of Constantin Dobrogeanu-Gherea. Even more prominent was Christian G. Rakovsky, who was the guiding spirit of the Rumanian Social Democratic party founded in 1893 and also played an active role in Bulgarian socialism. After 1917 he went on to play a leading role in Soviet affairs.

More extensive yet was the Russian influence on the Bulgarian Socialists whose leader for many years, Dimitur Blagoev, studied in Russia from 1878 to 1885 and is credited with establishing the first Social Democratic group in that country in 1884. He founded the Bulgarian Social Democratic party in 1891, and headed its Narrow wing until his death in 1924. Many of his fellow Socialists also had close Russian connections: Yanko Sakuzov who, as leader of the Broad wing after 1903, became Blagoev's chief rival; as well as Georgi Bakalov, Khristo Kabakchiev, and Vasil Kolarov, who were all closely associated with the Russian Socialist movement. Georgi Dimitrov was the only Bulgarian Socialist prominent before 1917 who did not have close Russian associations, and he made up for this by spending much of his long period of exile (1923–1946) in the Soviet Union. In Croatia, Slovenia, and Bosnia-Hercegovina, by contrast, the Social Democratic movement received its inspiration from Central Europe, and this was true to almost the same degree in Serbia and Greece.

In the two or three years following the Bolshevik Revolution, the Left wings of the various Social Democratic parties in Bulgaria (1919), Serbia (1919), Rumania (1921), and Greece (1924) became the nuclei of new Communist parties and henceforth had close relations with the U.S.S.R. All the more prominent leaders visited Russia at one time or another, and many lived there for long periods. Many also served as agents of the Comintern in various international activities, and particularly in the Spanish Civil War. A few rose to international prominence in the interwar period. The influence of communism within the Balkan countries was based primarily on its role of claiming to speak for the oppressed and discontented. Whereas the trade unionists were predominantly Social Democrats, the Communists drew their support from a wide variety of sources. The Magyars, Jews, and Slavs in Rumania; the Macedonians, Montenegrins, and Bosnians in Jugoslavia; the Macedonians in Bulgaria; and in Greece the new immigrants from Russia and Turkey—all these tended to find in the Communist party an outlet for grievances ignored or suppressed by the traditional parties. In all these countries there was also a substantial population of semiskilled workers on the border between village and urban life, and various categories of migrant and seasonal workers, to whom the Communists could appeal.

The electoral strength of the Communists was never great, except in the Jugoslav election of 1920 when they won 58 of 419 seats in the National Assembly. As parties under constant persecution they had limited opportunities for political maneuver. In 1936 the small Communist party in Greece held the parliamentary balance between the Royalists and the Liberals, but this was exceptional. The Communists also had some success in winning over splinter groups from the Socialist and Agrarian parties as a result of united-front tactics. They likewise exerted influence through the organization of strikes and revolts, and especially in the 1920's contributed substantially to the already considerable hazards of Balkan politics.

Perhaps the greatest impression made by Communist policy was in international relations. In an era of bitter enmities among the Balkan peoples, the idea of peace and friendship was attractive, and the Communist proposals for Balkan federation held out hope for resolving such controversial issues as the Macedonian question. The key to such influence as the Communists exerted nevertheless lay in the Soviet Union. In the 1920's the Soviet Union had little to offer the Balkan peoples. Its domestic system was neither stable nor prosperous enough to attract admirers, and in international relations it was regarded chiefly as a source of aggression and disturbance. At the same time, the radical transformation which Russia was undergoing doubtless served in some degree as a challenge to traditional political leaders in the Balkans, leading them in some instances to undertake reforms which they might not otherwise have considered.

This picture changed somewhat in the early 1930's, when the growing political stability and economic purposefulness of the Soviet government coincided with a period of depression and retrenchment in the West. The role of the Soviet Union in the League of Nations also relieved tension, and diplomatic relations were restored with Rumania and Bulgaria in 1934. Relations had been established with Albania as early as 1924, but were not renewed with Jugoslavia until 1940 and with Greece until 1941. These events did not greatly benefit the local Communist parties, however, and they were soon offset by the purge trials in the Soviet Union, and the German economic drive. On the eve of the Second World War, it could not be said that either the Soviet Union or the local Communist parties exerted any considerable ideological influence in these countries.

The events of the Second World War and after do not need to be recounted, but the relationship between Soviet military force and the influence of the Communist ideology deserves brief attention. In Rumania and Bulgaria it seems clear that the establishment of Communist regimes was entirely dependent on the presence of Soviet military power. In neither country did the Communist parties wield any considerable influence over centers of political power, or in the countryside through guerrilla operations, although they were substantially stronger in Bulgaria than in Rumania. In Jugoslavia and Albania, on the other hand, their strength was developed as a result of guerrilla operations and initially without Soviet assistance. In Jugoslavia, Tito's cadres proved to be sufficiently strong to withstand Soviet infiltration. The clumsy Soviet effort in 1948 to oust the Jugoslav Communist leadership proved to be a total failure, and Tito survived with aid from the West to implement his own version of national communism. In

Greece a strong guerrilla position was established by the Communists during the war, but in the absence of Soviet military support it was unable to retain its influence after the war despite persistent efforts.

Russian ideological influence in Rumania, Bulgaria, and Albania is now unrivaled, and all policies and institutions have been remodeled along Soviet lines. To the extent that this process is not yet completed, it is due to local conditions which can only be changed over a period of time. This is not to say that public opinion has been won over, however, and it may be questioned to what extent even the younger generation educated since 1944 is ideologically loyal. In the absence of an effective alternative, however, opposition to communism is limited to local efforts. In Jugoslavia the situation is more complex. The Communist party had primarily Soviet models in mind when it established its new institutions immediately after the war. Since the break with the Cominform, however, there has been considerable experimentation with alternative forms of administration as well as frequent consultation with West European Socialists. As a result, a peculiarly Jugoslav form of communism has been developed which combines highly centralized controls with some local administrative autonomy. In Greece, on the other hand, Communist influence has survived in the form of the Communist-sponsored Union of the Democratic Left, which won a quarter of the seats in the Greek parliament in 1958. It thus represents an important force to be reckoned with, and attracts the support of a variety of disaffected groups.

In reviewing the record since the beginning of the nineteenth century, one may conclude that until 1944 there was relatively little Russian influence on the ideologies of modernization actually implemented in the Balkans. During the first half of the nineteenth century Russian influence supported governments in the Danubian Principalities, Serbia, Montenegro, and Greece which were opposed to fundamental social change. Between the Crimean War and the First World War Russian radicals and Socialists had considerable influence on progressive thought in Bulgaria and Serbia, and to a lesser extent in Rumania, but this had only a negligible impact on government policies. This influence was chiefly as an interpreter of Western ideas, which also came to these countries in a more influential and effective form directly from the West. Even among the southern Slavs of the Habsburg Empire, where Russian sympathies were particularly strong, neither radical nor official Russia had much to offer in the way of programs of social and economic change. In the interwar period government policy in the Balkans paid little attention to Soviet models, and only after 1944 did these exert a determining influence north of Greece.

ECONOMIC GROWTH

In many respects the most direct and impressive aspect of modernization as a general phenomenon has been in the realm of economic growth. The Balkan countries have shared in this process, although in a rather modest way, and all branches of their economies have undergone a fundamental change. The peasant agriculture and handicrafts of the mid-nineteenth century have been supplanted to a considerable degree by modern technology. This transformation was brought about in part by free enterprise and in part by state initiative, and in both foreign capital played a significant role. The underlying social significance of this transformation has been the possibility of increased per-capita consumption along with the social and cultural benefits of a higher standard of living.

In this process Russia played almost no role until after the Second World War. The programs and technology of economic growth, as well as the bulk of the foreign capital, came from Western and Central Europe. Throughout this period Russia was a capital-importing country and, except for relatively modest financial operations in Turkey, Persia, and Mongolia, did not undertake foreign investments. Its financial operations in the Balkans were in fact limited to a few loans with a political aim: the financing of wars of liberation against the Ottoman Empire. Thus in 1830 Russia advanced 3,000,000 francs to Greece. Two years later Russia joined with the United Kingdom and France to guarantee a larger loan to the new Greek state, but no Russian capital was involved. Between 1867 and 1878 Russia advanced some 8,700,000 dinars to the Serbian government, in addition to military assistance. Russia also gave extensive assistance in the form of military supplies to Bulgaria in 1877–1878, but under the Treaty of Berlin that country was required to assume the costs of the Russian occupation and, after 1885, of the expenses of the Russian army in

Eastern Rumelia as well. These costs amounted to 56,300,000 francs, and Bulgaria continued payments on this debt until the First World War.

Apart from these limited financial operations, Russia appears to have had little direct share in the economic growth of this region. There was some effort by Russian banking concerns in the early 1880's to participate in the construction of railroads in Serbia and Bulgaria, but these efforts were not supported by the Russian government and they came to nothing. To this one may add several instances in which Russian economic institutions served as a model for those in this region. Thus it is clear that Prince Cuza, in promulgating the land reform of 1864, was influenced by the Russian emancipation of 1861. In Bulgaria, the fiscal system established after the liberation was based on the Russian model, and other examples of this type of influence could be cited. Yet by comparison with the extensive adaptation of institutions and methods in the economic sphere from European societies, Russia's role in this regard was small.

The relative absence of Russia from the Balkan economic scene before the Second World War is also reflected in its small share of the foreign trade of these countries. The following table reflects this situation, as well as the dramatic change which occurred after the Second World War.

Since 1944 Russia has played a major economic role in Rumania and Bulgaria, in Jugoslavia up to 1948, and in Albania since that date. The first impact of Soviet economic policy took the form of the removal of capital goods from Bulgaria and Rumania in compensation for war losses. In Bulgaria this amounted to relatively small enforced shipments of foodstuffs, but from Rumania capital goods valued at some $2,000,000,000 were removed by 1948. Both countries also had to pay occupation costs. In addition, sixteen Soviet-Rumanian and five Soviet-Bulgarian joint companies were established. These enjoyed various tax privileges, and turned over one-half of their earnings to the U.S.S.R. The Soviet share in these companies consisted of confiscated German assets, which in turn included the assets of other European countries which Germany had confiscated earlier in the war. The total removal of capital under these and various other operations has not been estimated, and perhaps cannot be, but in the first postwar

RUSSIA'S SHARE IN THE BALKANS TRADE
(In percent of total trade)

	1909–1912	1938	1957	Soviet bloc 1957
Albania	—	import 0.0 export 0.0	import 67.6 export 54.2	import 86.4 export 79.2
Bulgaria	import 3.9 export 0.2	import 0.0 export 0.0	import 55.4 export 57.2	import 72.7 export 78.8
Greece	import 19.4 export 2.0	import 2.0 export 0.3	import 2.0 export 4.1	import 4.6 export 8.5
Rumania	import 2.7 export 1.0	import — export —	import 55.9 export 50.5	import 70.8 export 66.3
Jugoslavia	—	import 0.1 export 0.0	import 10.4 export 12.3	import 20.4 export 24.0

—— = negligible, less than 0.1.
SOURCES: Bulgaria, Rumania, and Serbia for 1909–1912, from A. Zaleski, *Les courants commerciaux de l'Europe danubienne au cours de la première moitié du XIX* siècle* (Paris, 1952), p. 48; Greece for 1909–1912, from M. Dorizas, *The Foreign Trade of Greece* (Philadelphia, 1925), p. 124; remaining figures from United Nations, *Direction of International Trade, annual issue* (New York, 1959), *passim*.

decade it clearly amounted to several billion dollars in value, and by far the greater share was from Rumania.

The joint companies in Bulgaria and Rumania were dissolved between 1954 and 1956, with compensation for the U.S.S.R., and after the events of the latter year a new Soviet approach was attempted. The debts of Rumania ($717,000,000) and Albania ($105,500,000) were canceled. At the same time, Russia extended loans and credits in the amount of $47,700,000 to Albania, $192,500,000 to Bulgaria, and $100,500,000 to Rumania. Simultaneously, the terms of Soviet trade with these three countries reflect a significant and continuing price discrimination against them.

The net loss to Rumania and Bulgaria since the Second World War would appear to be considerable, although it cannot be estimated without more complete information. Albania is exceptional, as it was in fact a dependency of Jugoslavia until 1948 and received from its northern neighbor substantial economic assistance. Since that date, the task of supporting the Albanian economy has been shared by the Soviet Union and the people's democracies. Jugoslavia also is exceptional, as its economic relations with the U.S.S.R. and the Soviet bloc have for political reasons fluctuated so greatly. In the period up to 1948, the Soviet Union failed to gain any substantial hold on the Jugoslav economy, although about one-half of Jugoslav foreign trade was with the Soviet bloc. Trade relations were resumed, and Soviet credits extended, during the brief period of reconciliation between 1955 and 1957. More recently, however, economic relations between Jugoslavia and the Soviet bloc have again reached a low ebb.

In the aims and methods of their economic policies since the war, Albania, Bulgaria, and Rumania have followed closely the Soviet pattern. Industry, capital, and trade have been brought under state control. A high percentage of the national income is invested each year in industry, where production has increased rapidly. At the same time agriculture, which still employs the bulk of the population, and also consumer goods, have been neglected. The burden on private consumption resulting from this investment pattern is well known, and it may be questioned whether disposable income per capita has yet attained the prewar level. The new managerial elite, on the other hand, takes care of itself and enjoys many of the perquisites of power. There are also significant variations within the overall pattern. Bulgaria has hewn most closely to the Soviet line, and has even undertaken an economic reorganization à la Khrushchev despite the fact that the entire country is not much bigger than one of the larger Soviet *sovnarkhozy*. In Rumania the pace has been somewhat more relaxed. Albania, on the other hand, is a generation or two behind its neighbors in economic development and is in many respects unable to meet the requirements of the Soviet model.

The question of Russian economic influence on Tito's Jugoslavia is more subtle. Although the Jugoslav economy still resembles the Soviet pattern, it has evolved some unique solutions to the problems of a socialist economy. The similarity to the Soviet system lies in the degree of state ownership and control, the reliance on planning, the emphasis on producer goods at the expense of consumer goods and agriculture, and the creation of a small privileged group of managers in the environment of a generally low level of per-capita consumption.

The differences, however, are also striking. The new economic system developed since 1950 has aimed at a significant decentralization of planning, participation of workers in factory management, reliance on a monetary rather than an administrative regulation of prices, and on market incentives instead of collectivization in agriculture. It is also significant that from the start Jugoslav economic policies have been independent of direct Soviet pressures, and also that some of Khrushchev's reforms in industrial and agricultural production resemble (no doubt unconsciously) those of Tito in significant respects.

CULTURE AND INSTITUTIONS

Russia and the Balkans were equally indebted to the West in literature, the arts, education, and other institutions. At the same time, in these as in other fields, Russia played in some measure the role of mediator between the West and the Balkans. Two important distinctions must nevertheless be noted. In literature, music, and the performing arts, Russia became a major contributor to world culture, widely admired and imitated. In these matters Russia was not only an equal but also a teacher of the West in a significant sense. At the same time, the common link of religion with the great majority of the Balkan peoples, and of language with the southern Slavs, gave Russia a particular advantage as compared with the West.

Ecclesiastical relations may in fact be traced back to the early years of the Turkish conquest, when the only substantial contacts were those between the Russian Orthodox Church and the monasteries and clergy in this region. These contacts were supplemented by the intermittent diplomatic relations between Moscow and Constantinople after 1495. By the eighteenth century there was a recognition on the part of leaders of opinion, especially among the southern Slavs, that Russia was one of the principal enemies of the Ottoman Empire and to this extent a potential ally against Turkish oppression. The cultural relations among the monasteries of Moldavia, Wallachia, Bulgaria, and Serbia, and between these and the Russian church, served to keep alive this idea of a Russian presence. Nevertheless this was a political rather than an ideological influence, and neither Father Paisii nor Dositej Obradović, for example, drew significantly on Russian inspiration for their ideas, although the latter was friendly to Russia and headed the Serbian mission to Russian army headquarters in Wallachia in 1806–1810.

During the years of struggle against Turkish rule, Russian Orthodoxy was no doubt an active force assisting in the process of national liberation and guiding it along conservative lines. In some measure it served as a branch of the Russian government, but it could also act independently, as in the crisis of 1875–1878, to provide both moral and material support for the southern Slavs. After the Balkan peoples gained their independence, it is difficult to discern any substantial influence emanating from the Russian church apart from the normal maintenance of ecclesiastical relations.

The doctrine that Slavic culture was distinct from that of Western Europe, and should be preserved from contamination, was actively preached in Russia in the middle years of the nineteenth century. It was nevertheless an idea that had relatively little appeal even to the Serbs and Bulgarians, in competition with Western ideas and institutions, and to the Rumanians, Greeks, and Albanians it was meaningless. Panslavism, as the political aspect of Slavophilism, no doubt had its greatest influence in Croatia. In its formulation by Juraj Križanić, as publicized in the mid-nineteenth century, and in its espousal by such leaders as Ljudevit Gaj and Bishop Strossmayer, it represented the brightest hope for liberation from Habsburg rule. Their plans envisaged the union of the Catholic and Orthodox churches, however, and this idea never attracted Russian support. Panslavism also had a brief and dramatic period of influence among the Slavic peoples under Turkish rule in the 1870's and 1880's. Characteristic of the strengths and weaknesses of this movement was the activity of General Cherniaev in Serbia in 1876–1878. Apart from its temporary political significance, however, Panslavism had no more to offer than Slavophilism and remained an essentially sterile doctrine. It was nevertheless a source of considerable apprehension on the part of the Greeks, and served to exacerbate relations between them and the Slavic peoples to the north.

Although this particular effort to export Slavic traditions proved to be ineffectual and even self-defeating, the true greatness of Russian culture as expressed in literature had widespread influence in the Balkans. The Russian literary classics were translated into the Balkan languages, widely read by the educated public, and studied by writers. Russian plays and operas were frequently performed, and Russian music was also popular. Of particular relevance was the preoccupation of Russian writers with the social and moral questions peculiar to an era of rapid change. The problems were confronted in the Balkans about a generation later than in Russia, and the works of Turgenev and Dostoevsky, Chekhov and Gorky, undoubtedly held a special significance apart from their literary merit. Russian literature was perhaps most widely appreciated in Bulgaria, where similarities of language as well as a sense of cultural kinship were strongest. Among the leading writers, Petko R. Slaveikov, Ivan Vazov, Pencho Slaveikov, Aleko Konstantinov, and Elin Pelin in particular turned to Russia for inspiration. At the same time, much of Western literature also came to Bulgaria first in the form of Russian translations. In Serbia, one may cite the influence of Chernyshevsky and Turgenev on Laza Lazarević, of Gogol on Jakov Ignjatović, and of Lermontov on Jovan Jovanović Zmaj. In Croatia, there were translations of Tolstoy and Shevchenko by Avgust Harambašić, and influences of Turgenev in the work of Ljubomir Babić.

In the non-Slavic countries Russian literature played a lesser role, but it was by no means unimportant. Rumanian writers from Bessarabia were particularly subject to Russian influence. Constantin Stamati gained prominence as a translator and imitator of Derzhavin, Zhukovsky, Pushkin, and Lermontov. Bogdan Hasdeu wrote his early works in Russian, and Costache Negruzzi decided to undertake a literary career after meeting Pushkin during the latter's Bessarabian exile. After the middle of the nineteenth century Western literary models predominated in Rumania, but the influence of the Russian classics was never absent. In Greece one may cite the influence of Tolstoy on Kostis Palamas, of Turgenev on Gregorios Xenopoulos, and of Tolstoy and Dostoevsky on Constantine Theotokis.

Other Russian cultural influences must be sought primarily among the Slavic peoples, and date from the early eighteenth century. In 1724, Peter the Great sent to Serbia what would now be called a technical-assistance mission, headed by Maksim Suvorov, which established the first schools and initiated the study of grammar and language. In the nineteenth century, Vuk Karadžić maintained close relations with Russian scholars, although his own contributions were primarily of Western inspiration. In Bulgaria, the initiative of Vasil Evstatiev Aprilov in founding the first secondary school in 1835 was due to the influence of the Ukrainian scholar Venelin. The leading creators of the modern Bulgarian language, Naiden Gerov and Ivan Andreev Bogorov, relied extensively on Russian scholarship.

In noting briefly these influences on culture and institutions, which were significant primarily for Bulgaria and Serbia, it should not be forgotten that in these as in other matters the Balkan people looked primarily to the West. French and German were the foreign languages most widely studied throughout the Balkans, and education, scholarship, law, the press, literature and the arts, and political and social institutions were based primarily on European rather than Russian models. This was a reflection not of any lack of respect for Russian institutions, but rather of the recognition that it was in most respects Europe that set the standards in these matters for the whole world.

Russian influence on Balkan culture and institutions declined significantly after 1917. This was due in part to political reasons, as contacts between Russia and the Balkans were in considerable measure cut off between the wars, but it was due also to the fact that Soviet institutions were still in the process of formation and not yet ready for export. Since the Second World War, under very different circumstances, Russian culture and institutions have of course exerted a very pervasive influence in Albania, Bulgaria, and Rumania. Political and social institutions, as well as education, scholarship, literature, and the arts, have been extensively remodeled along Russian lines. A lively program of cultural interchange is maintained, with many Soviet specialists visiting these countries, and many students going to Soviet universities. Jugoslavia followed the same course until 1948, and probably went further than its neighbors in sending students to Russia and modeling its institutions after those in the U.S.S.R. Many of these institutions have remained unchanged since 1948, but the West has now replaced Russia as the principal source of inspiration. Jugoslav students and technicians now study in Central and Western Europe and in the United States, and Western books, plays, and motion pictures are preferred. Even in the field of ideology, Soviet influence is no longer prominent.

In Greece, Soviet culture and institutions have relatively few admirers. Indeed, the constitution adopted in 1952 goes out of its way to provide that all teaching in elementary and intermediate schools should be "on the basis of the ideological principles of Greek Christian civilization" (Art. 16, para. 2). Greece's cultural contacts have always been more cosmopolitan than those of its Balkan neighbors, and for most Greeks the bitter experiences in the wars of the twentieth century outweigh the memories of Russian assistance in the struggle for liberation. The range and intensity of Greek feelings on this subject are sensitively reflected in the novels of Nikos Kazantzakis, who spent two years in Russia as head of the mission in charge of evacuating Greek refugees after the First World War.

EXTENT AND NATURE OF RUSSIAN INFLUENCE

The relationship of Russia to the Balkans reflects, in microcosm, patterns that are characteristic of many other parts of the world. Every society tends to modernize in its own way, adopting the ideas and institutions essential to all social change but investing them with a spirit based on its own traditions and values. Political power aside, societies will tend to borrow from those who seem best able to meet their needs. But political power is in fact never absent, and it frequently tends to distort the natural flow of nonpolitical influences. It is therefore relevant to suggest answers to two questions raised by the role of Russia in the modernization of the Balkans. How has the relative influence in this region of Russia and of the countries of Western and Central Europe been affected by social change? What has been the relative role in Russian influence of forcible imposition and voluntary borrowing?

Throughout the period since Turkish rule, the extent and nature of Russian influence has depended on the balance of power, which in turn has reflected in a marked fashion the differing effects of social change within each of the powers. From the latter part of the eighteenth century, when Russia emerged as a major factor in Balkan affairs, until the Crimean War, Russia was the bulwark of the dynastic conservatism which still predominated in most of Europe and did not consider itself to be behind the times. Europe was not the static world which Nicholas I imagined it to be, however, and the ineluctable pressures of social change soon brought an end to the dynastic system which appeared to have survived so successfully the crisis of 1848–1850. Once again in 1876–1878 Russian troops were able to dominate the Balkans, but the political consequences of this war soon revealed the changes wrought by the unification of Germany and the beginnings of Austrian disintegration. Russia was now faced by a new Europe, with which it could compete neither in power nor in ideas. From 1856 to 1917 the official Russia of tsarist policy exerted less influence in the Balkans than the unofficial Russia of radical thought and of a literature concerned with social change.

Between the wars both Europe and Russia were in the throes of social readjustment, and the Balkan countries experimented with many half-solutions which met with little success. Neither the French system of the 1920's nor the German system of the 1930's offered a stable program for modernization, although if Europe had been led by competent statesmen a constructive program embracing Western, Central, and Southeastern Europe might well have been evolved. In Russia the unrest was even greater, marked by social experiments purchased at the cost of millions of lives and a political system held together by purges and labor camps. Not until after the Second World War was the Soviet system generally accepted as a viable alternative to the European approach to modernization, and by then it had to compete with a Europe that was again dynamic.

The social change characteristic of the modern world has had a twofold effect on Russian influence: it has affected Russia's relative power position, as well as her ability to make a substantive contribution to the modernization of Southeastern Europe. In terms of power, the effects of social change led to the relative decline of Russia as compared with Western and Central Europe between 1856 and 1944. Despite the strength of Russia's position in this region in terms of size, proximity, and historic relationships, she was unable to retain her influence because of the more rapid modernization of the rival powers. With the reconstruction of Russia after the Second World War, after a period of rapid if interrupted social change dating from the 1880's, Russia's relative strength again approximates that of the first half of the nineteenth century.

As a contributor to social change in Southeastern Europe, the delayed modernization of Russia deprived her of much of the influence which she could otherwise have exerted. Only in a few fields, such as literature and the performing arts, did Russian influence transcend the role of reinterpreting European achievements to an audience limited primarily to the southern Slavs. In such vital matters as political institutions, programs of economic growth, and technology, Russia made only a limited contribution before 1944. Since the Second World War, the significance of this contribution has grown as the gap between Russia and the West is closing.

A somewhat different question is that of the relative role of forcible imposition and voluntary borrowing in Russian influence in this region, although it is a reflection of the same forces of social change. Certainly there are significant aspects of Russian influence which are difficult to imagine in the absence of Russian power. The entire role of Russia as the liberator of Balkan peoples from Turkish rule was essentially a military proposition, implementing political programs which originated elsewhere. The generally conservative trend of Balkan governments in the first half of the nineteenth century, and most characteristically the support given to the boiars in Moldavia and Wallachia, was also a consequence of military power. Similarly, the degree of Russian influence in Bulgaria and Rumania since 1944, and in Albania since 1948, can be explained only by the unchallenged presence of Soviet power.

At the same time it is clear that some influences have also depended significantly on the unimposed example of Russia. Indeed, some of the most salient features of Russian influence in the latter half of the nineteenth century came from the unofficial Russia, not the Russia that controlled the armies. Although the national traditions and values of Russia differ significantly from those of the Balkan peoples, she has been confronted with many of the same problems of social change. In addition, the similarity of language and culture go a long way to explain Russia's special influence in Serbia and Bulgaria.

At the least, the Russian radicals served as intermediaries of European progressive thought, restating its conclusions in a manner that was frequently more relevant to Balkan problems. Many southern Slavs, in particular, first learned of Western thought from Russian writers, and then went on to study the originals. This may account for the apparent paradox that such leaders as Nikola Pašić and Stefan Stambolov, who were so imbued with Russian radicalism in their youth, went on to become bulwarks of stable government. It was not so much that they became conservative with age, as that the Russian radicals introduced them to the Western thought and institutions which guided them throughout their careers.

It was also no doubt natural, in view of the profound frustrations encountered by the Balkan peoples in their efforts to modernize, that Marxism—and more particularly its Leninist version—should have had a following among them. The idea that state socialism could provide a solution to their problems had particular influence after the solutions sponsored by Western Europe ended in a great depression and that of Central Europe in the Second World War. That the strength of communism reflected domestic discontents rather than Soviet pressure is illustrated by the fact that it achieved its greatest successes in war-ravaged Jugoslavia and Greece at a time when Russian power was temporarily in eclipse. Indeed, it is interesting to speculate whether communism would have as much support today in either Rumania or Bulgaria, were it not for the Soviet presence, as in Greece. Throughout the interwar period, Jugoslavia and Greece were the two countries in this region which were burdened with the most difficult social problems and at the same time with the most ineffectual and unimaginative governments. Jugoslavia, like other Communist states, also illustrates the fact that even so aggressive an ideology as communism cannot obliterate traditional attitudes and ways of doing things, and that there is such a thing as national communism which can evolve independently of and even in resistance to Soviet influence.

In the category of influences independent of politics one must also include literature and the arts, education, science, technology, and economic relations. Influences in this category may follow the flag, as they have in Rumania and Bulgaria since 1944, but they also move in the free market of ideas and interests. Where contributions of universal significance have originated in Russia, they have found as ready a reception in the Balkans as elsewhere. If such contributions were limited in the nineteenth century primarily to ideas, literature, and the arts, by the mid-twentieth they have increasingly included much more varied fields of knowledge and branches of technology.

The prospects for long-term Russian influence in the Balkans, apart from that which can be imposed by force, lie in the ability of the Soviet system to evolve original solutions to the myriad of problems confronted by societies undergoing modernization.

BIBLIOGRAPHY

There are no general accounts of Russian influence in the Balkans, treating all aspects of the subject for the entire period since Turkish rule. Even for briefer periods, or individual countries, few general works exist. Of these, the most important is B. H. Sumner, *Russia and the Balkans, 1870–1880* (Oxford, 1937), a pioneering achievement which sets a high standard for all work in this field. A valuable brief interpretation is Ivo J. Lederer, "Russia and the Balkans," in Ivo J. Lederer, ed., *Russian Foreign Policy: Essays in Historical Perspective* (New Haven, 1962), 417–451. The recent revival of Soviet interest in Balkan history is reflected in the numerous articles which have appeared in recent years in the *Uchenye zapiski* [*Studies*] and the *Kratkii soobshcheniia* [*Brief Communications*] of the Institute of Slavistics of the Academy of Sciences of the USSR, and in handbooks and symposia such as F. N. Petrov, ed., *Balkanskie Strany* [*The Balkan Countries*], (Moscow, 1946); V. Picheta, ed., *Slavianskii sbornik* [*Slavic Symposium*], (Moscow, 1947); S. M. Stetskevich, ed., *Ocherki istorii iuzhnykh i zapadnykh slavian* [*Essays on the History of the Southern and Western Slavs*], (Leningrad, 1957); S. A. Nikitin and L. B. Valev, eds., *Obshchestvenno-politicheskie i kulturnye sviazi narodov SSSR i Iugoslavii* [*Social, Political and Cultural Bonds Between the Peoples of the USSR and Jugoslavia*], (Moscow, 1957); and L. B. Valev, V. N. Kondratyeva, and S. A. Nikitin, eds., *Iz istorii russko-bolgarskikh otnoshenii* [*From the History of Russian-Bulgarian Relations*], (Moscow, 1958).

Among the relatively few general treatments of individual countries and regions, Charles Jelavich, *Tsarist Russia and Balkan Nationalism: Russian Influence in the Internal Affairs of Bulgaria and Serbia, 1879–1886* (Berkeley and Los Angeles, 1958), covers a broad range of political, ideological, and economic questions. A brief, but reasonably comprehensive, Soviet interpretation of Russian-Jugoslav relations is provided by V. G. Karasaev, *Istoricheskie sviazi narodov Sovetskogo soiuza i Iugoslavii* [*Historical Bonds of the Peoples of the Soviet Union and Jugoslavia*], (Moscow, 1956). Guides to bibliography and historiography should be sought in the standard reference works, but two items of particular relevance should be noted: A. Pogodin, *Ruska-srpska bibliografija 1800–1925* [*Russian-Serbian Bibliography, 1800–1925*], (Belgrade, 1932–1936), 2 vols.; and Stephen A. Fischer-Galati, "Slavic-Romanian Relations in Modern Romanian Historiography," Mid-European Studies Center, Mimeographed Series, No. 8 (New York, 1953).

The scarcity of general works is largely compensated for by the number of special studies available. Apart from the extensive literature dealing with the history of Southeastern Europe, the Eastern Question, Russian foreign policy, and related subjects, much has been written on specific aspects of Russian political and ideological influence in the Balkans. Less has been done, however, in the realm of economic and cultural influences. Much of this work is by Balkan scholars, particularly those of Bulgaria, Serbia, and Croatia. This work has produced many contributions to scholarship, even though it has been strongly influenced by the prevailing nationalist (and, more recently, Communist) bias. Russian research in this field is concentrated primarily in the latter part of the nineteenth century, in the 1920's, and in the period since the Second World War. Although these productive phases have tended to coincide with active Russian interest in the Balkans, the Russian publications include much valuable scholarship.

Useful work has also been done by European and American students of this subject. On the whole this work benefits from a relative freedom from immediate political concerns, apart from a general tendency to favor Balkan resistance to Russian political controls, and has produced some penetrating analyses of the Russian-Balkan relationship. If one may venture to criticize this body of scholarship as a whole, it would be essentially from two points of view. First, there has been a strong tendency to dwell on political and ideological influences to the exclusion of social, economic, and cultural. This can no doubt be explained by the difficult problems of sources and method, but every effort should be made to go beyond the traditional two-dimensional approach. Second, there is a tendency in many of these studies to ignore the larger context of Balkan relations with Europe as a whole, and to treat Russian-Balkan affairs as though they existed in isolation.

What follows is a limited review of the work of particular significance for the subject of the preceding essay. The limitations in my knowledge of Balkan languages has prevented me from making use of works in Albanian, Greek, and Rumanian.

Political Influences.—The story of Russian political and military policies in the Balkans is told in the general accounts and monographs dealing with Russian foreign affairs during the century and a half under consideration, too numerous to cite here. Attention should be called, however, to several recent contributions dealing with the latter half of the nineteenth century, the period that has attracted the most active interest on the part of historians: Charles and Barbara Jelavich, *Russia in the East, 1876–1880* (Leiden, 1959), a documentary study based on the papers of Giers, and their "The Danubian Principalities and Bulgaria under Russian Protectorship," *Jahrbücher für Geschichte Osteuropas,* IX (October, 1961), 349–366; Melvin C. Wren, "Pobedonostsev and Russian Influence in the Balkans, 1881–1888," *Journal* of *Modern History*, XIX (June, 1947), 130–141; and three studies by S. A. Nikitin, the leading Soviet student of Russian-Balkan relations: "Diplomaticheskie otnosheniia Rossii s iuzhnymi slavianami v 60–kh godakh XIX v." ["The Diplomatic Relations of Russia with the Southern Slavs in the 1860's"], *Slavianskii sbornik* [*Slavic Symposium*], (Moscow, 1947), 262–290; "Podlozhnye dokumenty o russkoi politike na Balkanakh v 70–e gg. XIX v." ["Spurious Documents Concerning Russian Policy in the Balkans in the 1870's"], *Isvestiia Akademiia nauk SSSR. Seriia istorii i filosofii* [*Bulletin of the Academy of Sciences of USSR. Series of History and Philosophy*] III (1946), 87–91; and his valuable *Slavianskie komitety v Rossii 1856–1876* [*The Slavic Committees in Russia, 1856–1876*], (Moscow, 1960), based on extensive use of Russian archives. Of the various accounts of Soviet policy in Eastern Europe since the Second World War, Zbigniew K. Brzezinski, *The Soviet Bloc: Unity and Conflict* (Cambridge, Mass., 1960) is the most valuable.

Of the available studies of Russian political influence in Rumania, the most comprehensive is Nicolas Iorga, *Histoire des relations russo-roumaines* (Jassy, 1917), which takes the story to the end of the nineteenth century. Individual periods and problems are discussed in I. Cheban, "O vzaimootnosheniiakh Moldavii s Moskovskom gosudarstvom v XV–XVIII vekakh" ["On the Relations of Moldavia with the Muscovite State from the Fifteenth to the Eighteenth Centuries"], *Voprosy istorii* [*Problems of History*], No. 2 (Feb., 1945), 50–71; Jean C. Filitti, *Les Principautés roumaines sous l'occupation russe* (*1828–1834*), (Bucharest, 1904); Barbara Jelavich, *Russia and the Rumanian National Cause, 1858–1859* (Bloomington, 1959); S. Graur, *Les relations entre la Roumanie et l'U.R.S.S. depuis le traité de Versailles* (Paris, 1936); V. Fedorov, "Russkaia voennaia missiia v Romynii vo vremia mirovoi voiny 1914–1918 godov" ["The Russian Military Mission in Rumania during the World War of 1914–1918"], *Voprosy istorii* [*Problems of History*], No. 8 (Aug., 1947), 94–99; and C. G. Rakovsky, *Roumania and Bessarabia* (London, 1925).

There is no general study of Russian-Bulgarian relations, although the *Istoriia na Bulgariia* [*History of Bulgaria*], (Sofia, 1954–1955), 2 vols., by the Bulgarian Academy of Sciences, devotes much attention to this subject from the Communist point of view. Dimitŭr Iotsov, *Rusiia i Bulgariia* (*vchera, dnes i utre*), *Diplomaticheski studii* [*Russia and Bulgaria* (*Yesterday, Today, and Tomorrow*), *Diplomatic Studies*], (Sofia, 1940) discusses selected problems in the diplomatic relations of the two countries. General accounts of briefer scope include James F. Clarke, "Russia and Bulgaria, 1878–1944," *Journal of Central European Affairs*, V (January, 1946), 394–398; E. Grimm, "K istorii russko-bolgarskikh otnoshenii" ["Concerning the History of Russian-Bulgarian Relations"], *Novyi vostok* [*The New East*], V (1924), 68–85; and I. N.

Shabatin, "Iz istorii velikoi russko-bolgarskoi druzhby" ["From the History of the Great Russian-Bulgarian Friendship"], *Zhurnal moskovskoi Patriarkhii* [*Journal of the Moscow Patriarchate*], No. 12 (Dec., 1948), 45–56. A number of special studies deal with the events following the war of 1878: N. R. Ovsianyi, *Russkoe upravlenie v Bolgarii v 1877–78–79 gg.* [*The Russian Administration in Bulgaria in 1877–78–79*], (St. Petersburg, 1906); P. Pavlovich, ed., *Avantiury russkogo tsarizma v Bolgarii: Sbornik dokumentov* [*Adventures of Russian Tsarism in Bulgaria: Collection of Documents*], (Moscow, 1935); Khristo N. Gandev, "K izucheniiu deiatelnosti russkogo okupatsionnago upravleniia v Vostochnoi Rumelii 1878–1879 g.g." ["Toward the Study of the Activity of the Russian Occupation Administration in Eastern Rumelia in 1878–1879"], *Zapiski nauchno-izsledovatelskago obedineniia pri russkii svobodnyi universitet v Prage* [*Reports of the Scientific Research Association of the Russian Free University in Prague*], VI (1938), 43–86; S. Sidelnikov, "Avantiura russkogo tsarizma v Bolgariia, 1878–1896 gg." ["The Adventure of Russian Tsarism in Bulgaria, 1878–1896"], *Uchenyi zapiski Leningradskogo gosudarstvennago universiteta. Seriia istoricheskikh nauk* [*Studies of the Leningrad State University. Historical Science Series*], No. 36, issue 3 (1939), 145–80; J. J. Mikkola, "Einige Bemerkungen über die Tätigkeit General Casimir Ehrnrooths als Bulgarischer Staatsmann," *Sbornik v pamet na Profesor Petr Nikov* [*Symposium in Memory of Professor Peter Nikov*], (Sofia, 1939), 301–307; C. E. Black, *The Establishment of Constitutional Government in Bulgaria* (Princeton, 1943); P. K. Fortunatov, *Voina 1877–1878 gg. i osvobozhdenie Bolgarii* [*The War of 1877–1878 and the Liberation of Bulgaria*], (Moscow, 1950); V. Konobeev, "Russko-bolgarskoe boevoe sodruzhestvo v voine 1875–1877 godov" ["Russian-Bulgarian Military Collaboration in the War of 1875–1877"], *Voprosy istorii* [*Problems of History*], No. 10 (Oct., 1951), 42–64; L. B. Valev, S. A. Nikitin, and P. N. Tretiakov, eds., *Osvobozhedenie Bolgarii ot turetskogo iga: Sbornik statei* [*The Liberation of Bulgaria from the Turkish Yoke: Collection of Articles*], (Moscow, 1953); and S. A. Nikitin and others, eds., *Osvobozhdenie Bolgarii ot turetskogo iga* [*The Liberation of Bulgaria from the Turkish Yoke*], Vol. I (Moscow, 1961), of a projected three-volume series. Valuable treatments of other topics include Charles Jelavich, "Russo-Bulgarian Relations, 1892–1896: With Particular Reference to the Problem of the Bulgarian Succession," *Journal of Modern History*, XXIV (Dec., 1952), 341–351; and James F. Clarke, "The Russian Bible Society and the Bulgarians," *Harvard Slavic Studies*, III (1957), 67–104.

The most comprehensive study of Russian-Serbian relations deals with the first half of the nineteenth century: Nil Popov, *Rossiia i Serbiia: istoricheskii ocherk russkago pokrovitelstva Servii s 1806 po 1856* god [*Russia and Serbia: A Historical Account of the Russian Protectorship of Serbia from 1806 to 1856*], (2 vols.; Moscow, 1869). There are also a number of studies limited to special periods: S. K. Bogoiavlensky, "Iz russkoserbskikh otnoshenii pri Petre Pervom" ["From Russian-Serbian Relations in the Time of Peter I"], *Voprosy istorii* [*Problems of History*], No. 8–9 (Aug.–Sept., 1946), 19–24; S. K. Bogoiavlenskii, "Sviazi mezhdu russkimi i serbami v XVII–XVIII vv." ["Relations between Russians and Serbs in the Seventeenth and Eighteenth Centuries"], *Slavianskii sbornik* [*Slavic Symposium*], (Moscow, 1947), 241–261; Vaso Trivanovitch, "Serbia, Russia, and Austria during the Rule of Milan Obrenovich, 1868–78," *Journal of Modern History*, III (Sept., 1931), 414–440; Wayne S. Vucinich, *Serbia Between East and West: The Events of 1903–1908* (Stanford, 1954); Illija Jovanović, Stevan Rajković, and Beljko Ribar, *Jugoslovenski dobrovoljački korpus u Rosiji: prilog istoriji dobrovoljačkog pokreta 1914–1918* [*The Jugoslav Volunteer Corps in Russia: Contribution to the History of the Volunteer Movement 1914–1918*], (Belgrade, 1954). On the controversial question of Soviet-Jugoslav relations since 1945, several useful monographs and collections of documents are available: Royal Institute of International Affairs, *The Soviet-Yugoslav Dispute: Text of the Published Correspondence* (New York, 1949); Milovan Djilas, "Yugoslav-Soviet Relations," *International Affairs*, XXVII (1951), 167–175; Adam B. Ulam, *Titoism and the Cominform* (Cambridge, Mass., 1952); Robert B. Farrell, *Jugoslavia and the Soviet Union, 1948–1956* (Hamden, Conn., 1956); and Vaclav L. Benes, Robert F. Byrnes, and Nicolas Spulber, eds., *The Second Soviet-Yugoslav Dispute: Full Text of Main Documents, April–June, 1958, With An Introductory Analysis* (Bloomington, 1959).

Russian political influence in Greece does not appear to have received much separate attention, although it is extensively treated in general works on diplomatic history and the Eastern Question. O. Shparo, "Rol Rossii v borbe Gretsii za nezavisimost" ["The Role of Russia in the Struggle of Greece for Independence"], *Voprosy istorii* [*Problems of History*], No. 8 (Aug., 1949), 52–73; and A. M. Stanislavskaia, "Rossiia i Gretsiia v kontse XVIII—nachale XIX v. Iz istorii politiki Rossii na Ionicheskikh Ostrovakh (1798–1807)" ["Russia and Greece at the End of the Eighteenth and the Beginning of the Nineteenth Centuries. From the History of Russian Policy in the Ionian Islands (1798–1807)"], *Istoriia SSSR* [*History of the USSR*], (Jan.–Feb., 1960), 59–76, may be cited as examples of recent Soviet treatments of this problem. See also Barbara Jelavich, "Russia, Bavaria and the Greek Revolution of 1862/1863," *Balkan Studies*, II (July, 1961), 125–150. E. Adamov, *Evropeiskie derzhavy i Gretsiia v epokhu mirovoi voiny* [*The European States and Greece in the Period of the World*

War], (Moscow, 1922), is based on the archives of the Russian foreign office. On Albania, in this as in other matters, Stavro Skendi, ed., *Albania* (New York, 1946) is the best guide.

Ideological Influences.—In the Balkans, as in Russia, the question as to what program of modernization should be adopted has been the subject of an extensive literature throughout the period under consideration. Of particular interest were such questions as how the peoples of the Balkans should attempt to match the achievements of Central and Western Europe, and what was the relevance of the Russian experience in this regard. In discussing these issues it is not easy to draw a clear line between ideological and political influences, but the attempt has been made in this essay to restrict the latter to the establishment and control of political power. This leaves to the realm of ideology not only abstract speculation but also the programs of those in office and in opposition.

The three principal aspects of Russian ideological influence in the Balkans—conservative, liberal, and Marxist-Leninist—have received unequal treatment. The conservative influences which predominated in the earlier part of the nineteenth century have been the subject of relatively little separate attention as they have concerned the Balkans, despite the extensive literature on the more general aspects of the subject. The Russian setting in this influence has been treated most recently in the chapter on foreign policy in Nicholas Riasanovsky, *Nicholas I and Official Nationality in Russia, 1825–1855* (Berkeley and Los Angeles, 1959), 235–265; and for the later period in Michael B. Petrovich, *The Emergence of Russian Panslavism, 1856–1870* (New York, 1956). Two recent articles discuss the significance of Križanić, about whom a large literature exists: Michael B. Petrovich, "Juraj Križanić: A Precursor of Pan-Slavism," *American Slavic and East Europe Review*, VI (Dec., 1947), 75–92; and V. I. Picheta, "Iurii Krizhanich i ego otnoshenie k Russkomu gosudarstvu (1618–1683 gg.)" ["Juraj Križanić and His Relationship with the Russian State, 1618–1683], *Slavianskii sbornik* [*Slavic Symposium*], (Moscow, 1947), 202–240. There are also studies of the popular Bulgarian tradition of respect for Russia: I. Trifonov, "Istorichesko obiasnenie na verata v deda Ivan (Rusiia) u Bŭlgariskiia narod" ["A Historical Explanation of the Belief in Grandfather Ivan (Russia) on the Part of the Bulgarian People"], *Biblioteka na Slavianska beseda* [*Library of the Slavic Society*], III (1908), 26–56; and of the general problem of the influence of Russian absolutism on the southern Slavs: N. S. Derzhavin, "Russkii absoliutizm i iuzhnoe slavianstvo" ["Russian Absolutism and Southern Slavdom"], *Izvestiia Leningradskogo gosudarstvennogo universiteta* [*Bulletin of the Leningrad State University*], I (1928), 43–82. Conservative as well as liberal influences are discussed in two useful general interpretations of Bulgarian and Serbian thought in the nineteenth century: B. Mintses, "Dŭrzhavnopravnite i sotsialno-stopanskite idei v bŭlgarskata doosvoboditelna literature" ["Constitutional, Social, and Economic Ideas in Bulgarian Pre-Liberation Literature"], *Sbornik na narodni umotvoreniia, nauka, i knizhnina* [*Journal of Folklore, Education, and Literature*], XVI–XVII (1900), 3–58; and Traian Stoianovich, "The Pattern of Serbian Intellectual Evolution, 1830–1880," *Comparative Studies in Society and History,* I (March, 1959), 242–272; and a recent anthology of Croatian writings about Russia spans a considerable range of opinion: Josip Badalić, ed., *Hrvatska svjedočanstva o Rusiji* [*Croatian Accounts of Russia*], (Zagreb, 1945).

The earliest liberal influences from Russia may be traced to the Decembrists, whose plans for the Balkans are discussed in B. E. Syroechkovsky, "Balkanskaia problema v politicheskikh planakh Dekabristov" ["The Balkan Problem in the Political Plans of the Decembrists"], in N. M. Druzhinin and B. E. Syroechkovsky, eds., *Ocherki iz istorii dvizheniia Dekabristov: sbornik statei* [*Essays in the History of the Decembrist Movement: Collection of Articles*], (Moscow, 1954), 186–275. The direct impact of the Decembrists in Rumania is discussed in S. Vianu, "Quelques aspects de l'influence exercée par la pensée progressiste russe sur la société roumaine de la fin du XVIII⁰ siècle," *Nouvelles études d'histoire* (Bucharest, 1955), 285–297; S. Stirbu, "Les rapports de collaboration entre Tudor Vladimirescu et les movements de libération des pays de l'Est européen," *Nouvelles études d'histoire* (Bucharest, 1955), 313–339; and Alfred Roth, *Theodor Vladimirescu und die Orientpolitik: Der Beginn nationalrumänischer Entwicklung und die Haltung der Anrainergrossmächte Russland, Österreich und Türkei 1821–22* (Leipzig, 1943). Russian influences in Bulgaria in this period are treated in James F. Clarke, "Serbia and the Bulgarian Revival (1762–1872)," *American Slavic and East European Review,* IV (Dec., 1945), 141–162; and S. S. Bernshtein, "Stranitsa iz istorii bolgarskoi immigratsii v Rossiiu vo vremia russko-turetskoi voiny 1828–1829 gg." ["A Page from the History of the Bulgarian Immigration in Russia at the Time of the Russian-Turkish War of 1828–1829"], *Uchenye zapiski instituta slavianovedeniia Akademiia nauk SSSR* [*Studies of the Institute of Slavistics of the Academy of Sciences of the USSR*], I (1949), 327–341.

The influences on the southern Slavs of Russian populism and radicalism has been the subject of much study. The principal problem of interpretation is whether one is to regard this influence as an aspect of Western liberalism, joining with more powerful direct influences from the West to make up the characteristic Southern Slav liberalism of the latter part of the nineteenth century, or as a more distinctive and exclusive Russian influence foreshadowing the advent of Marxism-Leninism. The present essay shares the former view, but most of the work in this field has been done by Russian or Balkan scholars who

favor the latter interpretation. The evolution of this latter view through
the years is reflected in V. Bogucharsky [Iakovlev], "Revoliutsionnoe
dvizhenie sredi balkanskikh slavian, russko-turetskaia voina i otnoshenie
k etim sobytiiam russkikh sotsialistov" ["The Revolutionary Movement
among the Balkan Slavs, the Russian-Turkish War, and the Attitude
to These Events of the Russian Socialists"], Chap. IX in his *Aktivnoe
narodnichestvo semidesiatykh godov* [*Active Populism in the 1870's*],
(Moscow, 1912), 262–294; K. A. Pushkarevich, "Balkanskie slaviane
i russkie 'osvoboditeli.' (Slavianskie komitety i sobytiia na Balkanakh
pered russko-turetskoi voinoi 1877–1878 gg.)" ["The Balkan Slavs and
the Russian 'Liberators.' (The Slavic Committees and the Events in
the Balkans before the Russian-Turkish War of 1877–1878)"], *Trudy
instituta slavianovedeniia Akademiia nauk SSSR* [*Transactions of the
Institute of Slavistics of the Academy of Sciences of the USSR*], II
(1934), 189–229; L. Erikhonov, *Russkie revoliutsionnye demokraty i
obshchestvennaia mysl iuzhnykh slavian v 60–70kh godakh XIX veka
[The Russian Revolutionary Democrats and the Social Thought of the
Southern Slavs in the 1860's and 1870's*], (Moscow, 1950); and S. A.
Nikitin, "Iuzhnoslavianskie sviazy russkoi narodnicheskoi pechati 60–kh
godov XIX veka" ["South Slav Relations of the Russian Populist
Press in the 1860's"], *Uchenye zapiski instituta slavianovedeniia Akademiia nauk SSSR* [*Studies of the Institute of Slavistics of the Academy
of Sciences of the USSR*], VI (1952), 89–122.

As regards Bulgaria, the general subject of Russian liberal influences
is discussed in C. E. Black, *The Establishment of Constitutional Government in Bulgaria* (Princeton, 1943). A number of other studies
complement and revise this treatment: D. Sheludko, "Liuben Karavelov
i Ukraina" ["Liuben Karavelov and the Ukraine"], *Sbornik v chest na
Profesor Iv. D. Shishmanov* [*Symposium in Honor of Professor Ivan D.
Shishmanov*], (Sofia, 1920), 158–170; G. Bakalov, "Russkaia revoliutsionnaia emigratsiia sredi bolgar" ["The Russian Emigré Revolutionaries in Bulgaria"], *Katorga i ssylka* [*Penal Servitude and Exile*], LXIII
(1930), 114–137, LXIV (1930), 105–120; G. Bakalov, "Chernyshevskii
na Balkanakh" ["Chernyshevsky in the Balkans"], *Katorga i ssylka*
[*Penal Servitude and Exile*], CXIII (1934), 22–32; L. B. Valev, "So-
tsialno-politicheskie vozzrennia Khristo Boteva" ["The Social and Political Views of Khristo Botev"], *Uchenye zapiski instituta slavianovedeniia Akademiia nauk SSSR* [*Studies of the Institute of Slavistics of
the Academy of Sciences of the USSR*], II (1950), 95–105; and I. V.
Kozmenko, "Peterburgskii proekt Tyrnovskoi konstitutsii 1879 goda"
["The St. Petersburg Draft of the Tirnovo Constitution of 1879"],
Istoricheskii arkhiv [*Historical Archive*], IV (1949), 184–324. Russian
populist influence in later years is discussed in Vivian Pinto, "The
Civic and Aesthetic Ideals of Bulgarian Narodnik Writers," *Slavonic
and East European Review*, XXXII (June, 1954), 344–366, which

draws on the same author's doctoral dissertation on "The Narodnik Movement of Bulgarian Literature and the Influence on that Movement of Russian Thought" (University of London, 1952).

The best brief account for Serbia is the recent article by Professor Traian Stoianovich cited above. Those wishing to probe the subject further should turn to the extensive literature on Svetozar Marković and Serbian socialism. Four recent articles of particular relevance may be cited: Jean Mousset, "Le socialisme serbe a la croisée des chemins: Bakuninisme ou Marxisme?" *Revue des études slaves*, XXIII (1947), 102–119; E. N. Kusheva, "Iz russko-serbskikh revoliutsionnykh sviazei 1870-kh godov" ["Russian-Serbian Revolutionary Relations in the 1870's"], *Uchenye zapiski instituta slavianovedeniia Akademiia nauk SSSR* [*Studies of the Institute of Slavistics of the Academy of Sciences of the USSR*], I (1949), 343–358; I. D. Ivanov, "Dokumenty o russko-serbskikh revoliutsionnykh sviaziakh 80-kh godov XIX v." ["Documents on Russian-Serbian Revolutionary Relations in the 1880's"], *Kratkie soobshcheniia instituta slavianovedeniia Akademiia nauk SSSR* [*Brief Communications of the Institute of Slavistics of the Academy of Sciences of the USSR*], XIX (1956), 64–77; V. G. Karasev, "D. I. Pisarev i Svetozar Marković" ["D. I. Pisarev and Svetozar Marković"], *Kratkie soobshcheniia instituta slavianovedeniia Akademiia Nauk SSSR* [*Brief Communications of the Institute of Slavistics of the Academy of Sciences of the USSR*], IX (1952), 24–33.

Marxist-Leninist influences have been the subject of much writing in recent years, principally by Soviet and Balkan scholars. Rather than citing examples of this literature, it seems best to refer to appropriate guides. The literature on Bulgaria is discussed in meticulous detail in Joseph Rothschild, *The Communist Party of Bulgaria: Origins and Development, 1883–1936* (New York, 1959). The fullest guide to recent Jugoslav work in this field is Jorjo Tadić, ed., *Ten Years of Yugoslav Historiography, 1945–1955* (Belgrade, 1955). On Greece, Dimitrios G. Kousoulas, *The Greek Communist Party since 1918* (unpublished doctoral dissertation, Syracuse University, 1957) provides a valuable introduction. Useful bibliographies are also available in the handbooks prepared by the Mid-European Studies Center: Stavro Skendi, ed., *Albania* (New York, 1956), Stephen Fischer-Galati, ed., *Romania* (New York, 1957), L. A. D. Dellin, ed., *Bulgaria* (New York, 1957), and Robert F. Byrnes, ed., *Yugoslavia* (New York, 1957).

Economic Influence.—Russian economic influence in the Balkans before the Second World War was slight, and the literature on the subject is correspondingly small. Indeed, there appears to be no special study of this subject. The most useful references to Russian activity are in several studies of more general aspects of Balkan economic life: Radoslave M. Dimtschoff, *Das Eisenbahnwesen auf der Balkan-Halbinsel. Eine politisch-wirtschaftliche Studie* (Bamberg, 1894); Mirko

Lamer, "Die Wandlungen der ausländischen Kapitalanlagen auf dem
Balkan," *Weltwirtschaftliches Archiv*, XLVIII (Nov., 1938), 470–524;
John A. Levandis, *The Greek Foreign Debt and the Great Powers,
1821–1898* (New York, 1944); E. Zaleski, *Les courants commerciaux
de l'Europe danubienne au cours de la première moitié du XIXe siècle*
(Paris, 1952); and Nicolas Spulber, "The Role of the State in Economic Growth in Eastern Europe since 1860," in Hugh G. J. Aitken,
ed., *The State and Economic Growth* (New York, 1959), 255–286.

Much has been written, on the other hand, about Russian economic
influences since 1944. This literature can best be followed in three recent general studies of Eastern Europe: Nicolas Spulber, *The Economics of Communist Eastern Europe* (New York, 1957); Irwin T.
Sanders, ed., *Collectivization of Agriculture in Eastern Europe* (Lexington, 1958); and Jan Wszelaki, *Communist Economic Strategy: The
Role of East-Central Europe* (Washington, D.C., 1959); which cite
the extensive Soviet and Balkan literature in this field. The question
of the terms of Soviet-Balkan trade has been explored recently in two
articles by Horst Mendershausen, "Terms of Trade between the Soviet
Union and Smaller Communist Countries, 1955–1957," and "The Terms
of Soviet-Satellite Trade: a Broadened Analysis," in *Review of Economics and Statistics*, XLI (May, 1959), 106–118, and XLII (May,
1960), 152–163, respectively; and by Jan Wszelaki, "Soviet Price Discrimination in Export to East-Central Europe," *Assembly of Captive
European Nations*, Doc. 207 (VI) Econ. (June 7, 1960).

Cultural Influences.—General treatments of Russian cultural influence in the Balkans in modern times are scarce, although if one may
judge from the papers on Russian influence on the South Slav literatures summarized in *IV Mezhdunarodnyi s'ezd slavistov* [*Fourth International Congress of Slavists*], (Moscow, 1962), I, 79–469, special
studies of specific authors and topics are now sufficiently numerous to
permit the elaboration of a general interpretation. Suffice it here to cite
a few titles that were found useful for this essay. For Rumania: Eu-
phrosine Dvoičenko-Markoff, "L'influence de la littérature russe sur
la littérature roumaine," *Communications et Rapports. IIIème Congrès
International des Slavistes* (Belgrade, 1939), 92–96; Eufrosina Dvoi-
chenko-Markoff, "Puškin and the Rumanian Historical Legend," *American Slavic and East European Review*, VII (April, 1948), 144–149;
and Sergiu Farcasan, "Constantin Dobrogeanu-Gherea: A Prominent
Representative of Rumanian Literary Criticism," *Rumanian Review*,
IX (Fall, 1955), 57–73. Russian literary influences in Bulgaria are extensively discussed in Nicolai Dontcheff, *Inflences étrangères dans la
littérature bulgare* (Sofia, 1934), 9–79; and more generally in N. S.
Derzhavin, *Plemenni i kulturni vruzki mezhdu Bulgarskiia i Ruskiia
narod* [*Ethnic and Cultural Ties between the Bulgarian and Russian
Peoples*], (Sofia, 1945); and in D. F. Markov, "Problema genezisa

sotsialisticheskogo realizma v bolgarskoi literature" ["The Problem of the Genesis of Socialist Realism in Bulgarian Literature"], *Issledovaniia po slavianskomu literaturovedeniiu i stilistike* [*Studies in Slavic Literary Scholarship and Stylistics*], (Moscow, 1960), 338–375. In regard to Jugoslavia, two valuable articles by M. N. Speransky are: "K istorii vzaimnootnoshenii russkoi i iugoslavianskikh literatur" ["On the Inter-relations Between the Russian and the South Slav Literatures"], *Izvestiia otdeleniia russkogo iazyka i slovesnosti* [*Proceedings of the Department of Russian Language and Letters*], XXVI (1921), 143–206; and "K voprosu o russkom vliianii v serbskoi leterature XVIII veka" ["On the Question of Russian Influences in Serbian Literature in the Eighteenth Century"], *Trudy instituta slavianovedeniia AN SSSR* [*Transactions of the Institute of Slavistics of the Academy of Sciences of the USSR*], II (1934), 24–33. One may also cite N. I. Kravtsov, "Gogol i bolgarskaia literatura" ["Gogol and Bulgarian Literature"], *Kratkie soobshcheniia institut slavianovedeniia Akademiia Nauk SSSR* [*Brief Communications of the Institute of Slavistics of the Academy of Sciences of the USSR*], VIII (1952), 22–42; D. F. Markov, "Maiakovskii i bolgarskaia revoliutsionnaia poeziia" ["Maiakovsky and Bulgarian Revolutionary Poetry"], *Kratkie soobshchennia instituta slavianovedeniia Akademiia nauk SSSR* [*Brief Communications of the Institute of Slavistics of the Academy of Sciences of the USSR*], I (1951), 9–28; J. Badalić, "Der Einfluss Tolstojs auf die kroatische dramatische literatur," *Festschrift für Dmytro Čyževskij* (Berlin, 1954), 59–68; and E. D. Goy, "The attitude of the Serbs to Turgenev's works in the nineteenth century," *Slavonic and East European Review*, XXXVI (Dec., 1957), 123–49; as examples of Soviet and Western literary scholarship relating to individual authors. Russian influences in Greek literature are treated briefly in D. C. Hesseling, *Histoire de la littérature Grecque moderne* (Paris, 1924).

THE INFLUENCE OF THE WEST

ON THE BALKANS

L. S. Stavrianos

ANTI-WESTERNISM OF BALKAN ORTHODOXY

The encounter between the West and the great non-Western majority of mankind seems likely to be viewed in retrospect as the central feature of modern history. The expansion of the West, and the response to that expansion, appear, at present at least, to be the unifying historical theme of the half millennium between the fifteenth and the twentieth centuries.

In the Balkan Peninsula the dynamism of the West assumes particular significance because it represents a reversal of the traditional historical pattern. Until modern times it was the Balkan peoples who provided leadership and the Westerners who were the "natives." In the first century B.C., for example, Greek traders used wine in northern and western Europe in the same manner that the Westerners later were to use rum and gin in Africa and the Americas. A contemporary Greek historian, Diodorus Siculus, describes how cheaply the Celts sold captives to get wine, "exchanging a servant for a drink." Thirteen centuries later, when the Westerners began their siege of Constantinople in 1203, they were awe-struck by the wealth and the magnificence of that ancient capital.

Those who had not seen [Constantinople] before, could not believe that there could be in all the world so rich a city. When they saw those high walls and those mighty towers with which it was surrounded, and those rich palaces and lofty churches, of which there

---

The author is indebted to the Carnegie Corporation of New York for financial assistance in conducting research in World History. This research greatly facilitated the preparation of this essay.

were so many that no man could believe it unless he had seen it with his own eyes; and when they beheld the length and the breadth of the city, which of all others was the sovereign, know well that there was no man so bold that his flesh did not creep, and this was no wonder that he was aghast for never was so great an undertaking entered upon by human beings since the world was created.[1]

About the fifteenth century A.D. this traditional relationship between the Balkans and the West began to be reversed. The first portent of what the future held in store is to be found in a letter written in 1444 by the Greek scholar, Cardinal Bessarion. Having lived many years in Rome, he was impressed by the advanced state of handicrafts in Italy. So he wrote to Constantine Palaeologos, then ruler of the autonomous Byzantine province of Peloponnesus (Morea), suggesting that "four or eight young men" be sent to Italy surreptitiously to learn Italian craft skills, and to learn Italian "so as to be conversant with what is said." Bessarion was particularly impressed by the water-driven saw mills which eliminated hand labor. He referred to "wood cut by automatic saws, mill wheels moved as quickly and as neatly as can be." Likewise he had in mind water-driven bellows when he wrote that "in the smelting and separation of metals they have leather bellows which are distended and relaxed untouched by any hand, and separate the metal from the useless and earthy matter that may be present." Bessarion also reported that in Italy "one may easily acquire knowledge of the making of iron, which is so useful and necessary to Man." The significance of this testimony is apparent. The technological advances made by medieval Western Europe had been of such magnitude that for the first time an Easterner was recommending that pupils should be sent to the West to learn the "practical arts."[2]

Bessarion's advice was not followed by his countrymen. Only a decade later their long-threatened capital, Constantinople, fell to the advancing Turks. Rather than going to school in the West, the Greeks and their Balkan fellow Christians now sank into oblivion as subject provincials of the Ottoman sultan. During the following centuries the Balkan peoples were to a considerable degree isolated, like the Russians during their period of Mongol domination.

---

[1] Mailhard de la Couture, ed., *Chroniques de Villehardouin et de Henri de Valenciennes, De la Conquete de Constantinople* (Paris, 1889), pp. 63–64.

[2] A. G. Keller, "A Byzantine Admirer of 'Western' Progress: Cardinal Bessarion," *Cambridge Historical Journal,* XI (1955), 343–348.

The iron curtain that cut off the Balkan Christians cannot be attributed exclusively to the Ottoman conquest. The profound anti-Westernism of the Orthodox Church also was in large part responsible. This anti-Westernism had its roots in the protracted conflict between pope and patriarch, in the barbarities of the Fourth Crusade, and in the merciless stranglehold of the Italian merchants on Byzantium's economy. Echoes of this anti-Westernism persist to the present day, as is attested by the Greek folk-saying:

Κάλλιο τοῦ Τούρκου τὸ σπαθὶ
παρὰ τοῦ Φράγκου τὸ ψωμὶ

[Better the sword of the Turk
than the bread of the Frank.]

After the fall of Constantinople, Mohammed II encouraged the perpetuation of this anti-Western sentiment by selecting for the patriarchal seat a strong enemy of the Latin church, Gennadius Scholarius. At the same time the liberal-minded Greek leaders were tending to emigrate to the West, leaving the conservatives entrenched. Thus Gennadius and most of his successors freely opposed the West as the home of Catholicism and Protestantism and as the birthplace of the Renaissance. They rejected vigorously everything the Renaissance represented—the exaltation of reason in place of dogma, the turn to Greek antiquity, and the preference for Plato to Aristotle. In fact, Gennadius anathematized the contemporary Greek philosopher, Pletho, precisely because he was a neo-Platonist and a champion of reason as against revelation. In short, Balkan Orthodoxy opposed the West not only because it was heretical but also because it was becoming modern.

The hostility of Balkan Orthodoxy to the West might be compared with the campaign of Russian Orthodoxy against Peter the Great. In fact, Patriarch Dositheus of Jerusalem actively fought against the tsar's Westernization program and particularly against his plan for an Academy of Sciences organized on Western lines. The Orthodox leaders failed in Russia because in that country the state power was arrayed against them. But in the Balkan Peninsula the government consisted of Ottoman officials who were uninterested, and of Orthodox bishops who were as much prefects as prelates and who comprised an integral element in Ottoman administration. There was no counterpart in the Balkans to the dynamic Westernization drive of the top government circles in Russia. Consequently the Orthodox hierarchy remained the masters of a Balkan theocracy during the centuries following 1453. One illustration was the execution of Patriarch Cyril Loukaris in 1638 when he collaborated with the Protestants and attempted, like Peter the Great, to open a window to the West. Another illustration, at a less exalted, grass roots, level, is the experience of a Croatian Franciscan monk who was sent in the mid-seventeenth century to convert the Serbians. The Franciscan reported a long discussion concerning the union of the churches with a Serbian monk, Gavrilo. The latter, when pushed to the wall, finally ended the conversation with the remark, "What you say is true, but I would rather become a Turk than join you Latins who hate and persecute us."[3] Little had changed between the mid-fifteenth and mid-seventeenth centuries.

ORIGINS AND PATTERN OF THE WESTERNIZATION PROCESS

Beneath the surface, however, the West by the seventeenth century was unobtrusively undermining the foundations of Balkan Orthodoxy. Despite the opposition of both church and government, Western forces were impinging on the peninsula, as they were to do later on other parts of the globe. At the risk of oversimplification, these forces may be defined as the economic, the scientific, and the political revolutions, which galvanized first Europe and then the rest of the world.

The economic, or more specifically, the Commercial Revolution, followed a well-known sequence of agrarian, commercial, industrial, and financial developments. These altered basically Europe's economy, and made it possible for the West to exploit the opportunities presented by the Discoveries. The Europeans gained control over world-trade routes and became the middlemen of a new global trade, as the Arabs and Italians had been of the earlier Eurasian commerce. This trade on a world-wide scale affected appreciably the domestic economies of many regions of the globe, including the Balkans. We shall see later that the impact during this commercial era was not as pro-

---

[3] Cited by L. Hadrovics, *Le peuple serbe et son église sous la domination turque* (Paris: Presses universitaires de France, 1947), p. 25.

found as in the later industrial period. Yet, in the Balkan Peninsula at least, it was sharp enough to set off a chain reaction with far-reaching repercussions.

The West's scientific revolution also affected profoundly the Balkans and the entire globe. It did so because it provided the foundation for not only the technological and military predominance of the West, but also for the intellectual. Being based on an objective methodology, science is universal and has secured general assent to its propositions. It is the one product of Western civilization that the non-Western peoples generally respect and seek. As Herbert Butterfield has noted, "when we speak of Western civilization being carried to an oriental country like Japan in recent generations, we do not mean Graeco-Roman philosophy and humanist ideals, we do not mean the Christianizing of Japan, we mean the science, the modes of thought and all that apparatus of civilization which were beginning to change the face of the West in the latter half of the seventeenth century." [4] The same point can be made concerning the Balkans. There science provided an intellectual meeting point with the West in place of the earlier intellectual deadlock. So long as Western civilization was essentially Catholic or Protestant, it was unacceptable to Orthodox peoples. When it became primarily scientific and secular, it was acceptable, and even desirable, to a constantly growing proportion of the population. Arnold Toynbee has observed in this connection that,

In the fifteenth century, Orthodox Christians had acquiesced in the political domination of the Muslim Osmanlis as a less odious alternative than a reception of the Western Christian way of life in the then current religious terms of acknowledging the ecclesiastical supremacy of the Pope. Toward the close of the seventeenth century the descendants of these same Orthodox Christians eagerly inscribed themselves as pupils in a new-model Western school in which Technology had been substituted for Theology as the obligatory principal subject. This revolution in the Orthodox Christian attitude toward the West [came] in response to the West's own revolutionary revaluation of traditional Western spiritual values. [5]

---

[4] H. Butterfield, *The Origins of Modern Science 1300–1800* (London: G. Bell, 1957), p. 179.

[5] A. J. Toynbee, *A Study of History* (London: Oxford University Press, 1954), VIII, 119–120.

Finally the West's political revolution also left its imprint on the Balkans and the entire globe. The essence of the political revolution was the ending of the concept of a divinely ordained division of humanity into rulers and ruled. No longer was government regarded as above the people, and the people as below the government. The political revolution resulted for the first time in history in the identification of government and people—the awakening and activation of the masses so that they not only participated in government but also considered it their inherent right to do so. This political revolution got under way with the English Revolution in the seventeenth century, developed much further with the American and French revolutions that followed, and then affected the whole of Europe during the nineteenth century, and the entire globe during the twentieth. De Tocqueville perceived the international nature of the political revolution when he wrote:

The French Revolution had no territory of its own; indeed, its effect was to efface, in a way, all older frontiers. It brought men together, or divided them, in spite of laws, traditions, character and language, turning enemies sometimes into compatriots, and kinsmen into strangers; or, rather, it formed, above all particular nationalities, an intellectual common country of which men of all nations might become citizens.[6]

These economic, scientific and political revolutions gave Western Europe its distinctive dynamism and thereby made it possible for this hitherto insignificant peninsula of the Eurasian land mass to transform the entire globe at an ever accelerating speed. The general manner in which this Westernization process operated has been described by Sir Henry Maine, the English jurist and historian who served in India between 1862 and 1869:

It is by indirect and for the most part unintended influence that the British power [in India] metamorphoses and dissolves the ideas and social forms underneath it, nor is there any expedient by which it can escape the duty of rebuilding upon its own principles that which it unwillingly destroyed. . . . We do not destroy in mere arrogance. We

---

[6] Cited by R. R. Palmer, The Age of the Democratic Revolution: A Political History of Europe and America, 1760–1800 (Princeton: Princeton University Press, 1959), p. 11. This study emphasizes the international aspects of the democratic revolution; see especially chap. i.

rather change because we cannot help it. Whatever be the nature and value of that bundle of influences which we call Progress, nothing can be more certain than that, when a society is once touched by it, it spreads like a contagion.[7]

This automatic and self-perpetuating feature of Westernization is evident in the Balkans as well as in India. We shall now see that the more the West intruded, the more it engendered new conditions and new social groups that demanded still further Westernization.

WESTERN INFLUENCE DURING THE OTTOMAN PERIOD

One of the earliest significant effects of the West upon the Balkan Peninsula was the introduction of some material goods which proceeded unobtrusively throughout the Ottoman period despite the anti-Westernism of Orthodoxy and Islam. The most important of these was corn, which appeared in the seventeenth century, and cotton, which was present earlier, though it did not become important in the Greek and Macedonian economies until the early eighteenth century. (It is undetermined whether cotton originally came from the West.) The new crops contributed to the rise of the onerous *chiflik* landholding system, which gradually replaced the more liberal *timar* system that had been established at the time of the Conquest. The cultivation of cotton and corn quickly spread over the Balkan plains areas (Durazzo plains, Epirote plain in Arta, Albanian coastal plains, Danubian Principalities, and the Peloponnesus) in response to the growing demand of Western cities for foodstuffs, and of Western industries for cotton. The resulting drive for maximum production of the new agricultural goods created a powerful incentive to scrap the old *timars* in which the peasant had enjoyed hereditary rights and the spahi had been limited to certain specified revenues. In their place arose the *chifliks*, which were the heritable and private property of their owners, and which depressed the formerly free cultivators to virtual serfdom. Consequently the *chifliks* allowed uncontrolled exploitation of the peasantry for the production of export commodities.

The expanding economy of Western Europe affected not only the

---

[7] Cited by G. Wint, *The British in Asia* (New York: Institute of Pacific Relations, 1954), pp. 53-54.

landholding system but also commerce and handicrafts. The exportation of the maize and cotton stimulated the growth of a class of native Balkan merchants and mariners. Foreign merchants and shipping conducted much of the export business but a considerable share fell to the new entrepreneurs. The result was the rapid rise of the Dubrovnik (Ragusan), Dulcignote, and Greek merchant fleets, and also the enrichment of the Greek and Macedonian merchants who controlled much of the overland trade up the Danube Valley into Central Europe. Furthermore the Anglo-French wars of the eighteenth and early nineteenth centuries disrupted commerce in the Mediterranean and ruined the Western merchants who had established themselves in various Balkan ports and had monopolized the overseas trade. Local merchants promptly took the place of the Westerners and exported Balkan products through overland trade channels into Central Europe. At first the Greeks, Jews, and Vlachs controlled most of the trade, but gradually the Serbs and Bulgars also participated in it.

The expansion of trade in turn stimulated the demand and the output of handicraft products. Important manufacturing centers appeared in various parts of the peninsula, frequently in isolated mountain areas where the artisans could practice their crafts with a minimum of Turkish interference. In Bulgaria and Greece particularly, village artisans turned out substantial quantities of woolen and cotton thread and textiles, stockings, clothes, carpets, silks, and furs. Most of the output was marketed within the empire, but certain products were also exported to foreign countries, mostly in Central Europe. The rise of commerce and industry stimulated the growth of a merchant marine. The most important maritime centers were along the Dalmatian coast (Trieste, Fiume or Rijeka, Senj, Spalato or Split, Carlobago or Karlopag, Ragusa or Dubrovnik, and Cattaro or Kotor), the Albanian and Epirote coast (Durazzo, Parga, Arta, and Preveza) and the Greek littoral and islands (Hydra, Spetsai, Psara, Galaxidi, and Crete). The new merchant marine exported Balkan products such as cotton, maize and other grains, dyeing materials, wine, oil, and fruits, especially currants. In return they brought back mostly manufactured goods and colonial products, particularly spices, sugar, woolens, glass, watches, guns, and gunpowder.

These developments in agriculture, commerce, and industry created a new Balkan world that was responsive to Western science and secularism. Or, to use Sir Henry Maine's words, Western influence now spread through Balkan society "like a contagion." This Western influence no longer was dependent upon its "bridgeheads" in Slovenia, Croatia and the Italian-held Greek islands. For centuries these outlying regions under Western rule had played a vital role as channels for communication and interaction. But now the initiative came from within the Turkish-ruled Balkans. The rising class of merchants, artisans, and mariners had a different attitude toward the West from that of the hitherto dominant Orthodox prelates. Some of these new elements had lived in Western cities where they usually were favorably impressed by the political institutions, the rule of law, the economic prosperity, and the intellectual life. Far from branding this Western civilization as "Latin" and therefore heretical and repugnant, they viewed it as a model to be imitated. While the Orthodox churchmen dismissed Western scientists as *antitheoi* or antitheists, and their teachings as *morosophia* or foolish wisdom, Adamantios Korais referred repeatedly to *Photismenē*, or "Enlightened," Europe. The latter viewpoint gradually became more acceptable, partly because of the undeniable advances of the West, but also because of the deterioration of the position of the Church. This involved, among other things, the secularization of the Patriarchate through the intervention of the Phanariotes, the tendency to regard the higher clergy as collaborators of the Ottoman regime, the decline in the quantity and quality of the Orthodox priests in some regions, and the abolition of the Patriarchate of Peć which alienated most Serbians.

The new positive attitude to the West led merchants throughout the Balkans to seek to bring Europe's Enlightenment to their enslaved and benighted countrymen. The Serbian merchants in southern Hungary, the Bulgarian merchants in southern Russia and the Danubian Principalities, and the Greek merchants scattered widely in foreign cities such as Trieste, Venice, Vienna, Budapest, Bucharest, and Odessa, all contributed greatly to the awakening of their countries. They did so by bestowing upon their native towns and villages lavish gifts of books, equipment, and money. Frequently they financed the education of young fellow countrymen in foreign universities. In addition they made possible the publication of books and newspapers in their native languages, and also the translation of the works of Voltaire, Locke, Rousseau, Descartes, Leibnitz, and others.

All this activity meant not only more education but a new type of education. It was no longer primarily religious. Instead it was deeply influenced by the West's Enlightenment. Amongst the Serbs, for example, we find Dositej Obradović, who declared in 1771 that he was beginning the writing of his adventures with two aims in mind:

First, to show the uselessness of monasteries for society; and second, to show the great need for sound learning, as the most effective method of freeing men from superstition and of guiding them to a true reverence for God, to rational piety and to enlightened virtue, whereby a man gifted with reason enters on the true path of his temporal and his eternal welfare.[8]

Likewise the contemporary Greek educator, Adamantios Korias, described to his countrymen the wonders of Paris, which he contrasted with the sad state of his homeland:

I have been in the celebrated city of Paris since the 24 of May [1788], the home of arts and science, the Athens of today. Imagine a city, much larger than Constantinople, with 800,000 people, all sorts of academies, public libraries, where science and art have been developed to perfection, where learned men are to be seen all over the city, in boulevards, market places, cafes, etc. In the latter place you will find political and literary newspapers written in German, English, and French, and in all other languages. . . . Such, my friends, is Paris. . . . all these blessings exist no longer in Greece but have instead been replaced by myriad evils. . . . instead of a Miltiades and Themistocles, whom Europe still admires, we are governed by scoundrels and stupid men as well as by an ignorant clergy who are even worse than our foreign tyrants the Turks.

The only way to national rebirth, Korais advised his fellow Greeks was to follow the example of the enlightened West.

What we have learned hitherto is good, and we ought to be grateful to those who taught it, since they taught everything they knew. But the present state of Hellas demands something better, more systematic, more profound, more useful; and this, without doubt, is to be found in the learning of Europe, which many of our intellectual heroes have acquired not long since.[9]

---

[8] Cited by G. P. Noyes, ed., *The Life and Adventures of Dimitrije Obradović* (Berkeley and Los Angeles: University of California Press, 1953), p. 23.

[9] Cited by S. G. Chaconas, *Adamantios Korais: A Study in Greek Nationalism* (New York: Columbia University Press, 1942), p. 28.

These economic and intellectual developments inevitably had political repercussions, as the "contagion" of Westernization spread still further through the Balkan world. The merchants who subsidized the translation of Locke or Newton or Voltaire were likely to support also movements for political liberation. It is no mere coincidence that Greek merchants organized the revolutionary Philike Hetaeria; that pig dealers were prominent in the Serbian revolt; and that "the history of the Bulgarian national revival is the history of the craft guilds."[10]

Behind this leadership provided by the merchants was the essential support of the peasants who became increasingly disaffected with the spread of the *chifliks*. In fact, a direct relationship exists between the growth of the *chiflik* system and the incidence of peasant revolts. Closely related to the peasant unrest was the armed resistance of the outlaws, known as *haiduts* in Bulgaria, *hajduks* in Serbia and *klephts* in Greece. Driven to desperation by the extortion and exploitation arising from the breakdown of Ottoman administration and the spread of *chifliks*, the bolder peasants took to the mountains and forests. These outlaws, for the most part, had no political consciousness or ideology, except where they were exposed to outside influences and ideas. But they did create a tradition of resistance and kept alive the idea of justice and freedom. They also provided a ready-made fighting force when various factors which they scarcely comprehended culminated in the series of national uprisings in the nineteenth century.

It was this combination of economic, intellectual, and political developments that made the Balkan peoples susceptible to Europe's ideologies and revolutions. The English and American revolutions were too remote to exert much influence, but the French Revolution, and Napoleon's exploits, struck a responsive chord in the new Balkans. Despite the relative isolation of the peninsula, revolutionary ideas and literature did seep in through various channels. The uprisings in Paris and the spectacular successes of French arms made the people more restless, more independent, and more determined to win their freedom.

Furthermore, all the powers in the Balkans during this period enrolled in their armies a number of recruits from the local populations.

---

[10] J. F. Clarke, "Bible Societies, American Missionaries, and the National Revival of Bulgaria" (Harvard University, unpublished doctoral dissertation, 1937), p. 118.

This military service under the French, British, and Russian flags was quite significant, opening new horizons for the recruits as well as instructing them in military techniques. For example, Sir Richard Church, who organized a regiment of the Duke of York's Greek Light Infantry while stationed in the Ionian Islands, reported on November 12, 1811, that he had been able to transform his men "from the most lawless of mankind, not only into good soldiers, but also into praiseworthy members of civilized society. . . . The number of recruits that flock to me from all parts of Greece is really extraordinary." [11] A contemporary Greek revolutionary described the over-all impact of the French Revolution upon the Balkan peoples as follows:

The French Revolution in general awakened the minds of all men. . . . All the Christians of the Near East prayed to God that France should wage war against the Turks, and they believed that they would be freed. . . . But when Napoleon made no move, they began to take measures for freeing themselves.[12]

Similar is the testimony of another Greek revolutionary, the colorful Theodore Kolokotronis, who, after being a klepht in the Peloponnesus, served under the British in the Ionian Islands and then played a leading role in the Greek war of independence:

According to my judgment, the French Revolution and the doings of Napoleon opened the eyes of the world. The nations knew nothing before, and the people thought that kings were gods upon the earth and that they were bound to say that whatever they did was well done. Through this present change it is more difficult to rule the people.[13]

We may conclude from the above that, in various direct and indirect ways, the economic, scientific, and political revolutions that transformed Western Europe also transformed the Turkish-ruled Balkans. The result was the passing of the age of theocracy and the advent of a new age of secular and national ideas and aspirations. This change made possible the appearance of revolutionary leaders like Rhigas, Karadjordje, Vladimirescu, and Rakovsky. It also led to the appearance during the course of the nineteenth century of a patchwork of nation-

---

[11] S. Lane-Poole, *Sir Richard Church* (London, 1890), p. 27.

[12] Ch. Photios [Chrysanthopoulos], *Apomnemoneumata peri tes Hellenikes epanastaseos* [*Memoirs of the Greek Revolution*], (Athens, 1899), I, 1.

[13] T. Kolokotrones and E. M. Edmonds, *Kolokotrones: Klepht and Warrior* (London, 1892), pp. 127–28.

states in the Balkan Peninsula that replaced the multinational empire of the sultans.

The several Balkan states did not appear simultaneously as the outcome of a coördinated peninsular revolution against Ottoman rule. Instead a series of independent uprisings spread over the whole of the nineteenth century. And in place of common effort there was continual rivalry and occasional open conflict. One reason for this dissension was that the speed of national revival varied greatly from people to people. Probably the most important single factor explaining the difference in speed was the degree of contact with, and influence by, the West. It is not accidental that the Greeks, with their unequaled commercial and cultural ties with the West, came first, and that the Serbians followed next because of their pig dealers and their numerous fellow countrymen across the Danube. The Rumanians lagged behind because the sharp stratification of their society and the commanding role of foreign elements in their administrative and economic affairs combined to minimize the impact of the West on the Rumanian people themselves. The Bulgarians were retarded because their geographic location hampered direct ties with the West, and the Albanians were virtually immune to Western influences until the twentieth century because of their primitive tribal organization and their religious divisions.

WESTERN INFLUENCE DURING THE NATIONAL PERIOD

The establishment of independent Balkan states during the nineteenth century did not mean the end of Western influence. Indeed the nineteenth century witnessed the high point of the West's impact, not only upon the Balkan Peninsula, but upon the entire globe. It was during this period that Europe's dynamism and expansionism was omnipotent and unchallenged. The world-wide repercussions are reflected in the striking differences between a map of the globe in, say, 1763, and one of the globe in 1914. In the earlier year, Europe's possessions in Eurasia were limited to insignificant coastal toeholds in Africa, India, and Southeast Asia. But by 1914 the European powers ruled directly the Indian subcontinent and almost the whole of Africa and Southeast Asia. In addition, they exerted decisive indirect control over the Far

East and Middle East through the familiar combination of extraterritoriality, capitulations, financial loans, debt commissions, spheres of influence, concessions, military missions, and, when necessary, gunboat diplomacy.

All this represented the high tide of European imperialism. The point that concerns us here is that this was a new type of imperialism. It differed fundamentally from all previous forms, which had exploited the colonies but had left their cultures basically unaffected. Tribute had shifted from one ruling group to another, but economies and institutions had remained essentially the same. The new imperialism, by contrast, engendered a thorough transformation of the subject territories. As Sir Henry Maine pointed out, this was not so much deliberate policy as it was the multifold and continuous impact of the dynamic industrialism of Western Europe upon the static, self-contained agrarian regimes of Africa and Asia.

This impact affected all aspects of the subordinate cultures: their traditional values and ways of thinking as well as their economic and social organization. When the Europeans first began their overseas expansion they were looked down upon as uncouth barbarians by Confucian mandarins, Hindu pundits and Muslim kadis. But before the end of the nineteenth century, Chinese students were studying in Europe, the Tanzimat movement was winning support in the Ottoman Empire, and the venerable Rammohun Roy in India was petitioning the English governor-general for "a liberal and enlightened system of instruction, embracing mathematics, natural philosophy, chemistry, anatomy, with other useful sciences, which may be accomplished . . . by employing a few gentlemen of talent and learning educated in Europe." [14] In short, the whole world, in varying proportions, feared, respected, admired, and imitated Europe, and it did so not only because of Europe's gunboats, factories, and bankers, but also for her science, schools, and political philosophies.

Arminius Vambery has described vividly, from first-hand observation, how crushing and all-pervasive was Europe's grip upon the globe:

When, comfortably seated in our well-upholstered railway carriage, we gaze upon the Hyrkanian Steppe, upon the terrible deserts of

---

[14] Cited by W. T. de Bary, ed., Sources of Indian Tradition (New York: Columbia University Press, 1958), p. 595.

Karakum and Kisilkum, we can scarcely realize the terrors, the sufferings, and the privations, to which travellers formerly were exposed.
. . . And great changes similar to those which have taken place in
Central Asia may also be noticed in greater or less degree in other
parts and regions of the Eastern world: Siberia, West and North China,
Mongolia, Manchuria, and Japan, were in the first half of the nineteenth century scarcely known to us, and . . . we now find that the
supreme power of the Western world is gradually making itself felt.
The walls of seclusion are ruthlessly pulled down, and the resistance
caused by the favoured superstitions, prejudices, and the ignorance of
the sleepy and apathetic man in the East, is slowly being overcome.
. . . present-day Europe, in its restless, bustling activity will take good
care not to let the East relapse again into its former indolence. We
forcibly tear its eyes open; we push, jolt, toss, and shake it, and we
compel it to exchange its world-worn, hereditary ideas and customs
for our modern views of life; nay, we have even succeeded to some
extent in convincing our Eastern neighbours that our civilisation, our
faith, our customs, our philosophy, are the only means whereby the
well-being, the progress, and the happiness, of the human race can be
secured.

For well-nigh 300 years we have been carrying on this struggle with
the Eastern world, and persist in our unsolicited interference, following
in the wake of ancient Rome, which began the work with marked per-
severance, but naturally never met with much success because of the
inadequate means at its disposal. . . . We may admire the splendour,
the might, and the glory of ancient Rome, we may allow that the glitter
of its arms struck terror and alarm into the furthest corners of Asia;
but in spite of all that, it would be difficult to admit that the civilising
influence of Rome was ever more than an external varnish, a transitory
glamour. Compared with the real earnest work done in our days by
Western Powers, the efforts of Rome are as the flickering of an oil-lamp
in comparison with the radiance of the sun in its full glory. It may be
said without exaggeration that never in the world's history has one continent exercised such influence over another as has the Europe of our
days over Asia.[15]

This brief survey of Europe's global impact in the nineteenth century provides the necessary background for the Westernization process
in the Balkans during the national period. What happened in the
Balkan Peninsula represents a microcosm of a world-wide process,
though, as we shall note later, there were local variations.

---

[15] Arminius Vambery, *Western Culture in Eastern Lands* (London: J. Murray,
1906), pp. 1–4.

The Balkans, like other regions of the globe, was vitally affected by Western diplomacy. In fact, the so-called Eastern Question, which runs like a red thread through European diplomatic history, was essentially the question of how the European powers should divide amongst themselves the Balkan territories of the declining sultan. But the several powers that had designs on the Balkan lands neutralized each other in the long run. In the Indian Ocean, the British navy was unchallenged and so the whole of the Indian peninsula fell under British rule. But the Balkan Peninsula was vulnerable not only to British warships but also to French warships and to Austrian and Russian land forces. Consequently the Balkan Peninsula was never taken over by any one of the European powers. It was not even partitioned amongst the eastern empires, as Catherine the Great and Joseph II had planned, and as did happen to Poland. Instead, only the outlying provinces and islands were nibbled away and held for periods varying from a few years to two centuries. The remainder of the peninsula, which was the heartland of the Balkan peoples, continued under the inefficient and weakening Ottoman rule. This explains why Serbs and Greeks and Rumanians won their autonomy or independence during the first part of the nineteenth century, while the Croats and Slovenes and Transylvanians remained under foreign rule until the First World War.

If the European powers did not annex the Balkan countries outright, they did influence decisively their foreign relations. This is reflected in the existence, at various periods, of "French," "British," "Russian," and "Austrian" political parties in the Balkan capitals. Also, at certain times, individual powers dominated some Balkan states, as when Serbia was Austria's "Tunis," or when Sir Edmund Lyons, British minister to Athens, declared in 1841: "A Greece truly independent is an absurdity. Greece is Russian or she is English; and since she must not be Russian, it is necessary that she be English."[16] The manner in which the powers strove to gain their diplomatic goals in the Balkans varied, according to circumstances, from troop crossings of the Danube and blockading of ports, to closing of markets to Balkan exports and granting or withholding of loans.

Turning from the diplomatic to the socioeconomic aspects of the

---

[16] Cited by L. Bower and G. Bolitho, *Otho I: King of Greece* (London: Selwyn and Blount, 1939), p. 106.

West's intrusion, the first point to note is the remarkable population increase in the Balkans from the early nineteenth century onward. Greater security probably explains the growth at the outset, but after 1878 it was caused by rising income and by a fall in the death rate brought about by the spread of Western medical knowledge and hygiene. Thus the Balkans now passed through the same phase of sharp population growth that Western Europe experienced a century earlier, and for the same reasons. The population of Serbia rose from 1,700,000 in 1878 to 3,020,000 in 1914, while that of Bulgaria, including Eastern Rumelia, increased from 2,820,000 in 1881 to 4,330,000 in 1911. Over a longer period the population of Moldavia and Wallachia rose from 1,500,000 in 1815 to 7,200,000 in 1912, and that of Greece from 750,000 in 1829 to 2,750,000 in 1912. The area of the latter country had increased somewhat in the interval, but the population per square mile jumped from 41 to 114, an almost threefold increase in less than a century.

This population spurt continued unchecked during the twentieth century. The inevitable result was growing population pressure on the arable land. The extensive land reforms following the First World War gave some relief, but only in some districts and for a short period. The accompanying table shows that by the 1930's the population pressure per unit of arable land was much greater in the Balkans than in most Western European countries.

This population pressure affected fundamentally the character of Balkan agriculture. It caused the small peasant plots to be divided and redivided among the numerous sons, to the point where most holdings in each Balkan country became too small to support a family. This meant that the Balkan countryside in the interwar period suffered from severe overpopulation: more people were engaged in agriculture than were needed for the prevailing type of cultivation. It has been estimated that in 1930 61.5 percent of the rural population in Jugoslavia was "surplus," 53 percent in Bulgaria, 51.4 percent in Rumania, and 50.3 percent in Greece. Furthermore this was a chronic problem; it did not represent passing unemployment as in the Western countries during the depression years. In other words, the majority of the people in the Balkan villages simply were not needed. In fact, they were an outright burden. If perchance they had disappeared overnight, the

DEMOGRAPHIC AND ECONOMIC INDICES OF BALKAN AND
SELECTED WESTERN EUROPEAN STATES IN THE INTERWAR PERIOD

Country	Average annual interwar population growth in percent[a]	Population density per square kilometer[b]	Percent of population dependent on agriculture[c] ca. 1938	Density per "arable-equivalent" land,[d] ca. 1930[e]
Greece	1.93	48	60	86.7
Jugoslavia	1.43	56	75	100.1
Bulgaria	1.30	59	80	95.4
Rumania	1.27	61	78	79.7
Italy	0.85	133	44	53.4
Germany	0.67	139	20	52.1
England and Wales	0.49	264	5	33.8
France	0.44	76	29	28.8

[a] D. Kirk, *Europe's Population in the Interwar Years* (Geneva, 1946), pp. 263 ff.
[b] *Ibid.*
[c] Based on W. E. Moore, *Economic Demography of Eastern and Southern Europe* (Geneva, 1945), p. 26; H. L. Roberts, *Rumania: Political Problems of an Agrarian State* (New Haven, Connecticut, 1951), pp. 355 ff.; J. Tomasevich, *Peasants, Politics and Economic Change in Yugoslavia* (Stanford, Calif., 1955); S. D. Zagoroff, *The Agricultural Economy of the Danubian Countries 1935–45* (Stanford, Calif., 1955) p. 11; *Economic Development in S.E. Europe* (London, 1945); *South-Eastern Europe: A Political and Economic Survey* (London, 1939), pp. 125, 139, 156, 167. Although these sources give different figures concerning population percentages dependent on agriculture, all give much higher percentages for the Balkan states than for the others.
[d] Density of population dependent upon agriculture per square kilometer of "arable-equivalent" agricultural land. "Arable-equivalent" is a statistical device to achieve a rough comparability between different types of land (arable, pasture, vineyards, etc.) used for agricultural purposes. This is necessary for meaningful comparison because a square kilometer of pasture obviously is not equivalent to a square kilometer of arable land.
[e] Moore, *op. cit.*, pp. 197 ff. Different figures on density of population dependent on each unit of arable land are given in Tomasevich, *op. cit.*, p. 309; *Economic Development in S.E. Europe*, p. 26; A. Pepelasis, "Socio-Cultural Barriers to the Economic Development of Greece" (University of California, Berkeley, unpublished doctoral dissertation, 1955), p. 34, and *Report of the FAO Mission for Greece* (Washington, D.C., March, 1947), p. 134. But again all sources agree that population pressure per unit of arable land is greater in the Balkans than in most Western European countries.

remaining minority would have been able to carry on the work and would have had more left to eat.

The Balkan governments did try to cope with the problem by encouraging industrialization. They employed various methods, including tariff protection, tax exemption, special railway rates, and lucrative concessions to foreign investors. As a result, Balkan industry expanded considerably. Western capital played an important role in this expansion, but its blessings were mixed. In Jugoslavia, for example, Jozo Tomasevich has acknowledged that "foreign capital was perhaps the most dynamic force in the development of Jugoslav transport facilities, mining and industry." But this capital infusion, Tomasevich pointed out, had serious drawbacks:

Judging from the profits derived by most foreign companies in Yugoslavia, there can be little doubt that the price paid to foreign investors for their services was too high. Nor can the cost be measured in terms of dividends alone. Part of the toll was taken in unsystematic development of the country's natural resources. Foreign investors pursued the most profitable and least risky enterprises, without respect as to how their exploitation would affect the general development of the nation's economy. The exploitation of forests, for example, was highly uneconomical, and the farming in the neighborhood of the Bor mines was impaired. Foreign capital kept the country producing raw materials and semifinished products, and it was difficult to persuade foreign investors to develop facilities for production of finished products. This, of course, reduced the country's possibilities of utilizing its labor.[17]

The basic difficulty with Balkan industrialization, however, was not the exactions of Western investors but rather the inadequacy of the rate of industrialization. In no country did the new factories and mines absorb a substantial share of the surplus rural population. In Jugoslavia, for example, the number of industrial workers rose from 200,000 in 1919 to 385,000 in 1938. But in the same period the population of the country rose from 11,600,000 to 15,600,000, an increase of 4,000,000, of whom about one-half were of working age. The same disproportion between industrial employment and population increase prevailed in the other Balkan countries.

We may conclude that the population problem in the Balkans was essentially the same as in the rest of the underdeveloped world. It was created by Western medicine and hygiene. In the West, the population increase was absorbed by concurrent industrialization, but efforts to stimulate a corresponding industrialization failed in the Balkans, as in other underdeveloped areas. Consequently the South Slavs, the

---

[17] J. Tomasevich, "Foreign Economic Relations, 1918–1941," in R. J. Kerner, ed., *Yugoslavia* (Berkeley and Los Angeles: University of California Press, 1949), p. 194.

Greeks, and the Rumanians, like the Chinese, the Indians, and the Egyptians, were forced to remain primarily hewers of wood and drawers of water vis-à-vis the industrialized West.

Western Europe influenced the Balkans in the realm of finance as well as demography. The new Balkan states soon found themselves in financial difficulties because of the expense of their military establishments, their burgeoning bureaucracies, and their railroad and other construction projects. By 1914 the Bulgarian public debt amounted to 850,000,000 francs, the Serbian 903,000,000 francs, the Greek 1,250,-000,000 francs, and the Rumanian 1,700,000,000 francs. These debt loads proved too heavy, so that before the First World War all Balkan governments except the Rumanian had to accept arrangements whereby their creditors were given a measure of control over the revenues pledged to the payment of the bonds they held. This indebtedness also imposed a constantly growing tax burden upon the peasantry. In Greece, for example, the average per-capita tax rose from 15.6 drachmas in 1875 to 37.63 in 1893. And yet the national debt during the same period more than trebled, so that by 1893, Greece's foreign indebtedness was consuming 33 percent of her budgetary receipts. Balkan financial dependence on the West continued undiminished during the twentieth century, particularly because of heavy borrowing to repair the damages of the First World War and to cope with the problems engendered by the great depression.

Railway building was another manifestation and instrument of Western intrusion in the Balkans. Construction began after the Crimean War, and reached its peak in 1868 when Sultan Abd ul-Aziz gave a concession for the building of a main trunk from Constantinople to the Austrian border. After many delays the project was completed in 1888 when the first through train rumbled over the tracks from Vienna to Constantinople. In the meantime other lines were being built to the north in Rumania and to the south in Greece. This railway building had extensive repercussions in the Balkan lands. The money spent in the process of construction undermined the traditional self-sufficient economy of the regions immediately affected. Also the railways made possible the importation of large quantities of cheap foreign machine-made goods. These were bought to an increasing degree by the peasants, who thereby became correspondingly less self-sufficient. At the same time European demand for Balkan agricultural products such as Rumanian grain, Serbian livestock, and Greek currants and tobacco increased. Railway and steamship transportation now enabled the Balkan peasant to produce for the European market, and he did so to an increasing extent as the nineteenth century progressed. If he had any hesitation about availing himself of the opportunity, he was soon forced to bestir himself by the growing demands of the tax collector. The tax burden, together with the cost of the manufactured goods now made available, compelled the peasant to earn a money income by increasing his production or by getting outside work or both.

This spread of the money economy in turn had far-reaching social consequences, many of them uncomfortable and unsettling for the peasants. The manner of everyday living changed considerably. Tea, coffee, sugar, and other commodities lost their character as luxury goods and passed into more common use. Town-made lamps replaced the home-molded candles, and the more prosperous peasants also bought furniture and household utensils. Iron and steel plows became more common, though the poorer peasants still used the home-made ironshod variety. A few householders began to buy ready-made clothing although most of them still wove their garments from purchased yarn. In some peasant homes even a few books began to appear that were not exclusively religious. The number of purchased articles may appear insignificant by urban standards, but they represented, nevertheless, a radical departure from the self-sufficiency of earlier decades.

The diffusion of the money economy also increased village contacts with the outside world and thereby affected the traditional pattern of village life. The peasant sensed that literacy was essential under the new order if he were to be able to deal with the townsmen. Hence he readily accepted elementary schooling for his children whenever it was made available. Once reading and writing became reasonably common, new ideas and ethics, new tastes and ways of living, began to alter the age-old peasant traditions. The younger generation was soon questioning the assumptions and attitudes upon which peasant life had been based. Age no longer was regarded as sacrosanct. A new spirit of individualism and a desire for self-advancement and for personally owned possessions undermined the solidarity of village life and even of the family. An indication of this trend was the gradual dissolution of the *zadrugas;* by 1914, the patriarchal families no longer were an important factor in Balkan economy or social organization.

Village solidarity was also shattered by the development of economic stratification. The peasant was frequently unable to meet his obligations because he lacked the knowledge and the capital to increase his productivity and because opportunities for outside employment were scarce. As his debts mounted he was forced to turn to a new figure in the village—the well-to-do peasant who was turning merchant and moneylender. Being unfamiliar with money matters, the peasant frequently overburdened himself with debts at usurious rates ranging from 10 to more than 100 percent. Peasant indebtedness early became a serious problem in the Balkan countries. The governments made some efforts to free the peasants from the usurers by providing credit at low rates. But the peasants usually were unable to provide the required security or found the formalities and legal expenses excessive for the small sums they needed. Thus it was the usurers who borrowed the government funds at around 6 percent and reloaned them to the peasants at double, triple, or several times that rate.

The spread of the money economy made the Balkan peasants subject to the vagaries of the national, and even the international, market and credit mechanism. No sooner did they begin to produce for the European market than they felt the crushing competition of overseas agricultural products. The Balkan peasants did not escape the effects of the long depression which all European agriculture experienced from 1873 to the mid-nineties. The twentieth century witnessed an increase in the vulnerability of Balkan agriculture to Western pressures. One example was the agricultural protectionism adopted by most European industrial states during the interwar years. This reduced substantially the market for Balkan agricultural products. Another example was the great depression, during which the prices of raw materials dropped more than those of manufactured goods. This created a price scissors that hit the Balkan economies especially hard.

Finally, the West affected the Balkan economy by making possible large-scale emigration at the end of the nineteenth century. During the preceding centuries, of course, there had been a good deal of emigration from the peninsula: Albanians to southern Italy, Serbs to southern Hungary, Bulgarians to the Danubian Principalities and to Russia, and Greeks to most of the surrounding countries. This early emigration, as we have seen, contributed in various ways to the national awakening of the Balkan peoples. The later emigration was mostly overseas, to the United States, Latin America, and the British dominions. It was a large-scale movement, especially from regions with poor soil, such as Montenegro and parts of Greece and Albania. It is estimated that by 1912 one-third of the able-bodied Montenegrin men had left their country permanently or temporarily. There was a large-scale exodus also from regions where much of the land was held in large estates, such as Slavonia and the Vojvodina. By contrast, emigration was comparatively light from Serbia and Bulgaria where land distribution was more equitable.

This emigration affected the Balkan countries both economically and culturally. In return for the exodus of able-bodied young males, they received a golden stream of remittances. In Greece, for example, the remittances in 1921 totaled 121,000,000 dollars. The economic results of this flow of dollars is reflected in the following conclusion of a Greek government commission that investigated the effect of emigration:

No one can deny that it is to [the emigrants] in great measure . . . that we owe the rise in the value of our paper currency almost to par. . . . Everyone mentions . . . that in these provinces, particularly in Peloponnesus, which are the oldest and most prolific sources of emigration to the United States, there has been a striking fall in the rate of interest and a proportionate rise in the value of agricultural real estate.[18]

Balkan emigration also had significant cultural repercussions, particularly because of the influence of emigrants who returned to their homeland. They returned for various reasons, including economic pressure during slump periods in the United States, desire to resume family ties or to marry and raise a family in the native land, and also preference for the more familiar and easygoing life of the mother country. It is estimated that of the more than half million Greeks admitted into the United States by 1931, about 40 percent, or 197,000, went back as repatriates. Upon their return many of them found adjustment difficult. They were oppressed by the poverty and the slow tempo of life. They found that, despite their money, they had gained little social prestige by their stay in America. A popular saying was,

---

[18] Cited by T. Saloutos, *They Remember America: The Story of the Repatriated Greek-Americans* (Berkeley and Los Angeles: University of California Press, 1956), p. 118.

"He left as a young donkey and returned as an older one." Also, the repatriates were usually besieged by poverty-stricken relatives and sometimes fleeced in shady business deals. On the other hand, many repatriates were able to settle down in towns and villages and contribute to their communities from the new skills and experiences they had acquired in America. At the time of the First World War Arnold Toynbee foresaw the leavening influence of these repatriates:

It is a strange experience to spend a night in some remote mountain-village of Greece, and see Americanism and Hellenism face to face. Hellenism is represented by the village schoolmaster. He wears a black coat, talks a little French, and can probably read Homer; but his longest journey has been to his normal school at Athens, and it has not altered his belief that the ikon in the neighbouring monastery was made by St. Luke and the Bulgar beyond the mountains by the Devil. On the other side of you sits the returned emigrant, chatting irrepressibly in his queer version of the "American language," and showing you the newspapers which are mailed to him every fortnight from the States. . . . His greatest gift to his country will be his American point of view.[19]

This "American point of view," to which Toynbee refers, was most pronounced and significant during the interwar years when so many emigrants were returning to their Balkan homelands. Its influence declined sharply during and following the Second World War, partly because of the drop in emigration and repatriation, and also because of the overwhelming impact of the war, the occupation, the resistance movements, and the postwar social and political upheavals.

The Western impact during the nineteenth century was not limited to the diplomatic, social, and economic spheres. Political institutions also were affected, and the results were not altogether positive. The pashas, the agas, and the other representatives of Ottoman authority were now gone. In their place were established Western-type state structures, with the usual bureaucracies, standing armies, centralized administrations, parliamentary bodies, and political parties. This attempt to graft Western institutions on a native stock produced serious tensions and maladjustments. The communal self-government that had existed under the Turks withered under the centralism of the

---

[19] N. Forbes, A. J. Toynbee, D. Mitrany, and D. G. Hogarth, *The Balkans: A History of Bulgaria, Serbia, Greece, Rumania, Turkey* (Oxford: The Clarendon Press, 1915), p. 249.

modern nation state. The latter also inflicted an excessive financial burden on the shoulders of the peasant. The modern state structure had developed in the West naturally and harmoniously with the growth of economic life, but in the Balkans it was superimposed with all its elaborateness and costliness upon underdeveloped agrarian economies.

It is true that the new national governments were not as arbitrary and unpredictable as the disintegrating Ottoman imperial regime. But they were fully as exacting, if not more so. They rapidly created large bureaucracies and armies, which, for the peasant, meant heavy taxes, burdensome service in the army, and periodic forced labor on roads and fortifications. In return for these onerous obligations the peasant received little from the state. No wonder that the animosity formerly held for the Turkish overlord was now turned against the bureaucrat, the tax collector, and the gendarme. Precisely this point was made by a Bulgarian novelist writing in 1892:

The peasant has but the vaguest idea of our transition from servitude to independent life; for him it matters little whether he pays tax to Akhmed, or Ivan. In fact, Ivan is often more distasteful to him than Akhmed, for Akhmed could be more easily fooled or bribed; Akhmed did not take his son off as a soldier whereas Ivan does: Akhmed was naive and spoke Turkish, while Ivan is to all appearance a Christian like him, speaks Bulgarian, yet exacts more from him than did Akhmed. The meaning of state, rights, and duties for the peasant add up to tax-payment and sending his son off as a soldier.[20]

On the surface the Balkan peoples enjoyed all the trappings of Western parliamentary democracy. "Conservative" and "liberal" parties contested periodic elections and conducted debates in national assemblies. But all this signified little, given the illiteracy of the peasant masses and the lack of strong middle-class elements. The similarity to Western political institutions and practices was more in form than in substance. This was so also during the 1930's when the misery and tension attendant upon the Depression led to the establishment of dictatorships in all Balkan countries. These regimes were modeled after the contemporary authoritarian governments in Fascist Italy and Nazi Germany. But again the similarity was superficial. The Balkan

---

[20] From Maksimov's novel *Tselina* [*Virgin Soil*], cited by V. Pinto, "The Civic and Aesthetic Ideals of Bulgarian Narodnik Writers," *Slavonic and East European Review*, XXXII (June, 1954), 357.

regimes lacked over-all mass support comparable to that enjoyed by Hitler. They did not possess an ideology that caught the imagination of the masses, with the exception of certain regions and disaffected groups. Nor did they have the efficiency and technical facilities necessary to indoctrinate the masses even if they had had an effective ideology. Thus the bulk of the people remained unaffected by native fuehrers like Carol, Metaxas and Stojadinović. David Mitrany stated:

The eastern dictatorships never rested on the support of strong sections of the masses. The villagers especially looked with bland peasant skepticism on the uniforms and parades and oratorical antics of these would-be-tribunes. The eastern dictatorships were never anything but bureaucratic and military regimes, as brittle as they were inefficient and oppressive.[21]

The following indictment of Rumanian political institutions by a citizen of that country is in large part applicable to the entire peninsula.

Unfortunately our glorious urban institutions, for all their liberal-democratic techniques, are pure falsehoods . . . we have introduced universal suffrage, but with ballot stuffing; we have ruined rural households in order to increase credit institutions, but have not permitted free competition among these institutions, but have favored some— those belonging to us—and have attacked others—those belonging to our adversaries; we have encouraged national industry, but not for the benefit of the rural population, as would have been right, since they made the sacrifices, but for the benefit of politicians who are pensioners of this national industry; we have centralized the administration of the country, but not in the hands of the party and its partisans; in a word we have aped the European bourgeoisie in form, but at bottom we have persisted in the sycophantic habits of the past. In this way we have transformed political life into a hopeless turmoil.[22]

There remains the influence of the West on the intellectual and general cultural development of the Balkans during the national period. This has so many variations and ramifications that only a schematic outline is feasible. First it should be noted that the West appeared to the Balkan peoples as something strange and foreign, so that

---

[21] D. Mitrany, *Marx against the Peasant: A Study in Social Dogmatism* (Chapel Hill, N.C.: University of North Carolina Press, 1951), p. 122.

[22] Cited by H. Roberts, *Rumania: Political Problems of an Agrarian State* (New Haven, Conn.: Yale University Press, 1951), pp. 115–116.

they normally talked of "going to Europe." In the eyes of most Balkan intellectuals this foreign "Europe" was advanced, superior, and worthy of emulation. A significant exception to this rule is the romantics and Slavophiles who championed the traditional patriarchal society as against capitalism and the centralized nation state. Typical of this attitude is the warning of the mid-nineteenth century Serbian writer, Laza Kostić: "Seek not salvation in the West, where the shopkeeper and the broker rule." [23] Also it should be noted that in the early nineteenth century, when communications were relatively primitive, Western influences frequently reached individual Balkan peoples indirectly through intermediaries. An example of this is the introduction of French language and thought among the Rumanians through Greek newspapers published in Vienna and Greek schools operating in the Principalities. Another example are the many Bulgarian students who accepted the scholarships of the Odessa Seminary for Bulgarian Students and of the Slavic Welfare Committee in Moscow. Most of these students imbibed in Russia not the principles of Orthodoxy and autocracy, but the writings, which they read in the original or in translation, of French philosophers, English constitutional historians, German philosophers, and Marxist socialists.

Whatever the mode of transmission, Western cultural influence was most diverse because of several determining variables. One of these was the particular people affected. For example, the Rumanians were in general more likely to be susceptible to French influences, and the Bulgarians to Russian. But there were many exceptions. We have seen that many Bulgarian students became Westernized in Russia, and many others at Robert College, and later played an important role in the history of their country. Another variable is the period, for this determined the nature of the Western influences and the degree of receptivity in the Balkans. The time factor obviously determined whether the Western ideas in question were those of Rousseau, Schiller, Darwin, Mills, Mazzini, Marx, or Hitler. Time also determined whether the party in power favored the propagation of this or that Western ideology. In nineteenth-century Bulgaria, for example, the Conservatives admired the highly centralized, bureaucratic Habsburg and German states, while the Liberals looked to Belgium, France, Italy, and

---

[23] Cited by T. Stoianovich, "The Pattern of Serbian Political Evolution 1830–1880," *Comparative Studies in Society and History*, I (March, 1959), 258.

England, and were disciples of Voltaire, Rousseau, Mazzini, Gladstone, and Bagehot. Turning to a contemporary example, it is self-evident what aspects of Western culture would be predominant in Greece today if that country were a "peoples' democracy" rather than a monarchy. Still another variable was the nature of the discipline or field of study. Among Serbian students, for example, it was long the custom to go to Vienna for medicine, to Germany for philosophy and law, to Germany or France for history, and to Russia for theology.

Finally, Western intellectual and cultural influence was throughout the nineteenth century a rather superficial affair, affecting only an insignificant minority. This remained true until the development of mass-communication media following the First World War, and especially the Second World War. Until that time most people were absorbed in their folk cultures and were largely unaffected by the culture of their own capitals, let alone those of London or Paris or Berlin. For example, of 100 Serbian army recruits examined about 1909, everyone knew Marko Kraljević, the legendary Serbian hero, 98 were familiar with Miloš Obilić, another medieval hero, but only 47 had heard of the reigning King Peter in Belgrade. Even the intellectuals, who may have studied abroad and adopted Western ideas, were rarely free to implement these ideas. Usually they had to choose between joining a party machine and forswearing their political principles, or maintaining their principles and forswearing a career. Those who chose the former course naturally had the greater impact on Balkan developments, as may be seen in the contrasting careers of Svetozar Marković and Nikola Pašić.

In conclusion: the Westernization process we have been examining did not affect uniformly all parts of the Balkan Peninsula. We noted earlier that the differential explains the variations in the speed of national revival in the eighteenth and nineteenth centuries. It also explains why the 1921 census in Jugoslavia showed that the regional illiteracy rates spread from 8.8 percent in Slovenia to 23.3 percent in the Vojvodina, 32.2 in Croatia, 49.5 in Dalmatia, 65.4 in Serbia, 67.0 in Montenegro, 80.5 in Bosnia-Hercegovina, and 83.8 in Macedonia. The independent variable behind these figures obviously is the length of exposure to European rule and influences. At the one extreme are the Slovenes, who were under Habsburg rule from the fourteenth to the twentieth centuries; at the other are the Macedonians who re-

mained under the Turks until the twentieth century. The Slovenes inherited from their rulers a relatively advanced system of public education, and habits of hard work, level-headedness and frugality that have
caused some of their fellow South Slavs to dub them "the Germans of
Jugoslavia." The Macedonians, by contrast, have been so retarded
that even the neighboring Serbs talk about people in Macedonia living *kao stoka*, like animals.[24] A revealing indication of the relationship
between Westernization and Ottoman rule is the following passage
that appeared in a Young Turk newspaper published in Cairo at the
turn of the century:

Five-and-twenty years ago, Sophia was full of crooked and dirty
streets, such as we still see in Adrianople, Yanina, Monastir, etc., without any features to commend itself either for beauty or convenience,
and with the exception of several places of worship, barracks, and
prisons, there was nothing to denote any degree of culture. Since
Sophia has been under Bulgarian government, one would scarcely rec-
ognise the place on account of the many improvements and changes
which have been made. It now possesses straight wide streets, public
squares, theatres, museums, zoological and botanical gardens, electric
light, tramways, telephone, etc. And not only Sophia, but also Varna,
Philippopolis, and other towns, have been Europeanised. Roumania,
Servia, and Greece, as well as Bulgaria, have been illumined by the
light of civilisation since they have become independent States. Crete
will soon follow suit. When we look round in our own land and see
how Adrianople, Brussa, Aleppo, Damascus, and Bagdad, all once cen-
tres of the empire, have failed to maintain their former glory and
beauty, and have become desolate through utter neglect of the spirit
of modernization, we pity them for the darkness and ignorance into
which they have sunk. At Brussa and Adrianople, situated at very short
distances from the capital, we still find the primitive waggons pulled
by oxen, and omnibuses, even, are an unknown convenience. But why
quote instances from provincial towns? Let us take Constantinople itself, with its million inhabitants, and in point of natural beauty excel-
ling all other capitals. On the roughly paved streets dirt and filth lie
deep, and dogs prowl about. Barracks abound, but the military are
only there to suppress revolts; for personal safety little or no provision
is made. Stamboul has no theatres, no botanical or zoological gardens
—modern institutions which have found their way even into Australia
and Siberia. . . . For God's sake let us have done with this slowness,
this negligence. Let us not turn our eyes away from the light of culture.[25]

---

[24] J. M. Halpern, *A Serbian Village*, p. 296.
[25] Cited by Vambery, *op. cit.*, pp. 343–344.

What pattern emerges from this survey of Western influence during the national period? A succinct answer has been given by the American anthropologist, Joel Martin Halpern, who spent 1953–1954 in the Serbian village of Orašac. His purpose was to examine the processes of social and cultural change, and after a careful study of all aspects of village life, he reached the following conclusions:

Over the past century and half there have been a number of important changes in Orašac. There was, first, an increasing centralization of power in the hands of the national government, with a subsequent decline in the importance of local authorities. Second, the villager has been drawn more and more into a cash economy, primarily on account of increasing taxes but also because the expanding towns required more food from the countryside, while the peasant himself has been developing new tastes and needs. Third, there has been the state's increasing regulation of the peasant's life, by taxes, laws, military service, and other obligations. Fourth, as a result of increasing participation in a cash economy, technology and the material culture of the village have begun to change at a faster rate than ever before. Fifth, changes are also reflected in the nonmaterial culture, as in the decline of the zadruga. Sixth, some villagers have begun to migrate to the town and to derive income from sources other than agriculture. Basically, these changes are all an outgrowth of the influence of the Western commercial and industrial revolution, which over the past seventy-five years has made an increasing impact on rural Serbia.[26]

This statement shows clearly that Westernization was a disruptive process. It did bring electricity, improved implements, security from epidemics, and even radio sets and movies. But it also brought constant change in values, institutions, and practices, and adjustment to this change was unsettling and uncomfortable. This bitter-sweet aspect of Westernization is evident in the following reminiscences of an Orašac peasant:

I was born in 1866. . . . We used to eat less than we do today. Our clothes were not good. We went without pants. There was no doctor, no railway, and there were dense forests all around. We used to cultivate with wooden plows. It wasn't until the reign of King Peter I that we had iron plows and wagons, better houses, and all the rest.

I remember once when Milan Obrenović came to our village in a horse-drawn carriage. He got out and walked through the village and talked to the people. At that time we paid one ducat for taxes on our property,

---

[26] Halpern, op. cit., pp. 302–303.

which amounted to thirty hectares. . . . We had no beds and used to sleep on the dirt floor around the hearth. . . .

I used to go to the fairs in Milanovac [about forty miles from Orašac] on foot. . . . In the old days, when I was twenty, I used to plow with six oxen. At that time we had a wooden plow, while today we use a steel one with two cows. We did not have brick houses, nor did we know how to build them. A recruit used to go serve in the army on foot while today they all go by train. Until 1905 we all went everywhere on foot.

We used to eat corn bread, and nobody ever smoked or cursed. People were healthier than they are today. Holy things were respected and kept. Today all is different. A new life is coming, when one has to work more and harder to have less.[27]

BALKAN WESTERNIZATION IN WORLD PERSPECTIVE

We noted earlier that the West's intrusion into the Balkan Peninsula was a local manifestation of a world-wide trend. This raises the question of regional variations. To what extent did Western Influence on the Balkans follow the over-all global pattern and to what extent did it differ?

To approach this problem meaningfully it will be necessary to exclude the non-Eurasian portions of the globe, that is, subsaharan Africa and the New World. Until the fifteenth century these areas had little or no contact with the great centers of civilization in the Eurasian land mass. The isolation retarded severely their rates of development. Consequently when Europe began its fateful expansion in the fifteenth century, the impact and the response were quite different in subsaharan Africa and the Americas from what they were in Russia, the Middle East, and South and East Asia. The difference was so marked that little can be gained by attempting to compare the effect of Westernization on the Balkan peoples, with that on the Bantus, the Aztecs, or the Plains Indians. For this reason the following comparative analysis of the Westernization process will be restricted to the Eurasian part of the globe.

Considering first the matter of timing, the Balkan Peninsula was one of the first regions to be influenced by the West. It followed Russia in this respect, for the borrowing of Western technical and material

---

[27] *Ibid.*, pp. 205–206.

knowledge became a fairly steadfast Muscovite policy from the time of Ivan the Great's marriage to Zoe Palaeologus in 1472. But Balkan Westernization did precede that of the Muslim Middle East, India and the Far East. There seem to be two principal reasons for this sequence. One, obviously, is geographic propinquity. We have seen that this factor explains why the Greeks and the Serbians felt the influence of the West before the isolated Bulgarians. In a larger setting this also explains why the Russian and Balkan peoples experienced Westernization earlier than did the Chinese and Japanese at the other end of Eurasia. The other explanation for the timing of the Westernization process is the attitude of the local population, and particularly the local ruling class. Peter the Great's ardent Westernism, for example, aided rapid diffusion of Western thought and technology in Russia, while the rigid seclusion policies of China and Japan greatly curtailed Western influence in those countries until the second half of the nineteenth century.

There was no counterpart to Peter the Great among the Balkan peoples, and yet they were relatively responsive to the West—certainly more so than the other ethnic groups in the Ottoman Empire. One reason for this is that the Balkan populations are mostly Christian and therefore more receptive to the Christian West than were the Muslim Turks and Arabs. The other reason is that a Balkan middle class appeared in the eighteenth and nineteenth centuries, and this class, as we have seen, naturally developed contacts with the West and a preference for its institutions and practices. The Muslim peoples had no such elements; instead, the Jews and the Christian Greeks and Armenians controlled most economic enterprises in the Ottoman Empire. It appears, then, that the explanation for the Balkan peoples' relatively early receptivity to the West is geographic location, Christian faith, and West-oriented mercantile groups.

Considering next the actual nature of the West's impact, we have noted that everywhere it resembled a pebble falling in a pool and stimulating a series of ever expanding circles. In all parts of Eurasia, Western intrusion was at first usually confined to some single specific field. But invariably it had repercussions in other fields, which in turn induced further impulses until an entire society was affected. More specifically, Western influence usually began in the military field. Non-Europeans were most impressed and alarmed by the West's superior military technology, and strove to learn the secrets of this technology as soon as possible. But Western arms required the development of certain industries, so that the original military objectives were perforce extended to new objectives in the economic field. But Westernization in tools led inevitably to modernization in ideas and values. Arms and factories required schools and science, as one Western borrowing continued inexorably to necessitate another. Military and economic change produced intellectual, social, and political change. New classes appeared which challenged the traditional society and ruling groups, and also challenged Western domination where it prevailed. This explains the intellectual ferment and the revolutionary movements that opposed tsardom in Russia, British control in India, and the direct Manchu rule and indirect Western control in China.

This general Eurasian pattern overlooks regional nuances and exceptions. In the Balkans the Westernization process during the Ottoman period differed considerably from that during the national period. In the earlier era the course of Westernization was affected by the existence of a foreign ruling group. It is true that a similar situation prevailed in British-held India, but the rulers there were themselves Westerners, and they encouraged the Westernization of the country, particularly in economics, administration, and education. In the Balkans, by contrast, the Turkish overlords, with their Islamic anti-Western bias and their general unprogressiveness, were either unresponsive or outrightly antipathetic to the West. Some Ottoman leaders, of course, did favor a certain degree of Westernization. Long before Selim III, Mahmud II, and the *tanzimat* movement, there was the Turkish encyclopedist and historian, Katib Chelebi, who warned his people in the mid-seventeenth century of the folly of ignoring Western science and philosophy. "Henceforth," he forecast, "people will be looking at the universe with eyes of oxen." [28] But Chelebi and the other Ottoman reformers were ineffective in the face of the Islamic superiority complex, the power of the vested interests supporting the status quo, and the reluctance of even enlightened Turks to risk the downward diffusion of Westernism in a multinational and ramshackle empire. Whereas Peter the Great strove desperately in Russia to pro-

---

[28] Cited by A. Adnan-Adivar, "Interaction of Islamic and Western Thought in Turkey," *Near Eastern Culture and Society,* ed. by T. C. Young (Princeton: Princeton University Press, 1951), p. 122.

mote the downward diffusion of Westernism, the Turks strove to block such diffusion in their empire. Accordingly Westernization in the peninsula came from the bottom up, not from the top down as in Russia and Japan. It follows that Westernization in the Balkans was essentially an antigovernment or anti-Turkish movement rather than anti-Western as in Russia and Japan. Korais wished to awaken his fellow countrymen in order to be rid of the Turkish incubus; by contrast, Ivan the Terrible and Emperor Meiji were interested in modernizing their realms in order to resist the encroachments of the West.

When the Balkan peoples won their independence, the process of Westernization became more similar to that in the rest of the world. The new nation states now were the innovators—the instruments of Westernization. It was these states that arranged for the construction of railways, the building of schools, the organization of armies with Western-trained officers, and the development of Western-type bureaucracies. The relatively static and self-contained Balkan world was thereby laid open to outside pressures, and the result was the gradual but irresistible Westernization trend as described above by Halpern.

The final point to note about Western influence in the Balkans is that it has been steadily increasing in intensity. This also is in accord with the world pattern. Hundreds of millions of people on all continents are today being politically activated, and their daily lives revolutionized, by Western ideas, Western industry, and Western material goods. The newspapers provide a stream of examples of this fateful trend that is enveloping the globe.

Outer Mongolia still lives by the social pattern carved across her terrain by the ruthless hand of Genghis Khan. But after nearly 700 years this remote Asian country stands on the brink of change. . . . What is happening in Outer Mongolia is simply this: the nation's Communist rulers have embarked on a program designed to catapult the country from the thirteenth to the twentieth century within not more than ten years. . . . The essence of the program is: full speed ahead in a plan to change a nation of nomads into a nation based on the agriculture of the plow and the industry of the production line. [Harrison E. Salisbury, in *New York Times*, August 3, 1959].

The Prado La Paz, a central boulevard (in La Paz, Bolivia) looks almost like the main street of a southwestern United States city when school lets out, except for Indian women in brown bowler hats and babies slung over their backs in colored ponchos. Bolivian girls wear their hair in pony-tails, dress in toreador pants or skirts, bobbysox and saddle shoes. Boys by preference wear blue jeans and black leather jackets. In an Indian market place an Aymara girl tending her mother's stand solemnly chews what turns out with a pink pop to be not the traditional coca leaves but bubble-gum. [*New York Times,* March 20, 1959].

It is a question of dignity. Arabs want to feel equal to other nations and must unite to do so. President Nasser has shown us how we can look you in the eye. We want to belong to a larger movement with a sense of purpose and direction. We cannot be happy when others about us in the Arab world are miserable. Our day is coming. Nothing can stop the Arabs from unity. You will see. [*Young men in Kuwait to American correspondent: New York Times,* May 2, 1959].

What we are witnessing today is a breathtaking acceleration of Western influence. Since the fifteenth century the West has been affecting profoundly the entire globe. But with the partial exception of the idea of nationalism, the Westernization process has been largely passive so far as the masses of the people have been concerned. They tended to be pawns rather than active participants. They were affected, but affected unwillingly, by forces that they dimly comprehended and that they found generally distasteful and disturbing. Until the twentieth century, only an insignificant leisure class was participating in the Westernization process. Only this handful comprehended the meaning of the West from their knowledge of European languages and literatures, and their travels in European lands.

Today, by contrast, a growing share of the masses is taking part actively and consciously. The explanation is partly the factories where they find employment and the highways that are ending their isolation. But equally important are the new mass media of tabloids, radio, and movies which are overshadowing the old class media of books and travel. Westernization has gained its present enormous impetus because it is dependent not on Oxford colleges and Paris salons, but on loudspeakers blaring out on illiterate yet responsive multitudes in village squares. New regimes and leaders are now purposefully exploiting the mass media to the utmost in order to mobilize popular support for their revolutionary programs. Nasser stated recently:

It is true that most of our people are still illiterate. But politically that counts far less than it did twenty years ago. . . . Radio has changed everything. . . . Today people in the most remote villages hear of what is happening everywhere and form their opinions. Leaders cannot govern as they once did. We live in a new world.[29]

Nasser's "new world" extends to the Balkan Peninsula. One illustration is the Bulgarian village of Dragalevtsy, studied intensively by the American sociologist, Irwin T. Sanders. When he first visited the village in 1934 he found only two radios, but on his return in 1944 there were more than one hundred. This meant that about one-third of the families were in contact with the government broadcasting system. Upon inquiry, Sanders learned:

Listening to the radio had become a new recreational pattern for many people. Over and over again I asked them what programs they preferred. The men, perhaps because they deemed it the proper answer, often said that they listened to the news. Quite a few were quick to add, "It's nothing but lies though." Many of the women preferred the folk music, and the young people jazz.[30]

Equally revealing is the following report made thirteen years later by an American correspondent in Sofia:

It is possible to hear American-style rock'n roll almost everywhere in Bulgaria, with the possible exception of remote villages. In many places the tunes are sung in English with the original lyrics, and played from arrangements straight from Tin Pan Alley. The rock'n roll rage is sweeping Bulgaria in spite of stern ideological proscriptions.[31]

Another illustration of the "new world" in the Balkans is the essays written by eighth graders (fourteen to fifteen years old) in the villages of Orašac on the subject, "What I Want to Be and Why."

I am determined, if they accept me as an apprentice, to study one of the metal-working trades, and as such I shall be useful to the Federal People's Republic of Yugoslavia. . . .

As soon as I finish I intend to study to be an electrician, and when I have finished learning my trade I shall take part with my friends in the electrification of the villages and cities as well as in the construction of new hydroelectric plants. . . .

When I was a little girl I was hardly able to wait for the time to start school. . . . As soon as I began elementary school I began thinking

---

[29] Cited by D. Lerner, The Passing of Traditional Society: Modernizing the Middle East (Glencoe, Ill.: Free Press, 1958), p. 214.
[30] I. Sanders, Balkan Village (Lexington, Ky.: University of Kentucky Press, 1949), pp. 206–207.
[31] New York Times, September 24, 1957.

about different occupations such as schoolteacher, doctor, engineer, craftsman, etc. Thinking about these occupations I wanted most to become a schoolteacher . . . because . . . by doing so I would spread the new culture to our people. The schoolteacher's work is to emancipate and to make the people literate.[32]

It might be asked at this point what the relationship is between the topic of this essay—"The Influence of the West on the Balkans"—and the described developments in two Communist-ruled Balkan states. The answer is that these attitudes and aspirations described by Sanders and Halpern—the interest in news, the craze for jazz, the determination to learn new professions and to participate in national reconstruction—all these represent the essence of Westernization. For Westernization is not merely the investment of capital, the building of railways, and the construction of factories. It is just as much a way of thinking and acting and looking at life. It is the acceptance of social change as desirable and inevitable. It is the belief that the individual can and should participate in, and contribute to, this change. It is the desire for new material goods and comforts, and the assumption that misery is not an act of God. It is, finally, the conviction that all citizens should have the opportunity to learn and to advance themselves, depending on their ability and desire rather than on their money or class. In short, Westernization replaces the isolation, ignorance, and acquiescence of traditionalism with the participation, knowledge, and initiative of modernism.[33]

Westernization (or modernization), as defined above, is today undermining traditional society in the Balkans more rapidly than at any time in the past. In the early nineteenth century the Westernization process advanced to a new stage with the establishment of independent nation states that accepted the goods, techniques, and institutions of the newly industrialized West. Perhaps the Balkan peoples at present are entering another stage with the appearance of regimes and leaders committed to economic and social innovation, and exploiting

---

[32] Halpern, *op. cit.*, pp. 256–257.

[33] The terms modernism (or modernization) and Westernism (or Westernization) are here used interchangeably. It should be noted, however, that in dealing with the twentieth century, modernism is preferable to Westernism, since the West frequently is equated with Europe. But the impulse for change today may come from the United States or the Soviet Union as well as Europe. See Lerner, *op. cit.*, p. 45.

the media for mass communication and indoctrination in order to attain their goals. The fact that this trend is world-wide and is gathering momentum raises questions concerning the future of all mankind. "It may well be," observes John K. Fairbank, "that the universality of scientific technology, its essential independence of any local culture, even that of its origin, is indeed drawing the world onto a common homogeneous plane of methods and practices (in the direction of a cosmopolitan or supra-national world civilization based on a single scientific value system)." [34]

BIBLIOGRAPHY

Western influence on the Ottoman Empire as a whole is somewhat peripheral to the topic of this essay but it constitutes the broader background that must be kept in mind. It is a subject that embraces much more than the well-known diplomatic encounters, capitulatory arrangements, or *Tanzimat* movement, as is indicated by recent studies such as Lewis V. Thomas, "Ottoman Awareness of Europe 1650–1800" (in manuscript); I. A. Abu-Lughod, "Arab Rediscovery of Europe 1800–1870" (Princeton University, unpublished doctoral dissertation, 1958); A. W. A. Qaysi, "The Impact of Modernization on Iraqi Society during the Modern Era: A Study of Intellectual Development in Iraq 1869–1917" (University of Michigan, unpublished doctoral dissertation, 1958); A. Adnan, *La Science chez les Turcs ottomans* (Paris, 1939); and M. Akdag, "Osmanli Imparatorlugunun kuruluş ve inkişaf devrinde Türkiye' nin iktisadî vaziyeti," ["The Economic Position of Turkey during the Foundation and the Rise of the Ottoman Empire"], *Belleten*, XIII (July, 1949), 497–568. The latter work emphasizes the injurious effect of Western trade upon the Ottoman economy and presents evidence suggesting a significant parallel between Ottoman and Spanish economic development.

For the circumstances under which Western Europe surpassed Southeastern Europe in early modern times, see A. G. Keller, "A Byzantine Admirer of 'Western' Progress: Cardinal Bessarion," *Cambridge Historical Journal*, XI (1955), 343–348; W. C. Barck, *Origins of the Medieval World* (Stanford, Calif., 1958); Lynn T. White Jr., "Technology and Invention in the Middle Ages," *Speculum*, XV (1940), 141–

[34] John K. Fairbank, "The Influence of Modern Western Science and Technology on Japan and China," *Explorations in Entrepreneurial History*, VII (April, 1955), 201.

159; and the same author's forthcoming book entitled *Medieval Technology and Social Change*.

The *chiflik* landholding system, whose growth owed much to Western-introduced staple crops and to Western markets for these crops, is analyzed in the following works: R. Busch-Zantner, *Agrarverfassung, Gesellschaft und Siedlung in Südosteuropa in besonderer Berücksichtigung der Türkenzeit* (Leipzig, 1938); J. Tomasevich, *Peasants, Politics and Economic Change in Yugoslavia* (Stanford, Calif., 1955); H. Inalcik, "Land Problems in Turkish History," *Muslim World*, XLV (July, 1955), 221–228; T. Stoianovich, "Land Tenure and Related Sectors of the Balkan Economy 1600–1800," *Journal of Economic History*, XIII (Fall, 1953), 398–411; and the same author's unpublished essay: "Lost Villages, Recolonization, and Peasant Servitude: A Balkan Example." The Stoianovich articles are especially important in showing the economic and political repercussions of the rise of the *chiflik* regime.

The most important single work on the rise of commerce and industry in the Balkans in the seventeenth and eighteenth centuries is the unpublished doctoral dissertation by T. Stoianovich, "L'économie balkanique aux XVII⁰ et XVIII⁰ siècles" (University of Paris, 1952). Material may also be found in H. A. R. Gibb and H. Bowen, *Islamic Society and the West*, Vol. I, Parts I and II: *Islamic Society in the Eighteenth Century* (London, 1950, 1957); F. Braudel, *La Méditerranée et le monde méditerranean à l'époque de Philippe II* (Paris 1949); and N. Svoronos, *Le commerce de Salonique au XVIII⁰ siècle* (Paris, 1952). Also, there are the economic histories of individual Balkan states, such as I. Sakazov, *Bulgarische Wirtschaftsgeschichte* (Berlin, 1929); and contemporary accounts by the consuls of foreign powers who followed economic developments—for example, F. Beaujour, *A View of the Commerce of Greece Formed after an Annual Average from 1787 to 1797* (London, 1800).

Little that is peninsular in scope has been written on the political and intellectual awakening of the Balkan peoples, which was to a considerable degree stimulated directly or indirectly by the West. Exceptions are the interesting study by N. Moschopoulos, *La Presse dans la renaissance balkanique* (Athens, 1931); the unpublished manuscript by T. Stoianovich entitled "Balkan Merchants, Officeholders, and Bourgeoisies: Prehistory of the Wars of National Independence," and L. S. Stavrianos, "Antecedents to the Balkan Revolutions of the Nineteenth Century," *Journal of Modern History*, XXIX (December, 1957), 335–348. Similar general studies are needed concerning the effect upon Balkan nationalism and Balkan social classes and institutions of Western ideologies, the development of commerce, and the rise of merchant groups at home and abroad. The studies now available on these subjects are national in scope, as for example the biographies of leaders such as Obradović, Karadžić, Korais, Rhigas, and Aprilov, and also the following representative works: N. Iorga, "Le Despotisme éclairé dans les pays roumains au XVIIIᵉ siècle," *Bulletin of the International Committee of Historical Sciences*, IX (1937), 100–115; D. Russo, *Studii istorice greco-române* (Bucharest, 1939, 2 vols); T. H. Papadopoullos, *Studies and Documents Relating to the History of the Greek Church and People under Turkish Domination* (Brussels, 1952); G. G. Arnakis, "The Greek Church of Constantinople and the Ottoman Empire," *Journal of Modern History*, XXIV (September, 1952), 235–250; E. P. Papanoutsos, *Neoelleneke Philosophia* [*Modern Greek Philosophy*], (Athens, 1953), Vol. I; C. Dimaras, *Historia tes Neoellenikes Logotechnias* [*History of Modern Greek Literature*], (Athens, 1948), Vol. I; R. Demos, "The Neo-Hellenic Enlightenment (1750–1821)," *Journal of the History of Ideas*, XIX (October, 1958), 523–541; G. Kordatos, *Koinonike Semasia tes Espanastaseos tou 1821* [*Social Significance of the Revolution of 1821*], (Athens, 1946, rev. ed.); L. Hadrovics, *L'église serbe sous la domination turque* (Paris, 1947); C. Jelavich, "Some Aspects of Serbian Religious Development in the Eighteenth Century," *Church History*, XXIII (June, 1954), 3–11; M. B. Petrovich, "The Rise of Modern Serbian Historiography," *Journal of Central European Affairs*, XVI (April, 1956), 1–24; S. Skendi, "Beginnings of Albanian Nationalist Trends in Culture and Education (1878–1912)," *Journal of Central European Affairs*, XII (January, 1953), 356–367; J. C. Campbell, "French Influence and the Rise of Roumanian Nationalism," (Harvard University, unpublished doctoral dissertation, 1940); J. C. Campbell, "The Influence of Western Political Thought in the Rumanian Principalities, 1821–1848," *Journal of Central European Affairs*, IV (October, 1944), 262–273; and J. F. Clarke," Bible Societies, American Missionaries and the National Revival of Bulgaria" (Harvard University, unpublished doctoral dissertation, 1937).

There is no adequate comprehensive study of the impact of the French Revolution and of Napoleon on the Balkans as a whole, although there is a considerable body of literature concerning the influence in specific localities. The following studies are of a general nature but superficial: N. Iorga, *La Révolution française et le sud-est de l'Europe* (Bucharest, 1934); F. Thierfelder, *Ursprung und Wirkung der französischen Kultureinflüsse in Südosteuropa:* (Berlin, 1943); *1789: Éveil des peuples: la révolution française, l'Europe centrale et les Balkans* (Paris, 1939).

Another fairly significant source of Western influence was the considerable number of local recruits in great-power armies that operated at various times on Balkan soil. This has been studied only piecemeal in the following: S. I. Samoilov, "Narodnoosvoboditelnoe vosstanie 1821 g.v. Valakhii" ["The National Liberation Uprising of 1821 in Wallachia"], *Voprosy Istorii* (October, 1955), pp. 94–105; N. I. Kaza-

kov, "Iz istorii Russko-Bôlgarskikh sviazei v period voiny Rossii s
Turtsiei (1806–1812 gg.)" ["From the history of Russo-Bulgarian ties
during the war of Russia with Turkey (1806–1812)"], *Voprosy Istorii*
(June 1955), pp. 42–55; P. K. Fortunatov, "Boevoi Russko-Bolgarskii
soiuz v voine 1877–1878 godov" ["The Russo-Bulgarian military alliance in the war of 1877–1878"], in *Osvobozhdenie Bôlgarii ot Turetskogo Iga* [*The liberation of Bulgaria from the Turkish yoke*], (Moscow,
1953), pp. 47–70; J. Savant, "Napoléon et la libération de la Grèce,"
L'hellénisme contemporain (July-October 1950), pp. 320–341; and A.
Bakalopoulou, *Ta Hellenika Strateumata tou 1821* [*The Greek Armies
of 1821*], (Salonika, 1948).

General studies of the early phase of Western diplomacy in the
Balkans are W. Fritzemeyer, *Christenheit und Europa* (Leipzig, 1931);
F. L. Baumer, "England, the Turk, and the Common Corps of Christen-
dom," *American Historical Review*, L (October, 1944), 26–48; and D.
Vaughan, *Europe and the Turk: A Pattern of Alliances 1350–1700*
(Liverpool, 1954). The effects of Great Power diplomacy on inter-
Balkan relations since the eighteenth century is traced in L. S. Sta-
vrianos, *Balkan Federation: A History of the Movement toward Balkan
Unity in Modern Times* (Northampton, Mass., 1944). The voluminous
literature on great-power diplomacy during the various Balkan crises is
given in L. S. Stavrianos, *The Balkans since 1453* (New York, 1958).

There is no comprehensive analysis of the socioeconomic impact of
the West on the Balkans during the national period. The following are
among the most important specialized studies: D. Warriner, "Some
Controversial Issues in the History of Agrarian Europe," *Slavonic and
East European Review*, XXXII (December, 1953), 168–186; I. Sakazov,
Bulgarische Wirtschaftsgeschichte (Berlin, 1929); J. Tomasevich, *Peasants, Politics and Economic Change in Yugoslavia* (Stanford, Calif.,
1955); R. Trouton, *Peasant Renaissance in Yugoslavia 1900–1950* (London, 1952); D. Mitrany, *The Land and the Peasant in Rumania* (London, 1930); H. L. Roberts, *Rumania: Political Problems of an Agrarian
State* (New Haven, Conn., 1951); Ch. Evelpides, *Oikonomike kai
koinonike historia tes Hellados* [*Economic and Social History of
Greece*], (Athens, 1950); G. Kordatos, *Eisagoge sten historia tes
hellenikes kephalaiokratias* [*Introduction to the History of Greek Capitalism*], (Athens, 1930), the latter being a Marxist interpretation. The
effect of socioeconomic change on the Balkan *zadruga* is described in
D. Novakovich, *La Zadrouga* (Paris, 1905); E. Sicard, *La Zadruga sud-
slav dans l'évolution du groupe domestique* (Paris, 1934); and the articles by P. E. Mosely, "The Peasant Family: The Zadruga or Communal
Joint-Family in the Balkans and its Recent Evolution," in C. F. Ware,
ed., *The Cultural Approach to History* (New York, 1940), pp. 95–108;
"Adaptation for Survival: The Varžić Zadruga," *Slavonic and East
European Review*, XXI (March, 1943), 147–173; and "The Distribution

of the Zadruga within South-Eastern Europe," *Jewish Social Studies Publication*, V (1953), 219–230.

For the West's financial role in the Balkans, see H. Feis, *Europe the World's Banker 1870–1914* (New Haven, 1930), chap. 12; D. C. Blaisdell, *European Financial Control in the Ottoman Empire* (New York, 1929); A. Levandis, *The Greek Foreign Debt and the Great Powers 1821–1898* (New York, 1944); K. C. Popov, *La Bulgarie économique* (Sofia, 1920); D. Kastris, *Les Capitaux étrangers dans la finance Roumaine* (Paris, 1921); M. Simitch, *La Dette publique de la Serbie* (Paris, 1925).

The West's role in Balkan railway construction is described in Feis, *op. cit.*, ch. 13; C. Jelavich, *Tsarist Russia and Balkan Nationalism* (Berkeley and Los Angeles, Calif., 1958), chap. 3; W. S. Vucinich, *Serbia Between East and West: The Events of 1903–1908* (Stanford, Calif., 1954); and A. J. May, "The Novibazar Railway Project," *Journal of Modern History*, X (December, 1938), 496–527, and "Trans-Balkan Railway Schemes," *Journal of Modern History*, XXIV (December, 1952), 352–367.

The extent and significance of Balkan emigration before the nineteenth century is analyzed in the Stoianovich studies listed above. The large-scale overseas emigration in the nineteenth and twentieth centuries is described in individual national studies, as for example, N. J. Polyzos, *Essai sur l'émigration grecque* (Paris, 1947) T. Saloutos, *They Remember America: The Story of the Repatriated Greek-Americans* (Berkeley and Los Angeles, Calif., 1956); C. A. Galitzi, *A Study of Assimilation among the Roumanians in the United States* (New York, 1929); Federal Writers' Project of the Works Progress Administration, *The Albanian Struggle in the Old World and New* (Boston, 1919).

The impact of the West on Balkan political institutions and practices is analyzed in the mentioned works by Roberts, Tomasevich, and also in T. Stoianovich, "The Pattern of Serbian Intellectual Evolution 1830–1880," *Comparative Studies in Society and History*, I (March, 1959), 242–272; A. Pepelasis," Socio-Cultural Barriers to the Economic Development of Greece" (University of California, unpublished doctoral dissertation, 1955); and the same author's "The Legal System and Economic Development of Greece," *Journal of Economic History*, XIX (June, 1959), 173–198; C. E. Black, "The Influence of Western Political Thought in Bulgaria, 1850–1885," *American Historical Review*, XLVIII (April, 1943), 507–520.

For the contemporary phase of the Westernization process, see I. Sanders, *Balkan Village* (Lexington, Ky., 1949); J. M. Halpern, *A Serbian Village* (New York, 1958); and D. Lee, "Greece," in *Cultural Patterns and Technical Change*, ed. by Margaret Mead (New York, 1952). For global perspective, these works may be compared with D. Lerner, *The Passing of Traditional Society: Modernizing the Middle*

East (Glencoe, Ill., 1958); L. S. S. O'Malley, *Modern India and the West: A Study of the Interaction of their Civilizations* (London, 1941); *Traditional Cultures in South-East Asia,* prepared for UNESCO by the Institute of Traditional Cultures, Madras (Bombay, 1958); J. Numata, "Acceptance and Rejection of Elements of European Culture in Japan," *Journal of World History,* III, (1956), 231–253; J. K. Fairbank, "China's Response to the West: Problems and Suggestions," *Journal of World History,* III, (1956), 381–406; K. Little, "African Culture and the Western Intrusion," *Journal of World History,* III, (1957), 941–964.

GREEK LITERATURE SINCE THE FALL

OF CONSTANTINOPLE IN

1453

C. A. Trypanis

Unlike the other Balkan peoples, the Greeks have a "literary memory" that reaches back far beyond the Middle Ages, extending to the origins of Western writing, the great Homeric poems.[1] No doubt each succeeding era brought with it a fresh social, political, and emotional life, which is reflected in contemporary writing (the most important changes occurred with the conversion of the Greeks to Christianity) but the thread of national, linguistic, and literary unity was retained uninterrupted—the oldest living tradition in the Western world.[2] Thus many of the major factors that determined the development of Greek letters in the period under consideration have their roots in the distant past, and are unintelligible without some knowledge of what happened

---

[1] I have been asked to give an outline of Greek literature and letters from the fall of Constantinople to the Turks in 1453 up to the present day. The space at my disposal is too limited to allow an adequate account of this important development in Balkan life, and so I shall touch on only a few salient features and mention only a few of the many important names.

The fall of Constantinople to the Turks is no real landmark in the development of Greek literature and letters. The roots of "modern Greek" literature lie deep in the Byzantine period, but I have been asked to take 1453 as my starting point. On the origins of "modern Greek" literature see E. Kriaras, *Anglo-Greek Review*, V (1950), 92 f., L. Politis, *Hellenika* XIII (1954), 400, and *N. Hestia*, LVIII (1955), 986 f., 1307, and 1554 f.; K. Th. Demaras, *Historia Neohellenikes Logotechnias* [History of Modern Greek Literature], (Athens, 1948), pp. 2 f. For a different point of view see D. Papas, "When Does Modern Greek Literature Begin? A Contribution to the Solution of the Problem of the Divisions of Medieval and Modern Literature," *Probleme der neugriechischen Literatur* (Berlin, 1959), I, 106–144.

[2] Cf. W. Miller, *A History of the Greek People 1821–1921* (London, 1922), p. 2 f.

in preceding centuries. Of these factors undoubtedly the most important is what is known as the "language question," the two rival schools of language in modern Greece (the "purist" and the "popular"), whose respective instruments are both ultimately derived, although by different routes, from the workshop of Homer and the other classics.

As for the development of the Greek language it must suffice to note that all major changes which lead from ancient to modern Greek (the change from a pitch to a stress accent, the main simplification in phonetics, grammar, and syntax) occurred roughly in the years between 300 B.C. and 300 A.D. (the so-called *koine* period of the Greek language); and that the further development, which occurred naturally throughout the Byzantine and succeeding centuries, gradually alienated the spoken tongue from the written language as taught in the schools of rhetoric, grammar, and theology of those days.[3] For the school curricula had been on the whole fixed at the end of antiquity according to the great "classical" writers, and they were more or less rigorously observed by the Byzantine and post-Byzantine Greeks up to the liberation of Greece in the nineteenth century, to the detriment of many written works and of education in Greece as a whole.

From the Fall of Constantinople to the Liberation of Greece (1453–1828)

Just as the transfer of the Roman capital from Rome to Byzantium in 330 A.D. (the founding of Constantinople) was, as stressed by Wilamowitz-Moellendorf, the great turning point in the history of the Mediterranean lands,[4] the fall of the city to the Turks in 1453 has rightly been seen as the Greek nation's most disastrous catastrophe. In fact, in view of the far-reaching effects it had on the whole of Europe, and of the preponderant position the Turks thereby secured for themselves in the East, it is a milestone in the history of the world. Already from the thirteenth century the economic and political decline in the Eastern Empire was evident, and this, together with the demand in the West

---

[3] A full bibliography and a clear account of it is in S. G. Kapsomenos, "Die griechische Sprache zwischen Koine und Neugriechisch," *Berichte zum XI. Internationalen Byzantinisten-Kongress* (München, 1958), pp. 1 f. See also A. Debrunner, *Geschichte der griechischen Sprache* (Berlin, 1954), II, 34 f.

[4] See N. H. Baynes-H. St. L. B. Moss, *Byzantium* (Oxford, 1948), p. xvii.

for Greek manuscripts and letters, drove a number of eminent Byzantine scholars to Italy and France. These were joined by others after the capital of the empire had fallen to the Turks. The services of men like Emmanuel Chrysoloras, Bessarion, John Argyropoulos, Demetrios Chalcocondylis, Constantine and John Laskaris in spreading the knowledge of Greek in the West (which was later to flow back to the Balkans) must not be forgotten. They stimulated the study of ancient philosophy, which resulted at the close of the fifteenth century in the great controversy over the merits of the Platonic and Aristotelian philosophies, championed by Gemistos Pletho and Georgios Gennadios.[5]

In the centuries when the Western world was enjoying the rich fruits of the Renaissance—the fruits that had been offered by Greek learning—when in Italy, France, Spain, and England kings and bishops were the patrons of art and letters, the Greek world lay crushed under the heel of an Asiatic conqueror mercilessly extinguishing every spark of life.[6] Its lands were devastated, its children seized and turned into Mohammedans (one-fifth of its males were for centuries collected every four years and carefully educated as Mohammedans, thus providing the sultan with a standing army and a devoted body of household slaves),[7] its women were cast into the harems of the Muslim pashas, its churches turned into mosques, and its schools banned.[8] Naturally, Turkish ferocity was not directed exclusively against the Greeks, but the agrarian populations (and such were on the whole the other Balkan peoples at the time) felt it much less. It was the city dwellers who were in the first instance affected, and thus the light of learning that had shone in the many great centers of the late Byzantine world, such as Constantinople, Trebizond, and Mistra, died out, and all literate as well as national life centered on the Patriarch in Constantinople. It was the Orthodox Church which became responsible during the first centuries after the fall for the preservation of education, however inadequate, and which succeeded in keeping

---

[5] See G. M. Hartmann, "Die Bedeutung des Griechentums für die Entwicklung des italienischen Humanismus," *Probleme der neugriechischen Literatur* (Berlin, 1960) II, pp. 3 f.

[6] See W. Miller, *The Ottoman Empire and Its Successors* (Cambridge [England], 1936) p. 21.

[7] See E. S. Forster, *History of Modern Greece* (London, 1941), p. 2.

[8] Cf. G. Finlay, *History of Greece* (Oxford, 1877) V, 162 f.

aglow the embers of Greek learning until the better years that were to follow.

The main factor in the survival and further development of Greek life and letters was for the most part the privileges granted to the Greek Orthodox Church by Mohammed II, the Conqueror, as part of his fiscal and anti-Western policy. The young sultan, whose political and military genius was matched only by his extreme cruelty, set on the throne of the Patriarch Gennadios Scholarios, the champion of the party in the Greek Orthodox Church which had opposed the union with Rome. This he thought—and again he was proved right—would dissuade the Roman Catholic West from embarking on a crusade to liberate the Orthodox Greeks from the infidels.[9] Moreover, by allowing the Church to organize and to a certain extent administer the conquered Christians, the sultan hoped to extract the taxes he desired from his Christian subjects. But whatever the motives of Mohammed may have been, the consequences of his actions were far-reaching and of fundamental significance for the survival and development of the Balkan peoples and of Greek literature and learning.

The period under Turkish domination (1453–1828) can best be examined if we treat separately the two areas of activity in Greek literature and letters, namely the Greek lands under Frankish rule (mainly as a result of the Fourth Crusade in 1204) and Constantinople and the Greek lands under Turkish domination.

The Greek Lands under Frankish Rule

The only Greeks who could obtain some degree of higher education were those living in the lands under Frankish, mostly Venetian, rule where the benefits of Western culture could be enjoyed.[10] Rhodes, Cyprus, Chios, Crete, and the Ionian Islands are the places where a literary life becomes manifest.

The fountainhead for these centers of learning was Venice, where a Greek community of merchants and men of letter appears as early

---

[9] Cf. K. Paparhegopoulos, *Ta Didaktikotera Porismata tes Historias tou Hellenikou Ethnous* [*The Most Instructive Conclusions from the History of the Greek Nation*], (Athens: Erevna, 1932), pp. 22 f.

[10] Cf. W. Miller, *The Latins in the Levant* (London, 1908), pp. 541 f., 605, 618 and *passim;* A. Mirambel, *La Litterature Grecque Moderne* (Paris, 1953), pp. 14 f.

as the middle of the fifteenth century. From modest origins this Greek element in Venice had reached a remarkable level of prosperity and influence by the turn of the seventeenth to the eighteenth century. It had a magnificent Greek church of its own (S. Giorgio dei Greci) and an important school built by the munificence of the Corfiote Thomas Flanginis. This became a center for the training of Greek teachers and clergy, many of whom on returning to their homeland brought with them Western thought and learning to benefit their less fortunate compatriots in the Balkans.[11] A number of Greek communities gradually appeared in other Italian cities, of which many sent back teachers and educated men to the Turkish-occupied parts of Greece. To this group belong Theophilos Corydaleus[12] (middle of the sixteenth century) whose books were studied in Greek schools up to the liberation of Greece in 1828, and Elias Miniatis (middle of the seventeenth century) the greatest preacher of the period under consideration.[13]

Of all the Greek lands under Latin rule, the place where Italian influence is most evident, and where important Greek literature flourished with a character of its own, was Venetian-occupied Crete.

Crete remained under Venetian rule from 1204 to 1669. In this period it developed a vigorous literary and artistic life, which was strengthened by the arrival of a number of Greek scholars and artists, who took refuge on the island after the fall of Constantinople in 1453. The climax of this development was reached in the first half of the seventeenth century. Many Cretan writers and painters became famous all over the Greek world, and even in the West, as can be seen from the example of Domenico Theotocopoulo, El Greco. Italy, through her literary and artistic splendor, was exercising a profound influence all over the civilized world in those days, and Crete also was greatly affected, particularly in her dramatic and epic poetry. The development of Cretan literature can now be followed in its main out-

---

[11] Cf. Miller, *The Latins* . . . , p. 541.

[12] See C. Tsourkas, *Les debuts de l'enseignement philosophique et de la libre pensée dans les Balkans* (Bucharest, 1948), pp. 27 f.

[13] The works of these (as well as of many other Greeks of the period) were also translated into other Balkan languages. Cf. Veselin Beshevliev, "Der Widerhall des neugriechischen Sprachkampfes und der neugriechischen Literatur im Bulgarien des vorigen Jahrhunderts," *Probleme der neugriechischen Literatur* (Berlin, 1960), II, 48–54.

lines thanks to the work done in recent times by Cretan scholars, notably S. A. Xanthoudidis. We can trace the progress in versification from the crude rhymed fifteen-syllable "political" lines of Georgios Choumis in his paraphrase of *Genesis* and *Exodus*, written early in the sixteenth century, to the finished handling of the same meter by Vincentsos Cornaros in his great romantic poem the *Erotokritos*, which probably dates from the middle of the seventeenth century. This, an epic-lyrical composition of 10,052 rhyming fifteen-syllable lines, is the masterpiece of Cretan literature. Its theme is the chivalrous love of the hero, Erotokritos, for Aretousa, and their final union after long and arduous adventures. The general trend of the story follows the French prose work *Paris et Vienne*, which the author of the Cretan epic most probably knew in an Italian version; but at the same time the influence of the Italian epic, in particular of Ariosto, is evident. The qualities which the poet celebrates are chivalry in love and valor in combat, expressed by dramatic rather than didactic means. The language, a developed form of the Cretan dialect, is vigorous and full of verve, rich in sound and imagery. For the Greeks, much of the charm of the poem lay in its national character, for elements of the classical tradition abound, and the contrast between Hellenes and "barbarians" is stressed. The *Erotokritos* soon became popular throughout the Greek world. Its chief characters became proverbial figures and were often represented in carnival processions; detached parts of it were sung as folk songs, and instances are known of all its 10,052 lines being recited by heart, even by illiterate peasants!

Cretan dramatic literature presents us with fairly rich material, but it was external Western influence far more than ancestral tradition which was responsible for its sudden flourishing in the sixteenth and seventeenth centuries. The most important work of this group of plays is *Abraham's Sacrifice*, a religious drama fashioned on the model of the *Isach* by L. Groto. The poet, probably Vincentsos Cornaros himself, superimposes a number of popular Cretan elements, gnomic sayings, similes, and the like, upon the fine character analysis of his verses. The longest and by far the grimmest Cretan tragedy, verging on the gruesome, is the *Erophile*, which was inspired by Giraldi's *Orbecche*. The poet, George Chortatzis, wrote this work before 1637 in characters of the Latin alphabet, yet another proof of the fusion of Greek and Italian culture in Crete. The *Erophile* is a blood-thirsty drama.

The heroine, daughter of a king of Egypt, falls in love with, and marries in secret, a prince of the court. Her father discovers this, kills the young man and offers her his head, heart, and hands. Erophile kills herself, and the king is slain by her serving maids. The dialogue is lively, and the choric songs and laments are not lacking in poetic force. Even so, one wonders how this melodramatic play captivated the imagination of the Greeks, and how some of its verses have passed on to the people. It seems as though it were a glorification of faith in love that secured its popularity in Crete and the Ionian Islands, where it was also later acted.

The Cretan plays included comedies, such as *Stathis* and *Fortounatos*, which though in the main borrowed from Italian and ultimately deriving from Plautine and Terentian comedy, are interesting because of their introduction of local color and characters. But the real gem of Cretan comedy is *Gyparis*, also by an anonymous author, and dating from about 1600. It describes in a masterly and humorous manner how two shepherd girls, who had previously scorned love, are converted to its cause.

Closely connected with the Italian pastorals, which flourished from the Renaissance up to the seventeenth century, is *The Fair Shepherdess*, a Cretan pastoral, published in 1627 by Nicolas Drymitinos. This poem, whose versification, the eleven-syllable line, is more Italian than Greek, was much read among the Greeks of the seventeenth and eighteenth centuries, who mistook its intentional artlessness for true simplicity, and were drawn more to the peaceful, idyllic setting than to the work itself. Large parts of it were sung by popular folk poets, who also readapted them to the traditional demotic fifteen-syllable line, one more proof that parts of literary works can easily be detached, readapted, and finally heard on the lips of the people as folk songs.[14] We have also from this period a few Cretan historical and didactic poems of little artistic merit, as well as some Cretan folk songs of remarkable vigor.

The language of the Cretans of the sixteenth and seventeenth centuries is striking in its unity and absence of obsolete forms; the goal toward which the Greeks had striven in vain for so many centuries seems to have been almost reached. Had Crete not fallen into the

---

[14] We find the same thing in some Acritic Ballads, cf. P. Kalonaros, *Basileios Digenes Akritas* (Athens, 1941), I, 33 f.

234 C. A. TRYPANIS

hands of the Turks in 1669, the course of Greek literature would probably have taken a very different turn.[15] The Cretan dialect, elevated
to a common Greek literary idiom, might well have prevailed, and
the harassing "language question" might have been solved much earlier. However, the Turkish occupation of Crete in 1669 brought about
the end of Cretan literature—a literature in which the tragic muse,
mute since the end of the classical period, had spoken again in Greek,
even if the Cretan dramas were mainly adaptations from Italian models. After the fall of Crete it was left to the Ionian Islands to continue
the Italian-influenced Greek tradition. This seems however to have
waned as the years went by, as the Italian language in its widening
sphere drew to itself many of the Greek writers of the "Heptanese."

Of the other Greek lands under Frankish occupation, in Rhodes and
Cyprus erotic lyric poetry (notably absent from Byzantine literature)
was composed, admittedly under Italian influence, but nevertheless in
the spoken idiom of the islands. At the same time the chronicles of
Makhairas, and *Boustronis,* written in Cyprus during the fifteenth and
the sixteenth centuries, are monuments of Greek vernacular and important historical sources.[16]

The Greek writing which appeared in the Frankish-occupied lands
are of great significance in the history of Greek literature; first because
they were written in the spoken idiom, as the traditional Byzantine
school system had virtually broken down in those areas; and secondly
since it was due to Frankish influence that rhyme was introduced to
Greek poetry. Rhyme is of Semitic origin,[17] but had to travel round
the southern Mediterranean to Spain, Provence, and Italy before being introduced by the Crusaders of the Fourth Crusade to the Greek
world. It is an interesting example of the powers of resistance of the
great Greek classical tradition that, although the Byzantine Empire
first embraced and then became a close neighbor of the Semitic lands
where rhyme was so richly employed, and although much of the early
Christian Semitic literature was translated into Greek, rhyme was

---

[15] Cf. A. Kampanis, *Historia tes Neohellenikes Logotechnias* [*History of Modern Greek Literature*], (Athens, 1948), p. 58.

[16] Cf. R. M. Dawkins, *Leontios Makhairas* (Oxford, 1932).

[17] Cf. W. Meyer, *Abhandlungen d. philos.-philol. Classe der k. Bayerischen Akademie der Wissenschaften,* XVII (1886), part I, pp. 308 f.

never used,[18] because it was not an integral part of Greek classical poetry (except of course as a rhetorical figure of speech, the *homoioteleuton*). It was left to make its way with the Crusaders to those parts of the Greek world where the traditional Byzantine school education had been abolished.

The Greek Lands under Turkish Rule

As for the Greek mainland, Constantinople occupies the center of the scene. The few learned men who remained in that broken world after the fall of the city clustered round the patriarch, and there laid the foundations of the new Greek national and literary life. During the first two centuries the picture is somewhat dark. Such schools as functioned were supported by the Church, and their main object was to educate men for the Church. On the whole they were a continuation, or rather they were a dim reflection, of the traditional Byzantine schools, but whether directly or indirectly, Western ideas were gradually introduced. Thus in the sixteenth and seventeenth centuries we find in Constantinople highly-educated men such as George Aetolos, and enlightened patriarchs such as Jeremiah II (1572–1595), or Cyril Loukaris (1621–1638), who took the lead in matters of Church and education, in spite of the combined attacks and intrigues of Turks and Jesuits.

THE MERCHANTS

By the middle of the eighteenth century the picture of the Greek world becomes brighter. The Greeks, through their resource and ingenuity (and by taking advantage of the decline of Turkish administration) succeeded in capturing for themselves nearly all the commerce and maritime trade of the eastern Mediterranean. Thus many a flourishing Christian community reëmerges, and even where only a minority, it is they who set the standards of civilization and culture.[19]

---

[18] There is only one remarkable exception, the *Akathistos Hymn* of the Greek Orthodox Church, probably composed at the end of the fifth century; cf. S. Mercati, *Encyclopaedia Italiana*, "Acatisto."

[19] It is significant for example that all doctors in the Balkans were Greek. The Southern Slav word for doctor was *Grk* = the Greek. See also T. Stoianovich, "Conquering Balkan Orthodox Merchant," *Journal of Economic History*, XX (June 1960) 296 f.

This new class of Greek merchants with their colonies and contacts with the West is perhaps the most important channel through which Western ideas and culture flowed into the Balkans.[20] This was achieved mainly by the establishment and support of Greek schools throughout the Balkan world (which functioned under the auspices of the Orthodox Church of Constantinople) and by the issue of educational works in Greek from the printing presses of Venice, Trieste, and Vienna, together with Greek newspapers from the same sources.

The Orthodox Church and its schools did not discriminate at the time between the various Christian nationalities under Turkish rule; generally they were all considered to be Orthodox children of the Church, who were to be helped and protected in both this and the other life.[21] No doubt the majority of priests, bishops, and teachers were Greek (the other Balkan peoples, being primarily rural, had on the whole neither the opportunity nor the traditions of the Greeks for education at that time),[22] but there was no exclusively Greek nor bigoted nationalist spirit in the Church or its schools in those days. This can be seen from the fact that neither in the Theological School of the Patriarchate (the central establishment of education in the Orthodox Church) nor later in the Athos Academy (the "Athonias" of Mount Athos) was there any discrimination between Greeks and non-Greeks, nor any bar against non-Greek students—in fact, a number of other Balkan nationals were educated there; and it can also be seen by the donations and legacies left to Greek schools by wealthy Slavs and Bulgarians who recognized the services rendered.[23]

---

[20] E. Turczynski, "Die deutsch-griechischen Kulturbeziehungen und die griechischen Zeitungen (1784–1821)," *Probleme der neugriechischen Literatur* (Berlin, 1960), II, 55–109.

[21] Already in 1844 Robert Cyprien said: "Man muss zum Lobe des Griechentums betonen, dass Bulgarien seine besten Patrioten unter den Philhellenen aufzuweisen hat. Überall dort, wo der griechische Einfluss stärker wirksam wird, bekommt der Bulgare ein lebendigeres und genaueres Gefühl für seine eigene Würde." Beshevliev, *op. cit.*, p. 49.

[22] Cf. Finlay, *op. cit.*, VI, 16.

[23] Cf. T. Evangellidis, *He Paideia epi Tourkokratias* [*Education during the Ottoman Domination*], (Athens, 1936), II, 336 f. See also Beshevliev, *op. cit.*, pp. 49 f.: "Von besonderer Bedeutung für die geistige Wiedergeburt der Bulgarn waren die griechischen Schulen in Kydonia (türk. Ayvali), auf den Inseln Chios, Andros, Syra, Chalki, auf dem Athos usw. Die Lehrer an allen diesen Schulen hatten ihre Ausbildung in Italien, Frankreich und Deutschland erhalten und waren wirkliche Humanisten von der Art der Italienischen. . . . Alle Bul-

Indeed the services were great, for these Greek schools flourished in Belgrade, Skoplje, Veles, Koritsa, Moschopolis (where a printing press was also established in 1743), Sofia, Varna, Karlovo, Bucharest, and Jassy, to mention only a few of the main centers on the periphery of the Greek world, and to say nothing of the numerous other schools in Macedonia and Epirus attended by Balkan peoples of all nationalities.[24] The standard of teaching varied greatly, but in some centers it reached significant heights. There were teachers such as Athanasios Psalidas in Yannina, who was a pupil of Kant and in direct correspondence with the great philosopher, to cite only one striking example.

Together with learning, Christian art was also fostered in those centers and filtered through to the Balkans until a second stream came to the northern areas from Russia.

THE FOLK SONGS

Before returning to Constantinople and to Phanariotes of the seventeenth and eighteenth centuries, a few words must be said about the Greek folk songs which flourished in the Turkish-occupied mainland, some of which are undoubtedly among the finest verse ever composed in Greek. Folk songs expressing the feelings of the people in their own spoken idioms were produced throughout the Middle Ages (the most important cycle being that of the "Acritis" ballads). Many of them still live with numerous variations on the lips of the peasants and sailors of Greece. The origin of a few can even be traced back to ancient Greece, as for example the "Chelidonisma," which was sung in spring to celebrate the return of the swallows.[25] The eight-

---

garen die eine höhere Bildung zu geniesen wünschten, konnten sie nur in den griechischen Schulen finden. . . . Die meisten hielten das Bewusstsein ihrer Volkszugehörigkeit lebendig und wurden Führer der nationalen Wiedergeburt des Bulgarentums, wie z.B. Raino Popowitsch, Christaki Pawlowitsch, Konst. Fotinoff, Dr. Iw. Seliminski, Gawr. Krastewitsch, Sawa Dobroplodni, Marko Balabanoff, Noefit Rilski, Iw. Dobrowski, u.a.m. Sie empfanden Hochachtung vor der griechischen Kultur und übernahmen manche Ideen und Anschauungen ihrer Lehrer, die sie auf bulgarischen Boden verpflanzten."

[24] Cf. Evangellidis, *op. cit.*, II, 339 f., 336 f., 378; and N. Moschopoulos, *La Presse dans la renaissance Balkanique* (Athens, 1921), pp. 122 f. Even after the liberation of Greece the University of Athens in its early years had a great number of Rumanian and Bulgarian students.

[25] Cf. C. Fauriel, *Chants populaires de la Grèce moderne* (Paris, 1824–1825), II, 256.

eenth century, however, is the period when the folk song truly flourished. A number of the earlier and later Greek folk songs have been
taken over by Greece's neighbors—Albanians, Southern Slavs, and Bulgarians—and some have even traveled to the north and west of Europe.[26] They fall into three main divisions: first the historical folk
songs, recounting historical events as they caught the imagination of
the people. The Acritic ballads, the Laments for the fall of Constantinople and certain klephtic ballads are among the most notable examples of this group. Secondly the Songs of Everyday Life—love
songs, lullabies, marriage songs, working songs, songs of exile, dirges
and carols; and thirdly, the *Paraloges*—short narratives of a swift epic
character—which often amount to summaries of folk traditions and
folk tales. The meter most frequently used is the fifteen-syllable line,
rhymed and unrhymed (the *Politikos Stichos*), which is broken up
into the other main forms of demotic meters to conform to the demands of music and dance. In these folk songs strong family feeling
predominates; death is personified in the form of Charos, who struggles with his victims, is sometimes worsted, but as a rule triumphs.
They are full of the breath of the forests and mountains, and like so
much of great Greek poetry personify trees, rocks, and rivers. Even
the mountains sing the prowess of the klephts, bewail their death, and
comfort the bereaved wives and mothers. They have been a constant
source of inspiration and rejuvenation to modern Greek poetry.

THE PHANARIOTES

We now return once again to Constantinople and the group of influential and educated Greeks who lived there in the seventeenth and
eighteenth centuries, known as the Phanariotes.[27] These Greeks,
through their intellect, education and wealth succeeded in occupying
high posts in the Turkish government—grand dragomans of the Porte,
dragomans of the Fleet, ambassadors to Western courts, and the like.
The creation of the positions of voivods, or Christian rulers, of Moldavia in 1712 and Wallachia in 1716 gave able Phanariotes further

---

[26] Cf. W. J. Entwistle, *European Balladry* (Oxford, 1939), *passim*.
[27] The name is derived from the quarter of Constantinople called *Phanari*,
where the Patriarch was established, and where most of the influential Greeks
lived.

opportunities of distinction, and the holders of these offices naturally chose their subordinates from among their own nation. After the Greeks, it was the Rumanians, who in spite of much justified criticism, benefited most by the Phanariotes. For the academies of Bucharest and Jassy (both Phanariote foundations), to say nothing of the many smaller schools, were the first direct contacts of the Rumanian people with Western culture. "They were for the Rumanians, who were then under profound Slavic influence, the first steps toward their emancipation."[28] But Phanariote influence was not limited only to Greeks and Rumanians. By the schools and printing presses they established and by the books they wrote they greatly helped Balkan education as a whole. For the Phanariotes were the first group of men in the Ottoman Empire to master French, the language of diplomacy, and having become acquainted with the great French writings of the time, were the earliest channel through which French thought and literature flowed to the Balkans—an influence which was later to become predominant.

The most distinguished Phanariote is Alexander Mavrocordatos, known to the Greek world by the title, *Ex Aporrheton* (the Secret Counselor). A Chiot by origin, he first directed the patriarchal school in Constantinople, and later was entrusted by the Porte with many important diplomatic missions, including the conclusion of the Treaty of Carlowitz (1699). He wrote a number of significant works, mainly in an austere, purist form of Greek, ranging from commentaries on Aristotle to his own interpretations of life and history. Many members of the Mavrocordatos family in later times also distinguished themselves in Greek letters, as indeed did a number of other Phanariote families who combined the missions of patron and author.

As for poetry, Caesarios Dapontes (1714–1789), at a time when knowledge rather than art was the order of the day, was greatly admired by his contemporaries. In his many thousands of verses he interwove personal experiences, for his life was full of adventure. Starting from the island of Skopelos, he reached Constantinople and the

---

[28] P. P. Panaitescu, "Perioada slavonă la Români," in *Revista Fundatiilor Regale*, XI (January, 1944), pp. 126 f. On the influence of the Academies of Bucharest and Jassy, where the teachings of Theophilos Corydaleus were discussed till the end of the eighteenth century see C. Tsourkas, *op. cit.*, pp. 61 f. See also N. Iorga, *Byzance après Byzance* (Bucharest, 1935), pp. 155 f.

Danubian principalities, landed in jail, and finally died as a monk on Mount Athos. The *Mirror of Ladies* and the *Garden of Graces* are his best-known works.

THE TEACHERS OF THE NATION

The combined efforts of the Church, the Phanariotes, and the wealthy merchants to stimulate education as a means of "resuscitation" for the Greek nation, resulted in a class of distinguished teachers found at the eve of the Greek War of Independence, and known to the Greeks as the "Teachers of the Nation." The debt owed to these men by the Greeks—indeed by the whole Balkan world—cannot be overrated. They prepared the Greek nation for the great struggle for liberation, without which no Balkan country would have achieved its national freedom from the Turkish yoke as early as it did. Representative are the two distinguished prelates Nikephoros Theotokis (1731–1800) and Eugenios Voulgaris (1715–1806), both natives of Corfu, who wrote in the literary language in defense of Greek orthodoxy, but also produced works of mathematics, physics, geography, archaeology and philosophy, in addition to translations. Many works of the Teachers of the Nation in Greek were translated into other Balkan languages and served for the enlightenment of these countries.[29] Their language may have been on the whole artificial, but their work was of inestimable value to the Balkan Greeks of those days. However, the greatest name among the forerunners of the Greek revival is that of Adamantios Korais (1748–1833), who, though born in Smyrna, where he received his first education, was of Chiot origin. He later distinguished himself as a student of medicine at Montpellier, and in 1788 moved to Paris, where he devoted his life to literary pursuits. Patriotism and a passion for learning were the two main features of his character. He first worked on the classical medical writers, and then edited with outstanding success the *Characters* of Theophrastus. This was followed by editions of Hippocrates, Longus, and Heliodorus, which established his international reputation as a scholar; he was invited to take part in the French translation of Strabo, prepared at the command of Napoleon. But his most important literary undertaking was the *Library of Greek Literature* (1805–1826), which consisted

---

[29] Cf. Beshevliev, *op. cit.*, p. 51.

of seventeen volumes of classical texts.[30] At the same time Korais prepared a second series, the *Parerga* (1809–1827), in nine volumes.[31] Later scholars have been lavish in their praise of Korais' ability; a great number of his emendations have been accepted, and many confirmed by manuscripts and papyri found later. Korais did not edit the Greek poets, because he considered them less important for solving the problems with which the Greek nation was faced. Moreover, in his fervent desire to help the Greeks, he embarked on a series of patriotic pamphlets, of polemical verse, dialogues, and political admonitions, many of which were included in the long introductions to the volumes of his *Library of Greek Literature*. Nor did he neglect the practical side of the Greek struggle for liberation. He was one of the founders of the "Philhellenic Committee of Paris" (1825), which gave financial support to the fighting Greeks; and he kept up a vast correspondence with most leading Philhellenes, scholars and statesmen, urging them to support the Greek cause.

Korais worked hard to improve the standards of Greek schools in Turkey, and to found libraries and scholarships for young Greeks to study in the universities of the West. He edited parts of the New Testament in order to enlighten the clergy of the Eastern Church, and proceeded to many other theological publications, in which he fought against old superstitions and prejudices. Korais exerted a far-reaching influence in the dispute over the modern Greek language. His main concern was to simplify the written Greek of his day by assimilating the literary tongue with the living idiom of modern Greece. In this endeavor he became the founder of modern Greek linguistic studies. His *Atakta* (1828–1835), in five volumes, are not only the first serious study of modern Greek, but also the first dictionary of that language. Still more linguistic material and a full grammar of modern

---

[30] The *Prodromos,* containing Aelian's *Varia Historia,* Heracleides Ponticus, and Nicolaus Damascenus, was followed by two volumes of Isocrates, six volumes of Plutarch's *Lives,* four of Strabo, the *Politics* and *Ethics* of Aristotle, the *Memorabilia* of Xenophon, with the *Gorgias* of Plato, and lastly Lycurgus' *Leocrates.*

[31] This included Polyaenus, Aesop, Xenocrates, Galen's *De Alimento ex Aquatilibus,* the *Meditations* of Marcus Aurelius, the *Tactics* of Onesander, five political treatises of Plutarch, Cebes, and Cleanthes with the *Encheiridion* of Epictetus, and two volumes of Arrian's version of his discourses. He also edited *Iliad* I–IV, translated Herodotus into modern Greek, and wrote valuable notes on Herodotus, Thucydides, Athenaeus, and Hesychius.

Greek are to be found in the nine volumes of his posthumous works (1881–1891). Perhaps no other scholar in modern times has exercised so much influence in so many fields as Korais. An unassuming man, he refused all honors offered to him by the universities and the academic bodies of France, including the invitation made by Boissonade in 1816 to join the Institute de France. Korais is undoubtedly the greatest letter writer in the Greek language. More than 5,000 of his letters have survived, some of which are of historical value, giving important information about the French Revolution. These have been translated into French by Quex de St. Hilaire.

Korais was not the only forerunner of the Greek revival who wrote and translated inspiring works. Other teachers, men of the Church and men of letters, many inspired by the French Revolution, taught, translated from the French, or wrote pamphlets or verse of their own to stimulate and prepare the Greek nation for its struggle for independence. Among them are Cosmas Aetolos (1714–1799) and Rhigas Pheraios (1757–1798), who both met with a martyr's death at the hands of the Turks. No verses of those days excited patriotic enthusiasm more, or enjoyed a greater popularity than Rhegas' *Thourios*. Full of the spirit of the French Revolution and freedom, that poem was sung by Greeks, Rumanians, Albanians, and Slavs with almost equal fervor, and many martyrs for liberty died with it on their lips ("Better enjoy one hour of freedom, than live for forty years a prisoner, a slave . . .").

Athanasios Christopoulos (1772–1847) and John Velaras (1771–1823) in a greater or lesser degree are influenced by the spirit of the Phanariotes, though the latter stands in sharp opposition to them in his use of language. Christopoulos, in spite of his artificiality and servile copying of the Anacreontics, marks a definite step in the evolution of personal Greek poetry. He uses a simple diction and has a notion of form, which brings his work to life, at least by comparison with the endless stilted lines of Dapontes. Velaras marks yet another step forward, for he is the first to link elevated poetry to the folk-song tradition, linguistically at least. A physician by profession (he was also the private doctor of Veli, the son of Ali Pasha of Yannina), he had a trained mind, and tried to apply even in poetry the extremist demotic linguistic ideas he had expressed in his small but important book on the Greek language, *Romeikē Glossa*. In spite of his admiration for the Greek folk songs, however, his poetry still displays the influence of the Anacreontics and of French drawing-room bucolics of the eighteenth century, as can be seen even from the names of his heroines—Daphne, Chloe, Phylle.

FROM THE LIBERATION OF GREECE TO THE PRESENT DAY (1828–1960)

The heroic efforts and sacrifices of the Greek nation in its struggle for independence (1821–1828) gave rise to a number of folk songs connected with individual warriors or groups of fighters or martyrs. With the liberation of Greece, however, all literary activity centers on the capital of the new state—as one would expect—at first Nauplia and then from 1834 Athens. All national literary forces converged there, the Phanariotes from Constantinople, the Greeks from other lands still under Turkish occupation, and many living in the Greek communities of the West.

New schools were established in the first years of the young Greek kingdom, which formed the foundation of all subsequent Greek education and influenced the development of modern Greek literature.[32] These new schools at first endeavored to blend the traditional Byzantine views in education with the romantic and utopian ideas imported with the first Greek king Otho (a Bavarian prince, son of Ludwig I of Bavaria) and his advisers. The Bavarians who came to Greece were imbued with an admiration for classical Greece, then prevalent in Germany. They therefore tried to orient Greek education toward a "classical" ideal, which disregarded the medieval and modern Greek elements in Greek language and life. Thus the secondary schools then established, the *hellenika scholia* and the classical gymnasia, as well as the "spirit" of the University of Athens (which was founded in 1837) came to enhance the conservative linguistic and literary views of the Phanariotes and the Church, and delayed the solution of the "language question" for more than fifty further years to the detriment of all

---

[32] A detailed account of these, as well as the many changes that were subsequently made, the addition of subjects, and the shifting emphasis toward science, the new types of schools, the commercial, agricultural, nautical, etc., schools, does not fall within the limits of this outline.

Greek writing. The intention of the first educational advisers were no doubt noble, but the harm that resulted to Greek literature and life was great and has not yet been fully overcome.

In dealing with modern Greek literature it is convenient to treat poetry and prose separately.

Poetry

THE GREEK ROMANTICS

It was in the mixed and unsettled society of the first years after the liberation of Greece that "The Romantic School of Athens" first appeared. Its founder and leading spirit was Alexander Soutsos (1803–1863). He had studied in Chios and later in Paris, where he came under the influence of the French Romantics, but his exuberant and patriotic writings never succeeded in capturing the spirit of their models. As a satirist, he is often terse and vigorous. The influence he exercised upon Greek poetry was felt for many years.

Other representatives of the earlier Romantic School (c. 1830–1850), Panagiotis Soutsos (1806–1868), Alexander Rizos Rangavis (1809–1892), George Zalocostas (1805–1858), Theodore Orphanides (1817–1886), Elias Tantalides (1818–1876), and John Karasoutsas (1824–1873), use mainly the "purist" language, and are boundlessly patriotic. Alexander Rizos Rangavis is perhaps the most striking figure of this group. A man of extraordinary versatility, he achieved considerable charm in the classicizing style. His products include ballads, hymns, odes, narrative poems, tragedies and comedies as well as several prose works.

Achilles Paraschos (1838–1895) is the leading figure in the second period of the school (c. 1850–1880). Alfred de Musset, Victor Hugo, and Lord Byron were his idols, but the rhetorical wealth and mock heroic patriotism of his verses prevented him from ever rising to significant level, though a spark of true poetry is often evident. All his contemporaries, however, George Paraschos (1822–1886), Angelos Vlachos (1838–1919), Alexander Vyzantios (1841–1898), Demetrios Paparrhegopoulos (1843–1873) and George Vizyinos (1849–1896), were overshadowed by his reputation, in spite of the greater sincerity and more delicate technique evident in many of their writings.

THE SCHOOL OF THE IONIAN ISLANDS

Parallel to the Romantic School of Athens another school of poetry flourished in the Ionian Islands, which remained under British rule till 1864. Its founder and greatest representative was Dionysios Solomos (1798–1857), a native of Zante. Like many of the Ionian aristocracy of his day, he was practically bilingual, and having received his education in Italy, wrote his first poems in Italian. He soon developed a preference for Greek, however. His early works in Greek were short lyrics, but the War of Independence stirred him to more ambitious projects. As the years passed, his philosophic approach to art and life deepened and expressed itself in verses of great delicacy and balance, unsurpassed to this day in modern Greek. From the "Hymn to Liberty" (the first stanzas of which became the Greek national anthem) to the "Free Besieged," which sings of the heroic resistance and sally at Mesolonghi in 1824, we can trace the development of a highly spiritual nature. Most of his mature work is known only from fragments, since the instability of his disposition and an ever-growing self-criticism seem to have prevented him from finishing any of his major writings.

In the struggle between the purist idiom (the *katharevousa*) and the spoken idiom (the *demotikē*) as the language of modern Greek literature, Solomos marks a turning point, for by choosing the latter he pointed the way which Greek poetry was to follow with the Demotic Movement of the eighties. Moreover, he introduced a number of Western metrical forms (the *sestina rima*, the *ottava rima*, the *terza rima*) which freed Greek poetry from the monotony of the fifteen-syllable line, the main metrical form till his days. Among the other poets of the Ionian School are George Tertsetis (1800–1874), Julius Typaldos (1814–1883), Gerasimos Marcoras (1826–1911), and Lorentzos Mavilis (1860–1912) (the greatest exponent of the sonnet in Greek), but Andreas Calvos (1792–1869) and Aristotle Valaoritis (1824–1879) are the most distinguished. Andreas Calvos drew his inspiration from the Greek classics and developed an austere and moralizing poetry in a classicizing form of the language, which exercised no notable influence on subsequent literature. Aristotle Valaoritis, on the other hand, though deeply romantic and often too grandiloquent, was greatly admired by his contemporaries, and among others influenced Costis Palamas in adopting the spoken tongue as the language of poetry. Thus Valaoritis became the link that connects the Ionian School with the New School of Athens.

The feeling that Greek literature, and in particular poetry, by employing a purist, classicizing form of the language and by indulging in the weaker side of the Romantic movement, was heading for sterility, stirred a group of young writers to form in the eighties the "New School of Athens." This reaction became more general and more violent and is known in the history of Greek literature and letters as the Demotic Movement. The first important document of this literary and cultural movement was the publication in 1888 by Psycharis of his 'My Journey', ostensibly a series of impressions of travel in Greece, but really intended to awaken the dormant linguistic consciousness of the Greeks. The battle flared up and a number of distinguished critics, authors, artists, and men of letters joined in, attacking fiercely the obsolete purist language of most contemporary writing. The movement did not limit itself to the linguistic side. It broadened into a reaction against the dead weight of the whole archaic tradition and preached a return of art, literature, and culture in general to the living roots of modern Greek life. This was greatly helped by the study of modern Greek folklore, which was then promoted by Nicholas Politis, and the historical research of Constantine Paparrhegopoulos, who had recently emphasized the continuity of Greek history and had drawn the nation's attention to its great immediate past. As might be expected, the Demotic Movement had a direct bearing on Greek education. The *Educational Society* which was later founded (1910) studied a number of problems connected with the introduction of the spoken idiom to the schools (the central figure in this development was the eminent Greek philologist Manolis Triantaphyllidis), and since 1918 the spoken idiom has gradually been introduced into the state schools by successive Greek governments with remarkable effects on the further development of Greek creative literature.[33]

THE NEW SCHOOL OF ATHENS

The founders of the New School of Athens had aspired to become the Greek Parnassians, masters of a restrained and objective art, which

---

[33] See also A. Steinmetz, "Schrift und Volkssprache in Griechenland," *Probleme der neugriechischen Literatur* (Berlin, 1959), I, 154 f.

would draw inspiration from contemporary Greece and use the living idiom. The central figure of this new school was Costis Palamas (1859–1943), a man of remarkable talent and wide reading. Born in Patras, he was educated at Mesolonghi and Athens, where he studied law. In 1886 he published his first collection of poems, *The Songs of My Country*, followed later by publication of ever-increasing importance. The most significant of these are the *Iambs and Anapaests* (1897), *Life Immovable* (1904), (where the personality of the poet is fully developed), the long epic-lyric poem *The Twelve Lays of the Gypsy* (1907), and the formidable historical epic *The King's Flute* (1910). When Palamas overcame the influence of the Parnassians he was the first poet to give full expression to the national sufferings and aspirations of the modern Greeks, for the writings of Solomos had been few and fragmentary. There are many facets to the poetry of Palamas. With his virile lyricism, metrical variety and robust and rich language he cast into verse Greek history, mythology, and philosophy, injecting many Western European and even Eastern ideas. His influence on later Greek literature was preponderant. His one play, the *Thrice Noble* (1903), has lyric rather than dramatic merits. He also wrote a few short stories, and as a critic he introduced higher standards to modern Greek literary criticism. In poetry Palamas' distinguished contemporaries George Drosinis (1859–1952), John Polemis (1862–1925), and Costas Crystallis (1868–1894), as well as his immediate successors John Gryparis (1872–1942), Constantine Hadzopoulos (1871–1920), Miltiades Malakasis (1869–1943), and Lambros Porfyras (1877–1940), have all felt and acknowledged their debt to the leader of the school. It was the poets of this school who explored the great phrastic and metrical possibilities of the spoken idiom, and who introduced symbolism and free verse into Greek poetry, which has much enriched it in the twentieth century. Of the women writers of the New School of Athens Myrtiotissa (Madame Theone Dracopoulos, b. 1883), Emily Daphne (1887–1941), and Maria Polydouris (1905–1930) are noteworthy for the elegance and passion of their verses.

After Palamas, the most important figure in Greek poetry is undoubtedly Aneglos Sikelianos (1884–1952). His first important work, *Alafroiskiotos* [*The Dreamer and Seer*], published in 1909, already reveals the full lyrical powers of the poet. It was followed by a group of outstanding lyrics and long works like the *Mother of God* and the

Easter of the Greeks, to culminate in the *Delphic Discourse* (1927). The Greek tradition is given there a mystic turn and a universal significance, the national, historic, and religious symbols being widened into a universal sphere. In the thirties and forties a second group of lyrics appeared, which displayed the full mastery of Sikelianos' art. They express with a rich and incisive language and forceful imagery the poet's belief in the beauty and harmony of the world. The tragedies of Sikelianos (*Sibylla, Daedalus in Crete, Christ in Rome, The Death of Digenis,* and *Asclepius,* which are introduced by the long dramatic poem *The Dithyramb of the Rose*) are more notable for their lyric than their dramatic qualities. In his maturer works Sikelianos is rightly seen as fulfilling in poetry the aspirations of the Demotic Movement of the eighties, which had also sought to combine Greek tradition with Western thought. Although occasionally the power of his inspiration drives Sikelianos to an elaborate grandiloquence which blunts the poetic effect, some of his finer lyrics are among the best verse in twentieth-century Western literature.

The one great Greek poet who remained untouched by the influence of Palamas and the New School of Athens is Constantine Cavafis (1868–1933). A son of Alexandria, Egypt, both by birth and by spiritual inclination, his main theme is the tragic glory of Hellenistic Greece and its decadence, but in his work historical memories and personal experiences are inextricably blended. In no other Greek poet is the tragedy of life so sensually expressed, nor sensuality felt more tragically, though elements of relief abound, exquisitely lyrical, and often ironical. His writing, symptomatic of the present form of Western culture, has been universally acknowledged.

Of the many other poets who wrote in Greece since the end of the First World War four only can be mentioned here: Costas Karyotakis (1897–1928) is a pessimistic (and often sarcastic) poet. Nikos Kazantzakis (1885–1957), better known as a novelist, is also the author of the formidable "epic" poem (33,333 lines long), *The Odyssey:* its hero, a "modern Odysseus" wandering in the world of thought, appears to be haunted by the idea of nihilism; although the size and style of the work are overwhelming, there are long passages of great beauty, and a use of language of extreme wealth and vigor.[34] George

---

[34] Kimon Friar's English translation of Kazantzakis' *Odyssey* became a bestseller in the United States in 1959–1960.

Seferis (b. 1900), a genuine symbolist, who records with true poetic feeling the fate of modern man is rightly considered the greatest living Greek poet. Odysseus Elytis (b. 1912), is a lyricist whose verses are full of the light and color of the Aegean islands.

Modern Greek poetry is mainly lyrical; little satirical and hardly any dramatic verse of lasting merit has been written. The satires of Andrew Lascaratos (1811–1901) and George Souris (1853–1919)—who created a peculiar form of political satire in his weekly paper *Romios*, which he wrote single-handed for a great number of years—must be recorded, but they have lost much of their stinging flavor for contemporary readers.

From Homer to the present day not a single generation of Greeks has lived without expressing its joys and its sorrows in verse. It is a happy augury that in the last hundred years better poetry has been written than in fourteen preceding centuries and that in the last fifty years, by the surrender of its political or purely national aspirations, Greek poetry has achieved universal validity and a European significance.[35]

Prose

MODERN GREEK PROSE 1821–1888

In the first decades after the liberation of Greece prose was confined mainly to journalism and scholarship. The few writers of creative literature turned to the West for their models, and were attracted first by Sir Walter Scott, whose reputation was paramount on the Continent at the time, and later to Alexander Dumas, Father, some of whose works were translated into modern Greek by John Skylitsis.

This accounts for the popularity in Greece of the historical novel between 1821 and 1888. Its most distinguished representatives, all of whom employed an austere purist form of the language, were Alexander Rizos Rangavis (1809–1892), Emmanuel Rhoides (1835–1904), Spyridon Zambelios (1813–1881), and Demetrios Vikelas (1835–1908). Rangavis' novel *Lord of the Morea*, dealing with the Frankish occupation of the Peloponnesus (Morea), Rhoides' vivid historical satirical novel *Pope Joan*, and Vikelas' romance *Loukis Laras* dealing with the

---

[35] See *Times Literary Supplement*, August 5, 1955 (Special Autumn Number), p. xxv.

massacre of Chios by the Turks in 1822 deserve special mention. The short story in the purist language was also cultivated in this period, especially by George Vizyinos (1849–1896) and John Kondylakis (1861–1920).

The same period witnessed the development of a remarkable classicizing style by distinguished scholars. Two works of major importance stand out: *The History of the Greek Revolution* by Spyridon Trikoupis (1788–1873), and *The History of the Greek Nation* by Constantine Paparrhegopoulos (1815–1891), both of which represent independent research and scholarly accuracy, and are written in a balanced and flowing style. Alongside them may be mentioned the writers of memoirs of the Greek War of Independence, and especially the *Memoirs* of General John Makriyannis, who employs a vivid demotic idiom and shows keen objectivity.

MODERN GREEK PROSE 1888–1920

With the publication in 1888 of John Psycharis' *My Journey,* and the development of the Demotic Movement, modern Greek prose underwent a momentous change. The outcome of the resulting long and bitter linguistic and literary battle was complete victory for the use of the vernacular not only in poetry, but also in all prose works of an imaginative character. The prose writers of that period, turned to their "living roots" for inspiration, finding them in the life of the Greek village. Greece in the eighties of the nineteenth century was still inhabited mainly by agricultural and seafaring communities, and had no large towns except Athens. So the character of this new prose, which turned to the Greek countryside for inspiration, became preponderantly "pastoral," and this tendency continued till the turn of the century, when a more developed urban life made itself felt.

A forerunner of the "pastoral" trend is Paul Kalligas (1814–1896), a distinguished jurist, who in his novel *Thanos Vlekas,* published in 1855, described in an austere classicizing language the unsettled conditions of the Greek countryside in the days following the liberation of Greece. But the novel found no successors till after the eighties when Alexander Papadiamantis (1851–1911) and Andreas Karkavitsas (1866–1922) emerged, with their tales of villagers and fisher folk. Alexander Papadiamantis, a native of Skiathos, is undoubtedly the greatest modern Greek short-story writer. In a personal and slightly archaic idiom he examined the psychology of the simple island folk and described some moving incidents in their lives. His most arresting work, *The Murderess,* is more a short novel than a long short story, and deals with an old woman of Skiathos, who suffered so much herself and saw her daughters and all the women of the island so full of misery that she decided to kill all baby girls she could lay her hands on. *The Murderess* is one of the outstanding books in modern Greek literature. Among the other short stories of Papadiamantis, *Dream on the Waves, Under the Royal Oak, The Poor Saint* and *Full of Nostalgia* could be singled out. The short stories of Andreas Karkavitsas, though different in style, are of almost equal charm, but his greatest achievement is his realistic novel *The Beggar.* Another important contemporary work is the novel *Life and Death of Karavellas* by Constantine Theotokis (1872–1923), notable for its forceful realism and psychological insight. The "pastoral" short story also was cultivated by G. Drosinis, A. Eftaliotis, J. Vlachoyannis, Ch. Christovasilis, A. Travlandonis, D. Tangopoulos, and Z. Papandoniou.

The great social and economic changes Greece underwent at the end of the nineteenth century soon found reflection in her literature. The expanding middle class and the ensuing development of city life fostered the rise of an "urban" literature hitherto unknown. This was also aided by Greek translations of French novels of big-city life, notably those by Emile Zola. Thus the urban novel was introduced into Greek literature by two writers of different background and genius: John Psycharis, whose cosmopolitan background was appropriate for the development of such a literary genre, and Gregorios Xenopoulos (1867–1951), the gifted and prolific writer of Zante. The novels by Psycharis (the most successful of which is *The Dream of Yanniris,* published in 1897) exercised a great influence upon his contemporary Greek writers. But they are faulty in construction, the heroes never come to life, and the deep egotism of the author make them difficult to enjoy. Xenopoulos, on the other hand, who had to earn a living from his writing, serialized many of his works in Athenian newspapers, and so often had to pander to the taste of his readers. Of his many books the best are *The Honest and Dishonest* and *The Rich and the Poor.* The *Red Rock (Photeine Sandri)* and *Stella Violanti,* however, were his two best sellers. Psycharis and Xenopoulos were followed in their urban writings by Constantine Christomanos (1867–

1911), the friend and secretary of the Empress Elizabeth of Austria-Hungary, whose *Wax Doll* is full of delicacy and true feeling. At the same time Constantine Hadzopoulos (1871–1920) gave Greek literature its one symbolist novel before 1920, *Autumn*.

MODERN GREEK PROSE 1920–1960

The end of the First World War saw the rise of a group of young writers such as D. Voutieridis, Petros Pikros, Thrasos Kastanakis, Nikos Nicolaidis, and Photis Kondoglou, who paved the way for the prose writers of the thirties, when prose in the vernacular achieved maturity, and novels of universal significance appeared for the first time in Greek. Side by side with these have been written important short stories, historical biographies, travel impressions, and critical literary essays. An influence on many of these writers was the Scandinavian Knut Hamsun, whose works were translated into Greek and greatly admired between the wars.

Only a few of the many important writers of the thirties, forties and fifties can be mentioned here. The first to take the literary scene by storm was Stratis Myrivilis (b. 1892 in Lesbos). This he achieved with his book *Life in the Tomb*, a series of war impressions from the Macedonian front in the form of letters from a dead friend of the author to a girl in Lesbos. Myrivilis writes in a lively and robust demotic, in which dialectal and lyrical elements abound. The *Life in the Tomb* was followed by a second and maturer novel, connected with the Asia Minor campaign which ended in the Greek defeat of 1922, *The Teacher with the Golden Eyes*, and by shorter stories of power and originality. In 1955 he published the long novel *The Mermaid Madonna*, which treats of the life of a group of Greek refugees from Asia Minor in a small village of Lesbos, and which concludes what modern Greek criticism calls "the war trilogy of Myrivilis." He is undoubtedly the greatest living master of the "pronounced" demotic. Together with Myrivilis, Elias Venezis (b. 1904 in Asia Minor) made his appearance with a striking book on his life as a prisoner of the Turks in 1922–1923, *Number 31328*. Other important longer and shorter publications followed, the most significant of which is his long novel of childhood memories from Asia Minor, *Aeolia*. The style of Venezis is less arresting than that of Myrivilis, and his mood on the whole is much more "nostalgic," but clarity, beauty, and humanity are characteristic of his writings. One of he most gifted authors of the thirties is Cosmas Politis (P. Taveloudis) who in his *Eroica,* a book on the actions and reactions of a gang of children, as well as in his later novels *The Lemon Grove* and *Gyri,* has proved himself a master of the long narrative. The psychological probing of his heroes and his descriptions of natural beauty rank among the best in modern Greek. Next to him ranks George Theotakas, whose long novel *Argo* together with his many other writings—essays, short stories, travel books, plays —shows him to be an author of ability and versatility, and one of the best writers of a flowing and simple demotic. Other authors include A. Petsalis, A. Terzakis, P. Prevelakis, M. Karagatsis, S. Melas, C. Ouranis, T. Stavrou, and Clearete Dipla-Malamou. Most of these started their literary career in the thirties, but many are still writing and showing consistent development. Of the authors after the end of the Second World War, M. Lymberaki, A. Angeloglou, R. Roufos, N. Kasdaglis, S. Plaskovitis, and A. Kovadjis may be singled out.

The most striking achievement of recent years, however, is that of Nikos Kazantzakis (1883–1957). Born in Crete, he was educated in Athens and in Paris, where he studied law. Kazantzakis was endowed with extraordinary spiritual alertness, and left a work of impressive volume and variety. He published philosophic essays (the most important of which is *Salvatores Dei*), tragedies, travel books, and epic and lyric poetry. His *Odyssey* we have already mentioned; he also translated into Greek some Western classics, notably Dante's *Divine Comedy* and Goethe's *Faust.* However, his greatest achievement was undoubtedly in the field of the novel, in which he attained an international reputation. A number of the most important (*Alexis Zorbas, Christ Recrucified, Freedom and Death, The Poor Man of God,* and *The Last Temptation*) have been translated into many leading European languages. In his writings one can follow influences varying from primitive mysticism to the most highly developed realism, knit together by the extraordinary power of Kazantzakis' personality. Through his work, in which humane ideas abound, a deep pessimism, occasionally reaching the boundaries of nihilism, can be traced. Kazantzakis is one of the great masters of Greek demotic prose, whose wealth and vigor he has explored to a remarkable degree.

A survey of modern Greek prose would not be complete without mention of the *Chronographema,* which in many instances achieved real literary merit in modern Greece. This is a column in some Athenian newspapers that treats daily events in a humorous or lyrical manner. At the hands of writers like P. Nirvanas, S. Melas or P. Palaeologos it transcended the boundaries of journalism and achieved true literary distinction. In the development of modern Greek literature and letters a significant part is played by some literary periodicals. In the nineteenth century such publications as *Pandora* (1851–1872) and *Hestia* (1876–1894) were leading. These were followed by the main instrument of the demotic struggle, *Noumas* (1903–1929), *Nea Hestia* (founded in 1927 and still appearing every fortnight), *Nea Grammata, Anglohellenike-Epitheoresis,* and others. It is greatly due to *Nea Hestia* and *Nea Grammata* that modern Greek writers have found a forum for expressing their views and presenting their new work to the public.

MODERN GREEK DRAMA

The purist language was unsuited for the production of living drama. Hence, although numerous plays were written in the nineteenth century in verse and prose only three names of the older dramatists stand out: Demetrios Vernardakis (1834–1907), Spyridon Vasiliadis (1844–1874), and Demetrios Coromilas (1850–1898). The employment of the demotic and the choice of the themes relating to contemporary life have given plays fresh vitality and have done much toward the development of a national drama. Xenopoulos was the inaugurator of this. Together with him were J. Kambisis (1872–1902), S. Melas (b. 1883), T. Moraitinis (1875–1952), N. Laskaris (1868–1945), P. Horn (1881–1941), D. Bogris, Th. Synadinos, A. Terzakis, and G. Theotokas. A number of the most distinguished poets like C. Palamas, A. Sikelianos, and N. Kazantzakis have also written for the theater, but their plays are, as mentioned, more notable for their lyrical than their dramatic qualities.[36]

In concluding this brief outline the remarkable vitality shown in the face of the greatest difficulties should be stressed. Not only did Greek literature survive the Turkish and Frankish domination of the Greek world, but with an admirable power of renewal it gradually emerged

---

[36] On the Greek theater see M. Valsa, "Le Théâtre Grec Moderne de 1453 à 1900," *Berliner Byzantinische Arbeiten,* XVIII (Berlin, 1960).

from a regional and dialectal literature, smothered under the weight of the classical Greek and Byzantine traditions, into a living national literature, and, once the initial difficulties of the "language question" were overcome, into a literature of universal significance.[37] At the same time, the services rendered by Greek letters to the whole Balkan world should not be forgotten. They helped the survival of Orthodox Christianity throughout the dark centuries of Turkish domination, and for centuries were the main channel through which modern Western thought flowed into a great part of the Balkan Peninsula. Moreover, by educating a number of distinguished men of all Balkan nationalities and by inspiring the Greeks in their War of Independence they helped the Balkan peoples as a whole to shake off the Turkish yoke. Had it not been for Greek literature and letters, the Greek struggle for independence would never have come to fruition when it did, and had Greece not taken the lead the whole Balkan Peninsula would have probably remained under Turkish rule for many more years. The future of Greek literature is assured by the wealth and variety of the younger talent now appearing on the literary scene.

BIBLIOGRAPHY

The bibliography on the subject is so vast that it could easily fill a volume. Here only a few important general books are mentioned, in which the reader can find much further bibliography.

Apostolakis, G. M. *Ta Demotika Tragoudia* [*Folk Songs*], (Athens, 1929).
Apostolakis, G. M. *To Keftiko Tragoudi* [*The Klephtic Song*], (Athens, 1950).
Bóerje K. L'Histoire de la littérature néo-grecque (Stockholm, 1962).
Demaras, K. Th. *Historia Neohellenikes Logotechnias* [*History of Modern Greek Literature*], (Athens, 1956).
Dieterich, K. *Geschichte der byzantinischen und neugriechischen Literatur*, Vols. I–V (Leipzig, 1909).
Hesseling, D. C. *Histoire de las Littérature Grecque Moderne* (Paris, 1921) (translated from Dutch).
Jenkins, R. *Dionysios Solomos* (Cambridge, England, 1940).

---

[37] See *Times Literary Supplement*, August 5, 1955, p. xxv.

Kampanis, A. *Historia tes Neas Hellenikes Logotechnias* [*History of Modern Greek Literature*], (Athens, 1948).

Mirambel, A. *La Littérature Grecque Moderne* (Paris, 1953).

Panagiotopoulos, I. M. *Ta Prosopa kai ta Keimena* [*Persons and Texts*], Vols. I–V (Athens, 1942–1948).

Sachines, A. *Anazeteseis* [*Quests*], (Athens, 1945).

Sachines, A. *Synchrone Pezographia mas* [*Our Contemporary Prose*], (Athens, 1951).

Sachines, A. *Pezographia tes Katoches* [*Prose of the Occupation*, i.e., during the Axis Occupation], (Athens, 1948).

Sachines, A. *To Historiko Mythistorema* [*The Historical Novel*], (Athens, 1957).

Trypanis, C. A. *Medieval and Modern Greek Poetry* (Oxford, 1951).

Voutierides, E. *Historia Neohellenikes Logotechnias* [*History of Modern Greek Literature*], (Athens, 1924–1927), Vols. I–II.

Voutierides, E. *Syntome Historia Neohellenikes Logotechnias* [*Short History of Modern Greek Literature*], (Athens, 1933).

No collections, selections, or special editions of texts are given in this bibliography. The reader may find all he needs by consulting the books cited. As for the influence of Greek schools on Balkan education, attention should be drawn to T. Evangelides, *He Paideia epi Tourkokratias* [*Education During the Ottoman Domination*], (Athens, 1936), Vols. I–II.

Some translations into English of modern Greek prose and verse:

Abbott, G. F. *Songs of Modern Greece* (London, 1900).

Bien, P. A. *God's Pauper* by N. Kazantzakis (Oxford, 1962).

Bien, P. A. *The Last Temptation* by N. Kazantzakis (Oxford, 1961).

Brooke, E. M. *"Argo" by G. Theotokas* (London, 1951).

Brown, D. *Modern Greek Stories* (London, 1920).

Dalven, R. *The Complete Poems of Cavafy* (New York, 1961).

Dalven, R. *An Anthology of Modern Greek Poetry* (New York, 1950).

Durrell, L. *Six Poems from the Greek of Sikelianos and Seferis* (London, 1946).

Durrell, L. *"Pope Joan" by E. Rhoidis* (London, 1954).

Edmonds, E. M. *Greek Lays, Idylls and Legends* (London, 1886).

Fotheringham, D. R. *War Songs of the Greeks* (London, 1907).

Friar, K. *The Odyssey by N. Kazantzakis* (New York, 1959).

Griffin, J. *"Christ Recrucified" by N. Kazantzakis* (London, 1954).

Griffin, J. *"Freedom and Death" by N. Kazantzakis* (London, 1956).

Keeley, E. Ph. Sherrard, *Six Poets of Modern Greece* (London, 1960).

Marshall, F. H. and J. Mavrogordato. *Three Cretan Plays* (London, 1929).

Mavrogordato, J. *The Poems of C. P. Cavafy* (London, 1951).
Michalaros, D. A. *"The Grave" by C. Palamas* (Chicago, 1930).
Phoutrides, A. E. *Life Immovable* (Cambridge, Mass., 1919); *A Hundred Voices* (Cambridge, Mass. 1921); *"Trisergeni" by K. Palamas* (1923).
Rick, A. *The Mermaid Madonna* by S. Myrivilis (New York, 1959).
Scott-Kilvert, E. *"Aeolia" by E. Venezis* (London, 1949).
Stephanides, Ph. and G. C. Katsimbalis. *Poems by Costis Palamas* (London, 1925); *Modern Greek Poems* (London, 1926).
Spanos, W. D., *Red Rock* by G. Xenopoulos (New York, 1955).
Warner, Rex. *Poems, George Seferis* (London, 1960).
Wildman, G. *"Zorba the Greek" by N. Kazantzaikis* (London, 1952).

Selections from the works of a modern Greek lyric poet of wide range —Sotiris Skipis—are given in translation in *Patterns from a Grecian Loom*, (1928); good translations of Greek poems, and other literature, can be also found in the periodicals *Anglo-Greek Review* and *Horizon*.

NATIONALISM AND THE MUSES IN BALKAN

SLAVIC LITERATURE IN THE MODERN PERIOD

Albert B. Lord

Nationalism and its relationship to modern Balkan Slavic literature has been chosen as a focus for this contribution because nationalism was the common impulse that brought the modern manifestations of this literature into being. There were times indeed in some of them when it seemed that nationalism would hopelessly distort them as literature. And it could be argued that while they owed their existence to nationalism, eventually they reached their greatest excellence in spite of the extremes of nationalism or when nationalism was least self-conscious.

No special or subtle meaning for the term "nationalism" is used in this contribution. Nationalism is here thought of as an awareness of the ethnic group as a historical entity, implying a desire for political identity and self-expression. It normally displays an honest and justifiable pride in the accomplishments and aspirations of the group, but does not close its eyes to the group's faults, nor does it feel that only in the group lies salvation, justice, truth. This is nationalism at its normal best. Unfortunately, it sometimes develops, perhaps often unwittingly, into chauvinism. It then soon palls in literature because it becomes banal and must be fed on its own slogans; it becomes an empty "beating on the tupan."

A writer who writes about his native land and its peoples is not necessarily nationalistic. Ivo Andrić, for example, writes of the local scene in considerable detail and with depth of perception, but he should not be classified as "nationalistic." He is concerned primarily with something more than the national group. Moreover, a single patriotic poem by a writer should not mark him as "nationalistic" unless it be his only creation. We shall, as a matter of fact, try to separate the "nationalistic" writings of a single author from his other works. Finally, it should be understood clearly that it is not our intention to brand patriotic or nationalistic literary products as *per se* inferior. Many good poems would have to be eliminated were we to allow nationalism to blind us to literary values.

The nationalistic trends of the late eighteenth and of the first half of the nineteenth century in the political sphere manifested themselves on the literary scene in at least four clearly defined but not unrelated ways. Chronologically first came the appearance of a history of the national group as a unit in its contemporary world with its roots in the past, its own authority for existence as a national entity. Usually this history was written in the language of the national group itself; in only one instance (Slovenian) was it in another tongue.

In Bulgaria, the most clear-cut instance, Paisii Hilendarski's *Slavianob'lgarska istorija* [*Slavonic-Bulgarian History*] was finished in 1762, and was an influential document in Bulgaria's struggle for national awakening. It is the landmark from which one usually dates the beginning of modern Bulgarian literature. The book was the response to a feeling that a national spirit was needed; it was itself nationalistic. Paisii was an Orthodox monk; the nationalist movement from the very beginning was connected with the Bulgarian Church, because the movement was directed in part against the Greek Church and Hellenization.

Among the Serbs one might point to the history by Djordje Branković in the early eighteenth century (he was still writing on it at the time of his death in 1711) as the beginning of a reawakening of national consciousness, but it is more usual to think rather of the work of Jovan Rajić, an Orthodox monk and archimandrite, who in 1794–1795 published a history of the Bulgars, Croats, and Serbs (*Istorija raznih slavenskih narodov, napače Bolgar, Horvatov i Serbov* [*History of Various Slavic Peoples; Namely Bulgars, Croats and Serbs*], I–IV). As can be seen from the title, Rajić wrote of the Bulgars and Croats as well as of the Serbs, but the emphasis is, nevertheless, on his own group. The book is itself an indication of national awakening and, like Paisii's history, also nationalistic in content and spirit.

The case of the Croats does not fit the pattern precisely. The work to which one must turn in the eighteenth century is the famous *Razgovor ugodni naroda slovinskoga* [*Pleasant Conversation of the Slavic People*] by the Franciscan monk Andrija Kačić-Miošić in 1756. Like Rajić, Kačić did not limit himself to his own national group, the Croats, but included all South Slavs and even the Albanians. This is the least nationalistic of these histories. It is not strictly a history of the Croat group, but it belongs with the South-Slavism or the Pan-Slavism of the Dubrovnik and Dalmatian literatures on one side and with the larger allegiances of the Illyrian movement on the other.

The Slovenes are also somewhat atypical. They can point to a history filled with the feeling of brotherhood, namely, Anton Linhart's *Versuch einer Geschichte von Krain und der übrigen südlichen Slaven Oesterreichs*, published in Ljubljana in 1788. But this work is not in the Slovenian language. The first Slovene history written in Slovenian was by the priest Anton Krempl, *Dogodivšine štajerske zemle z' posebnim pogledom na Slovence* [*History of Styria with a Special Look at the Slovenes*], published in Graz in 1845. In his history of Slovenian literature (*Pregled slovenskega slovstva* [*Survey of Slovenian Literature*], (Ljubljana, 1934), pp. 113–114) Anton Slodnjak links Krempl's work in national spirit with that of Linhart and in manner with Kačić's *Razgovor*.

A second typical development of nationalism among the Balkan Slavs was a concern for a native literary language and a reformed orthography. At both ends of the South Slavic spectrum, that is to say in Bulgaria and in Slovenia, the situation had almost reached the point that one could speak about the struggle of the native language for its very existence. Greek was coming close to exterminating Bulgarian from literary and even economic life, and German and Italian were doing the same for Slovenian. We have just noted that the first history of Slovenia, or more specifically of Krain, was written in German.

If we proceed from east to west, we find that in Bulgaria the development of the modern literary language was closely allied with the establishment of schools and the growth of education. The language of Bishop Sofronii Vrachanski's *Kyriakodromion*, published in 1806 in Rimnik in Wallachia (the first printed Bulgarian book), was close to the modern tongue. This collection of sermons by a friend and close associate of Paisii carried forward in the realm of the literary language the nationalist cause and showed the need for more books in the vernacular. In 1824 Pet'r Beron published in Brashov his famous *Bukvar s razlichny pouchenija* [*Primer with Various Instructions*], the first modern Bulgarian schoolbook. In 1835 Aprilov, an emigrant in Odessa, born in Gabrovo, founded in his native city the first secular school in Bulgaria. Here Neofit Rilski taught from his own *Bolgarska grammatika* [*Bulgarian Grammar*], printed in Kragujevac in 1835. These were the early steps, taken under the influence of nationalism, that were to lead to Bulgarian literature.

The development of a modern literary language among the Bulgarians was comparatively simple, if viewed from the standpoint of the situation among the Serbs and Croats. The Serbo-Croatian-speaking lands had not only the many dialects and subdialects recognized by the linguists, but also had to contend with at least four literary languages, each with some tradition and claim to greatness. In Serbia there was the *Slavenoserpski* of Novi Sad, Orthodox, cultured, Russian, stamped with classical conservatism. Its exponents among the clergy and cultured classes had no really strong counterpart in Bulgaria. The Russian influence in the Serbian group was felt as being benign and superior. Raising its banner against this sacred cultural language marched the vernacular of Dositej Obradović and of Vuk Karadžić. A third entry in the lists was the literary *kajkavski* tradition in Zagreb. The fourth was the highly developed medium of the Dubrovnik-Dalmatian literary language, especially as used by Gundulić.

Dositej's, and more especially later Vuk's, struggle was with a group which was nationalist and Serbian as well, but also religious and ultraconservative. The vernacular in Serbian literature in Serbia proper, or among the Serbs in Hungary, was really triumphant only around the middle of the nineteenth century. Montenegrin writers such as Milutinović (if I may class him as Montenegrin) did not write in *Slavenoserpski*, although their orthography was antiquated. Vidaković and Jovan Sterija Popović used the vernacular, although they had begun their careers by writing *Slavenoserpski*. Sterija even satirized those who spoke the artificial tongue. In Serbia the most influential writer to aid Vuk was the younger poet Branko Radičević.

In Croatia the story was somewhat different, of course. The conflict there was not between an artificial sacred language and the vernacular. This conflict had been waged earlier, and the vernacular was already in use. The question was rather *which* vernacular dialect would be *the* literary language for all Croats (and for all Serbs and Slovenes as well, after 1835). Both *kajkavski* and the Dubrovnik-Dalmatian *štokavski* (as it had replaced and absorbed *čakavski*) had a tradition as a literary language, although that of the coast was older and more illustrious. Actually there was no conflict, because these two were not competing with one another. Ljudevit Gaj (1809–1872) and the Illyrians wished to have *štokavski-jekavski*, namely the same dialect advocated by Vuk in Serbia, become the literary language for all. Some of the Illyrians, like Ivan Mažuranić, preferred to see the language of Gundulić continue as the Croatian literary language. He compromised in his *Smrt Smailage Čengića* [*The Death of Smailaga Cengić*], and shortly after that he gave up writing literature almost entirely.

The Serbs and the Croats fostered a nationalism which was aimed, like that of the Bulgars, against foreign domination. But among the Serbs the question of the literary language was a religious as well as a literary question, and the Croats realized that it was so looked upon by them. On the other hand the problem of a literary language that could be understood by all South Slavs was not new for the Croats and Slovenes. It was a problem that the Protestants had tried to solve, as had also the representatives of the Catholic Counter-Reformation. It would seem that Croatian nationalism versus Serbian nationalism and vice versa was already operative in this struggle for a literary language. The Croatian poet Petar Preradović, a Serb from a Croatian enclave, wrote in the literary language proposed by the Illyrians; for he had joined the movement. His poem "Hrvat ili Srbin" [Croat or Serb"] reflected the opposing nationalisms, at the same time advocating brotherly coexistence and coöperation.

The Illyrian movement held dangers for the Slovenes and their language as well, because Gaj suggested that they too write the literary language of the South Slavs rather than Slovenian. Slovenian had been having its troubles in maintaining itself against German, and its proponents did not look kindly upon the Croatian suggestion. Moreover, they now had in Prešeren their own famous and great poet, and he wrote Slovenian. Only Stanko Vraz of the prominent Slovenes abandoned Slovenian for Croatian. He even moved to Zagreb. The national awakening in Slovenia had come before the Illyrian movement, and by the time of Gaj a Slovenian literature was already under way. Marko

Pohlin had published a Slovenian grammar (in German!) in 1768, which he followed by other works on the language and literature.

A third typical development of nationalism was the establishment of newspapers and other periodicals in the national language and for the national group. The schools and the press were the natural media for nationalism. In Slovenia we find that Pohlin's work led to the beginning of a secular poetic almanac, *Pisanice* [*Colored Eggs*], in 1779, which lasted for three years. Its first title was *Skupspravljanje krajnskeh pisanic od lepeh umetnost* [*A Collection of Krainian Colored Eggs of the Beaux Arts*], but it later became *Krajnske pisanice od lepeh umetnost* [*Krainian Colored Eggs of the Beaux Arts*]. In 1797 there appeared the first Slovenian periodical, *Lublanske novice* [*Ljubljana News*], founded by a Franciscan monk Valentin Vodnik. Another almanac was started in 1795, the *Velika praktika ali kalender* [*The Great Almanac or Calendar*], which became the *Mala praktika* [*The Little Almanac*] after 1798 and lasted as such to 1806. The most famous of the periodicals or almanacs for literary content was the *Krajnska čbelica* [*The Little Bee of Krain*], which began to be published in 1830. Such periodicals were among the most valuable contributions of nationalism to literature, because usually the best poets and writers of the day contributed to them and edited them.

This was true of the Croatian Illyrian *Narodne novine* [*National News*], with its weekly literary section *Danica* [*The Morning Star*], which first began to appear in 1835. Its editor was Ljudevit Gaj, and it was the organ of Illyrianism. Even more exciting than *Danica* from the literary point of view was *Kolo*, which was started in Zagreb in 1842 by Stanko Vraz and others. Another Croatian magazine of the time was *Iskra* [*The Spark*], but the only work of importance which it printed (its editor was Dimitrije Demeter) was the *Smrt Smailage Čengića* of Mažuranić, Demeter's son-in-law. Both *Danica* and *Kolo* were organs of nationalism and Illyrianism.

The oldest "periodical" among the South Slavs was the *Slavenoserpski magazin*, edited by Zaharije Orfelin and printed in Venice in 1768 —only one number appeared. It was printed at the same press, founded in 1758, which had printed *Plač Serbiji* [*Lament for Serbia*], in 1761 and *Pjesn istoričeskaja* [*A Historical Song*], an art poem about Kosovo, in 1762. Both poems are of interest and importance in the development of nationalism among the Serbs, especially the cult of Kosovo. In 1791, *Serbskija novini* [*Serbian News*] appeared in Vienna, and in 1792 a more serious journal, *Slaveno-serbskija Vjedomosti* [*Slaveno-Serbian News*], edited by Stefan Novaković. It expired in 1794. Also in Vienna appeared, in 1813, *Novine serbske* [*Serbian News*], of Dimitrije Davidović, the first Serbian daily. A group of nationally minded Serbian men of letters gathered around this paper which was to have great significance for Serbian literature. The Slovene Kopitar, at that time censor for Greek and Slavic books in Vienna, was active with it from the beginning. Through the paper he became acquainted at the end of 1813 (the first copy of the paper came out on August 1 with Vuk St. Karadžić who had just arrived in Vienna in the autumn of 1813 and had come to know people in the newspaper's circle. From this point Serbian nationalism and Serbian literature developed together both with greater strength for at least nine years. The *Novine serbske* of Vienna ceased to exist in February of 1822. In January, 1834, a new *Novine serbske*, under the same editorship, that of Davidović, appeared in Kragujevac. This was the first daily to be published on Serbian soil. In 1835 two political papers were begun in Pest by Teodor Pavlović, *Serbski narodni list* [*Serbian National Newspaper*] and *Serbske narodne novine* [*Serbian National News*], which lasted until 1848. The new *Novine serbske*, which was eventually transferred from Kragujevac to Belgrade, ceased to exist in 1839. These were the beginnings.

Bulgaria was the last to have a periodical press. The first publication, *Liuboslovie*, was produced by Konstantin Fotinov in Smyrna in 1844, after a trial copy had been printed in 1842. It lived for two years. This and the other periodicals that followed it were nationalistic but not especially literary. They were intended for the instruction of people who had not gone far in learning; they were educational, giving space to history rather than to literature. And in this, incidentally, they were not unlike the *Slavenoserpski magazin* of Orfelin, which in its turn followed a Russian model. Fotinov's title *Liuboslovie* is his version of *Philologia*.

The second and third periodicals in Bulgarian literary history were both founded by Ivan Bogorov, one in Leipzig and the other in Constantinople. *B'lgarski orel* [*The Bulgarian Eagle*], which appeared in 1846 and was supposed to come out twice a month, actually was published three times in two years, the second time with the title *B'lgarski naroden izvestnik* [*Bulgarian National Newspaper*]. It expired from lack of funds. But *Tsarigradski vestnik* [*Constantinople Newspaper*], which began in 1848, lasted for thirteen years, for the first four of which Bogorov was its editor. Both these periodicals were more nationalistic than Fotinov's *Liuboslovie.* The *Tsarigradski vestnik* was of considerable political importance, since it was published during the time of the conflict with the Patriarchate.

In addition to these periodicals, Bogorov contributed to Bulgarian cultural life several works on modern Bulgarian language of which he was a champion, and especially in 1844 his *P'rvichka b'lgarska grammatika* [*First Bulgarian Grammar*], printed in Bucharest. (Actually it was the second grammar, since Neofit Rilski's appeared in 1835.) We can credit Bogorov also with the first printed collection of Bulgarian folk songs and proverbs, his *B'lgarski narodni pesni i poslovici* [*Bulgarian Folk Songs and Proverbs*], printed in Pest in 1842 and containing twelve songs and two hundred proverbs.

The fourth phenomenon, and one of the most important, associated with nationalism among the Balkan Slavs was an interest in their own folk poetry. This poetry was significant for establishing the literary language, especially among the Serbs and Croats, because it represented—and was—the literary language of the people. The language of the folk poetry was already a literary language and really needed little, if any, modification. What was needed was only for the men of letters to recognize that they had a literary language at their disposal, if they wished to use it. In reality, they desired rather to make a literary language *out of* the folk poetry language—and that is something different. But, important as the influence of the folk poetry on the literary language was, it was only one of the results of the awakened national interest in folk literature.

Nevertheless, even in this realm the folk poetry was useful; for it provided, especially for the lyric poets, models for imitation and development. At least one generation, rebelling against an older classical or hieratic language, found directness of expression, and ease of composition in the style of the people and in the native meters. Into the molds of the folk poetry they poured their feelings about everything, including their nation. Excited, too, by the idea that the people celebrated the brave deeds of past and present in epic verse, they began to write in imitation of it, sometimes remembering what they had heard at home in the village. And on the wave of interest, the village singers themselves, with the aid the local schoolteacher or priest afforded, perhaps even led by them, produced a host of new songs for avid collectors. These were not (or not yet) new folk songs, although they entered the collections as such. They were a new category of art song. And they were nationalistic.

Actually, the interest in folk poetry and in its collecting came from outside. True, our oldest manuscript collections from the Dalmatian coast seem to be local products from Dubrovnik and Perast in the Bay of Kotor. The oldest of them belong to the first half of the eighteenth century, though some of them were written down in the sixties of that century. They remained unpublished until later in the nineteenth century.

The two songs in Kačić's *Razgovor,* which he tells us are presented as they are sung by the people and therefore cannot be taken as very accurate, seem scarcely to be considered by Kačić as national products of which one should be very proud. That was in 1756, but the pre-Romantic influence of Ossian and Percy was not to be felt in the Balkans until later in the century and then indirectly through Fortis in Italy. He tried to get information about epic singing or about folk poetry in general from an evidently not too enthusiastic or well-informed group of local intelligentsia in and around Split. At any rate, they provided him with material from Kačić and with one rather inferior oral poem that was to become famous throughout Europe, ironically enough, namely the "Hasanaginica" ["The Wife of Hasanaga"], later translated by Goethe. Another indirect effect of the Ossianic movement was the request of the German scholar Johannes Müller to Djuro Ferić in Dubrovnik for information about epic singing. Ferić replied in 1795 in Latin hexameters, translating for him some material from Kačić and some lyric songs. But to the request for the originals and for more material, Ferić turned a deaf ear. Clearly the folk poetry among the literate Slavs was still at this period looked upon as inferior, and they could not understand the interest of Italian and German scholars in their own barbaric heritage. In 1762 and in a later edition in 1779, M. A. Reljković in Slavonia included two folk songs, or two ballads, in his *Satir* [*Satyr*], themselves not nationalistic, but used here to illustrate a moral and social lesson in a book intended for educational enlightenment.

In Slovenia the earliest manuscript collection by the discalced Carmelite Marko Pohlin (1735–1801) was never published and was eventually lost, although some of its contents survive—in German translation! Once again the local interest was not strong enough to bring it to publication in Slovenian, but German interest was stronger. Pohlin knew Ossian in German translation, and we may think of his lost *Zakotnikova zbirka* [*Retired Man's Collection*] of around 1775 as the first direct effect of the Ossianic movement among the South Slavs, at least so far as collecting is concerned. This little collection contained five songs, and in 1780 Linhart published two of them in German in his *Blumen aus Krain*. Valentin Vodnik (1758–1819) and the group around Žiga Zois (1747–1819) were interested in folk poetry, and Vodnik began systematically to collect. His collection, on which he was still working at the time of his death in 1819, contained three narrative songs and one hundred and forty *poskočnic* or dance songs. The Czech Čelakovský in his *Slowanské narodny pjsnie* [*Slavic Folk Songs*] (1822–1827) included twelve Slovenian songs. *Kranjska čbelica* [*The Little Bee of Krain*], after publishing translations of Serbian folk songs in its second volume in 1831, included some Slovenian songs in the third and fourth volumes in 1832 and 1833. In 1839 in Ljubljana the Pole Emil Korytko published *Slovenske pesmi krajnskiga naroda* [*Slavic Poems of the Krain Folk*], which he followed with a second volume in 1840, a third and fourth in 1841, and a fifth in 1844. Stanko Vraz published in Zagreb in 1839 *Narodne pesni ilirske* [*Illyrian Folk Songs*]. But we are by now, of course, well beyond the influence of Kopitar and Vuk Karadžić on the Serbian scene. Except for a small group of enthusiastic Slovenes there seems to have been no strong nationalist movement involving the folk poetry until later.

The first Bulgarian folk poems to be published were brought out by Vuk Karadžić first in his 1815 *Narodna srbska pjesnarica* [*Serbian Folk-Song Book*] and then in the *Dodatak k Sinktpeterburgskim sravniteljnim rječnicima sviju jezika i narječija s osobitim ogledima bugarskog jezika* [*Supplement to the St. Petersburg Comparative Dictionaries of All Languages and Dialects with Particular Examples of the Bulgarian Language*], in Vienna in 1822. Between 1822 and 1827 Čelakovský included also some of the Bulgarian songs from Karadžić in his *Slowanské narodny pjsnie*. It is to be noted, of course, that these publications are outside of Bulgaria and were done by foreigners. The Bulgars themselves began to publish folk poetry in some of the journals mentioned earlier, such as the *Tsarigradski vestnik* (begun in 1850), the *B'lgarski knizhitsi* [*Bulgarian Pamphlets*], (begun in 1858), and the *Dunavski lebed* [*Danubian Swan*], (begun in 1860). Folk poems also appeared in Stanko Vraz's *Kolo*, in *Moskvitsanin* (Moscow, 1845), and elsewhere. The first separate published collection, as already mentioned, was Ivan Bogorov's *B'lgarski narodni pesni i poslovici*. In the thirties the Russian Jurii Venelin had stirred up a good deal of enthusiasm in Moscow and in Odessa for Bulgaria and Bulgarian folk poetry (as well as Serbian) which he collected in manuscript. The second published collection was that of Hadži Hajden Jovanovich, *Novi Bolgarski narodni pesni* [*New Bulgarian Folk Songs*], published in Belgrade in 1851. In 1855 the Russian P. Bezsonov put some Bulgarian songs, partly from previous publications and partly from manuscript collections in the Moscow *Vremennik* [*Chronicle*]. It was not until 1860 with the publication in Belgrade of S. Verković's *Narodne Pjesme Makedonski Bugara* [*Folk Songs of the Macedonian Bulgars*], and the monumental collection of the Miladinovci brothers, *B'lgarski narodni pesni* [*Bulgarian Folk Songs*], published in Zagreb in 1861, that the serious collecting began. It is significant how much interest came from outside Bulgaria—from Serbia, Czechoslovakia, Slovenia, and Russia.

Vuk Karadžić and the group working around and through him in Vienna, especially the Slovene Kopitar, played the most vital role in connecting the folk poetry with the national awakening. The feeling of nationalism was strong among the Serbs as among the other groups even without the influence of the folk poetry. That is to say, national awakening did not come *through* the folk poetry. The folk poets did not suddenly break forth of their own accord in songs of *national* greatness, of Serbdom. But once national feeling and a revival of the sense of the dignity and importance of Serbia in the world came into contact in Vienna with the reverberations of the Ossianic movement, it was inevitable that nationalism and the folk poetry in Serbia should eventually meet. In 1814 and 1815 the national feeling of the Serbs in Vienna at least was not strong enough to touch their pocketbooks to the extent of subsidizing more than one volume of Vuk's poems. Or perhaps it would be fairer to say that while nationalism was itself rife, particularly after 1803 and even after 1813, the patriotic Serbs did not yet see the national possibilities of the folk epic and even tended, from their position in Vienna or in Novi Sad, to look down upon these humble peasant products. Nationalism comes into Serbian folk poetry only after the appearance of Karadžić's *Narodna srbska pjesnarica* [*Serbian Folk-Song Book*] in 1815 with its four epics of the Serbian uprising which he had written down from Filip Višnjić. In 1814 Vuk had published one song about an event of 1806, but it was not nationalistic. Indeed, how slightly nationalism was connected at that time with the folk epic can be seen from Vuk's remark in the preface to his *Mala prostonarodna slaveno-serbska pesnarica* [*A Little Slavo-Serbian Folk-Song Book*].

Ovde, osim ljubovni i nježni pesana, koe se ženskim glasom pevaju imaju neke osobito na kraju, koese mužestvenim, poznatim Serbskim glasom, uz Gusle pevaju; i koe u sebi kao neke povesti soderžavaju. Ovakovi pesana ja bi mogao i više ovde dodati, ali se bojim da i ovo nebude mnogo; a da mi kakav od nove mode Serbljin nerekne: Gle šta e ovome palo n um te sljepačke pesne izdae. A meni se čini, dasu ovake pesne sodržale, i sad u narodu prostom sodržavaju, negdašnje bitie Serbsko, i ime.

[Here except for love songs and tender songs which are sung by women's voices, there are, especially at the end, some sung by men in the well-known Serbian manner to the *gusle*, and that contain some sort of story. I could add more of such songs here, but I am afraid that even these may be too many, and that some new-fashioned Serb may say: "Look what has come into this fellow's head! He has published blind beggars' songs!" But it seems to me that such songs have retained, and even now among the common folk still retain, former Serbian events and glory.]

Actually the song of the "Death of Kulin-kapetan" was of a simple traditional nature. A raven reports to the wife of the hero his death at the battle of Mišar.

The Serbs were soon to learn the lessons of Grimm, Herder, and Kopitar. Certainly the new songs of Filip Višnjić in Vuk's 1815 book began to indicate that folk epic could deal with contemporary events. It was not until the twenties and thirties, however, that nationalism and the folk poetry were really wed, never afterward to be divorced. And I suspect that the real moving spirits here were concerned less with the Serbian uprisings and more with the organized guerrilla warfare of the Montenegrins. There are indications that the Vladika Petar Petrović Njegoš I, as well as his more famous nephew, was given to

writing down and to composing on his own "folk" epics on the Montenegrin struggles. Some of these it would seem came into the hands
perhaps directly of Sima Milutinović, who, though a Serb born in
Sarajevo, was much inspired by Montenegrin heroism. It should be remembered that he published in 1837 a history of Montenegro in which
he included some epic songs. His own collection came out first in 1823
and then again in a second edition in 1837.

Vuk's Leipzig edition appeared in three volumes in 1823, and in it he
began at Kopitar's urging to give more information about the singers
and the circumstances of the songs. The fourth volume of the Leipzig
edition did not appear until 1833 with a variety of heroic songs from
different periods, but the third volume (in 1823) had included the
newer songs. While we are considering these early collections we
should not forget Petar Petrović Njegoš II's famed *Ogledalo Srpsko*
[*The Serbian Mirror*], which appeared in Belgrade in 1845. Taking
some songs from Karadžić's Leipzig edition, Book III, he expanded
his Montenegrin collection to include the newer Serbian songs as well.
Although this is the first actual publication of folk epic by Njegoš, he
had begun to write an epic of his own as early as 1833 using the Montenegrin folk songs as raw material. This was his *Glas Kamenštaka* [*The
Renown of the Rock Dwellers*], which he broadened in 1835 to form
the epic *Slobodijada* [*Song of Freedom*], not published until after his
death in 1851. These collections of Vuk, Milutinović, and Njegoš were
decisive for the role of the folk epic in the nationalist movement in
Serbia and Montenegro.

Of course, the very fact of publication of folk poetry is of itself a
patriotic act in a period of nationalism. The songs, regardless of their
content, enter the national picture by the force of public interest in
them. In the older songs, usually songs of local heroes, pride in the
deeds of one's ancestors is fostered. Folk epic seems most often concerned with local heroes, especially among the South Slavs. The
fourteenth-century Marko Kraljević is of this sort, although tradition
has accumulated around him much older folklore themes. What few
poems there are on the Kosovo battle in 1389 are concerned with individuals and not with the grand panorama of the Serbian nation and
its allies drawn up or engaged in mortal combat with the assembled
Turkish hosts.

Nationalism takes such traditional material and transforms it into national legend. The battle of Kosovo takes a larger place in *discussion* of Serbian folk epic than it does in the traditional epics themselves. Even the musical instrument used to accompany folk epic, the *gusle,* becomes a sacred national symbol. Marko Kraljević is elevated from the rank of popular folk hero to the grand national hero of the Serbs and of the Jugoslavs. This is the way of nationalism with the older songs. Instead of being merely a champion of the poor or of the oppressed, Marko becomes the champion of the Serbs, or of the Bulgars as the case may be. These sentiments are infused into the tradition by the collectors and local intellectuals. And some of the folk poets vie with their literate brothers in producing nationalistic folk epics.

This is especially apparent in the new songs. Although Višnjić's poems on the Serbian uprising appear in a nationalistic period and are not without traces of it, it is really to Njegoš, or one should say to the two Njegoši, that one must turn for examples of patriotic heroic nationalist epics. Its beginnings are even more appreciably felt here than in the older Vuk material.

The story has yet to be written of the state of oral epic tradition in the Balkans, particularly in the Slavic Balkans before 1814. When it is we shall know how strong the Kosovo tradition was; we shall know what other older songs were deeply rooted in tradition and what may have been written in the last years of the eighteenth and the early years of the nineteenth century, in Novi Sad and Cetinje. Did the *rodoljupci* in those cities, reading in Branković's or in Rajić's history or hearing the heroic boasts of the Montenegrins, pen patriotic poems in folk meter? Were these read to an admiring and zealous audience who then passed them on to the traditional singers? Were some of them, indeed, ever in the repertory of the real bards? How many songs of Montenegrin sallies came into being in the nineteenth century not because of the heroic tradition of epic song itself but because there was in the air a feeling that heroic epic glorifies the deeds of great men and because Montenegrins and Serbs were beginning to feel their own greatness? Is it possible that without nationalism the epic tradition of the Balkans would have died out by, say, the end of the nineteenth century? Did nationalism give it a longer lease on life by providing new subjects and giving it a respectability in the new era of education?

Strangely enough the tradition which remained liveliest as tradition, comparatively untouched by written influence, was that among the

Muslimized Slavs in Montenegro, Bosnia, Hercegovina, and the Sandjak. Some Muslim songs were included in Vuk's earliest collection, and after all the "Hasanaginica" is a Muslim ballad, yet it was not until the end of the century, understandably enough, that the Muslim songs were collected in any systematic way and in any great number.

To sum up, we have seen nationalism awakening the Slavs of the Balkans to a sense of identity, moving them to look backward in their history to the great deeds of the past which they recorded in prose and collected in verse, encouraging them to use their native tongue, the living language of their people, and make of it or revive in it a new literary language, to establish schools and write textbooks, and to start periodicals and almanacs. Some of these were merely organs of nationalism, while others became distinguished literary vehicles. The prose of the first half of the nineteenth century appeared in these periodicals as did a surprising amount of verse. Nationalism brought this all into being, gave it a goal, and provided subject matter for a large segment of literature and thought. In reviving the past and emphasizing history, both heroic and literary (such as the Dubrovnik-Dalmatian literature, which was being hunted out in manuscript and largely published now for the first time), nationalism turned the thoughts of poets and dramatists to choose historical subjects for their novels and poems, going back to Kosovo or again to the battle of Siget in 1566. It set a tone which has lasted even to today and which has come alive in the sculpture of Ivan Meštrović (such as his Marulić in Split and his Marko Kraljević in Belgrade).

Of the literary figures of the first half of the nineteenth century few devoted their entire work to overt nationalism. For the most part all of them wrote works that were nationalistic only by inference or that were purely literary in character. Ljudevit Gaj in Croatia is an exception. The Illyrian movement consumed him and everything he did, and he produced nothing purely literary. But other figures of the Illyrian movement were not so completely enveloped in its message. Thus, for example, Stanko Vraz found a guiding principle in the movement, a principle of South Slavic unity and an idea of Panslavism. In this spirit he edited the magazine *Kolo* (1842 to 1851) in which he included serial surveys of Russian, Polish, and Czech as well as the South Slavic literary scenes. He translated into Croatian and published in *Kolo* Pushkin's *Pikovaia Dama*, Byron's *The Prisoner of Chillon*, Mickiewicz's *Trebine*, and *Slávy Dcera* by the Czech Panslavist Ján Kollár. In *Kolo* he also presented a group of Bulgarian folk songs, together with a review of publications up to that time and a sketch of the Bulgarian language. One of the most valuable services of this magazine was a listing, sometimes with fuller comment, of the literary publications of each year both domestic and foreign. He published Croatian as well as Bulgarian folk songs. In the true spirit of Illyrianism, Vraz—like Ljudevit Gaj in *Danica Ilirska* [*The Illyrian Day Star*]—published works of the Dubrovnik and Dalmatian writers of the Classical period: for example, *Suze i Tužbe Radmilove* [*The Tears and Complaints of Radmil*] of Ivan Gundulić. Otherwise one must confess that the verse published in *Kolo* has always a patriotic tinge. Examples would be Petar Preradović's "Sbogom!" ["Farewell!"], Oriovčanin's "Smert Graničara" ["The Death of the Border Warrior"], D. Demeter's "Grobničko Polje" ["Graveyard Field"], or Ivan Kukuljević-Sakcinski's "Koraljke" ["Coral Necklaces"]. Stanko Vraz himself is fired by patriotic zeal in some of his lyrics, such as "Pali smo" ["We Have Fallen"], "Plač i uteha" ["Weeping and Consolation"], and "Hrvat pred otvorenim nebom" ["The Croat beneath the Open Sky"], (1848), and his "Kajite se" ["Repent"], recalls a famous passage in Mažuranić's *Smrt Smailage Cengića*.

Vraz, outside of the journal, in which he showed himself to be a discerning literary editor, wrote not only patriotic verse but also excellent love lyrics, some of the best of which (in both categories) appeared in his *Djulabije* [*Rose Apples*]. In a somber poem under the title "Ispovjest," ["Confession"], he expressed the feeling that love alone would crown him and lead him after death to paradise, that the laurel wreath of fame would never decorate his grave. In other words the romantic lyric was a form in which he was skilled in spite of the fact that Croatian was not his native tongue. His "Lijepa Anka" ["Beautiful Anka"], "O Ponoći" ["At Midnight"], are excellent examples. The influence of Byron in the Romantic ballad can also be seen in such poems as "Stana i Marko" ["Stana and Marko"], "Hajduk i Vezir" ["The Hajduk and the Vizier"], "Junak Hranilović" ["The Hero Hranilović"], and "Zora i Bogdan" ["Zora and Bogdan"]. Vraz was a true man of letters who found a vital focus for his creative talent in the Illyrian movement, partly at least because it included much that was the best in other Slavic literatures, past and present. In fact, what appeals to us most in Vraz in our day are his touching and lively love lyrics and, to a lesser degree, his romantic ballads.

Byron's influence was likewise deeply felt in the works of Vraz's younger contemporary, Petar Preradović, also a devoted Illyrian. He produced lyric and epic poetry and two dramas worthy of mention. Two years after Sterija Popović wrote his *San Kraljevića Marka* [*The Dream of Kraljević Marko*], Preradović began to write his *Kraljević Marko*, a play in verse and prose. The opening scenes remind us of the Dubrovnik pastoral plays, whereas the body of the action leans in the direction of Byronic rebellion, which ends with the calling forth of Marko from the dead to lead his people. Illyrian also and also Byronic is his other drama, *Vladimir i Kosara*, whose subject is from the *Ljetopis popa dukljanina* [*The Chronicle of the Priest of Duklja*], the famous legend of St. Vladimir. Vladimir is imprisoned by the Bulgarian emperor Samuel, saved from prison by the emperor's daughter Kosara, who falls in love with him and becomes his wife with her father's permission, only later, after Samuel's son and successor has treacherously slain her husband, to become a nun. The play itself is an act of Illyrian piety. *Kraljević Marko* has been praised extravagantly and damned almost as eloquently—it is at times a moving piece in the romantic tradition. Preradović wrote a number of lyric songs often of a patriotic character, such as his famous "Zora Puca—Bit' Će Dana" ["Dawn is breaking—'t will be day"], which first appeared in the *Zora Dalmatinska* [*Dalmatian Dawn*] in 1844, "Putnik," ["The Traveler"], and "Pozdrav domovini" ["Greeting to the Homeland"]. With other Illyrians he sang of Slavdom in his "Duh slavjanski" ["Slavic spirit"], "Zvanje slavljanstva" ["The Call of Slavdom"], and "Slavjanstvu" ["To Slavdom"]. One of his longish poems on the celebrated Sts. Cyril and Methodius is the "Slavjanski dioskuri" ["The Slavic Dioscuri"]. His "Kosovo polje" ["Kosovo field"], is in the more generally nationalistic rather than Illyrian stream, coming, as we have seen, from the same source of folk poetry as the inspiration for his drama *Kraljević Marko*. But his famous and moving "Miruj, miruj, srce moje" ["Quiet, quiet, my heart"], is not in patriotic vein, nor is his epic on Adam and Eve *Prvi Ljudi* [*The First People*], published in 1862. To Preradović nationalism was perhaps a mixed blessing, but he wrote some memorable verses both within and outside its framework.

The case of Ivan Mažuranić and the Illyrian movement is strange and interesting. He was a true Illyrian, a classicist with deep admiration for Gundulić and the other Renaissance writers of the coastland, a patriot who sought nothing more than the continuation of the older tradition of literature. At the request of the *Matica Ilirska* he completed Gundulić's *Osman*, a task particularly to his liking. And in 1846 he wrote at the urging of others his *Smrt Smailage Čengića*, taking a recent event in Montenegrin history as his subject and using the eight- and ten-syllable lines of the Montenegrin folk poetry. Yet he could not wholly abandon the classical tradition, and it shines frequently through. Shortly after this he gave up writing, out of a dissatisfaction with this work which soon (and in part incidentally through Stanko Vraz) gained great praise.

In Croatia writers seem to have shown less interest in the folk epic, or folk poetry in general, than in Serbia. This is not to say that the Croats did not collect and publish folk poetry, of course, but this was an activity of scholars rather than of writers. One can point to an anthology in Zagreb in 1848 by Lavoslav Župan, *Narodne pjesme, sabranje svijuh do sad izdatih i više nikada još neizšavših pjesamah hrvatskih, dalmatinskih, bosanskih i srbskih* [*Folk Songs, A Collection of All Hitherto Published Songs and of Several Never Yet Appeared of the Croats, Dalmatians, Bosnians, and Serbs*], the *Bosanski prijatelj* [*Bosnian Friend*], published in Zagreb in 1850 and 1851 by Jukić Banjalučanin; Luka Marjanović's *Hrvatske narodne pjesme* [*Croatian Folk Songs*], in Zagreb in 1864; Fran Kurelac's *Jačke ili narodne pesme* ["*Jačke*" or *Folk Songs*], also in Zagreb in 1871; Pavlinović's *Narodna pjesmarica* [*Folk-Song Book*], published by the *Matica Dalmatinska* in Zadar in 1879, to say nothing, of course, of the splendid publications of the *Matica Hrvatska*, beginning in 1896. The Slovene Vraz imitated or used the style of folk poetry and so did Preradović, but in a special way neither was typically Croatian. Mažuranić was not a whole-hearted imitator of folk poetry. As early as 1868 Franjo Marković introduced for the first time on a grand scale the iambic pentameter or hendecasyllable to Croatian literature in *Kohan i Vlasta* and to dramatic verse in 1872 in *Karlo Drački* and *Benko Bot* (see introduction by Nikola

Andrić to *Kohan i Vlasta,* 5th ed. *Matica Hrvatska,* Zagreb, 1923, p. ix).
The pull of foreign models was stronger than that of peasant poetry
from the homeland.

The Illyrian movement with its Panslavism already contained ideas
broader than those of Croatian nationalism. It brought its adherents
into contact with Polish, Czech, and Russian literature, and through
romanticism with the literatures and literary movements of Western
Europe as well. While the cause of Croatian freedom was not to be
forgotten, on the purely literary scene the excitement of intellectual
and artistic adventure like that being lived elsewhere was also attractive to Croatian (and other South Slavic) writers.

It is true that Croatian history plays a large role in the literature of
the period. Šenoa, the most outstanding representative of the second
half of the century both of romanticism and of realism in Croatia
sought themes for some of his most significant novels in Croatian history, such as his *Zlatarovo Zlato* [*The Goldsmith's Gold*] and *Seljačka
buna* [*The Peasant Uprising*]. Yet although Šenoa wrote often of the
past, as in those historical novels, he also wrote about the present conditions in Zagreb or in Croatia, as for example in his stories *Prijan
Lovro* [*Friend Lovro*] or *Kanarinčeva ljubovca* [*The Canary's Love*].
As writers now in the seventies and eighties moved from romanticism
to realism, the focus of nationalism was shifted from a contemplation
of the glories or sufferings of the past to an analysis of the oppressive
evils of the present.

The patriotic poem no longer holds an important position in Balkan
Slavic literatures. Such poems continue to be written, of course, after
the middle of the century, but they are not especially significant. We
can point to Mažuranić's *Hrvat* [*Croat*] in 1858, a reworking of his
Ilir [*Illyrian*] of 1835 (!). But such products after romanticism are no
longer in the center of the stage. For one thing, prose has become the
medium for social criticism and for historical realism. In Croatia this
prose is nationalistic as in Šenoa's and certainly in Kumičić's novels in
the eighties and nineties, because it criticizes the ruling classes, the
foreigners, even when dealing with the past in the historical novels.
Particularly from the sixties Croatian literature began to grow up. We
can see this maturing in Šenoa's famous article "Naša Književnost"
["Our Literature"] which appeared in Vienna. True, this document is
a cry for nationalism and more nationalism, for tendentiousness of the

Polish variety. But it is also a cry for something new in literary themes. He writes:

Everyone knows, that two thirds of our original stories tell of the Turkish war. Of course, it is more difficult to study the other periods of our history; the persons and cultural situation must be drawn more exactly; in it phrases such as 'the holy cross and golden freedom' are not sufficient. This indifference to our history, to the temper and historical development of the people, has led our story writers to base their stories and plots on foreign models, and instead of sharply delineating characters, they describe a hundred times the sun, the moon, the stars, and all the heavenly bodies in phrases rude to the Croatian ear; in a word, the whole story has nothing typical in it, and might have happened rather in Tartary or in Tunguzia than in Croatia.

Šenoa, as we know, practices what he preached. Only in one respect did he fail, perhaps, to do so, and this was in regard to "foreign models." One example of the influence of foreign writers on Šenoa is the relationship between *Prijan Lovro* and Stendhal's *Le Rouge et le Noir*. Šenoa's "Naša književnost" [Our Literature"] is strongly nationalistic even from its opening sentences:

Indeed every honest Croat must be very troubled when he looks at the present state of our literature. No matter how great a patriot [*rodoljub*] he may be, no matter how great an optimist, he will not be able to avoid the truth that our writing [*knjiga*], with rare exceptions, is languishing in sluggishness and lethargy, that scarcely anything written among the Croats today is of great value for the spiritual emancipation of our people!

In the name of nationalism Šenoa is calling for new life in literature, for greater reality, for a closer tie with the people. If we could discount the nationalism (which in the last analysis we cannot do, of course), we might discern a call for the romantic historical novel of Western Europe, written in Croatian with Croatian background. This is indeed what follows, at any rate.

It is interesting to compare this document of Šenoa's with Kumičić's "O romanu" in 1833. In less than twenty years Croatian literature had gone a long way. Much credit for it is due to Šenoa himself and his writings in the seventies. What strikes one immediately in reading is that one does not come upon the word "Croatian" for many pages. Kumičić is not appealing for nationalism. He is concerned with Zola and naturalism and the need for this type of writing in Croatia. He acknowledges Šenoa's own contribution to naturalism in his *Mladi gospodin* [*The Young Master*]. The talk has turned from Croatia and nationalism to foreign models, especially Zola, and literary theory as such. Our conversation with Kumičić is artistic and almost nonpolitical. Not that his own writing, any more than that of his younger contemporary Djalski, who published his famous story "Illustrissimus Battorych" ["The Illustrious Battorych"] in *Vijenac* in 1884, is not deeply involved with Croatia and her people. But from a literary point of view it has come of age and is already, in spite of nationalism, in the stream of European letters. It may not be great literature, but in its techniques it is neither backward nor provincial. And it is in this spirit that Croatian literature enters the twentieth century and the movement of the "Moderna." Like the rest of European literature Croatian literature, perhaps less nationalistic than national, concerns itself with form and style and literary movements. The "Moderna" is not a break with the past, but a logical continuation, reaction, and development from the realism and naturalism of the end of the nineteenth century.

The realists also wanted Croatian art to be on the same level as that of the rest of Europe. To a degree, then, one can mark a change in nationalism and perhaps a move away from its extreme forms. Literature, though never entirely free from it, reached the point at which it was not subservient to it either. The twentieth century brought greater freedom from nationalism in literature than there had ever been before, both in Serbia and in Croatia. But one could already see some concern with other than nationalistic matters in the late period of romanticism and in the realistic period.

After the folk poetry had its initial impact and its meters and language were introduced and took root in literary poetry, in reaction to the Dalmatian classicism in Croatia and *Slaveno-serbski* or antique classicism in Serbia, a new period began to experiment with meter and language. Thus in Serbian literature Kostić in the sixties was already trying out new verses and coining new words, deeply involved with Western literary models and artistic concepts.

But before looking more closely at Kostić, we should review briefly the course of Serbian literature and its relationship to nationalism from the time of Dositej and Vuk, that is to say, the two or three generations before Kostić. Dositej died in 1811, and Vuk in 1864. Kostić was born in 1841 and died in 1910; the first work of his to be considered, the play *Maksim Crnojević*, was written between 1862 and 1864, but was not published until 1872.

Obradović was a widely traveled, wise, clear-headed and gentle person, a *rodoljub* whom love led to instruct his people. He wrote in the vulgar tongue, with some admixtures of *Slaveno-serbski*. In 1809 he wrote in *Domaća pisma Dositija Obradovića* [*Domestic Letters of Dositej Obradović*], Beograd, 1899, Srpska Književna Zadruga No. 51, p. 194) a poem beginning:

> O može li ko na svetu kao ja znati
> kako je lepa naša srbija mati!
> Svak bi živ zaželio u Srbiju doći
> niti bi kad pomislio opet natrag poći.
>
> [O, can anyone on earth know as I do
> how beautiful our Serbian mother is!
> Everyone would long to come to Serbia,
> nor would he ever think of returning whence
> he had come.]

But his *Život i priključenija* [*Life and Adventures*], an autobiography finished in Leipzig January 1, 1789, breathes a cosmopolitan air of which future generations might well be envious. He was a good Serb but not an extremist.

The same might be said of Vuk Karadžić. His contributions to the literary language and the orthography are too well known to be recited here. Something has already been said about Serbian folk poetry and Karadžić's collecting of it. It seems that the nationalism that enters the traditional material during the second quarter of the nineteenth century is not of Vuk's doing to any great extent. One should look rather to the Montenegrins for this more extreme phase of nationalism. Here we have classed Sima Milutinović-Sarajlija and the two Petrović Njegoši. But it should be pointed out that in addition to *Slobodijada* (written in 1835, but published after his death) and *Ogledalo Srpsko* (1845), models of heroic nationalism, Petar Petrović Njegoš II (1813–1851) also wrote *Gorski Vijenac* [*The Mountain Wreath*], (1847), which at its greatest moments rises above heroic nationalism to problems of general humanity, and *Luča mikrokosma* [*The Ray of the Microcosm*], (1845). He was conversant with other literatures, knew Milton's *Paradise Lost* (in French), and Dante's *Divina Commedia*. He translated fragments of the *Iliad* and of the *Slovo o polku Igor'eve*.

Although he was deeply concerned in Montenegrin history and the fate of his country, he strove to acquaint himself with the epics of other peoples. Considering the time and the place, his *Luča mikrokosma* is an extraordinary accomplishment.

In lyrics and the epic, and in Serbia proper or at least among the Serbs in the Vojvodina, Branko Radičević (1824–1853) is a northern counterpart of Njegoš. In his narrative poems "Put" ["Journey"], 1947) and "Hajdukov grob" ["The Grave of the Hajduk"], (1849) his descriptions of Montenegro and of Montenegrin life are strongly influenced by Byron. The romantic heroism is at moments close to caricature, even where satire may have been intended, one hopes, as in parts of "Put." His nationalism is revealed particularly in what might be called the "Kosovo cult." Of a different caliber, of course, is his support of the language and orthographic reforms of Karadžić. His satirical remarks in "Put" about the old Slavic letters are telling. Radičević's strength is greatest in his lyrics, which are too personal and direct for nationalism to penetrate. Indeed, the influence of Byron and of Schiller and the romantic movement, and the satirical element in some of his poems, begin to place Serbian literature in the first half of this century in a broader framework than nationalism ordinarily would allow.

Of peculiar interest in our study of nationalism in Serbia is the figure of Jovan Sterija Popović (1806–1856). This idealist and educator from Vršac in the Vojvodina in 1830 found the literary genre that was most congenial to his nature, namely satirical comedy. During the thirties and forties he produced a number of plays which became part of the regular repertory of the Serbian theater. He had had a hand in founding and developing that theater. One of his plays, *Lahan,* calls to mind Ibsen's *The Enemy of the People.* But perhaps most germane to our subject is the play that was not produced until 54 years after it was written and 48 years after the death of its author. And it was not published until five years after it first appeared on the stage. From its title, *Rodoljupci* [*The Patriots*], one might suppose that it would have been popular in 1850. It was really, however, a satire on false patriotism. It showed up the shallowness and selfishness of many patriots who felt they would profit from the freedom of their country but who were unwilling to do anything except talk. They were noisy but impractical, and even while they made grand speeches about nationality and Panslavism they were secretly taking pay from the Hungarians once they discovered that their own cause was likely to be lost. They preached the heroic ideals of the political poster of the "Montenegrischer Mensch" as depicted, for example, in Radičević's Byronic "Hajdukov grob." Zelenićka at one point nobly plots the attack on Sentomaš from the distance of Vršac and takes a heroic stand in a room at home. But when she hears that the Hungarians have taken Sentomaš and will be in Vršac in a couple of days, she hides under the bed and then packs with her speech-making nephew to flee for Belgrade. This is what Sterija in a preface to the play calls "the private history of the Serbian movement." He is sure that history will tell the good things about the movement, but this play is for the instruction and guidance of the true patriots in judging the false and empty *rodoljupci* around them. The play was written by Sterija after he had retired to Vršac following the bitter disillusionment of the events of 1848. It is a bright moment, even though it is not great literature. It is unfortunate that his contemporaries were not able to benefit from it.

Sterija Popović affords us the earliest example in Serbian literature of a play about the battle of Kosovo in his *Miloš Obilić* in 1828. As Svetislav Šumarević points out in his book *Pozorište kod Srba* [*The Theater among the Serbs*], (Beograd, 1939, p. 147), until then the Serbs had fewer plays about the fall of the Serbian empire than the English, for whom Goff had written such a piece. The information for the events seems to have come from Rajić's history, which had a second edition in 1823—significantly enough also the date of the Leipzig edition of Vuk's *Srpske narodne pjesme* [*Serbian Folk Songs*]. The play, *Miloš Obilić*, a landmark in the "cult of Kosovo," is inferior as theater to another play of Sterija's which appeared in 1830 and was probably the first play in Serbian literature on a theme from the folk epic, namely *Nahod Simeun* [*The Foundling Simeun*]. This might be called a landmark in the "cult of the folk poetry." The influence of Shakespeare is apparent in Sterija at an early date and in this play, the action of which has been modified from that of the folk poem. *Miloš Obilić* was presented in 1840 in Zagreb, where it was well reviewed in *Danica Ilirska* [*The Illyrian Morning Star*]. It should be noted that the Belgrade Theater in 1841 was opened with another historical play by Sterija, *Smrt Stefana Dečanskog* [*The Death of Stefan Dečanski*].

And so the panorama of figures in Serbian literature continues with poets and dramatists, all honest patriots. Among the poets Jovan Jovanović Zmaj is the most prolific and perhaps the best beloved by the Serbs, especially as a children's poet. He wrote some moving poems on personal losses, and many nationalist verses. Even in one of his poems on the death of his wife, Jovan Jovanović Zmaj includes a note of nationalism: As he points out the peaks of Bosnia, from the heights of Fruškagora, he says ". . . i tam Srbin zivi" ["there, too, the Serb lives"], to which his dying wife exclaims: "Je li . . . Srbin živi" ["Is it so . . . the Serb lives"]. One would prefer the overt kind of patriotic song to this dubious intrusive element in family elegiac. One does not object, however, to the satirical songs "Jututunija and Jututunci" with their humor. Nor does one find fault with such poems as "Bildung" and "Nek se znade da smo slavni" ["Let it be known that we are glorious"], in which he exhibits Sterija Popović's kind of criticism of the imitators of Austrian culture and of the false patriots, the braggarts of heroism, who set out for the pub rather than for battle.

The Serbian poet, dramatist, and story writer Djuro Jakšić, places the same emphasis on national glory and shows the same interest in historical drama as Sterija. Jakšić's epics are only in part based on folk epics, for example, *Nevesta Pivljanina Baja* [*The Bride of Bajo Pivljanin*], *Osmanaga,* and others. But his best contributions to literature outside of the patriotic and nationalistic are some of his lyric poems, such as "Na Liparu" ["In Lipar"], "Ponoc" ["Midnight"], "Potok žubori" ["The Brook Murmurs"], and "Kroz ponoć" ["Through the Still of the Night"]. Among the poems that merit attention as artistic products in spite of national, perhaps even nationalistic references, would be his "Put u Gornjak" ["The Road to Gornjak"]. Jakšić has a better claim to fame for his lyric poetry than for his dramas. His three long-winded dramas were not composed on themes from folk poetry, as Sterija had done and as Kostić was doing, but on subjects from Serbian history. His *The Migration of the Serbs* was first published in Novi Sad in 1863; his *Jelisaveta, Montenegrin Princess* was printed in 1868 and staged in 1870; *Stanoje Glavaš* was presented in 1878 and printed in 1883. The stage, of course, has always been an excellent medium for nationalism.

A contemporary of Jakšić in Serbia was Laza Kostić (1841–1910). His play *Maksim Crnojević,* completed in 1864, harks back to the epic song, "The Wedding of Maksim Crnojević," in Vuk's classical collection. Here is an excellent example of the connecting of folk poetry and the cult of the folk epic on the stage. At first Kostić had tried to write on the subject of Vladimir and Kosara, the same theme that Preradović had used, but Kostić soon abandoned it in favor of a subject on Car Uroš, taken from old Serbian literature and history. But he eventually abandoned this for the folk-song theme.

With *Maksim Crnojević* Kostić was building on foundations set in 1830 by Sterija Popović in his *Nahod Simeun*. The folk epic involved is not an especially nationalistic poem. Kostić has stressed some nationalist sentiments. Ivo Crnojević appeals to Maksim to conceal from his blood brother Miloš his deep love for Andjelija, daughter of the Doge of Venice, for the sake of "the Serbian race and the glory of the Serbian faith." But nationalism is not Kostić's main concern. To emulate Shakespeare was his goal even at the age of twenty-two or twenty-three when he wrote this drama. Actually the folk epic has been changed considerably by Kostić, in his attempt to make a Hamlet of Maksim. At moments Kostić's skill with the verse and with the language, coupled with a penetrating knowledge of Shakespeare, confronts the audience with exciting and fine poetic drama. At other times subplots evaporate rather amusingly and one wishes that the Shakespearean influence had not dictated their inclusion. But the real difficulty in the play is motivation. The folk epic is not too satisfactory on this level either. What is significant for us, however, is not the weakness of the motivation, a fault stemming from the epic, but the strength and quality of the foreign influence.

Kostić's patriotism appears also in his poem "Jadranski Prometej" ["Adriatic Prometheus"], which, however, is put in a section of its own and not included in the section of "rodoljubive pesme" ["patriotic poems"] in the 1951 edition of his poems and dramas. He had before written the poem "Prometej" picturing the effect on Zeus of the giant's laugh as the eagle ate at his vitals. Now he transformed that poem into the figure of the Adriatic giant preyed upon by the double-headed eagle of Austria.

> Na hladne grudi stene prikovan,
> Prometej srpski, prigrlivši kam,
> Na raspetiju mre vekovitu.
> Kakav je greh te večno s njega mre?
> Nek reče Sila, neka kaže Vlast:
> "Kakav je greh?—Što htede sve da sme!
> Slobodu htede, htede sunčev žar:
> a svu slobodu za se treba car!"

[Chained to the cold breast of the cliff,
The Serbian Prometheus, embracing the stone,
On everlasting cross lies dying.
What was his sin from which eternally he dies?
Let Force say; let Power speak:
"What was his sin? He willed to dare all!
He wanted freedom and the sun's heat:
but the emperor needs all of freedom for himself!"]

One of the forces leading away from the nationalistic trend in literature is the influence of foreign writers and foreign literary movements.
Croatian literature began to feel this influence during the romantic
period with writers like Franjo Marković and Šenoa, and Serbian literature can point to Branko Radičević and Laza Kostić. The mere fact
of outside influence and foreign models is a counterforce to nationalism, but the character and quality of the influence determine the
direction it may take and the depth to which it may go. Shakespeare's
influence, for example, led among other things to a concern with psychological study of character. *Hamlet* and *Richard II* were influential
in this respect, and Kostić's youthful *Maksim Crnojević* is an example.
Nationalism can play only a secondary role in such plays, at the most.
On the other hand, while it is not difficult to move from a Byronic
Prometheus as depicted in Kostić's "Prometej" to the personification
of a national Prometheus in his "Jadranski Prometej," the grandeur
of the idea raises nationalism above itself into more general realms
from which the idea came and in which it belongs.

Realism and social criticism also tend away from nationalism or to
focus elsewhere. Satire is frequently related to realism, especially as
it moves into social criticism, and while it is an effective tool against
one's foreign enemies and oppressors it is also useful against domestic
foes, and can be a two-edged sword. Social criticism is directed toward
the general human sphere or toward a concern for social problems not
limited to any one national group. It is not by chance that two of the
calls for realism in Serbo-Croatian literature, that of Kumičić in Croatia
and that of Svetozar Marković in Serbia,· were made by men whose
political philosophies were Socialist. The inspiration for one came from
France, that for the other from Russia. While they were both concerned about the literature of their own people, Croats or Serbs, they
were interested in bringing their native literatures to share in and to
reap the benefits from larger literary movements in Europe and Russia.

But actually this concern was only a continuation of a trend that is almost a law or principle in South Slavic literature, namely, that it is drawn into the intellectual and spiritual life both of Europe and the East on whose both fringes it finds itself. The South Slavic literatures "belong," and this is the burden of the present essay. They are not merely nationalistic, although sometimes even their friends unwittingly have the contrary impression.

Serbian realism, to return to the particular, is related to Russian realism as well as to that of the West. Gogol and Turgenev, to say nothing of the influence of Chernyshevsky and other social reformers and critics, join here with Flaubert and Zola. There is a strong satirical strain apparent in Jakov Ignjatović (1824–1888), Radoje Domanović (1873–1908), and Stevan Sremac (1855–1906), reminiscent of the comedies of Sterija Popović and some of the poems of Jovan Jovanović Zmaj. There is also a strong conservative element in Laza Lazarević (1851–1890) and Bora Stanković (1876–1927), who find in social change, particularly the social change in Serbia, a disrupting and debilitating force in the lives of men and women. They look with some nostalgia at the stability and moral strength of the patriarchal life and with disapproval and some shock at the newer influences as they affect the younger generation.

Serbian realism is essentially a realism of the village and small-town life, and it is concerned with people and their relationship to one another, especially of families. One thinks of Sofka and her family, for example, in Stanković's famous novel *Nečista Krv* [*Impure Blood*], (1911). Like Croatian literature, Serbian literature enters the twentieth century on a wave of realism, which continues strong in the short story particularly but also to some extent in the novel. Poetry in Serbia, however, takes a different path from what we find in Croatia. There is no movement in Serbia to correspond to the Croatian "Modena." Poetry during the second part of the nineteenth century was dominated by Zmaj and Vojislav Ilić, and after the turn of the century by Jovan Dučić (1874–1943). Aleksa Šantić (1868–1924) and Milan Rakić (1876–1938) came into prominence, as lyricists. All these poets, in spite of divergence in their individual characteristics (and their lives, some of which were led outside the Balkans), indulged in patriotic verse at one time or another as a normal genre for poetry. Ilić and Dučić had been influenced by Pushkin, and Dučić had himself been a follower of

Ilić in his younger years. But later as he traveled in the West he became well acquainted with French poetry as did Rakić, who was especially impressed by Baudelaire. Perhaps Rakić and Dučić came closest to the poets of the "Moderna," but they are not so interested in form as such. Skerlić in his *Istorija nove srpske književnosti* [*History of Modern Serbian Literature*], says (p. 439) of Rakić:

During recent years Rakić, who has been at a post in Kosovo, has written a certain number of patriotic poems, in which, together with Aleksa Šantić, he has resurrected the old patriotic [rodoljubiv] poetry, and he has shown how even this can be made very literary and artistic. His patriotism is deep in his heart and in full harmony with his spirit; he has contemporary patriotism, without slogans and without posing, rational and discrete, which is a component element of the developed soul and ripe thought of modern man.

Rakić wrote only forty or fifty poems, and seven of them he grouped together under the heading "Na Kosovu" ("On Kosovo"). The most patriotic stanzas of the most patriotic of these, "Na Gazi Mostanu," are the following:

> Danas nama kažu, deci ovog veka,
> Da smo nedostojni istorije naše,
> Da nas zahvatila zapadnjačka reka,
> I da nam se duše opasnosti plaše
>   Dobra zemljo moja, lažu! Ko te voli,
> Danas, taj te voli, jer zna da si mati,
> Jer pre nas ni polja ni krševi goli
> Ne mogoše nikom svesnu ljubav dati!
>   I danas kad dodje do poslednjeg boja,
> Neozaren starog oreola sjajem,
> Ja ću dati život, otadžbino moja,
> Znajući šta dajem i zašto ga dajem!

> [Today they tell us, children of this age,
> That we're unworthy of our history,
> That a western river has seized upon us,
> And that our souls fear to face danger.
>   O my good land, they lie! Who loves you
> Today, he loves you, knowing that you are his mother,
> Because before us neither fields nor bare rocks
> Could give a conscious love to anyone!
>   And today when we reach the final battle,

Unadorned by the lustre of the halo of yore,
I shall give my life, o my fatherland,
Knowing what I give and why I give it!]

This is the modern patriotism of which Skerlić wrote.

Slovenian literature in the nineteenth century presents an excellent example of a national literature with a clear sense of national identity but with a minimum of exaggerated nationalism. France Prešeren (1800–1849), whose poetry was a boon to a feeling of Slovenian identity because it was written in Slovenian, wrote little that might be termed "nationalistic." In his "Zdravljica" ["The Toast"], for example, he is as much concerned with Slavdom as with Slovenes alone. Here he was influenced by Čelakovský and Kopitar and Matija Čop. He wrote a poem in German, "An die Slowenen, die in deutscher Sprache dichten." His lyricism is personal rather than narrowly patriotic as is abundantly clear both from "Sonetni venec" ["The Sonnet Wreath"], the acrostic to Julija, and from his narrative poem, "Krst pri Savici" ["The Cross at Savica"].

There are some Slovenian patriotic poems, for example, Urban Jarnik's (1784–1844) "Na Slovence" ["To the Slovenes"]. Jovan Vesel Koseski (1798–1884) wrote "Kdo je mar?" ["Who is dearer?"] in 1846, the last lines of each stanza of which are: "Mi zapojmo: rodovine/ je slovenski oratar; Ta pogumni koremine / je slovenski oratar," ["We sing: The Slovene ploughman is of our race; And the Slovene ploughman is of sturdy stock"].

A novel departure in Slovenian literature is the use of folk-tale themes in literary short stories. This is a peculiarly Slovenian aspect of the influence of folklore in the early half of the century. The folk tale, as it were, replaces the folk epic and provides narrative material. France Levstik (1831–1887), one of whose chief contributions to Slovenian nationalism was a purifying of the Slovene language, wrote the tale "Martin Krpan z Vrha" ["Martin Krpan of Vrh"] (1858), which is an example of a highly successful adaptation of a folk tale. Janez Trdina (1830–1905) collected Slovene folk tales, which were published in eight volumes, *Bajke in povesti* [*Fairy and Folk Tales*], (1904–1910). He also collected information on folk customs, printed in 1912 in the tenth volume of his collected works under the title *Isprehod v Belo Krajino* [*Wandering in Bela Krajina*].

Patriotic poems are found especially in the verses of Simon Jenko (1835–1869) and Josip Stritar (1836–1923). Jenko wrote a group of such poems under the title "Solze Slovenčeve" ["The Tears of the Slovenes"], the leading example of which is "Slovenska Zgodovina" ["Slovenian History"]. It begins:

> Bridka žalost me prešine,
> ·Ko se spomnim domovine,
> vsemu svetu nepoznane,
> od nikogar spoštovane.

> [A bitter sorrow pierces me,
> when I think of my homeland,
> unknown to all the world,
> by none honored.]

But side by side with these one must place his other poetry, lyrical, sensitive. Compare, for example, the last stanza of *Obrazi XV:*

> Šepetanje tajno
> nosi zrak čez njivo,
> sluku nerazumno,
> srcu razumljivo.

> [A secret murmuring
> the breeze carries over the fields,
> incomprehensible to the ear,
> comprehensible to the heart.]

An example of Josip Stritar's patriotic verse in his "Mojemu narodu" ["To my people"] (1869), which begins:

> Narodi boje bijejo krvave,
> oblastno zemljo z mecem si delijo.

> [The peoples fight bloody battles,
> They divide a mighty land with swords.]

The last lines echo this:

> Tvoj bode venec zmage nekrvave:
> naprej moj rod—"Naprej, zastava Slave!"

> [Yours be the crown of bloodless siege:
> Forward, my people—"Forward, banner of Glory!"]

The quotation at the end is from the national hymn by Jenko! But this poem is not typical of Stritar. More valuable are his *Dunajski soneti,*

[Danubian Sonnets], which are satirical and aimed at the conservative "Staroslovenci." Here are the last six lines of the sixteenth sonnet:

> Dve stranki imate sedaj v Ljubljani—
> ker tretja noče se še prav roditi—
> ni mesta mu na tej, ne óni strani.
>
> Tam národ svoj bi moral zatajiti,
> a k vam svobodoljubje njemu brani;
> težkó človeku je Slovencu biti!
>
> [There are two parties now in Ljubljana—
> because a third will not be born aright—
> there is no place for him on this or on that side.
>
> There he would have to defraud his own people,
> but this side forbids him liberalism toward you;
> it's hard for a man to be a Slovene!]

Yet in his novels Stritar takes his reader away from the local scene. In *Zorin* (earlier called *Eveline*) Rousseau's influence is evident. The hero says: "For a long time, my friend, I have especially loved Rousseau. I feel my whole being as somehow related to his. (Translated from *Zgodovina*, II, 322). Goethe too affected him profoundly. So here also, foreign influence is deep.

Another voice heard in Slovenia from outside is that of Sir Walter Scott. In 1868 Fran Levec called the prose writer Josip Jurčič (1844–1881) "naš Walter Scott" ["Our Walter Scott"], (*Zgodovina*, II, 302), because of his novel *Deseti brat* [*The Tenth Brother*], (1866).

But it is not the purpose of this essay to give a detailed survey of Slovenian literature. From the point of view of the problem of nationalism it presents the normal graph, as it were, of a small national literature struggling successfully against a larger one (German) to maintain itself in an essentially bilingual (or multilingual) country. Like its big sister literatures, Croatian and Serbian, it was saved from too extreme nationalism by foreign influences in romanticism, realism, and modernism. It had its internal faction. It was moved by Illyrianism or by outside forces from the northwest that preached Panslavism, but it was not engulfed by them. Its nationalism was strong enough to combat them, but wise enough to benefit from them as well.

As one reaches into the period of realism, already apparent in Jurčič's novels and stories, writers are even more concerned with native Slovenian subjects, in part from history, in part from contemporary life. Examples are Janko Kersnik (1852–1897) and Ivan Travčar (1851–1923). Anton Aškerc (1856–1912) added a bitter note in his satirical poems, and a new flavor in South Slavic literature in his Oriental motifs, as in his poem "Firduzi in Derviš" ["Firdusi and the Dervish"] (from *Lirske in epske poezije*, 1896) [*Lyric and Epic Poems*]. Aškerc's intensity in his epics, or more properly perhaps his ballads and romances, was employed in the struggle against Germanization and especially in the internal conflict on the side of the Young Slovenes against the "Staroslovenci."

The most important literary periodical for the younger group was *Ljubljanski Zvon* [*The Ljubljana Bell*]. In 1902 Aškerc gave up its editorship in favor of the new and still younger writers Cankar and Župančić. This new group, like the Moderna writers in Croatia, emphasized art and form.

Finally, in Bulgaria, as in Slovenia, nationalism in the normal and best sense played no small role. We have already seen it at work in establishing schools and periodicals, and in collecting folklore. Its early writers were educators; frequently they spent part of their lives in exile, in the Bulgarian colonies in the cities of Russia, Rumania, or Serbia. After the religious and educational poems from Neofit Rilski (1793–1881) to the Metropolitan of Trnovo (1835) or of Neofit Bozveli, one of the earliest poems (1837) is an ode to the Russian Venelin by G. T. Peshakov and a lament on the same man's death (1839). The first patriotic poem seems to be "Pohvala na drevnite Bolgari i na otechestvoto im," ["Encomium—the Ancient Bulgars and Their Fatherland"], (1840) by Sichan Nikolov (1806–1889). "Otechestvo" ["Fatherland"], (1849) by Hadzhi Naiden Iovanovich (1805–1862) has little but its sentiments to recommend it. More melodious were Stefan Izvorski's (1815–1875) "Ah, B'lgariia, moia dusho" [Ah, Bulgaria, my soul"], (1853) and Ivan Bogorov's "Otechestvo" ["Fatherland"], (1842). Dobri Chintulov (1822–1886) of Sliven added several others, such as, "Bulgaria, mila maiko!" ["Bulgaria, dear mother!"], "Stani, stani, iunak balkanski" ["Arise, Arise, Balkan Hero"], "K'de si viárna ti liubov narodna?" ["Where Are You, True Love of Our People?"], and "Viat'r echi, balkan stene" ["The Wind Howls, the Balkan Groans"]. Although a number of his poems are of this patriotic stamp, there are some with other subjects, such as his "Stara maika se proshtava s's sina si" ["The Old

Mother Says Farewell to Her Son"]. Naiden Gerov (1823–1900) of Koprivshtitsa composed "Stoian i Rada" (1842), a ballad in folk style, but using tonic instead of syllabic verse. It was the first Bulgarian poem to be printed separately. After 1853 he wrote a rousing poem which begins:

> Vik se vika ot balkana
> Ta se slusha po sveta:
> b'lgarin't na krak stana
> ta si iska svoboda.
>
> [A cry resounds from the Balkan mountains
> and it is heard throughout the world:
> The Bulgar rises to his feet
> and demands freedom.]

Of interest here is his poem recalling Simeon and reflecting a "cult of the *gusla*":

> Pred tvoi dnes az stoia oltar
> na tebe v'piia, Guslane,
> razkrii tvoite shtedri dlani,
> izlei na mene svoia dar,
> moiata gusla naglasi,
> kato dostoino da uspeia
> az Simeona da v'zpeia.
>
> [Today I stand before your altar,
> unto you I cry, O great singer!
> Open your preserving hands,
> pour forth your gift upon me!
> Give voice to my *gusla*,
> that I may worthily succeed
> in hymning Simeon!]

These patriotic songs culminated in the intense poems of Khristo Botev (1847–1876), whose fiery revolutionary poetry and short life are well known in Balkan circles.

In prose this patriotic spirit is represented by a correspondingly strong *feuilleton* tradition from the time of P. R. Slavcikov (1827–1859), Liuben Karavelov (1835–1879), and Botev himself. From the middle of the century up to at least 1878 social reform or social comment was implied and frequently overtly stated in much of the literature. Through Karavelov and Botev the Russian social reformers and revolutionaries

had their influence. Yet the pictures of Bulgarian life given by Karavelov in his "Maminoto detence" ["Mama's Boy"] or in the romantic
"Doncho Vojvoda," for example, are valuable in themselves even
without any message. This is, of course, especially true of Ivan Vazov's
(1850–1921) novels and stories. But his experience of literature was
great—Russian (for example, Nekrasov, Gogol) and French (Victor
Hugo)—and in the last analysis Vazov was primarily a writer, not a
journalist. His influence on all writers after 1878 was healthy. Both
Iordan Iovkov (1850–1937) and Elin Pelin (1878–1949) were indebted to him and also to French and Russian literature. These men,
too, were writers, and interested in ideas that go beyond the nation to
all mankind. In this they went back also to the influence exerted by
Pencho Slaveikov (1866–1912) and others in the periodical *Mis'l*
[*Thought*] around the turn of the century who had sought to direct
literature toward art and philosophy and to free it from the bonds of
tendentiousness and dogma. In the poetry of P. K. Iavorov (1877–1914)
we find such freedom, and great diversity of form and experimentation
in verse. For example, *S'brani s'chinenija*, I (Sofia, 1959), 202:

DVE DUSHI

Az ne zhiveia: az goria. Neprimirimi
v g'rdite mi se borjat dve dushi:
dushata na angel i demon. V g'rdi mi
te plam'ci dishat i plam me sushi.

[TWO SOULS

I do not live: I am consumed by fire. Irreconcilable
within my breast contend two souls:
soul of angel and of devil. In my breast
they breathe flames and flame withers me.]

Different as the two writers are, one can move with ease from the
stanza of Iavorov just quoted to almost any of the stories of Elin Pelin
in *Pod manastirskata loza* [*Under the Monastery Arbor*], or elsewhere.
Both were Bulgarian to the hilt, but both were men of letters in the
supranational realm of the arts.

Bulgaria, then, also shared in this century with the rest of our Western world the hopes and experiences of literature.

In sum, when the national awakening came in Serbia, Croatia, and
Bulgaria there was a kind of classicism that had become or was striving
to become traditional—a classicism that was based on foreign models

in one way or another. There was the Hellenism of Bulgaria, the Greek and especially Latin classicism of the Serbs coupled with a Church classicism in a Slavic language, and the Dalmatian-Dubrovnik classicism in Croatia coupled also with Italian influence and the ancient classics. Nationalism rebelled and brought in folk language, folk poetry as models, patriotic, nationalistic themes, patriotic papers and magazines and other periodicals, and patriotic literary societies. There was an interchange between the folk poetry and literature. Literature took on the language and style and subjects of the poetry, and the foundation was laid for the historical poem, the historical drama, the historical novel, or the drama, poem, or novel based on a folk theme. On the other hand the nationalism that led to recording of folk poetry and to a widespread interest in it, also led to the introduction of national themes into the folk poetry, which was previously local and not nationalistic. But the folk theme and the historical subject can appeal for only a limited time, and soon the present scene, realistically treated, replaced the historical and romantic. With experimentation in forms and meters, with the growing influence of Western European and Russian literary trends, the Balkan Slavic literatures, whether they were accessible to the West or not (and, of course, they were not), once again reached a position abreast of the other literatures of Europe, no longer really separated by nationalistic barriers. Today, indeed, as has been true for some time, the gulf between Balkan Slavic literature and that of the West, or of European literature including Russian, is chiefly, perhaps even solely, caused by language.

Perhaps the time has come for the interested world to cease thinking of Balkan literatures—and I speak particularly of Balkan Slavic literatures—as "nationalistic literatures." The modern literatures of the Balkan nations came into being, as we have seen, together with the awakening of their peoples to a group identity or to a new realization of group identity. Politically and socially nationalism was important and necessary. It helped in fostering the use of the everyday language rather than a hieratic language or someone else's language for literature and in giving a new start to the literature itself. But nationalism was noisy and soon became banal, empty, unworthy in the spiritual and intellectual growth of unusually talented peoples. The Balkan Slavs have produced literatures that can be truly called by that name—literatures that are not mere slogans and self-congratulatory speeches.

We should try to save these literatures from their most avid supporters, the nationalists of the Balkan Slavs both at home and abroad, who are well-intentioned but not too wise. The Balkan Slavic literatures, if they are not crammed down our throats by nationalist groups, and if we can avoid the patriotic and the quaint—which is what usually gets into anthologies and translations—can stand well on their own feet. There are exciting discoveries to make for those who want to learn the languages so that they may venture therein. If they can get beyond Kosovo and its cult, beyond the nationalistic "folk" epic to the true oral epos of the South Slavs, and to a gifted group of men of letters in all genres they will find the effort rewarding.

BIBLIOGRAPHY

Although the books about and translations of South Slavic literature in English, French, German, and Italian are increasing slowly, the material available is far from being adequate. The following general surveys in WESTERN LANGUAGES of the modern literatures in Serbocroatian, Bulgarian, and Slovenian are useful:

Serbocroatian Literature

IN ENGLISH
Barac, Antun. *A History of Yugoslav Literature* (Belgrade, 1955).
Kadić, Ante. *Contemporary Croatian Literature* ('s Gravenhage, 1960).
IN FRENCH
Savković, Miloš. *La Littérature yougoslave moderne* (Belgrade, 1936).
IN GERMAN
Gesemann, Gerhard. *Literaturen der slavischen Völker: Die serbo-kroatische Literatur* (Wildpark-Potsdam, 1930).
IN ITALIAN
Cronia, Arturo. *Storia della letteratura serbo-croata* (Milan, 1956).
Maver, G. "Letteratura serbo-croata," in Pellegrini, Carlo, ed., *Storia delle letterature moderne d'Europa e d'America*, Vol. VI (Milan, 1960), pp. 99–176.

Bulgarian Literature

IN ENGLISH
Manning, C. A. and R. Smal-Stocki. *The History of Modern Bulgarian Literature* (New York, 1960). (Inadequate and tendentious)

IN FRENCH

Dontchev, Nikolai, *Études bulgares* (Sofia, n. d.).

IN ITALIAN

Salvini, Luigi. *La Letteratura bulgara dalla liberazione alla Prima Guerra Balcanica (1878–1912)* (Roma, 1936).

Damiani, Enrico. "Letteratura bulgara" in Pellegrini, Carlo, ed., *Storia delle letterature moderne d'Europa e d'America*, (Milan, 1960), VI, 179–229.

Slovenian Literature

IN GERMAN

Slodnjak, Anton. *Geschichte der Slowenischen Literatur* (Berlin, 1958).

The following books in SOUTH SLAVIC LANGUAGES are recommended to cover the history of the respective literatures:

In Serbocroatian

Barac, Antun. *Jugoslavenska književnost* [*Jugoslav Literature*], Zagreb, 1954 (English translation listed in preceding section).

Barac, Antun. *Hrvatska književnost od preporoda do stvaranja Jugoslavije* [*Croatian Literature from the Revival to the Formation of Jugoslavia*], (Zagreb, 1954–1960), 2 vols.

Ježić, Slavko. *Hrvatska književnost od početka do danas, 1100–1941* [*Croatian Literature from the Beginning to the Present, 1100–1941*], (Zagreb, 1944).

Skerlić, Jovan. *Istorija nove srpske književnosti* [*History of Modern Serbian Literature*], 3d ed. (Belgrade, 1953).

Stanojević, Stanoje, ed. *Narodna enciklopedija srpsko-hrvatsko-slovenačka* [*The National Encyclopedia of the Serbs, Croats and Slovenes*], (Zagreb, 1925–1929) 4 vols.

The following works treat special periods or movements:

Marjanović, Milan. *Hrvatska moderna* [*The Croatian Modernist Movement*], (Zagreb, 1951), 2 vols.

Skerlić, Jovan. *Srpska književnost u XVIII veku* [*Serbian Literature in the Eighteenth Century*], (Belgrade, 1923).

Skerlić, Jovan. *Omladina i njena književnost 1848–1871* [*The Younger Group and its Literature, 1848–1871*], 2d ed. (Belgrade, 1925).

Gligorić, Velibor. *Srpski realisti* [*The Serbian Realists*] 2d ed. (Belgrade), 1961).

In Bulgarian

Angelov, B. *B'lgarska literatura* [*Bulgarian Literature*] part ii (Sofia, 1924).

Penev, Bojan. *Istoriia na novata b'lgarskata literatura* [*History of Modern Bulgarian Literature*], (Sofia, 1930–1936), 4 vols.

Konstantinov, G. *Nova b'lgarska literatura* [*Modern Bulgarian Literature*], (Sofia, 1947).

Dinekov, P. *P'rvi v'zrozhdenci* [*The First Writers of the Revival*], (Sofia, 1942).

In Russian

Beliaeva, Ju. D., et al. *Ocherki istorii bolgarskoi literatury XIX–XX vekov* [*Sketches of the History of Bulgarian Literature of the Nineteenth and Twentieth Centuries*], (Moskva, 1959).

In Slovenian

Grafenauer, Ivan. *Zgodovina novejšega slovenskega slovstva* [History of Modern Slovenian Literature], (Ljubljana, 1909–1911), 2 vols.

Janež, Stanko. *Zgodovina slovenske književnosti* [*History of Slovenian Literature*], (Maribor, 1957).

Legiša, Lino, ed. *Zgodovina slovenskega slovstva* [*History of Slovenian Literature*], (Ljubljana, 1956–1961), 3 vols.

THE SOCIAL FOUNDATIONS

OF BALKAN POLITICS,

1750–1941

Traian Stoianovich

The Estate or Traditional Society

Social differentiation arises under four principal conditions: when one people conquers another and forces it to perform manual labor and fulfill some secondary military functions, while it itself specializes in the art of government and conquest, or when a functionally specialized foreign social group settles in a hitherto undifferentiated society; when religious differences are introduced into a society or community; when a people enters into frequent cultural intercourse with societies in which social differentiation has already occurred; and when a society is sufficiently large to require and support the division of labor, and is psychologically oriented to allow the attachment of different rewards to different functions and talents, thereby fostering the unequal distribution of wealth and the development of differences in the style of life of various groups within the society. Unless, however, the differentiation is released from ethnic, religious, and other traditional restrictions, the society acquires an estate basis. Social classes do not

The title of my report for the Conference at Berkeley was "The Dynamics of Balkan Classes." For reasons of space the present essay, an otherwise expanded version of the original report, does not include the sections on class values and styles, nor on the ecology of classes and the relation between class, nation, and culture. I am indebted for many ideas formulated herein to the thought and writings of Fernand Braudel, C. E. Labrousse, and the late Georges Lefebvre. I am grateful to Alexander Vucinich for carefully reading my manuscript and to Irwin T. Sanders, Leften S. Stavrianos, Jozo Tomasevich, Basil Laourdas, Wayne S. Vucinich, Charles Jelavich, and Peter F. Sugar for several useful comments on the preliminary or final draft.

arise until the fourth condition is fulfilled and the individual is rewarded on the basis of competitive ability.

In the Balkans, as in the West, social mobility became more intense during the sixteenth century, and both the total and relative membership of several different social or professional and economic categories —merchants, craftsmen, and public officials—grew considerably. Balkan social differentiation, however, was less the product of the discovery and exploitation of a new world than the outcome of a new political situation: the conquest of the entire peninsula by the Turks and the attendant religious differentiation (the introduction of Islam as the religion of the dominant political elements), the inclination of Ottoman administrators to patronize the cities (where the Turks or Muslims were generally numerous) and neglect the rural areas (where they were often few), and their skill in uniting a vast area—the Balkans, Anatolia, and the Fertile Crescent—and exploiting it to their own advantage.

The new ruling class altered the medieval social order of traditional rights and duties to suit their own aims but retained the basic estates structure. The revised social order was not recognized by a written constitution, nor was it the object, to our knowledge, of a clear theoretical statement, except in regard to some of its parts. It was developed instead on an *ad hoc* basis and was occasionally modified. From the reign of Süleyman the Lawgiver (Magnificent) to the end of the eighteenth century, however, it remained a society of six fairly distinct social estates (excluding slaves, who, in keeping with traditions of Roman law, were not considered persons): the *asker* or military and governing estate; the *ulema* or Muslim judicial, educational, and ecclesiastical order; the *beledy*[1] or urban civil estate of the non-Muslim

---

[1] For a detailed discussion of the *asker* and *ulema* and a brief identification of the *beledy*, see: [Ignatius Mouradgea] d'Ohsson, *Tableau général de l'Empire Othoman*, 4 vols. in 5 (Paris, 1788–1820), IV, part 2, pp. 483–613. The seventeenth-century Ottoman historian and minor army official, Hadji-Khalifa, divided human society into four "pillars": *ulema, asker, tajjar,* and *rayah*. The *tajjar* were the traders and artisans. It seems to us, however, that Ottoman Muslim traders and artisans fell into a special category, since they were as much a part of the *asker* as of the trading community. For a brief analysis of Hadji-Khalifa's views, see: Erwin I. J. Rosenthal, *Political Thought in Medieval Islam* (Cambridge, England: University Press, 1958), pp. 229–233. For additional details on Ottoman estate society, see Sherif Mardin, "The Mind of the Turkish Reformer, 1700–1900," *Western Humanities Review*, XIV (Autumn, 1960), pp. 420–425.

millets or religious communities; the armed rayah or privileged Christian peasantry; the disarmed rayah or pariah pseudo-estate; and the self-governing foreign communities (and their Ottoman protégés), which enjoyed extraterritorial rights and were protected by treaty.

Since the study of sixteenth-century Ottoman institutions by Albert Howe Lybyer, the military and governing estate has been known as the "Ruling Institution." The Ruling Institution was the executive arm of the government. No distinction was made between civil government or civil institutions and military government. All government was military government, and the Ruling Institution was subject to military discipline. The Ruling Institution and the Defense Arm were one and the same, and the Turkish name for both was *asker* (from the Latin *exercitus*).

In the sixteenth century, the *asker* was made up of Muslim Turks, of renegades and converts to Islam, of Christian peasants and former nobles in possession of military fiefs, and of Christian troops (*martolosi*) used to garrison the fortresses of the north. The Ruling Institution, or *asker*, was internally stratified but advancement from the lowest to the highest position was possible. Conversion to Islam was necessary, however, for the exercise of all but the lowliest functions. Christians in the *asker* were thus tempted to apostasize, and the Christian element declined in importance after 1600.

The franchised Christian peasantry, who performed internal security functions in return for exemption from some taxes and a guarantee against the spread of the seignorial regime to their communities, possessed some of the attributes of the *asker*. Privileged individuals and franchised communities, and sometimes franchised federations of rural communes (such as the *eparchia* and *knežina* federations of the Greeks and Serbs), existed among all Balkan nationalities. Toward the end of the sixteenth century, however, privileged pastoral-military (*voynuk*) villages began to vanish, and the Turks repeatedly tried to rid the Serbs and Bulgarians, and later the Greeks, of their special immunities. Not with complete success, however. The free communes or *eleftherochoria* of the Greeks and Macedo-Vlachs and the *knežinas* of the Serbs persisted into the nineteenth century.

Unlike the privileged Christian rayah, who were almost invariably herdsmen, the pariah rayah were generally tillers of the soil, bound to land or master. Some of the rayah, largely descendants of non-Turkish peasant converts to Islam, were Muslim. But unlike the unprivileged Christian rayah, the Muslims could be assimilated into the *asker*. The unprivileged, or pariah, rayah were Orthodox Christian (and, in the western provinces, Roman Catholic) peasants of South Slavic, Albanian, and Greek—but rarely Macedo-Vlach—nationality. They could escape from their servile condition in life only by fleeing into the hills and woods and becoming outlaws or by running away, in violation of the law, to some distant town or region and seeking the protection of friendly notables or of other lords.

Charged with satisfying the wants of the towns, the *beledy* estate fulfilled its economic functions as if it were part of a larger order to which were also admitted both underpaid soldiers and profit-minded members of the *asker*. In matters not pertaining to business, however, these Muslims reverted to the military estate. The non-Muslim *beledy*, on the other hand, were separated into three principal groups, each organized as a *millet*: Jews, Orthodox Christians, and Gregorian Armenians. Each religious subgroup had its own judicial, educational, and ecclesiastical organization, and was free to make decisions on education, religion, and intracommunity law to the extent that such acts did not infringe upon the rights of other *millets*, guild law, or the primacy of the Muslim religion. The three principal non-Muslim religious groups thus had an institution corresponding to the Muslim *ulema*. However, they had only a truncated governing estate, consisting of primates who exercised administrative powers but were subordinate to the *asker*, advisers to the Ottoman government and secretaries to Ottoman officials, and high officials appointed to the vassal principalities of Wallachia and Moldavia. As the auxiliary *"asker"* or armed rural rayah did not form part of the *beledy*, the latter lacked an autonomous executive arm. The pariah rayah, on the other hand, were subject to the religious, moral, and judicial decisions of the *beledy* community of their faith (unless they chose to submit to the military law of the *asker* or the normal law of the *ulema*) but did not share in the privileges of the *beledy*.

The full-time *asker* corresponded to a kind of aristocracy of the sword, the *ulema* to a nobility of the robe, the *beledy* and part-time *asker* of the towns to a Third Estate divided into several different religious communities, the privileged rayah to a kind of yeomanry, the pariah rayah to a quasi-order of serfs. The *ulema* enjoyed "the noble privilege of immunity from taxation" and the *de jure* right of hereditary transmission of property and, in part, of privilege. The *asker* lacked a *de jure* right of this kind but did exercise its own justice (like the *ulema*) and was exempt from some forms of taxation, while its upper echelons even succeeded in maintaining property and privilege in their families by resorting to bribery or force, or by making the right marriage. Some members of the *asker* managed to transfer one or more of their sons to the *ulema;* others had their land recognized as inalienable ecclesiastical property but kept the revenues derived therefrom as a family right.[2]

The German-Imperial (Austrian) internuncio to the Porte, Baron Herbert, thus rightly advised his government in 1779:

Having hardly entered Turkey [at Belgrade], I recognized the futility of a prejudice that prevails in Christendom. They think there is no nobility in Turkey and that no distinction exists between the children of a vizier and the children of a picklock (*crocheteur*). Precisely the contrary is true. The sons of pashas are called *Bey*, or noble of the first rank, and [the dignity is extended to] their descendants. A person with an ancestry of several pashas is very highly esteemed and arrives at honors with greater ease. The same is true of the charges of the Robe. They are also very careful in their marriage alliances, whereas they consult only their taste in choosing concubines. The former pasha of Belgrade, for example, is the son of a Kapudan Pasha. His son already holds an office of distinction, while his daughter is the spouse of the Reis Efendi [who has been just] dismissed. In this matter, then, [things] are as with ministers among us.[3]

Duplicating a comparable Russian and western European current,[4] the tendency toward the inheritance of social status gained momentum during the seventeenth and eighteenth centuries. The "captains" of the

---

[2] Albert Howe Lybyer, *The Government of the Ottoman Empire in the Time of Suleiman the Magnificent* (Cambridge, Mass.: Harvard University Press, 1913), pp. 195, 203; G[uillaume] A[ntoine] Olivier, *Voyage dans l'Empire Othoman, l'Egypte et la Perse, fait par ordre du Gouvernement, pendant les six premières années de la République*, I (Paris: H. Agasse, Year IX), 276–277, 284.

[3] Haus-, Hof- und Staatsarchiv (Vienna), StA. Türkei V/18, dispatch from Baron Herbert to Count Cobenzl, dated Belgrade, August 12, 1779. The dispatch is written in French.

[4] For a concise statement and interpretation of the analogous situation in the West, see the important study of R. R. Palmer, *The Age of the Democratic Revolution: A Political History of Europe and America, 1760–1800*, I (Princeton, N.J.: Princeton University Press, 1959), esp. p. 29.

marches of Bosnia-Hercegovina acquired *de facto* hereditary status before the end of the seventeenth century. Urban notables (*ayans*) and powerful lords of the valleys (*derebeys*) similarly succeeded in making their authority and wealth hereditary. The central government, however, refused to legalize the accomplishments of the military aristocracy. A portion of the *asker* was consequently almost always in revolt from the close of the sixteenth to the middle of the nineteenth century.

In the latter part of the eighteenth century, the Ottoman "Fronde" acquired serious size. Under the influence of the Enlightenment, the new *frondeurs* planned to "improve" or "rationalize" the estates organization. Enlightenment did not deter them, however, from enlisting the services of the riffraff of the empire to consolidate their power, augment their properties, and legalize their social status: to "rationalize" the estates system. As in the past, therefore, their movement was fundamentally an aristocratic reaction, a coalition and conspiracy of aristocrats and brigands, against the little people and against the central government.

The growth of status consciousness and the drift toward the hereditary transmission of social status among the dominant (Muslim) political class were matched by a similar trend among the *beledy*. The Phanariotes, who were Christian bankers, publicans, and diplomats, as well as administrators of the civil and financial affairs of the Greek Orthodox Church and governors of the Danubian Principalities, constituted the highest echelon of the Greek Orthodox *beledy*. Members of a special satellite nobility of the robe, they enjoyed the title of bey or prince, while their wives were addressed as *domna* or *archontissa* (*Lady Archon*).[5]

An English physician who traveled widely in Greece during the Napoleonic Wars, Henry Holland, found that "family antiquity and connections" had "a good deal of weight" among the Greeks and procured respect "independently of mere wealth." Furthermore,

even the dejected political state of the Greeks [had] not precluded the use of certain titles, applied as distinctions to particular classes of society. Those who [held] the situation of Archons, or other magisterial office, were generally spoken of and addressed with the epithet of

---

[5] Joseph Gottwald, "Phanariotische Studien," *Leipziger Vierteljahrsschrift für Südosteuropa*, V (1941), 50.

Eugenestatos or *Entimotatos;* a merchant with that of *Timiotatos;* a physician as *Exochotatos;* and a schoolmaster with the long prefixture of *Sophologiotatos,* which was given with all due forms of usage.[6]

Bishops, Phanariotes, and "primates of the towns and richer [intra-imperial] merchants" knew that the Greek rayah, no less than the Slavs, regarded them as "friends to tyranny" and "Christian Turks." They consequently feared social revolution quite as much as did the rebellious aristocracy of the sword, and did not want a war of national independence unless they could be "certain of benefiting by the change."[7]

In spite of the traditionalist and antirevolutionary views and attitudes of the dominant Muslim and satellitic Christian oligarchies, social and national revolution was realized in Šumadija and in Attica, the Peloponnesus (Morea), and the islands of the Aegean, and its impact was felt from the Adriatic to the Euxine. The inquiry now naturally turns to the human and institutional factors that permitted the rise of a revolutionary situation.

FROM DUAL SOVEREIGNTY TO MULTIPLE SOVEREIGNTY

Revolution ensues from the discontent of the masses only when a capable and zealous minority imbued with a chiliastic social myth challenges the myth of the dominant political class and resolutely leads the discontented against the existing political and social order. The dominant political class consists of the groups in authority. The revolutionary minority constitutes a new political class, radically different from both the dominant and the satellitic or dependent political class.

A new political class does not arise unless there is first a condition of *anomie,* a loss of faith in the old norms and values, a feeling of lethargy among part of the dominant political class, a sentiment among another part that the country is "going to the dogs," and volitional or uncon-

---

[6] Henry Holland, *Travels in the Ionian Isles, Albania, Thessaly, Macedonia, &c. during the Years 1812 and 1813* (London, 1815), pp. 153, 165.

[7] The reference to "Christian Turks" is from William Martin Leake, *Travels in the Morea,* 3 vols. (London, 1830), II, 177. The other quotations are from J. C. Hobhouse, *A Journey through Albania, and Other Provinces of Turkey in Europe and Asia, to Constantinople, during the Years 1809 and 1810* (London, 1813), II, 597.

scious action by a third group to take it along that path.[8] But *anomie* alone is not sufficient to create a revolutionary situation, which develops—in contrast to the coup d'état or "palace revolution"—only after the manifestation of a socially significant structural change. The latter almost invariably assumes two aspects, at once complementary and contradictory: enlightenment (or rationalism) and "revolution." On the one hand, the dominant class is forced—partly by conviction and partly by circumstances beyond their control—to pursue policies or express views at variance with and destructive of the old social myth. The weight of the old myth, however, prevents them from executing the new policies with energy and without the old ethnic, religious, or class prejudices. Secondly, a new social element emerges. The *homines novi* lack power at first but pursue similar (actually different) goals (which they recognize for what they are) with energy and conviction, at a new tempo, and without the old prejudices.

The new charismatic leadership is transformed into a revolutionary political class as soon as it devises a plan for the transfer of power from the traditional leaders to itself. To continue to exist as such, it must create and perpetuate a condition of dual sovereignty until it is strong enough to expel its rivals from power. It must deny the legitimacy and contest the authority of the legal political class and resort to legal, extralegal, and illegal methods to gain public acceptance of its own theory and authority. The old authority, however, invariably enjoys the advantage of traditional and institutional supports and is secure so long as it does not lose control of the police, army, and public administration, or of the chief instruments of communication and transportation. The "new men," on the other hand, have but one initial advantage, their own absolute conviction in the truth and worth of their social myth, their charisma. Not until they infiltrate a strategically or tactically important preëxisting institution, or succeed in forming efficient and reliable political and military authorities of their own,

---

[8] For a discussion of the sentiment that a country is "going to the dogs," see: H. N. Brailsford, *Macedonia: Its Races and Their Future* (London: Methuen, 1906), pp. 28–29. For an introduction to Emile Durkheim's concept of *anomie*, see: Emile Durkheim, "On Anomie," in C. Wright Mills, ed., *Images of Man: The Classic Tradition in Sociological Thinking* (New York: George Braziller, 1960), pp. 449–485, and the chapter on *anomie* in Robert K. Merton, *Social Theory and Social Structure: Toward the Codification of Theory and Research* (Glencoe, Ill.: The Free Press, 1949).

are they fully ready to test the mettle of the ruling class. The road to revolution thus passes through *anomie*, transvaluation, and dual sovereignty, all happening before the complete transfer of power from one political class to another.

When conditions of transvaluation, dual sovereignty, and revolution arise simultaneously in several different parts of the world, the transvaluating culture in the forefront of human evolution—the "psychohistorical focus" [9]—exerts a preponderant influence upon the others, forcing them to move in directions they never may have taken had they occurred as isolated "revolutions." The isolated revolutions tend to look backward, toward the restoration of some ideal past. The clustered revolutions are inclined to follow, with varying degrees of exactness, the lead of the dominant revolution.

The Political Class of the French Revolutionary Cluster

The Balkan historian Nicholas Iorga conceded that the Greek revolution of the 1820's was the product of Muslim-Christian hostility and of revived memories of Greek achievements in antiquity and of the glories of Byzantium. He insisted, however, upon the prevalence in the revolution of a second and ultimately more important tendency. Anticipating the concept of the "Western Revolution," so admirably exposited by R. R. Palmer and Jacques Godechot, Iorga characterized the Hellenic movement as largely a product of

the Western spirit, borne by Phanariote philosophes of the Principalities, by Greek merchants scattered throughout the world, as far as Marseilles and Philadelphia, by navigators of the Aegean islands of Hydra, Psara, and Spetsai, by middlemen grown rich in the Mediterranean trade during the Continental Blockade, by free Greeks under English protection in the Republic of the Ionian Islands, by vestiges of the French domination in these islands and along the mainland coast, and, finally, by the exhortations of the Greek colony in Vienna, whence [the Greco-Vlach patriot] Rhigas [Pheraios] had once issued his [Greek] 'Marseillaise.' [10]

Indeed, both the Serbian and Greek revolutions—known to traditionalist historians as simple wars of national independence—properly

---

[9] Zevedei Barbu, *Problems of Historical Psychology* (New York: Grove Press [1960]), p. 10.

[10] N[icolae] Iorga, *Essai de synthèse de l'histoire de l'humanité*, IV (Paris: J. Gamber, 1928), 184–185.

belong to the French (or Western) revolutionary cluster. Some of their leaders, it is true, found more inspiration in native legend or history, and many klephts and *hajduks* (outlaws) in their own craft and prowess, than in the principles of the French Revolution. Many leaders aimed to restore medieval power or the grandeur of antiquity; some favored the retention of "Turkish" manners and Ottoman ways. But the "new men"—some *hajduks*, rural and semiurban merchants who did business with the West, and the new Western-oriented secular intelligentsia—gave their support to Peterism, Josephinism, or Jacobinism. The bulk of the new merchant and intellectual class resided abroad either permanently or temporarily, but many gladly contributed part of their wealth and much of their talent to the cause of modernism or of bourgeois-national (and even democratic) revolution.

While some of the new men placed a high value upon liberty and sometimes upon equality, a segment of the dominant political class espoused the idea of enlightenment. Thus, enlightenment with a small "e" and the spirit of the eighteenth-century Enlightenment spread, during the reign of Selim III (1789–1807), to some high Ottoman officials who favored central government, as well as to a few members of the rebel aristocracy. Among these officials were Ebu Bekir Ratip Efendi, special emissary to Vienna in 1793 and foreign minister in 1795; Hadji-Mustafa, governor of Belgrade; Mustafa Bayraktar, governor of Rushchuk (Ruse); Seid Mustafa, teacher at the School of Engineering in Istanbul; and "Englishman" Mahmud, foreign minister from 1800 to 1805. Selim and his enlightened officials hoped to rationalize the institutions of government. But rationalization requires the creation and maintenance of order. Order was what they could not create because they were too few and the unenlightened were too many.

More numerous and in many ways more open to the values of the Enlightenment were the Phanariote "nobility of the robe" and part of the Orthodox upper clergy. As men of the Enlightenment, the Phanariotes embraced at least a modicum of secularism, defined by one student of historical psychology as the displacement of emotionality from the religious to the political field.[11] As Voltairians, they tended to regard religion as a useful tool for the preservation of order. But an act of their own making, the abolition in 1766 of the Serbian patriarchate,

[11] Barbu, *op. cit.*, pp. 48–49.

unintentionally provoked "disorder" by weakening the hold of the secular-directed church upon the Serbians under Ottoman rule and promoting the diffusion of disbelief in traditional religion and of faith in human (bourgeois) reason—a second secularism to counter the first —among educated Austrian (Hungarian) Serbs.

Since Muslim and Christian "rationalists" both were largely opposed to the downward transmission of enlightenment, its propagation among the sons of rural merchants was left to the philanthropy and self-interest of the institutionally less privileged Balkan merchants (Ottoman, Habsburg, and Russian subjects) themselves. The latter provided money to found schools or hire itinerant teachers, cultivated some interest in foreign literatures and in medicine, mathematics, physics, politics, philology and history, and—when they acquired sufficient wealth—sent their sons to study in the higher schools of Italy, Austria, Hungary, Germany, Russia, and sometimes France.

The expansion of Greek and Serbian commerce during the eighteenth century and the emergence of a class of merchants in constant intercourse with Europe and Russia led not only to the growth of a Westernized and secularized Greek and Serbian intelligentsia but, according to Dr. Holland, to a corresponding depreciation—at least among the Greeks—of the social status of the lower clergy, simply because the new merchants were better educated than the priests and because they were wealthy while the priests were poor:

This class of men [the priests] labours under disadvantages throughout every part of Greece. . . . The general smallness of their stipends brings most of them from an inferior class of society; their means of education are limited both by habit and necessity; and they but seldom enjoy the opportunities of traveling obtained by other Greeks. There are many exceptions to the statement, yet it may be said generally that a smaller proportion of the literature of the country has come from the Greek clergy, than from other classes of the community.[12]

A Greek or Serbian priest who was honored by the people normally won his laurels as a warrior, as a priest-klepht, and was distinguished only rarely for his piety or for qualities springing from his calling. He was accepted by the people because he was one of them and was respected because he was often brave. But the lower clergy failed to provide intellectual leadership and, being no braver than the rest of

---

[12] Holland, *op. cit.*, p. 167.

the people, played only a modest role in the subversion of the old society.

The protopope, on the other hand, merits more serious consideration, both as a representative of the well-to-do peasantry, or nascent rural middle class, and as an able defender of middle-class ideals. Such an interpretation is suggested in any event by the moderating influence in the Serbian revolution of the protopope Matija Nenadović. He argued that the church cannot flourish without the support of the state, nor the state thrive without the aid of the church, while the supremacy of either would lead to the ultimate ruin of both.[13]

The satellitic Christian oligarchy was basically hostile to a radical alteration of the status quo. In response, however, to the gradual abolition of *voynuk* villages, the Islamization of the *martolosi,* and the reduction of the privileges of village and *knežina* chiefs, many members of the franchised Serbian rayah were drawn to the *hajduk* life after the seignioral reaction of the late sixteenth century. The general effect upon *knežina* headmen, unmistakably distressed by the shrinking of their ancient immunities, was to bring them closer to the people. The Serbs were thus provided with a more "national" leadership— plebeianized *knezes* (*knežina* chiefs) and *hajduk*-merchants. The alienation of the satellite political class of the Greeks, less "peripheral" than its Serbian counterpart, did not occur for the most part until the latter half of the eighteenth century, when the privileged rayah of the Peloponnesus and expatriate Phanariotes transferred their loyalty to intellectually "enlightened" but socially conservative Russia. Political leadership gradually passed into the hands of new merchants, outlaws, disgruntled elders, and intellectuals—all uprooted men who had broken with custom or were denied the privileges or economic freedoms they craved.

The new merchant class originated in the physically remote and naturally protected highland or woodland cantons and in the agriculturally least promising of the Aegean islands. Cities provided the best opportunities for commerce, but the urban orders and guilds jealously guarded their prerogatives against the unwelcome incursions of the rural and semiurban merchants. The latter therefore became muleteers, cattle traders, wool, cotton, and wheat exporters, and commission

---

[13] Matija Nenadović, *Memoari* [*Memoirs*], (Belgrade: Prosveta, 1947), pp. 52–57.

agents, bringing the goods of their communities and of neighboring rural areas to the cities of Europe, Russia, and the Mediterranean.[14] Necessity made them look to the West, travel in the West, sell to the West, buy from the West, and learn the virtues, vices, and science of the West.

Rural merchant, *hajduk*, and peasant—Westernized elements and elements indifferent to the West—were all unfavorably disposed toward the Ottoman city, which they regarded as the sanctuary of monopoly capital, of estate society, and of the machinery of military and legal repression. Many members of all three social groups probably agreed with the Greek or Greco-Vlach klepht Stergios, who drew a sharp line of demarcation between the advocates of privilege and the partisans of freedom, the men of the towns and the men of the "solitudes," the denationalized collaborators who "submit to the Turks" and the freemen who prefer to "live with the beasts." [15] Many likewise may have shared the animosity of the Serbian patriot-intellectual Vuk Karadžić for the few Serbians (and other Christians) who dwelt in Ottoman towns. Karadžić, in any case, deplored their observance of Turkish manners and their habit, in time of war or trouble, of seeking refuge among the Turks or fleeing with their moneybags to Austria, instead of uniting with the Serbian peasantry.[16] The dominant political class was partly empire-oriented, the satellitic provincial oligarchy was commune or clan-oriented. The merchant-*hajduk*-intellectual element valued a third way of life: the nation.

Apart from their inclination to accept the national ideal, the vast majority of rural and semiurban merchants were revolutionary in two further respects: in their cultivation of the acquisitive values and their plea for a government of law. As they extended their trade and increased their wealth, however, they provoked the envy of the insurgnt aristocracy and monopolistic guild merchants of the cities and thereby unwittingly aggravated the very conditions of insecurity they yearned to escape.

During the Austro-Turkish war of 1788–1791 and for more than a

---

[14] Traian Stoianovich, "The Conquering Balkan Orthodox Merchant," *Journal of Economic History*, XX (1960), 234–313.

[15] P. S. Spandonidis, "Le clèfte," *L'Hellénisme contemporain*, 2d ser., VIII (1954), 7, n. 2.

[16] Vuk Stefanović Karadžić, *Danica* [*Morning Star*], II (Vienna, 1827), 101.

decade thereafter, the insurgent Ottoman nobility recruited the dregs of Balkan society—brigands, adventurers, underpaid soldiers, and destitute craftsmen—to despoil and expropriate the peasantry and well-to-do rural merchants. The terror of the brigands and aristocrats infused fear into the hearts of all real and potential victims, and the fear, or collective emotionality, spread from the land of Souli in Epirus, across Macedonia and Bulgaria, to the shores of the Serbian Danube.

The reaction of the Serbs was very much like the response of the French to the "Great Fear" of 1789. Relying upon their experience as soldiers and noncoms in Austrian volunteer detachments during the war of 1788–1791, the rural merchants and *hajduks* of Serbia—joined by the frightened *knezes*—organized the terrified peasantry into a "national guard" and led them first against the brigands of Pasvanoglu, then against the brigand deys of Belgrade, and finally against the empire itself. Serbian merchants and *hajduks* thus became the agents of revolution, a revolution to which a number of Vojvodina intellectuals, inspired partly by the French Revolution, intended to give a liberal direction.

Between 1806 and 1809, Russia entered into war against Turkey and reached an understanding with France, Napoleon recovered the Ionian Islands and brought the Illyrian Provinces into the French Empire, and a series of rebellions broke out in the Peloponnesus, in the Serbo-Croatian (Habsburg) province of Srem, in the Serbo-Rumanian (Habsburg) Banat, among the Serbs of Bosnia, in the former bailiwick of Pasvanoglu in western Bulgaria, and among the Slavs, Greeks, and Vlachs of Macedonia and Thessaly. It seemed as if the Serbian revolution might become a Balkan revolution.

But all the rebellions failed, and the Balkan revolution never came. The reasons for the failure are many: poor leadership, inadequate arms, Russian preferences for the traditionalist leadership of Montenegro to the revolutionary leadership of Serbia, the mistaken belief of the French that Serbia was the tool of Russia, and the preference of many Greek traders for the art of making money (in the caravan trade between the eastern Mediterranean and central Europe, or as blockade runners and privateers) to the art of making revolution. A further reason was the occurrence of the Banato-Syrmian, Macedo-Thessalian, and Bosnian rebellions in confessionally and ethnically mixed areas without a well-defined national consciousness. The rebel chieftains of

Thessaly and Macedonia could summon the people to stand up boldly "like Christians and Romei" (Romans), but they could not call upon them to bear themselves "like Hellenes and Greeks." [17] They could not base their appeals upon the new charismatic ideology.

The view that a Balkan revolution never came may be further from the truth, however, than the thesis that it occurred in two phases, first as a "democratic revolution" (1788–1808) and then as a "Thermidorean reaction" (1809–1830). The "democratic revolution" had the widest repercussions among the Serbs, although it also spread, at least briefly, among the other Balkan peoples. In Serbia, the "Thermidorean reaction" was interrupted by Restoration and terror in 1814 and by the renewal of insurrection in 1815. It was subsequently consummated in the establishment of "one-man rule." In Greece, the "Thermidorean reaction" appeared in the form of a slackening of interest in revolution between 1808 and 1818. When new recruits were drawn to the cause of revolution after 1818, it was often with the understanding that the revolution would be made to follow a conservative course,[18] that it would begin as a "Thermidorean reaction."

The new political class which carried out the revolution in Serbia was made up of many *hajduks,* of some intellectuals, and of "the better people, who were able to feed and arm two, ten, or twenty serving companions (*momaks*)." These "better people" were "*knezes,* merchants, priests, *kmets* [village chiefs], and property holders with large households and cattle, mills, and other revenues, who were called *gazdas.*" [19] Similar elements entered into the formation of the political class of the Greeks. But the Greek mercantile element was wealthier than its Serbian counterpart, and the Greek political class included a larger oligarchical and pseudo-aristocratic element. Having more to lose than the Serbians, the Greek political leadership tended to be more conservative.

The difference between the Serbian and Greek revolutions is reflected also in the fact that the first began in a time of war and of general political and social fermentation, while the Greek revolution of 1821 started in a time of peace and of general political and social reac-

---

[17] John W[ortley] Baggaly, *The Klephtic Ballads in Relation to Greek History (1715–1821),* (Oxford: Basil Blackwell, 1936), pp. 78–101.

[18] C. W. Crawley, "John Capodistrias and the Greeks before 1821," *Cambridge Historical Journal,* XIII (1957), 179.

[19] Nenadović, *op. cit.,* p. 311.

tion. To the extent that it formed part of a larger world movement, the Greek revolution was clustered as closely around the romantic-inspired "classical reaction"—of which philhellenism was both a symptom and cause—as around the French Revolution. But the effect of the "classical reaction" was to reinforce the internal tendency of the revolution—inherent, in fact, in all revolutions—to express itself as a "Restoration," "Reconquista," or "Great Retreat."

Although the Greek revolution was intrinsically more conservative than the Serbian, both revolutions were profoundly social. Both effected the almost complete transfer of property and property rights from the formerly dominant political class to the new political classes and to the peasantry, both accepted the theory of nationality, and both generated a current in favor of a new social order guaranteeing the security of property and founded upon the principles of freedom of contract, equality before the law, and social mobility on the basis of free political and economic competition.

The Multiclass and Multiparty Society

It would be an error to suppose that the old order immediately vanished, since internal and external events alike dictated against the quick formation of a free society. From a struggle for freedom, the Balkan revolutions were transformed into a contest for power between the advocates of oligarchy and the partisans of monarchy. The native antiliberal currents were reinforced by the general European reaction of the post-Napoleonic era and by the returning tide of conservatism after the brief revolutions of 1830–1832.

To combat royal or princely prerogatives, the oligarchs defended the principles of limited monarchy and legal domination, or government of law. In essence, however, they desired the transfer of monopolies to themselves rather than their abolition, and therefore sought to give reality to what John Stuart Mill later described as the "theory of dependence and protection."

According to Mill, the "theory of dependence" holds that

the lot of the poor, in all things which affect them collectively, should be regulated for them, not by them. They should not be encouraged to think for themselves, or give to their own reflection or forecast an influential voice in the determination of their destiny. [At the same time] the relation between rich and poor . . . should be only partly authoritative; it should be amiable, moral, and sentimental: affectionate tutelage on the one side, respectful and grateful deference to the rich. The rich should be *in loco parentis* to the poor, guiding and restraining them like children.[20]

In defense of the "theory of dependence," a portion of the new political class of patriarchal Serbia demanded the concentration of political authority and economic power in the hands of an "enlightened" oligarchy of well-to-do landowners, public and church officials, and military commanders. This group also sought a constitution limiting the powers of the prince but regarded liberal agitation for a representative assembly as a kind of "game of children." [21] The theory of dependence found even firmer support among the members of the new Hellenic political class—the *tzakia* (*djakia*), or "hearths." But nowhere in the Balkans was political and social conservatism stronger than in Bosnia, Albania, and the Danubian Principalities, areas in which social revolution was avoided during the nineteenth century either because peasants, local lords, and government officials were all of the same religion or because religious divisions among the peasantry prevented the latter from putting up a united front against their oppressors.

The theory of dependence and protection was derived from the old regime and from the Enlightenment. Balkan liberalism, on the other hand, was the offspring of the Western Revolution and of new economic conditions. Enlightened conservatives and liberals were united in their zeal to discover "the white world" (*beli svet*)[22] beyond their geographic or temporal frontiers, but conservaties lacked faith in the people and did not believe in the possibility of a remedy for the "dark world" [23] of peasant life. The liberals, on the other hand, borrowed from Herder, Hegel, Mazzini, and the early Slavophiles of Austria,

---

[20] John Stuart Mill, *Principles of Political Economy, with Some of Their Applications to Social Philosophy*, ed. by W. J. Ashley (New York, Bombay, and Calcutta: Longmans, Green, 1909), Book IV, chap. 7, p. 753.

[21] Traian Stoianovich, "The Pattern of Serbian Intellectual Evolution, 1830–1880," *Comparative Studies in Society and History*, I (March, 1959), 244–245, 254.

[22] Nenadović, *op. cit.*, pp. 171, 155–156.

[23] The term "dark world" was used by the Bulgarian *Narodnik* writer K. Maksimov. See: Vivian Pinto, "The Civic and Aesthetic Ideals of Bulgarian Narodnik Writers," *Slavonic and East European Review*, XXXII (June, 1954), 357.

Hungary, and Russia the idea of an eternal "national genius" (*Volksgeist*) as the guiding principle of historical development.

By founding intermediate and higher schools at home and sending qualified students to the universities and higher schools of Europe and Russia, Balkan conservatives unintentionally helped transform the Balkan intelligentsia from a tiny ineffectual group in each country into an influential "educated class." Still more important in facilitating and hastening the growth of a liberal intelligentsia were the loosening of family, clan, and patriarchal ties, the expansion of a money and exchange economy, the rise of a class of "national" urban merchants and shopkeepers, and the evolution of the new quasi-states into political organisms with most of the characteristics of the modern political state.

Allying themselves with the cause of the growing class of merchants and market-oriented peasants, the "educated class" propagated their social theory, after 1848, under somewhat more propitious circumstances. In Greece, Serbia, and the Danubian Principalities, they organized themselves into liberal political clubs and waged a successful struggle, during the 1850's, against the politics of reaction which triumphed after the failure of the revolutions of 1848. In the sixties and seventies, Bulgarian exiles in Serbia and Rumania repeated the achievements of their neighbors.

In Albania, Macedonia, and Bosnia-Hercegovina, the resistance to liberalism was inexorable until the turn of the century. The rural and semiurban Orthodox merchant class of these areas did not allow their faith to become a serious impediment to innovation, but they could not hurdle the obstacle of Muslim traditionalism. However, the Bosnian rural merchantry united with the Christian peasantry in 1875 to do what the Christians of Serbia and Greece had accomplished a half-century earlier. But when Bosnia-Hercegovina was transferred to Austro-Hungarian administration, the new government continued to favor the old Muslim landowning class as landowners while relegating the functions of administration to a new official class of non-Bosnian origin. The Dual Monarchy thus frustrated both the economic and political ambitions of the Bosnian rural and semiurban merchant class. Liberal theory consequently failed to obtain a firm foothold in Bosnia-Hercegovina until the economic and educational improvements introduced by the Habsburg Monarchy allowed the emergence, toward 1900, of a native intelligentsia.

The new Bosnian intelligentsia did not actively champion the cause of the peasantry but acted nevertheless in the interest of the nation as a whole. They were resolved to remove the new official class from power and to prevent the old official (Muslim landowning) class from restoring its ancient authority. The assassination of Archduke Francis Ferdinand, *cause célèbre* of the First World War, was the most spectacular expression of their first goal. The most articulate statement of their second objective has come from the pen of one of their members, the now internationally famous writer, Ivo Andrić.

In one of the tableaux of his *Bridge on the Drina,* a novel published in 1945, Andrić animates an excitable Bosnian liberal who chides a Muslim fellow student for planning to major in Oriental languages at the University of Vienna:

Disconcerted by the new times, you no longer know your exact and rightful place in the world. Your love for everything oriental is only a contemporary expression of your "will to power"; for you the eastern way of life and thought is very closely bound up with a social and legal order which was the basis of your centuries of lordship. That is understandable. But it in no way means that you have any sense for orientalism as a study. You are orientals but you are making a mistake when you think that you are thereby called upon to be orientalists. In general you have not got the calling or the true inclination for science. . . . You are the only nobles in this country, or at least you were; for centuries you have enlarged, confirmed and defended your privileges by sword and pen, legally, religiously and by force of arms; that has made of you typical warriors, administrators and landowners, and that class of men nowhere in the world worries about abstract sciences but leaves them to those who have nothing else and can do nothing else. The true studies for you are law and economics, for you are men of practical knowledge. Such are men from the ruling classes, always and everywhere. . . . The conditions which at one time made you what you are have changed long ago, but that does not mean that you can change with the same speed. This is not the first, nor will it be the last, instance of a social caste losing its reason for existence and yet remaining the same. Conditions of life change but a class remains what it is, for only so can it exist and as such it will die.[24]

Even before the diffusion of nineteenth-century liberalism to all parts of the Balkans, a following was created in several areas, particularly

---

[24] Ivo Andrić, *The Bridge on the Drina,* trans. from the Serbo-Croat by Lovett F. Edwards (New York: The New American Library [published as a Signet Book by arrangement with Macmillan], 1960), pp. 327–329.

in the countries and regions where liberal theory had already taken root and where the people's sympathies went out to unofficial Russia, for the ideology of radicalism, better known today as "democracy." Where anti-Russian sentiment was strong and pro-Russian feelings were relatively mild, as in Rumania and Greece, radicalism was weaker. Where liberalism was late in coming but there was strong pro-Russian or pro-Serbian sentiment, as in Bosnia and Montenegro, radicalism and liberalism developed almost simultaneously.

Bertrand Russell rightly maintains that, in the less advanced countries, "theory inspires practice." [25] But theory inspires practice nowhere if its only justification is the caprice of a few intellectuals. In fact, the diffusion of a new social theory is dependent upon the presence and interaction—Zusammenhang—of two different sets of objective conditions, one favoring the rise of a new intelligentsia and the other inviting the new intellectual class to advance a specific theory.

An educated class tends to separate into two or more parts whenever it expands beyond the faculty of the political and social order to sustain all its members with public or private functions corresponding to their educational achievements. The overexpansion of an educated class is normally the result of a sudden diffusion of educational opportunities to new social strata, or of a socially unjustifiable emphasis upon a few sectors of learning at the expense of the rest. The latter fosters the growth of an overexpanded educated class in an undereducated society.

During the latter half of the nineteenth century, educational opportunities were extended rapidly to the market-oriented peasant—although the education of most peasants, and of women in particular, was sadly neglected—and even more quickly to the urban sector of Balkan society. But the natural disdain for manual labor—or rather for new forms of labor—of a society without a strong middle-class tradition diverted students from the practical and technical arts to the study of law, history, and literature.

The smallness of the literary public forced the literati into politics, journalism, and polemics. Students of law were sucked even more ir-

---

[25] Bertrand Russell, *History of Western Philosophy and Its Connection with Political and Social Circumstances from the Earliest Times to the Present Day* (London: George Allen and Unwin, 1940), pp. 624–625.

retrievably into the vortex of politics. Far from being peculiarly Balkan, this pattern of intellectual evolution was then typical of all less advanced societies that consciously or subconsciously aspired to enter the mainstream of human history.

In the politically and socially more advanced provinces of the Balkans, an "educated class" (liberals) grew up, between 1830 and 1870, at the side of the "governing class" (conservatives). After 1860, part of the new educated class acquired some or all of the attributes of the governing class. Another part, however, failed to obtain this right, simply because the number of competitors far exceeded the number of available functions.

The least favored members of the educated class were the newest and youngest, not because of a special plot against youth but because the older members were naturally reluctant to relinquish their posts of public trust to their inexperienced and unemployed rivals. Historically, the older members were liberals, but their age and position in life, as well as their new awareness that profound social changes are not the result of a momentary operation, made them conservative in spite of their theory. Their theory was a reflection of the structural innovations of the era in which their movement came into being, their practices were in closer conformity with their new station in life.

In the year of the Paris Commune, the new intelligentsia—urban youth in their teens and twenties, numerically small but ideologically influential—rebelled against the authority of their "fathers," rejected their idealism, insisted that theory must flow out of the newest social reality, defended the concept of "self-government," rebuked the imperialist states, and organized themselves into radical clubs and "communes." A decade later, the radicals of Serbia organized their own political party, giving it a popular basis by taking it to the people, by establishing clubs or party cells among the peasantry. The other parties were thereupon compelled to extend their own political organizations into the rural areas so as to compete against their new opponents.

The decline of estate society and of clan and familial authority, and the rise of individual conscience, are the factors lying behind the generational conflicts, or struggles between youth and age, of the nineteenth century. In this era of rapid social change, the education of each new generation differed from that of the preceding one in form no less than in content. Bound both by the community of age and of a common education, every new generation sought to constitute itself as a separate political party.

The epithets applied to the various Balkan parties suggest that party members and outsiders alike were consciously aware of the two agents —age and education (more broadly, culture)—that united and divided them. Conservatives were known as "Old Turks" and liberals as "Young Turks." Serbian and Bulgarian radicals of the seventies took pride in the name *šestidesjatnik*, "man of the sixties," borrowed from the generation of Russian radicals who were their chief source of inspiration. Some of them called themselves "Communists," in recognition of their attachment to the ideas of the Paris Commune. When, at the turn of the century, the Serbian Radical party split into two factions, the members of the parent group were identified as the "Old Radicals" and those of the splinter group as the "Young (Independent) Radicals."

A close biotic relationship often exists between party leaders and parties. The Radical party of Serbia, for example, was organized by Nikola Pašić. Upon his death, thirty-five years later, the party lost its will to survive. The Liberal party of Eleftherios Venizelos, organized after the "Young Turk" revolution of 1908, similarly ceased to be a vital force after the death of its founder. The significance of the death of a party leader, when it comes after a full life, lies in its symbolization of the approaching end of the generation that made and nurtured the party and, therefore, of the party itself.

Party friction and fission precede, accompany, and follow the death of an old party leader. The fault lies not with the leader—except in the sense that age deprives him of his former energy—but with the loss of a following, as his generation disappears. But a party can sometimes acquire personal continuity beyond the lifetime of a single leader, if the leader grooms a member of his family for the succession. A remarkable example of personal continuity of this kind is offered by the Bratianu family of Rumania, which preserved the Liberal party as a political force—in spite of its uncertain and fluctuating ideology— for almost a century.

Useful in explaining the rise of a new intelligentsia or the formation of new political parties, the concept of conflict of generations does not adequately explain why a particular generation adopts one theory as against another. The source of new social theory is a new social situation, and the new situation which inspired the diffusion of radical theory in the Balkans was the subjection of the new states, especially after the Crimean War, to the economic and political imperialism of the European powers, of which an important consequence was the impoverishment of a portion of the Balkan peasantry and artisan class.

The Balkan states could not protect themselves against the competition of European manufactures, either because existing treaties forbade them to erect protective tariffs and obliged them to exhaust their limited capital resources in the building of railroads (instead of allowing them to develop their industry), or because the bulk of their exports was earmarked for one or two European countries, which could deprive them of a market if they tried to assert their economic independence. The adoption of new industrial techniques and the pursuit of a more coherent economic program were therefore delayed until the end of the century. In the meantime, the old craft industries stagnated or declined.

The comparative security of person and property after 1830, the relative absence of war between 1830 and 1910, and the introduction of medical and hygienic improvements permitted the rapid growth of population. But the slowness and dependent nature of industrial progress, imposed or sustained by the imperialist states, made the pattern of demographic growth assume the form of rural overpopulation. Economic imperialism thus helped create a situation in the Balkans of too many peasants with too few head of cattle on too little land.

The well-to-do official and landowning class, on the other hand, profited from the export of raw materials to the industrial economies of the West. Investing their profits abroad and in domestic banking enterprise, they modified their theory of "dependence and protection" to conform with the ideology of their social counterparts in western and central Europe. In other words, they embraced the cause of positivism.

The champion of positivism in Greece was the party of Charilaos Trikoupis. In Rumania, both the Liberal and Conservative parties accepted some aspects of positivism. In Turkey, the new ideology—in fact, the old ideology of enlightenment—was given practical application by the foreign-dominated Council of Administration of the Ottoman Public Debt. The theoretical Ottoman positivists, on the other hand, were in exile in Paris and Geneva. The Serbian positivists organized themselves in the 1880's as a separate political party of "Progressists." Known also as "Young Conservatives," the Progressists were the sons and grandsons of the "Old Turks" and "Constitutionalists." The chief interpreters of positivism in Bulgaria were first the Liberals and then the Democrats, who split off from the former in the 1890's. After 1894, however, the Russian-oriented Conservatives likewise adopted portions of the positivist philosophy, partly in imitation of Russia itself.

The Progressists or politically conservative positivists were the exponents of a triple slogan: "progress," "order," and "European culture." In general, they encouraged the investment of European capital in Balkan railroads, mines, banks, and municipal utilities, defended the interests of the "capital-collecting" classes (large landowners, great merchants, high officials, and bankers), and sought to "Westernize" their countrymen. Convinced that industrialization was an automatic process to be achieved only after a long period of capital accumulation, they believed in befriending the capitalist powers that played a dominant role in their national economy (Austria, Germany, France, Italy, or Britain) or the paramount power in the world economy (Britain). They were sometimes scornfully called "Germanizers" or "Englishmen."

The goal of the Radicals, on the other hand, was the amelioration of the economic position of the most fortunate and most enlightened portion of the peasantry and the creation of new opportunities for the most ambitious industrial elements. Placing a high value upon man as a producer, they accepted the principle of industrial protection. Along with the radical Liberals and Old Conservatives, they preferred the capitalist powers that played a secondary role in their economy (Russia, France, or Germany).

The Liberals were divided in outlook but could sometimes be distinguished from the Progressists and Radicals by their distrust of centrally controlled economic action and by their subordination of the idea of social justice to the principle of economic and political freedom. The picture is often obscured, however, by the fact that party names do not coincide exactly with—and sometimes belie—party philosophies.

After 1870 or 1880, all political groups sought to create the impression that only their theory had its source in popular needs or demands. Under normal circumstances, the party struggles may have been less tumultuous or violent, but the international economic crisis of 1873–1896 provoked an outburst of political Darwinism. Since political victory meant the gain, and defeat meant the loss of favors, functions, and contracts, victory was always preferable. In a period of economic troubles, it was vital. Political contests thus became part of a fierce and relentless "struggle for life." [26]

In the Darwinian struggle between one party and the others and between the parties on the one hand and the monarchs on the other, principle was sacrificed at the altar of political expediency. In 1883, when the peasantry of eastern Serbia rebelled against the decision of the government to deprive them of their arms, one of the members of the Central Committee of the Radical party was prepared to aid the government against the rebels, another advised King Milan that the Radicals, "like all other pink parties," would learn moderation if placed in positions of authority, and a third volunteered to foment discord within the party in order to prevent it from coming under the control of extremists.[27]

But Milan preferred nonparty or "neutral" government to party rule and endeavored to undermine confidence in the party system. His son and successor, Alexander, had similar inclinations and succeeded in creating a coterie of subservient politicians known as Court Radicals. The two monarchs desired nonparty government because Serbian parties were a fair reflection of current public opinion and could not be manipulated easily from above, even though individual political leaders were corruptible.

In Rumania, where the parties represented the landowners or the town dwellers, the king gladly accepted the two-party system, since neither Liberals nor Conservatives had broad public backing and thus could be granted and deprived of favors more or less at will. A multiparty system would have reduced the efficacy of royal manipulation and might have brought to the fore the "condition of Rumania" question—the problem of the landless peasantry.

In Bulgaria, a grave "condition of the nation" question did not yet

---

[26] J. Hogge, *La Serbie de nos jours. Etude politique et économique* (Brussels: Librairie Falk fils, 1901), part I, p. 72.

[27] Dragoslav Janković, *O političkim strankama u Srbiji XIX veka* [*Political Parties in Nineteenth-Century Serbia*], (Belgrade: Prosveta, 1951), pp. 148–150, 239.

trouble the security of the state, but the Bulgarians lacked political experience and only a small number of them was politically oriented. Strong-man (Liberal) Stefan Stambolov, who freed the country from Russian tutelage, was thus allowed to become dictator (1887–1894), and the Stambolov dictatorship was followed by the covert but more effective dictatorship of Prince Ferdinand.

Whether under Stambolov or Ferdinand, the expression of public opinion at the polls—at least during the 1880's or 1890's—was always a farce, sometimes with tragic innuendoes. Prefects, municipal councils, and political machines hired bands of toughs and rumor mongers to create an atmosphere of fear. Many peasants were thus dissuaded from exercising their right to vote.[28] According to one report, only 5 percent of the electorate cast a vote during the Stambolov regime, although the official records showed the participation of two-thirds of the eligible voters.[29]

Bulgarian Liberals and Conservatives desired to create a "rational" society. The only elements of the bourgeois rational society which seeped down to the peasant, however, were the power of the state to recruit, punish, and tax. By their idealization of the "rational" society and unconcern for the day-to-day world of the peasant, the parties lost the confidence of the people. Unable to fall back upon the people and afraid of losing or never obtaining a sinecure, the Bulgarian political class readily accepted the royal policy of rewarding the politically subservient with the "spoils" of public office.

The economic crisis of the eighties and nineties discouraged any other kind of solution. To the international crisis, moreover, was added a local crisis in agriculture and commerce, resulting from the loss, after Bulgarian liberation in 1878, of a part of the Ottoman market for Bulgarian farm products. The commercial sector was thus temporarily closed to new talent, while the demand for intellectuals with a humanist education rose less quickly than the supply. Factors of this nature encouraged the acceptance of authoritarian rule, even by individuals

---

[28] Aleko Constantinov, *Baï Gagno le Tartarin bulgare*, trans. from the Bulgarian by Matei Gueorguiev and Jean Jagerschmidt, with preface by Louis Léger (Paris: Ernest Leroux, 1911), pp. 181–223. For similar practices in Greece, see: Baron D'Estournelles de Constant, *La vie de province en Grèce* (Paris: Librairie Hachette, 1878), pp. 63–70.

[29] Edward Dicey, *The Peasant State: An Account of Bulgaria in 1894* (London: John Murray, 1894), p. 149.

and groups that had vigorously opposed authoritarian principles in the preliberation era. As a result, parties were oriented around powerful political personalities or around wirepullers, "political bosses" who were more concerned with the manipulation of men and the organization of a political machine than with the reification of ideas.

The British historian R. W. Seton-Watson has even observed a connection between the assertion of monarchical authoritarianism in the new Bulgarian state and the investment of foreign capital, the spread of political corruption and "commercial and financial Panamism," and the fragmentation of parties into a large number of quarreling political machines. The "scarcely veiled invitation to every public man" was "Go get rich," the *mot d'ordre* of François Guizot in the bourgeois monarchy of Louis Philippe. "Foreign bankers, notably those of Budapest, obligingly facilitated the process" of corrupting officials by providing the monarch with needed funds. In return, the bankers were allowed to strengthen their grip upon the country's economy. Seton-Watson's comments upon the proclivities of Prince (later Tsar) Ferdinand are well worth citing:

[He] made it his business to pry into the personal activities of his ministers, and his dossier of compromising documents [was] the envy of every criminal investigation department in Europe. The great Stambolov himself displayed a brutal shamelessness in using his official position to acquire a private fortune; but his successors sought to veil their rapacity under a thin veneer of external rectitude. . . . In short, Ferdinand set himself to create a system by which the individual might grow rich and prosper exceedingly, so long as he remained the faithful servitor of the throne, but risked immediate disgrace and ruin if he ventured to assert his independence. Thus there was always a waiting list for the post of Premier, and whenever Ferdinand had had enough of one politician and his following, he merely had to turn to a rival group and entrust it with the "making" of an election and a majority.[30]

Monarchical authoritarianism and the "spoils" system prevailed also in Greece, while the relations between Trikoupis and George I were not unlike those between Stambolov and Ferdinand. Such, in any case, is the verdict of at least one student of Greek political life:

Although the King's nominal authority was limited by the Greek Constitution, he was jealous of his own pre-eminence in the affairs of

[30] R. W. Seton-Watson, *Europe in the Melting-Pot* (London:Macmillan, 1919), pp. 357–358.

the kingdom. It has even been said that he never allowed a promising political leader to become too powerful. Trikoupis, a man of extraordinary gifts, caused him anxiety in this respect. But Trikoupis was handicapped by a custom which weakens the authority of Prime Ministers. As Venizelos has explained, "he fell into the error of thinking that, to remain in power and so carry out his programme, it was necessary for him to give way to the system of changing the personnel of the civil service when a new Government came into office." [31]

When other means of maintaining themselves in power threatened to fail, kings, ministers, national deputies, prefects, and other administrative and elective officials had recourse to *"ein bisschen Hokuspokus."* [32] Details regarding this "hocus-pocus" are not easily available. But part of the hocus-pocus apparently included verbal compacts between public officials and bands of brigands, the former promising not to pursue or indict the latter for acts of ordinary brigandage if they agreed to perform an act of political murder or some other political villainy, when called upon.

The actual recrudescence of brigandage should be blamed, at least in part, upon the economic crisis. Once the brigands were available, unscrupulous officials naturally made use of them. Having little reason for expecting justice from many of their officials, innocent peasants sometimes took flight to the hills. As the number of brigands grew in the countryside, the number of receivers of stolen goods grew in the towns. Such, in any case, appears to have been the sequence of events in Serbia. [33]

Political brigandage was incompatible, however, with the "progressist" idea—adopted in the 1890's even by parties without the "progressist" label—of progress through order. Steps were therefore taken to eliminate it. It was not eliminated altogether, but after 1894 it was partly expelled beyond the frontiers of Serbia, Bulgaria, Greece, and Montenegro to Crete, Macedonia, Old Serbia, Bosnia-Hercegovina, and Armenia.

---

[31] S. B. Chester, *Life of Venizelos* (London: Constable, 1921), p. 127.

[32] The expression *"ein bisschen Hokuspokus"* was apparently employed by a Serbian prefect. See: Herbert Vivian, *Servia, the Poor Man's Paradise* (London, New York, and Bombay: Longmans, Green, 1897), pp. 24–25.

[33] *Ibid.*, pp. 25–27, 177–184; Velibor Gligorić, *Srpski realisti* [*Serbian Realists*], (Belgrade: Prosveta, 1954), pp. 223–257. A similar situation appears to have prevailed in Greece. Cf. Alfred Fouillée, *Esquisse psychologique des peuples européens*, 4th ed. (Paris: Félix Alcan, 1903), pp. 41–42.

In 1893, several Macedonian patriots founded the Internal Macedonian Revolutionary Organization (IMRO) with the object of fighting for Macedonian autonomy. In the following year, however, the Bulgarian Crown created a rival organization, the Supreme Macedonian Committee. The latter got rid of Bulgarian officials who were opposed to unilateral territorial aggrandizement, carried on propaganda to associate all Bulgarians with the nationalist and imperialist aims of the Bulgarian state, and committed numerous acts of terrorism in Macedonia, not only against the dominant Turks but even against Greeks, Serbians, and unsympathetic Macedonian Slavs.

To protect their own partisans in Macedonia, the Greek and Serbian governments, aided by semiofficial groups, created "violence-using" and "protection-producing" [34] agencies of their own. Greek and Serbian guerrilla bands were smuggled into the province to fight against the Bulgarian guerrillas. Brigandage—with nationalist colors—was thus compressed, after 1894, into the unredeemed European, Mediterranean (Crete), and Asiatic (Armenia) territories.

The "violent way of life" was fortified by both the *kirjali* (pure brigand) and *hajduk* (brigand of the "Robin Hood" and mixed villain-hero type) traditions. It also found a stimulus in the idea of "propaganda of the deed," first systematically diffused into the Balkans by students under the sway of Russian radicalism. Individuals attracted to the violent way of life were thus of several different kinds: high school students and young "intellectuals," disgruntled army officers, intellectuals dissatisfied with their official public roles, social revolutionaries, pure patriots, nationalist extremists, and real gangsters. What most of them had in common was that they were, in one way or another, marginal men.

Under such diverse influences, violence-using enterprises were formed by government and semiofficial agencies, by nonofficial groups, and by mixed organizations. The Supreme Committee was of the first type, IMRO—until its infiltration by the Supremists—was of the second type, and the Union or Death society of Serbia, formed in 1911 and implicated in the assassination of Archduke Francis Ferdinand, was of the third type. The official violence-using enterprises were so-

---

[34] On the general subject of "protection-producing" and "violence-using" enterprises, see: Frederic C. Lane, "Economic Consequences of Organized Violence," *Journal of Economic History*, XVIII (1958), 401–417.

cially conservative. The nonofficial and mixed types included both conservative and radical wings and were subject to fissiparous tendencies. The conservative members of IMRO thus joined the Supremists, while a segment of the radical wing went over to socialism or communism. The Union or Death society split into a radical wing known as the "Black Hand" and a conservative faction known as the "White Hand." The first was headed by the Chief of Serbian Intelligence, who was executed by the "White Hand" in 1917. The second was led unofficially by the Prince-Regent (later King) Alexander Karadjordjević.

To the political corruption, financial Panamism, authoritarianism, and terrorism of the *fin de siècle* was added anti-Semitism. Anti-Jewish feeling was not new in the Balkans, but until 1880 it was based primarily upon religious and only secondarily upon economic considerations, except in Rumania, where the Jews were moneylenders and middlemen. After 1880, it acquired a more distinctly economic basis in the area south of the Danube and Sava—the Balkans proper—and a racist, as well as religious and economic, basis in the area to the north.

The Jewish population of Moldavia and Wallachia was already considerable in 1821, when the peasant-national rising of Tudor Vladimirescu assumed an anti-Semitic as well as anti-Hellenic turn. The influx of Jews from Russia after the pogroms of the eighties augmented the Jewish population of Rumania still further. At the end of the century, two-fifths of the urban element was Jewish.

The business culture of the nineteenth century required the talents of the people of the Book. The Congress of Berlin (1878) therefore obliged the Balkan states to abolish all legal restrictions against Jews. Already entrenched in business, the Jews of Rumania thereupon advanced in the liberal professions. But their successes not only gave rise to a new wave of anti-Semitism but made the non-Jewish *Kleinbürgertum* of the country fiercely anti-intellectual.

Many Rumanian peasants moved into towns during the latter half of the century, opened small shops, and began to send their sons to higher schools. In prosperous times, there may have been room for both Jews and Rumanians. But the closing decades of the century were a time of crisis. Confronted with the competition of Jewish shopkeepers and forced to accept the services of Jewish lawyers, doctors, actors, and bankers, the Rumanian town dwellers blamed the depression upon the egoism and avarice of the Jew. Rumanian writers expounded anti-Semitic themes with a partly racist bias.

Even in Serbia, where there were no Jews in the villages and few Jews in the towns, there was an upsurge of anti-Semitism. In 1882, the Liberal newspaper *Srpska nezavisnost* [*Serbian Independence*] called for the formation of an anti-Semitic association to prevent the immigration of Russian Jews, "these grasshoppers," into the country. Almost simultaneously, the Radical organ *Samouprava* [*Self-Government*] denounced the Russian pogroms but printed an article under the caption, "We Don't Want the Jews." "Let the Progressist Club buy the kingdom of Jerusalem if it wants," polemicized *Samouprava*. "We are sorry for the Jews expelled from Russia, but we are too small and too weak to receive them." The Socialist newspaper *Borba* [*Combat*] denounced religious anti-Semitism but justified anti-Semitism as a national, social, and economic protest against the role of the Jews in protecting and disseminating the capitalist business culture.[35]

Serbian anti-Semitism had both a religious and economic basis. Primarily, however, it was a manifestation of liberal, radical-populist, and socialist discontent with the Austrophilism and "Germano-Westernism" of Milan and the Progressists, and of hostility to the royal-Progressist policy of opening the country to foreign capital without adequately protecting national interests.

Several forms of political Darwinism that we have discussed—and a few that we have not—may have betrayed a certain Balkan style. The fact of violence and political Darwinism, however, was not peculiarly Balkan. The anti-Semitic, anti-Serbian, and anti-Byzantine half-Jew of Croatia, Josip Frank, would have shuddered at being called a Balkanite. Houston Stewart Chamberlain, Edouard Drumont, Karl Lueger, Konstantin Pobedonostsev, and Prince Meshchersky were not Balkanites, but they were all anti-Semites. The *fin de siècle* was in fact a time of race-thinking and anti-Semitism on both sides of the Atlantic. Russian Panslavism, Pangermanism, Zionism, the "white man's burden," and Abd ul-Hamid's Panislam and anti-intellectualism were products of the same epoch. Political opportunism (or *trasformismo*) was no less common to France, Italy, and the United States than to the Bal-

---

[35] Jean Mousset, *La Serbie et son Eglise* (*1830–1904*), (Paris: Institut d'Etudes slaves, 1938), pp. 253–257, 352–354.

kans, and Panamism was of extra-Balkan origin. The embodiment of the authoritarian personality in persons in authority was not confined to Stambolov, Ferdinand, or George I. Bismarck, Wilhelm, Boulanger, Pelloux, von Taaffe, Abd ul-Hamid, Porfirio Díaz, Khuen-Héderváry, Benjamin von Kállay, and the Russian tsars—all contemporaries of the Balkanites—were no less authoritarian, and the emperor cult of Japan in its modern (pre-1945) form was developed during the very same period. Political assassination and organized (official and private) violence—both in this period and in the 1920's and 1930's—were a "universal" rather than peculiarly Balkan phenomenon.

Since political Darwinism was international in character and occurred almost everywhere simultaneously, it should perhaps be explained in terms of a common cause. We offer three explanations, each of some validity. If one accepts the principle of struggle as nature's way of regulating relations between one force and another or between man and man, one may reasonably infer that political Darwinism is a natural consequence of political organization. This explanation unfortunately does not tell us why there was more political Darwinism in the eighties and nineties than in some earlier or later periods. More satisfactory, and certainly more historical, is the opinion that the added part of political Darwinism was produced by the introduction of political participation on a mass scale before the dissipation of parochialism or the widespread diffusion of political education. Without a third factor, however, the political Darwinism may not have been quite so immoderate. This was the world economic crisis of 1873–1896, part of a larger cultural crisis, that culminated in a perceptible modulation of the key, speed, and rhythm of human behavior, in a quick transition from one type of economic regime (early industrial capitalism in western or commercial capitalism in eastern Europe) to another (mature industrial capitalism in western and early industrial capitalism in eastern Europe).

In the Balkans as in other parts of the world, many persons reacted sharply against authoritarianism and makeshift politics. Agitation for reform was carried on in particular by several populist muckrakers, among them Milovan Glišić and Svetolik Ranković of Serbia and Aleko Konstantinov and Tsanko Tserkovski of Bulgaria. More influential in the long run as a purifying force, however, were satirists, scientists, and scholars like Jovan Cvijić, Stojan Novaković, Alexander D. Xenopol, and Nicholas Iorga, gifted literary critics—the outstanding example was Bogdan Popović—and the new generation of "Modernist" poets: Kostes Palamas, Pencho Slaveikov, Petko Todorov, Aleksa Šantić, Milan Rakić, Jovan Dučić, and Vladimir Nazor. To the aestheticism or art for art's sake of the Symbolists and Decadents, the Balkan "Modernists"— in this they resembled Charles Péguy of France—added a deep sense of ethical and national value.

But the reactionary forces were too potent to be eliminated without the threat or use of force. Such force was exerted in all Balkan countries between 1899 and 1910, starting with peasant protest and rebellion in Bulgaria (1899–1900) and followed, in 1903, by a Socialist demonstration and military coup d'état (and the murder of Alexander Obrenović) in Serbia, antigovernmental manifestations in the Habsburg provinces, and insurrection in Macedonia. In 1905, Prince Nikola was obliged to grant his Montenegrins a constitution in order to quiet popular grumbling against his authoritarian methods and to weaken opposition to his policy of concessions for Italian commercial and finance capitalism. The Bosnian labor disturbances of 1906, the Rumanian agrarian risings of 1907, the "Young Turk" revolution of 1908, and the Greek military coup d'état of 1909 and resulting Venizelist government of 1910, continued the cycle of events which necessitated or inspired political reform. All Balkan governments moved in the direction of removing some obvious political abuses and improving parliamentary institutions and practices. Serbia even laid the foundations for political democracy.

Balkan political improvements were in some degree the result of renewed prosperity and in particular of the enrichment of a segment of the peasantry. The investment of foreign capital, the amelioration of transportation and communications, and the impoverishment of part of the peasantry materially aided the "embourgeoisement" of another part. By 1900, there was in the area south of the Danube and Sava a fairly large class of gazdas or kulaks, peasants who were not mere subsistence farmers but market-oriented cultivators and farm managers. The marginal peasant, on the other hand, emigrated to Europe or America.

In Serbia, the gazdas—peasants with ten hectares or more of land— increased from 7 percent of the total landed population in 1889 to more than twice this in 1897.[36] The rural and urban "middle classes" thus included, at the close of the century, at least a fifth of the total population. The new prosperity helped the Serbian middle groups to counter the economic warfare of imperialist Austria with success and to discover new markets for their products, diversify their exports, form new political alliances, and, in conjunction with the other Balkan states, drive the Turk to the Bosporus. In Greece, the progressist policies of Trikoupis and the subsequent conditions of world-wide prosperity allowed the growth of an even more substantial middle class, predominantly urban and larger than its Serbian counterpart.

On the eve of the Balkan Wars, the economies of the Balkan states were sounder than ever before, and more persons than ever before were playing the political game in accordance with the same rules. The accumulation of capital and the rise, after 1890, of a fairly large and self-confident rural and urban intermediate class encouraged the Balkan governments to pursue industrialization with greater vigor. The psychological effects of economic well-being were perhaps the most important of all, for the spirit of self-confidence not only spurred the Balkan peoples to the fuller realization of their national ambitions but reduced the need for acrimony in politics and created a more propitious atmosphere for the successful functioning of the multiparty system and eventual realization of political democracy.

Social Disamalgamation

The expected did not happen. The century of relative peace (1830–1910) was succeeded by a decade of war (1911–1922). War made possible territorial aggrandizement, but territorial aggrandizement resulted in the addition of dissident national minorities, which were opposed to making the enlarged states work, and of several sub-nationality groups, which were ethnically and linguistically close to the dominant nationality of the "old" kingdoms but considered themselves culturally different, if not superior.

War was followed by a period of reconstruction (1919–1924). If all had gone well and reconstruction had been followed by two decades of

---

[36] Janković, *op. cit.*, pp. 150–152; Nikola Vučo, *Privredna istorija Srbije do prvog svetskog rata* [*Economic History of Serbia to World War I*], (Belgrade, 1955), p. 178.

uninterrupted economic growth, the problems arising from cultural and economic heterogeneity would probably have lost part of their gravity. But the fall of world farm prices after 1925 seriously hurt the agrarian sector of the Balkan economy, while the world economic crisis of the thirties not only provoked a crisis in Balkan industry but aggravated the crisis in Balkan agriculture.

The world economic crisis was part of a greater crisis, a moral crisis, the crisis of a world experiencing fundamental change at a heretofore unprecedented pace. Among the upper segments of society, the moral crisis was punctuated by alternating sentiments of overconfidence and deep anxiety. Among the lower social strata, the general reaction was one of resentment, overt or latent. In some societies, the anomic tensions found expression in suicide. In others, in gang war, genocide, or class war.

Among the political leaders of the victorious Balkan states, the crisis took the form of megalomania, indifference to foreign (and domestic) public opinion, and exaggerated self-esteem:[37] a typical fantasy of wish-fulfillment. Their egocentrism and autodependence hindered them from taking systematic measures to persuade the younger generations "to follow the path which [was] being traced under their very eyes."[38] By neglecting to create an acceptable political tradition for the future, they failed to perform the primary function of a dominant political class: the preservation and slow modification of the existing political and social structure.

The multiparty system was not only retained but further complicated by the formation of several parties of "social integration."[39] This occurred not only in defeated Bulgaria, where defeat was in itself suffi-

---

[37] Stephen Graham, *Alexander of Yugoslavia: The Story of the King Who Was Murdered at Marseilles* (New Haven, Conn.: Yale University Press, 1939), p. 264; R. H. Bruce Lockhart, *Retreat from Glory* (New York: G. P. Putnam, 1934), p. 268.

[38] Count Carlo Sforza, *Europe and Europeans: A Study in Historical Psychology and International Politics* (Indianapolis and New York: Bobbs-Merrill, 1936), p. 198.

[39] For a discussion of the concepts of parties of "social integration" and "individual representation," see: Sigmund Neumann, "Toward a Comparative Study of Political Parties," in *Modern Political Parties. Approaches to Comparative Politics*, ed. by Sigmund Neumann (Chicago: University of Chicago Press, 1956), pp. 403–405. See also: Seymour Martin Lipset, *Political Man. The Social Bases of Politics* (Garden City, N.Y.: Doubleday, 1960), pp. 86–91.

cient to discredit (but not destroy) the older political tradition, but also among the victors. The parties of integration were the peasant, Communist, and "integral nationalist" parties. All three types had existed in the prewar era, at least as tendencies, but they succeeded in winning a wide following only after 1918.

Driven by the "spirit of 'groupism,'" the parties of integration aimed to reorient society around a new ideology, perform a catharsis, and create a homogeneous millenarian culture, or revert to "a pre-individualistic social order of a community type."[40] The Communists expected to do this through the class struggle. The peasantists did not have a clear program but sought to preserve and reintegrate peasant culture, "the culture of the heart and soul."[41] Fundamentally anti-clerical but not antireligious, they regarded the peasant struggle against the city in pseudo-Manichean terms: as a holy war between good and evil.[42] The program of the integral nationalists was also exclusivist but was directed less against the city than against competing nationalities, which were to be divested of their political and economic influence in the interest of the charismatic nationality. The supporters of the integral nationalist movements were generally drawn from marginal groups and from certain dominant elements that were afraid of losing their power to dominate.

There were in addition, in several of the Balkan countries, some parties of special integration, chiefly Roman Catholic, Muslim, and reform socialist (Social Democratic) organizations. In theory, the parties of special integration rejected some large aspect of the existing social order. In practice, however, they conformed to the basic tenets and requirements of the status quo.

The liberal, conservative, and progressist parties were basically parties of "individual representation." Even the Radical party of Serbia (and, after 1918, of the Serb-Croat-Slovene state) and the less influential "radical" parties of the other Balkan states, which initially had been constituted as parties of integration, behaved primarily like parties of

---

[40] On the "spirit of 'groupism'" and social reversion, see: Barbu, *op. cit.*, p. 53.

[41] This, in particular, was the aim of the founder of the Croatian Peasant party. Cf. D[inko] Tomašić, "Ideologies and the Structure of Eastern European Society," *American Journal of Sociology*, LIII (1947–1948), 370.

[42] Graham, *op. cit.*, p. 132; Joseph S. Roucek, *The Politics of the Balkans* (New York and London: McGraw-Hill, 1939), p. 124.

individual representation. Unlike the parties of integration, the latter tended to represent individuals rather than well-defined social, religious, or cultural groups, and had no fundamental quarrel with the essence of the existing social regime. Even parties of individual representation, however, were not free of "integral" or "groupist" tendencies. Even they catered to special sectional or subnational interests.

None of the parties remained immutable, least of all the peasant parties. The latter declined as organs of peasant integration to absorb some of the characteristics of the parties of national integration and individual representation. Founded to combat the urban middle classes, the peasant parties of Rumania and Jugoslavia (Kingdom of the Serbs, Croats, and Slovenes) reached an understanding with one or more bourgeois parties—notably, with the National party of Iuliu Maniu of Transylvania, or with the Independent Democrats of Svetozar Pribičević. Moreover, they were infiltrated by lawyers and businessmen, who obtained key posts in the party organization and subordinated the social program of the peasantry to the waging of a political struggle against the upper and middle strata of the "old kingdoms" in behalf of the middle strata of the new territories.

De-peasantized through the "embourgeoisement" of their leaders and principal followers, they tried to maintain their hold over the poorer peasants through their folk ideology. Favorably disposed toward the *mystique* of soil and people in the humanist form given to it by Jules Michelet and Jovan Cvijić, the Croatian Peasant party—or certain elements within it—succumbed to the less innocuous Germano-Fascist ideology of blood and soil. While some of the older bourgeois intellectuals were suspicious of the "Byzantine" character of Serbian culture, certain younger intellectuals who made their way into the Croatian Peasant party discriminated between "peaceful *zadruga* culture" and "turbulent patriarchal culture," identifying the first with the "democratic" familial and communal organization of the Croatian "Slavs" and the second with the "authoritarian" familial and communal organization of the Serbian "Uralo-Altaics." The National Peasants of Rumania idealized their "Daco-Roman" folk culture, denounced Jewry, and upheld the Rumanian middle class and well-to-do peasantry of Transylvania against the Magyar and German minorities and against some of the upper and middle elements of the old kingdom. In Greece, where the peasantry constituted only half the population, peasant parties had little chance of success. Here also, however, there grew a "*mystique* of the people," which was mingled with the "*mystique* of the Hellenic Idea." Both ideologies preached the isolation of Hellenism from the rest of the world by an irreversible historic process that made of Greece and Greeks an inimitable metaphysical entity.[43]

Communist groups rose to prominence during and immediately following the First World War and then again during the depression and international political crisis of the thirties. The Communist parties were especially popular in Serbia, Bulgaria, Macedonia, Montenegro, and Bessarabia. In the years immediately following the Second World War, they had the backing of 10 to 20 percent of the electorate—at least in Bulgaria and Jugoslavia. Between the early twenties and 1935, however, they were forced underground and lost most of their popular support. After adopting "popular front" programs in 1935, they succeeded in restoring part of their former strength, both among the peasantry of the depressed provinces and among the university youth and workers of the large urban centers.

Integral nationalist groups similarly succeeded in winning a public in the years following the First World War and during the great depression, especially in the provinces which had formerly been part of the Dual Monarchy. The out-and-out integral nationalist movements were brought up on ancestor worship and necrolatry, xenophobia, the cult of violence, and the authoritarian way of life. They were anti-Semitic, fundamentally anti-Slavic, anti-Communist, and anti-intellectual. For example, the terrorist *Ustaši* of Croatia traced their ancestry to the anti-Semitic, anti-Serbian, and pro-Habsburg Pure Party of Rights of Josip Frank. Having plotted and executed the assassination of King Alexander of Jugoslavia with the aid of IMRO fellow terrorists and of Fascist Italy and authoritarian Hungary, they had recourse, during the Second World War, to a policy of ruthless genocide against the Serbians of the new puppet state of Croatia. As allies of Germany and Hungary, they found it expedient to insist upon the Germanic and Avaro-Turkic origins of the Croats. It is improbable, however, that the integral nationalist movements enjoyed the support of more than 10 percent of the population in any of the Balkan countries except

---

[43] On the Greek "*mystique* of the people," see: Nicolas Svoronos, *Histoire de la Grèce moderne*, in paperback series *Que sais-je?* No. 578 (Paris: Presses Universitaires de France, 1953), pp. 111–112.

Rumania, where the competing groups—especially the Iron Guard and the National Christian party—won the endorsement, by 1937, of more than a fourth of the articulate public.

Exact statistical information on the class origins of the Balkan integral nationalist groups has not yet been gathered or published, but it is relatively certain they obtained recruits from marginal elements of all classes. It is also fairly clear that the bulk of their leadership was attracted from the section of the population that we shall call the "middle sectors" or "middle groups." [44] A large segment of the ordinary membership—how large has not been ascertained—also came from the middle groups.

The most penetrating analysis of the situation and psychology of the Balkan (specifically Jugoslav) middle groups of the interwar era is found in a short essay by the Serbian social scientist and Agrarian leader, Dragoljub Jovanović.[45] He made no distinction between "middle classes"—*classes moyennes*—and "middle groups," and our view is that the two may be used almost interchangeably. The first term, however, draws attention to the fact that the groups in question are distinct from other social classes, the second emphasizes their lack of a *common* social consciousness in spite of their intermediate position in society. Both emphasize their middleness. Both are descriptively correct.

The middle sectors comprised the social strata that had mastered the techniques or routines which facilitate the duties of the policy-making or political class. They were the *policy-conforming* elements, the elements that, after the policy makers, had benefited the most from the process of social, cultural, political, and economic rationalization. Included in their midst were the relatively well-to-do peasants who produced for a market, the nonmarginal craftsmen and traders, clerical workers from the rank of rural scribe to that of ministerial secretary, lower and middle-ranking public functionaries, technical specialists, representatives of the liberal professions, priests and protopopes, gendarmes and noncoms, and officers unable to advance beyond the rank of major or colonel.

---

[44] For the use of these and similar terms, see: John J. Johnson, *Political Change in Latin America: The Emergence of the Middle Sectors* (Stanford, Calif.: Stanford University Press, 1958).

[45] Dragolioub Yovanovitch, "Les classes moyennes chez les Slaves du Sud," in *Inventaires III. Classes moyennes,* publication of the Centre de Documentation sociale de l'Ecole Normale Supérieure (Paris: Félix Alcan, 1939), pp. 217–250.

Although they constituted a quarter of the Greek, Jugoslav, Rumanian, and Bulgarian population and were probably able to sway another quarter, the middle groups were considerably weaker than their numbers would indicate. Stratified internally and divided professionally into very diverse elements, they were separated in every country by cultural differences and in several of the countries by religious and national distinctions. They were weakened still further by their inability or lack of desire to halt the spread of monopoly and bureaucratic capitalism.

The biggest capitalist in the Balkans was the state. In Jugoslavia, the state owned many forests, railroads, mines, lumber mills, banks, spas, sugar refineries, and armaments factories. It owned and operated all radio stations and PTT (Post Office, Telephone, and Telegraph) lines and offices. It also owned some textile manufactures and most river boats and harbor facilities. The state industrial monopolies were reinforced by state sales and trading monopolies. In the other states, especially Rumania, a comparable situation existed.

As in prerevolutionary Russia, the industrial, commercial, and financial community, known in most of the Balkans as the *čaršija*, was closely associated with the state administration. Far from being an autonomous force, capitalism was dependent upon the largess of government bureaus and ministries, and government officials were rarely "large" unless business was kind in turn.

When a political party or coalition was turned out of office, there was either a turnover of government contracts or a gesture by business in favor of the party in power. The segment of the business community that profited most from the patronage of the state became a partisan, the neglected segment became a critic, of the state. Some elements—minorities and subnationalities—even called for territorial reorganization as a means of achieving the transfer of power from the business and political classes of the old kingdoms to those of the annexed territories. The business class was thus fragmented into advocates and opponents of the existing state regimes.

The capitalist class was dependent upon the state, the state was dependent upon foreign capital. The Balkan countries sought to reduce the role of foreign and increase the participation of domestic capital, but foreign investments were high in all sectors of economic enterprise except agriculture and amounted, in the mid-thirties, to no less than half the total joint-stock investment in industry. Foreign capital was distributed ecologically into an Italian zone of economic penetration along the Mediterranean periphery, a Central European zone in the north and west, and a West European zone in the center, south, and east. Moreover, some countries (or their subjects) held a preponderant share of the capital invested in certain sectors of the economy: Britain, France, Belgium, and Austria in mining and banking, Hungary and Italy in the building industry, Hungary, Italy, Czechoslovakia, and Poland in consumer goods, Sweden, Switzerland, Belgium, and the United States in the electrical field, and Britain and Germany in heavy industry.

The satellitic nature of the Balkan economy was further accentuated by the inadequate diversification of exports and export markets. In 1937, for example, two products—wheat and petroleum—accounted for 72.7 percent of all Rumanian exports; three products—tobacco, currants, and raisins—accounted for 60.8 percent of all Greek exports; three products—tobacco, wheat, and eggs—accounted for 53.7 percent of all Bulgarian exports; and five products—lumber, corn, wheat, iron ore, and copper ore—accounted for 52.1 percent of all Jugoslav exports.[46] The acceptance by the Balkan countries, during and after 1934, of clearing agreements with Germany resulted in an increasing diversion of their trade to that market. The German annexation of Austria and dismemberment and partial annexation of Czechoslovakia intensified this tendency still further, so that after 1938 two-fifths or more of the import-export trade of the Balkan states was with Germany.

Part of the Balkan business and political class thus came to the conclusion after 1934 that economic progress and well-being for the middle and upper social strata were not conceivable unless the Balkans were constituted as an integral part of a Central European *Grossraumwirtschaft*. By 1938, this view found its way into the writings of a well-known Croatian and one-time Jugoslav minister of agriculture, Otto Frangeš.

Convinced that the accumulation of capital is far easier on large than on tiny properties, Frangeš regretted the postwar subdivision of large estates among the Balkan peasantry. While an advocate of industrialization, he believed that efforts to industrialize should be concentrated

---

[46] Ernst Wagemann, *Der neue Balkan: altes Land, junge Wirtschaft* (Hamburg, Hanseatische Verlagsantalt [1939]), pp. 115–116.

338 TRAIAN STOIANOVICH

upon the most highly capitalized sector of the economy—mining and forest-product industries—and upon the production of consumer goods and goods that do not require highly skilled labor. He advocated in particular the intensification and diversification of agriculture. Lacking confidence in the human factor, he did not believe in the early possibility of Balkan economic autonomy. Being a "realist" and progressist, he urged the Balkan states to accept the principle of a Middle European political-economic *Grossraum*. This "grand space" of Middle Europe, he vaguely hinted, would be divided into two principal areas, a central or dominant German space and a dependent, peripheral, or satellitic space. Since, however, the scarcity of capital and skilled labor and of ferrous metals and coking coal would not permit the Balkan states to become an independent force, they should profit from the benefits conferred upon self-sufficing geosocial units by integrating themselves more fully into the German-dominated Middle European *Grossraum*.[47] In nearly every respect, the Frangeš recommendations duplicated the policy recommendations for the Balkans of the director of the German Institute for Business Research, Ernst Wagemann.[48]

While the idea of a Middle European *Grossraum* may have appealed to the more well-to-do rural and urban elements in the territories of the former Habsburg Monarchy, economic nationalism was more attractive to comparable social elements in the old kingdoms.

[47] Otto von Frangeš, "Die treibenden Kräfte der wirtschaftlichen Strukturwandlungen in Jugoslawien," *Weltwirtschaftliches Archiv*, XLVIII (September, 1938), esp. pp. 327–330; Otto von Frangeš, "Die Donaustaaten Südosteuropas und der deutsche Grosswirtschaftsraum," *Weltwirtschaftliches Archiv*, LIII (March, 1941), pp. 284–316. A partial development of his ideas was also published in French under the title, "L'Industrialisation des pays agricoles du Sud-est de l'Europe," *Revue économique internationale*, 30e année, III (July-September, 1938), 27–77. For comments on Frangeš as "Minister against Agrarian Reform," see: Hermann Wendel, "Dictatorship in Yugo-Slavia," in *Dictatorship on Its Trial, by Eminent Leaders of Modern Thought*, ed. Otto Forst de Battaglia, trans. by Huntley Paterson, with an introduction by Winston S. Churchill (London, Bombay, Sydney: George G. Harrap, 1930), p. 352. For an elaboration of the concepts of dominant and dominated economies, see: François Perroux, "Esquisse d'une théorie de l'économie dominante," *Economie appliquée*, I (April-September, 1948), 243–300.
[48] Wagemann, *Der neue Balkan;* see also: Henry L. Roberts, *Rumania: Political Problems of an Agrarian State* (New Haven, Conn.: Yale University Press, 1951), pp. 216–218. For a succinct analysis of Wagemann's views on demography, see: Fernand Braudel, "Les 'Seuils' d'Ernst Wagemann," *Annales (Economies—Sociétés—Civilisations)*, XV (1960), 494–503.

The leading exponent of economic nationalism in Rumania was the politician-economist Mihail Manoilescu, who correctly maintained that the world was divided into economically advanced and economically retarded societies and that economic principles and policies conducive to economic growth in the first did not necessarily work in the interest of the second.

Without going into an analysis of his mathematical theory, criticized by many economists, we ought to state his general argument. Manoilescu contended that the various sectors of the economy are distinguishable from each other not only in naturally expected ways but by different degrees of per-capita labor productivity, as measured in terms of purchasing power. Because labor productivity is ordinarily higher in industry than in agriculture, free trade between agricultural and industrial countries results in a specific advantage for the industrial states. To compensate for this disadvantage, agricultural countries should create a protectionist system in favor of those economic activities which labor is most productive. This can be instituted, however, only if horizontal social conflicts or class struggles are eliminated, and the latter can be realized only if society is reorganized on a vertical (estate or corporate) basis. Finally, conflict between the vertical units can be checked only by the institution of authoritarian government.[49]

During the thirties, the Rumanian government embarked upon a program of more intensive industrialization in order to cope with the economic crisis. In its search for economic revival, it adopted several of Manoilescu's suggestions. State economic controls were extended, the position of industrial and trading monopolies was strengthened, the trappings of corporatism were mounted, and the authority of the state was formally augmented, even as Rumanian society became more disamalgamated. The program was carried out in such an inefficient and piecemeal fashion, however, that the country failed to create an autonomous national economy and was drawn instead into the orbit of the German *Grossraum*.

Greece, Bulgaria, and Jugoslavia likewise tried to solve the economic crisis by fostering industrial development. In all four countries, how-

---

[49] Roberts, *Rumania*, pp. 192–198; Mihail Manoilesco, "Arbeitsproduktivität und Aussenhandel," *Weltwirtschaftliches Archiv*, XLII (July, 1935), 13–43; Carl Brinkmann, "Mihail Manoilesco und die klassische Aussenhandelstheorie," *Weltwirtschaftliches Archiv*, XLVIII (September, 1938), 273–286.

ever, the governments were afraid that an overly rapid increase in the number of industrial workers might lead to their overthrow and the establishment of a new social regime. They were consequently convinced that industrialization must be accompanied by the creation of a homogeneous middle class.

This dual policy ripened into a conscious goal between 1933 and 1938. The execution, if not the authorship, of the policy is associated with the names of John Metaxas, King Boris, King Carol, and Milan Stojadinović. In Jugoslavia, the second part of the policy was probably even inaugurated with Alexander's dictatorship of January 6, 1929, for one of Alexander's aims was to encourage intermarriage, or the normalization of libidinal relations, between members of the various sub-nationalities. If this had been achieved, the Serbian and Croatian middle strata might have coalesced into a more homogeneous social group.

In none of the Balkan countries was the dual policy of industrializing and creating a unified middle class pursued so consciously as in Jugoslavia, although the objective everywhere was the achievement of "national rebirth." When Stojadinović assumed the reins of government after the depression of 1926–1935, he pursued a program in many ways similar to that of Russia's Count Witte—minus railroad building—after the depression of the eighties, combined with some aspects of Stolypin's program and perhaps of the economic thought of Keynes, Rathenau, and Hjalmar Schacht. Prime Minister from June, 1935, to February, 1939, he discarded deflationist monetary policies in favor of more elastic credit, reduced the land tax, reduced peasant debts by one-half, encouraged the growth of rice and cotton, promoted the development of the textile industry, and laid the foundations for a chemical and metallurgical industry. Aiming to prevent revolution from below, he wanted to be recognized as *vodja* or *Führer* in order to carry out a revolution from above. To consolidate the revolution in favor of the middle elements, he tried to form an organic union of the Serbian, Slovenian, and Muslim Bosnian upper and middle groups by transforming the (Serbian) Radical party into a movement of social integration known as the Jugoslav Radical Union. To placate the Croatians, he negotiated a concordat with the Vatican, a project originally entertained by the late King Alexander himself.

The endeavor to find a cure for *anomie* through the institution of mesocracy—the use of the leadership principle in behalf of the bourgeois ethos—did not succeed. Denouncing the concordat as antinational, the Serbian Orthodox clergy aroused such a popular outburst against it that it had to be withdrawn.[50] The demonstrations proved that the middle elements were more divided than ever before, but they showed even more clearly the disamalgamation of the dominant political class, now fragmented as a result of the structural and conjunctural crises into three or four different groups: traditionalists, mesocrats, and democrats and Communist fellow travelers.

In Greece, Bulgaria, and Rumania, the antidemocratic forces grew progressively stronger after 1933. In the first two countries, however, the opposition organized popular fronts in 1935 and 1936 to combat the authoritarianism of Boris and Metaxas. The attempt to stem the tide of authoritarianism failed, partly because the old political leaders had neglected the job of creating competent successors. Authoritarianism was also encouraged by the fact that the Greek and Bulgarian kings— the former recalled to the throne in 1935 by plebiscite—probably conformed to the father image of a sizable number of their subjects.

In Jugoslavia, authoritarian and antiauthoritarian tendencies grew simultaneously. Alexander did not conform to the father image of the Serbians and conformed still less to that of the Croatians. Following his assassination in Marseilles in October, 1934, the nominal political leadership of the country passed into the hands of his cousin and chief regent, Prince Paul. But to both Serbians and Croatians, Paul was a "foreigner." English in his tastes and with many personal and ideological ties with Russian tsarism, he readily succumbed—like a few members of the English aristocracy—to the antidemocratic appeals of nazism. Disappointed in the overly cosmopolitan regent, many Serbians began to regard themselves as a people without a true father and therefore responded more ardently both to the appeals of democracy and to those of other authoritarians.

After 1936, Serbian Democrats, Agrarians, and even some Radicals formed a common front with the Croatian Peasants of Vladimir

---

[50] For a brief discussion of the concordat and the popular outburst, see: Robert Lee Wolff, *The Balkans in Our Time* (Cambridge, Mass.: Harvard University Press, 1956), p. 124.

Maček against the Radical Union of Stojadinović. Stojadinović was a "realist," [51] ready to enter into diplomatic relations with all states. But Paul would not let him recognize the Soviet Union, the people would not let him recognize the Vatican, and Hitler's annexation of Austria frustrated his hopes of being able to use Mussolini against Hitler and Hitler against Mussolini. Failing to realize his foreign policy aims, widening instead of narrowing the gap between Serbs and Croats, and provoking instead of dissipating internal opposition, Stojadinović was forced to resign early in 1939.

But while one "realist" was removed, "realism" prevailed as a policy. Maček, for example, secretly bargained with Italy to sever Croatia from Jugoslavia and then resumed negotiations with Belgrade for Croatian autonomy within Jugoslavia,[52] reaching an understanding that did not even include fringe benefits for his erstwhile Serbian allies. Another "realist," Dragiša Cvetković, succeeded Stojadinović and appointed the former ambassador to Berlin, Cincar-Marković, to head the foreign ministry. Cincar-Marković was a cynic who regarded the Balkans as "comically backward" and Germany as the proper ruler of Middle Europe.[53]

Jugoslavia's economic servitude to Germany, born of the policy of "realism," was much aggravated during the ministry of Cvetković. The harvest of 1940 was inadequate even for the needs of the home market, but the Jugoslavs had to provide their northern neighbor with grains in order to obtain the imports required to keep their new industry in operation. While this may have been of some benefit to the producers of the fertile northern provinces, it meant a tightening of the belt for urban workers and for the consumers of the depressed areas, as the price of bread went up sharply during the winter and spring of 1941.[54]

As the government of Prince Paul prepared to go to Vienna in March 1941 to sign the Axis Tripartite Pact, the Serbs made individual protests and joined public demonstrations against a policy that deprived them of economic satisfaction no less than of political freedom. The malcon-

---

[51] Constantin Fotitch, *The War We Lost: Yugoslavia's Tragedy and the Failure of the West* (New York: Viking Press, 1948), pp. 12–13.

[52] Hugh Gibson, ed., *The Ciano Diaries, 1939–1943*, with an introduction by Sumner Welles (Garden City, N.Y.: Doubleday, 1946), pp. 84–91.

[53] Rebecca West, *Black Lamb and Grey Falcon: A Journey through Yugoslavia*, 2 vols. (New York: Viking Press, 1941), II, 1133.

[54] *Ibid.*, p. 1134.

tents and demonstrators were officers and simple soldiers, Orthodox priests, public officials, humble town folk and peasants, and textile workers and liberal and Communist high school and university students of the capital.[55] Taking advantage of the popular fermentation, a military junta under Air Force Brigadier-General Bora Mirković deposed some of the subservient "realists," forced Paul into exile, and proclaimed Alexander's son, Peter, king.

The coup d'état hastened still further the fragmentation of the upper and middle groups. The Croatian element that aspired to the role and functions of a ruling class remained neutralist or pro-Axis, the Serbian big-business and high-ranking officer class continued to be tied to a policy of "realism," and the younger Serbian military officers and civil servants of the middle ranks questioned the wisdom of "realism" but lacked a positive policy. The old political class ceased to know how to rule, the middle groups ceased to know to what to conform.

Cracked almost beyond repair before the German invasion, the Jugoslav social structure fell apart as the Germans rolled in. A segment of the middle and upper groups collaborated with German or Italian fascism or with the invading authorities, another part was taken captive or went into exile, a third group resisted but soon fell into the errors of "realism," and a fourth element was destroyed by the genocide policies of the *Ustaši*.

The old leaders were gone or at least partly discredited. The story of the future is the tale of new men and of a new social structure. In proportion to the total population, the faithful of 1941 were no more numerous than the merchant-*hajduk*-intellectuals of 1804, but like the faithful of 1788 and 1804, many leaders of 1941 were militarily well-trained—this time in war-torn Spain—and were able to mobilize many "floaters" to their side. The story of 1941 really begins in the thirties, with the adoption by the Communists of the policy of popular fronts, with the emergence of a unified Communist party under the charismatic leadership of Josip Broz Tito, and with the transfer of the allegiance of the radical youth and ultrademocratic intelligentsia—and particularly of the youth and intelligentsia of the so-called dominant nationality—from the old order to the *homines novi* and to a new social myth. When the old political class defaulted, a new political class was ready to seize power.

---

[55] *Ibid.*, pp. 1136–1137; *New York Times*, March 22–31, 1941.

On the basis of our study of the Balkan social structure and structural and conjunctural crises, we should like to suggest the following hypothesis: In the estate society, the process of revolution is initiated by the occurrence of a change in one of the vertical groups that deëmphasizes its vertical nature and gives it a horizontal (class) organization. In the class society, it starts after a change in one or more of the horizontal groups stimulates a condition of general social disamalgamation.[56] In either case, the revolution assumes a violent character when the tendency to move from one form of social structure to another is first unwittingly aided by the old political class (through their enlightenment or rationalism) and then obstructed by a combination of dominant and marginal elements (an aristocratic or mesocratic reaction and a real or quasi-conspiracy between local brigands or terrorists and foreign or quasi-foreign states).

Occurring during an unfavorable political or economic conjuncture, the aristocratic or mesocratic reaction is inspired by fear that the social structure will be altered to the detriment of the formerly satisfied social strata unless a homogeneous middle class is created or society is stratified vertically on a stricter or sounder basis, or unless the horizontal basis is wholly subordinated to a new vertical (corporate) structure. The social reaction in turn generates a "great fear," a fear of the brigands, of the terrorists, of the mesocrats and aristocrats, of foreign (or quasi-foreign) invasion, of most of the compromised institutions of the *ancien régime*. This "complex pattern of fear" preceded the Serbian rising of 1804, was present in the abortive Greco-Vlach rising of 1807 and in the Greek insurrection of 1821, led in Jugoslavia to the political-economic fermentation of the winter and spring of 1941, was the most important factor in the winning of recruits to Tito's Partisans and National Liberation movement, and was no less important in generating the Greek civil war after the Second World War.[57]

---

[56] For a similar theory of social restructuring and revolution, which unfortunately came to my attention only after the completion of my own study in its present revised form, see: Henri Janne, "Un modèle théorique du phénomène révolutionnaire," *Annales* (*Economies—Sociétés—Civilisations*), XV (1960), 1138–1154.

[57] For a very interesting and illuminating discussion of the "complex pattern of fear" during the Greek civil war, see: Frank Smothers, William Hardy McNeill, and Elizabeth Darbishire McNeill, *Report on the Greeks: Findings of a Twentieth Century Fund Team Which Surveyed Conditions in Greece in 1947* (New York: The Twentieth Century Fund, 1948), pp. 41–49.

The revolutions we have briefly examined were influenced by outside forces. They were "revolutions from without," [58] just as the English Revolution (1640–1660) was a revolution from the Netherlands, the American Revolution a revolution from England, the French Revolution a revolution from England and America, the "October Revolution" a revolution from the pages of the Paris Commune. In other words, they were all fundamentally revolutions provoked by "a structural crisis," properly speaking the only kind of social revolution. They were revolutions born of the failure of the old political class, of the economic and political fluidity of the middle and marginal elements, of the misery and fears of the peasantry, and of the rise of a new political class armed with the qualities missing in the old one and imbued with an ideology imported from abroad but modified to suit the needs of special national conditions.

---

[58] For a stimulating discussion of the so-called "revolution from without," see: Theodore H. Von Laue, "Die Revolution von aussen als erste Phase der russischen Revolution 1917," *Jahrbücher für Geschichte Osteuropas*, ser. 2, IV (1956), 138–158, and Palmer, *op. cit.*, I, 12–13

CHANGES IN THE ECONOMIC STRUCTURES

OF THE BALKANS,

1860–1960

Nicolas Spulber

This essay attempts to put into focus the basic characteristics of the economic development of the Balkans from 1860 to 1960.[1] Wide territorial and population displacements, absence of uniformity in the underlying statistical computations and in the data available from country to country and from period to period raise numerous and often insuperable difficulties with respect to the construction of long-term series and of uniform tabulations. This explains the resort to different indicators from one period to the next and the lack of completeness of some tables.

EARLY EFFORTS OF MODERNIZATION

The accession to political independence of the nuclei of the main Balkan countries (the Peloponnesus, the Danubian Principalities, Serbia, and Bulgaria) occurred at different dates (Greece in 1830; Rumania and Serbia, 1878; Bulgaria, 1908). It was the decay of the Turkish Empire, not their political status, which set for all of them the benchmarks at which they could enter into economic contact with foreign countries, engage in *de facto* autonomous economic policies and enact integrated domestic economic measures. Thus most of the area was opened to economic contacts with the West in 1830, began to

---

[1] I am indebted to my colleague, Professor Elmus R. Wicker, for helpful criticism of an earlier draft. I am also thankful to the graduate faculty of Indiana University for a grant covering cost of secretarial help and graph drawings.

enact autonomous economic policies within each of the mentioned national units by 1860 and completed the movement toward economic independence around 1880 or 1890. Truly enough, the secession from the Ottoman Empire opened the door to the spreading influence of other great powers. But these influences remained diverse in nature and different in scope and often neutralized each other. British influence was decisive (though not always reaching the same intensity) in Greece; Russian and German influences were significant in Bulgaria; German economic penetration was asserting itself on a wide front in the Principalities; Austro-Hungarian influence was overwhelming up to 1903 in Serbia. As we shall see subsequently, the progressive liquidation of the Ottoman Empire and the falling apart of the Dual Monarchy after the First World War finally opened for the Balkan countries the possibility of rounding out their territories and of acquiring exclusive control over their economies.

Within this framework, what was the extent of economic development of these small nuclei of Balkan countries from 1860 onward? There was identity of purpose between the individual countries. Their purposes were to create modern armies and administrations, to fulfill their "national aspirations"—which, alas, often meant the acquisition of the same pieces of territory—and to become integrated into the broad currents of capitalist growth and industrialization embracing Western and Central Europe. To encourage industrialization they resorted to tariffs, subsidies, state purchases of products of the domestic industry; moreover, they facilitated the growth of an integrated banking system and created favorable conditions for foreign investments.

The tasks were undertaken in the face of different factor endowments and different underlying social and economic structures. The largest and the best endowed of the four was Rumania. The population of the Principalities reached 4,500,000 in 1880 and 7,300,000 in 1913, compared to 1,900,000 and 3,000,000 in the same years for Serbia (the heart of interwar Jugoslavia), 2,800,000 and 4,500,000 for Bulgaria, and 1,700,000 and 2,700,000 for Greece. In Rumania and in most parts of Greece latifundia were the predominant form of ownership; in Bulgaria and Serbia small-scale holdings were typical. Given these differences in form of land ownership, Rumania was able to export a far larger share of its agricultural output than its neighbors whose soil was widely mortgaged to subsistence farming. However, notwithstanding the differences in forms of ownership, productivity per capita and yields per acre were distressingly low throughout the area. The incredible task of advancing toward modernity had thus to be undertaken on the one hand with an inefficient agriculture, hardly fit to compete on the world markets, and on the other hand, with only incipient towns most of whose artisan population was severely hit by the loss of its former Turkish markets. As soon as they could, the national governments set out to accomplish this task by further depressing consumption in villages, by borrowing heavily abroad and by expanding continuously the economic activity of the state.

The survey of the various indicators available suggests that significant economic growth was achieved in the area from 1860 to 1913. Rising trends in budget receipts and expenditures, in foreign as well as in domestic public indebtedness, in foreign trade turnover, in private foreign capital inflow, in the development of industry, transportation and of the credit system, all seem to point in this direction. Over-all budgetary receipts more than doubled between 1885 and 1913 (see graphs and Table 1), with per-capita taxation doubling. Foreign and domestic debt increased significantly, the former more than two and one-half times. Foreign loans extended between 1880 and 1890 served mostly for construction or purchase of foreign-owned railroads, construction of bridges, ports, and other public services. By 1913, more than 8,200 kilometers of track were laid, forming the main arteries of the railway system of the area as it operates today. The remainder of the loans was spent for military equipment and for various administrative purposes. Foreign trade more than doubled in these countries except Greece (see Table 1). This was accomplished notwithstanding the damaging competition of American wheat exports after 1875 which led to the virtual elimination of these countries from the Western markets. Rumania, Bulgaria and Serbia turned more heavily toward the Central European markets and toward protectionist measures at home. Emulating Hungary, Rumania enacted from 1887 on laws of "encouragement" of domestic industries. After 1894 Bulgaria enacted a similar set of laws. In both countries the state granted to industry numerous privileges such as free land grants for buildings, tax reduction or outright tax exemptions, duty-free imports or freight reduction on the state-owned railways. Using more devious means Serbia also

TABLE 1

ECONOMIC INDICATORS FOR 1890, 1900, 1910, 1913

(In millions of pre-1934 dollars)

Year	Budgetary receipts				Foreign debt				Foreign-trade turnover (Imports plus exports)			
	Rumania	Serbia	Bulgaria	Greece	Rumania	Serbia	Bulgaria	Greece	Rumania	Serbia	Bulgaria	Greece
1890	52.6	8.7	13.5	18.2	169.5	64.9	22.1	124.1	121.6	16.0	29.6	41.2
1900	53.3	12.6	10.3	19.6	259.0	84.5	55.6	139.5	94.6	22.9	19.1	44.6
1910	117.4	18.7	24.5	27.5	303.6	135.7	103.2	145.4	195.5	34.9	58.3	58.1
1913	135.9	16.7	18.5	23.7	326.7	189.8	174.7	219.9	233.1	36.2	58.1	56.1

SOURCES: *Statistisches Jahrbüch für das Deutsche Reich*, Berlin, 1904, 1905, 1912, and 1913; also miscellaneous national sources.

provided measures of encouragement to industry; however it did not enact comprehensive protectionist measures until after its break with Austria-Hungary in 1903. Greece reluctantly resorted to protectionism and industrialization. Officially bankrupt in 1893 and a loser of the 1897 war, Greece did not start to encourage industrial expansion until around 1910.[2]

In the stated conditions, industry developed between 1890 and 1910 more significantly in Rumania than in the other Balkan lands. Industrial growth in Rumania may be attributed to several factors: its relatively larger domestic market; its better endowment in raw materials— notably in oil, whose output rose from 8,000 barrels in 1860 to 383,000 in 1890 and 13,500,000 in 1913; its somewhat better accession to natural transportation facilities; and its larger volume of foreign trade, due partly to depressed consumption levels in the countryside. Rumania's industrialization may be crudely illustrated by the following figures: In 1860 that country had 12,800 handicraft workshops and small plants, half of which were flour mills. By 1887, 83 factories were in operation, each with a capital stock of more than 10,000 dollars, or with more than 25 gainfully employed. This "big industry" grew under the laws of encouragement to industry to 182 plants in 1902 and 472 plants in 1910 with a capital stock valued at 56,000,000 dollars. Total employment in "big industry" numbered 48,700 persons in 1910. To this total should be added 7,500 employed in the oil industry and 18,500 gainfully employed in railway transportation. By 1915 the capital stock of the Rumanian industry had grown to 130,000,000 dollars.[3] In Bulgaria, "big enterprises" defined there as consisting of plants with a capital stock valued at more than 5,000 dollars each, or with more than 20 gainfully employed, grew from 72 in 1894 to 103 in 1900 and 345 in 1911. In these enterprises 16,000 workers were employed. The capital

---

[2] The literature on this score is extremely abundant. See notably N. P. Arcadian, *Industrializarea României* [*Industrialization of Rumania*], 3d ed. (Bucharest, 1936); Christo T. Russeff, *Die Fortschritte der staatlich unterstützten Fabriksindustrie in Bulgarien* (Halle, 1914); D. Kyriazi, *Zur Entwicklung des Gewerbes im heutigen Griechenland* (Leipzig, 1926); and Wayne S. Vucinich, *Serbia Between East and West* (Stanford, Calif., 1954).

[3] See Virgil Madgearu, *Evoluția Economiei Românești dupa Războiul Mondial* [*Evolution of the Rumanian Economy after the World War*], (Bucharest, 1940), p. 20. For additional data, see Arcadian, *op. cit.*, *passim*.

stock of these industries was valued at more than 18,000,000 dollars.[4] Industrial growth spurted in Serbia after 1903 and in Greece after 1910. The former counted 80 factories of some significance in 1900, and 170 in 1910.[5] In 1917, Greece counted 282 "large" factories with more than 25 workers and an industrial labor force of 23,700.[6]

Tariffs and subsidies, state purchases of industrial products, provided only some of the conditions necessary for industrial growth. Another factor of primary importance was the mentioned development of an integrated banking system centered mostly on the national banks established after 1880. Commercial banks started to develop either after 1890 or, sometimes, after 1900. Following the classic Central European pattern these banks became the promoting factor in industry, buying and selling industrial shares, encouraging new foundations or mergers, providing patronage and advice. The penetration of foreign capital, both in banking and directly in industry, reached enormous proportions. In Rumanian industry, for example, 100,000,000 dollars out of the 130,000,000 dollars of capital invested in 1915 was either owned or made available by foreigners.[7]

Notwithstanding the growth, the attempts to integrate these small countries into the broad currents of capitalist economic expansion embracing most of Western and Central Europe can be viewed as only moderately successful. The archaic Ottoman domination had a paralyzing effect up to the moment when these countries acquired effective

---

[4] See Akad. Nauk S.S.S.R., *Istoriia Bolgarii* [*History of Bulgaria*], (Moscow, 1954), I, 446. See, also, Zhak Natan, "Kum vuprosa za purvonachal'noto natrupvane na kapitala v Bulgaria" (*"On the Question of the Primitive Accumulation of Capital in Bulgaria"*), *Izvestiia na ikonomicheskia institut*, Bulgarska Akademiia na Naukite [*Bulletin of the Economic Institute, Bulgarian Academy of Sciences*], 1954: 1–2 (Sofia, 1954), *passim*.

[5] See Jozo Tomasevich, *Peasants, Politics, and Economic Change in Yugoslavia* (Stanford, Calif., 1955), pp. 691–695.

[6] See X. E. Zolotas, *Griechenland auf dem Wege zur Industrialisierung* (Leipzig, 1926), p. 22. See, also, the study of G. Charitakes, "Le mouvement industriel en Grèce pendant les annees 1915–1925" in *Les Effets économiques et sociaux de la guerre en Grèce, Histoire Economique et Sociale de la Guerre Mondiale (Serie Grecque)*, ed. André Andréades et al. (Paris: Carnegie Foundation, 1928).

[7] See Madgearu, *op. cit.*, p. 20. For summary data on foreign capital in banking, see V. Colocotronis, *L'Organisation bancaire des pays balkaniques et les capitaux étrangers* (Paris, 1934), *passim*.

economic autonomy (that is, up to 1860). The Turkish occupation left
an almost insuperable backwardness in the Balkan villages. But the
independence *per se* did not and, it can be argued, could not provide a
sufficient impetus either for sustained growth, or for systematic spreading of development outside a few privileged centers. Some of the
Balkan lands included in the Austro-Hungarian Empire, such as
Slovenia or Croatia, for instance, made much more significant progress
than Montenegro (who enjoyed an independence with historically
insignificant results) or Serbia, which nearly collapsed in the process of
maintaining its national identity. Transylvania had an industrial and a
banking system in far better shape than that of the so-called Old
Rumanian Kingdom (i.e., the Principalities), independent for all practical purposes since 1860. Small Slovenia counted in 1913, 367 big
plants as against only 172 for Serbia. Transylvania counted 60 big mining and metallurgical enterprises in 1910, each with more than 20
workers and a labor force of 19,700, plus 322 other big industries with
33,300 gainfully employed. This matched very well the industrial labor
force of the Old Kingdom. Whatever were the failures of the Dual
Monarchy, the countries included in it clearly benefited from the
advantages of a large market and cheap credits channeled through the
great Vienna or Budapest banks. Hence they could develop a better-
structured industry of efficient operation. The effort made by each of
the four small countries to establish modern armies, administrations,
and public-utility networks on the basis of massive foreign borrowing
had many negative aspects. External control was exercised in the name
of the foreign lenders directly on the revenues of *ad hoc* created state
monopolies (for tobacco, matches, salt, alcohol) and indirectly on the
whole budgetary revenues and expenditures of most of these countries,
notably since 1890. Much of the foreign borrowing, coinciding with
political interests of the great powers or representing simply speculative investments by international operators, was secured at higher and
higher cost and was often wasted for onerous and utterly unproductive
purposes. Deficit financing was used to nourish plethoric bureaucracies
and impatient armies who promoted aggressive militarist policies in the
area under the cover of "nationalist aspirations." Much of the progress
achieved was ultimately destroyed by the Balkan wars. The transportation network, developed at relatively high costs remained far behind

the growth of railways in West and Central Europe. By 1913, the length of track per 1,000 inhabitants or per unit of surface was roughly three times smaller in the area than in the West. The merciless squeeze of the peasantry, notably in Rumania, undertaken by both landlords and state, under a system rightly called by David Mitrany "Raubwirtschaft," led finally to serious and costly social upheavals.[8] The multiplication of state intervention in the economy was of little help in the formation of an independent national entrepreneurial class. The expansion of the state activities facilitated both the proliferation of a corrupt administration trafficking in influence, and the devolution of entrepreneurial tasks to "pariah" groups of nonethnic origin, persecuted, despised, but ready to pay heavily for the official "protection." The, so to speak, "competitive independence" of the small Balkan lands pushed relentlessly toward the building of ever higher barriers among them instead of facilitating the move toward a broader unity of the area and perhaps toward a more rational utilization of its resources.

The penetration of capitalist economic relations appears to have been stronger in some areas than in others; for example, in the Dual Monarchy and in parts of the Old Rumanian Kingdom, clearly less all-embracing and tardier in Serbia, northern Bulgaria and southern Greece, and finally even less decisive in the mountainous parts of the peninsula, that is, in Bosnia-Hercegovina, Montenegro, Macedonia, Albania (entirely left under the Turkish rule) and southern Bulgaria. The barrenness of the soil, the lack of readily accessible resources, the scanty transportation system and, finally, the great weakness of the developing centers of the area themselves, left thus the heart of the Balkans to slumber in the most primitive conditions. Certainly in retrospect political autonomy was a positive step, especially when we compare its achievements to the overall conditions prevailing under the Ottomans. But one wonders if independence and its fruits would appear to us just as positive, if these small countries would have seceded in these crucial formative years from a more advanced political-economic entity such as for instance the Austro-Hungarian Empire, notwithstanding the latter's ultimate historical failure.

---

[8] See David Mitrany, *The Land and the Peasant in Rumania, the War and Agrarian Reform (1917–1921)*, (London and New Haven, 1930), pp. 571 ff.

INDEPENDENCE, AND OBSTACLES TO DEVELOPMENT

The First World War changed profoundly the political setup and the economic framework of the area. Two countries emerged far stronger than previously: "Greater Rumania" doubled its former territory, population, and industrial capacity; the united South Slav lands aggregated around Serbia constituted five times as large a territory and four times as great a population as prewar Serbia. Rumania and the united South Slav lands were accounting now for 295,000 and 249,000 square kilometers, and for a population of 16,200,000 and 12,400,000. As compared to them, the other Balkan states remained very small. Bulgaria shrunk to 103,000 square kilometers with a population of 5,100,000; Greece increased but only slightly, to 130,000 square kilometers and to a population of 6,000,000. Finally Albania entered the scene after the First World War as an independent entity with a territory of 28,000 square kilometers and a population of less than 800,000.

All the area was badly shattered and disorganized by the great war. Rumania and the united South Slav lands were beset by the difficult problem of fusing into a whole disparate provinces cut for centuries by both natural and man-made barriers, historic, religious, national, or economic in nature. The mistrust of the Transylvanians in the expanding economic and political power of the ruling circles of the Old Rumanian Kingdom was more than matched by the deep hostility of the Croats to the expanding power of the Serbs. Wide regional differences, old centrifugal interests, poor transportation systems, all seemed to lend little cohesion to the kingdom of Serbs, Croats, and Slovenes. Greece, which had engaged in an additional war with Turkey, had to absorb within the framework of its pauperized economy, a large influx of refugees expelled from Anatolia. Finally, all these countries entered the interwar period saddled with the heavy burden of some of the debts of the Ottoman Empire, of the Austro-Hungarian Empire, or of both.

The underlying social and economic structures became everywhere quite similar after the enactment throughout the area of comprehensive land reforms. Roughly 80 percent of the labor force of Rumania, Jugoslavia, and Bulgaria remained engaged in agriculture. The percentage rose even higher for Albania, while it fell to 50 percent for Greece, a country traditionally dependent on trade and sea shipping. Except perhaps in Albania, which persisted essentially as a tribal society, these reforms led to a wide fragmentation of land and to an impressive rise in small subsistence farming accounting for at least two-thirds of the landholdings and for at least one-third of the cultivated land. Given the rapid rate of increase in population and in the labor force, and given the limited capacity of labor intake in industry, increasing pressures on land, productivity margins, and so forth, were accumulating in the countryside. Efforts were made to expand both the cultivated area and the yields but these efforts did not always meet with success. During the interwar years, the area under grains was expanded by 10–20 percent in Rumania, Jugoslavia and Bulgaria, and by as much as 70 percent in Greece where about only one-fourth of the surface of the country is cultivable. In spite of these increases, output fell in Rumania in the 1930's to 90 percent of prewar, due to lagging crop yields and to low productivity per capita. The other main Balkan countries registered increases in yields ranging from 10 to 50 percent, so that certain of their outputs, particularly grains, rose by 30–70 percent over prewar. But even with these advances crop yields and per-capita productivity remained everywhere extremely low by Central or Western European standards. The output increases were secured in the face of an over-all growth in population of 25–30 percent. But, given the decrease in the actual share of exports in agricultural production, the share available for domestic consumption increased in all these countries except Rumania.

Although the largest part of the population was dependent on agriculture, and although agricultural output might have been increased significantly by improving farming methods (notably in respect to crop rotation and the types of seeds used and by increasing investments in fertilizers, irrigation, and storage facilities) little was done with or without governmental help. Except in Greece where the influx of refugees forced the government to turn its attention to agriculture, in the rest of the area the governments failed to help this sector either directly or indirectly. Faced with a falling demand for agricultural produce on the world markets and with the drives toward self-sufficiency of the advanced countries (and on the other hand, incapable either to stop the process of splitting up of landholdings in agriculture or of reducing the demographic pressures), the governments of the area turned their hopes toward industrialization and toward wider state intervention in the economy. As usually happens, however, sharp differences arose about what course industrialization should take. The agrarian parties confusedly aimed at the development of competitive industries close to agriculture and exposed any other policy as a devious plan of "monopoly capitalism." The other parties aimed at developing fully integrated industrial complexes within each national entity without regard to actual factor endowment. After 1930, the Crown—in Rumania and Jugoslavia particularly—chose this second road.

The drive toward autarky and industrialization in fact had begun already in the twenties under rather unfavorable conditions. The end of the war had witnessed the exacerbation of nationalistic and xenophobic policies in the area, and a somewhat haphazard extension of the sphere of the state in industry, banking, transportation, and trade. Under the slogan of "nostrification" directed mostly against the previously dominant nationalities as well as against the new or old minorities,[9] the nationalist leaders cut off many valuable contacts with the Central European banks and enterprises, and many "national" firms were ruined in the process. The state took over the mines, the biggest metallurgical works (in Rumania as well as in Jugoslavia), river and maritime shipping, the railroads, lumber mills, and various other types of enterprises.[10] All of these countries resorted further to borrowing abroad in order to stabilize the currency and restore confidence, to refund some of the prewar or war obligations, to purchase the railroads, or to establish some state institutions. While it is almost impossible to get an accurate figure of the amount of indebtedness thus incurred, the total foreign debt had generally doubled or tripled by the turn of the thirties as compared to prewar.[11] In order to foster industrialization,

---

[9] See L. Pasvolsky, *Economic Nationalism of the Danubian States* (New York, 1928), *passim*.

[10] See my study, "The Role of the State in Economic Growth in Eastern Europe Since 1860," in *The State and Economic Growth*, ed. Hugh G. J. Aitken (New York, 1959), pp. 255–284.

[11] The foreign debt was estimated to have increased in the twenties for Rumania to 678,000,000 dollars, for Yugoslavia to 692,000,000 dollars, and for Greece to 790,000,000 dollars. The estimates for Bulgaria are extremely contradictory as they include or exclude reparations and occupation debts. See U.S. Department of Commerce, Bureau of Foreign and Domestic Commerce, *Rumania: An Economic Handbook* (Washington, D.C., 1924), p. 47; Mirko Lamer, *Weltwirtschaftliche*

the Balkan states further increased the scope of their traditional protectionist policies and continued by legislation to encourage domestic industry. Unfortunately, the slogan of "nostrification" discouraged foreign capital at the very moment when foreign investors were ready and willing to invest. Instead of welcoming foreign investments, the Rumanian Liberal party of the Bratianu launched a policy called *Prin noi înşine* ("Through ourselves"). Simultaneously the Serbs did all they could to limit the influence of the Croatian banks and to cut off their useful connections with Vienna's industrial and banking spheres.[12]

The great depression of the thirties further accented the tendencies toward self-sufficiency: more protectionist measures and legislation to encourage national industry were enacted. The Balkan governments snagged their own drives, however, with erroneous fiscal, monetary, and lending policies. Following the then fashionable standards, these countries tried to balance their budgets by cutting expenditures and increasing taxes.[13] State financial institutions, developed especially for providing credits to private industry, reduced their loans. Truly enough, the cut in expenditures tended to affect economic and education expenditures, while military outlays continued to absorb from 25 to 33 percent of the ordinary budget. If one is tempted to ponder too much about the wisdom of these measures, let me add that the governments were not always successful in their efforts of balancing budgets at lower levels, so that the multiplier effect of the budgets remained positive in most cases. Furthermore, sustained state demand for the products of some domestic industries, reorganizations and mergers, increase in scale and renewal of equipment, led to increased efficiency

---

Verflechtungen Südslaviens (Zagreb, 1933), p. 48; Bickham Sweet-Escott, *Greece, a Political and Economic Survey* 1939–1953 (London and New York, 1954), p. 12. See also *Statistical Yearbook of the League of Nations, 1930–1931* (Geneva, 1931), pp. 217–218.

[12] For the background of the so-called "Croatian Question," see Rudolf Bičanić, *Ekonomska podloga Hrvatskog pitanja* [*Economic Basis of the Croatian Question*], (Zagreb, 1938).

[13] As the League of Nations (*World Economic Report 1938/39* [Geneva, 1939], p. 45) candidly puts it: "In every country for which statistics are available, the total income, when measured in money values, declined seriously during the depression. With this decline in national income there was a decline in the yields of taxation; and, in spite of almost universal attempts to offset this tendency by raising existing rates or by introducing new taxes, there was, in most cases, a serious decline in the revenue of the states."

in some industries. During the late 1930's new branches were established particularly with a view of raising the national military capabilities. In this respect, the state tended again to expand vigorously its
sphere of operation.

According to national statistics, net output of industry computed
at 1938 or 1939 prices rose as compared to 1929 (the last year before
the world depression) by 32 percent in Jugoslavia, 43 percent in Rumania, 75 percent in Greece and 143 percent in Bulgaria (see
graphs.)[14] The increase in plant capacity is hard to ascertain because
of the wide reorganizations and consolidations taking place during the
depression. A crude indicator of this growth is given by the fact that
industry proper (with more than 10–15 workers) doubled its employment capacity[15] (see Table 2). In spite of this growth, the contribution
of industry to national income remained by 1938 of the order of 20–25
percent, marking a relative increase of only 3–5 points as compared to
1926 (see Table 4). The railroad network expanded very little during
the interwar years. Nevertheless rolling stock, passenger and freight
traffic grew appreciably. In terms of the structure of the labor force,
few noteworthy changes were registered as compared to 1920. Agriculture still absorbed 76–80 percent of the labor force in the main Balkan
countries, while industry occupied only 8–10 percent of the gainfully
employed (see Table 5). The effects of industrialization were reflected
in a very limited way in the volume and structure of foreign trade.
Barely 2 percent of the area exports were manufactured goods (see
Table 6).

---

[14] See Stevan Stajić, "Realni nacionalni dohodak Jugoslavije u periodima 1926–
1939, 1947–1956" ["The Real National Income of Jugoslavia in the Periods
1926–1939 and 1947–1956"], in Ekonomski problemi [Economic Problems], (Belgrade, 1957), p. 33; M. G. "Venitul National" ["National Income"], in Enciclopedia Romăniei [Encyclopedia of Rumania], (Bucharest, 1940), IV, 941–966;
National Bank of Greece, I Directives for Economic Policy (G. J. Pesmazoglu) and
II Greek Economy in 1949, annex to first report (Athens, 1950); Dr. As. Chakalov,
Nationalniiat dokhod i razhod na Bulgariia 1924–1945 [National Income and Out-
lay of Bulgaria], (Sofia, 1946), p. 114.

[15] Given the shifts in pattern of business connections, industry tended to develop
faster in and around the capital cities. Industrial employment grew faster in Bucharest and in the Old Kingdom, or in Belgrade and in Serbia, than in the rest of the
country; conversely, employment stagnated or decreased in some of the newly
acquired provinces.

The ratio of foreign trade to national income was reduced significantly by: the breakdown of the traditional trade patterns after 1929, the subsequent increasing resort to clearing systems, the placing of transactions on a bilateral basis, the wide use of import and export licenses and of restrictive quotas. Worsening terms of trade and unfavorable balances for invisible transactions conditioned sharp drops in trade throughout the thirties. In the late twenties, the total trade turnover of Rumania, Jugoslavia, Greece, and Bulgaria was 350,000,000, 270,000,-000, 260,000,000, and 105,000,000. In 1934, this turnover fell for the same countries to 154,000,000, 85,000,000, 80,000,000, and 34,000,000. "Greater Rumania" traded less than the Old Kingdom whose trade turnover reached 157 million dollars in 1913. Small Albania, a semi-colony of Italy since 1928, traded in 1934 for a total of only 3,700,000 dollars.[16] The fall in the value of exports, of receipts from services and from remittances, the impossibility of securing new foreign loans, forced all these countries finally to default on their foreign debts. It is in this environment that Germany renewed its penetration into the area and revived its notorious theories of "Grossraumwirtschaft." The Balkan countries were attached through bilateral strings and high clearing prices to the German war machine, in a period in which, alas, the world market had virtually fallen apart.

One may view the period 1925 to 1935 as the acme of the independence of these countries: by 1925 the French influence was on the wane; by 1935, the German penetration was only beginning to assert itself in force. Unfortunately, it was in this particular period that the impact of the world depression on these countries was the greatest. A gigantic backlog of backwardness, increasing demographic pressures, consistently erroneous economic policies, insuperable nationalist barriers to fruitful coöperation in the area, all but arrested the process of economic growth. After hovering around the level reached in 1929, the per-capita income by 1939 grew 2 percent in Jugoslavia, 8 percent in Rumania, 11 percent in Greece, and 35 percent in Bulgaria. Even then the per-capita income may be estimated to have fluctuated to between 70 dollars (Greece) and 130 dollars (Bulgaria). This fact illustrates that the area remained, along with a few other countries, the most depressed part of Europe.

---

[16] All these figures are in pre-1933 dollars.

SELECTED ECONOMIC INDICATORS
FOR
1885-1913, 1926-1939, 1939 & 1948-1958

RUMANIA (up to 1913 Old Kingdom only)

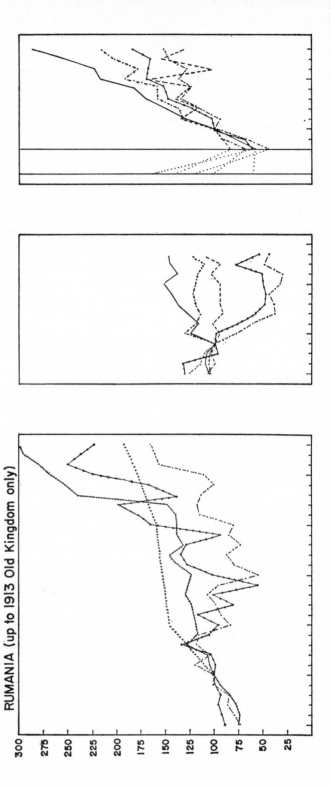

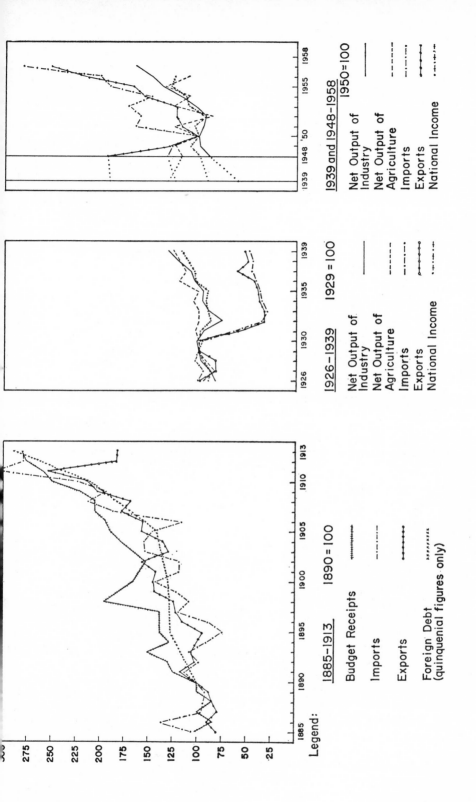

Legend:

1885-1913	1890=100
Budget Receipts	┼┼┼┼┼┼┼
Imports	─ ·· ─ ·· ─
Exports	●─●─●─●
Foreign Debt (quinquenial figures only)	∙∙∙∙∙∙∙∙∙

1926-1939	1929 = 100
Net Output of Industry	────────
Net Output of Agriculture	─ ─ ─ ─ ─
Imports	─ · ─ · ─
Exports	●─●─●─●
National Income	─ ·· ─ ·· ─

1939 and 1948-1958	1950=100
Net Output of Industry	────────
Net Output of Agriculture	─ ─ ─ ─ ─
Imports	─ · ─ · ─
Exports	●─●─●─●
National Income	─ ·· ─ ·· ─

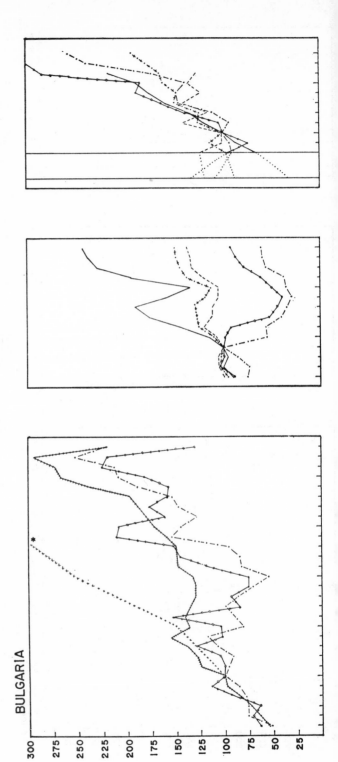

SELECTED ECONOMIC INDICATORS
FOR
1885–1913, 1926–1939, 1939 & 1948–1958

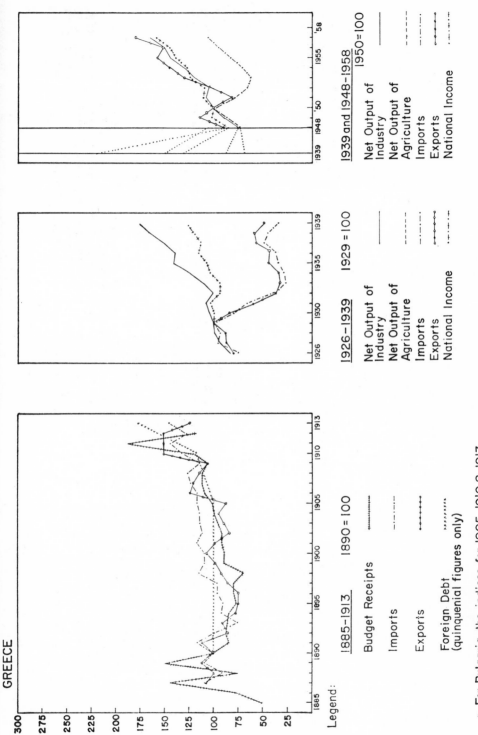

GREECE

Legend:

	1885-1913	1890 = 100
Budget Receipts	··········	
Imports	─·─·─	
Exports	●─●─●	
Foreign Debt (quinquenial figures only)	··········	

	1926-1939	1929 = 100
Net Output of Industry	──────	
Net Output of Agriculture	─·─·─	
Imports	─·─·─	
Exports	○─○─○	
National Income	─··─··─	

	1939 and 1948-1958	1950=100
Net Output of Industry	──────	
Net Output of Agriculture	─·─·─	
Imports	··········	
Exports	○─○─○	
National Income	─··─··─	

* For Bulgaria the indices for 1905, 1910 & 1913 were 319, 466, & 790 respectively.

TABLE 2

Plants[a] and Gainfully Employed in Industry Proper
(Selected years 1910–1957)

	1910[b]		1920		1928		1938		1948		1957[c]	
	Plants	Employed	Plants	Employed	Plants	Employed	Plants	Employed	Plants	Employed	Plants	Employed
Rumania	1,239	111,900	2,747	157,400	3,966	206,500	3,878	373,000	3,834	458,000[d]	1,940	935,500
Jugoslavia	1,140	...	1,855	174,900	3,038	278,600	2,976	301,000	...	452,000	2,370	812,400
Bulgaria	345	15,800	500	...	500	...	1,314	103,000	623	196,400	741	357,600

a "Plants" with more than 10 workers up to 1948; with more than 15 workers for 1957.

b Prewar data include for Rumania: 847 plants with 58,800 workers for the Old Kingdom and 382 plants with 53,000 workers for Transylvania; for Jugoslavia: 172 plants for Serbia, 322 for Croatia, 367 for Slovenia, and 279 for the rest of the country.

c 1956 for Bulgaria.

d Estimated.

SOURCES: 1910: Rumania: Arcadian, *op. cit.*, pp. 169 ff.; Jugoslavia: Tomasevich, *op. cit.*, p. 171; Bulgaria: *Istoria Bolgarii*, Vol. I, *op. cit.*, and L. Pasvolski, *Bulgaria's Economic Position* (Washington, 1930), p. 29. 1920 and 1928: Rumania: Arcadian, *op. cit.*, pp. 169 ff.; Jugoslavia: S. M. Kukoleca, *Industrija Jugoslavije 1918–1938* [*The Industry of Jugoslavia*], (Belgrade, 1941), p. 74; Bulgaria: Pasvolski, *op. cit.*, p. 214. 1938: Rumania: *Anuarul statistic al Romaniei 1939 şi 1940* [*Statistical Yearbook of Rumania 1939 and 1940*], (Bucharest, 1940), p. 347; Jugoslavia: Kukoleca, *ibid.*; Bulgaria: *Statisticheski godishnik 1939* [*Statistical Yearbook 1939*], (Sofia, 1939), p. 387. 1948 and 1957: For all: Spulber, *op. cit.*, chap. iii, *passim*; and B. Kisewetter, *Statistiken zur Wirtschaft Ost- und Südosteuropas* (Berlin, 1955), p. 10. For Rumania also: *Anuarul statistic al R.P.R. 1959* [*Statistical Yearbook of the Rumanian People's Republic*, 1959], (Bucharest, 1959), pp. 98–101. For Jugoslavia also: *Statisticki godisnjak FNRJ 1958* [*Statistical Yearbook of Yugoslavia*, 1958], p. 138. For Bulgaria also: *Statisticheski godishnik na narod. Rep. Bulg. 1956* [*Statistical Yearbook of the Bulgarian People's Republic*, 1956], p. 38.

TABLE 3

Shifts in the Employment Structure of Industry

(Absolute figures and percentages of total employment in key industries in or around 1938, 1948–1950, 1956–1958)

Industry	Rumania						Jugoslavia						Bulgaria					
	1938		1950		1958		1938		1950		1958		1938		1950		1958	
	000	per cent	000	per cent	000	per cent	000	per cent	000	per cent	000	per cent	000	per cent	000	per cent	000	per cent
Mining	69	18.5	46.6	7.2	69.2	7.0	58	19.2	79.7	12.6	84.9	10.4	11.0	10.6	4.6	2.3	24.3	6.8
Machinery and metal-working	51	13.6	154.8	24.1	241.4	24.6	...		190.0	30.1	256.5	31.5	6.0	5.8	23.9	12.1	57.7	16.1
Chemicals	28	7.5	13.1	2.0	29.0	2.9	12	3.9	19.1	3.0	26.5	3.2	4.0	3.8	1.7	0.8	9.5	2.6
Construction materials	...		36.3	5.6	64.1	6.5	...	...	38.3	6.0	41.1	5.0	...	...	9.0	4.5	17.6	4.9
Wood-working	63	16.9	52.5	8.2	98.5	9.1	76	25.2	94.5	15.0	85.0	10.4	6.0	5.8	41.3	21.0	46.8	13.0
Textile	74	19.8	85.0	13.2	113.0	11.5	61	20.2	84.9	13.4	118.6	14.5	32.0	31.0	37.6	19.1	58.6	16.3
Leather	13	3.4	35.4	5.5	42.9	4.3	6	2.0	18.5	2.9	24.8	3.0	4.0	3.8	2.6	1.3	6.2	1.7
Food processing (and tobacco)	38	10.1	67.7	10.5	90.3	9.2	40	13.2	51.8	8.2	85.0	10.4	33.0	32.0	38.0	19.3	63.1	17.
Total industrial employment	373	100.0	640.4	100.0	979.2	100.0	301	100.0	629.2	100.0	812.4	100.0	103.0	100.0	196.4	100.0	357.6	100.0

sources: As in Table 2.

TABLE 4

CHANGES IN THE STRUCTURE OF NATIONAL INCOME
1926, 1938, 1948, 1957
(In percent)

		Income by industrial origin[a]			
		1926	1938	1948	1957
Rumania	Industry	21.1	25.5	35.8	52.3
	Construction	3.1	2.9	3.5	7.7
	Agriculture	60.2	53.2	47.1	28.7
	Transportation	3.6	5.4	4.8	5.9
	Trade	12.0	13.0	8.8	5.4
	Other				
Jugoslavia	Industry	17.4	20.3	29.4	38.3
	Construction	1.6	1.8	5.4	3.7
	Agriculture	53.4	52.2	44.5	32.1
	Transportation	4.8	5.5	3.5	5.2
	Trade	12.5	11.8	12.2	13.3
	Other	10.3	8.4	5.0	7.4
Bulgaria	Industry	14.8	20.2	31.9	...
	Construction	0.8	1.7	4.6	...
	Agriculture	71.4	63.1	52.2	...
	Transportation	2.2	2.9	2.6	...
	Trade	10.8	12.1	8.7	...
	Other				
Greece	Industry	...	20.0	24.3	22.4
	Construction	...	...	...	4.0
	Agriculture	...	40.8	40.0	35.8
	Transportation	...	6.0	6.7	5.9
	Trade	...	11.9	11.2	12.0
	Other	...	21.3	17.8	19.9

[a] Underlying data: Rumania and Jugoslavia at 1938 prices; Bulgaria at 1939 prices; Greece 1938 at 1938 prices; others at 1954 prices.

SOURCES: For Rumania 1926, 1938: M.G., "Venitul National," *op. cit.*; 1948 and 1957: *Anuarul statistic al R. P. R. 1959* (as in table 2), p. 83.

For Jugoslavia: Stajić, *op. cit.*

For Bulgaria 1926, 1938: Khristo Popov, *Sushtnost, methodologiia i izchislenie na narodniia dokhod* [Nature, Method and Computation of National Income], (Sofia, 1951), p. 134; 1948: *Planovo stopanstvo* [*Planned Economy*] Year VIII, No. 11 (Sofia, 1953), p. 21.

For Greece: Pesmazoglou, *op. cit.*; *Yearbook of National Accounts Statistics, 1957 and 1958* (Geneva, 1958 and 1959), pp. 89, 93.

TABLE 5

STRUCTURE OF THE LABOR FORCE IN SELECTED YEARS

(In percent)

		1910[a]	1920	1939	1949[b]	1955[c]
Rumania	Agriculture	79.5	...	80.0	73.8	69.2
	Mining and industry	8.0	...	9.1	12.1	13.1
	Trade	2.7	...	2.9	2.0	2.6
	Other	9.8	...	8.0	12.1	15.1
Jugoslavia	Agriculture	...	78.9	76.3	78.3	70.4
	Mining and industry	...	9.9	10.0	12.0	13.1
	Trade	...	4.3	4.2	9.7	3.2
	Other	...	6.9	9.5	...	13.3
Bulgaria	Agriculture	81.9	82.4	80.0	81.8	71.8
	Mining and industry	8.0	8.1	8.0	8.4	12.1
	Trade	3.1	2.7	3.1	2.3	3.0
	Other	7.0	6.8	8.9	7.5	13.1
Greece	Agriculture	46.0	49.6	...	55.6	...
	Mining and industry	26.4	16.2	...	16.1	...
	Trade	11.1	8.1	...	9.0	...
	Other	16.5	26.1	...	19.3	...

[a] Rumania, 1913; Bulgaria, 1910; Greece, 1907.
[b] Rumania, 1950; Jugoslavia, 1948; Bulgaria, 1949; Greece, 1951.
[c] Rumania and Bulgaria, 1955; Jugoslavia, 1953.
SOURCES: 1910: *Statistical Yearbook of the League of Nations 1930/31* (Geneva, 1931), pp. 44–45; for Greece also: Andreades, et al., *op. cit.*, pt. IV, p. 11.
1920: Bulgaria and Greece: *Statistical Yearbook of the League of Nations*, pp. 44–45; for Jugoslavia: Božidar Jurković, *Das ausländische Kapital in Jugoslavien* (Berlin, 1941), p. 108.
1939: Spulber, *op. cit.*, p. 5.
1949 and 1955: *Economic Survey of Europe in 1957* (Geneva, 1958), chap. vii, p. 61; for Rumania also: *Anuarul statistic al R. P. R. 1959*, p. 87; for Jugoslavia also: P. F. Meyers and A. A. Campbell, *The Population of Yugoslavia* (Washington, 1954), p. 73; for Greece also: Bickham Sweet-Escott, *op. cit.*, p. 177.

368 NICOLAS SPULBER

TABLE 6

STRUCTURE OF FOREIGN TRADE IN 1938, 1948, 1956

(In percent)

Type of goods		Imports			Exports		
		1938	1948	1956	1938	1948	1956
Rumania	Manufactured goods	68.3	47.4	43.1	1.9	7.2	19.6
	Raw materials and semi-manufactured goods	27.3	48.2	50.3	64.3	44.1	57.2
	Foodstuffs and live animals	4.4	4.4	6.6	33.8	48.7	23.2
Jugoslavia	Manufactured goods	44.8	58.7	33.8	0.8	14.6	27.3
	Raw materials and semi-manufactured goods	50.1	35.9	33.1	49.5	36.0	35.4
	Foodstuffs and live animals	5.1	5.4	33.1	49.7	49.4	37.3
Bulgaria	Manufactured goods	68.0	39.1	59.6	2.0	1.1	18.8
	Raw materials and semi-manufactured goods	31.5	51.5	38.7	66.6	10.4	36.9
	Foodstuffs and live animals	0.5	9.4	1.7	31.4	88.5	44.3
Greece	Manufactured goods	41.8	49.7	42.0	...	...	...
	Raw materials and semi-manufactured goods	29.6	26.8	37.8	25.1	15.9	30.3
	Foodstuffs and live animals	28.6	23.5	20.2	74.9	84.1	69.7

SOURCES: 1938: Spulber, *op. cit.*, p. 8.
1948 and 1956: For Rumania and Bulgaria: *Economic Survey of Europe* (Geneva, 1958), pp. A-53 and 58; for Rumania also: *Probleme economice* [*Economic Problems*], Bucharest, X (Dec. 1957), 32, 33; for Jugoslavia: *Jugoslovenski pregled* [*Jugoslav Review*], (April, 1957), pp. 48 ff.; for Greece: Bickham Sweet-Escott, *op. cit.*, pp. 185, 186.

ECONOMIC GROWTH DURING THE 1950's

The Balkan countries emerged in the aftermath of the Second World War profoundly shaken politically and socially, and widely disorganized or utterly destroyed in certain regions—notably in parts of Jugoslavia and of Greece. The civil war in this latter country further annihilated a great share of human and material resources. Enormous

efforts were made, with and without help from the outside, to overcome war destruction, restore economic processes, and foster sustained
economic growth. The Communist parties which gained control in all
of the Balkans except Greece, swept away some of the social and
economic barriers in the countryside, limited sharply or annihilated
in some instances the basis of private ownership in agriculture, and in
the process opened the way to a wide reorganization of this key sector
of their economy. Industry, banking, transportation, and trade, were
completely nationalized. By 1948 or 1949, all former private enterprises were taken over, merged, reconditioned, and reorganized as autonomous state firms.[17]

Along with this restructuring of the economy, the Communists
stepped up sharply the rate of investment. From 20 to 30 percent of
the "net material product"—that is, net national product excluding
services—was methodically earmarked in each of the Communist-controlled countries for gross fixed investment. With some 10–15 percent
going for other government uses, the share of private consumption was
reduced in these countries to 55–70 percent of the yearly product. All
Communist Balkan countries then set out to reproduce in miniature the
Soviet economy. By a quirk of fate, communism at the moment of its
expansion became more hypernationalistic than all the supernational-
ists of the interwar period put together. The attempt to reproduce in
microcosm the Soviet economy implied a given pattern of investment
and a sustained effort of developing within each national entity a whole
set of industrial branches hardly, if at all, developed by them until
then. All these countries, including Jugoslavia—which broke away from
Soviet dogma in many respects but not in this one—started to channel
50–60 percent of their investments to industry. Out of these investments, the lion's share has been allocated to ferrous mining and metal-
lurgy and to machine construction. The rest of the 40–50 percent has
been split up between the other sectors, with a share usually of 8–13
percent of the total (that is, 1.5–3 percent of the national product)
going to agriculture.

The stepping up of the share of investment in income to roughly
four to five times its prewar rate, the increase in the share of industry
to at least half of all investments (to 10 or 15 percent of the total prod-

---

[17] For details for the subsequent discussion, see my book *The Economics of
Communist Eastern Europe* (New York, 1957), notably chaps. ix and xii.

uct, as compared to at best 2 percent during the late thirties) has led to impressive increases in output and employment in industry in general, and in output and employment particularly in the so-called key branches.[18] Between 1950 and 1958, the labor intake in the medium and large industry in Rumania, Jugoslavia, and Bulgaria roughly equaled the total industrial employment in these countries in 1939. In 1958, total industrial employment varied between two and a half and three times its prewar level. The leading machinery and metal-working branches increased their employment capacity five to nine times in the same period. In 1958, Bulgaria was producing 211,000 tons of steel, as against 6,000 in 1938; Rumania 934,000 as against 284,000 previously; Jugoslavia, 1,120,000 as against 230,000. Other key industrial outputs, such as electricity and cement, have increased in an impressive way. Output and employment in the consumer-goods branches, and particularly in textile and food processing, have also increased, but relatively less. It should be noted moreover in this connection that a large share of the textile output in Rumania and Bulgaria represents only contract work for the Soviet Union: Soviet raw materials are processed in these countries and reëxported to the U.S.S.R.

While heavy industry has become the top priority sector, agriculture has developed under the sign of low investment priority, heavy taxation of the remaining private holdings, and forced collectivization—except in Jugoslavia where the drive toward collectivization collapsed in 1951. According to the plans drawn for this sector, the areas sown for bread grains were to be reduced, while larger yields were to be secured through increased use of fertilizers and through wide mechanization. The land removed from grain was to provide an increase in land for industrial crops along with an expansion in fodder needed for an increasing livestock population. But on numerous counts the results were quite different from those expected throughout the 1950's, and particularly so in some bad years. As compared to prewar, wheat output has hardly increased in Rumania, Jugoslavia, and Bulgaria; corn output has decreased in most years (except in 1955 and 1957 in Rumania); potatoes have increased only slightly, while the outputs of industrial plants or fodder have hardly kept up with the scheduled needs. The lack of stable fodder supplies has, among other factors, hampered the development of livestock, which has progressed only slightly as com-

---

[18] For employment data, see Tables 2 and 3.

pared to prewar. As before, agriculture is still afflicted by low crop yields and low productivity per capita. Improvements in this respect have been extremely small. The per-capita supply is generally lower in the area than before the war. In order to cope with the needs of an expanding population and with the needs arising from the trend toward urbanization, these former grain-exporting countries had to change in numerous postwar years into grain importers. The glowing plans of increasing outputs by applying "modern techniques" have been thwarted by the small amount of investment left to this sector, the poor state of the equipment available, and last but not least, the reluctance of the peasants to work in and for the collectives. Most of the livestock continues to be raised on the small private plots left to the (collectivized) peasant homesteads: the collectives themselves have failed to keep up with the scheduled goals both in quantity and quality of livestock output.

The industrialization plans of Rumania, Bulgaria, Albania, like those of other Central European countries under Soviet influence (Poland, Czechoslovakia, East Germany) and partly also like those of Jugoslavia even though the latter cut its ties with the Soviet bloc, followed basically the same strategy of economic development, placed the same sector emphases, and led to increases in the same type of outputs. Since each of these countries aims at "all-round" development, each stressed the necessity of developing the same type of goods within its economy, even those whose cost previously appeared prohibitive. Now the attempt to solve the problems of industrialization in each nation separately necessitates the abandoning of international specialization and a lowering of the efficiency investment. Countries lacking basic resources on which to erect the industrialization structure are placed in a precarious position from the outset, since their planned development lessens their ability to export and to make good their deficiencies through import.

Soviet Russia's position as related to this scheme of development is shaped by its large foreign-trade possibilities as supplier of raw materials and as net importer of manufactured goods. As the industrialization on parallel lines of these various countries continued, they have had to enter into heavier and heavier competition among themselves both for the Soviet Union's raw materials and for the Soviet Union's (and China's) markets. This fact put serious brakes on the future industrialization plans of the Balkan countries—the least suited for competition within the bloc—and forced them to search eagerly for other markets in the nonbloc underdeveloped areas. There has been much talk about simultaneity in the launching of the long-term plans of all Soviet-bloc countries, consideration at the planning stage of the other countries' availabilities and structure of investment and outputs, limitation of autarkic tendencies, and coördination of key tasks. However, relatively little has been achieved in this direction. Each of these countries remains deeply committed to the dogma of the "undisputed priority" of heavy industry as the basis of "Socialist construction" in each unit. Few departures have been made from this dogma. Although a Council of Mutual Economic Assistance (CEMA) has been established in order to coördinate both the output and the foreign-trade plans of the Soviet Union and of the east-central European countries pertaining to its zone of influence, the Council has not modified the previously devised system of negotiation and establishment of trade relations on a bilateral basis. Planning of output and trade are drawn in the area within the framework of each "sovereign" state: coördination is achieved only piecemeal through laborious negotiation both in and outside the CEMA.

There can be little doubt that the enacting of wide nationalizations and the channeling of the available savings according to planned targets have placed powerful resources and tools in the hands of these states. It is possible in these conditions to increase capital formation at a rapid pace and to achieve economic growth according to the priorities set by the planners. However, the methodical implementation of the Soviet strategy of industrialization and the sharp reduction in the share of consumption which it entails at least for decades, creates imbalances and strains in the economy which at certain junctures assume an explosive character (such as the upheavals in Poland and Hungary in 1956). The keeping of consumption at very low levels in spite of rapid expansions in total product, the often ensuing corrosion of the will to work and the breakdown in the system of incentives, are inevitable aspects of the thrust of industrialization in the Soviet bloc.

While Rumania and Bulgaria have relied essentially on their own investment capabilities to carry out their plans and have received in fact only small credits from the Soviet Union, Jugoslavia and Greece have received substantial United States aid representing in some years for the former up to 5 percent of its gross yearly product and for the latter up to 15 percent. It must be noted, however, that Jugoslavia was placed in a very difficult situation after its expulsion from the Soviet bloc in 1948, and before its full readjustment to the international market in 1953, while Greece had for its part been devastated by the civil war. The data available suggest slower increases in both total product and industrial output for Jugoslavia and Greece than for Rumania, Bulgaria, or Albania. The underlying computations at prewar prices for the latter countries are open to numerous criticisms and, therefore, the data must be viewed with some suspicion. It is clear that for the area as a whole the fifties have been a period of growth at rates probably never matched in the past. High investment rates, plus generous outside help for some of these countries, have rendered the period a decisive one in the development of the area. In comparing the trends of net material product and of import and export indices (see graphs) one may note the growing dependence of Jugoslavia and Bulgaria on imports. Worsening terms of trade for all have enforced, moreover, the tendency toward a more rapid rise in exports, especially since 1953. The latter have started to reflect clearly by now the significant effort of industrialization undertaken in the area (see Table 5).

CONCLUSIONS

The following concluding remarks can be made as to the nature, scope, direction and limitations of the over-all process of economic development of the Balkans since 1860 on the basis of an examination of the changes or lack of changes in the economic structures of the area:

Changes have taken place in industry with respect to employment capacity, pattern of activity, and size groups of plants:

Industrial employment capacity within the same territory has roughly doubled in the interwar period and has again approximately doubled between 1948 and 1957. The ratio of the labor force in industry proper to total population has shifted slightly.

The pattern of industrial activity has changed significantly in most of the areas both in terms of employment and of output. Within the total industrial labor force, the shares of employment in machinery construction and in the metal-working industries have increased considerably, while those for textiles and food processing industries have appreciably decreased (see Table 3). The ratios of the gross value of output of capital goods to total value of industrial output have risen concurrently in the area except for Greece.

Considerable change has occurred in the relative position of the size groups of plants. The number of plants with more than 50 workers has grown as compared to prewar; those with more than 500 workers take now a far larger share in total employment than previously. Some very large plants—with more than 5000 workers each —are now in operation (in Rumania, for instance).

The process of industrialization has been accompanied by a systematic expansion in state ownership and state economic activity. Weaknesses of private entrepreneurship as well as great national emergencies such as wars or depressions have furthered this expansion. Only during short intervals in the interwar period have contrary tendencies manifested themselves with sufficient vigor. The processes of industrialization and of state expansion would most probably have ceased to grow together as higher levels of development were reached. The postwar development does not contradict this hypothesis. The all-embracing nationalization of 1948–1950 was not an "organic growth" of past processes. It evidently had its source in a set of completely different factors from those which have fostered the growth of the state sphere in the past.

On the basis of numerous criteria—such as growth in capital formation, growth in income, growth in industrial output—the 1948–1960 period can be characterized as a period of vigorous growth at rates unsurpassed by these countries in the past. Growth has been achieved in the Communist-controlled countries through a sharp increase in the rate of investment and through an allocation of resources leading to unbalanced sectoral growth. These, of course, are tenets of the Soviet strategy of industrialization. Following this strategy the Communist countries have attempted to achieve high rates of growth by increasing capital–labor ratios and productivity in industry, while agriculture is left far behind. It can be expected that during the sixties labor intake in industry will grow at relatively lower rates as related to total population growth, while capital intensity will further increase in the key

branches. Because of these factors the shifts in the pattern of employment of the total labor force will probably remain relatively small. The
share of the population employed in agriculture will continue to be
large and, furthermore, some areas will continue to remain primitive.

The fact that these economies are small—having a small domestic
market because of size of population and level of its income—has hampered substantially their development. How much more might one have
expected before 1914 from the then Balkan lands, backward specks of
land with minute populations, poorly located in relation to the world
commercial centers, and poorly endowed? Size and endowment have
barely changed in the period 1948–1960 as compared to the interwar
years. The former is a period of growth, while the latter was a period
of near-stagnation. "Size" up to a point can thus be offset by the capacity of the state to depress brutally consumption levels and to step
up considerably the investible resources. In the period 1948–1960 "location" has changed since the Balkans have now open before them the
sheltered Russian and Chinese markets. Even a very high ratio of investment to domestic product is unable to propel into sustained growth
small countries such as Bulgaria and Albania. Their efforts, without
massive outside help, can lead only to limited results. As the intra-
planned economies market becomes glutted with the same products,
the absurdity of pursuing economic development on strictly the same
pattern by each of these countries will become increasingly obvious
during the sixties.

Political, historical, and nationalistic factors stand in the way of a
more efficient allocation of resources in the Balkans through a broad
division of labor within the area. It is apparent that the creation of
Soviet microcosms in each national unit—whatever its size of resources
might be—leads to strains, duplication of the same facilities and hence
waste of resources, and to misconceptions as to what development
should mean not only in terms of rates of growth, but also in terms of
the welfare of the population.

POLITICS IN A SMALL STATE:

THE BALKAN EXAMPLE

Henry L. Roberts

In his introduction to a recent study Hugh Seton-Watson remarks: "Of all my travels I think the most enlightening were in the Balkans, whose combination of intellectual subtlety and crudity, of tortuous intrigue and honest courage revealed more truths about the political animal man than are to be found in most textbooks of political science." [1] This curiously revealing quality of Balkan politics has been experienced by many Western visitors and has undoubtedly been an important, if not always conscious, motive for further study of—and often passionate identification with—the tangled vicissitudes of this area.

There are perhaps two principal reasons why the life of the Balkans seems to provide such insights into the nature of politics and politicians. The first is the peculiar combination they present of the familiar and the unfamiliar, the recognizably European and the specifically Balkan. It is this, one may suppose, that leads to the impression of startling contrasts in behavior which Seton-Watson mentions. To the attentive Western observer the phenomena of Balkan politics give fuller meaning and clarity to one's whole political vocabulary, to such terms and categories as law, representation, party, leadership, or community. It is not that political life is more primitive or simpler, but rather that the shift in meaning and emphasis gives us a stereoscopic sense of seeing politics in three dimensions.

One of our principal imports from the Balkans has been its rich treasury of political aphorisms, jokes, and cartoons. These pungent

---

[1] Hugh Seton-Watson, *Neither War Nor Peace: The Struggle for Power in the Postwar World* (New York: Praeger, 1960), p. 15.

commentaries about political life gain their force and clarity precisely from this dissonant quality: a sharpened sense of reality through a distortion of familiar appearances. This effect is not the result just of difference. We do not seem to get the same *political* perceptions from a study, say, of the nilotic tribes of the Sudan or even of the advanced cultures of Eastern Asia: there the dissimilarities are too great.

A second reason is the sense, perhaps an erroneous one, that these smaller political entities in the Balkans are somehow more graspable than such vast political complexes as the United States or the highly articulated societies of Western Europe. It often seems, in studying the politics of the Balkans, that there are only a relatively small number of people who count politically. At times a single individual could almost stand for a social category. Mr. X and Y, by their ownership of the only two steel plants in the country are, in effect, Heavy Industry. A group of people arguing in one corner of a room at a reception are the Intellectuals. Count K. is the archetype of all *eminences grises,* and so on. This is undoubtedly an optical illusion that could lead to some dangerous simplifications, and yet, by following the actions of a relatively manageable number of people one does get a vivid sense of the movement of politics.

Strangely enough, however, this illuminating quality of Balkan politics seems, in the final analysis, to cast light on other areas more than on the Balkans themselves. As Seton-Watson suggests, the Balkans have been important to him for a general understanding of man and politics. Certainly one feels a more acute perception in dealing with American and Western European politics after some exposure to Balkan politics. And yet Balkan politics themselves remain obscure. The whetstone stays dull though it sharpens the knife.

The reason is not particularly mysterious: study of the Balkans forces us to pay more critical attention to the meaning and application of analytical categories that were, on the whole, developed in our own societies, and hence makes better tools of them. But the Balkan reality itself, the extent to which it can be explained by these tools remains uncertain.

So it is that the Balkans have been a marvelous training school for political scientists and diplomats,[2] and yet our understanding of Balkan

---

[2] I am grateful for Mr. Rothschild's observation in his comment on the first draft of this essay: " 'The Balkans as a testing ground' is not, of course, a new image.

politics still leaves much to be desired. We can hardly claim a satisfactory grasp of many vital features of Balkan politics in their evolution during the past century and a half: the actual functioning of political institutions, the full meaning of elections and electoral procedures, the reality and measure of public opinion, the background and recruitment of political leadership, and indeed the whole relationship of national political structure to peasant communities or local politics.

Yet it is clear that there is no easy answer for this difficulty, which confronts the Balkan student of Balkan affairs as much as it does his Western colleague. Indeed, the Balkan scholar may suffer an additional disadvantage. In times past at least, he was obliged to go to the West to pick up the tools of political and historical analysis, which he then brought back to apply to his own nation. Often this meant that he might not be as surefooted and critical about these Western tools as his Western colleague; at worst there was the temptation to use them as magical devices for purposes of incantation and ritual. All students of the Balkans have, in their reading, encountered the disconcerting phenomenon of a Balkan scholar using some wholly inapposite formula or principle from a Western writer to buttress an observation about the local scene, feeling that somehow this provided weight and authority for his position.

There is probably no solution except much more spade work at the level of raw data, whether of the written word or as immediate experience, and through it the development of appropriate tools of analysis and classification. We may be reluctant to realize how culture-bound our measuring instruments are in the social sciences. But it is well to recognize that we do not possess universal measurements, on deposit in some bureau of standards and applicable to all societies, but that there has been a close interplay between our intellectual categories and the societies out of which they have emerged as a means of ordering and, hopefully, controlling experience.

Given this perspective, the present essay could hardly hope to present any general interpretation of Balkan politics. Nor, regrettably, was

---

In the non-academic world, for example, a significant proportion of American governmental and semi-governmental personnel at present attempting to cope with the problems of the Afro-Asian countries received its training, so to speak, for such work in the Balkans, which have thus retrospectively become the original underdeveloped area. Soviet Russian foreign missions manifest a similar tendency."

it possible here to attempt even a modest contribution to the spade work that is so necessary. Rather, in the hope of stimulating future exploration, it is limited to some speculations on a single but possibly fruitful question: the influence of the Balkan states' position as "small powers" in the nineteenth and twentieth centuries upon the operation of their domestic political systems and upon the style and attitudes of the politicians themselves. It is the thesis of this essay, at least as a hypothesis warranting testing, that this factor of smallness has had significant and continuing effect.

On the face of it there would be good reason to suspect the existence of such an influence. Their relatively small size and population, the proximity of far larger and more powerful neighbors, their location in a region of prolonged and intense international pressures, and the fact that from their very origins as independent sovereignties the histories of the Balkan states have involved relations between great powers and small powers—all this would suggest more than casual consequences for domestic politics.

And yet these consequences are not as easy to identify and demonstrate as it might seem. For one thing it is always hard to sort out and evaluate the possible causes for anything so complex as a pattern of political life. Obviously many features of Balkan politics may be entirely unrelated to the size of these states; other essays in this volume indicate at least two other important influences: the impact of the West and the domestic social structures. Moreover, the wide diversity of political behavior within the different Balkan states, not to speak of other small powers, would indicate that, whatever the influence may be, it can find a variety of expressions.

There is, of course, no lack of easy generalizations about this presumed relationship between small-power status and domestic politics, but it is doubtful whether these advance our understanding very much, if only because most of them have arisen from an effort to place some kind of blame for the frequently untidy state of Balkan affairs. Thus, spokesmen for the Balkan states, taking off from Lord Acton's too frequently quoted observation about the corrupting effect of power, have been inclined to argue that the greed and ambition of the large neighboring states have constantly thwarted or upset the efforts of the Balkan states to establish orderly political communities. This argument is not without weight. It is not difficult to cite occasions when invasions or periods of occupation completely upset domestic political life. The periods of Nazi and Soviet occupation or hegemony are but recent, and spectacular, examples. Nevertheless, this argument is not wholly persuasive. In the first place, the historical image it creates of great-power policies and appetites is overly simplified and does not do justice either to the complexity of considerations that have determined the foreign policies of great powers or to the ambiguous effects of great-power intervention. It was, after all, a Russian occupation that brought the first constitutional instruments, the *Règlements Organiques,* to the Danubian Principalities. Moreover, it is by no means certain that the ups and downs of Balkan political life are attributable to these external influences. For example, it is doubtful that the breakdown of constitutional regimes in Balkan states during the interwar period is directly or chiefly the consequence of great-power interference. It has been suggested that the international developments leading to the Anschluss and the destruction of Czechoslovakia prompted King Carol II to establish his dictatorship in the spring of 1938.[3] While the climate of the times probably encouraged such a step, Carol had not been a friend of the parliamentary system and his move to personal rule antedated the downfall of Austria. In the case of the somewhat earlier establishment of authoritarian regimes in Jugoslavia and Bulgaria, however, the reasons appear to have been largely domestic.

In contrast to the picture of the Balkans as Sisyphus laboring vainly against inroads by the great powers, there is the theme of Balkan "immaturity" and "irresponsibility." Proceeding from the view that impotence, not power, corrupts, it is argued that, because of the long experience of subjugation and dependence, Balkan politics in the emerging national states were chaotic, chauvinistic, and lacking in measure and balance. Hence, the great powers, by necessity concerned with areas of potential danger, were obliged to come in as trouble shooters, whether competently or incompetently. Again this argument has some weight. One can think of the efforts of the European powers to handle the Macedonian problem, of the intervention in 1878 to remove discriminatory provisions in the Rumanian constitution, of the labors of the Conference of Ambassadors during the First Balkan war, of the insist-

---

[3] See, for example, Emil Ciuria's essay in *Captive Rumania,* edited by Alexander Cretzianu (New York: Praeger, 1956), pp. 12–13.

ence upon minority protection in the treaties after the First World War. And yet this picture of the Balkans as juvenile delinquents is equally unfair and rather less attractive esthetically.

When confronted with such conflicting interpretations it is tempting to say "the truth lies somewhere in between." But this is to say little, if anything. If we examine the thesis that the possession of power corrupts, and its reverse, that being impotent corrupts, the only middle ground between the two appears to be "it all depends," and we are likely to conclude that somehow the problem was put wrongly in the first place.

On reflection it would seem that we are misplacing ethical categories when we attribute vice to great powers and virtue to small powers, or the reverse. The possession of power in itself means nothing unless it is placed in the complex setting of the purposes for which it is employed and its function in providing a correspondence between national responsibilities and national capabilities.

When we speak of great powers and small powers, what do we have in mind? A difference in degree or a difference in kind? Are the relations between the Balkan states and the neighboring great powers simply a case of weaker and stronger, or is there a significant qualitative distinction to be made, expressible in such terms as "dependence" or "tutelage"? One has the sense that more than mere degree is involved, but it seems difficult to arrive at any simple formulation that can tell us, without gross historical simplification, what makes a small state "small" and a great power "great." It is true, of course, that in the nineteenth century the structure and practices of the European states system, and the relative ranking of the powers, were such that a fairly clear line was drawn between those states that "counted" and those that did not. And certainly the subjective views of the statesmen themselves were influenced by such diplomatic custom. Even so, it is not easy to define the real difference between, say, Italy's and Rumania's status in the alliance system that had its center in the power of imperial Germany. Moreover, the claims that Ionel Bratianu made for Rumania at the Versailles Conference were essentially those of a power demanding "equal status," and while not wholly successful, he was remarkably adept, despite the organization and procedural devices of the conferences, in acting as something other than the spokesman for a "small" power. It must be granted, however, that his success in this instance lay in the fact that not only Austria-Hungary and Germany, but also Russia were in a state of collapse or internal convulsion.[4]

The foreign minister of Poland in the nineteen-thirties, Jozef Beck, attempted a definition by means of a threefold distinction: at the one extreme the world powers, self-sustaining and with interests extending far beyond their own frontiers; at the other extreme dependent small powers, client states unable to hold their own and requiring the support of the large states; and in between such a state as Poland, self-reliant but without global or imperial interests and concerned only with problems in its immediate neighborhood.[5] This convenient definition, while having the merit of pointing out the significant fact of differences in the extent of responsibilities, will hardly do. Poland, in fact, could not be self-sustaining; nor is it realistic to assume that even a very small power can be indifferent to developments far beyond its own frontier, since they may come to affect it. Ethiopia and Spain, so it turned out, could not safely be considered as beyond Poland's range of proper concern.

Perhaps the most we can say is that a small power is (and is so regarded by others and itself) a state lacking any hope of successfully defending itself against a great power, unable through its own resources to take the initiative in determining the course of international politics, and only marginally capable of throwing effective weight in the scales of the balance of power. On the whole, the small state is an object rather than a subject in international relations, and its resources, manpower and territory, while of value to the great powers as assets to be gained, or withheld from others, are not of sufficient magnitude in themselves to permit an independent role. In this respect its position is like that of a pawn in a chess game, not in the usual sense that it may be moved about and sacrificed by the player (all chess pieces are so manipulated by the player), but in the limitations in the *types* of moves it can make vis-à-vis the major pieces.

It is true of course that even the limited capability of a small power may, under special circumstances, be of considerable importance. Jo-

---

[4] For a recent discussion of Bratianu's role, see Sherman David Spector, *Rumania at the Paris Peace Conference* (New York: Bookman Associates, 1962).

[5] Colonel Joseph Beck, *Dernier rapport: Politique polonaise 1926–1939* (Neuchâtel, 1951), p. 270.

seph Rothschild has suggested [6] that "in certain marginal but crucial situations such as a delicate balance between hostile alliance systems, a small state, its relative weight having been automatically increased by the general equilibrium, may exercise exorbitant blackmail power over its big ally by threatening to commit suicide." One may wonder, however, whether this opportunity for exploiting—whether through blackmail or tilting the scales—an evenly balanced great-power stand-off is as great, objectively or subjectively, as it may appear. While Bratianu made a number of paper gains between 1914 and 1916 through exploiting the "balance" between the Central Powers and the Entente, he was able to cash in on these only because of the temporary destruction of any coherent balance of power in 1918–1919. It might be argued that Prince Milan of Serbia took the plunge into war against Turkey in 1876 because of a stalemate among the great powers, and yet his actual reason for doing so seems to be chiefly his fear of losing his throne if he failed to take action. On the whole one may doubt whether the threat of suicide by a small power has been, in fact, frequently resorted to, or even seriously contemplated. It does not ring true psychologically, and such an imputation of motives seems rather to represent a transferral of the fears that may be held by a great power regarding its small ally.

Apart from these marginal situations, there is little doubt that this relative inability, through their own resources, to determine, or even effectively to contend for, a favorable situation for themselves in the international scene does strongly influence the diplomatic style and strategies of small powers.[7]

On the level of technique we can observe a variety of devices: Balkan diplomacy has discovered an astonishing assortment of ways to stall for time; the maneuvers of Bulgaria and Rumania in the First World War are most instructive in this regard. The reliance upon legalisms, often with the most marvelously ingenious hair-splitting, is necessary both to ward off the brute pressures of the great powers and also to have a case "for the record" in the event of catastrophe. One can trace this distinctively protective function of legalisms from the parti-

---

[6] In his valuable comment on the original draft of this essay.

[7] For a recent and thoughtful discussion of the role small powers can play in international crises see Annette Baker Fox, *The Power of Small States: Diplomacy in World War II* (University of Chicago Press, 1959).

tions of Poland [8]—and Poland's status in the years just before and after 1773 shows many striking parallels to the situation in the Balkans a century or more later—down through the aftermath of the Soviet occupation of Eastern Europe in 1945. Balkan statesmen are often skillful at what is called, in alpinism, "chimneying": working one's way up a crevice between two opposing cliffs by wedging oneself between both sides. Such devices are in some measure, of course, the stock in trade of all diplomats, but, as Mrs. Fox observes, while they usually are "of peripheral importance to the great power, supplementing its military strength, they may be essential to the small state, substituting for the military power which it lacks." [9]

Perhaps of more fundamental importance than the techniques are the *kinds* of policy choices that have been open to the Balkan states. In speaking of the diplomacy of the great powers we refer to such possible policies as "splendid isolation" or "intervention," "gaining hegemony" or "redressing the balance of power," "forming a coalition" or "operating through the European Concert." Now obviously none of these majestic choices has had much meaning for the Balkan states (except, of course, in the setting of intra-Balkan diplomacy, where there has been a real, if limited, game of power politics within the larger European framework). Their practical choices have been of a different order. While Montenegro, thanks to its terrain, could at times be "isolationist," all other states were too exposed to be able to withdraw from the field of encounter. The ideal situation for a Balkan state was, of course, to have the great powers in its immediate neighborhood either seriously preoccupied elsewhere or in a state of collapse—as in 1919—but such situations were infrequent and temporary and lay beyond the power of the Balkan states themselves to bring about. If the great powers were locked in stalemate, the best hope of the Balkan states was to have a partial "power vacuum" in their area which would give them a degree of real, if precarious, independence. Indeed, it was such continuing stalemate that gave the Balkans the opportunity to emerge as independent states in the nineteenth century. Had either Russia or Austria-Hungary been unhampered the outcome would have been different. The danger of the stalemate, of course, was that the

[8] Herbert H. Kaplan, *The First Partition of Poland* (New York: Columbia University Press, 1962).

[9] Fox, *op. cit.*, p. 185, n. 4.

great powers might try to resolve it, not by permitting a low-pressure buffer zone, but by partition. The specter of an Austrian-Russian agreement to divide the Balkans along a north-south line hung over the peninsula through much of the nineteenth century and into the twentieth, and reappeared briefly in the abortive Nazi-Soviet negotiations of November, 1940. Although there were always serious difficulties in the way of such a partition, it can certainly not be dismissed as having been an evident impossibility.

If one great power or grouping of powers came to be in the ascendency, it was incumbent upon the Balkan states to climb on the bandwagon or at least to be ready to hedge. Thus, in the nineteen-thirties we find King Carol in Rumania and Prince Paul and Stojadinović in Jugoslavia working to improve their relations with the ascendent power of Nazi Germany, even though their countries were beneficiaries of the Versailles settlement. And while at the time these steps were often attributed to political or ideological affinities, the evidence seems reasonably clear that the guiding impulse was in the realm of foreign policy.

But the action of coming under the aegis of a great power, either as protection against another great power or to avoid isolation, was always in danger of producing the situation against which Machiavelli warned: "A prince ought to take care never to make an alliance with one more powerful than himself for the purpose of attacking others, unless necessity compels him, as is said above; because if he conquers, you are at his discretion, and princes ought to avoid as much as possible being at the discretion of anyone." [10]

Certainly the smaller powers who felt compelled to join the Axis found themselves in this uncomfortable plight, and the successes of the Third Reich, so long as they continued, promised only to diminish the real independence of its small allies.

It is not inevitable that a small power will follow this path, even though the penalty for not doing so may be catastrophe. One apparently spectacular exception was the *coup d'état* of General Simović in March, 1941, at a time when Hitler was master in Europe, an act which Winston Churchill hailed with eloquence: "Early this morning the Yugoslav nation found its soul. . . . This patriotic movement arises from the wrath of a valiant and warlike race at the betrayal of their

---

[10] Nicolo Machiavelli, *The Prince,* chap. xxi.

country by the weakness of their rulers and the foul intrigues of the Axis powers."[11]

While the immediate result was a crushing German attack, one may feel that this *beau geste* by Jugoslavia is unmistakably at variance with the prudential concerns of small-power diplomacy outlined above. But the case is not a simple one. After the *coup d'état* the new government attempted to remain on good terms with Germany, and indeed one may wonder whether the purposes of the *coup* were those Mr. Churchill attributed to it. It can be argued that they arose more from domestic differences and were not chiefly an expression of foreign policy.[12] Even so it remains a remarkable event, and one that we must consider again presently in connection with domestic politics.

It is true, of course, that the foreign policies of the Balkan states have been strongly influenced, and complicated, by intra-Balkan relations: it was never just a question of relations between great and small powers. Indeed, it may be suggested that the perennial precariousness of international relations in the Balkans is a consequence of an overlapping of two power systems: the competition of the great powers for influence in this strategic area and the mutual rivalry of the emergent Balkan sovereignties, which could lead to common action between two or more Balkan states as in 1876 and 1912, or to conflict, as in 1885, 1913–1918 and 1941. This double set of wheels within wheels often led to a clashing of gears which made it difficult to achieve even a clear-cut lineup of powers and hence to rather dangerous uncertainty at all levels. For example, Austrian hostility to Serbia after 1908 suggested a rapprochement with Bulgaria, Serbia's rival in Macedonia; but such a rapprochement was not compatible with good Austrian-Rumanian relations because of the Rumanian-Bulgarian conflict over southern Dobrudja, itself an item in the internal Balkan power balance. Such curious self-contradictions may be found in the efforts of all the powers, great and small, to devise a consistent policy or set of alliances.

Still, despite the undoubted importance of small-power relations and their ability to set off conflicts, these relations, whether positive or negative, always lay under the shadow of the great powers, which

---

[11] Winston Churchill, *The Second World War*: III: *The Grand Alliance* (Boston: Houghton Mifflin, 1950), p. 168.

[12] For a discussion of this see Jacob Hoptner's *Yugoslavia in Crisis, 1934–1941* (New York: Columbia University Press, 1962).

were seen as being ultimately decisive. It is worth noting that the Balkan alliance of 1912 was explicitly under the aegis of Russia and, though events turned out otherwise, was not intended to stand as a self-sufficient entity. After the First World War the two combinations affecting Balkan states, the Little Entente and the Balkan Entente, were not directed against any great power. There was clearly the sense that the arithmetic sum of capabilities of the small states did not add up to great-power status.

In general, then, the foreign-policy choices before the Balkan states have been difficult and dangerous and within a frame of alternatives different from that of the great powers. This in turn seems to have produced, or at least contributed to, a different outlook on the nature of international politics. For whereas a larger power may have the hope of its foreign policy corresponding to its general political preferences in choosing friends and enemies, this is a luxury a small power cannot afford except at serious risk to its national existence.

Consequently we find the diplomacy of the Balkan states driven to two polar, but related positions, which we may call the "cynical" and the "utopian." On the one hand, since the small state must be sensitive to the shifting tides of power, be ready to abandon one ship and try to climb aboard another, this necessarily results in a rather special view of the world. It is nicely expressed in the Balkan diplomatic saying: "We have three kinds of friends: our friends, our friends' friends, and our enemies' enemies." It is also observable in the wisdom of the Cypriot saying: "When the rock falls on the egg—alas for the egg! When the egg falls on the rock—alas for the egg!"

It is frequently a cause of real misunderstanding between great powers and their small allies. Thus, as Mrs. Fox has observed:

In World War II, when the small states' leaders did examine their position in the balance of power, their perspectives on Germany and Russia almost without exception differed from those of the West and not primarily for ideological reasons. For them Germany was a valuable counterweight against the equally threatening Russians, and they were quite unable to obtain acceptance of this idea in the West, even as they failed every time in their several efforts at mediation to shorten the war. The longer the war lasted, the more precarious did they view their position, for they regarded the threatened extinction of Germany and the expansion of Communist Russia as two sides of a single catastrophe. Because of their views on the dual character of the war, they could not share the Western Allies' preference for final, unconditional, and total victory over Germany.[13]

The present author recalls a conversation he had with a Rumanian officer in Bucharest in the late autumn of 1944. The officer urged that since Nazi Germany was clearly facing defeat, the United States should at once make peace with it and join in a common alliance against the Soviet Union. To an American, at this time, such a proposal seemed shocking; from the perspective of Rumania this was the only course of common sense.

As against this rather hard-bitten view of international politics and preoccupation with power, we also find a "utopian" position which attempts, in a way, to escape from the uncomfortable world of power politics which is so perilous to the small state. This position has found its most striking, and at times constructive, expression in the support given by statesmen of small powers, including the Balkans, to the League of Nations and to the United Nations, and more particularly to the efforts to devise ways of controlling aggression. One thinks at once of Beneš, Titulescu, Politis. It would be interesting to have a full picture of the contribution of such men—in ideas, formulas, and formulations—to the various efforts to outlaw war, define aggression, and develop the scope of international law. It must be considerable. One has the impression, too, that scholars from the Balkans have been relatively active in developing approaches to international affairs—functional, economic, or legal—that seek to blunt or circumvent the problem of power.

The use of the term "cynical" and "utopian" for these two polar positions should not be taken to suggest that they are somehow distorted or inappropriate. They are not. In the first place, they are derived from the realities of the situation in which the Balkan states found themselves and represent an effort to achieve an adequate response to that situation. It would be inappropriate for a Balkan statesman to try to model himself after a Palmerston or a Lord Salisbury. Moreover, inasmuch as the situation of small powers—the problem of the weaker coping with the stronger—is an important part of the totality of international politics, the insights and attempted solutions of the statesmen

---

[13] Annette Baker Fox, *op. cit.*, p. 182.

of the Balkans are of more than local interest. They can be most illuminating to any student of international affairs.

But if, in the realm of Balkan foreign policy, we find these significant consequences of smallness, the further effects on Balkan domestic politics are less obvious. Indeed, the question may be raised whether there is any necessary connection between behavior in external affairs and behavior at home. The statement is often made that the one colors the other; for example, that if a society embarks on an aggressive or warlike foreign policy, this will cast a shadow over domestic practices, or, conversely that a democratic society, if it is to be true to itself, must work for, or at least not against, freedom and independence in the world at large. But this may represent a misplaced notion of unity and consistency. An unscrupulous politician may be a good husband and kind father, and it is possible to argue that there is no simple correlation between political behavior on different levels. As Barrington Moore has put it: "The connection between the internal organization of a society and its foreign policy is a complex question that cannot yet be answered on the basis of simple formulas. Athens engaged in foreign conquest perhaps more than did warlike Sparta, and the Japanese, despite the militaristic emphasis of their society, lived in isolation for centuries until the time of their forced contacts with the West." [14] Marxists have gone further to argue that, in the capitalist world at least, there is an inverse relation: that domestic liberty is possible only because of exploitation and aggression beyond the frontiers. In this "safety-valve" view nineteenth-century English liberalism can be understood only in connection with Ireland, India, and a colonial empire.

While we cannot attempt here to resolve this problem in its general form, it is clear that we must be careful in drawing broad conclusions about domestic Balkan politics from any selected set of examples. Still, it may be worthwhile to examine one or two examples, if only to raise some questions.

In 1907 Rumania experienced a violent peasant uprising. Among radical and reformist political groups in the country, whether populist or Socialist, there was great sympathy for the unhappy situation of the Rumanian peasantry and much criticism of the existing social and political order. And yet, when the explosion occurred, the principal con-

---

[14] Barrington Moore, Jr., *Soviet Politics—The Dilemma of Power* (Cambridge, Mass.: Harvard University Press, 1950), p. 396.

cern of these groups was for the quick reëstablishment of domestic order, for the simple reason—as they stated explicitly—that if the revolt got out of control Rumania might face an occupation by one of the neighboring great powers, Austria or Russia.[15] This attitude on the part of Rumanian political radicals stands in sharp contrast to those radicals in Russia who were defeatists at the time of the Russo-Japanese war, precisely because an external disaster might increase revolutionary possibilities at home. It may be that the Rumanian radicals lacked the zeal and intense political convictions of their Russian counterparts, but it seems more likely that the difference is a reflection of the size and vulnerability of the two countries. Rumania's tribulations as a small, exposed power were something not even the radicals could neglect or overlook.

No nation, no matter how large and secure, can be completely indifferent to the external repercussions of domestic events (witness the American concern about foreign reactions to the Little Rock episode). Nevertheless, the weight given to this consideration can obviously vary enormously from country to country.

In Rumania at least this inhibiting or dampening effect of worry about foreign affairs appears to be a fairly consistent strand in domestic politics. In the nineteen-twenties the National Peasant party was quite sensitive to charges by the Liberals that its reform program threatened to weaken the country's standing internationally; in the late nineteen-thirties and early nineteen-forties the democratic opposition to the dictatorial regimes of King Carol and Antonescu was restrained by the dangerous developments abroad.

A close examination of each of the Balkan countries would probably reveal traces, more or less important, of this same kind of preoccupation. It is interesting, for example, that in the nineteenth century the emerging Balkan states, of whose ebullient nationalism so much has been made, should nearly all have placed non-native rulers on their thrones. Whether the reason was fear of local rivalries (and the Obrenović-Karadjeordjević feud in Serbia showed the dangers of competing native dynasties) or the felt need to secure useful connections abroad, the presence of foreign monarchs would suggest a continuing, if not easily defined, connection between the operation of the domestic po-

---

[15] Henry L. Roberts, *Rumania: Political Problems of an Agrarian State* (New Haven, Conn.: Yale University Press, 1951), p. 19.

litical system and external concerns. For a time, in Greece, the political groupings themselves were known as the French party, or the British party, or the Russian party—a fairly clear sign of the lack of autonomy of local politics.

From these examples one is tempted to draw the conclusion that in the Balkans, with their perennial vulnerability to, and relative help-lessness against, external dangers, domestic politics could not be played as an autonomous or self-contained game, that there was rather a tend-ency to restrain or inhibit the force of political and social impulses. Unhappily for this conclusion, political caution and moderation can hardly be regarded as the hallmarks of Balkan domestic politics. The Balkans have a rich history of violent and intemperate political actions, many of them in complete disregard of foreign considerations, The Simović *coup d'état* of 1941 has already been mentioned, as a striking, even reckless, example of flying in the face of common prudence. The overthrow of rulers, the occasional rashes of political assassination, the presence of political parties having extreme programs and advocat-ing extreme measures to achieve these programs—all these would seem to have little to do with the cautious concerns of a small power. More-over, the intensity and expression of such impulses have been notice-ably different in each of the Balkan states.

Nevertheless, there may be some connection between these two anti-thetical types of political behavior. Just as in the field of foreign policy there appear to be underlying bonds between what we have called "cynical" and "utopian" outlooks, so in domestic politics we may sug-gest that extreme prudence and extreme recklessness are not unrelated, that they are opposite responses to the perils, frustrations, and harass-ments of political action within a weak state under constant external pressures that may at any time limit or destroy freedom of action, even domestically.

It would require careful historical investigation to trace and identify all the cumulative consequences of this condition, which has certainly prevailed throughout the independent existence of the Balkan states and, in a different form, during the period of Ottoman hegemony. It is perhaps not fanciful to see its effects in the very style and comport-ment of many Balkan politicians, those alternations in behavior that Seton-Watson referred to in the introduction cited above. One is tempted, too, to speculate about such men as Ionel Bratianu, Nikola

Pašić, or Thomas Masaryk, men of commanding personality and vigor, who could surely have played major roles in world history had their stage of action been a great power. What were the effects on such men, and upon their behavior as political figures, of this limitation to their role? In Bratianu's dealings with the diplomats representing the great powers one can sense an almost constant irritation. Did this in turn find expression in political relations at home? Unfortunately, these questions can only be raised here, not answered.

If we turn to the question of violence and intemperance, it is clear that the Balkans, for all the familiar stereotypes of terrorism, factionalism, conspiracy, and *coup*, have no unique claim to these forms of political action. While some of them may have indigenous roots going back to the heroic outlawry of the Ottoman era, others are derivable from French Jacobinism, German Marxism, and Russian anarchism. Nor can we point to political assassination as a characteristic peculiar to Balkan history. Around the turn of the twentieth century, for example, there was a widespread rash of assassinations which included the Balkans but many other nations as well: President Carnot of France (1894); Premier Canalejas of Spain (1912); King Carlos of Portugal (1908); King Humbert of Italy (1900); the Empress Elizabeth of Austria-Hungary (1898); Minister of the Interior V. K. Plehve and President of the Council of Ministers P. A. Stolypin of Russia (1904, 1911); King George of Greece (1913); King Alexander of Serbia (1903); Premier S. Stambulov of Bulgaria (1894); Minister of War Mahmud Shevket Pasha of Turkey (1913); and, to round out the picture, President McKinley of the United States (1901).

As for the last forty years it has been great powers, not the small, that have established some of the most hideously violent forms of government known to history.

In other words, we cannot simply identify political violence and intemperance with the Balkans as small, insecure powers. They obviously have shared the varying impulses toward violence, whether rational or irrational, prevailing in the world at large. Nonetheless, within this more general pattern of behavior the fact of smallness does seem to give a special and possibly distinguishing flavor to such actions. Three examples may be offered for consideration.

As we have observed, during much of their modern history the Balkan states as weak powers were clients of neighboring great powers, in a condition of greater or lesser dependence. Under these circumstances domestic disputes, whether dynastic, oligarchic, or party-political, often led to efforts by the opposition to gain support from outside —at the Porte, in St. Petersburg, or in Vienna. In consequence the dividing line between opposition and treason could easily become blurred, more so than in the case of a great power where the necessity, or the temptation, to look to outside support was by its nature less compelling. The hectic politics of the Principalities in the Phanariote period, of Bulgaria in the years after 1878, of Serbia before 1903, provide numerous examples of this phenomenon, for which the term treason is not wholly appropriate and yet which clearly had a disturbing effect on local politics. The twentieth century, of course, has presented us with new forms of political treason identified with the totalitarian movements of the Left and Right,[16] and it is not easy to say whether in the interwar years the Balkan states, enjoying somewhat more independence than before 1914, were more seriously afflicted than other European nations with this particular manifestation of political pathology. One has the impression that some of the extreme fascists or Communists in the Balkans were perhaps less inhibited in contemplating or undertaking treasonous activities than were their counterparts in Western Europe, but this is a subject for further inquiry.

A second set of examples may be found in those instances where the freedom of domestic politics is curtailed or suppressed, prhaps brutally, for the sake of defending the nation's security, only to have it turn out that the latter effort is not equal to the task in any event. The resultant sense of futility may then feed back into a further poisoning of domestic politics. A poignant example is King Carol's overthrow of the parliamentary system and the establishment of a "strong" monarchy, an act followed shortly by the militarily unopposed territorial losses of 1940. The frantic and savage turmoil that led immediately to the Antonescu dictatorship was certainly in part a reaction to this double frustration, itself a consequence of Rumania's impotence vis-à-vis Soviet Russia and the Axis powers.

A third and related set of examples comprise those actions which seem to emerge from a desperate mood of rebellion against the hope-

---

[16] See Margret Boveri, *Der Verrat im 20. Jahrhundert*, 4 vols. (Hamburg, 1956–1960).

less lack of correspondence between ends and means, between purposes and capabilities, actions whose rational purpose is singularly
difficult to ascertain. Now obviously in great states we find many
instances of irrational political behavior resulting from the psychological instability of persons in positions of power, and at times whole
social groups can behave in a demented fashion. One may suggest,
however, that in the Balkans these tendencies have sometimes been
reinforced by the fact of national weakness. It is in this setting that
political assassination, which as we have noted is not a regional peculi-
arity, may most fruitfully be analyzed. In what measure have assassinations in the Balkans shown, or failed to show, a traceable connection
between political ends and political means? To take the most fateful of
modern assassinations, the shooting of Archduke Francis Ferdinand at
Sarajevo, can we find a real political purpose behind that act? If not,
is it explainable in terms of the idiosyncrasies of a few plotters, or does
it reflect a somewhat more deeply rooted political impulse? [17]

These examples are here offered only as suggestive, not as a con-
clusive demonstration, but we may at least put forward the proposition
that the principal effect upon domestic Balkan politics of being a small
power has been to create, especially in times of crisis, a polarization
between a retreat to politics of impotence and a rage at the impotence
of politics.

But even if this double typology—of "cynical" versus "utopian"
foreign policy and "prudent" versus "reckless" domestic politics—has
some validity, it does not explain why political behavior moves toward
one rather than the other pole. It is certainly plausible to argue that a

---

[17] In commenting on an earlier draft of this essay, Mr. Rothschild remarked:
"When one compares the size of Serbia, for example, on a political map of
Europe in 1914, with the territory indicated as inhabited by South Slavs on
ethnographic maps of the same year, one becomes aware of a dimension in which
the assassination of Francis Ferdinand was neither more nor less of an *acte
gratuit*—if I understand this term correctly—than, say, Bismarck's distortion of
the Ems telegram in 1870. In each case something was to be gained by war and
the consequent restructuring of the European power system. That the First World
War was so much more destructive of human life than the Franco-Prussian one
is hardly the responsibility of Gavrilo Princip." I would agree that the term *acte
gratuit* is not really applicable; both were politically motivated acts. Nor can one
fairly judge by the ultimate consequences of such acts. I would argue, however,
that it is easier to follow Bismarck's line of reasoning, to discern just what he
planned to have happen as the result of his act, than it is in the case of Princip, or
his co-conspirators.

nation's status as an irredentist or a satisfied power, its stake in preserving or upsetting the status quo, would be influential in this regard.[18] And yet when we come down to cases the picture is not simple. While it is true that the three men mentioned earlier—Beneš, Titulescu, and Politis—represented states that were beneficiaries and supporters of the Versailles settlement of 1919, it is also true that Colonel Beck of Poland, another such beneficiary, was definitely "cynical" and anti-utopian in his approach to foreign policy. Nor does there appear to be any simple correlation between external status and ambitions and internal political behavior. Certainly the differing styles of Serbian and Rumanian politics, for example, are to be sought in their domestic history and culture rather than in their external successes and failures, which on the whole corresponded fairly closely in the nineteenth and first third of the twentieth centuries. Perhaps the most we can say is that while the political behaviors of the Balkan states are the product of a vast complex of factors—as are those of any nation—the tendency toward polarization which has been discussed here does determine a certain field, a frame of alternatives for both foreign and domestic politics, which is characteristic of the Balkans as small powers.

---

[18] Again I am most grateful to Mr. Rothschild for his observations on this important point.

THE BALKANS:

HERITAGE AND CONTINUITY

John C. Campbell

In the long sweep of Balkan history the period since the Second World War may appear but an episode, on which we have so little perspective as to render conclusions risky if not impossible. It is especially difficult to see through the dust raised by the issue of Communist domination that has been fastened on a large part of the area during these years, and of the propaganda and distortions of truth which have accompanied it. Perhaps we can best give the period a critical evaluation if we look at some of the main elements of continuity in Balkan life and history since the end of the Ottoman era and at what has happened to them in the last fifteen years of revolutionary change. Put in the starkest political terms, such an inquiry raises, though it is not likely to answer, the question: Will the Communist empire absorb the Balkans, or will the Balkans absorb and "Balkanize" communism?

To approach the subject in that way is not to minimize the fact that in this second half of the twentieth century no small border area determines its own fate. Obviously the conflict, balance, or reconciliation of great powers and blocs will have greater significance than whether Balkan peasants accept or resist collectivization. Nevertheless, the Balkan area presents its special points of interest: first, because the continuation of a general equilibrium of military power between the giants, whether by mutual fear of destruction or by agreed limitation and control of armaments, leaves the struggle to be waged on all other levels in critical areas throughout the world; second, because through the area which we are considering here as a historical unit run the lines which divide the Communist empire from the free world and from the one successful experiment in national communism.

With those thoughts in the background, let us narrow the focus to the local scene and consider the Balkans today, the elements of continuity and of transformation, the elements of unity and of difference, and the lessons—if there be any—of history. The generalizations will be broad, perhaps superficial. How future historians will interpret these past fifteen years it would be foolish to guess. But the historians of today, in this volume and elsewhere, have given us a picture of the Ottoman era and of the age of nationalism, and this perhaps, together with the impressions of the past few years, will provide enough raw material for cautious speculation.

NATIONALISM

With the decline of Ottoman power and the rise of national states the Balkan Peninsula lost whatever unity it had—the unity of subjection to an outside power. The facts of geography and the nature of the Ottoman system had kept the region a mosaic of different nationalities; together with the particularism which the new nationalism introduced, they left its peoples exposed to their own internecine conflicts and to the influence or domination of the great powers of Europe.

Thus there emerged in the nineteenth and twentieth centuries the classic model of what the world has come to know as Balkanization—a group of small, unstable and weak states, each based on the idea of nationality, in an area in which nation and state did not and could not coincide; all with conflicting territorial claims and with ethnic minorities that had to be assimilated or repressed, driven into unstable and changing alignments among themselves, seeking support from outside powers in order to protect the national existence or to satisfy national ambitions, and in turn being used by those powers for the latters' own strategic advantage. It was the balance among competing powers, in the last analysis, that allowed the Balkan nations to enjoy any independence at all.

This system, or lack of system, is too familiar to require any detailed description of how it worked. It has its parallels elsewhere—in Asia, the Middle East, and now perhaps Africa. One can even speak, loosely, of the Balkanization of the world. But meanwhile what has happened in Southeastern Europe? The international anarchy of which the Balkans provided only the most extreme and grotesque expression found its logical outcome in two great periods of war, from 1912 to 1922 and from 1939 to 1945. Whether the old pattern would recur after the experience of the Second World War depended upon the will of the victors and upon the new forces and new leadership emerging in the region itself. It was the first factor, of course, which was largely responsible for the second. In all but one country the leaders who won their way to power did so with the support of the Soviet Union, while in Greece the direct military intervention of the British defeated a Communist bid for power, and Anglo-American support in the civil war of 1946–1949 preserved for the Greek people the opportunity for self-government on Western lines.

Yet this apparently clear pattern of the determination of the future of the Balkan nations by outside forces beyond their control does not answer all questions. What kind of system has developed in the Soviet-controlled countries? Why was one Balkan Communist state able to assert its national independence? What are the durable elements that have survived the imposition of Communist rule and may outlive it? How far will the Balkan nations be able to work out their relationships among themselves? Perhaps the historian and the so-called political scientist had best leave these speculative questions alone, since evidence is inadequate, confused, often contradictory, and such as to stimulate impressions rather than to compel firm conclusions. But the questions are big and vital enough to warrant a tentative discussion among those who by scholarship or by experience find themselves at home in the recent history of the Balkan peoples or in their more distant past.

Let us consider first the general subject of the political configuration and international relations of the region, then subsequently the transformation of society under the impact of postwar developments.

The force of nationalism, which in a generally liberal and democratic form had inspired the Balkan peoples in the long struggle for freedom and independence, had finally helped to open the gates to Hitler and during the war had continued to consume the nations themselves in the fires of hatred and massacre. The worst carnage was in Jugoslavia, but the same spirit was in evidence elsewhere, as in the Bulgarian occupation of neighboring lands and in the mutual oppression of Hungarians and Rumanians in Transylvania.

We can only guess what would have happened had Communist rule not imposed itself on all these nations and established a discipline which suppressed their conflicts. Had anything like the prewar regimes been restored, either through the return of old politicians from exile or through the emergence of new nationalist leaders, it is difficult to see how bitter and destructive national conflicts could have been avoided. Certainly the exiles, with a few exceptions, gave little sign of the conciliatory and constructive spirit that would have been necessary to build a new order in the Balkans—the agreement on federation reached by the Greek and Jugoslav governments-in-exile in 1942 was the only concrete gesture in that direction. Thus, not only did the nationalist forces in all nations except Greece (some democratic and some not so democratic) lack the power to act after the war—the Soviet Union saw to that—but they also gave every evidence of lacking the capacity to rise above the conflicts of the past. This is not to say that the imposition of Communist domination was a fortunate thing for the Balkan peoples or that some kind of democratic federalism could not have been worked out in due course with the help and advice of the West; only that the Communists in one sense served as the agents of history in bringing to an end a system that had outlived its time.

Since 1945 the great question has been: How has the force of nationalism, which cannot be abolished by fiat, manifested itself under the new conditions? Is it still a major factor in the attitudes of the governments and of the population? In particular, how does it affect (a) the cohesion of the states themselves, (b) their relations with each other, (c) their relations with the Soviet Union, and (d) the global conflict between East and West?

On the surface, both in Jugoslavia and in the countries of the Soviet bloc, there is an enlightened policy on nationality questions and national minorities. According to the theory, with the destruction of the power of the old ruling classes and with the building of socialism, there is no more room for bourgeois nationalism. Recognition is given to the fact of ethnic differences through such devices as the federal system in Jugoslavia, the creation of the Magyar Autonomous Region in Rumania, and legislation which permits to minorities the use of their own language and the flowering of their cultures. Because life is "Socialist in content," culture and even political organization can be national in form. In practice, the regimes, through their monopoly of political power, have suppressed the manifestations of nationalism in its old forms.

We know that in Jugoslavia the ill feeling between the Croats and Serbs has not disappeared; it is merely kept under the surface; it even shows up from time to time in incidents and in disagreements within the framework of the Communist system itself. We know that popular attitudes of Rumanians and Hungarians in Transylvania have not been transformed by the official fiction that all are now working in harmony to build socialism. Because public discussion of such matters is taboo, the evidence must come mainly from the personal reports of refugees and of Western visitors and from occasional official references to the existence of "rotten" conceptions left over from the past or introduced by contacts with the capitalist world. But it would not do to exaggerate these influences. The Communist regimes have had real success in taming nationalism on the local scene and controlling the disruptive effects of the grievances of national minorities.

Whatever the methods, the experience of the past fifteen years in this regard has been remarkable, as even non-Communists will attest. To a large extent it is because new and fundamental issues have been posed. The Communists, in attempting to remold men's lives, have dealt with their subjects by class and by mass, not as members of this or that ethnic group; and the anti-Communists, the great majority of the population, have clung to their national feelings as a refuge and protection against Soviet domination and the system itself rather than as a cause for fighting each other on issues of ethnic prejudice or discrimination.

The picture is roughly similar in the relations between satellite states of the Soviet bloc. It is decreed as a matter of Communist dogma that no national conflict, no territorial disputes, can mar the fraternal co-operation of Socialist states. Hungary, for example, does not quarrel with Rumania over Transylvania, nor does Rumania challenge Bulgaria's right to southern Dobrudja. If there are such disputes, they are not allowed to come out into the open. Here again, it is a combination of official policy and popular attitudes that has, so far as we can see, taken the edge off these quarrels. It is the overshadowing presence of the Soviet Union which is bound to dominate the thinking of these peoples. Their continued national existence depends on how their relations with the Soviet Union work out over the long run. They are no longer so inclined, even were they able, to indulge in the national rivalries, ambitions, claims, and counterclaims which absorbed their energies before 1939.

They have been allowed, even goaded, to revive this game, however, in the one instance where it served Soviet purposes that they should do so. That is in their relations with Jugoslavia. Tito's break with the bloc has provided interesting evidence of the potentialities and the limitations of the role which local national rivalries and territorial disputes can play in the relations between Communist states.

The dispute between the Jugoslav and Soviet Communists which produced the break in 1948 turned on the question of nationalism, however much Tito and his colleagues chose to deny it. They declared their continued devotion to Marxism-Leninism, but they would interpret it for themselves and they, not Stalin, would govern Jugoslavia. This was national self-determination, not by popular plebiscite but by the decisions of Communist leaders responsive to national feelings and unwilling to subordinate national interests as they saw them to a higher authority of world communism in Moscow.

The evidence seems to show that in this assertion of independence, which has been maintained ever since despite the experiments in reconciliation of 1955–1957 and 1962–1963, Tito has had the support of the peoples of Jugoslavia. They gave this support, moreover, not so much as Serbs, Croats, Slovenes, Montenegrins, and Macedonians, but primarily as Jugoslavs. This is not to say that the nationality policy of the regime had effaced ethnic loyalties within the country and created a real consciousness of Jugoslav nationality—few of its subjects think of themselves first and foremost as Jugoslavs—but the common dislike and fear of Russia did bind them together. The state, once the overpowering influence of Moscow was removed, did not fly apart. It was held together mainly by the strength of the local dictatorship, but also to some extent by the solidarity of the Jugoslav peoples in support of the country's national independence. The contrast between this crisis and that of 1941 is unmistakable.

The break between Stalin and Tito brought with it, or rather brought to the surface, some of the historic national disputes which had plagued the Balkans in times past. Stalin, seeking all possible means to unseat the Tito regime, encouraged the loyal satellites to revive and press claims which had been smothered by officially imposed silence during the period of fraternal solidarity in the building of socialism and resisting the "imperialists." The Jugoslav-Bulgarian conflict over Macedonia was publicly revived, with revelations of the continuing disputes between the two Communist parties that had been going on since 1941 and had been taken on several occasions to Stalin for decision. The Hoxha regime in Albania, which until 1948 had been in effect a satellite of Jugoslavia, attempted to stir up trouble in the Kosovo-Metohija region, and the Jugoslav government gave signs of treating the Albanian minority there in the old prewar fashion. Rumania and Hungary, though having no territorial claims on Jugoslavia, took security measures against their own Jugoslav minorities, of which the most drastic was the removal of large numbers of Serbs from the Rumanian Banat to distant eastern reaches of the country.

For a time it looked as if the Balkan countries were returning to the old pattern of national conflict covered only by new and rather transparent propaganda charges about loyalty and disloyalty to the precepts of Marxism-Leninism. The notable fact, however, is that it did not go beyond propaganda warfare and frontier incidents. That result we can attribute to the ability of Jugoslavia to hold its own (though it could hardly expect to do much in the way of a counteroffensive), to the hesitation of the Soviet leadership to push matters to extremes, and to the general international situation. The Soviets had good reason to hesitate. There was danger in giving full rein to the forces of nationalism in the Balkans, even though they might be temporarily exploited to advantage. And by late 1949 the conflict with Jugoslavia was more than an affair within the Communist family; the United States was virtually certain to support Jugoslavia if the territorial disputes passed to the stage of armed hostilities.

The other and even more dangerous aspect of the exploitation of Balkan national disputes lay in the fact that the line between the Soviet and the non-Soviet world, about which there may have been some uncertainty in the case of Jugoslavia, ran clearly and distinctly along the frontiers of Albania and Bulgaria with Greece and Turkey. In the 1946–1949 period the Soviet Union and its Balkan satellites had supported a Communist rebellion in Greece centering largely in the northern provinces, which had been the object of conflicting national claims in the past. Stalin, however, had played this game with some caution, not committing the Soviet Union to support the idea of detaching Macedonia and western Thrace from Greece and apparently hoping eventually to bring all of that country, not just the northern regions, into the Soviet corral. He put limits on his support of Tito's territorial ambitions in Greek Macedonia, as in the Trieste area. Then, with the extension of American protection and effective support to Greece, the courageous fighting of the Greek forces, and the defection of Tito, the military adventure came to an end.

Since 1949 the line between the blocs has been frozen—even the frontiers of isolated Albania, which now finds itself at odds with its former protector, the Soviet Union, as well as with its old enemies, Jugoslavia and Greece, and looks for help to Communist China. National conflicts and territorial claims are at the bottom of these ideological disputes, but because both the Soviet Union and the NATO powers are so well aware of the risks involved, local nationalistic drives either as an instrument of great-power policy or as a factor drawing the great powers into conflict are not permitted to make the Balkans again Europe's powder keg. In this respect the Balkan states today, including neutralist Jugoslavia, do not have even the degree of independence in foreign policy that they enjoyed before the last war.

Indeed, the nature of the world balance of power and the revolution in weapons in recent years have robbed Southeastern Europe of much of the strategic significance it had in former centuries. The Soviets will undoubtedly keep up the pressure on Jugoslavia and seek to draw Greece and Turkey out of NATO by threats, blandishments, and subversion, while the West would like to see the Balkan satellites enjoy greater independence and eventually find their future outside the Soviet military bloc. But this area is now but one part of the long frontier zone extending from the North Cape all the way to Japan and has been for some time overshadowed by the more critical points in Central Europe and the Middle East. Strategic positions remain important on both sides, but if basic changes are to take place in the status of the Balkan countries, this is more likely to come about through political developments both international and local than through a feeling of compulsion on either side to improve its strategic position through the use of force.

THE TRANSFORMATION OF SOCIETY

The main theme of Balkan history since the end of the Ottoman era, as
other contributions to this volume have shown, is modernization: the
growth of industry, the reform of agriculture, the increase in literacy
and participation in national affairs, and the growth of a Europeanized
intelligentsia and of commercial and professional classes. The pace has
often been halting and slow but the direction has been clear. In the
Balkans, where the great majority of the population was a primitive
and static peasantry, the heart of the change has been the process of
drawing these people into new ways of life through transforming their
status and methods as farmers, organizing them in political parties, or
attracting them to the cities where they or their children turned to
industrial work, law, politics, or business. In some areas, of course, that
process is still in its beginnings.

We are especially concerned now about the character and the forms
which this general trend has taken in the nations under Communist
rule. How does the pattern differ from what went before, and how does
it differ from that of Greece today? What significant differences are
there between individual states? Does the experience of Jugoslavia
show which elements stem from communism as a system and which
from Soviet dictation? Finally, do local Balkan factors have the staying
power to resist or to outlast the period of imposed "socialism"? A brief
essay can only point to some trends and suggest developments to
watch.

The main elements in the Communist pattern were industrialization
at a forced pace and the directed social revolution which accompanied
it. Industrial growth fostered by the government was nothing new. It
had been a characteristic of the prewar period evident in high tariffs,
subsidies, and some state planning and state-owned enterprises, backed
by theories of autarky and the desire for a stronger bargaining position
with the industrial states. Bulgaria and Greece showed considerable
gains in the interwar period, partly because their starting base was so
small, while Jugoslavia and Rumania made relatively little progress.
The record everywhere was spotty and uneven, marked by intervals of
stagnation, for these countries were especially vulnerable to world eco-

nomic conditions, to rapid and often unexpected political changes, and to shifting attitudes toward foreign trade and foreign capital. The peasant parties, whenever they could make their influence felt, remained generally hostile to the favoring of industry. World depression and the local arms race helped to keep governments in debt and increasingly dependent on Germany, which was interested in political domination and in exploitation of agriculture and raw materials.

After 1944 the advent to power by a revolutionary party brought with it the seizure of the "heights" of the respective national economies, the dispossession of the old owners domestic and foreign, and the adoption as fundamental policy of centrally planned, rapid expansion of industry. The early years saw considerable economic chaos and confusion, because of the problems of recovery created by the war, the depredations of the Russians, the inexperience of the new planners and managers, and the general social upheaval. Despite all that the Balkan states, following the Soviet model, embarked on a remarkable industrial growth which in fifteen years has brought them to new and higher levels of production, though at heavy human and economic cost.

Given the unreliability of available statistics in the Communist countries and the risks of putting variously derived figures into the same mold, it is not easy to demonstrate the exact progress of industrial growth. The figures we have, together with the corrective commentary provided by those experienced in their interpretation, give a general picture sufficient for our purposes. The charts accompanying Mr. Spulber's discussion of economic trends indicate it clearly.

Rumania's industrial production, if we use the League of Nations figures, grew 35 percent between 1929 and 1939. In 1948 it was still below the prewar level. Thereafter, according to the official figures, it leaped rapidly to 290 (1938 = 100) in 1955 and 425 in 1958, a rate of 10 percent annually in recent years. A few concrete figures give more substance to the statistics in percentages. Crude steel production was 277,000 metric tons in 1938, 950,000 in 1958. Electric power went from 1.15 billion kilowatt hours in 1938 to 6.8 billion in 1959. Petroleum production, already on the decline in 1938, is now well above the highest prewar level (1936) although not expanding rapidly.

In Bulgaria the rise in percentage terms has been greater than Rumania's largely because the starting base was lower. Less affected

by wartime losses and postwar "takings" by the Russians, production of
Bulgarian industry by 1948 was already well above the prewar level; by
1955 it was more than five times as high (538 on a basis of 1938 =
100); by 1958 it was 803. Coal production (mostly lignite) was 4,000,-
000 metric tons in 1943, roughly the same in 1948, then jumped to 10,-
400,000 in 1955 and has been rising rapidly ever since. Electric power
rose from .2 billion kwh in 1938 to 3.87 billion kwh in 1959.

In many respects industrialization went too far and too fast during
the Stalin period. The rate was beyond the capabilities of countries
generally poor in industrial resources and skills, for the Balkan states
were the poor relations in the Communist family as they were in prewar Europe. Adjustments have since been made in some of the more
extreme and uneconomic goals and methods copied from the Soviet
model and by a more rational economic planning based on local
resources and on a rough division of labor among the satellite states.
Both Bulgaria and Rumania will probably pay more attention in the
future to agriculture, and to those industries to which they are best
suited, such as oil and petro-chemical (rather than steel) in Rumania.

Nevertheless, the expansion of industry, even of heavy industry, will
go on. Some of the early investments have begun to pay off. The people
have not benefited much in consumption goods or an easier life, but
industrial growth is a reality. There is a new class of managers, who are
privileged, and a new class of proletarians, who though underprivi-
leged are in some ways better off than they were as peasants. This
part of the Communist system—state ownership, central control and
planning, and rapid industrialization—is now well established and not
really challenged, for the Balkan peoples had no strong tradition of
industrial growth through private enterprise.

The experience of Jugoslavia offers some interesting points of difference. There the initiation of the new "Socialist" order followed the
same lines. The first Jugoslav national economic plans were the most
ambitious in the Communist bloc, as befitted the doctrinaire and self-
confident Jugoslav leadership. Then came the break with Stalin, the
rupture of economic ties with the bloc, and the necessity of carrying
on with local resources plus what could be obtained in trade and aid
from the West. The basic concentration on industry remained. Industrial production in 1951 was already almost twice that of 1947, three
and a half times that of 1938.

Yet the new circumstances brought about modifications both of goals and of practices. The Jugoslav leaders postponed or abandoned the more grandiose industrial projects of their original five-year plan, and they introduced real decentralization of authority and a much greater recognition and use of incentives and the free market. The rate of industrial growth, especially heavy industry, slowed down in the early 1950's, compared to that of Rumania and Bulgaria, but this was followed by a steady gain of more than 10 percent annually in the late 1950's. To provide greater investment in agriculture and in some consumer-goods industries, modification of former policies gave the people something more than impressive statistics to eat and to wear. The result was that, after some very difficult years, Jugoslavia had its own "economic miracle" in 1959, thanks to a bumper harvest as well as to the industrial program. Elements of uncertainty and weakness remained, as a sharp downturn in growth in 1961 and 1962 made evident, but the economy seemed strong enough to maintain its forward rhythm.

To what can Jugoslavia's relative progress be ascribed? To the wisdom of its investment policy, to the new economic institutions, to the fact that Jugoslavia's socialism is national rather than Moscow-directed, or to Western aid? There is insufficient evidence to justify conclusions on this point and sufficient doubt about the future of the Jugoslav economy to curb any predilection for prophecy. The Jugoslav experiment, however, is one which could have a great influence on the Balkan future because it is a system that has cut itself off from integration in the Moscow-dominated bloc, established normal economic relations with the West, and made adaptations (for example, in agricultural policy) to Balkan conditions.

Greece, which has kept its prewar political and economic system, has not matched the other Balkan states in rate of industrial growth but has made considerable progress nonetheless, partly because of infusions of American aid. By 1951 the basic transport system was restored and improved, and industrial production was 30 percent higher than in 1938, and since then the annual increase has ranged between 5 and 10 percent, less than in the Communist countries to the north but still substantial. The basic poverty of the country has remained a real limitation on its development, private Greek capital has tended to seek investment elsewhere than in industry, and the emphasis of United States aid programs has been on agriculture; and the fact that successive Greek governments have had to face democratic elections has prevented the kind of forced-draft industrialization which the satellite regimes have put through at the expense of the freedom and the living standards of their peoples.

The main element in Balkan society throughout history, numerically at least, has been the peasant mass. The peasants, who as late as the 1930's still constituted 70–80 percent of the population except in Greece, were largely excluded from the body politic except when called upon to fight the foreign enemy. They were the victims of oppression by other classes, of misgovernment, and of the cruel nationality struggles such as those which plagued Macedonia for many years. Peasant parties were often unrepresentative of peasant interests in their leadership or in their policies. The peasant was the forgotten man of Balkan politics, but the peasant mass had remained the basic repository of national consciousness and continuity throughout the centuries.

In the years of independence before the First World War and in the interwar period the trend to modernization largely bypassed the peasantry, though from its ranks came most of the new "bourgeois" leadership in politics, in the government bureaucracies, and in the new industries. The winds of modernization blew but lightly over the countryside, and the governments, by design or by neglect, did not exert themselves sufficiently, at least not in time, to attack the problems of a backward agriculture and to bring the peasants into the mainstream of public life.

While some of the reasons for that situation were political, the basic difficulties were social and economic. Only in Rumania and in some parts of Jugoslavia was a main part of the problem the need for land reform through breaking up large estates, and it is a notable fact that the socially necessary and impressively drastic Rumanian land reform of the period immediately after the First World War could not by itself give the country a modern and prosperous agriculture. More often the problem was general poverty and backwardness, lack of credit, and excessive division and parcellization of the ownership and use of land. Where the average output of a Balkan peasant was roughly one-tenth of the output of a farmer in Western Europe, the lack of capital and of modern skills made it impossible to bring agriculture to the point where it could rapidly improve itself or provide adequate backing for the growth of industry. Overpopulation on the land was a continuously depressing factor which was overcome neither by emigration (largely cut off after the First World War), nor by industrial growth, nor by government policy.

The peasants were not immune, however, to new hopes and ambitions. Where they were caught up in the whirlwinds of the Second World War, the reaction of many was defensive: to cling to their land and survive; but that of others, especially from the poor and devastated areas, was revolutionary: to look for a new deal. Jugoslavia, where the many forcibly uprooted peasants became a significant element in Tito's partisan armies, was the most striking example. The new deal they got was not what they hoped for, except for the favored few who temporarily gained by the new land reforms of 1945 or by the confiscation of properties of Germans and collaborationists.

Whoever took power in the Balkans at the end of the war had to cope with the old problems of a backward agriculture and a backward peasantry, compounded in countries like Greece and Jugoslavia by the serious economic losses caused by the war and its aftermath. Greece, which is in a separate category anyway because agriculture plays a relatively smaller part in its economy, has been able with American assistance to bring its agricultural production up to and beyond the prewar level without drastic changes in organization. Although wide variations persist in different parts of the country, in general Greece has successfully begun to readjust the imbalance between population and developed resources, which plagued it for so many years; its farmers and tobacco-field workers, while still at the bottom of the social scale, can look forward to gradual economic progress within the limits of the country's basic poverty in arable land. It is in the Communist countries that the more interesting questions have presented themselves.

On gaining control of the state apparatus the Communist regimes directed their economic policies first to the destruction of the former "ruling classes," then to reconstruction, and finally to the application of Socialist doctrine based on the Soviet example, although these different phases cannot be neatly separated in time or in content. The heavy concentration on the growth of industry relieved some of the pressure of overpopulation in the countryside—and incidentally created a stronger working class, one of the political aims of the new order. So far as agriculture itself was concerned, for immediate political as well as doctrinaire reasons the Communists put the emphasis on socializing it through the creation of collective and state farms rather than on the economic and technical measures needed to make it more productive.

The record of the satellite regimes in agriculture, from the standpoint of production, has to be considered one of relative failure, a charge that can also be made against the Soviet Union itself. For more than a decade after the end of the war, while total population increased, the satellite regimes were unable to lift production up to the levels of the 1930's. That formerly food-exporting countries should have become dependent on food imports was not unexpected, in view of the growth of cities and the broader internal market. But that per-capita and even overall output should go down at a time of general expansion of the economy was extraordinary.

One obvious explanation for the stagnation of agriculture was its low priority in the various national economic plans. The great bulk of investment went to industry. Almost every policy was calculated to depress the situation of the peasant, who was subjected to compulsory deliveries of produce at low fixed prices, heavy taxation, and eventually forced collectivization, whether the purpose was to break him as a political opponent or to squeeze him for the benefit of the industrialization program.

Such policies have been rather consistently applied in the satellite states, though with alternating forward leaps and intervals of consolidation. Bulgaria has led the way in the drive to socialized agriculture, with the process now virtually complete (more than 90 percent of the arable land in the Socialist sector). Rumania moved more deliberately, collectivizing first the flat lands of the Dobrudja and the Danubian plain obviously suited to large-scale cultivation while proceeding more slowly in dealing with the independent-minded peasantry of Transylvania, but the pace was accelerated after 1956 and had reached the point by the spring of 1962 where almost all the arable land was said to be in the socialist sector. The lesson seems to be that, whether the peasants like it or not, the regimes have the capacity to force them into various types of coöperatives, collectives, and state farms roughly parallel to the Soviet forms. The peasants have had neither the economic power nor the political organization to put up a resistance that could do more than delay the process.

The developments in Jugoslavia provide a contrast, considering the basic similarity both in the original approach and in the long-term goals. The Tito regime reached the height of its campaign to collectivize agriculture between 1949 and 1953, as if to prove under Stalin's criticism the purity of its devotion to socialism. By that time, however, under the stress of economic necessity and strong peasant resistance, it felt compelled to make compromises in order to lift production and reduce the country's critical dependence on help from abroad. Basic decisions were then taken which abandoned the policy of force and permitted peasants to withdraw from existing collective farms if they wished. All but a handful did.

The developments of the early 1950's represented a great victory for the peasants of Jugoslavia but were also a tribute to the regime's realism. Peasant resistance, combined with the government's mismanagement of agriculture and seriously adverse weather conditions in 1950 and 1952, had brought matters to a pass where the Communist leadership, anxious to avoid strife and the use of force at a time when the country was under severe outside pressure, was ready to sacrifice doctrines for economic results. It contented itself with urging voluntary participation in coöperatives "of the general type," which left to the peasants private ownership of their land (though limited to 10 hectares per holding). Within a few years the regime had also come to the point where it was ready to invest considerable sums in agriculture, curbing some of its more ambitious industrial projects. Experiments with Italian wheat and American hybrid corn, with some United States and United Nations technical assistance, turned out well, and suddenly, with a break in the recurrent biennial cycle of bad weather, Jugoslavia by the end of the 1950's no longer needed the annual shipments of United States surplus commodities which in recent years had included nearly one million tons of wheat. The good luck did not hold, as climatic conditions played tricks both with planners' projections and with farmers' hopes, and American help was again sought. But the future of agriculture was still promising.

Jugoslav officials now believe that their agriculture has turned the corner, that production will rise steadily, that dependence on outside help is a thing of the past, that the poorer areas can be brought nearer to the level of the more advanced and more fertile northern areas, and that the economy is strong enough for the first time to withstand another drought like that of 1950. While that may be too optimistic a view, Jugoslavia does seem to have evolved a pattern which holds the promise of lifting Balkan agriculture out of its age-old backwardness with a system based largely on incentives and independent ownership rather than coercion and collectivism. True, the peasants have not lost their distrust of the regime, but they are more reconciled to it as a permanent fact of life than they ever have been and are not doing badly from an economic standpoint.

In the Soviet Balkan satellites the production curve, if we can believe the official statistics, is not so very different, although the sharp fluctuations from year to year make comparison difficult. They have finally passed the prewar levels, as Jugoslavia has. They also have more machinery, more fertilizers, more diversified crops, better techniques; and agriculture now, as in the U.S.S.R., has a higher priority than it had in Stalin's day. On both sides of the iron curtain it looks as if Balkan agriculture, though still far behind Western Europe, may be at the point of emergence into a period of steady growth.

The main difference is the one already mentioned: that Jugoslav peasants have succeeded in maintaining or regaining a status of independence which most Bulgarian and Rumanian peasants have lost. The existence of an independent peasantry in a Socialist state, as in Jugoslavia or Poland, may seem anomalous, but that fact can have real significance if voluntary coöperative organization and technical advances can be combined with individual initiative to give them a rising prosperity to go with their relative freedom. Even if agriculture in Rumania, Bulgaria, and Albania does not stagnate or collapse, the Jugoslav experience will be favorably known in those countries. Collectivization of farms is the one major change in economic and social life which has not been and will not be willingly accepted. Peasants are not so important numerically as they used to be, nor are they likely to have a decisive voice in political decisions, but they can sabotage or slow down the success of policies and programs. The conflict between orthodox and national Communists may well be sharpened if the unwillingness of the Balkan peasant to be a socialized serf shows up increasingly in the production statistics and leaves its mark on political developments.

The temperature of the cold war and the state of tensions within the bloc probably will determine whether the pressure on the peasants in the satellites, and the collective system into which they have been forced, will ever be relaxed, or whether the Soviets will insist that it be maintained at all costs. Private property and a relatively free market in agriculture provide such a striking example of revisionism that they may exert great pressure to put Poland back on the road to socialism in the countryside. Jugoslavia cannot be as easily subjected to Soviet pressure. The question which hangs over the Jugoslav peasants is that of the intentions of the regime itself. As Communists the leaders still regard a socialized agriculture as a necessary part of the economic system they will ultimately establish, but they have set no date and are not likely to. Meanwhile they have come to accept a compromise with doctrine which, along with their other compromises and experiments in industrial organization and political institutions, makes Jugoslavia a contrast and a challenge to its neighbors of the Soviet bloc.

Fifteen years of rapid economic development and revolutionary change have inevitably transformed Balkan society. The breaking down of old class distinctions and the creation of new ones; the new mobility of the population, forced or voluntary; the uprooting and atomization of society in the political interest of the Communist leadership; the imposition of new forms of social organization and activity; the effort to sever the cultural links with the past and with the Western world and to indoctrinate a new generation—all this seems to have left little of the Balkan legacy, especially if we concede that much of it was bound to disappear, though more gradually, even in the absence of the Communist-imposed revolution.

General rejection of or disillusionment with the new institutions that have been built by the regimes on the ruins of the old—and this is true even in Jugoslavia, although much less than in the satellites—raises some interesting questions about the shape of Balkan society in the future. Perhaps intelligent discussion of those questions must await more data on personal and social attitudes of the recent past and on evidence which only the future can provide. The key may lie with the intelligentsia which the new generation is producing. So far as society does not bear a made-in-Moscow stamp, it is this class now in the making which is likely to give it shape.

The peasantry, as we have said, can play a role of passive resistance but hardly one of leadership. The new urban proletariat, if the Hungarian events of 1956 can be taken as a clue, may exert itself to win greater rewards and a voice in the management of industry. Both will continue to harbor strong national feelings against foreign domination, and in that sense may look to the past. But the initiative and the leadership will have to come from the new intelligentsia. Much of the youth today seems afflicted with a cynicism and a spirit of rejection of both past and present that is not surprising in view of the travail through which these nations have passed in the past few decades. As the world moves in the direction of a more uniform and mechanistic society, few historic institutions may remain in the Balkans except as curiosities for tourists and folklorists. It is, nevertheless, of some interest that as the Balkan social revolution passes into its Thermidor the "new class," including elements of the old educated class which have made a difficult but nonetheless real adjustment to new circumstances, may well preserve some links with the past, particularly those imbedded in national cultures which survived other periods of war, social upheaval, and foreign domination.

The Balkan Future

The theme of Balkan development before the end of the Ottoman era, we have seen, is evolution from a static to a modern society largely by the process of borrowing, adaptation and, in some areas, direct imposition. The channels through which outside influences have come—from Central Europe, from the West, or from Russia—have been mainly determined by the balance of power and the changing political alignments. Political forms have tended to change with the shifts in the strength of various foreign influences which have put their imprint on the social structure, on the drives of classes and groups for political power, and on the way in which old institutions gave way to new.

It is not easy to disentangle the foreign and the local influences or to find the balance between them in explaining how and why the traditional Balkan institutions began to disappear. But the fact that people had begun to abandon old habits and to question old values did not make them entirely suited to new values and institutions developed in other countries under different conditions. It seems as if, coming on the scene as independent nations so late in the day, they have never had the time to work out a combination of borrowed and native institutions that would give them a modern society with reasonably stable and adaptable systems of government based generally on the consent of the governed.

Western political institutions sat rather lightly on the Balkan peoples. Their monarchies did not develop like the constitutional monarchies of the West, nor did their parliamentary systems have the long background of gradual growth and basic popular acceptance necessary for them to work. In the interwar period there was a degree of political stability on an ostensibly democratic basis for the privileged classes both old and new, but the system was unable to survive the challenge of extremist ideologies appealing to the mass, the dislocations of the Second World War, and the disruptive effects of social and national conflicts. The monarchies became unpopular dictatorships and were probably doomed whether Communist regimes took power or not. Even in Greece, which still has a king, the monarchy itself has been at critical times a divisive issue in Greek politics rather than a symbol of national unity.

The imposition of Communist rule cut off the opportunity to see whether democratic institutions could have been restored and strengthened in the Balkan countries after the war. One may be permitted to doubt that they would have been. There were men of democratic faith briefly on the scene, yet their ability to contain within a democratic political system the new social forces was by no means assured. As we look to the future, we should not underestimate the appeal which free political institutions have had and will have, especially for peoples who had had some experience with them followed by the experience of living under Communist rule. Yet it would be a mistake to see the future only as a choice between two clear alternatives, Western constitutional democracy and communism. The question is what modifications of the one or the other, or what third alternative, will fit Balkan conditions and will be politically feasible.

Similarly, on the question of how peace and security might be organized in the Balkans, plans for federation were liberally discussed during the Second World War and are still mentioned by those intrepid souls who have expressed themselves on how Southeastern Europe should be organized when the Soviet tide recedes. A more conservative approach seems in order now, one which assumes that there will be no basic change for sometime in the *de facto* boundaries of the Soviet bloc in this part of the world, that it will not be possible for the Soviets or for the West or for the Balkan nations themselves to organize the whole area. Whatever changes come to pass in the status of the Balkan nations and in their relations with each other are likely to be gradual and due less to revolutionary crises, internal or international, than to internal forces that grow stronger or weaker with the passage of time. Let us consider, among those forces, nationalism, the idea of Balkan unity, and the attraction of the West.

A permanent fact, to repeat a point already made, will be the continuing existence of national cultures deeply rooted in the people. Centered in the common language and experience of each nation and in some, though probably a declining, degree on religion, this consciousness and pride of nationality provides a haven and a means of resistance to Sovietization or Russification. So far as we have evidence, the Soviets are not going to be able to make "the new Soviet man" out of the youth of Rumania, Bulgaria, and Albania, no matter how much indoctrination is administered, if that means going against their national feelings. And such feelings inevitably will find political expression, though rarely in such extreme form as in Hungary in 1956.

Rumania and Bulgaria have in their history experienced long periods of foreign domination to which they adjusted without losing their existence as nations. Their peoples do not now openly challenge the existing order, and the regimes are notoriously subservient to Moscow. From one standpoint the regimes have to cling to the Moscow connection because it is what keeps them in power. Yet from another standpoint they have a common interest with the people in the preservation of nationality and in giving some substance to the national sovereignty they nominally represent. The regimes have to govern; they cannot ignore entirely the motive forces that lie in the mass of the people. Traicho Kostov, for example, was not just an isolated phenomenon. For leaders who speak and act for a nation, Communists though they be, the rule that the only test to be applied in the art of governing is loyalty to the U.S.S.R. is not always easy to accept or to apply. If we knew the whole story of relations between the satellite regimes and the Kremlin and not just the final communiqués of conferences held in brotherly harmony, we might find that a kind of lower-key Titoism is a recurring fact of life in the Socialist camp.

Wide differences of national attitudes and character among the various Balkan nations cannot be overlooked. There were many reasons why Jugoslavia could win outright independence, while Rumania, Bulgaria, and Albania could not. Geography was one, circumstance another, leadership a third. But one should not ignore the history and character of the Serbs, which are not the same as those of the more stolid Bulgarians and of the more supple Rumanians. Jugoslavia has only a limited attraction to Rumanians, Bulgarians, and Albanians. They do not yearn for Tito's leadership. But Jugoslavia is an example of which they are acutely aware. What Jugoslavia has won is bound to be a goal toward which they and their successors will strive, cautiously and each in his own way.

Khrushchev himself knows and has made clear that the Soviet Union cannot reimpose on Eastern Europe the rigid control of Stalin's day. The Soviet bloc cannot be a monolith. It will be subject to extraordinary stresses and strains, and its Balkan appendages, albeit small and relatively unimportant, cannot but be affected. The strength of national feeling and solidarity may determine how they are affected.

Will solidarity go further? Will it bring the Balkan nations to cooperation with one another on behalf of common interests? While geography and ethnic diversity have shaped their history, which has been one largely of conflict and disunity, there exists also a tradition of regional unity grounded in common periods of subjection, in religious ties, in the infrequent but still significant coöperation among the respective movements for national liberation in the nineteenth century, and in the basic similarities of peasant societies under the impact of the winds of change. Unfortunately it has been a tradition unable to assert itself against the forces of division, internal and external, as was illustrated by the collapse of the Balkan League in 1913 and the inability of the movement for Balkan unity in the 1930's to do anything to arrest the quarrels and the weaknesses which helped to bring subjection to Hitler and the horrors of the war period.

The idea of Balkan unity has been a tender flower at best. In the interwar period it lived mainly on intellectual enthusiasm and may have had some vague popular support, but it never developed the political strength to influence the basic decisions of governments. How, then, can we expect it to exert much influence in a situation where the peninsula is split three ways? The region now includes a group of three states which are allowed only the unity that comes from their incorporation in the "Socialist camp," a national Communist state intent on avoiding close alignment with states of any bloc, and a member of NATO. And yet the idea of common interests and unity is not to be dismissed without further thought. It has had its adherents among Communist leaders who may well have had their own Balkan reasons for their views, not just a purpose of conforming to Soviet policies and tactics. Indeed, during their long years in the wilderness of ineffective agitation between the wars, Balkan federation was the great issue they discussed and debated and put into their programs. Federation was the Communists' answer to the nationality conflicts, just as it was the answer of some of the intellectuals and the peasant leaders. Tito, between 1944 and 1948, toyed with the concept of Balkan federation; and Georgi Dimitrov was bold or injudicious enough to talk about it publicly, probably without foreseeing the vehemence of Stalin's reaction.

Since 1948 all concrete plans for union or federation, but probably not the basic idea, have receded into the background. The temporary reconciliation of 1955–1957 undoubtedly awakened Jugoslav hopes of close relations with Balkan neighbors within a new and loosely organized Communist bloc that would give scope to the development of national communism, or independent roads to socialism as the official statements put it. Even the dashing of those hopes, we may surmise, has not killed the idea entirely. As for Greece, which has had normal and friendly relations with Jugoslavia since 1949 but remains anchored in the Western world, any thought of closer alignments with Balkan states which live under Communist rule carries too much danger to be regarded as a serious proposition.

The Khrushchev policy of detente and of neutral or "de-atomized" zones recently raised the question in a new form. The proposals of the Rumanian government for some kind of entente including Jugoslavia, Bulgaria, Rumania, Albania, Greece, and Turkey must be considered as a part of Soviet strategy to weaken the West, and were naturally rejected by Greece and Turkey although Tito was receptive. They represent, nevertheless, a recognition of greater Balkan unity as a concept that in itself has some reality. It can scarcely have great political significance until there is a substantial change in circumstances in East-West or in Soviet-Jugoslav relations. But if such changes develop gradually as the years pass, the theme of unity may have a role to play, not merely as an instrument of strategy on one side or the other but as something of value for the Balkan peoples themselves.

Finally, there is the influence of the West, defined as more than the urge to modernization and economic advance, which can come from the East as well. We have seen that Western political institutions did not strike deep root (except possibly in Greece) and that those leaders and classes which espoused them were swept aside. There remains, nonetheless, a reservoir of cultural and other factors which draw the Balkan peoples toward Western Europe and America in spite of all that has happened. Western influence, after all, was extruded from the countries north of Greece by force and not by the conscious action of peoples. And the fact that the West stands as the antithesis and the opponent of Soviet rule creates a negative attraction on those who do not like what they have now. So long as the West maintains far higher living standards than the Balkan nations, those who are aware of it through travel and in other ways can hardly fail to question the Soviet system on its own promise of a better material life.

The opening of Jugoslavia to Western influences since 1948, which have given the leadership at least a few moments of worry and have led to periodic warnings to the party and to the youth not to relax ideological discipline, illustrates how they can make themselves felt, even without any basic change in the nature of the regime. Peoples who have enjoyed independence in the past and have been a part of the European community do not easily in their minds repudiate those ties despite fifteen or more years of contrary indoctrination.

The Western powers cannot act with military force in the region except in defense of Greece and Turkey, or of Jugoslavia, and the limitations on political action are severe indeed; but they should not and cannot remain unconcerned with the existence of Western influence and Western attachments which, like the force of nationalism and the idea of Balkan unity, can have a long-run bearing on the Balkan future.

Which of the three segments into which Southeastern Europe is now divided, if any, represents the future is a question that cannot be answered. We can be fairly sure that Greece and Jugoslavia will not be swept into the Soviet bloc if the West is successful in maintaining and building further its material and political strength. Whether the present satellites will move in the other direction obviously depends on the evolution of Soviet policy and on relations within the bloc. But the play of local forces in the Balkan area within those limits may not be a negligible factor in the equation.

It is here that Greece and Jugoslavia, their societies built on a closer adherence to traditions of freedom and independence which have some meaning in Balkan history and on fruitful association with the West, may exert some attractive force. Those two countries, of course, are very different, but they have maintained a friendly and close relationship for the past ten years despite the obscurity into which the Balkan alliance, concluded with considerable fanfare in 1954, has fallen. Both societies are in a transition phase and both are evolving in ways which may take some of the edge off the ideological differences which have separated them. It is incumbent on the West, therefore, to do everything possible to help them to become real going concerns, increasingly solid in their economic and social structure, and impervious to disruption by Soviet threats and blandishments. To do so may require faith and hope as well as increased effort on our part. But are these not also essential ingredients of our efforts for the survival and growth of freedom in the West and in the world?

HISTORICAL STUDIES IN THE BALKANS

IN MODERN TIMES

George C. Soulis

One of the principal features of Europe's intellectual life in the nineteenth century is the astonishing flowering of the study of history. It is therefore with good reason that this century has often been referred to as the age of historicism. This return to the past was dictated mainly by the two dominant movements of the past century—romanticism and nationalism. The romantic movement with its eyes nostalgically turned toward the past opened the road to historicism, while the growth of national life, which the French Revolution and Napoleon had each fostered in their different ways, gave unparalleled impetus to historical studies throughout the continent.

Since the past is the main source from which every nationalistic movement draws its inspiration and stamina, it became necessary to study national history, illuminate its glorious periods in the most striking light, and trace it in unbroken continuity as far back as possible. On the other hand, history could serve nationalism either as a potent instrument for increasing national consciousness and securing national unity, or by supplying the necessary justification by arguments for national aspirations and irredentist claims.

Thus, with the rise of nationalism in the Balkans we notice, as one would expect, the growth of an intense interest in national history. Roughly until the middle of the nineteenth century, the writing of history among the Balkan peoples was totally in the hands of patriots rather than of trained scholars, and it was characterized by a romantic and uncritical spirit, which was unable to distinguish legend from historical fact or make critical use of the available sources. History was regarded by those amateur historians merely as a tool for stimulating national feelings and achieving national independence. The critical

historical method, which was taking definite shape in Western Europe
early in the nineteenth century, left the Balkans practically completely
untouched in the period before the second half of the same century.
This is understandable if one bears in mind that educational facilities
hardly existed above the elementary level, and those which did exist
were of a rather general encyclopedic nature; facilities for even the
most primitive scholarly activity were thus completely lacking.

For this reason, one must view the work of these amateur historians,
who preceded the beginnings of modern historiography in the Balkan
countries, with sympathy and understanding. Their work must not be
scorned altogether, because although confronted with enormous problems, they succeeded in preparing the ground for a more reflective
state of mind, nourished by systematic contact with the historical science of the West which, in time, laid the foundations for critical historiography in the Balkan countries.

The present essay is limited to a brief survey of historical studies in
the Balkans since the appearance of critical historiography as the
Western world understands it, followed by some general observations.
I shall omit any discussion of the preceding stage, except in a paren-
thetical way when necessary. One must not, however, form the false
impression that the appearance of critical historical scholarship marked
the end of historical works written in a romantic and uncritical spirit.
These continued to appear, and they have always constituted the bulk
of the entire historical output in the Balkan countries.

The Jugoslavs and the Greeks were the first among the Balkan peoples to come into direct and more intimate contact with the West. Their
geographical proximity to the West rendered both of them more susceptible to Western influences. Thus it is not surprising that nationalism made its first appearance in the Balkans among these two peoples,
and as a result they were the first to struggle for independence from
the Ottoman yoke.

In surveying the course of historical studies among the Jugoslavs in
modern times, two main centers are distinguishable—Zagreb and Belgrade (other smaller ones being Ljubljana, Novi Sad, Skoplje, Sarajevo,
and Dubrovnik)—from which the bulk of Jugoslav historical scholarship emanated. For geographical, political, and cultural reasons, Zagreb
played the role of pioneer in the development of critical historical

scholarship among the Jugoslav peoples. Being part of the Habsburg Empire and enjoying a much higher educational level than any of the other peoples of the Balkan peninsula, the Croats were the first to become acquainted with the new methods of historiography, as practiced in the countries of Central Europe. The foundation of the Društvo za povestnicu Jugoslovensku [Jugoslav Historical Society] in 1850 by Ivan Kukuljević-Sakcinski (1816–1889) and the appearance of its journal *Arhiv za povestnicu Jugoslovensku* in the following year mark the dawn of modern historiography among the Jugoslavs. A solid basis for the development of historical studies was provided, however, only a generation later when Bishop J. Strossmayer established the Jugoslavenska akademija znanosti i umjetnosti [Jugoslav Academy] in 1867 and the University of Zagreb in 1874. Patterned after the Vienna Akademie der Wissenschaften, the Jugoslav Academy was from the beginning oriented toward historical and philological studies under the guidance of Franjo Rački (1828–1894), who can justly be considered the father of modern Croat historiography. The impressive output of historical source material and studies, which has appeared both in the periodical and the serial publications of the Academy (*Rad, Starine, Djela*), as well as in special collections of archival material, indicates the leading role which this institution has played in the development of historical research in modern Croatia. In stressing the role of the Academy one must not neglect the contribution made by the University of Zagreb where the teaching of history was entrusted to such excellently trained scholars as Tadija Smičiklas (1843–1914), and his pupil Ferdinand Šišić (1869–1940), the latter being undoubtedly the greatest historian the Jugoslavs have produced so far. Šišić distinguished himself by his numerous studies on particular problems of Croatian history and his editions of pertinent texts, and as the author of a scholarly and impartial synthesis on the history of the Croats (*Hrvatska povijest* [*Croatian History*], Zagreb, 1906–1913, 3 vols.; one volume, covering the period to 1102, translated as *Geschichte der Kroaten*, Zagreb, 1917).

The Serbs, having been less fortunate than the Croats, had to wait longer to witness the establishment of critical historical scholarship in their midst. Critical examination of historical sources was introduced first by Ilarion Ruvarac (1832–1905) who, by dismissing a number of unauthenticated stories (such as, that Montenegro had never submitted to the Turks) made a serious attempt to divorce historical truth from legend and patriotism. The tradition of Ruvarac's work was carried on in a more vigorous manner by Stojan Novaković (1842–1915), who holds a position in Serbian historiography as important as that held by Rački in Croatian historiography. As was true of Rački, a whole generation of historians grew up under Novaković's influence, which dominated historical studies in Serbia until recently.

The Srpska kraljevska akademija [Serbian Royal Academy; after the Second World War called Srpska akademija nauka (Serbian Academy of Sciences)], which was founded in 1888 as successor to the Srpsko učeno društvo [Serbian Learned Society], displayed the same historical and philological orientation and coördinated all serious historical work, most of which eventually appeared in its periodical (*Glas, Spomenik*) and serial publications. These series apparently followed the example of the Zagreb academy.

The University of Belgrade (founded in 1905 as successor to Velika Škola) included among its teaching staff the historians St. Stanojević (1874–1937), V. Ćorović (1885–1914), and J. Radonić (1873–1956) to mention only some of the better-known names, whose works and influence are responsible to a large extent for making Belgrade the primary center of historical scholarship in Jugoslavia since the end of the First World War.

The Greeks, being the first of the Balkan peoples to win complete independence (1830) were in a more fortunate position to organize their intellectual life on a national basis. Shortly after the establishment of the new state in 1837, a university and an archaeological society [Archaiologike Hetaeria] were founded in Athens. The University of Athens was the first institution of higher learning in the Balkans and the Near East. It included among its first faculty a number of German and English scholars who, in their philhellenic enthusiasm, came to assist in the revival of learning on the soil of the classical land. These professors of the university along with their native Greek colleagues, most of whom were trained in Germany, brought to Greece the fruits of Western critical scholarship. The newly-born state was caught in the midst of the classical revival in the West, which brought the study of ancient Greece to the front of scholarly research. Thus, Greek historiography, as well as all other aspects of Greek intellectual life, were from the beginning oriented toward the classical past. The various facets of the Greek tradition from antiquity to the present were looked upon as the unbroken record of national history. For this reason, the theory advanced by J. Ph. Fallmerayer in his *Geschichte der Halbinsel Morea während des Mittelalters* (Stuttgart, 1830–1836, 2 vols.) that the modern Greeks are not the descendants of the inhabitants of classical Greece, but hellenized Slavs, who had invaded the depopulated land in the Middle Ages, was received with great hostility by the Greeks. It became the task of both patriots and scholars to disprove Fallmerayer's theory. A critique of Fallmerayer's views, which found them exaggerated, appeared in 1843 from Constantine Paparregopoulos (1815–1891). One may disagree with some of Paparregopoulos' interpretations of the sources, which he studied carefully, but one cannot deny that this study is written in the manner of critical scholarship. In this way Paparregopoulos may be considered as the father of modern Greek historiography. He taught history at the University of Athens for many years and produced his voluminous *Historia tou Hellenikou Ethnous* [*History of the Greek Nation*], (Athens, 1860–1872, 5 vols.), followed by an abridgement, which has also appeared in French, under the title *Histoire de la civilisation hellénique* (Paris, 1878). Thus Paparregopoulos attained the position of the national historian of Greece, and his work is considered as a kind of national testament to this day. He looked upon the Greek civilization from its remotest age up until the Revolution in terms of unbroken continuity, as the national history of Greece.

One of Paparregopoulos' pupils, Spyridon Lampros (1851–1919), was the first Greek historian to be trained extensively abroad as a historian. Upon his return to Greece he introduced at the University of Athens the systematic study of palaeography, and began to publish great quantities of Greek texts and documents. Lampros, who distinguished himself as the most prolific modern Greek scholar, published numerous studies on the history of medieval and modern Greece. He also produced a synthetic work *Historia tes Hellados* [*History of Greece*], (Athens, 1886–1903), 6 vols., covering the history from antiquity to 1453. Lampros' many-faceted influence on the development of modern historiography in Greece has never been properly evaluated. His numerous editions of texts and his critical historical studies have served as models to Greek historians to this day. As a professor of history at the University of Athens, he taught several generations of

Greek students and acted as the mentor of practically all those historians who have achieved renown in later years. His ability for organization was an important factor in promoting historical scholarship. Since
Greece lacked an institution similar to the Zagreb and Belgrade academies of science—the Akademia Athenon [Athens Academy] was not
founded until 1926—which would guide and patronize historical research, the responsibility for such a task was left in the hands of a few
individual scholars, among whom Lampros was the most distinguished.
He founded several learned societies, such as the Philologikos Syllogos
Parnassos [The Parnassus Philological Society], and the Historike kai
Ethnologike Hetairia tes Hellados [Historical and Ethnological Society
of Greece], in whose journals historical writing found both encouragement and an outlet.

Until the Balkan wars, the intellectual home of most of the unredeemed Greeks was Constantinople, where the Hellenikos Philologikos
Syllogos [Greek Philological Society] founded in 1861 played the role
of an academy of science. A glance at the contents of the thirty-four
volumes of the society's journal published between 1861 and 1921, reveals the institution's contribution to modern Greek historiography.

The Rumanians, claiming direct descent from the Roman legions
settled in Dacia by the Emperor Trajan, were preoccupied from the
beginning of their modern historiographical endeavor with the idea
of showing to the world the unbroken continuity of their tradition and
of stressing its Latin character. Michael Kogálniceanu (1817–1891)
and Bogdan Petriceicŭ Haşdeu (1836–1907) are the pioneering figures
of modern Rumanian historiography, but its real father is the Moldavian, Alexander Xénopol (1847–1920), who taught history at the University of Jassy. Moved by the idea of the unbroken unity of Rumanian
history and the continuous presence of the Rumanians in Dacia since
the times of the Emperor Trajan—which idea was denied by R. Rösler
in *Romanische Studien* (Leipzig, 1879), and which is still disputed by
Hungarian scholars to this day—Xénopol set about to produce a synthetic work similar in magnitude to that of Paparregopoulos on Greek
history. His six volume *Istoria Rominilor din Dacia Traiana* [*History of
the Rumanians of Trajan Dacia*], (Jassy, 1888–1893); a two-volume
abridgement has appeared in French: *Histoire des Roumains de la
Dacie Trajane depuis les origines jusqu'à l'union de principautés en
1859* (Paris, 1896), viewed the entire pageant of Rumanian history

with the eyes of a Rumanian patriot, but also with a critical mind. It was the first attempt to give a comprehensive picture of the history of the Rumanians free from any land divisions and demarcations of time. Far from remaining merely a national historian, Xénopol, who was a man with a strong philosophical disposition, dealt also with problems of the philosophy of history. His best-known book in this respect is *Les lois fondamentales de l'histoire* (Paris, 1899).

Xénopol's mantle soon fell upon the shoulders of his pupil, Nicholas Iorga (1871–1940), who is the greatest historian any Balkan country has produced so far. For this reason the name "the Giant of Southeastern Europe" is a fitting tribute to the stature of this scholar. Iorga is responsible for the high scholarly level achieved by Rumanian historiography before the Second World War. The leading position which Rumanian historiography assumed during that time in the Balkans is due to a large extent to Iorga's work and influence. He broadened the outlook of the Rumanian historians by helping them to see the whole of Southeastern Europe as a historical entity, and by encouraging them to examine its historical problems within the framework of universal history. His genial influence, however, extended far beyond the frontiers of his own country. There is hardly a Balkan historian of some consequence who has not been influenced or instructed by Iorga's work.

Although Iorga distinguished himself as historian, editor, journalist, literary critic, university professor, and political figure (he published about 1,200 books and 23,000 articles and reviews!) his fame rests primarily on his work in history.

Trained in the great French historical tradition at the École des Chartres and at the École Pratique des Hautes Études in Paris and at the University of Leipzig under Karl Lamprecht, Iorga returned to his native country, where he became professor of general history at the University of Bucharest at the age of twenty-three. There is hardly any aspect of Rumanian history, which he did not study in the course of his half-century of historical activity, and besides the numerous volumes containing archival material and studies on special problems, he left behind two comprehensive accounts of the general course of Rumanian history. His *Geschichte des rumänischen Volkes im Rahmen seiner Staatsbildungen* (Gotha, 1902, 2 vols.; an abridgement subsequently appeared in various Western languages), unlike Xénopol's work, examines the medieval period thoroughly and emphasizes political as well as social, economic, and cultural aspects of Rumanian history, aiming at presenting a complete picture of the whole living past of the nation, even beyond its Dacian frontiers. This same view is further developed in the crowning achievement of his historical career, his ten-volume *Istoria Românilor* [*History of the Rumanians*], (Bucharest, 1936–1939); a French edition with some differences appeared almost simultaneously under the title: *Histoire des Roumains et de la romanité orientale* which, despite some shortcomings in historical analysis, is a stupendous work and a monument of historical writing.

In studying the "Romanité orientale" as a historical unity and the history of the Byzantine and Ottoman empires, in both of which Iorga distinguished himself, he saw clearly the interdependence of the national histories of the various Balkan countries. He not only stressed in several of his works the importance of the common Byzantine and Turkish heritage which all Balkan peoples share, but tried to advance his views in more concrete fashion by establishing in 1913 the Institut pour l'étude de l'Europe sud-orientale, which issued first a *Bulletin* (10 vols., 1914–1923) and later the *Revue historique du Sud-Est Européen* (23 vols., 1924–1946).

In his wish to provide Rumanian historians with a broader view of history, extending beyond the Balkan area, Iorga was instrumental in establishing the École Roumaine en France and the Scuola Romena di Roma which in the prewar era had become centers of historical research. On the other hand the Rumanian Academy [Academia Româna; after the Second World War: Academia Republicii Populare Române] which since its foundation displayed a predilection for historical studies, fell under Iorga's direct influence.

Iorga's strong personality and prolific production tend to overshadow the important work of other Rumanian historians—such as D. Onciul (1856–1923), Ion Bogdan (1864–1919), V. Parvan (1862–1927), and C. Giurescu (1875–1918)—who have contributed greatly to the development of more vigorous critical methods of historiography in their country, based mainly on those practiced at the time in Austria and Germany.

From the large number of excellent historians of the generation which reached maturity in the period between the two World Wars— some of whom at times were critical of their master, N. Iorga—one must mention especially P. P. Panaitescu and C. C. Giurescu, the latter being the editor of the prewar *Revista Istorică Română* and the author of *Istoria Românilor* [*History of the Rumanians*], (Bucharest, 1934–1942, 3 vols., covering the history to 1821), which today is undoubtedly the most authoritative and dependable history of Rumania.

The Bulgarians entered the stage of critical historical scholarship later than any of their neighbors, with the exception of the Turks. The belated growth of national feeling and the lack of political self-rule for the greatest part of the nineteenth century is largely responsible for this situation.

The foundations of modern Bulgarian historiography have been laid by Marin Drinov (1838–1906), who was the first Bulgarian historian to achieve European reputation as a scholar. Trained in Russia, where he lived most of his life as a professor at Kharkov University, he played an important role in the development of the intellectual life of his native country, where he even spent the critical years of 1877–1884 in various official capacities. In 1869 Drinov founded in Braila, Rumania, the Bulgarsko knizhovno druzhestvo [Bulgarian Literary Society], which in 1911 grew into the Bulgarska akademiia na naukite [Bulgarian Academy of Sciences]. He also founded the Society's journal *Periodichesko spisanie* (published from 1870–1876 in Braila and from 1882–1910 in Sofia) which became the main Bulgarian journal for historical and related studies. In his historical studies Drinov touched upon many problems of medieval and modern Bulgarian history, but he failed to produce a systematic account of the entire course of Bulgarian history. This task was undertaken by a young Czech historian, Constantine Jireček (1854–1918), whose name is closely connected with the development of modern Bulgarian historiography. Jireček, who has remained without peer as a historian of the Balkan Slavs, exercised a genial influence on Bulgarian historiography, not only by writing his *Geschichte der Bulgaren* (Prague, 1876), which was the first scholarly history of Bulgaria, but also by his presence in the newly-born Bulgarian state, where he guided its cultural development between 1879–1882 in various official capacities, including that of the Minister of Education.

But the most eminent and the first specially trained historian Bulgaria produced was undoubtedly Vasil N. Zlatarski (1866–1935). Like Drinov, Zlatarski was also trained in Russia primarily as a Byzantine and Slavic scholar under V. Vasil'evskii and V. Lamanskii, which provided him with a solid foundation for treating the medieval history of his native country in a broad framework, as can be judged from his great work *Istoriia na Bulgarskata durzhava prez sriednitie viekove* [*History of the Bulgarian State during the Middle Ages*], (Sofia, 1918–1940), 3 vols., covering the history to 1280. Zlatarski's work extends into the modern period, but his main contribution has been always to the medieval history of his country. As professor of Bulgarian history at the University of Sofia, a position he held from the establishment of this institution in 1904 to his death in 1935, and as the main force behind the historical activities of the Bulgarian Academy and the Sofia Istorichesko druzhestvo [Historical Society] which he had founded in 1905, he determined the course of modern Bulgarian historiography. He formed a whole generation of historians, who proved worthy continuators of his work, especially in the medieval field. The best-known among them are P. Nikov (1884–1938) and P. Mutafchiev (1883–1943), the latter also being the author of an *Istoriia na Bulgarskiia narod* [*History of the Bulgarian Nation*], (Sofia, 1943–1944), 2 vols., covering the period to the end of the fourteenth century.

The growth of nationalism among the Turkish people, culminating in the revolt of the Young Turks in 1908, created the conditions necessary for a more critical approach to the study of their national history, following the example of Western scholarship. As Western ideas penetrated Turkey the traditional historians, the *vaq'anuvis,* whom the Ottoman State had maintained in continuous succession from an early age, gave way to more modern ideas of writing history. Thus in 1910 the Tarihi Osmani encümeni [Ottoman Historical Association] later changed to Türk tarih kurumu [Turkish Historical Society] which was founded to acquaint Turkish historians with the standards and techniques of their colleagues in the West, issued the first historical journal, properly speaking, in Turkey—*Tarihi-i-Osmani encümeni mecmu'asï* later known as the *Türk tarih encümeni mecmu'asï.* The *Türk tarih kurumu* has now become the main center of historical studies in Turkey and its *Belleten,* published regularly since 1937, is the most important historical Turkish journal.

Much of modern Turkish historiography, however, is preoccupied with excessive nationalistic tendencies, especially with respect to the obscure problems of the rise of the Ottoman Empire. Here H. A. Gibbons who, in his book *The Fountain of the Ottoman Empire* (Oxford,

1916), saw the empire as a European creation and a continuation of Byzantium, drew the Turkish scholars' animosity similar to that which Fallmerayer or Rösler engendered from the Greek and Rumanian scholars. In many ways the central figure in contemporary Turkish historiography, and certainly the best-known scholar outside his own country is Mehmed Fuad Köprülü, who has been active in politics also, as have so many Balkan historians in the past. All Turkish historians of the younger generation, some of whom occupy today the chairs of history at the Universities of Ankara and Istanbul, have been directly or indirectly influenced by Köprülü's teaching and scholarship.

The Albanians, being the last of the Balkan peoples to develop a national consciousness and to organize an independent political life, did not succeed in the prewar era in developing any organized intellectual life. Facilities for higher education and research were virtually nonexistent, and persons with a university training in history were few in number. Albanian historical writings have never achieved a level of critical scholarship. The pertinent papers included in such reviews as *Hylli i Dritës* and *Leka* are generally amateurish. There is much to be desired, even in the historical writings of Fan Noli and A. Gegaj, both of whom studied and worked abroad. In recent years historical studies have been, for the first time, organized to some degree—but with a Marxist orientation—by the Instituti i Shkencavet [Scientific Institute], established in Tirana in 1947.

From the very beginning modern historiography has turned its attention to the publication of source material. Since its conclusions had to be based on the evidence and on a critical appraisal of the available sources, it is easy to understand why the idea of editing texts and documents attracted the historians of the last century. Such a task was the surest foundation for all further investigation. Thus it became one of the primary duties of the historians and their colleagues in related fields to collect and edit critically the available sources pertaining to their national history. And so the famous collection of the *Monumenta Germaniae Historica* grew up, which quickly found imitators among the various European nations including the Balkan countries. Thus the Jugoslav Academy at Zagreb produced the *Monumenta spectantia historiam Slavorum meridionalium* (Zagreb, 1876 ff.), the *Monumenta historico-iuridica Slavorum meridionalium* (Zagreb, 1877 ff.), and the

Codex diplomaticus regni Croatiae, Dalmatiae et Slavoniae (Zagreb, 1904 ff.) edited by T. Smičiklas, to mention only the most important and most extensive of such collections. The Serbian Academy published the valuable collections of source material included in the multi-volumed *Zbornik za istoriju, jezik i književnost* [*Miscellany for History, Language and Literature*]; (first section: *Spomenici na srpskom jeziku*, Belgrade, 1902 ff.; second section: *Spomenici na tudjim jezicima*, Belgrade, 1904 ff.; third section: *Fontes rerum Slavorum meridionalium*, Belgrade, 1923 ff.) To those collections one must add the *Gradivo za zgodovino Slovencev v srednjem veku* [*Source Material for the History of the Slovenes during the Middle Ages*], (Ljubljana, 1903 ff.) edited by the foremost Slovene historian Franc Kos (1853–1924), and continued after his death by his son Milko Kos. In the postwar period, and with even greater intensity, the Jugoslavs continued to publish source material from the earliest times of their history down to Tito's resistance movement.

Greece, unfortunately, does not present us with systematic collections of sources. Whatever has been done has been in a haphazard way and has been the work of individual scholars rather than that of learned societies. Here the name of S. Lampros, mentioned earlier, stands out as an editor of texts, and also that of C. Sathas, who edited the *Mesaionike Bibliotheke* [*Medieval Library*], (Venice, 1872–1894), in 7 vols., and *Documents inédits relatifs à l'histoire de la Grèce au Moyen Age* (Paris, 1880–1890), in 9 vols. The *Mnemeia Hellenikes Historias* [*Monuments of Greek History*], (Athens, 1932 ff.) of the Academy of Athens, and the smaller collections of documents concerning Macedonia put out by the Hetairia Makedonikon Spoudon [Society for Macedonian Studies] at Thessalonica, should also be mentioned here.

Of all the Balkan countries the Rumanians again have been the most productive in this respect. Th. Codrescu's pioneering collection *Unicariul sau colectiune de diferite acte care pot servi la istoria Romîni-lor* [*Historical Miscellany, or Collections of Various Acts Relating to Rumanian History*], (Jassy, 1852–1896), in 25 vols., is not without merit, but the monumental collection *Documente privitore la istoria Romînilor* [*Documents Relating to the History of the Rumanians*], (Bucharest, 1876–1938), in 21 vols., originated by Eudoxiu Hurmuzaki and published under the auspices of the Rumanian Academy, contains an invaluable, though incomplete, collection of materials gathered from various sources covering the period from 1199 to 1849. A supplement is the work of G. Petrescu, D. A. Sturdza, D. C. Sturdza, and G. Colescu-Vartić, *Actes et documents relatifs à l'histoire de la régéneration de la Roumanie* (Bucharest, 1888–1909), in 10 vols. Several volumes with source material have also been edited by Iorga.

The most spectacular effort, however, in the publication of Rumanian historical sources has been made by the postwar Rumanian Academy, which inaugurated in 1951 the publication of a most comprehensive collection of documents relating to their national history, a multivolumed (incomplete) collection entitled: *Documente privind istoria Rominiei* [*Documents Relating to the History of Rumania*]. The same institution is contemplating a corpus of all the narrative sources of Rumanian history, parts of which have already appeared (e.g., *Letopiseţ cantacuzinesc* [*Annals of the Period of the Cantacuzenes*]). In its ambitious program the Academy also plans to put out a corpus of inscriptions and of various legal codes used in the past in the Rumanian lands.

The Bulgarians have fared less well in the publication of collections of sources. The *Bulgarski starini* [*Bulgarian Antiquities*], (Sofia, 1906–1936), in 13 vols., and the *Dokumenti za Bulgarskata istoriia* [*Documents for Bulgarian History*], (Sofia, 1931 ff.), both published by the Bulgarian Academy of Sciences, are the only extensive collections of sources. Recently the same institution has made a more systematic effort in this direction by inaugurating an ambitious series *Izvori za Bulgarskata Istoriia* [*Sources for Bulgarian History*], (Sofia, 1954, ff.) of which only two volumes have appeared so far, one covering Greek and one Latin sources.

It is only in recent decades that Turkish historians have begun to exploit the rich Ottoman archives, which, when published systematically, will vastly increase our knowledge of the history of the Ottoman Empire and of its Balkan subjects.

In Albania it is only recently that the Scientific Institute at Tirana has promised to undertake publication of source material. The texts and documents concerning the history of Albania, which we have now, have been the work of foreign scholars.

The amount of source material published by native Balkan scholars is impressive but by no means exhaustive, and together with the numerous sources which foreign scholars have edited, provides a firm foundation for analytic studies and synthetic works.

Many individual problems and particular periods of the national histories of the Balkan peoples have been studied by native scholars in a most thorough and competent fashion. Much less has been accomplished in terms of great syntheses. If one excludes the histories of Rumania by Iorga and Giurescu, all other important and strictly scholarly synthetic works, such as those by Šišić and Zlatarski mentioned above, cover only the early period.

In surveying the accomplishments of modern Balkan historiography it is evident that the medieval period has attracted more serious attention than the later periods. The history of the Balkans under Turkish rule has been studied very little. No one denies the importance of this period for the understanding of the evolution of the Balkan peoples, but before the Turkish archives are properly exploited it would be premature to attempt to write the history of this period. It is true that we possess many other historical sources for this period, but the importance of the Turkish archival material can hardly be overestimated. The latest periods which cover the national revolutions and the struggles for political independence have been studied more carefully and the pertinent source material more systematically edited.

The reason for the special emphasis on the medieval period by the most competent Balkan historians must be examined, in my opinion, in close connection not only with nationalism which discovered in it a glorious historical past, but also with the development of Byzantine studies since the latter part of the last century. The establishment of Byzantine studies in the West as a separate discipline, and their astonishing flowering, had a great impact on Balkan historiography. Since the medieval past of all the Balkan peoples was directly connected with Byzantium, and its study cannot yield adequate results without a thorough knowledge of the Byzantine sources, it is not surprising that most prominent Balkan historians were primarily trained as Byzantine scholars in the West or in Russia. Having acquired the necessary scholarly methods and techniques in an established discipline, they were able to apply them to the study of their national history. Byzantine studies also exercised a genial influence on the Balkan historians, in enabling them to broaden the narrow outlook they held on the history of their countries, occasioned by nationalism, and helped them to look upon the Balkan Peninsula as a unit with a common heritage. Iorga was the first Balkan historian to grasp the significance of this outlook, and he advocated by work and deed the idea that the Byzantine and Turkish heritage which the various Balkan peoples shared made imperative the study of national history on a broader basis, which would view the various common Balkan traditions as one whole. Iorga succeeded in imbuing the younger generation of Rumanian historians with these views. The contents of two excellent Rumanian journals, the *Revue historique du Sud-Est Européen* (23 vols., 1924–1946) and *Balcania* (8 vols., 1938–1945)—the latter being published by the *Institutul de Studii și Cercetări Balcanice* [Institute of Balkan Studies and Research], its activities ending in 1948—testify to the importance of the contribution of the Rumanian scholars in this respect.

On the other hand, the movement to encourage Balkan coöperation, which grew after the First World War, also fostered a common inter-Balkan outlook among the native historians, which best found expression in the ambitious Jugoslav journal *Revue internationale des études balkaniques* (6 vols., 1935–1938).

In surveying the over-all picture of the development of modern Balkan historiography one immediately notices that the interest of the Balkan historians has remained basically within the boundaries of national history. Even when they dealt with problems outside the orbit of national history, as they did mainly when writing on Byzantine, Ottoman, and general Balkan history, they viewed these problems in connection with the history of their own countries. With a few notable exceptions—such as N. Iorga, and A. Andreades, whose *Histoire de la Banque d'Angleterre* (Paris, 1904), 2 vols., is still considered one of the standard books on the subject—the scope of the Balkan historians has hardly extended beyond the areas directly related to the history of their native country, and even when it did so, no significant contributions resulted.

The Balkan historian is confronted with a number of problems unknown to most of his Western colleagues, which render his task more difficult. The inadequate library and research facilities in the Balkan countries are well known. With the exception of the Library of the Rumanian Academy and the Gennadeion in Athens, the Balkan libraries cannot supply all the necessary books even for the study of national history proper. Most Balkan archives are badly organized, and thus not easily accessible to scholars for research purposes.

Besides, the preoccupation of every Balkan historian with the history of his native land renders him susceptible in varying degrees to influences from modern political antagonisms. It suffices to mention only the much debated controversial questions of Transylvania, Dobrudja, and Macedonia, in order to show that even historians of Iorga's stature were unable always to keep a cool head. The force of nationalism in the Balkans often has proved much stronger, when it relates especially to territorial problems, than even the most rigorous Western training in critical and objective historical scholarship. The Balkan historian never separates in his mind his scholarly work from his country's political life, in which he often actively participates. One may recall in this connection the political careers of Novaković, Lampros, Iorga, and Köprülü.

Another general characteristic of Balkan historians is that their minds tend to become encyclopedic. It is difficult for a competent scholar in the Balkans to remain restricted exclusively to his own specialty. The lack of a sufficient number of well-trained and talented scholars in any of these countries would demand from the historian of ability with a good Western training a much more active and extensive participation in the several aspects of his country's intellectual and cultural life. Therefore it is not surprising to find in the Balkans professional historians who, while teaching at the university, are also seriously engaged in literary criticism, in play-writing, or in publishing a newspaper or a magazine.

Since research centers for historical studies with a permanent staff of scholars were almost unknown in the Balkans until after the Second World War, a professorship of history at a university was practically the only scholarly position to which a historian could aspire. Even the position of a history professorship in the Balkan universities would not always be conducive to scholarly work, because the main purpose of the philosophical faculties of the Balkan universities, to which the chairs of history are attached, has been to produce high-school teachers, most of whom would be expected to teach their young pupils their national history as a religion rather than as an objective account of the country's evolution.

In spite of these difficulties many Balkan historians have made notable contributions. They have produced, on the whole, better monographic studies than great synthetic works. Of all the peoples of the Balkan Peninsula in the era before the Second World War the Rumanians succeeded best in attaining a high level of historical scholarship, which yielded rich results. The last war and its aftermath put an end to this preëminent position of Rumanian scholarship, a position which is now held by the Jugoslavs. Most of the important historical research emanating today from the Balkans comes from Jugoslavia. The postwar reorganization of the Jugoslav academies and the creation of a number of historical institutes with permanent research staffs has provided, for the first time in the history of that country, young historians with a fine opportunity to devote themselves completely to their scholarly pursuits. However, as one might expect as the result of political conditions, the main emphasis is on the social and economic aspects of history. This same system of organization of historical studies has been adopted by the other satellite countries in the Balkans, but here the even stricter attachment to the Marxist interpretation of history has produced a greater amount of biased historiography.

BIBLIOGRAPHY

G. Cahen, "Bulgarie," *Histoire et historiens depuis cinquante ans,* I (Paris, 1927), 72 ff.
J. C. Campbell, "Nicholas Iorga," *The Slavonic and East European Review,* XXVI (1947–49), 44 ff. By far the best account in English of Iorga's personality and historical work.
J. F. Clarke, "Zlatarski and Bulgarian Historiography," *ibid.,* XV (1936–37), 435 ff.
P. Constantinescu-Iaşi, "L'apport des historiens roumains à l'historiographie universelle depuis le 23 Août 1944," *Nouvelles études d'histoire présentées au Xe Congrès des sciences historiques, Rome 1955* (Bucharest, 1955), 3 ff.
J. Deny, "Turquie," *Histoire et historiens . . . ,* I, 438 ff.
E. Driault and M. Lhéritier, "Grèce," *ibid.,* 192 ff.
I. Duichev (Dujčev), "Pregled na bŭlgarskata istoriografiia" ["Survey of Bulgarian Historiography"], *Jugoslovenski istoriski časopis,* IV (1938), 40 ff.

————. "Die bulgarische Geschichtsforschung während des letzten Vierteljahrhunderts, 1918–1942," *Südost-Forschungen,* VII (1942), 546 ff.

I. Duichev, "Übersicht über die bulgarische Geschichtsschreibung," *Antike und Mittelalter in Bulgarien* (Berlin, 1960), 51 ff.

"Historical Studies in Turkey," *The Times Literary Supplement,* April 23, 1954, p. 270.

E. Haumant, "Yougoslavie," *Histoire et historiens* . . . , I, 455 ff.

N. Iorga, "Roumanie," *ibid.,* I, 320 ff.

K. Key, *An Outline of Modern Turkish Historiography* (Istanbul, 1954).

M. Kos, "Pregled slovenske historiografije" ["Survey of Slovenian Historiography"], *Jugoslovenski istoriski časopis,* I (1935), 8 ff.

J. Macůrek, *Dějepisectví evropského východu* (Prague, 1946).

V. Mošin, "Les études byzantines et les problèmes d'histoire inter-balkanique," *Revue internationale des études balkaniques,* I (1935), 314 ff.

V. Novak, "Jugoslovenska istoriografija izmedju dva svetska rata i njeni savremeni zadaci" ["Jugoslav Historiography between Two World Wars and Its Present Tasks"], *Istoriski časopis,* I (1948), 199 ff.

————. "Outline of Yugoslav Historiography," *Ten Years of Yugoslav Historiography, 1945–1955* (Belgrade, 1955), 11 ff.

P. Panaitescu, "Rumänische Geschichtsschreibung, 1918–1942," *Südost-Forschungen,* VIII (1943), 69 ff.

Marin Pundeff, "Bulgarian Historiography, 1942–1958," *American Historical Review,* LXVI:3 (April, 1961), 682–693.

M. Sakellariou, "Neollenikes historikes spoudes" ["Studies of Modern Greek History"], *Nea Hestia,* XXXIII (1943), 26 ff.

F. Šišić, "Hrvatska historiografija od XVI do XX stoljeca" ["Croatian Historiography from the Sixteenth to the Twentieth Century"], *Jugoslovenski istoriski časopis,* I (1935), 22 ff.; II (1936), 16 ff.

J. W. Thompson, *A History of Historical Writing,* II (New York, 1942), *passim.*

P. Topping, "Greek Historical Writing on the Period 1453–1914," *Journal of Modern History,* XXXIII (June, 1961), pp. 157–173.

INDEX